THE CULTURAL DYNAMICS OF SHELL-MATRIX SITES

THE CULTURAL DYNAMICS OF SHELL-MATRIX SITES

Mirjana Roksandic,

Sheila Mendonça de Souza,

Sabine Eggers,

Meghan Burchell,

and Daniela Klokler

UNIVERSITY OF NEW MEXICO PRESS • ALBUQUERQUE

Library of Congress Cataloging-in-Publication Data

The cultural dynamics of shell-matrix sites / edited by Mirjana Roksandic,
Sheila Mendonça de Souza, Sabine Eggers, Meghan Burchell, and Daniela Klokler.
    pages cm
  Includes bibliographical references and index.
  ISBN 978-0-8263-5456-3 (cloth : alkaline paper)
  ISBN 978-0-8263-5457-0 (electronic)
  1. Kitchen-middens—Analysis. 2. Kitchen-middens—Social aspects. 3. Fish
remains (Archaeology) 4. Human remains (Archaeology) 5. Excavations
(Archaeology) 6. Social archaeology. 7. Coastal archaeology. 8. Ethnoarchaeology.
I. Roksandic, Mirjana. II. Souza, Sheila Mendonça de. III. Eggers, Sabine, 1961–
IV. Burchell, Meghan. V. Klokler, Daniela.
CC77.S5C85 2014
  930.1—dc23
                          2013046744

This book is composed in Minion, designed by Robert Slimbach, and released
in 1992. It was inspired by classical, old style typefaces of the late Renaissance,
a period of elegant, beautiful, and highly readable type designs.

CONTENTS

ILLUSTRATIONS

FIGURES

vii

TABLES

Cultural Dynamics of Shell-Matrix Sites: Diverse Perspectives on Biological Remains from Shell Mounds and Shell Middens

Mirjana Roksandic, Sheila Mendonça de Souza,
Daniela Klokler, Sabine Eggers, and Meghan Burchell

Shellfish fill a particular niche in subsistence economies; however, the reasons why people gather and consume shellfish are contingent on environmental and historical circumstances and are sanctioned by cultural practices. Cheryl Claassen (1991) challenged "normative thinking at shell bearing sites," and economic models such as the "optimal foraging theory" and "central place models" of shellfish collection. Claassen's voice (1991, 1998), while certainly not the only one, was prominent in shifting the focus of research from food refuse to symbolic, deliberate, and ritual usage of shells in the archaeological context.

Shell-matrix sites are complex structures that challenge our ability to excavate, record, and, eventually, interpret past human behavior, unless they are excavated with the utmost, or even obsessive, attention to detail (chapters 2, 7, and 9). Even in their most basic form—as evidence of food refuse (chapter 6)—they often involve a lot of "dirt moving" that needs careful deciphering. However, the attention to detail comes with high revenue. Shell-matrix sites are sensitive to environmental fluctuations and provide a wealth of information about the past use of natural resources. In addition to information about subsistence practices, they represent conspicuous markers on the landscape, are bearers of human burials in environments that are otherwise not conducive to skeletal preservation, and provide focal points covering large areas of past landscapes (chapters 1, 3, 7, 8, 11, 12, 21, 22). They were often both used and deliberately built for burial purposes, connecting us with the very notion of the ritual, social memory, and identity (Burchell 2006, 262). Individual shells and accumulations of shells often carry symbolic meanings we can only extrapolate from more modern usages: the shell as a symbol of birth, female sexuality, and rebirth; shells to remember distant sounds of the sea; or shells as symbols of life, fertility, and peace (Hamell 1992; Saunders 1999, 248; Stiner 1999).

Whether shell mounds are remains of subsistence activities, platform structures for safer and more adequate living/settlement, sacred mounds, or territorial markers, the sheer variety of shapes and sizes, chronologies, functions, different types of material culture, and/or activities that take place in them calls for a truly multidisciplinary approach as the only way to grapple with the complexity inherent in these sites. An arsenal of different disciplines—from micromorphology, geochemistry, biological anthropology, paleobotany, ethnoarchaeology, zooarchaeology, geoarchaeology, and biogeochemistry to symbolic analysis and semantics—has been applied in recent years to excavations and analyses of these sites. The result of this vigorous research comes in thousands of specialized reports and papers, focusing on a particular method, material, or aspect of a site or a region. Many new initiatives and innovative approaches remain isolated as a consequence of increased field compartmentalization and lack of awareness between different disciplines and different research traditions. This isolation is further aggravated in the case of non-Anglophone academia, often published in less accessible or less well-known journals, and neglected even when it is at the vanguard of research.

Our book attempts to redress these two issues by compiling very different approaches to shell-matrix-site research in a single volume, and by emphasizing research from areas underrepresented until now in the Anglophone literature, notably Brazil, Argentina, and Portugal. By examining various aspects of this most abundantly present material in shell-matrix sites, the authors had to demonstrate anthropogenic activities and aim to understand cultural phenomena. Although by no means comprehensive, the chapters deal with several key areas of active research: the Northwest Coast of Canada (chapters 15, 17, and 18), California (chapter 1), Florida and the southeastern United States (chapters 3, 4, and 5), Brazil (chapters 7, 8, 11, 12, 13, 16, 21, and 22), Patagonia (chapters 14 and 20), Portugal (chapters 6, 9, 10), and Scotland (chapter 19), and discusses more than 220 sites in ten countries on four continents. Each of these geographic areas has recognizable "signature questions" that arose through a combination of research history and site- or region-specific problems and manifestations of shell-matrix sites. Combining these diverse perspectives in one volume can help inform the practice of archeology and invigorate research, not only in the regions represented here, but also in other areas of the world.

As with all edited volumes, this book is a compromise between our personal ideals and the research focus of the contributors, but the goal we set out at the beginning of our work on this volume remained unchanged. For all five of us (three biological anthropologists: MR, SMS, and SE; one geoarchaeologist: MB; and one zooarchaeologist: DK), the concept of the book was based on a relatively simple fact: shell-matrix sites are composed of biological remains deposited by cultural activities. This volume explores our ability to interpret culture and the meaning of middens and mounds, and aims to promote interregional understanding of the problematic faced by all researchers on biological phenomena associated with these very complex structures.

With the aim of covering as much of the worldwide distribution as possible (respecting the page limits of our publishers) and presenting novel methodological approaches and interpretations, we left it to the authors to decide the style of writing, the paper length, and the number of illustrations necessary to demonstrate their procedures and results. The idea was to give as much free flow to the book as possible, recognizing that some approaches are more descriptive, while others need more graphs or figures.

In order to maintain academic standards, all papers were reviewed by at least one of the coeditors, one internal (any of the participating authors) and two external reviewers, and in the final stages by MR before they were accepted for publication. We worked intensively with the authors to maintain coherence in content and style, while allowing and even favoring individual expression. The chapters presented here are therefore deliberately unequal in content, focus, method, length, and approach. Our buzz word was diversity: of thought, of geographic area, of method, of theoretical perspective, of anything under the sun that has relevance to archaeology, and we hope we succeeded in conveying the vibrancy and diversity of this field of study.

Research presented in the following 22 chapters is often concerned with new perspectives on different regional syntheses (17 chapters) of which one is continent-wide (chapter 5), but it also includes several site-specific studies (chapters 2, 6, 9, 10, 11, and 20) demonstrating particular new developments. Most of the chapters represent the reevaluation of data in light of current developments: a new understanding of site formation (chapters 1, 2, 3, and 7), rarely used methodologies (chapters 9, 10, 18, 20, 21, 22), changing paradigms in the discipline (chapters 4 and 7), or changing regional perspectives (chapters 4, 5, 7, 10, 12, 13, 14, 15, 16, 17, 19). All of them focus on understanding past human societies as dynamic living anthropological entities.

The volume is organized into three thematic sections. The first part of our volume, "Typology and Function," examines questions stemming from interest in site formation and interpretation of function, covering the coasts of the United States, Brazil, Australia, and Portugal. The authors examine different factors associated with the accumulation of shellfish and discuss the symbolic nature of some of the structures. These concerns are important in discussing mobility and settlement patterns (chapters 1, 5, and 6). While subsistence practices are assumed, the emphasis is on the intentional construction of sites and the formation of anthropogenic landscapes (chapters 2, 3, 4, and 7). Instead of simply representing components of the archaeological matrix, equated with food by-products, shells are seen as indicators of communal events, as building materials for large-scale platforms, and as protection and tombs for the deceased.

The second section, "People and Burials," features research on the study of human remains from burial grounds in Brazil, Portugal, and Argentina. Research covers issues of demography (chapter 12), cultural and biological networks (chapters 13 and 14), burial (chapters 8, 9, and 10), and ancestral rituals (chapter 11). Site formation processes, while not the focus, represent an important component of three of the chapters (9, 10, and 11). Two apply archaeothanatology (Duday 2009) for the reexcavation of burials preserved in breccia (chapter 9) and the evaluation of discarded photographic evidence (chapter 10). Notably, authors demonstrate techniques and approaches that allow us to capture data from older excavations using recent methodologies.

The final portion of the book, "Subsistence and Ecology," focuses on economic resources and subsistence strategies. These studies often incorporate more regional and long-term approaches in the investigation of resource acquisition, processing, and use. Patterns of foraging behavior (chapters 15, 16, and 19) and sustainability (chapter 17) are investigated based on studies of faunal remains, while seasonality and resource use are explored through chemical analyses (chapters 18 and 20). Paleobotanical studies (chapters 21 and 22) underscore the importance of plants for these groups in daily and sacred aspects of life, an element that sometimes gets overlooked by the massive presence of animal remains in the sites. As can be seen, sites range from extreme adaptations to the coast, to a more generalized hunter-gatherer economy.

Rather than providing conclusive answers, by comparing experiences of researchers dealing with different materials, geographic settings, and intellectual traditions, we hoped to inspire a more vigorous cross-disciplinary communication among scientists studying shell-matrix sites in different regions of the world. This undertaking was a concerted effort of many individuals. Each of the editors brought with her different experiences of archaeology and of shell-matrix sites, as well as her own connections with colleagues, research areas, and traditions. During the past two years, we worked extensively with authors to unify the volume while preserving the freedom and the diversity of approaches. This effort would not have been possible without the help of our research colleagues, reviewers, and publisher. We would like to express our thanks to all contributors for their endurance during both internal, external, and finally publisher external review. We especially thank our obliging colleagues who graciously agreed to serve as external reviewers and who have to remain anonymous. We would like to thank John Byram and the University of New Mexico Press for their guidance during book writing and to their external reviewers, whose insights necessitated some important changes that we strongly believe made the book more relevant. We would also like to acknowledge the University of Winnipeg and the University of Sao Paolo for providing funding for the initial copyediting and for the indexing of this volume, respectively. Finally, we, the authors and editors alike, are grateful to our copyeditor Stephanie Armstrong for her help with rendering some of the EAS phrases into proper English, for generally keeping track of all the changes, and for maintaining her own and our sanity in this complex process that involved truly intercontinental communication.

PART I: TYPOLOGY AND FUNCTION

FACTORS INFLUENCING THE FORMATION OF LARGE SHELL MOUNDS IN CALIFORNIA'S SANTA BARBARA CHANNEL REGION

Todd J. Braje, Jon M. Erlandson, and Torben C. Rick

SUMMARY

From San Francisco Bay to the Santa Barbara Channel, the California coast is well known for its large prehistoric shell middens and mounds created by sedentary hunter-gatherer populations who harvested rich marine, estuarine, and terrestrial habitats. Except for the very large shell mounds that once lined San Francisco Bay, most of California's largest shell middens are considered distinct from megamiddens that have been identified in many parts of the New and Old Worlds. Here, we examine large shell middens of the Santa Barbara Channel region, including the Northern Channel Islands, focusing on factors that contributed to the creation of massive accumulations of shell refuse at some sites. Population size, sedentism, freshwater availability, and a long occupational history are key variables contributing to the formation of large shell mounds, but the long-term productivity and resilience of intertidal habitats, the dietary importance of shellfish, and other factors are also important.

INTRODUCTION

First coined in the late 1970s, the term *megamiddens* usually refers to large coastal shell mounds created by complex or sedentary coastal hunter-gatherers around the world. The most recognizable of these may be from the megamidden period defined for the west coast of South Africa, dating between about 3,000 and 2,000 years ago (Jerardino 1998; Mitchell 2002, 10). In the New World, another widely recognized series of large shell mounds has been identified in coastal Brazil (see Gaspar et al.; Klokler; and Okumura and Eggers, chaps. 7, 11, and 8 in this volume), with the largest of these Brazilian sites estimated to contain some 2.5

billion shellfish, and dated to after about 5,000 years ago when eustatic sea-level rise began to slow and shorelines stabilized. Along the southwest coast of Mexico, Barbara Voorhies and Douglas J. Kennett have investigated a series of large mounded shell deposits up to 7.0 meters deep, with dense midden deposits dominated by marsh clam shell and dated between about 5,000 and 3,500 years ago (Kennett, Voorhies, and Martorana 2006; Voorhies and Gasco 2004). Kennett and colleagues (2006) argued that these sites are key to understanding the transition from hunter-gatherer populations to maize-based agriculturalists in the region.

In the United States, large shell mounds dating between about 7,200 and 2,400 years old have been identified in southeastern and midwestern sites (Sassaman 2004, 255–58). This time period is often called the Shell Mound Archaic and usually refers to interior, freshwater shell mounds, although large coastal shell rings and mounds have also been identified along the Gulf and Atlantic coasts (e.g., Thompson and Pluckhahn 2010). In some cases these shell mounds may have been created as midden deposits and tied to the stabilization of sea levels and river morphology and the increased productivity of shellfishing during summer months (Steponaitis 1986). However, a growing number of researchers argue that many of these large shell mounds and coastal shell rings were intentionally constructed as part of ceremonial and burial landscapes that evolved in complexity through time (e.g., Claassen 1996; Russo 1994). From its foundation in the Middle Archaic, shell mounding traditions in the American Southeast extended into the Historic period. At European contact, the Calusa of southwestern Florida constructed massive shell mounds, which served as living and ceremonials platforms (Widmer 1988), and represent the fruition of thousands of years of coastal hunting and gathering, sociopolitical evolution, sea-level rise, and the construction of anthropogenic landscapes.

In California, the most widely recognized large shell mounds come from the San Francisco Bay area. In the early 20th century, Nels C. Nelson (1909) recorded 425 shell middens along San Francisco Bay; some of these were very large shell mounds, the earliest of which are now known to date to about 4,000 years ago (Broughton 1994a, b, 376; Lightfoot and Luby 2006). The Emeryville shell mound, for instance, was 300 meters long, 100 meters wide, and nearly ten meters deep (Broughton 1994a, b; Schenck 1926). San Francisco Bay shell mounds vary tremendously in size and shape and have been regarded, primarily, as refuse debris, or kitchen middens. Many of the mounds contained human burials, however—thousands of them in some instances—and certainly served a ceremonial function, but the absence of definitive living surfaces and domestic structures dissuaded most archaeologists from suggesting ritual or symbolic motivations for their construction. Edward M. Luby and Mark F. Gruber (1999) linked the mounds to mortuary feasting practices, however, which may have intensified in the Late Holocene (Lightfoot and Luby 2006).

The shell middens of southern California's Santa Barbara Channel area have also received considerable archaeological attention, with more than a century of research. Renowned for their antiquity, preservation, density, and research value, the larger Santa Barbara Channel middens have not been discussed as part of a broader phenomenon of megamiddens or huge shell mounds found in South Africa, South America, the American Southeast, San Francisco Bay, or other regions. In the following sections, we examine the large middens of the Santa Barbara Coast and Northern Channel Islands, focusing on several factors that contributed to the creation of very large accumulations of shell refuse at some sites, and the unique geographic and cultural variables of the Santa Barbara Channel region that helped shape these sites.

ENVIRONMENTAL AND CULTURAL OVERVIEW

The Santa Barbara Channel is a unique geographic area of the California coast, trending east-west for approximately 130 kilometers, bordered by Point Arguello to the west and Point Dume to the east (Figure 1.1). With its protected shoreline, offshore islands, estuaries, and sandy beaches, the area has long attracted human settlement (Erlandson et al. 2011). Historically, the central California coast and Santa Barbara Channel contained one of the most productive fisheries in the world, fueled by strong upwelling of nutrient-rich marine waters, numerous estuaries along the mainland coast, a complex combination of oceanic currents, and extensive nearshore kelp forests. These variables encouraged high primary marine productivity that supported complex food webs, including a diverse array of marine plants, shellfish, fish, seabirds, and marine mammals harvested by humans for over 10,000 years (Schoenherr, Feldmeth, and Emerson 1999). When combined with a wealth of terrestrial plant and animal resources, especially along the mainland coast, these marine resources supported relatively large human populations for millennia.

The Santa Barbara Channel area is characterized by a Mediterranean climate with cool, wet winters and warm, dry summers. Along the mainland coast, the Santa Ynez Mountains rise sharply from a relatively narrow coastal plain, reaching heights of approximately 1,000 meters. This mountainous terrain provides a variety of stacked environmental zones within a relatively small area, including marine, estuarine, coastal plain, riparian, and montane habitats that support a diverse array of flora and fauna (Erlandson 1994, 23). On the mainland, the coastal plain is dissected by numerous canyons containing perennial and seasonal streams, which had productive estuaries at their mouths at various times in the past. The lack of rainfall during the summer and early fall puts a premium on perennial water sources, near which year-round human settlements tend to be located.

The four Northern Channel Islands (Anacapa, Santa Cruz, Santa Rosa, and San Miguel), ranging in size from about 2.6 to 249 square kilometers, are located between about 20 and 44 kilometers from the mainland coast. The Northern Channel Islands were never connected to the mainland during the Quaternary, making them somewhat distinct from the adjacent mainland. The islands contain a more limited terrestrial fauna and flora, for instance, lacking the diversity and productivity of many of the economically important land animals and plants common on the mainland (Schoenherr, Feldmeth, and Emerson 1999, 7–17). The islands also are considerably more arid than the mainland with smaller, less reliable freshwater sources, especially on the two smallest northern islands of Anacapa and San Miguel (Schoenherr, Feldmeth, and Emerson 1999).

At European contact in AD 1542, the Santa Barbara Channel and Northern Channel Islands were occupied by the coastal and island Chumash, who were complex, sedentary, maritime hunter-gatherers (Arnold 2001; Kennett 2005). With over 13,000 years of human occupation in the area (Erlandson, Rick, and Peterson 2005; Erlandson et al.

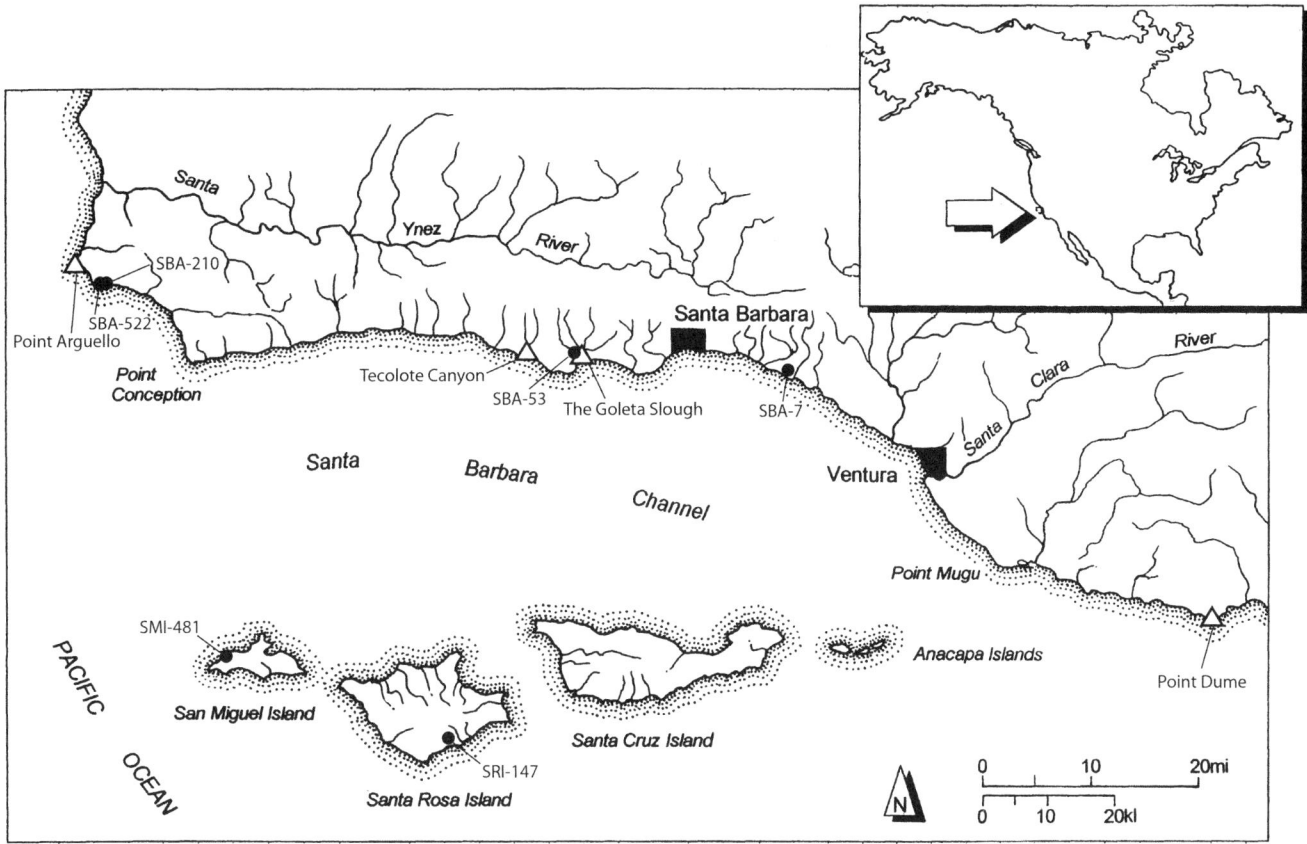

1.1. Map of the Santa Barbara Channel, the Northern Channel Islands, and the major sites discussed in this chapter.

2011; Johnson et al. 2002), the Chumash developed a complex exchange network between the islands and mainland; sophisticated sewn plank boats; shell, bone, and stone hunting and fishing tackle; a shell bead currency; and a hierarchical sociopolitical system (Arnold 2001; Gamble 2008; Kennett 2005; Rick 2007). Subsistence economies on the mainland focused on both terrestrial and marine resources with acorns, small seeds, deer, elk, small game, fish, shellfish, and sea mammals providing the bulk of the diet. With fewer terrestrial resources, the island Chumash focused more heavily on marine hunting, fishing, and shellfish foraging, along with trade with their mainland neighbors for terrestrial resources not available on the islands.

LARGE SHELL MOUNDS OF THE
SANTA BARBARA CHANNEL REGION

Overview of the Mainland Coast

Along the mainland coast, historic construction, agricultural development, coastal erosion, and other disturbances have damaged or destroyed many of the largest

archaeological sites (Reeder, Rick, and Erlandson 2011), so we rely primarily on the accounts of early archaeologists to identify and quantify large coastal shell middens. Even by the mid-1920s, when David B. Rogers (1929) began the first relatively systematic and well-documented archaeological research along the Santa Barbara Channel, historic construction, looting, and agricultural development had damaged portions of some sites. Rogers and other early archaeologists also tended to underestimate the size of many coastal shell middens, focusing their mapping and excavation efforts on the densest and most conspicuous central portions of sites. Therefore, the best place to begin is with the ethnographic record and early European accounts of mainland Chumash population centers.

In AD 1769, Captain Gaspar de Portolá, Father Juan Crespí, and a company of Spanish soldiers marched through the Santa Barbara Channel region on the first land expedition through Alta California (Gamble 2008, 1). Crespí noted numerous densely populated coastal Chumash towns and villages, which grew in size until they reached the Goleta Slough, the social and political center of the Chumash world. The expedition noted large settlements clustered around substantial estuaries at Goleta, El Estero (Santa Barbara), Carpinteria, and Mugu Lagoon, as well as the open coastline of Ventura and Santa Barbara counties where the Chumash utilized a diverse range of marine, freshwater, and terrestrial habitats. The Chumash fished in kelp forests and the open ocean from canoes and inshore along rocky intertidal habitats, collected shellfish at low tide, hunted sea and land mammals and birds, and collected a variety of seeds, acorns, and other terrestrial flora.

A number of scholars have attempted to reconstruct Chumash populations at European contact using historic accounts, mission records, and archaeological data (e.g., Brown 1967; Erlandson et al. 2001; Gamble 2008; Johnson 1988), with estimates ranging from 15,000 to 25,000 people. Regardless of the actual numbers, historic documents and archaeological research along the mainland coast demonstrate that the Chumash lived in permanent settlements at historic contact that ranged tremendously in size and density, and achieved some of the highest hunter-gatherer population densities ever recorded (Gamble 2008). In total, archaeologists and historians have identified at least 25 historic Chumash villages along the mainland coast between Point Conception and Malibu, with 20 identified between Point Conception and Ventura (Figure 1.2; Gamble 2008; King 1975). Most or all of these sites contained large accumulations of midden refuse, house features, sweat lodges, dance floors, cemeteries, and other activity areas. At nearly all of these sites, there is no clear evidence of intentional mounding of midden debris as living surfaces or as burial mounds, but these Late Holocene and historic villages contained large accumulations of shell refuse, sometimes reaching five to six meters deep. At the village of Noqto, however, there is evidence of intentional midden engineering and the creation of artificial terraces on which rows of houses were built.

The settlements at the Goleta Slough provide an excellent example of the large shell mounds that are or were associated with these Historic Period settlements. Since most of these villages contain earlier occupations, dating back to the Middle or Early Holocene in many cases, these sites are likely where the largest mainland Santa Barbara Channel shell mounds formed. The settlements at Goleta Slough and the village of Helo' on Mescalitan Island provide an excellent example of this pattern.

The Goleta Slough, Mescalitan Island, Helo', and the Aerophysics Site (CA-SBA-53)

The Goleta Slough captured the attention of a number of early European explorers, as the population center of the Chumash world. Juan Rodríguez Cabrillo led the first European expedition to visit the area, which sailed north from Mexico in AD 1542 and named three villages situated around the expansive lagoon (Gamble 2008, 84). A more detailed account of the area was provided by the Portolá expedition in AD 1769, when five large villages or towns were described, with a total population for the area of some 2,000 (Brown 1967, 29). Helo' was probably the largest of these towns and was situated on Mescalitan Island in the middle of the lagoon (Gamble 2008, 18). A Franciscan priest, Father Crespí, described Helo' in AD 1769, writing:

> On that island [Mescalitan Island], which is very green and covered with trees, we saw a large town, in which there were counted more than a hundred houses. This estuary spreads out to the west, forming many marshes and lagoons upon whose banks there are other towns, but we could not learn with certainty how many there were. Nevertheless, some of our soldiers said there were four, making with that of the island, five, the latter appearing to be the largest. [Bolton 1926, 156–57]

Mescalitan Island has been heavily modified since Cabrillo and Portolá first visited, most of it being bulldozed and used to fill wetlands for the construction of the Santa Barbara Municipal Airport, but a number of archaeological investigations have helped to reconstruct the long history of human settlement and use of this location (see Gamble 2008).

When visited by the Spanish, the Goleta Slough contained a large lagoon between 4 and 11 feet deep at high tide and separated from the ocean by a sandspit (Gamble 2008, 19). We may never know the exact number of sites that once existed along the Goleta Slough, but early Spanish maps depict five large historic villages and several smaller sites scattered along the margins of the lagoon. Numerous earlier sites also exist in the area, the oldest dating to the Early Holocene (Erlandson 1994, 179; Erlandson, Rick, and Vellanoweth 2008). In total, archaeologists have recorded approximately 25 sites on or near the shores of the Goleta Slough (Glassow, Johnson, and Erlandson 1986; Rogers 1929; Wilcoxon, Erlandson, and Stone 1982). Mescalitan Island, containing the large historic Chumash settlement of Helo', was 21 meters tall and a little less than a kilometer wide, and contained at least two springs and a diverse flora including oaks and grasslands (Gamble 2008, 19). Crespí commented several times on the population of Helo', suggesting that 800 people lived in 100 houses on Mescalitan Island (see Glassow, Johnson, and Erlandson 1986; Gamble 2008, 87).

Mescalitan Island is one of the most extensively

1.2. Map of the historic Chumash villages on the island and mainland based on ethnographic and archaeological records (adapted from Johnson 1988).

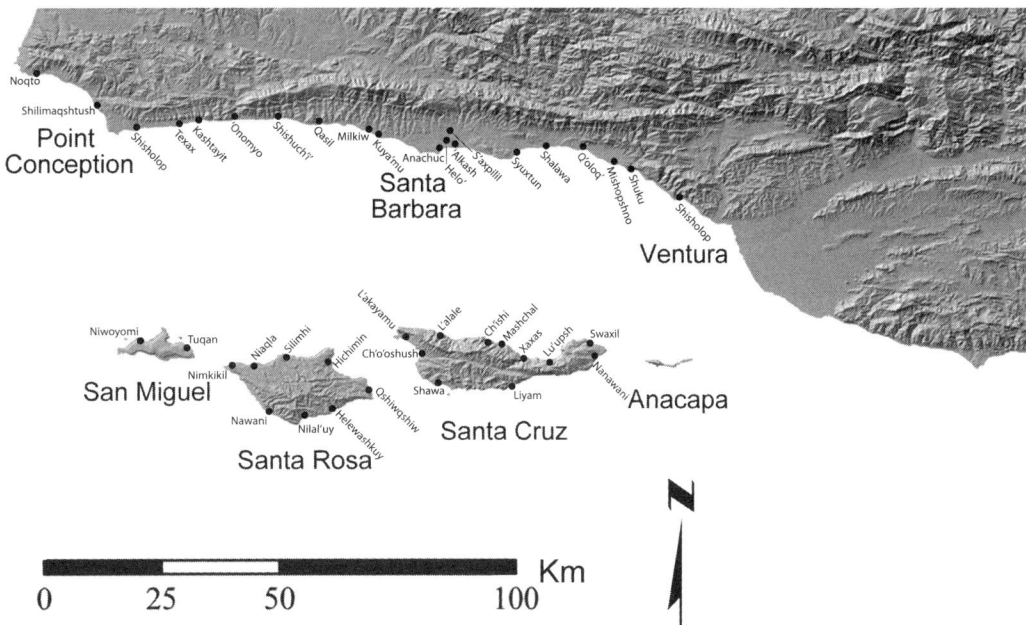

excavated (and looted) archaeological sites along the Santa Barbara Channel. While excavation techniques, research objectives, and record-keeping methods have varied tremendously, formal archaeological projects began in 1875 with the Wheeler Expedition, part of the U.S. Geographical Surveys west of the 100th meridian, and focused on artifact collections and cemetery excavations. Their work produced an abundance of finely made artifacts and burial goods, leading them to dub the site the "Big Bonanza." The collections are housed at the Smithsonian Institution, where they remain largely unstudied due to the lack of provenience information. Modern archaeological investigation at the site has documented a variety of house floors, cemeteries, residential features, and large midden deposits (Gamble 2008, 89–92). In 1986, Michael A. Glassow and colleagues wrote that the site of Helo' and Mescalitan Island once contained "one of the two or three greatest concentrations of midden deposits anywhere within the Santa Barbara Channel" (Glassow, Johnson, and Erlandson 1986, 9). Unfortunately, development projects beginning in 1941 mined much of Mescalitan Island for fill and removed over 75 percent of the island and most of the archaeological deposits before archaeologists could fully record the depth and density of the sites (Glassow, Johnson, and Erlandson 1986, 10).

Helo', Mescalitan Island, and the Goleta Slough settlements suggest how many of the large shell mounds on the mainland were formed. The largest sites were clustered around productive estuary or marine habitats, with nearby freshwater sources. The dense populations at many of these permanently occupied mainland villages would have resulted in the rapid accumulation of midden debris. Helo' is an excellent example of these processes occurring within a circumscribed environment, demonstrating a number of similarities to Northern Channel Island shell mound sites that will be discussed below. Mescalitan Island contained a large population at historic contact, which probably could not have been achieved without the freshwater springs on the island, the large estuary, and oak groves surrounding it, as well as access to extensive kelp forest and pelagic fisheries outside the mouth of the estuary. The occupants likely sacrificed mobility for the protection and safety afforded by the island, which may have been an important draw, especially in the last 1,500 years when Chumash population growth accelerated and violent conflict increased (Lambert 1997).

Although generally not as large as the Late Holocene shell middens, a few Middle Holocene middens on the Goleta Slough also contain large shell refuse deposits that show a deeper antiquity to the formation of these mainland middens. One of these is CA-SBA-53, the Aerophysics site, located on the ancient shoreline of the Goleta Slough. Excavated by David B. Rogers (1929) and by William M. Harrison and Edith S. Harrison (1966; see also Glassow 1996; Rick and Glassow 1999) in the 1950s, shell midden deposits once covered an area of at least 245 x 150 meters and were more than one meter deep. The site contained abundant artifacts, estuarine and open-coast shellfish species, and the remains of terrestrial and marine mammals, birds, and fishes. Thought to be a residential base, this site exemplifies the creation of large shell midden deposits on the mainland coast beginning at least by 5500 cal BP (Rick and Glassow 1999).

Another very large mainland shell midden, CA-SBA-7 was located at the mouth of the Carpinteria Slough and included the historic Chumash town of Mishopsno. Rogers (1929, 48) described this site as one of the largest along the Santa Barbara Coast, stating that it covered a large triangular area extending for more than 1.2 kilometer (~3/4 of a mile) north to south and east to west. CA-SBA-7 is poorly known archaeologically and has been largely destroyed by urban development, but it once contained multiple components that may have spanned the Early, Middle, and Late Holocene (Rogers 1929). The vast size of the shell midden is consistent with a series of large settlements located in optimal estuarine locations, with sequential occupations whose midden deposits overlap horizontally to create a huge multicomponent site.

Two very large shell middens from the northern Santa Barbara Coast, CA-SBA-552 and CA-SBA-210, also grew to substantial sizes over a long occupational period, these in a nonestuarine, outer-coast environment. The sites are located between Point Arguello and Point Conception on either side of the mouth of perennial Agua Vina Creek, along a south-facing stretch of rocky coast. This setting provides some relief from the dense fogs that often shroud the coast north of Point Conception, as well as protection from the strong northwesterly winds and waves that batter the area (Glassow 1996, 86). Archaeological investigations in the 1970s established that both sites contain dense multicomponent shell midden deposits more than five meters deep, leading Glassow (1996, 86) to conclude that "few other sites in southern California contain midden deposits as deep" as these two sites. CA-SBA-210, the historic village of Noqto where test units were excavated to depths of 5.6 meters and 4.2 meters before sterile sediments were reached, encompasses an area of over 19 hectares (190,000 square meters). Human occupation began roughly 5,000 years ago and extended into historic times. At CA-SBA-552, roughly twice the size of CA-SBA-210, midden deposits reached a depth of at least 5.2 meters and the lower four meters appear to have accumulated prior to 7,000 years ago. Glassow (1996, 88) suggested that these two sites operated as a single community for millennia, with the emphasis of human settlement shifting between the two at different times. At the historic village of Noqto, which in AD 1769 had between 60 and 100 inhabitants and

12–14 houses (Gamble 2008, 71), midden deposits appear to have been used to create artificial terraces to accommodate an orderly arrangement of houses and other activity areas. A cemetery was located on the uppermost terrace, where the dead were interred in the shell midden. At these two large sites, the size, depth, and volume of shell midden deposits appear to be related to recurring occupation of an optimal location during nearly 9,000 years, a heavy reliance on shellfish as a source of protein that complemented abundant terrestrial plant foods (Erlandson 1994, 261; Glassow 1996, 125), long-term ecological stability and resilience, and the high productivity of mussels and other intertidal shellfish populations along a rich stretch of rocky coast.

Overview of the Northern Channel Islands

Like the mainland coast, the archaeological record on the Northern Channel Islands contains a long and continuous sequence, but limited historical development and a dearth of burrowing animals on the islands have fostered better site integrity (Erlandson et al. 2011; Rick et al. 2005). The islands have been the focus of archaeological investigations for more than a century. Research has increased over the last 20 years, resulting in some of the highest resolution data sets for coastal hunter-gatherers anywhere in the world. The rise of sociopolitical complexity along the channel has been one popular avenue of research (e.g., Arnold 2001; Kennett 2005; Rick 2007) and has resulted in the documentation of at least 21 historic island Chumash villages, all with large accumulations of shell midden and other domestic features (Johnson 1982).

The archaeological record suggests that the last 3,500 years (Late Holocene) in Chumash history was a critical period of reorganization and intensification of island settlement, subsistence, and sociopolitical patterns. It was during this period when island population growth accelerated (Erlandson et al. 2001) and numerous relatively large, coastal, multifamily villages were established, many persisting into historic times (Rick et al. 2005). These Late Holocene villages are clustered near springs located along rocky shorelines and kelp forests—some of the most productive marine habitats on the islands—along with sandy beaches that served as canoe landings. Village formation, nearshore and open-ocean fishing, trade, and bead production all intensified during the Late Holocene and may have been accelerated by cooler sea-surface temperatures and drought conditions between 800 and 650 cal BP (Kennett 2005), resulting in the accumulation of massive kitchen middens that are often several meters deep (e.g.,

1.3. Overview photograph of the 30-meter-high dune in the western portion of CA-SMI-481 at Otter Point (photo by J. M. Erlandson and adapted from Erlandson, Rick, and Peterson 2005). For scale, see two individuals standing atop the dune.

CA-SCRI-240 and CA-SCRI-333 on Santa Cruz Island; Arnold 2001; Wilcoxon 1993).

The accumulation of large shell mounds on the Channel Islands seems to have occurred earlier and in distinct ways from portions of the mainland coast. Notable exceptions, such as the Aerophysics (described above) and Vandenberg sites, indicate some early formation of large middens on the mainland. Since the mainland Chumash had greater access to terrestrial plants and animals, small seeds and other terrestrial flora were a major part of the subsistence economy, especially until about 5,000 to 6,000 years ago. As a result, shell midden or mound building may not have accelerated as quickly on the mainland, in many cases, until the Late Holocene. With a less diverse and productive terrestrial flora and fauna on the islands, the formation of massive shell mounds seems to have begun by the Middle Holocene (7500–3500 cal BP) in some optimal locations. Another possibility is that the larger land area and wider distribution of freshwater on the mainland allowed people to move settlements more easily than on the islands, resulting in smaller sites. Complicating the picture, however, are historical disturbances and bioturbation, which have destroyed many mainland sites or created palimpsests that make it difficult to determine precisely when sites formed on the mainland. Below, we describe two sites, one from San Miguel Island and one from Santa Rosa

Island, to illustrate the formation of large shell middens on the Northern Channel Islands.

Otter Point (CA-SMI-481), San Miguel Island

In the 1920s, Rogers (1929) surveyed the shoreline of San Miguel Island and described the entire north coast as one vast and nearly continuous shell midden. Later surveys recorded scores of discrete sites along this north coast, including several very large shell middens. One of the largest of these is CA-SMI-481, located in a large dune complex with at least ten discrete archaeological deposits spanning about 7,300 years. Located on the northwest coast of San Miguel Island at Otter Point, the site extends for nearly a kilometer from east to west, including a series of shell midden deposits in a 30-meter-high dune, several nearby smaller dunes capped with shell midden, and a meter-thick midden on the tip of the point (Figure 1.3). This is one of the largest and densest archaeological sites on San Miguel Island, covering an area more than 600 meters long and up to 420 meters wide (Rick 2007).

The site extends from Otter Point on the west to an intermittent, freshwater drainage, Otter Creek, on the east and includes two protected, sandy coves (Amphitheater Cove and Otter Harbor). The Otter Point area and CA-SMI-481 were likely continually reoccupied because of the abundance of marine resources including intertidal shellfish, nearshore and kelp-forest fish, and marine mammal populations aggregated on offshore rocks. Otter Creek also has one of the more reliable freshwater sources on the island, an invaluable commodity on the arid Channel Islands.

Several dense accumulations of shell midden, some several meters thick, exist in this area, but most individual components are between about 0.4 and 1.0 meter thick. Starting about 7,300 to 6,500 years ago, the pace of dune building on San Miguel seems to have increased (Erlandson, Rick, and Peterson 2005, 1233), perhaps linked to the warming and drying of the Altithermal or slower sea-level rise and accelerated coastal erosion. Continued reoccupation of Otter Point and the large dune provided well-drained dune soils, access to freshwater and a wealth of marine resources, and good visibility of the surrounding viewshed, the total area visible with the human eye from a fixed location (see Kennett 2005, 104–8). Intensified human occupation also led to higher rates of refuse disposal, which helped stabilize the sand dune and create a massive shell midden with discrete occupational lenses, now visible in eroding exposures of the dune. The deposition of shell and other organic, nutrient-rich debris encouraged vegetation growth, helped create paleosols, and stabilized sand dunes.

This process is not unique to Otter Point or to San Miguel Island and is seen in several areas around San Miguel and the other Northern Channel Islands, albeit at smaller scales in most locations. These sites may have only been abandoned when nearby freshwater springs and shellfish beds were buried under beach or dune sand (Erlandson, Rick, and Peterson 2005, 1233) from episodic dune building that may have accelerated in the Late Holocene with increased anthropogenic impacts on terrestrial flora from vegetation stripping and burning (Johnson 1972).

CA-SRI-147, Santa Rosa Island

CA-SRI-147 is a large habitation site located at the confluence of two freshwater drainages in Jolla Vieja Canyon that flow to the south coast of Santa Rosa Island. A total of 45 sites have been recorded in the canyon, most of which are relatively ephemeral, positioned to access freshwater, and date to the Late Holocene. About four kilometers inland, as the canyon winds its way north to northwest from the south coast, a series of smaller drainages flowing from the hills to the north and west merge into a substantial confluence flanked by several caves or rock shelters. This location was the site of several substantial Middle to Late Holocene occupations (Braje et al. 2007; Kennett 2005, 144–45).

The first subsurface archaeological investigations at CA-SRI-147, a site measuring 200,000 square meters in

area, were conducted by Phillip M. Jones (1956) in the early 1900s, who described the site as "a large rancheria of great interest" (Orr 1968, 233). Jones spent three days excavating at the site, collecting a variety of artifacts and exhuming numerous burials. Subsequent visits by Phil C. Orr of the Santa Barbara Museum of Natural History revealed Jones's extensive excavations and several deep stratified middens in open air, rock shelter, and cave settings. Orr (1968, 229–33) described habitation debris and human remains in every cave, one of which contained the only petroglyphs (incised dots and lines) on Santa Rosa Island. Although many of the cultural deposits have been damaged by early excavations and severe erosion, intact deposits, some several meters thick, are currently exposed in the canyon walls. Recent archaeological work has documented a three-meter-deep shell midden exposure in the eastern branch of the canyon wall at the main confluence of the drainage (Kennett 2005). Radiocarbon dating at this location revealed a nearly continuous occupational history beginning about 7,200 years ago until about 400 years ago, when most of the site activity was relocated to the coast (Braje et al. 2007).

The midden deposits at CA-SRI-147 are densely packed with a variety of shellfish species including abalones, California and platform mussels, sea urchins, and turban snails, and smaller amounts of fish bone, all of which were laboriously transported up the canyon and processed on site. Although this location may have facilitated access to inland terrestrial plant communities (Kennett 2005, 145), it may have been situated primarily to access potable water. The site occupants would have weighed this advantage against the travel costs to and from productive shellfish beds and access to other marine resources. The site was likely abandoned or infrequently visited when marine resources near the mouth of the canyon were depleted, which increased travel costs (Braje et al. 2007). Increased population growth and conflict along the Santa Barbara Channel may have also driven the Chumash to occupy large coastal villages with better viewsheds (Kennett 2005).

DISCUSSION AND CONCLUSIONS

California's Santa Barbara Channel contains a remarkable record of human occupation, spanning the last 13,000 years (Erlandson et al. 2011; Johnson et al. 2002) and culminating in the densely populated, complex, and sedentary maritime Chumash societies recorded by the Spanish (Arnold 2001; Gamble 2008; Rick 2007). Although there has been little recognition that the Chumash and their ancestors intentionally created large shell mounds or megamiddens similar to those in San Francisco Bay, the southeastern United States, or Brazil, our review of the largest sites on the mainland and islands demonstrates that they are comparable in size to many megamiddens found in other parts of the world, and many contain house pits, cemeteries, dance floors, sweat lodges, and other discrete activity areas (Erlandson, Rick, and Vellanoweth 2008; Gamble 2008; Rogers 1929). Like many megamiddens elsewhere, the large shell middens in Chumash territory were created in prime resource locations, the result of intensive and long-term marine foraging, food processing, residential activities, and the disposal of vast quantities of faunal and other debris.

The physiography, climate, hydrology, and ecology of the Santa Barbara Channel played a critical role in the formation of these large shell middens. The arid and Mediterranean climate of the Santa Barbara Channel, where dry summers encouraged settlement at perennial springs or streams, may be the single most important factor in the formation of these large middens. Relatively steep topography and narrow coastal plains on the islands and mainland also contributed to this pattern, providing ready access to multiple ecosystems and encouraging sedentism in optimal coastal locations. These ecological factors encouraged the aggregation of large populations at central locations, where long-term foraging resulted in the accumulation of dense refuse and the formation of large shell mounds.

A highly productive coastal ecosystem, with its long history of marine upwelling, dense offshore kelp forests, and a variety of terrestrial plant foods, also provided the resource base to support large, dense, and sedentary populations. These large human populations clearly influenced the structure of nearshore fisheries and ecosystems (see Rick et al. 2008), but California's kelp forest, rocky shore, and estuarine ecosystems—along with the people who harvested these resources—appear to have been deeply resilient, allowing long-term human harvests in particularly rich localities. In many cases, this environment focused settlement near productive rocky-shore habitats, along sandy beaches and protected coves for boat landings, and around mainland estuaries with a rich mix of terrestrial and marine resources. For the maritime Chumash, the use of seaworthy boats also increased mobility, resource exploitation territories, and trade opportunities, allowing some groups to sustain themselves at large coastal villages for long periods of time.

Finally, many of the large Santa Barbara shell middens have multiple occupations, where people repeatedly used favorable landforms and optimal locations over the millennia. In some cases, the deposition of cultural materials may have helped stabilize these landforms, creating a feedback loop and resulting in sites such as the impressive Otter Point case where at least ten components spanning the past 7,300 years built up over an area almost a kilometer long.

These processes seem to have worked in a similar fashion along both the mainland coast and the Northern Channel Islands, but there are some differences in the records. The heavier emphasis on shellfish as a meat source on the Channel Islands, where terrestrial flora and fauna are less diverse and productive, created some larger, deeper, and denser shell middens than along the Santa Barbara Coast proper. Shellfish collecting was also relatively intensive along stretches of rocky coast north of Point Conception, where rougher waters limited offshore fishing, leading to the accumulations of vast shell midden deposits in some favorable locations.

The Chumash and their ancestors did bury their dead in coastal shell middens (Rogers 1929), but archaeologists working in southern California have generally focused shell midden research on questions of subsistence and economics. This focus may be one reason that the area has not been recognized as a megamidden landscape. Megamidden archaeologists generally have focused on the ceremonial nature of large shell middens, as burial sites, platforms for elite individuals, evidence of feasting activities, or sociopolitically delineated space, although some large shell middens have been explained as the unintentional outcome of subsistence activities (e.g., Kennett, Voorhies, and Martorana 2006). Even those large shell middens lacking human burials or domestic features likely served a ceremonial function, as places where the ancestors lived, ate, gathered, interacted, and performed activities both mundane and symbolic. Shell middens, especially large and obvious ones, would provide powerful connections to the past and present, to places of memory and meaning.

Ultimately, the large coastal shell mounds of the Santa Barbara Channel area offer an interesting comparison to other such sites around the world. The Chumash and their ancestors created massive accumulations of shell, at times interred their dead in these middens, and likely saw these as an important part of the anthropogenic landscape. The megamiddens of the Santa Barbara Channel do not appear to have been built primarily as ceremonial centers, however, but were probably the outcome of millennia of concentrated subsistence-related activities by sedentary, complex, maritime hunter-gatherers. While their formation and distribution followed a unique trajectory, they are an important element in understanding the processes of coastal adaptations and economic intensification of complex hunter-gatherer-fishers around the globe. It is important to remember, however, that the Santa Barbara Channel record demonstrates that large shell mound sites around the world represent a continuum of mounding activities that occurred for a variety of purposes and under unique geographic, cultural, and environmental conditions.

ACKNOWLEDGMENTS

We are indebted to Mirjana Roksandic, Sheila Mendonça de Souza, Sabine Eggers, Meghan Burchell, and Daniela Klokler for inviting us to participate in this volume and for their editorial comments and assistance in the revision and production of our chapter. Our research has been supported by a variety of individuals and institutions, including funding from the National Science Foundation, Channel Islands National Park, Western National Parks Association, and our home institutions. We are also indebted to Channel Islands National Park and the National Marine Fisheries Service for logistical support, especially Bob DeLong, Ann Huston, Kelly Minas, and Ian Williams.

CHAPTER TWO

THE KEY MARCO SITE, A PLANNED SHELL MOUND COMMUNITY ON THE SOUTHWEST FLORIDA COAST

Randolph J. Widmer

SUMMARY

The Key Marco site is a large, 13.5-hectare planned village site on the southwest Florida coast, intentionally constructed from marine shell. The site has 61 mounds with a volume of over 240,000 cubic meters of shell, including a distinct elite residential precinct with 37 house mounds and a ceremonial precinct containing six temple mounds constructed of marine shell. Thirteen shell ridges, separated by canals, radiate from the elite residential precinct. The shell ridges and mounds form the bases for structures. All structures on mounds and ridges were built on pilings. The site has an occupational span from 5000 BP to contact period with approximately 1,500 years in its present configuration, with a population of 500. Most function-based typologies of shell-matrix sites in Florida are constructed from inadequate excavation strategies, and therefore do not reflect the inherent complexity and intentionality of these structures. I propose a functional typology that aims to allow easy identification of the level of intentionality and complexity associated with these sites.

INTRODUCTION

One of the greatest problems in southeastern United States prehistoric archaeology is classifying and ascertaining the function of large shell-bearing sites. Elsewhere (Widmer 1989) I have proposed a typology of shell-bearing archaeological sites that categorizes the types of shell deposits that can be found in the coastal areas of the southeastern United States, demonstrating that there is a wide range of contexts for these sites. The short typology presented here, based on the understanding of site formation processes and functions, allows us to discern the level of complexity and intentionality in the shell mound, and the variation in the purported usage of these sites.

Shell Midden Sites

A shell midden site is one in which the shell remains are secondarily deposited from food consumption activities *and* in which there is no evidence of other functions at the site. In other words, the site is a task-specific area associated exclusively with mollusk consumption activity. The percentage of shell comprising the site sediment is unimportant. These sites should be void of vertebrate faunal remains and have only a few artifacts.

Shell Midden

This is a discrete lens or deposit of shell, void of vertebrate faunal remains, secondarily discarded from food consumption activities localized at a site.

Shell-Bearing Midden Site

This type of site is composed of secondary refuse, which includes shell, discarded from a wide range of activities, including food consumption, craft, and domestic discard activities.

Shell-Bearing Midden

This type of deposit is composed of secondary refuse, including shell, discarded from a wide range of activities, including food consumption, craft, and domestic discard activities that are localized at a site.

Shell-Bearing Habitation Site

These sites are formed primarily of shell, usually secondarily deposited from food consumption. However, the shell deposits may be natural in deposition or natural (non-food remain) shell culturally transported into the site. The shell is used as fill for floors, causeways, platforms, and mounds. Often these sites may start out as shell-bearing middens, which are temporarily utilized and transformed into platforms or mounds for habitations. Primary and secondary shell material may then be added to them, either as midden or as fill. This type of site is extremely complex because it contains the greatest number of different formation processes. These sites are common on the southwest Florida coast and have received the most archaeological attention.

Unfortunately, a shell midden or shell-bearing midden classification is often assigned to an archaeological site without any actual excavation, and even when only limited testing is conducted, a shell midden interpretation of the shell deposits typically results without any empirical evidence to support the assessment (Claassen 1991; Widmer 1989). Fortunately, most early researchers in southwest Florida recognized to some extent that the large sites located there were shell-bearing habitation sites rather than the accumulation of food refuse. The original excavator of the Key Marco site clearly maintained that the site was an intentional construction with multiple functions. He even provides the reasons for their construction and notes that they became culturally patterned:

> We have seen how, for many reasons, it was necessary for the key dwellers to build their mound-like homes or islands, out in the seas. . . . they developed the habit of erecting great mounds for special structures of this kind to such extent, that it became fixed; so customary traditionally, that whithersoever they or rather their descendants went thereafter, they continued the practice as an essential tribal regulation." [Cushing 1973 (1896), 402]

This view was shared by Ales Hrdlicka (1922), who conducted the first extensive survey of southwest Florida and characterized the archaeological sites along this archipelago. He clearly indicates that the shell heaps, as he calls them, were intentionally constructed and not solely midden accumulations:

> The remains in question are of two or possibly three classes. The first are simple shell heaps, composed principally of oyster shells, with a larger or smaller admixture of conchs, a few clam shells, turtle shells and bones of fish and various game animals. These heaps contain none or but little sand or soil; they are generally in the form of more or less pronounced, extensive and generally parallel ridges, the troughs between which served frequently—if not invariably—as canals which facilitated the approach with canoes. They are from such evidence as could be gathered poor to almost sterile in archeological or skeletal remains of the Indians. Their role was doubtless in the main that of platforms for habitations and for protection against the overflowing waters during storms. They were built expressly for these purposes, and that partly of dead shells brought to the spot from the beach and the oyster bars, and partly by the refuse shells and bones of the habitations.

> Besides these ridges there are found in this region occasional isolated good-sized shell mounds. These are usually oval, but may be almost circular in outline, have more or less conical form with blunt or flat top, and range from about ten to near thirty feet in height. The material of which they are built is much the same as that of the shell heaps. The object of these shell mounds has not been determined. It is possible that some served as points for observation, or signaling, or for ceremonial observances, and some perhaps also for habitations and burials. None of these mounds have apparently as yet been explored. [Hrdlicka 1922, 27–28]

In his synthesis of the archaeology of south Florida, John Goggin classified the southwest Florida shell-bearing sites as shell works. He differentiated these shell deposits from shell middens, although they are constructed from shell midden material:

> Shell works are planned groups of simple to complex structures built with shell midden material. A large midden deposit generally forms a pediment upon which elaborate series of ridges and mounds are laid out. At some places the pediment may be wholly or partially lacking and shell ridges, mounds and causeways can be found in swamps. . . . It is most probable that shell works were deliberately constructed by Indians after some preconceived plan. Utilizing the immense quantities of available shell refuse the elaborate ridges and mounds were most likely formed to serve(s) (sic) as pediments for houses or temples. Ramps, causeways, and canals gave access to these structures. [Goggin 1949, 396–97]

However, because of the limited archaeological work at the time of his synthesis, site function was problematic. "It is not possible to determine the exact function of any of these sites. None have been completely excavated and few have been adequately surveyed" (Goggin 1949, 397).

Margo Schwadron (2010, 183) agrees with Hrdlicka (1922) and considers conical mounds to be purposely constructed ceremonial monuments. Schwadron (2010, 193, 207) recorded postmolds at the Fakahatchee and Dismal Key sites in the Ten Thousand Islands, clearly indicating the existence of a domestic structure on shell deposit. Based on her detailed mapping of the shell works in the Ten Thousand Islands, Michael Russo (2004, 2006) also considers a non-midden context for shell deposits at the Horr's Island site, also in the Ten Thousand Islands.

SITE FORMATION PROCESSES AND SHELL-BEARING SITES

In south Florida, much of the confusion and uncertainty about site formation processes and site function results from the use of small, one-meter-square test pits used to collect data from the sites (Marquardt 1992; Schwadron 2010). The small area of the excavations and the limited number of such tests preclude the ability to find floor plans of structures. These limited tests do often reveal postmolds (Schwadron 2010, 193, 207).

However, when extensive area excavations are conducted in these shell-bearing sites, structures are uncovered that would have otherwise been missed (Russo 1991; Widmer 1996). Therefore, the real issue is a lack of extensive excavation area at these large shell-work sites. Test pitting is inadequate for determining the existence of structures and the full range of features that are found at these sites, and therefore cannot provide any meaningful assessment of site type.

Recently, William H. Marquardt (2010a, 562–63) has taken a revisionist view of shell-work function, going so far as to suggest that none of the mounds and shell works of the southwest Florida Coast in the period from AD 500 to AD 900 functioned as temple mounds. He dismisses clear evidence of spires, cemented into place to siphon large *Busycon* shell in stratigraphic layers, as intentional constructions and instead considers them nothing more than refuse accumulations. Of course, once again his conclusion is based on his experience with data derived from one-meter-square test pits, rather than from extensive block excavations designed to uncover house floor plans and features, not to mention the lack of detailed sedimentological studies of the

various strata. However, as I will point out in this chapter, this position is incorrect, and indeed the prevalent characterization of these southwest Florida shell-bearing sites and their shell works as planned, intentionally constructed settlements is actually correct.

The real issue with investigating shell-bearing habitation sites in the southeastern United States is developing a research and excavation strategy to adequately determine the site formation processes and to actually demonstrate the functions that these sites fulfilled. Over the last 40 years, I have developed a strategy for just this purpose, combining three approaches: (1) extensive stratigraphic excavation of a large contiguous area that differentiates and collects distinct sedimentary deposits; (2) detailed mapping of sites together with spatial analysis of the resulting topographic features; and (3) the use of soil sedimentary samples and flotation samples, collected not only from features but from every excavation provenience. It is one thing to make field assessments of sedimentological differences of strata encountered, but this is only useful for distinguishing stratigraphy, not for characterizing their formation processes or deposition type, that is, fill, midden, or natural beach wash, that have been discussed and systematized above.

This approach to soil sampling is crucial for characterizing deposit types because "the key to understanding these site formation processes is to evaluate and interpret the composition of the sediments by virtue of standard sedimentologic and taphonomic indices" (Pickering 1998, 26), a study that he performed on sediments from the Key Marco site. The combination of all of these lines of evidence permits a very robust reconstruction of the community layout of the Key Marco site.

In this chapter I will demonstrate that the Key Marco site (8Cr48), a southwest Florida shell works, is indeed an intentionally planned and constructed, hierarchically organized settlement with residential houses and temple mounds associated with its shell features. I will discuss the community layout along with the methods and data that allowed for this reconstruction.

SETTLEMENT PATTERNING AT THE KEY MARCO SITE

The Key Marco site, 8Cr48, is one of a number of large shell-bearing sites on the southwest coast of Florida. Sites in this area are planned village communities with various layouts. The Key Marco site is one that is in the southern archipelagos of islands along the southwest Florida coast

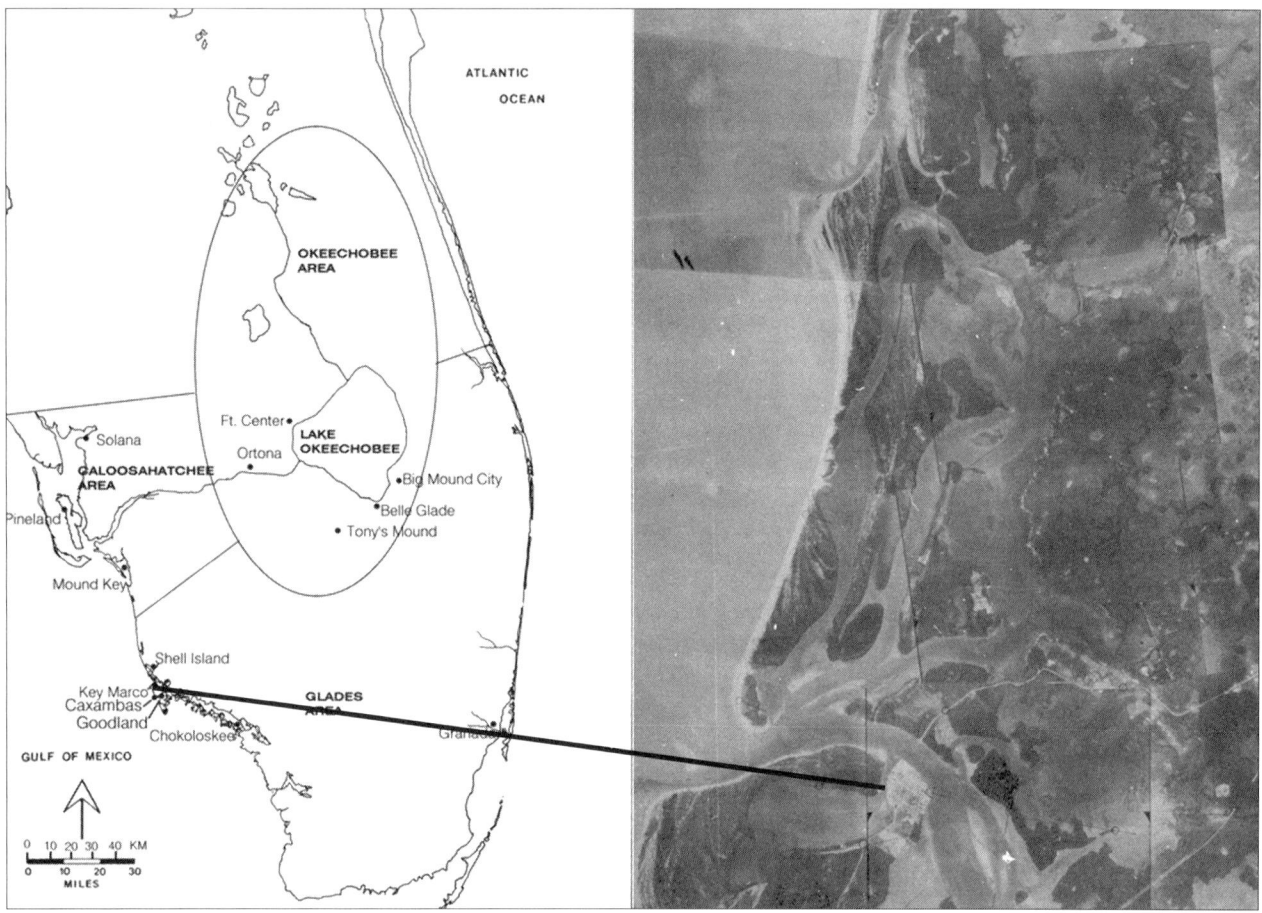

2.1. Location of the Key Marco site.

referred to as the Ten Thousand Islands. It is located on the northernmost island known as Marco Island (Figure 2.1). Today, the term *Key Marco* is used to refer to an island adjacent to and south of Marco Island, known as Horr's Island on official Coast Guard charts of the region. This renaming was done by real estate developers. There has been much confusion of the term *Key Marco* because the area where the site is located has never been given this name except by the archaeologist who excavated there, Frank Hamilton Cushing (1973 [1896]). The area of the site was officially known as Marco, Collier City, or Olde Marco. The name Key Marco actually refers to the prehistoric archaeological site that was located on Marco (which is the location of the site and different from Marco Island).

Today, the site is unrecognizable in comparison with the prehistoric archaeological site that was mapped in 1895. The site has been leveled to a uniform elevation of around two meters. The taller mounds and ridges that originally existed at the site were leveled and pushed into the adjacent low-lying areas. A series of modern canals was also dredged through the site, and the dredge spoil was utilized to fill in low-lying areas. Now, the site is completely developed with single-family homes, shops, restaurants, apartments, and condominiums built upon its surface (Figure 2.1).

The archaeological significance of the site cannot be overestimated. In 1895, Frank Cushing excavated a muck pond in the southwest corner of the site. From this location he collected over 1,000 wooden artifacts, many of them representing spectacular works of art unparalleled in the eastern United States to this day. His artist, draftsman, photographer, and surveyor, Wells Sawyer, created an extraordinarily detailed topographic map. However, subsequent to this initial excavation the site was largely ignored by archaeologists; the reason, I suspect, is the disdain for excavating dense shell-bearing sites.

We are very fortunate to have this incredibly detailed topographic map of the original archaeological site prior to modern development, but one issue that must be

2.2. Comparison of Key Marco site in 1895 (A) with today (B). (C) Surfer map of Key Marco site to generate site volume. (D) Location of excavations on the Key Marco site.

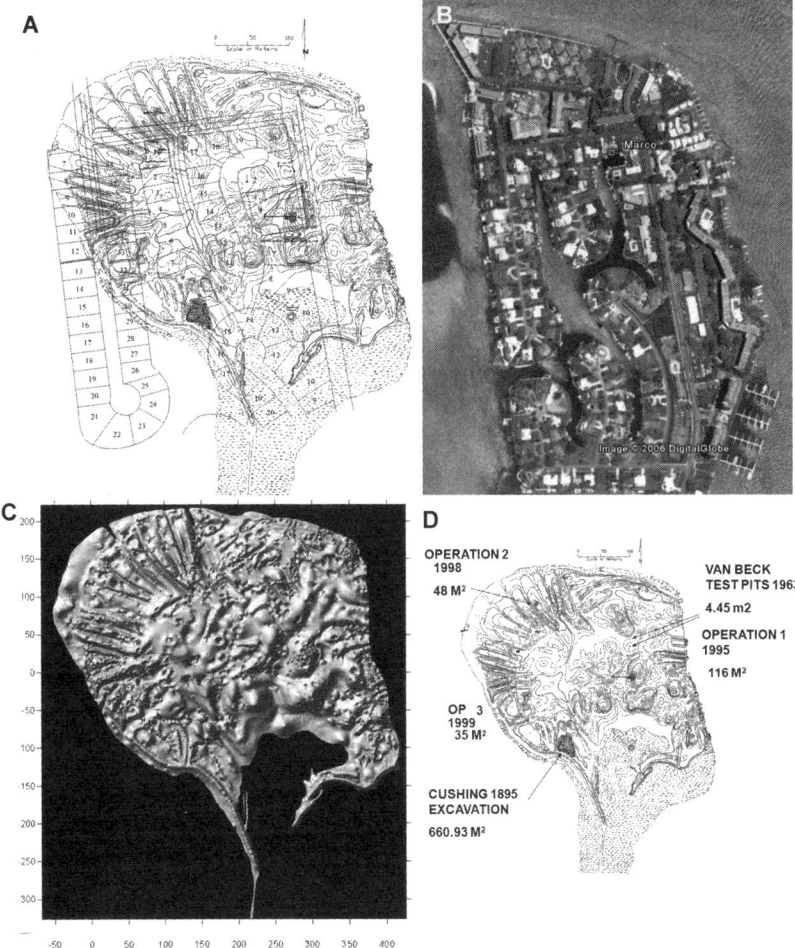

addressed is the correlation of the detailed topographic map, prepared by Wells Sawyer in 1895 (Cushing 1973 [1896]), with the existing topography and landform of this northeast area of Marco Island. The site has been dramatically modified and disturbed since the initial excavation took place 100 years earlier. A digitized AutoCAD vector contour map of the Wells Sawyer map was created from the original map and then a layer containing the modern streets and corrected plat map was superimposed onto it. This was done to determine where the original Sawyer map features are located today and to determine the original size of the site, 13.48 hectares (Figure 2.2). Following this, the X, Y, and Z vertices from the AutoCAD contour map were converted into the Surfer mapping program so that a three-dimensional contour map could be made and, more important, so that the volume of the site, 240,367.42 cubic meters, could be calculated (Figure 2.2c).

As mentioned, the most famous archaeological excavations at the site were conducted in 1895 by Frank Cushing.

He excavated the entire muck pond, an area of 660.93 square meters, which he referred to as the "Court of the Pile Dwellers" (see Figure 2.2d). Clarence B. Moore (1900, 1905, 1907, 1919) also excavated in the pond after Cushing, finding nothing left. No excavations were conducted at the site subsequent to Moore until the early 1960s, when John C. and Linda M. Van Beck (1965) excavated two test pits at the site, totaling an area of 4.45 square meters. Unfortunately, they did not have access to the Cushing report and the Wells Sawyer map, and so thought they were on a different archaeological site. Their excavation locations have been placed on the AutoCAD map (Figure 2.2d).

I began excavation at the site in 1995, when development of a condominium provided the archaeologists access to an empty lot prior to construction. Similar situations arose in 1998 and again in 1999. These excavations have been referred to as Operations, 1, 2, and 3, respectively, with areas of 116 square meters, 48 square meters, and 35 square meters for each of the operations, yielding a total of 199

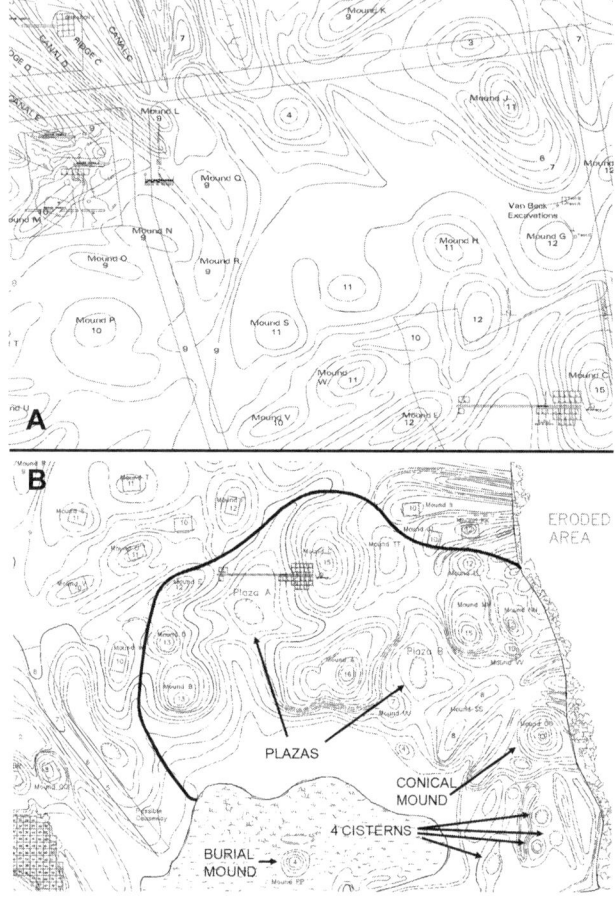

2.3. (A) Location of Operations 1, 2, and 3 excavations on the
Key Marco site. (B) Location of mounds and features in the
ceremonial precinct at the Key Marco site.

square meters. In all, a total of 864.38 square meters has
been excavated at the Key Marco site, most of which was
from the "Court of the Pile Dwellers." These excavations
were in three types of topography as mapped by Sawyer
(Cushing 1973 [1896], 421, plate 30). Operation 1 was situated on a large mound in the southeast area of the site,
Operation 2 was placed on one of the shell ridges in the
northwestern area of the site, and Operation 3 was located
on one of the smaller mounds adjacent to the ridge area
of the site. These three excavations provide excavation
data from three distinct topographic features of the site.
Figure 2.2d indicates the location of these excavations,
their year of execution, and the area excavated, and
Figure 2.3a provides a more detailed map of their excavation location and layout.

It was possible to ascertain the nature of the construction, the stratigraphy, the function of the mounds and

ridges indicated on the map, and the degree of disturbance
to the Key Marco site from the Operations 1, 2, and 3 excavations utilizing the research strategy outlined above
(Figure 2.3a). Excavations at Operation 1 were on the eastern slope of Mound C, the second tallest mound at Key
Marco with an original height of 4.57 meters (15 feet). Excavations revealed important characteristics of the mound
construction. The upper 2.5 meters of the mound had been
truncated and pushed west to fill in the low-lying area,
only to have dredge fill from the adjacent canal dumped
there as well.

Three superimposed platforms remained intact
(Figure 2.4). These were composed of marine and estuary
shell along with sand. This fill was void of midden refuse,
except for a single deposit, and so these constructions were
intentional and not the result of food refuse disposal. This
observation was confirmed by the detailed soil sedimentological study conducted on the Operation 1 sediments
(Pickering 1998). Of particular interest was one platform
level consisting of large unaltered *Busycon* and *Pleuroploca*
gastropods, intentionally placed spire to siphon in adjoining rows to create a MacAdam-like fill for mound construction. This is a type of compacted surface that traditionally uses stones that are tamped down to create a
uniform hard-packed surface (similar to the surface of
modern roads). These shells were intentionally placed in a
concretelike matrix and were so tightly packed that it was
impossible for a backhoe to penetrate beneath their surface. Interestingly, a similar *Busycon* layer was encountered in the Van Becks' 1963 excavation in Test Pit C in the
adjacent Mound G at precisely the same level as was found
in Mound C (Van Beck and Van Beck 1965), also confirming the contention that this was an intentional platform
construction rather than food refuse, as has been incorrectly suggested by Marquardt (2010a, 562–63). This *Busycon* layer was so compacted that they had to terminate
their excavations.

In addition to this *Busycon* layer, pen shells were then
deposited onto the slopes of the platforms, which were created largely by surf clams (*Spissula*). This would have given
the platform a nacreous appearance from its sides. This
field assessment of deposit type was confirmed by a sedimentological study (Pickering 1998) that clearly indicated
that none of the platform strata resulted from food refuse,
nor could they be classified as a midden in context (Pickering 1998, 91–94). The site is stratigraphically complex, with
at least 50 distinct strata encountered in each of our operations. Furthermore, midden material is not found on
mounds or ridges but instead in the swales, canals, and

2.4. Postmolds and mound stratigraphy at Operation 1.

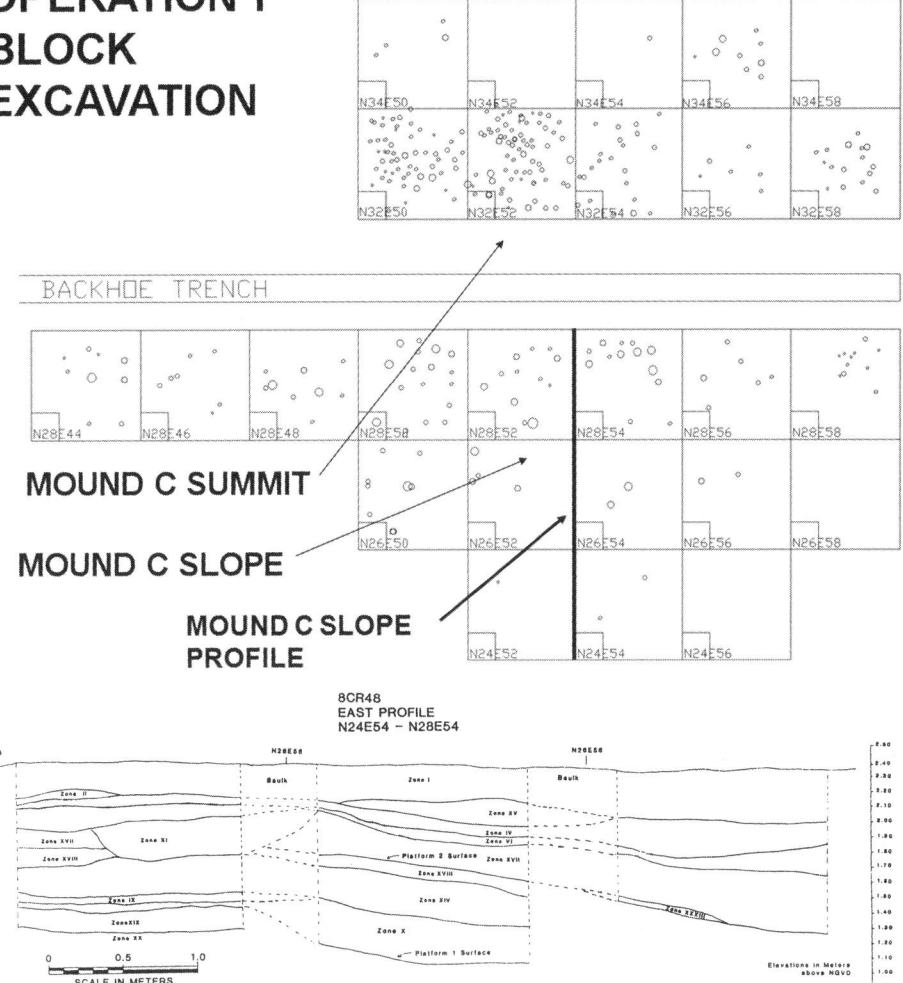

lower-lying areas. The Mound C excavation revealed a long, continuous, and uninterrupted occupation from around at least AD 500 to contact. In addition, valuable exotic materials such as a *Busycon* shell cup, an articulated section of shark steak, yellow and red ocher, and an unused chert projectile point were found in the platform fill. The latter three offerings were not native to the site area and had to be imported from farther north. This finding suggests that this structure functioned as a temple mound. Postholes, 31 of them in the platform summit, indicate that a structure, presumably a temple, was erected on the platform summit. Adjacent midden areas were encountered, indicating that the subsistence at the site was predominately based on fish, both marine and estuary (Widmer 1988; Wing 1965).

Our Operation 2 excavations focused on the linear shell ridges radiating northwest out from the center of the site.

Excavations there revealed numerous postmolds, indicating structures on the surface of these ridges (Figure 2.3b). Compacted calcitic mud surfaces were also recovered, but postholes penetrated this stratum, denoting a lack of definable floor area. This therefore indicates that a floor was prepared below an elevated structure set up on piles. Once again, the shell ridges were intentional shell constructions containing no midden material. Midden material was instead located in the adjacent canals west of the ridge. The sequential layering of shells, with their distinct postmold origins, is indicative of repeated building episodes (Figures 2.5 and 2.6a). The fact that the elevation of these ridges tapers or slopes from the interior of the site to its exterior margin suggests that they accreted in a linear fashion from the interior through time as the population at the site grew (Figure 2.6). Interestingly, postmold diameters from these excavations are identical to those for

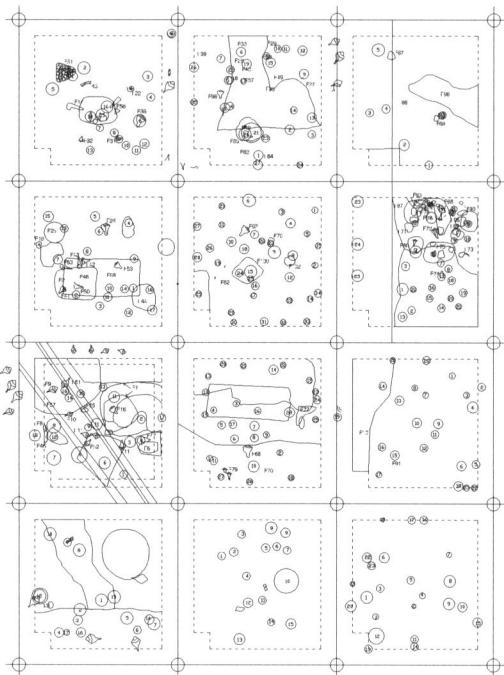

2.5. Postmolds and features at Operation 2.

2.6. (A) Photograph of postmolds in shell strata at Operation 2.
(B) Postmolds and features at Operation 3.

Operation 1, revealing that a systematic size was used for building posts (Figure 2.5).

Operation 3 focused on a low mound located at the interior edge of the shell ridge (Figure 2.3a). Once again, the excavations exposed how sequential structures were repeatedly built on the mound. They also revealed an extremely artifact-dense midden, ironically not containing any shell in its sedimentary matrix. Instead, a dark, charcoal-colored, organic-stained sand was deposited on top of the canalward slope of the shell mound. The postmold diameters here are identical to those from Operations 1 and 2 (Figure 2.6b).

Furthermore, we were also on the edge of a buried canal that paralleled a ridge somewhere west of our Operation 2 excavation. The canal, similar to Canal D adjacent to Ridge C, contained no water that was extended to the current water table, a depth of 2.3 meters, even in our deepest excavation. This deep dry canal currently without water in it suggests that if these canals contained water, it would have been during a higher sea level, perhaps the one documented for the region at around AD 450. If so, this would indicate that these features were constructed at that time.

The next step in the analysis of the site was to label the mound, ridge, and canal features on the Sawyer map and then incorporate the findings of our excavations together with the topographic features. We identified and labeled 50 mounds. We then prepared a histogram of the mound heights. These mound heights fall into three distinct spatial groups that have been described as a Ceremonial Precinct, an Elite Precinct, and a Non-Elite Precinct (Figure 2.7). There are 6 mounds in the Ceremonial Precinct, with elevations from 3.9 to 4.8 meters (13 to 16 feet); 36 mounds in the Elite Precinct having mound heights of 2.7 to 3.6 meters (9 to 12 feet); and 19 mounds in the Non-Elite Precinct with mound heights of 1.2 to 2.4 meters (4 to 8 feet). These precincts extend from the southeast area of the site to the northwest area of the site, in that order. I am suggesting that each of these mounds contained a structure on its summit. Furthermore, all of these mounds, except those in the Ceremonial Precinct, were residential house mounds (Figure 2.8).

Two distinct characteristics of the Ceremonial Precinct are the existence of a tall conical mound 4.8 meters (16 feet) in height, the tallest and only such conical mound, and the pairing of the large temple mounds, a feature observed in the ethnohistoric documents of the region. Four cisterns are located in the extreme southeast corner of the precinct and indicate the importance of fresh water to this site. Two plazas, labeled Plaza A and Plaza B, are found separating the mounds in this precinct. Another ridgelike feature on the southwest margin of the Ceremonial Precinct seems to function as a wall or barrier to this precinct since it lies directly next to a causeway that leads into the site from its southern edge (Figure 2.3b).

The Elite Precinct consists of relatively tall house mounds, ranging in height from 2.7 to 3.6 meters (9 to 12 feet), that are distributed in two arcs, one adjacent to the Ceremonial Precinct and the other adjacent to the Non-Elite Precinct. There are also two plazas located in the area, labeled Plaza C and Plaza D. The causeway into the site from the southern edge leads directly into the southwest portion of this precinct. Two mounds flank each side of this causeway and more than likely controlled access into the site.

The Non-Elite northwestern arc of the site is composed of a series of radial shell ridges and canals. There are 14 of these ridges and canals, and these have been labeled A through N, respectively, from the northeast to the southwest. These ridges were densely occupied as witnessed from the postmolds in Operation 2. I have therefore modeled 70 houses on these 14 ridges, an average of 5 per ridge (Figure 2.8). This frequency is based on the spacing between structures actually recorded in our excavation, of course projecting the housing over the entire length of the ridge. The structure size was also determined through excavation. It is suggested that the houses had a population of five individuals, a figure consistent with ethnographic studies of similar types of societies.

It is probably the case that the ridges grew out from the interior of the site as the population increased through time. This outward growth is more than likely what accounted for the lineal expansion. This would explain the increased elevation of the ridges toward the interior edge of the sites. I suggest that each of these ridges represents the residential unit associated with a lineage and that the heads of these lineages resided on the mounds that form the arc within the Elite Precinct (Figure 2.8).

By adding up the number of mounds from the Elite and Non-Elite precincts, and multiplying this number by an average household size of five, a population figure of 510 is calculated for the Key Marco site. This figure might be a little high, but a population of around 500 is not unreasonable (Table 2.1).

CONCLUSIONS

The Key Marco site was a planned community laid out from the start with three distinct regions: a Ceremonial Precinct, an Elite Precinct, and a Non-Elite residential precinct. The

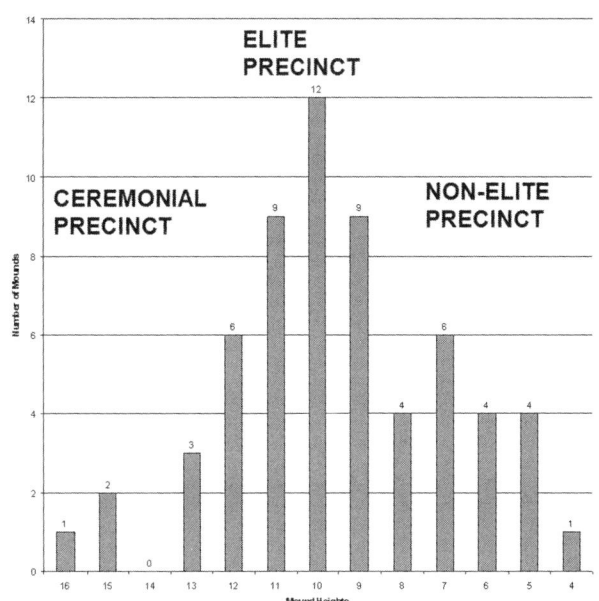

2.7. Histograms of mound heights at the Key Marco site. These fall into three spatially distinct groups.

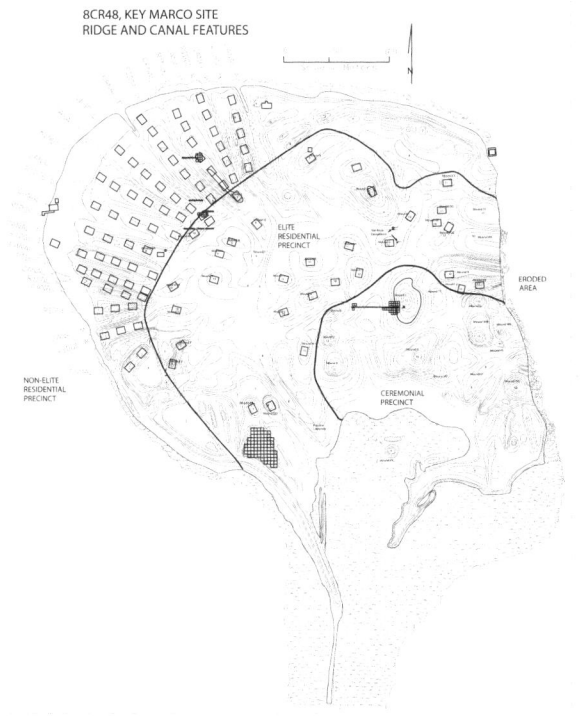

2.8. Location of distinct precincts at the Key Marco site.

Table 2.1. *Population estimates for the Key Marco site, 8CR48*

MAXIMUM NUMBER OF RESIDENCES AND POPULATION

Site Location	Ceremonial Precinct	Elite Precinct	Non-Elite Precinct	Total
Number of Residential Houses	-------------	32	70	102
Population (Based on an average of 5 per household)	------------	160	350	510

Ceremonial Precinct, located in the southeast margin of the site, is characterized by paired large temple mounds. An adjacent band of mounds to the northwest, the Elite Precinct, contained residential structures on their summits that more than likely functioned as houses for lineage heads. Northwest of these mounds, a series of 14 canals and ridges radiated out from the southeast. These ridges contained houses for non-elites living at the site, and each ridge was probably associated with a lineage. These mounds and ridges were intentional, deliberate constructions of shell and sand, and were not midden accumulation, nor did the construction utilize midden material (Klokler, chap. 11 in this volume). A population of about 500 resided at the site, and it had a continuous history of occupation from at least AD 500 to the contact period. No early 16th-century Spanish artifacts have been recovered or reported for the site.

CHAPTER THREE

RINGED SHELL FEATURES OF THE SOUTHEAST UNITED STATES

Architecture and Midden

Michael Russo

SUMMARY

Late Archaic (3000–1000 BC [5000–3000 BP]) shell rings are found along the coast from South Carolina to Mississippi, while Woodland (500 BC–AD 1000 [2500–1000 BP]) ring middens are best known along the northwest Florida coast. Though their occupations were widely separated in time (Table 3.1), because both site types—Archaic shell rings and Woodland ring middens—contain shell deposited in circular formations, their functions are typically assumed to have been the same: accretional quotidian midden accumulations of short- or long-term occupational sites. However, I suggest that the distributional characteristics of the shell (amounts and types of shell, artifact and faunal inclusions, features) in the two types of rings differ significantly. While both ring types represent middens of sorts, different consumption, social, and semiotic patterns are reflected in the depositional patterns of their discarded materials.

INTRODUCTION

Shell rings are Late Archaic circular or quasi-circular deposits of oyster shell averaging 2 meters in height and nearly 100 meters in diameter (Table 3.2). *Ring middens* are Middle Woodland deposits of organic midden soils with variable amounts and kinds of shell and other debris averaging more than 120 meters in diameter but less than 1 meter in depth (Table 3.3). Both ring types are primarily coastal phenomena (Figure 3.1), although Woodland ring middens largely lacking shell have been identified inland from the coast (Milanich et al. 1984; Pluckhahn 2003), and Archaic shell rings have been found along one freshwater river (Randall 2008). Both coastal ring site types have been interpreted as village sites with ceremonial aspects (e.g., Russo 1991, 1996, 2004; Russo, Hadden, and Dengel 2009; Russo, Schwadron, and Yates 2006; Russo et al. 2011; Thompson 2006; Trinkley 1985; cf. Middaugh 2009; cf. Saunders, chap. 4 in this volume), while others suggest

Table 3.1. Cultures and periods related to coastal shell rings and ring middens

Culture	Period	BP	AD/BC	Region
Late Archaic	Late Archaic	5000–3000	3000–1000 BC	SE US coast
Deptford	Early Woodland	2500–1800	500 BC–AD 200	NW Florida
Swift Creek	Middle Woodland	1900–1600	AD 0–400	NW Florida
Santa Rosa/Swift Creek	Middle Woodland	1850–1400	AD 150–600	NW Florida
Weeden Island	Late Woodland	1400–1000	AD 600–1000	NW Florida

Table 3.2. Archaic shell rings: shape, diameter (length), height (thickness), and primary shell species

Site No.*	Ring Name	Shape	Diameter (m)	Height (m)	Shell
9GN57	Cannon's Point	C	79	1.8	Oyster
9GN76	West	U	58	0.7	Oyster
9LI1231	St. Catherines	Circle	70	1.5	Oyster
9LI1648	McQueen	Circle	71	0.5	Oyster
9MC23	Sapelo 1	Circle	80	2.7	Oyster
9MC23	Sapelo 2	Circle	75	0.9	Oyster
9MC23	Sapelo 3	Circle	55	0.9	Oyster
9MC87	Busch Krick	C	?	2.4	Oyster
38BU7	Sea Pines	Circle	60	1.0	Oyster
38BU8	Skull Creek 1	Attached	55	2.1	Oyster
38BU8	Skull Creek 2	Attached	43	2.1	Oyster
38BU21	Guerard Point	Circle	80	0.7	Oyster
38CH7	Hankel	C	62	2.4	Oyster
38CH12	Lighthouse Pt.	Circle	76	3.0	Oyster
38CH14	Horse Island	C	61	3.0	Oyster
38CH23	Buzzards Island	Circle	80	2.0	Oyster
38CH24	Stratton Place	C	57	0.6	Oyster
38CH41	Auld	Circle	73	1.8	Oyster
38CH45	Sewee	Circle	75	3.2	Oyster
38CH60	Crow Island	Circle	70	1.0	Oyster
38CH77	Skidaway	C	77	2.3	Oyster
38BU1866	Coosaw 1	Attached	60	1.7	Oyster
38BU1866	Coosaw 2	Attached	60	1.7	Oyster
38BU1866	Coosaw 3	Circle	60	0.6	Oyster
38BU1866	Coosaw 4	Circle	60	0.5	Oyster
38BU300	Barrow	C	60	2.0	Oyster/periwinkle
38BU301	Patent	C	60	1.0	Oyster
38CH42	Fig Island 1	Attached	157	6.0	Oyster
38CH42	Fig Island 2	Circle	82	2.1	Oyster
38CH42	Fig Island 3	C	49	1.9	Oyster
38BU29	Chester Field	C	75	3.2	Oyster
8DU7510	Rollins	C/Attached	235	3.5	Oyster
8DU7478	Oxeye	Circle	160	3.0	Oyster

Site No.*	Ring Name	Shape	Diameter (m)	Height (m)	Shell
8SJ2554	Guana	U	170	1.3	Oyster/clam
8MT13	Reed	U	250	1.7	Oyster
8CR209	Horrs Island	U	160	4.5	Oyster
8LL717	Bonita Bay	U	230	1.1	Oyster
8SO2	Hill Cottage	U	140	4.2	Oyster
8OK102	Meig's Pasture	C	77	0.9	Oyster
8WL90	Buck Bayou	C?	120	1.2	Oyster
22HC30	Cedarland	C	165	4.0	Oyster
22HC35	Clairborne	C	200	2.0	Oyster
Average GA/SC			**69**	**1.8**	
Average FL/MS			**173**	**2.5**	
Average Total			**96**	**2.0**	

* Prefix numbers indicate the state: Georgia (9), South Carolina (38), Florida (8), Mississippi (22).

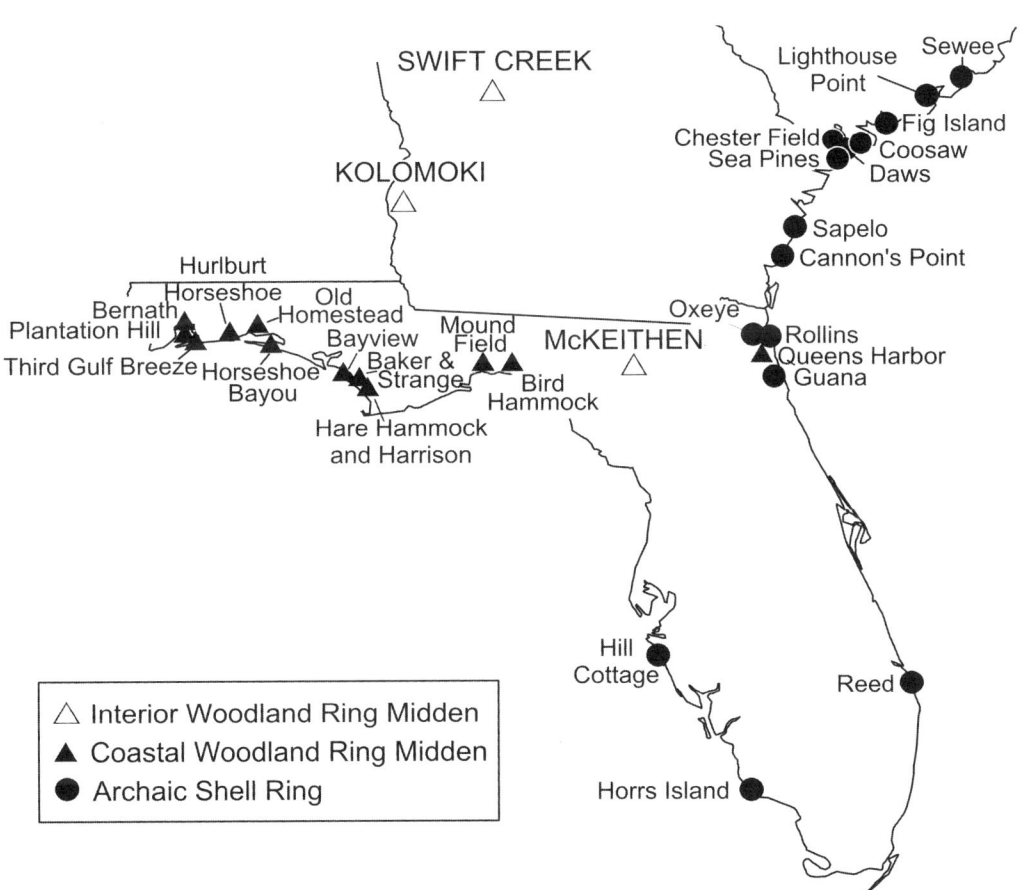

3.1. Archaic shell rings and Woodland ring middens in the southeast United States.

Table 3.3. Woodland ring middens: shape, diameter, height, and primary shell species (Russo, Schwadron, and Yates 2006)

Site No.	Ring	Shape	Diameter (m)	Height (m)	Shell
8By23	St. Andrews [c]	Quasi-circular	52	1.2	?
8By27	Laughtons [c]	Circle	?	?	?
8By29	Baker [a]	Circle	80	0.5	Oyster
8By49	Bear Point [c]	Circle	?	?	?
8By73	Callaway Fox [a, c]	"Rectangular"	120	1.2	Oyster, scallop
8By74	Imperial Oaks [a, c]	Circle	?	?	?
8By137	Bayview [c]	Circle	220	1.0	Oyster, scallop
8By1347	Hare Hammock [c]	Circle	240	1.0	Conch, whelk, scallop
8By1355	Stranges [c]	Circle	220	0.7	Oyster
8By1359	Harrison [a]	Circle	80	0.7	Conch, whelk
8Fr364	Pickalene a, [c]	C	32	?	?
8Ok380	Hurlburt [c]	Crescent	210	0.3	Oyster
8SR8	Third Gulf Breeze [a]	C	115	1.0	Oyster
8SR67	Plantation West [c]	Circle	110	0.4	Oyster
8SR986	Bernath [b]	C	75	0.3	?
8Wa8	Mound Field [c]	Circle?	135	1.0	Oyster, conch, clam
8Wa30	Bird Hammock [a, c]	C	130	1.0	Oyster, scallop, clam
8Wa52	Snow Beach [a]	C	90	0.7	?
8Wl36	Horseshoe Bayou [b]	C	135	0.8	Rangia, oyster
8Wl58	Old Homestead [b]	C	70	?	Rangia, oyster
Average WI			170	0.9	
Average SC and SR/SC			92	0.7	
Average Total			124	0.8	

[a] Swift Creek (SC)

[b] Santa Rosa/Swift Creek (SR/SC)

[c] Weeden Island (WI)

there is no material evidence for ceremony (DePratter 2010; Marquardt 2010a, 2010b; Marrinan 2010).

ARCHAIC SHELL RINGS

Rejecting antiquarian notions of rings as forts, gaming arenas, dikes, and fish traps, most archaeologists have implicitly assumed or explicitly inferred that people inhabited rings and that the circular distribution of shell arose as epiphenomena of their occupants' patterns of consumption and refuse discard (Marrinan 1975; Michie 1979; Russo 1991; Trinkley 1985). People lived in circles, and their distribution of garbage reflected their living pattern (Figure 3.2). Most who bring up the topic of houses, and not many do, hypothesize that houses were placed around the edges of the plaza next to the shell ring. As the shell

debris accumulated, the ring builders had to move their domiciles to the top or laterally away from the rising piles of shell (Figure 3.3) (Edwards 1965; Russo 1991; Thompson 2006, 273; Trinkley 1985, 1997).

Unfortunately, most rings lack evidence of house structures or have yielded evidence only below the actual shell ring, suggesting, at least to some archaeologists, that domiciliary structures were only present at the initial occupations of the site before the extensive piling of shell occurred and were abandoned as shell impinged upon them (Russo 2004; Thompson 2006; cf. Trinkley 1985). No evidence of house structures has ever been identified on ring tops or within the shell deposits constituting the rings (Russo 1991, 2004; Saunders and Russo 2002; Thompson 2006). Rather than topside living, shell is seen as having been placed behind or beside houses whose front entrances faced the plaza (Figure 3.4). Periodic lateral moves of houses around the edge of the plaza characterized habitation until mounded shell to the sides and behind the houses reached a point that available house sites on a level with the plaza became unavailable. At that point, houses either had to be moved in toward the plaza, forming a new, smaller concentric zone of habitation (Thompson 2006), or the plaza had to be raised. In the case of Horrs Island, the plaza was raised over decades and perhaps centuries, ultimately reaching two meters in thickness. Evidence for sequential plaza revitalizations is found in a series of lateral and vertical shifts of stone-lined hearths, one atop another and thousands of postmolds around the edges of the plaza. Coincident with the rising ring of shell, the plaza level kept pace by infilling with sand (Russo 1991, 1994). In these cases of vertical and lateral house movements, the question of why shell was mounded in the shape of rings is answered—because the houses had been placed in circles. The rings appear solely to have been the epiphenomena of house discard.

But are the shell rings just aggregated house middens? Some rings reach heights of three to six meters, reflecting level of maintenance efforts beyond those of mere practical discard. If shell-ring function is reflected in its constituents and depositional traits, note needs to be taken of the differences between shell ring-midden and the typical shell midden that is not placed in a ring. The type of midden found at Archaic shell rings differs from the typical quotidian "dark-earth midden" that constitutes most "sheet"

midden coastal Archaic sites consisting of organically stained dark soil with variable kinds of refuse from daily living activities (e.g., pottery, lithics, shell, shell tools, bone, charcoal, ash). In contrast to such house middens at non-shell-ring sites, all Archaic shell-ring deposits are made up primarily of oyster shell (*Crassostrea virginica*) with relatively few other faunal, artifact, or soil inclusions by volume (Russo 1991; Saunders 2004a; Saunders and Russo 2002). Reflecting the relatively depauperate nature of shell ring midden deposits, colloquially, archaeologists have referred to the large piles of oyster shells that make up the rings as *clean* shell (Figure 3.5).

Many archaeologists working on Archaic rings recognize that these differences may reflect at least the possibility of a site's use in feasting ceremonies (Russo 2004; Sanger and Thomas 2010; Saunders 2004a; Saunders, chap. 4 in this volume; Thompson and Andrus 2011). While all researchers agree that the piling of shell in the ring had the practical advantage of getting rid of refuse, the piling of shell in great amounts and in iconic circular shapes of variable and sometimes prodigious heights is seen by some as having been motivated by primarily social rather than practical imperatives.

WOODLAND RING MIDDENS

Woodland ring middens differ from Archaic shell rings in constituents and traits that more cleanly fit archaeologists'

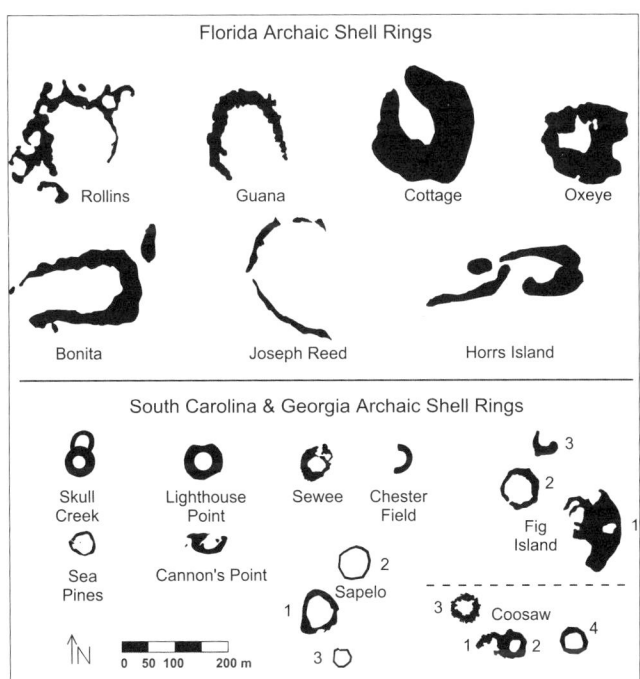

3.2. *(left) Archaic shell-ring footprints based on sketched or mapped topography and/or shell distribution.*

3.3. *(above) Archaic shell ring resulting from gradual garbage accumulation in the domiciliary zone (after Thompson 2006, 273; Trinkley 1997). Note the frequent movement of houses upward and laterally to accommodate rising midden (illustration, Gary Whitely).*

3.4. *Archaic shell ring as a circular village with trash thrown behind houses (illustration, Gary Whitely).*

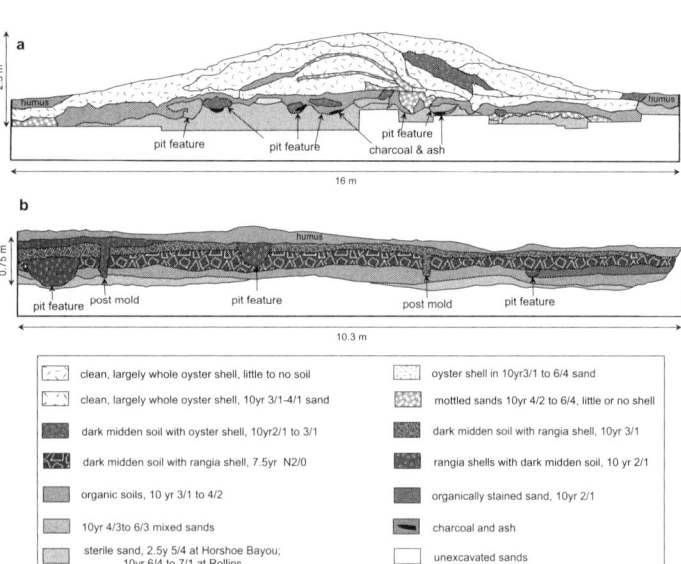

clean, largely whole oyster shell, little to no soil		oyster shell in 10yr3/1 to 6/4 sand	
clean, largely whole oyster shell, 10yr 3/1-4/1 sand		mottled sands 10yr 4/2 to 6/4, little or no shell	
dark midden soil with oyster shell, 10yr2/1 to 3/1		dark midden soil with rangia shell, 10yr 3/1	
dark midden soil with rangia shell, 7.5yr N2/0		rangia shells with dark midden soil, 10 yr 2/1	
organic soils, 10 yr 3/1 to 4/2		organically stained sand, 10yr 2/1	
10yr 4/3to 6/3 mixed sands		charcoal and ash	
sterile sand, 2.5y 5/4 at Horshoe Bayou; 10yr 6/4 to 7/1 at Rollins		unexcavated sands	

3.5. *(a) Late Archaic depositional sequence showing predominant oyster-shell deposits (Rollins shell ring, Trench 1, south profile [Russo and Heide 2003, 37; Saunders 2004a, 254]). (b) Santa Rosa/Swift Creek depositional sequence showing predominant dark-earth midden with shell (Horseshoe Bayou ring midden, Trench 2, north profile [Meyer, Thomas, and Dicks 2001, 31]).*

de facto conceptions of coastal habitation refuse—organic soils with variable amounts of shell inclusions and mundane artifacts (e.g., Bense 1969; Doran and Piatek 1985; Marquardt 2010a; Moore 1902, 1918; Penton 1970; Russo, Hadden, and Dengel 2009; Russo, Schwadron, and Yates 2006; Russo et al. 2011; Stephenson, Bense, and Snow 2002; Thomas et al. 1996; Willey 1949a). The darkened soils of coastal ring middens are presumed to have derived from large amounts of organics (e.g., charcoal, other vegetal matter, degraded bone and shell, vermin, and feces) and also contain pottery, lithics, and shell tools, in addition to the well-preserved bone and shell food remains. Features such as pits, hearths, and posts may be found within or below these ring middens. The accumulation of this kind of midden and its features are typically seen as resulting gradually from daily maintenance activities.

In northwest coastal Florida, the successive Swift Creek and Weeden Island cultures constructed ring middens often at the same or nearby sites. These cultures are distinguished primarily by different pottery series. The complicated stamped wares of the early Swift Creek were ultimately replaced by incised Weeden Island wares. New data suggests that these two cultures may also be distinguished by their ring-midden size, with Weeden Island almost twice the size of Swift Creek ring diameters, supporting the long-held belief based on more numerous sites that Weeden Island populations were larger (see Table 3.3; Figure 3.6).

George W. Percy and David S. Brose (1974) posited the idea that Woodland ring-midden sites were villages, each serving a small number of nuclear families, and that each village site was associated with an adjacent lineage burial mound. The exact size, shape, and contents of the ring sites were not described, nor were specific ring sites identified. At the time, in fact, only one ring, the Swift Creek/Weeden Island–period Bird Hammock, had been extensively reported (Bense 1969; Penton 1970). As more Woodland ring middens were subsequently identified west of the Apalachicola River, the model was extended to cover the entire Florida Panhandle coast (Milanich 1994). Seven Swift Creek–era (called Santa Rosa–Swift Creek in the western Panhandle) and three Weeden Island ring middens were excavated or mapped in the intervening years (Bense 1998; Russo, Hadden, and Dengel 2009; Russo, Schwadron, and Yates 2006, 68–69; Russo et al. 2011; Stephenson, Bense, and Snow 2002, 319, 334; Thomas and Campbell 1993).

The shell in these ring-midden deposits differs from that in Archaic shell rings in a number of ways. The primary shell in the Woodland ring-midden deposits can consist of

3.6. Coastal Woodland ring-midden footprints and mound orientations. Note that some shapes are based on the extent of pottery or midden below surface, some on surface midden, and others on topography.

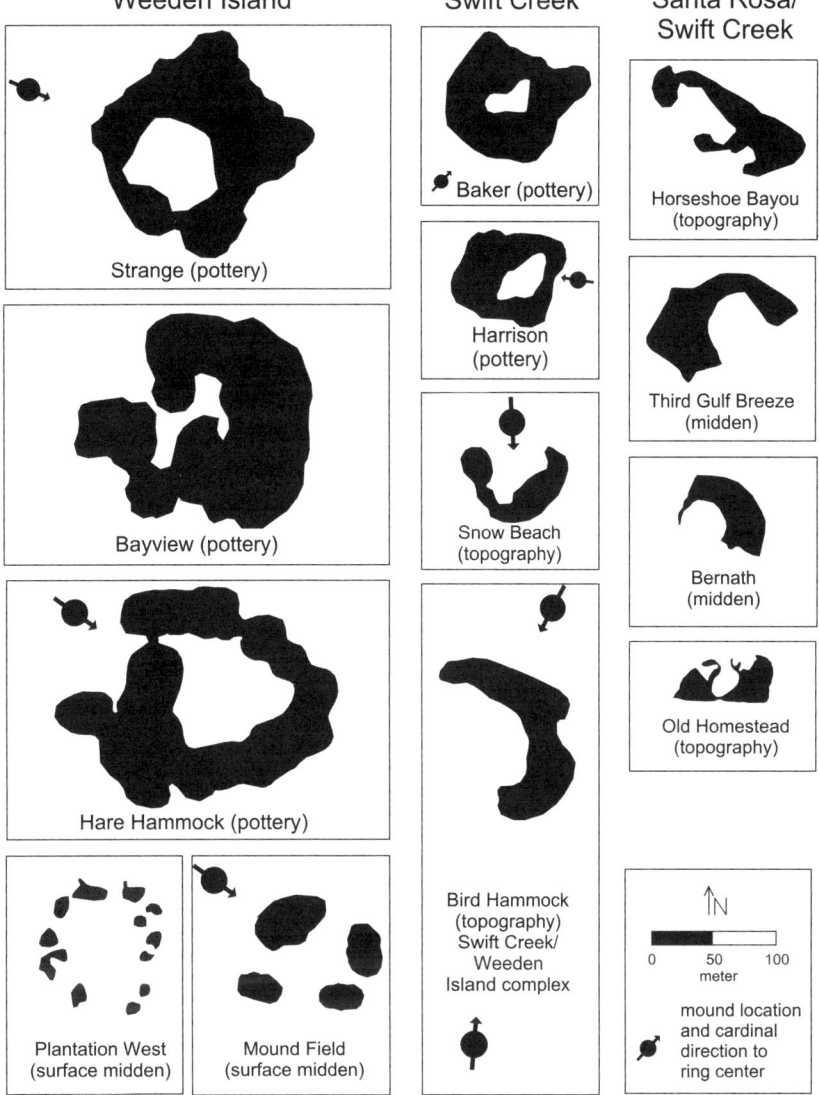

Weeden Island

Strange (pottery)

Bayview (pottery)

Hare Hammock (pottery)

Plantation West (surface midden)

Mound Field (surface midden)

Swift Creek

Baker (pottery)

Harrison (pottery)

Snow Beach (topography)

Bird Hammock (topography) Swift Creek/ Weeden Island complex

Santa Rosa/ Swift Creek

Horseshoe Bayou (topography)

Third Gulf Breeze (midden)

Bernath (midden)

Old Homestead (topography)

↑N

0   50   100
        meter

mound location and cardinal direction to ring center

multiple species, not necessarily oyster, and the rings are topographically lower to the point they may not be mounded at all (see Table 3.3) (Bense 1994; Russo, Hadden, and Dengel 2009; Russo et al. 2011). For example, at the Bernath site, a Santa Rosa–Swift Creek ring midden, no elevated midden or mounded shell was identified. The primary evidence for the presence of ring midden was "a sandy soil" that had been stained dark from organic matter. Shell was present in particular areas, but the archaeologist emphasized that the ring was not, strictly speaking, a shell midden (Bense 1994, 264). At Hare Hammock, the greater part of the circle of midden that constituted the ring contained little or no shell (Russo, Hadden, and Dengel 2009).

The fact that Woodland ring middens are viewed as having been made through the gradual accumulations of habitation debris might seem to exclude any ceremonial functions for the rings. But the unusual Bernath site suggests otherwise. An extensive cemetery in its plaza suggests that it was a place of ritual and ceremony where "public social, religious, and political events" were staged (Bense 1994, 6–7). At Old Homestead, another Santa Rosa–Swift Creek ring midden, unusual Basin Bayou wares and cooking features found along the plaza/ring interface suggested intensive food preparation in the plaza for ceremonial purposes (Thomas and Campbell 1996, 149–50). It has been hypothesized that these special wares and those at the Plantation West Weeden Island ring (Doran and Piatek

1985, 90, 97, 121) indicated that the rings may have functioned as residences for leaders or shamans who led ceremonial activities in relation to nearby burial mounds. At the Harrison Ring and Mound complex (Russo, Hadden, and Dengel 2009), new unpublished data has revealed that the ring midden and plaza are abundant with debitage and discarded materials (e.g., ocher, crystal quartz, exotic ground and carved stones) more commonly associated with the mortuary contexts of nearby mounds.

Because there are so few investigations of either Swift Creek or Weeden Island coastal ring-midden plazas, our understanding of ring and plaza functions has been hindered. We do not know the extent of either the ceremonial or the mundane practices that may have taken place. Most of the larger studies have focused on establishing cultural chronologies, quantifying relative subsistence contributions, and interpreting environmental changes (e.g., Thomas and Campbell 1993, 561–69). But by contrasting the dark-earth Woodland ring middens and their varied artifact and soil inclusions with the most often heterogeneous Archaic shell rings can provide insight into the varied social practices that characterize each distinct ring-site type.

CLEAN SHELL AND FEASTING

Clean Shell

Evidence of feasting and, by extension, ceremony is found at Archaic shell rings in the large individual piles of oyster shell that make up the rings (Russo 2004). In the context of rings and other shell sites, shell piles lacking little else by volume other than largely undamaged shell have been referred to as *unconsolidated, whole, unbroken, loose,* or *clean* (e.g., Bullen and Bullen 1956; Edwards 1965; Russo 2004, 43; Walker 1992, 281). These related terms are informal but widely understood in the southeast United States. The various terms, each with its own nuance, recognize that the shell may represent deposits that were relatively undisturbed before or after they were laid down. The term *whole* reflects observations on the size and condition of the shell specimens. *Unbroken* further implies an absence of pre- and post-depositional effects (e.g., no trampling). *Loose,* on the other hand, suggests not only an absence of trampling, but a lack of soil that might bind the shell specimens together. However, shell may also be considered *loose* even when soil is present if the soil consists of large particle sizes (e.g., sandy-skeletal) with few fines or organics to bind the matrix. *Unconsolidated,* a term borrowed from geology, affirms the absence of a binding medium as well as an absence of compaction, while connoting great

porosity (that is, voids between shells). These concepts are rarely defined in great detail or with precision by the archaeologists using them, but they have been and can be generally subsumed, under *clean* shell, a term with its own particular connotations of white or light color of the shell, a condition often juxtaposed against darkly stained shell resulting from burial within organic soil matrices (e.g., Aten 1999, 140; Bullen and Bullen 1956, 8; Sassaman 2003, 88–90; Saunders, chap. 4 in this volume).

Archaeologists have noted that the synonymic but subtly distinct use of these terms can make comparative analyses problematic (Russo 2004; Russo and Heide 2003, 42, 43, 47; see also Marquardt 2010a, 555; Thompson and Andrus 2011, 343). On one extreme, essentialists suggests that *clean* shell should simply not refer to shell containing *any* other debris, soil, or artifacts (Marquardt 2010a, 554, 557). The point is well taken since no shell midden is known to lack any and all inclusions—all shell is "unclean" to some extent. But adherence to such a strict definition would leave archaeologists wanting a similarly useful term to differentiate among the various conditions and constituents of shell middens and the natural and cultural processes behind their making. Contextualizing the term might be the better strategy. For example, for the upper, mounded clean-shell deposits at Archaic shell rings, I have attempted to deconstruct the meaning behind the informal use of the word *clean*:

> These massive, unconsolidated strata of shell are typically identified as "clean" or "loose," having little to moderate amounts of soil, but always containing mostly shell with oyster usually dominating (i.e., low equitability and diversity) and with little to no evidence of hearths, pits, crushing, or other human activities aside from garbage disposal (e.g., Russo 1991; Saunders 2002b; Waring and Larson 1968). They variably contain charcoal, artifacts, and other faunal remains, but not in the relative abundances of other midden deposits in the ring. [Russo 2004, 43]

Of course, deposits of clean shell can result from many cultural practices and natural processes, including shell processing at collection sites, daily discard in refuse areas restricted to shell, storage for future use in tool manufacture or construction, burial in oblation or tribute, or disposal in heterogeneous middens where biodegradation leaves behind only the most durable of refuse: shell (Marquardt 2010a, 555; Russo 1991, 147, 269, 408; 2002, 91; 2004, 44; Russo, Hadden, and Dengel 2009, 92, 106; Torrence

1996). The reason that shell deposits may persist as or develop into clean shell must always be inferred by the archaeologist. One must necessarily obtain measures of inclusions, organic soils, or the relative abundances of soils, and distributional patterning to establish a foundation for inference. In the absence of evidence for differential biodegradation of all but shell in clean-shell deposits, inferences explaining clean shell are most readily directed to social practices behind their discard. By definition, all shell middens are cultural constructions.

One obvious social practice at Archaic shell rings included the community's placement of large piles of mostly oyster shell around a central public plaza. I have suggested that the "clean" aspect of the shell deposits resulted from the rapid deposition of large amounts of oyster shell. "If shell is deposited quickly, as opposed to the gradual accumulation of daily meals discarded underfoot, relatively less evidence should be found of crushing, windborne sand, surface fires, artifacts, fauna drawn to exposed shell (e.g., land snails), and other subaerial indicators of human and natural activity" (Russo 2004, 43). This commonsense concept of rapid shell deposit is widely recognized and is often differentiated from the gradual, daily accumulations of household or kitchen midden that can result in an assemblage consisting of greater amounts of artifacts, broken debris, organic debris, and "organic midden soils" (e.g., Bullen and Bullen 1956, 8; Marquardt 2010a, 555; Russo and Heide 2003, 41–42; Thompson and Andrus 2011, 319; Walker 1992, 281). The greater variety of material inclusions in the gradual midden results from the extended time and the multiple activities involved in its accumulation. For example, whereas a meter of shell discarded in a single spot may have resulted in a single day from a large-scale feast, a meter of shell in a gradually accumulated kitchen midden may have taken decades or centuries to accumulate. Given time constraints alone, the number and variety of activities and materials reflected in a rapid one-day deposit are potentially less than those in a series of gradually accumulated deposits extending over centuries. Understanding the concepts and manifestations associated with rapid versus gradual shell midden accumulation is critical to understanding the processes behind the formation of both Archaic shell rings and Woodland ring middens as well as shell middens in general.

Feasting

Feasting is a multifunctional event that serves to provide and redistribute food and, at the same time, to establish and reinforce social relations through ritual and ceremonial practices. Archaeologically, feasting can be seen as the extraquotidian preparation, display, consumption, and discard of food. Socially, feasts can reify kin, societal, and political relations. Social goals behind feasts may include the gain and maintenance of position, prestige, and political capital. *Solidarity feasts*, particularly those among egalitarian groups, may or may not have promotional aspects to them (Hayden 2001), but, if structurally allowed, individuals can vie for power and prestige through feasts (Russo 1991, 2004). That is, feasts can provide opportunities for gaining social status even among societies that may be otherwise egalitarian outside ceremonial contexts. Under the social and ritual aegis of feasts or other ceremony, hosts may have the opportunity to gain and/or maintain prestige or power that intentionally results in a material record on the landscape of that gained prestige. Feasting houses, display structures, public exhibits of great quantities of food, and even the plazas themselves are examples of such ceremonial structures (Heckenberger 2005; Malinowski 1929; Russo 2004; Saunders 2003; Thompson and Andrus 2011). If persistent, these material and landscape architectures may serve to instill corporate memory of the ceremony or its participants and, in the process, be signified or perceived as monuments.

Ethnographically, village plazas can serve as the location of daily meals as well as periodic public feasts (e.g., Chagnon 1992; Malinowski 1929). That is, plazas may be situationally mediated between sacred and mundane activities. As such, refuse from feast foods and the sumptuary meals of daily life may be lost underfoot or intentionally discarded at the same locations, which, in the case of ring villages, most agree, is the ring of midden that encircles the plaza. This intermixing of two types of social food consumption in the same activity and discard areas can make the discernment between feasting and quotidian food refuse difficult for the archaeologists, particularly if the same food types are used in both daily and ritual consumption. Under these constraints, in the absence of distinctive ritual pottery or other artifacts associated with the refuse, it is the context and quantities of food that hold a potential for separating feasting from quotidian food remains (Hayden 2001, 50; Russo 2004; Thompson and Andrus 2011).

COMPARING ARCHAIC AND WOODLAND RING SITES

Organic Midden Soils and Clean-shell Midden

Both Archaic and Woodland rings have organically stained midden soils with variable amounts of shell in lenses, pits, and scatters. At Woodland rings, these midden soils and features hold most of the site's shell deposits. At Archaic rings, these kinds of midden deposits are typically found only in the lowest levels (see Figure 3.5a), with piled clean shell making up most of the volume above them. While both ring types may contain posts and hearths within or below their dark-earth midden levels, in Archaic rings these features have not yet been found in the overlapping piles of clean shell that constitute the major volume of the rings (see Figure 3.5a) (Calmes 1968, fig. 3.2; Russo 1991, 271; Russo and Heide 2003, 41–43; Saunders 2002b, 106, 110; 2003; Saunders and Russo 2002).

At some Archaic rings, thin layers of dark earth and shell are found within the clean-shell deposits and overlying the clean-shell piles on top of today's surface of the rings. These are typically interpreted as humus/shell zones denoting long-term exposure to natural processes of wind-borne sedimentation and biological decomposition on top of the ring after site abandonment (Russo 1991, 110; Russo and Heide 2003, 10–12; Saunders 2002b, 106; Waring and Larson 1968, 272). Because these humic layers may resemble the color and organic content of midden soils, some have suggested that humic surfaces were living surfaces. But the steep grades of some of these deposits suggest pedogenic rather than anthropogenic processes (Calmes 1968; Russo 1991, 110; 2004; Waring and Larson 1968).

Although abundant with shell, most Woodland ring middens generally lack the large pilings of clean shell that give Archaic shell rings their height and conspicuous forms. For example, the Bird Hammock ring midden is made mostly of "dark midden," not shell (Nanfro 2004, 26; see also Bense 1969, 19). The Plantation Hill West ring-midden deposits consist of "highly organic midden soils, shell, and ceramics" with no apparent mounds of clean shell above the surrounding landscape (Doran and Piatek 1985, 38, 121). The ring midden at Mound Field yielded scattered shells or small lenses of shell intermixed with mostly organic soils (Willey 1949a, 60). A few areas of the Bayview and Hare Hammock ring middens yielded dense amounts of shell, but always in dark organic midden soils (Russo, Hadden, and Dengel 2009; Russo, Schwadron, and Yates 2006). Judith A. Bense (1998, 264–67) described the Bernath ring as totally lacking shell except in refuse pits. In short, coastal Woodland ring middens usually contain only "lenses and areas of more and less shell" (Bense and Watson 1977, 22; see also Doran and Piatek 1985, 25–46).

The shell contents of the Woodland ring middens correlate to their proximity to different environments and may change through time as the environments change (Russo, Hadden, and Dengel 2009; Russo et al. 2011;

Thomas and Campbell 1993, 564–69). Typically the variably predominant shell species in Woodland-period rings included oyster, whelk (*Busycon* sp.), scallop (*Argopectin irradians*), conch (e.g., *Strombus alatus*), and/or rangia clam (*Rangia cuneata*). The relative abundances of these shellfish in ring middens have been cited as having been affected by changing sea levels and a site's proximity to changes in bay/ocean environments (Thomas et al. 1993, 2001). In contrast, coastal Archaic shell rings are always and only dominated by oyster shell deposits. Rather than switching species, Archaic shell-ring builders may have simply abandoned the rings under changing environmental conditions that resulted in a reduction in local oyster populations (Russo 2010; Thomas 2010).

I conclude from these observations that, in addition to the artifacts unique to each period, the primary *material* differences between Archaic shell rings and Woodland ring middens lie in the amounts of shell relative to soil and other debris. Among the 42 known Archaic shell rings that have been examined internally, the tallest deposits consist mostly of clean, relatively unbroken oyster shell that range in height/depth from one to six meters, averaging over two meters (Table 3.2). Among the Woodland ring middens with sufficient internal structural data for assessment, the thickest shell deposits consist of a variety of species and range from 30 to 120 centimeters, averaging 80 centimeters deep in dark organic soil matrices (Table 3.3).

Ring Heights

The hypertrophic mounding of shell up to six meters high at Archaic rings results in distinctive and easily observed circular and quasi-circular shapes. Without the aid of excavation or mapping, 19th-century antiquarians easily identified the shapes of these rings of shell along the coasts of South Carolina and Georgia and recognized them as features uniquely distinct from the thousands of other earth and shell mounds that covered the eastern United States (e.g., Drayton 1802; McKinley 1873; Moore 1897). Identification of the larger Archaic shell rings in Florida, however, had to wait until the late 20th century, due in part to their enshrouding in heavy vegetation that blocked the observation of the rings' shapes within a single view, as well as, in some cases, the partial burial beneath mangrove and marsh sediments (Beriault et al. 2003; Kennedy 1980; Russo 1991; Russo and Heide 2002; Russo and Saunders 1999; Saunders and Russo 2002). The greater height of Archaic rings resulted from repeated, sequential collocation of shell piles around a central open area or plaza. As the ring increased in height, easy, direct access to the outside of the ring was inhibited at some point by the ring wall, as more shell piles were placed to close the gaps between individual piles. This pattern of placement was undoubtedly intentional and had the effect of physically and visually isolating the central plaza from the outside world.

In contrast, easily recognizable, closed-circle, topographically prominent rings are rarer among Woodland sites, in part, perhaps, because middens accumulated more gradually, not as intentionally mounded depositions. This low topographic relief allowed continued pedestrian access to the plaza by their ring-midden builders, more trampling, and greater compaction and breakage than found in the mounded Archaic shell rings (cf. Stephenson, Bense, and Snow 2002, 342). For example, Daniel Penton (1970, 27) described the Swift Creek/Weeden Island Bird Hammock ring as a midden accumulation that "crudely resembled a midden 'ring.'" A half-century earlier, Clarence B. Moore (1918, 564) described the same site, presumably in a better state of repair, as "humps, rises, and low ridges between two mounds." At Plantation Hill West, the configuration of the Weeden Island ring midden was indiscernible in walkover surveys (Piatek 1981; Prokopetz 1975; Tesar 1973). Its ring shape was finally recognized only when the distribution of unmounded surface shell deposits was mapped (Doran and Piatek 1985). Similarly, neither the Old Homestead nor the Hurlburt Horseshoe sites were initially recognized as ring shaped, largely because of the low topography in parts of their middens (Thomas 1983, 68; 1985, 16, sec. 3). Ultimately, subsurface and more systematic investigations permitted the identification of the ring-shaped midden distribution (Thomas and Campbell 1993; Thomas et al. 1996). At both the Bayview and Hare Hammock sites, antiquarians and archaeologists failed to perceive ring structures (Geo-Marine 2006; Knudson 1979; Moore 1902, 1918; Thomas and Campbell 1985, 208, 221) until systematic surveys finally revealed circular distribution, not of elevated midden or shell, but of ceramics within the middens, parts of which contained little or no shell (Russo and Lawson 2007; Russo, Schwadron, and Yates 2006).

Ring Expanses and Shapes

Both Archaic shell rings and Woodland ring middens range between 70 and 250 meters across. But patterns in sizes and shapes can be seen among various cultures. Swift Creek ring middens are generally smaller than the later Weeden Island rings, and South Carolina and Georgia shell rings are smaller than Florida rings (see Figure 3.2 and Tables 3.1 and 3.3). In addition, while both Archaic and Woodland ring types are typically closed circles or C-shapes, one form apparently unique to the Florida Archaic shell rings is U-shape. (cf. Milanich et al. 1984; Pluckhahn 2003 for non-shell-bearing inland Woodland U-shaped middens). Moreover, Archaic shell-ring complexes consist of penecontemporaneous multiple rings that may or may not be attached to one another, traits unknown to Woodland ring sites (Calmes 1968; Heide and Russo 2003; Russo, Cordell, and Ruhl 1993; Saunders 2003; cf. Russo, Hadden, and Dengel 2009 for a rare multi-ring/multi-mound Woodland complex, albeit of two temporally and culturally distinct occupations). There may be many possible reasons for multiple ring sites, including village fissioning, renewal, and political and social restructuring as well as multiple quotidian and ceremonial uses for each separate ring (e.g., Heckenberger 2005; Russo 2004).

Plazas

The relatively shell-free, level areas that ring middens and shell rings circumscribe have been interpreted as plazas by most archaeologists, who have commonly suggested that plazas at both ring types were intentionally kept free of refuse to facilitate public activities and rituals, such as dancing, games, and feasting, and that the resultant cleaning efforts ended up as midden contributions in the surrounding ring (Bense 1992, 1998; Russo 2004; Stephenson, Bense, and Snow 2002, 344; Thompson 2006, 193; Trinkley 1985; cf. Marquardt 2010a). Certainly in contrast to the surrounding ring of shell-bearing midden, there is relatively little debris in the typical plaza. However, as evidenced by features and artifacts, many ring sites have revealed that a variety of activities occurred in the public forum of the plaza.

At the Archaic Stratton Place, posts and pit features suggesting cooking activities were found along the edge of the plaza near the shell ring. Only highly fragmented pottery was found in the center, suggesting that if the plaza was not routinely kept free of debris, then, perhaps, it was only periodically used for relatively debris-free activities (Trinkley 1985, 116–17). At the Archaic Horrs Island ring that was occupied by people who did not use pottery, similar pit and post features were found along with stone-lined hearths around the edges of the plaza with only thinly scattered bones of small fish being recovered from an otherwise featureless sandy matrix generally lacking artifacts (Russo 1991). Within the plaza at Sapelo, dark midden soils with crushed shell and lithic flakes suggested that living activities included cooking and flint-knapping within the plaza (Thompson 2005, 193, 218). At the St. Catherines shell ring, large postmolds suggestive of structures were found both around the outside edge and in the center of the circular plaza, with a five-meter-wide featureless zone between the two areas of posts (Sanger and Thomas 2010, 58–60).

Fewer studies have been undertaken of the coastal Woodland ring-midden plazas. Of the ring midden sites that have only been systematically shovel tested, plazas have yielded relatively little pottery or other artifacts (e.g., Doran and Piatek 1985; Russo, Hadden, and Dengel 2009; Russo, Schwadron, and Yates 2006; Russo et al. 2011). These absences help distinguish the plazas from the ring middens, but provide little insight into the plaza activities. Large block excavations within plazas, until recently, have only been conducted at three Woodland ring middens. At Old Homestead, postmolds, dark midden soils, and abundant pottery indicated habitation along the outside perimeter of the plaza next to the ring (Thomas et al. 1996, 149–51), while at the Horseshoe Bayou ring, post and pit features in the ring midden itself implied habitation (Thomas, Campbell, and Cannon 2001). At Bernath, 17 human burials (one extended, the others flexed or bundled) were identified within the plaza. A hearth and multiple refuse pits were also identified in the plaza (Bense 1998, 263–69). Excavations as yet unpublished from the Swift Creek–period Harrison Ring, revealed pit features and posts around the outside edge of the plaza, with pits also found in the central plaza area.

Together, these data from both Archaic shell rings and Woodland ring middens suggest the multiple-uses of plazas at both ring types. But plazas are rarely if ever used for the large-scale quotidian refuse disposal that characterize the surrounding shell-bearing rings.

Artifacts

Most artifacts from Archaic shell rings and Woodland ring middens consist of utilitarian shell and bone tools, chipped and ground lithics, lithic debitage, and pottery. Some Archaic rings lack pottery because they were occupied before pottery was adopted in the region. But pottery is abundant or present at 40 of the 46 recorded Archaic shell rings (Russo 2006, 36) and at all known Woodland ring middens. At two noncoastal Weeden Island ring-midden sites that consist of multiple earthen mounds connected with middens surrounding central plazas, the concept of *elite* or *prestige* pottery (higher quality or specially designed pottery) has been forwarded as being restricted to burial mounds and high-status positions along the ring middens (Kohler 1978; Milanich et al. 1984). As the names

imply, elite or prestige potteries reflect inferred social status to their owners or users. The application of the elite/prestige pottery concept, however, while applied to coastal Woodland mounds, has been less often used to analyze ring middens along the coast. At the coastal Homestead Ring, elite status has been assigned to the Basin Bayou pottery found within the ring, suggesting that special ceremonies and people occupied the ring (Thomas et al. 1996). At the Weeden Island Hare Hammock ring, a predominance of elite pottery was found on the northern side of the ring with utilitarian wares dominating the southern side (Russo et al. 2009), while at the Weeden Island Strange's Ring a few miles away elite pottery was concentrated on the eastern side of the ring (Russo et al. 2011).

Among Archaic shell rings, such socially imbued wares have not been hypothesized, in part because Archaic cultures in the regions are typically seen as strictly egalitarian. As such, *elite* or *prestige* wares, by definition, cannot exist. However, recently archaeologists have challenged this concept, suggesting that under the context of ceremony and ritual, prestige wares can be found even among egalitarian societies (Russo 2004). At the Archaic Rollins, Guana, and Coosaw shell rings, greater percentages of decorated wares are found than are found in other non-ring contemporary domestic sites, suggesting the rings' ceremonial aspects or otherwise special use (Saunders 2004; Saunders, chap. 4 of this volume).

Shell tools appear to be most common during the Archaic in Florida, particularly in south Florida where they are found at 80 percent of the rings (Russo 1991, 2006, 41). Among Woodland rings, shell tools are rarer, in part because rings are farther north and are nearer to lithic quarry sources, and in part because trade networks were more robust during the Woodland, thus diminishing the need for shell tools (see below). In total, only 21 of 46 Archaic rings have been reported to yield shell tools, while Woodland ring middens have rarely been noted to yield abundant, if any formal tools (e.g., Russo, Hadden, and Dengel. 2009; cf. Russo 2006). It is possible that the relative rarity of shell tools may, in part, be due to archaeologists' failure to recognize tools made from shell, especially nonce tools with no formal shapes apparent. Early archaeologists also discarded most shells because they were too abundant and too bulky to collect, thus confounding our assessment of relative use of shell tools at ring sites. Lithic debitage and ground stone objects are limited and relatively rare at both ring types, but only in relation to other artifacts such as pottery (Russo 2006, 38). Lithics of any sort have only been recovered from 13 of 46 Archaic rings (Russo 2006, 38). At

Woodland rings, neither ground nor chipped stone artifacts are as abundant as pottery, but lithic tools and debitage are far more common than at Archaic rings. This relative abundance may be due to the established trade patterns between coastal Woodland populations and noncoastal groups who could provide the coastal settlements with raw lithic resources not found on the coasts. Ground stone tools, chipped lithics, and various mineral resources have been identified at most Woodland ring middens, and, in fact are among the most common objects used to identify coastal rings as special-use sites, not just refuse sites.

Bone tools are frequently found at Archaic sites. Recovered from 26 of the 46 shell rings, bone points or awls are the most common carved tools. In contrast, only two Woodland rings have yielded bone tools of any kind. Of these, only the Old Homestead ring midden, the most extensively excavated of all coastal Woodland ring middens, has produced a substantial number of bone points (Mikell 1996, 119–31). This finding suggests that bone points may have been commonly used at Woodland ring middens, but more extensive excavations may be needed to recover them, a fact that may hold for all types of artifacts described here as rare.

Exotic artifacts hundreds of miles from their sources have been recovered from both Archaic and Woodland rings. Exotic stones at Archaic shell rings include fragments of soft soapstone from carved vessels and bannerstones. Other relatively rare artifacts include greenstone, quartz, and ochre. At Woodland rings, these exotics as well as others including mica have long been linked to ritual burial contexts of funerary mounds, but rarely to the ring middens that have been placed next to them. As noted above, this is, in part, likely due to the relative rarity of ring midden excavation. More recently, rare minerals, stones, and common funerary objects have been found to frequently occur in various ring midden contexts, including pits, living floors, and middens. Some ring middens, in fact, seem to contain more of these rare objects, albeit most often fragmentary, than the associated burial mounds commonly supposed to have been their exclusive domain (Russo, Dengel, and Shanks 2013).

CONSUMPTION AND CEREMONY AT RING SITES

Quantified data on shell rings and ring middens is spotty, sometimes lacking even nominal descriptions of size and shape of the ring features. While some rings have yielded large amounts of pottery or other artifacts, others with precise measures of topography and shell distribution have not yet been investigated with the goals of recovering comparative assemblages of artifacts, identifying features, or revealing activity contexts. The following analysis is necessarily generalized with respect to the varied characteristics found at each type of ring. The interpretations I present are inferences drawn from the factual data described above through bridging arguments made with ethnographic analogy, spatial theory of circular social formations, and feasting theory (Grøn 1991; Hayden 2001; Russo 2004).

Shell Rings as Habitation and Ceremonial Sites

Both Archaic and Woodland coastal peoples used shell to make tools and ornaments, and to trade for interior goods such as minerals and stone. But, most conspicuously, shellfish was the source of daily food, feasting food, and ritual offerings. Shell resulting from these uses ended up in middens of varied forms, including pits, anthropomorphous sheets, mounds, and circularly-shaped sheet and mounded midden deposits. Within these forms, it is not always easy to ascertain from which activities shell and other constituents were derived. Distinguishing between quotidian and more specialized uses of shell is largely an empirical task dependent on observations and interpretations of archaeological contexts.

At Archaic shell rings, the large, rapidly deposited shell piles arranged in their various semicircular patterns are observable units of construction that suggest activities and purposes far different from those found at contemporary non-ring midden sites. At no other kind of Archaic site is midden of any type amassed in such quantities and heights into uniquely iconic geometric forms. Unlike other Late Archaic shell-bearing sites such as temporary camps where shell may have been lost or tossed underfoot, or shellfish processing stations where flesh was removed for transport to consumption sites and shell left behind, shellfish processing, consumption, and discard at ring sites was performed around the ring plaza, the center of community interaction. The plaza was the public forum open to the daily observation of inhabitants and, periodically during intergroup ceremonies, to observation and participation by guests. At Archaic shell rings, community members continually kept the plaza surface free of shell while building the midden higher, all the while maintaining its ring shape. The ring followed a prescribed architectural plan that was adhered to as episodic deposition continued over generations, decades, and, in some cases, centuries.

Ethnographically, in segmentary and band societies, social consumption of food in ritualized venues outside the daily norm of household consumption is one definition of feasting (Hayden 2001, 28). If that food is somehow special, for instance, if it is extranutritional, rare, or consumed only in specific locales, the chances increase that it may be identified by archaeologists as ritual or feasting remains (Hayden 2001). In the southeast United States, in fact, feasting sites have been typically interpreted by the unusual character of midden remains (e.g., a high proportion of bone from nutritionally valued parts of a deer) and/or their socially signified locale (e.g., on top of a flat-topped mound) (Knight 2001; Van Derwarker 1999; Widmer 2002, 391). Such elite feasts are common to hierarchically organized societies that practice unequal access to food. However, feasts geared toward a special few and based on relatively rare foods may not be sustainable for a mass community of hunter-gatherers—by their very definition, if foods or food cuts are rare, they are likely insufficiently accessible to everyone in a community.

Among egalitarian hunter-gatherer communities, of which the Archaic ring builders are typically classified, larger feasts involved a greater percentage of, if not the entire, community membership (Russo 2004). Brian Hayden (2001, 49–52) suggests that one purpose of large-scale feasts is to strengthen the bonds among members. Archaeologically, such feasts may be "minimally distinctive" in that the participants do not feast on special foods, but on ordinary and/or otherwise abundant fare; participants contribute roughly equally to the feast; and ostentatious display is minimized. That is, the remains of the feast may be similar to types of deposits found in daily refuse heaps. The primary difference may only be in the size of the deposits (Hayden 2001, 51; Russo 2004), and, as such, the chances of distinguishing feast from daily refuse are diminished if the two types are intermixed into the same middens. However, if the large quantities of durable feast-food refuse, such as shell, are discarded in separate locations from quotidian middens, and are deposited rapidly, they may be distinguishable from smaller, slowly accreted household midden deposits not only by their larger amounts, but by less non-feasting-related debris. It is an archaeological axiom that daily living sites have greater diversity in terms of artifacts and ecofacts reflecting a greater diversity of activities, while special sites are less diverse in material remains. If context is controlled, the discard of special activities, large-scale, rapidly deposited feasting remains are potentially distinguishable from smaller, slowly accumulated remains.

The greater volume of oyster shell at Archaic shell-ring sites was derived from large-scale consumption activities that led to oyster shell being piled quickly and higher than at primary quotidian middens at other site types. Piled in this manner, a tall circle of shell with relatively few inclusions arose. Rather than hauling the shell away from the public site of the feast to a distant refuse dump, the feasters built an edifice whose form was maintained and magnified on their territory with each successive feast. Such oyster feasting became a normative behavior for many Archaic coastal occupants across the southeastern U.S. seaboard (see Figure 3.1).

Conspicuous consumption by large numbers of people at the venue of oyster feasts resulted in large quantities of refuse. The overt, practical purpose of Archaic shell-ring construction was, of course, to dispose of these massive amounts of food refuse. Thus shell rings were refuse dumps, which over millennia have resisted biodegradation. While their fastest periods of growth occurred when they functioned as ceremonial sites, if feasts were not taking place, other daily activities were, at least at some of the rings (Russo 1991; Thompson 2006; Trinkley 1985). That is, as evidenced by the circular distribution of quotidian features that include houses, hearths, and organic middens mostly below or along the plaza edge, many Archaic shell rings initially started out as circular habitation sites. At these sites, the pattern of living shifted as shell deposition increased the height and width of the ring to a point of critical mass where further shifting was not an option if plaza size was to be maintained (Thompson and Andrus 2011, 317). Archaeologists have suggested that at this point, or for environmental or social reasons (e.g., climate change, fissioning), the ring may have been abandoned and taken on the more singular function of monument (Marquardt 2010a).

Were rings consciously built as monuments from their beginning, or were they so designated only after abandonment? Shortly after their initial placement on the landscape, shell-ring forms were maintained to a point that ultimately exceeded the simple practicality of garbage management. In some views, this architectural construction that exceeds practical purpose is the archaeological definition of monument (Marquardt 2010a, 552; Trigger 1990, 119). There is no practical reason to pile a continuous ring of shell at exceedingly steep angles and greater heights that overflows onto and buries living space while restricting ease of physical access to the world outside the ring.

If a monument is a memorial to events, persons, or ideas, monument construction was likely manifested in Archaic shell rings. The conspicuous consumption of large amounts of oyster during site feasts was matched by the conspicuous display of the food refuse from those activities. The greater volume of shell was not isolated in a separate garbage dump or hidden from daily view by burial in pits. The mounds of food refuse that made up the Archaic shell rings were intentionally placed, shaped, elevated, maintained, and viewed daily, in part to serve a memorial purpose.

Ultimately, one likely continuing and lasting objective of Archaic shell-ring construction was the memorialization of the feasts, their associated ceremonies, their participants, and the host or host community who sponsored the feasts. Ring construction reified these memories upon the landscape, and, in this sense, rings were functioning monuments not only after abandonment but beginning at or near their initial construction episode. It is rare to find subsequent cultures reusing the Archaic rings as living sites (cf. Russo 1991). This avoidance suggests either persistent recognition of the shell-ring sites as memorialized features, altered landscapes at the shell rings that precluded reuse of the sites, or changed environments that precluded subsequent intensive reuse due to unavailable resources. Since post-Archaic sites are often found adjacent to Archaic shell rings, the persistence of shell rings as recognized monuments remains a possibility (Russo 1991, 2010; Russo, Heide, and Rolland 2002; Thomas 2010).

Ring Middens as Habitation and Ceremonial Sites

Coastal Woodland ring middens differ from their Archaic shell antecedents in that they are often less prominent. The shell refuse found at ring middens is intermixed within dark organic midden soils. The piles of ring-midden shell deposits are relatively small, are often discontiguous, and lack the greater, mounded deposits of clean shell common to Archaic shell rings. These differences suggest that Woodland ring middens were formed through the accretion of refuse whose ultimate forms were not intended, planned, or strictly maintained as conspicuous landscape features. The organic midden soils contain mundane pottery, ash lenses, garbage-filled pits, hearths, and posts. The lumpy character of ring middens with gaps between denser piles of shell-bearing midden may reflect household trash piles behind domiciles located around a central plaza (Bense 1998; Percy and Brose 1974; Russo, Hadden, and Dengel 2009; Russo, Schwadron, and Yates 2006; Stephenson, Bense, and Snow 2002; Thomas et al. 1996).

Whether overtly conspicuous or not, the ring midden may have served as a boundary between the public/sacred plaza and the natural world (Bense 1998; Means 2007). Kin group or village burial mounds are found near many coastal Woodland ring middens, the latter of which are commonly interpreted as the remains of villages. The proximity of the mounds to the public forum of the plaza leaves open the possibility that Woodland rings were also special places where burial-related ceremony and ritual occurred. What is the case for ceremony? If death, burial, or memorial feasts occurred, no specialized areas restricted for feast refuse have yet been identified at any ring midden, though some have suggested that individual lenses and pit features may be feast deposits (e.g., Nanfro 2004). But food remains are not the only materials left behind by feasting ceremonies. At some ring middens, evidence for feasts has been linked to special pottery discarded underfoot and in exhausted cooking pits within the plaza. Researchers have suggested that the rare pottery types represent special containers in which feast foods were displayed and consumed by an elite or specialized segment of society (e.g., Doran and Piatek 1985; Thomas et al. 1996, 149–53). If such elite feasts were so restricted, of course, they would have been much smaller affairs than the community-wide solidarity feasts that I have suggested occurred at Archaic shell rings. If Woodland ring middens were built primarily from the refuse of daily food and these occasional small-scale feasts, feast refuse might be expected to be less abundant than that found at Archaic rings for similar lengths of occupation and use. This expectation is supported by the relatively lower relief and discontiguous aspects of Woodland rings.

A number of possibilities may account for the paucity of mounded clean-shell deposits at Woodland ring middens:

1. Large-scale feasts of shellfish were not held at Woodland ring villages;
2. Any large-scale feasting refuse has been intermixed with quotidian midden materials and rendered archaeologically indiscernible;
3. Feast refuse was discarded away from the ring; or
4. The conspicuous display and memorialization of feasts was not practiced at Woodland ring villages.

There is some evidence that shellfish feasting of various scales did occur at ring-midden sites. As discussed, a number of investigators have identified clean-shell deposits in pits within plazas. Rather than displaying and memorializing their feast through the mounding of feast refuse as did Archaic shell-ring builders, Woodland ring builders may have buried the remains of sacred feasts for the dead in sacred contexts of the central plaza separate from the quotidian refuse in the ring middens. Archaeologists working on coastal ring middens nearly universally see the plaza as a sacred place kept free from the profane pollution of quotidian activities by periodic sweeping and the relegation of all daily refuse to the mundane ring midden surrounding the plaza. That is, ring midden sites are defined into two basic zones: the sacred plaza and the secular ring midden. Whether or not this model has fidelity is an empirical question. But associations of ceremonial artifacts with some of the central plaza pit features have been noted (Thomas et al. 1996), and ceremonial objects have been recovered from the Swift Creek–period Harrison plaza (Russo, Dengel, and Shanks 2013), not to mention the burials within the Bernath plaza.

So-called sacred and secular objects in and of themselves cannot be used to define sacred/secular places. Context must also be discerned. Although Woodland ring-middens sites may have been places of daily living, evidence other than food remains suggests that ceremonial activities were also practiced, some of which were geared toward the burial mound lying just outside the village. These conspicuous burial monuments have been more extensively reported than the ring middens with which they are associated (Moore 1902, 1918; Willey 1949a). We know from burial mounds that usual food (shellfish) generally considered quotidian in the ring-midden contexts was offered in oblation or otherwise ritually within and atop individual burials. Also included in the mounds are utilitarian pottery vessels of types common at the ring middens as well as special ornate vessels found only in burial contexts. Exotic stones, including unshaped and shaped quartz, ochre, greenstone, and mica, were commonly placed as burial objects. Many of these largely ornamental artifacts, such as ochre (and the stone manos used to grind it), chipped quartz, mica fragments, and greenstone celts, are also found in the ring middens (usually fragmented), suggesting that preparation and display of the material destined to be burial goods occurred at the ring-midden sites next to the mounds (Russo et al. 2011). That is, we may infer that ceremonially oriented activities occurred at the ring middens, even though evidence of feasts possibly associated with the ceremonies is often equivocal. The presence of whole, fragments, or debitage of elite pottery and rare stone and mineral artifacts in ring middens and plazas suggests that practices oriented to the elite and the dead were the foci of ceremonial and other social activities held at the ring villages (Russo, Hadden, and Dengel 2009; Russo et al. 2011; Thomas and Campbell 1996). The ritual burial of exotic and other objects in pits separate from the quotidian ring refuse supports the idea that some of these artifacts were held sacred, requiring

discard rituals distinct from everyday discard into the mundane ring midden (Walker 2001).

The connection of coastal Woodland ring-midden sites to ritual activities, or at least their setting within a ritualized landscape, is supported by the observation that sterile areas, or what could possibly prove to be processional paths leading to the mound, lie between the mounds and the ring (Russo, Dengel, and Shanks 2013; Russo, Hadden, and Dengel 2009; Russo et al. 2011). This ritual focus on ceremonies and construction of monuments to the dead is distinct from the Archaic focus on the celebration of food as a central ritual activity. That is, Woodland ring occupants did not build circles of shell as monuments to feasts and/or their attendant ceremonies. Their monuments were the burial mounds and plazas where ritual attentions were paid to their contemporary kin and ancestors (Mikell 1992, 218; Pluckhahn 2003; Stephenson, Bense, and Snow 2002). At coastal Woodland burial mounds and ring plazas, food remains, when they are found, are relatively small ritual offerings (Moore 1902; Willey 1949a). On the other hand, Archaic shell-ring builders rarely, if ever, participated in the kinds of fetishes of the dead that were to mark the later coastal Woodland-period mound/ring-midden sites. Only three Archaic shell-ring complexes are known to be associated with mounds, which may or may not contain burials, and formal burials at ring sites are relatively rare (Russo 2006). At Archaic shell rings, memorialization of the feast was the lasting result of whatever ceremony the feast may have attended. At Woodland rings, any feast was ancillary to the mound and the ceremonies associated with funerary and ancestral rites.

MULTIPLE FUNCTIONS AND SOCIAL ORGANIZATION AT RINGS

If, as I suggest, the variations in height and content of Archaic and Woodland rings were due to different social and ceremonial practices, questions arise: Why the different ring shapes? Why circles? Why C-shapes? Why U-shapes? On a practical level, because the shell in shell rings was placed as a continuous ring, blocking all but one way in and out, the openings in C- and U-shaped rings seem to reflect a purposely constructed feature designed to facilitate ingress and egress into the plaza. Among Woodland ring middens, the open ends are often nearest the nearby burial mound, suggesting processional paths for egress to the mound monument. But Woodland rings middens can also have a number of gaps or areas with less midden and multiple pathways in and out of the plaza (Figure 3.7) (Russo et al. 2011)—a

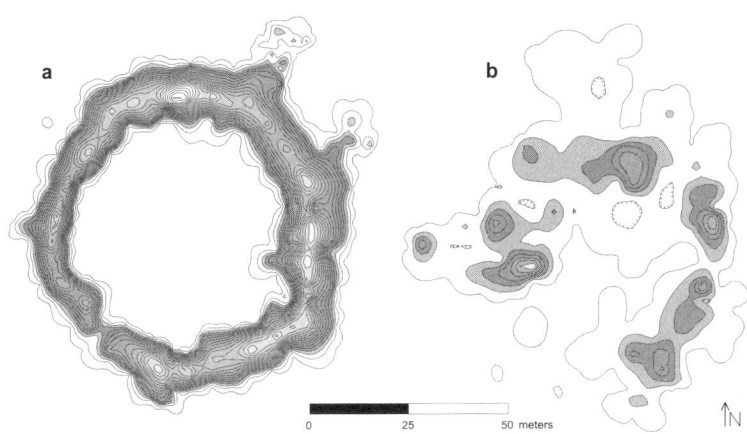

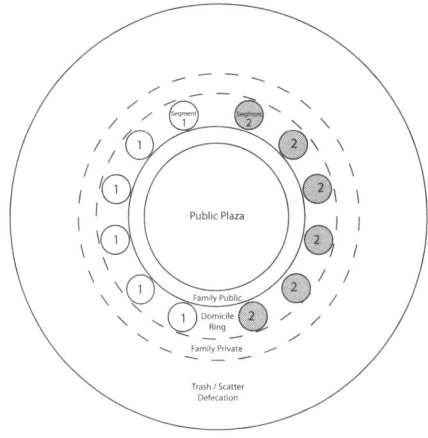

3.7. Shell thickness at the Archaic Fig Island 2 shell ring (a) and the Swift Creek Harrison ring midden (b). Note the tightly restricted and continuously mounded ring at Fig Island versus the scattered, gap-filled, low-relief shell at the Harrison ring midden.

3.8. Combined diametric and concentric model of ring communities (after Grøn 1991; Means 2007; Portnoy 1981; Trinkley 1985).

pattern found among ethnographic cultures where access in and out of the village occurs at gaps between houses (e.g., Fraser 1968, fig. 73).

If the single openings in C- and U-shaped villages represent entranceways to the plaza and the surrounding houses (Grøn 1991; Russo 2004), the question arises as to how people entered and exited closed or circular rings. Some closed circular Archaic shell rings, such as the six-meter-high Fig Island 1 and possibly the two-meter-high Fig Island 2 circles, required shell ramps to gain access to the top of the ring from the exterior, but it is less apparent how the plaza was accessed from the top of the ring. It is difficult to envision people actually living along the plaza edge of some of these closed rings where access is so restricted. Efforts to get in and out of the plaza over steep and loosely packed shell-ring walls would have been laborious and destructive to the ring. Thus, purposes other than daily living seem likely for the closed shell rings with high shell walls. However, other tall-walled "closed" circles have only nominal mounding on one side of the ring, with much lower levels on the opposite site, thus allowing easier ingress and egress (Russo 2004, 2006; Russo and Heide 2002).

Ethnographically based models of non-shell-bearing circular villages suggest that the population size, the sizes and numbers of houses, the socially prescribed spacing between the structures, and the kinds of activities planned for the communal plaza are the primary factors behind the size of circular villages (Means 2007, 52). The plaza facilitates socially integrative public, religious, economic, and

political rituals for the entire community, and domiciles are located around it under socially prescribed rules (e.g., Heckenberger 2005).

Two idealized templates—diametric and concentric—have been modeled for ring communities. Diametric patterns in circular communities segment villages along kin, cardinal directions, or cosmological lines. On a structural level, this segmentation may manifest as two separate kin groups occupying opposite sides of a ring, for example, one on the north side of the ring and one on the south side (Figure 3.8) (e.g., Fabian 1992). Alternatively, in concentric models, different activity areas are found in concentric zones expanding out from the village center or the public, often sacred, plaza. Surrounding the plaza is the family or house zone where domiciles are constructed and family activities occur. With house entrances facing the plaza, public family activities occur in front of the house. Private family activities occur behind the house, constituting a separate concentric activity zone. In some models, the area behind the private family zone is another activity ring or zone where the outermost limit of artifact deposits is located. In other models, this zone and/or a concentric area outward from it constitutes the village midden where refuse disposal and defecation take place (Means 2007, 57; Portnoy 1981).

A similar concentric model has been formulated for Archaic shell rings. Concentric rings are believed to fall into four zones from the innermost to the outermost. These are the *interior* (plaza), the *interior edge of the ring* (read "house ring"), the *shell midden ring* (limit of artifact and trash scatter), and the *exterior edge of the ring* (read "defecation zone") (Trinkley 1985, 108). The difference between Michael B. Trinkley's Archaic shell-ring model and the ethnographic models of ring villages is that houses and cooking facilities are posited to have occurred on the shell ring, thereby conflating the two zones of houses and midden within a single concentric circle of activity. According to Trinkley, Archaic shell-ring builders are thought to have lived within the trash zone surrounding the plaza, atop of the shell midden and/or otherwise surrounded by most of their trash. This model for shell-ring occupation, however, is not universally accepted. With less formal models, other shell-ring archaeologists have suggested that the apparent habitation activities found in the trash (shell midden) zone result from the expanding shell deposits covering former house locations, not from living on the trash. In these models, as trash accumulates around them, houses are moved to the inside of the ring toward the plaza, or the trash zone is expanded outward and/or upward, keeping the trash zone and the ring for houses still relatively close but in separate concentric zones (Russo 1991, 2004; Thompson 2006, 273). However, because there is virtually no direct evidence of house structures at any shell-ring site (e.g., Thompson 2006, 264; Trinkley 1985; cf. Russo 1991), where, when, and if people lived in houses at shell-ring sites is still a matter of some debate.

Tables 3.1 and 3.3 provide data on the shapes and sizes of Woodland and Archaic rings. Archaic rings can occur in complexes of multiple rings, but, whether attached or separate, the most common shapes are circles and half-circles (C-shapes) in Georgia and South Carolina, and U-shapes in Florida. The circle is a practical shape to facilitate equal oral and visual communications among all community members (Grøn 1991). Such equality in observing and being observed is not found in the square, the rectangle, or even the U-shape, where individual households, physically blocked by houses on either side of them, may be invisible to other houses down the line. Circular rings are ideally shaped for egalitarian organization where all community members practice routine public social activities as equals and in view of all others (Russo 2004; see also Grøn 1991; Trinkley 1985).

Ethnographically, however, circular village forms do not necessarily equate only with egalitarian social organization. Circular settlement plans are also commonly associated with segmentary and hierarchical societies, wherein kin or gender groups, sodalities, or other social factions may be aligned opposite each other and/or along cosmological demarcations. Without additional materials and

features denoting social complexities (and few studies have even attempted to identify the differential distributions of goods and features at either Archaic or Woodland rings), shape alone is not a sufficient marker to determine social organization. There are some indications, in fact, that circular shell-ring builders as well as U-ring builders were more complexly organized than strict egalitarianism allows. When a diametric model is applied, many of the larger and U-shaped Archaic rings seem to reflect dual social organization (Russo 2004). For one, the larger sizes of U-shaped rings suggest larger occupying populations than found at individual circular rings and, perhaps, greater organizational needs to diffuse social tensions that arise concomitantly. The larger plazas could have served to increase space among community factions to alleviate potential conflicts (Means 2007, 53). I have also suggested that the open-ended nature of the U also allowed the physical expansion of the village on its open ends as populations increased (Russo 2004). In contrast, with no method to increase the living area in circular rings, population increase and conflict mitigation at circular Archaic rings may have only been possible through fissioning (e.g., Chagnon 2013). Among Archaic circular ring-building societies, this resulted in sites with multiple rings or more numerous, closely spaced ring communities as opposed to U-shaped ring sites that typically consisted of larger, but more widely spaced communities (see Figure 3.1) (Russo 2006, fig. 17).

In comparison, burial mounds associated with Woodland ring middens have yielded pottery and interment patterns suggesting different statuses among community members, at least in death (Moore 1902, 1918; Willey 1949a). Because recent investigations have found some of the same status markers in ring middens, however, archaeologists have suggested that status distinctions also existed in life. Exotic goods found within rings may reflect higher status for their holders, and specific locations of elite pottery at Woodland rings may mark specific locations in the ring middens where high-ranked individuals resided (Doran and Piatek 1985; Kohler 1978; Milanich 1994; Russo, Hadden, and Dengel 2009; Russo, Schwadron, and Yates 2006; Thomas et al. 1996).

No such pottery status markers have been identified at Archaic shell-ring sites, though efforts have been made to find them (Russo, Heide, and Rolland 2002). But I have suggested that evidence of status distinctions can be found at many Archaic shell-ring sites in the distribution of shell. The shell in circular middens is most often highest or most voluminous opposite the section of ring wall containing the least volume. Similarly, in C- and U-shaped shell rings, the greatest heights and volumes are found opposite the ring openings. Assuming that each area around the plaza was occupied or maintained by particular families, I have posited that the families who had the social resources to gather and pile more shell for public display (that is, those with more kin, more debt holders obliged to them, or greater social status that would lead to more food gatherers coming to their assistance) could gain and/or maintain status, however transitory, during the feasting ceremonies.

In ethnographic descriptions of non-shell-bearing circular and quasi-circular villages, high-status positions are marked by larger dwellings, elevated structures, higher topographies, or other displays of power, such as elaborate buildings, ostentatious presentations of foods, display of special objects, or placement of totems. Typically, the highest status positions are those opposite the entrance into the village (Grøn 1991; Means 2007; Russo 2004). In Archaic circular shell-ring settlements, the locations of these high-status positions are the places where the largest piles of shell are found, suggesting status distinctions for those locations situated around the plaza (Russo 2004, 2006; Russo, Hadden, and Dengel 2009).

CONCLUSION

This book is intended for a global audience, and, I suspect, such an audience might question the necessity of proclaiming as midden the various circles of shell that have obviously been deposited as middens by the various cultures discussed. I have stressed the point that both Archaic and Woodland rings are indeed middens, in part because I wanted to note that other than simply trash piles, middens can serve multiple purposes such as monument construction, symbolic signification, and territorial and social status marking. But I also emphasize that the Archaic- and Woodland-period rings are middens, because some researchers have suggested that Archaic shell rings are neither middens nor ceremonial sites, but rather holding tanks or freshwater reservoirs made of shell mined from distant shell middens (Marquardt 2010a, 2010b; Middaugh 2009). Evidence for the use of shell rings as reservoirs is insubstantiated, however. As I have argued here, the many rings discussed retain all the characterstics of shell middens. But they also served various and multiple purposes beyond the sole one of residential discard dumps.

To this latter point, some have argued that shell mounds of any shape or size, including ring shapes, cannot be viewed as monuments because shell is first and foremost trash, and unless it can be proven that it is not trash, it cannot be presumed to be ritual or ceremonial (Marquardt 2010a). Such essentialism, of course, fails to aknowledge the complex relationships among humans, materials, and landscapes that allow for multiple functionalities of any and all materials within a cultural system. It also fails to acknowledge that ceremonialism is not presumed for all shell deposits, but is obtained through the gathering and interpretation of evidence, including materials and social and archaeological contexts. The evidence at the various sites described above demonstrates that ring sites are indeed made from "kitchen" trash and are thus middens. But they were also placed and mounded to demarcate rings and memorialize social events and people. Thus rings are social constructions, parts of monumental sites consisting of the ritualized ring midden, the sacred public plaza, and/or mounds serving burial and other functions.

CHAPTER FOUR

SHELL RINGS OF THE LOWER ATLANTIC COAST OF THE UNITED STATES

Defining Function by Contrasting Details, with Reference to Ecuador, Columbia, and Japan

Rebecca Saunders

SUMMARY

There are over 40 known Archaic period (10,000–2500 BP) shell-ring sites along the lower Atlantic coast (Figure 4.1). Unequivocal radiocarbon dates indicate that these Archaic rings were constructed in the Late Archaic period, between 5000 and 3400 cal BP. Archaic-period ring-shaped settlements are present throughout much of the coastal Southeast; indeed circular settlements persist in the prehistory of the Southeast (Russo 2010; chap. 3 of this volume) and are present elsewhere in the United States (e.g., Means 2007) after the Archaic period. However, the Archaic-period shell-ring sites on the lower Atlantic coast form a distinctive subset. The overall configuration of these sites—especially the height and character of the shell deposits—is unique.

I argue in this chapter that many (although not necessarily all) of these constructions, built by fisher-gatherer-hunters, functioned as ceremonial centers, among the first of such centers in the southeastern United States (Saunders and Russo 2011). Like ceremonial centers built by small-scale societies in other parts of the New World (see, e.g., de Boer 1997), as well as the Old (Spielmann 2008), these centers served as integrative facilities that brought dispersed bands together to share information, to exchange mates, and to trade, all accompanied by religious ritual, dancing, and feasting.

ARCHAIC SHELL RINGS ON THE LOWER ATLANTIC COAST: DEFINITIONS, DESCRIPTIONS, AND OTHER DETAILS

Archaic shell rings are variations of U-shaped or circular constructions ranging in height from less than one meter to more than six meters; rings occur as single structures or sites may contain a number of rings. The Fig Island Shell Ring Complex, in South Carolina, is one of the most elaborate of the ring complexes (Figure 4.2). Interior diameters of shell rings vary from less than 40 to more than 200 meters. With some exceptions, ring walls are composed overwhelmingly of whole oyster (*Crassostrea virginica*) shell. The deposits are remarkably free of organic soil; thus there is little organic staining on the shell. This leaves the shell with a very clean appearance. Shell hash is usually present, and the deposits usually contain literally millions of tiny fish bones (for shell, see Russo, chap. 3 in this volume, Table 3.3). Artifacts, overwhelmingly pottery, are also present.

Early researchers (e.g., Moore 1897; Waring 1968; Waring and Larson 1968) were struck by the contrast between the character of the midden in the relatively rare rings (Figure 4.3), and the broken oyster and dark organic soil that characterizes the contemporaneous sheet middens—generally considered residential sites—that line the lower Atlantic coast. Other contrasts with contemporaneous shell sites include the formal layout of rings in comparison to amorphous sheet middens, and the maintenance of ring sites: the interior "plaza" and the area immediately outside of the ring wall are relatively free of contemporaneous shell and other organics.

Construction of shell rings ensued at the beginning of the Late Archaic period, around 5000 cal BP, at a time when local populations had abandoned their Middle Archaic subsistence strategy, which involved a fairly equitable reliance on both terrestrial and estuarine resources. In its place, Late Archaic people focused on a few estuarine resources. Most shell middens of this culture (and indeed,

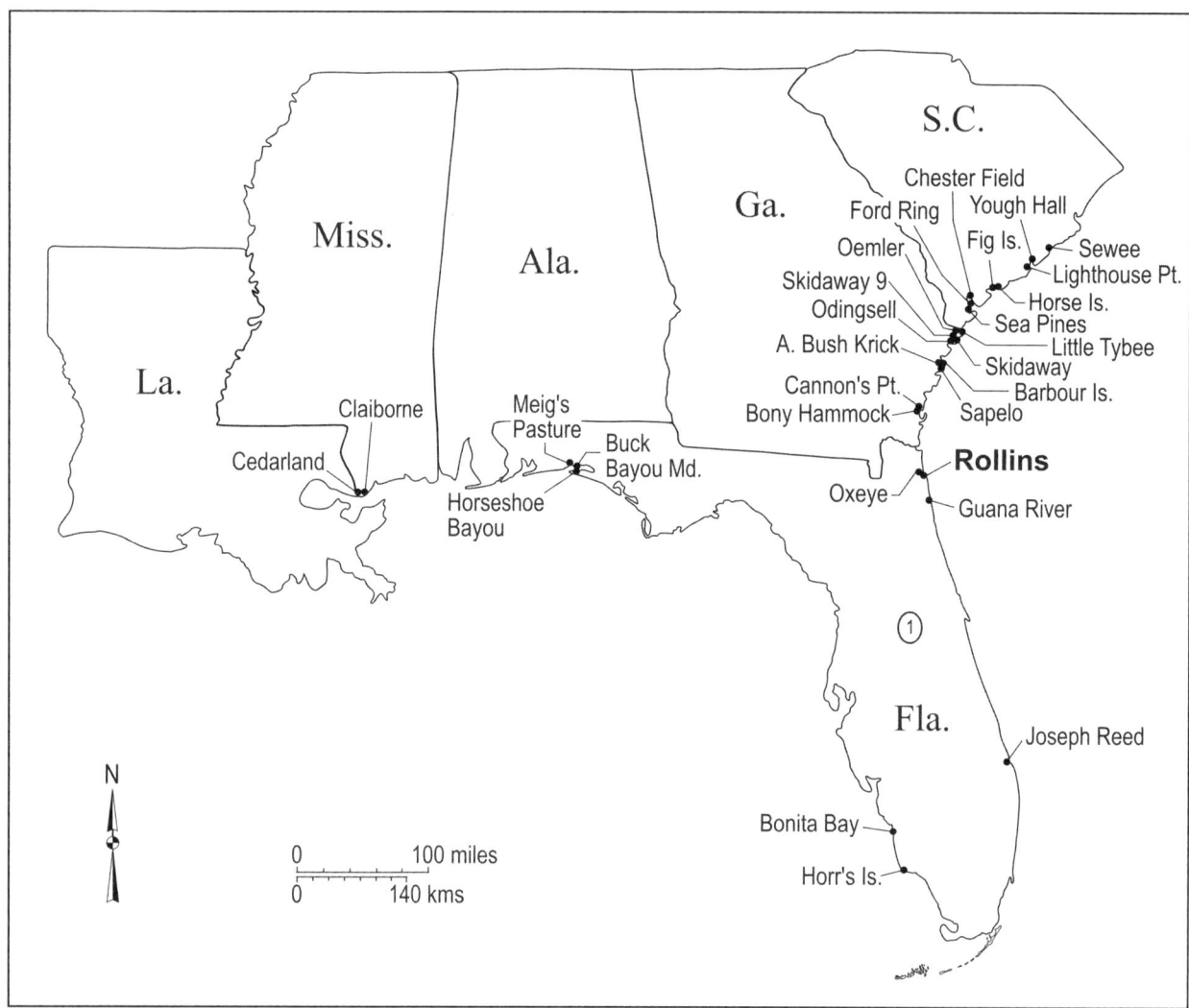

4.1. Archaic shell-ring sites along the lower Atlantic and Gulf coasts. Circle indicates approximate location of possible rings on the St. Johns River.

of subsequent coastal cultures) contain oyster and only traces of other bivalves and gastropods (see Russo, chap. 3 of this volume, Table 3.3), as well as a limited number of species of small, net-able fishes especially saltwater cat-fishes (Ariidae) and herrings (Clupeidae) that appear in large schools in the coastal estuaries.[1] Shell rings are no exception. Furthermore, just as these societies looked only eastward for subsistence resources, they also turned their collective backs on trade with the interior. On the stone-poor coast, Middle Archaic sites contain many more lithic artifacts than Late Archaic sites (of any configuration). Indeed, in the absence of sustained trade with the interior, ceremonial centers may have become necessary for information exchange, communal revitalization ceremonies, and the exchange of mates.

In this respect, it is important to note that Archaic-period shell rings have a very discrete distribution—they are a coastal phenomenon. There are huge freshwater shell midden sites dating to the Late Archaic in the interior southeastern United States, along the Green, Tennessee, and Ohio Rivers, as well as along the Lower Savannah River in Georgia, and the St. Johns River in Florida, but none of these assumes a ring shape. An exception to this coastal distribution apparently existed along the middle St. Johns River, where Jeffries Wyman (1875) described a set of four U-shaped freshwater shell monuments, spaced some 20–30 kilometers apart (Randall 2008, 15). All of these have been destroyed or heavily disturbed by shell mining. However, Asa Randall (2008) identified the remnants of one of Wyman's rings at the Silver Glen Run site on the west side of Lake George. If his reconstruction of this highly disturbed site is correct, at over 7 meters tall and 400 meters in length, this construction would have dwarfed the largest coastal rings.

Geographically at least, the St. Johns freshwater shell rings are part of a suite of huge (up to eight meters in height) mounds of freshwater shell that began to accrue along the river's edge by 7,000 years ago. Over thousands of years of use, these mounds became complex configurations of shell fields, shell "midden-mounds," some of which became "specialized mortuary facilities" (Sassaman 2008, 7) and shell ridges, along with sand and shell burial mounds (Wheeler, Newman, and McGee 2000). The intricate stratigraphy of the larger shell midden-mounds, and especially those used as mortuaries, are reminiscent of Brazilian *sambaquis*:

> Proportions of soil, sand, shell, and the kinds of cultural inclusions and features in sambaquis . . . are variable . . . Larger shell mounds typically have horizontally and vertically complex stratigraphy, including alternating sequences of shell deposits, narrower and darker layers of charcoal and burned bone that mark occupation surfaces, and clusters of burials, hearths, and postholes descending from these surfaces. Food refuse is present in sambaquis, along with a set of feature types that are commonplace in residential occupations. [Gaspar et al. 2008, 319]

This description would fit quite comfortably in a characterization of a St. Johns River shell mound.

Although once considered habitation sites, Maria Dulce Gaspar and colleagues (2008, 320; compare Gaspar 1998 for the domestic view) argued that sambaquis, "particularly the massive ones," were mortuary structures, in use for millennia (Gaspar et al. 2008, 324). In this, the trajectory of the interpretation of sambaquis is similar to interpretations of the structurally and functionally similar shell mounds of the interior U.S. Southeast and midcontinent. Until quite recently, all of these southeastern U.S. shell mound sites were considered the result of the gradual accumulations of refuse of transhumant hunter-gatherers (Claassen 2010).[2] In all of these cases, interpretations of function are turning to the sacred, or to a combination of sacred and secular, although these reappraisals are not without critics (Marquardt 2010a, 2010b).

While interpretation of shell rings has also followed this secular-to-sacred route, the function of rings appears quite distinct from the function of shell mounds. Many rings were deposited rapidly (see below) and none was a mortuary. Isolated human bone has been recovered from rings, but it is rare, and there is no indication that deposition was patterned; that is to say, bone is not found in only one particular location within a ring.

As noted, the term *shell ring* is something of a misnomer, as many rings are U-shaped rather than donut-shaped. The second of three rings at the Fig Island Ring Complex in

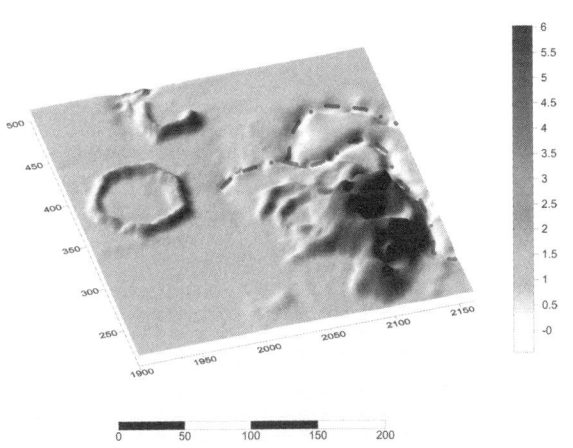

4.2. *Surfer 3D surface map of the Fig Island Ring Complex. All elevated areas are built of oyster shell, except for the sand mound immediately south of the largest ring. The dot-dashed line indicates a tidal creek. North follows left axis. Horizontal and vertical scales in meters.*

4.3. *Fig Island Ring 1 profile showing the jumbled shell with little soil that is characteristic of shell-ring deposits. South profile of Fig 1, Unit 1, 0–100 cm.*

South Carolina was once considered the quintessential "circular" shell ring. However, close-interval mapping revealed that the ring is actually hexagonal (Russo 2002). This configuration suggests that the ring was built in segments; indeed, mapping at other ring sites, such as Guana and Rollins in Florida, may indicate that these rings also were built of conjoined linear segments rather than in a continuous arc (see also Russo 2008). Within the segments, it appears that, like earthen mounds, shell rings were built by "haystacking"—creating piles of shell and then infilling. This produces distinct peaks within the ring.

The segmentary nature of the rings suggests, as Katherine Spielmann (2008) pointed out for the Ohio Hopewell and British Neolithic segmented enclosures, that the sections in the lower Atlantic shell rings replicate the social structure of the group that constructed them—that rings were microcosms or sociograms that express in a material way the social relations within the broader community. In the case of rings, "microcosm" may be more appropriate because, as will be seen, it is likely that rings express not only the relationships in "This World" (the expression of the earth in its relationship to the Upper and the Lower [or Under] realms in the Southeastern Indian worldview [Hudson 1976, 122]), but also those within the cosmos. This is not to suggest that the segments necessarily reflect segmentary lineages, just that some kind of societal divisions are expressed in the discrete linear subdivisions of the rings.

Michael Russo has juxtaposed to scale the extant maps of ring sites in South Carolina, Georgia, and Florida, and this graphic provides a good overview of the variability of ring footprints across space (Figure 4.4; also see Russo 2006 for a compendium of maps and other information). As can be seen, site configuration at many rings is quite complex; configuration does not conform to expectations of small egalitarian settlements (as argued by Trinkley 1985). The Rollins Shell Ring in northeast Florida, for instance, is a U-shaped structure with an interior "plaza" some 250 meters by 100 meters in diameter (Figure 4.5). On the western and northern sides of the ring, where elevation is highest (up to four meters above the plaza), there is a series of smaller enclosures, or "ringlets." Indeed, the ringlets at Rollins are as large as independent rings mapped in Georgia and South Carolina (Figure 4.4). It may be no coincidence that some of these relatively small ring sites in Georgia and South Carolina have multiple rings (see below). Four rings are present at the Coosa Shell Ring Complex (Heide and Russo 2003); there are three at Sapelo and Fig Island. Two remain at Cannons Point, and the Ford Shell Ring site has two overlapping rings. At Fig Island, the aforementioned hexagonal Fig Island 2 ring was connected with the arc-like Fig Island 3 ring by a 30-centimeter-thick shell causeway complete with ramps to the tops of the rings (Figure 4.2). At six meters above the surrounding marsh, Fig Island 1 is the tallest known coastal ring. Like Rollins, it has smaller enclosures on the north and west sides; alone among the lower Atlantic rings, Fig Island 1 may have a sand mound along its southwestern flank (Russo 2006).

DETAILS ON DATES AND DIFFERENCES

The only preceramic ring, Oxeye Island, on the northeast Florida coast, has basal dates of 5030–4835 1 cal BP (Table 4.1). A radiocarbon sample taken directly above this basal date, near the top of the ring wall (10–15 centimeters below surface [cmbs]), produced a date of 4820–4650 1 cal BP. These date ranges miss overlapping at one sigma by 15 years, and so may indicate rapid construction, but may also suggest that the ring was deposited over many generations. However, other rings have top and bottom dates that are statistically indistinguishable at one sigma. These include: two of the three Fig Island rings and Ringlet C at Fig Island 1; the Rollins main ring; Rollins Ringlet D; the Sewee Ring; and Coosa Ring 2 (the other Coosa rings do not have top and bottom dates).

It is unclear why some sites have multiple rings; however, sites with multiple rings contain mostly closed rings (e.g., circles) rather than open crescents.[3] One might suppose that a ring was abandoned when it became too small for its function, yet at Coosa, all three mapped rings are close to the same size; thus, a small ring was not abandoned for a larger one. Indeed, in some cases, the closed rings are contemporaneous, while in others, construction appears successive. At Coosa, for instance, Rings 1 and 3 appear contemporaneous, with basal dates of around 3900 cal BP, but Ring 2 was begun around 3600 cal BP. Fig Island Rings 2 and 3 (there is no basal date for the huge Fig Island 1 ring) are contemporaneous, but the tremendous difference in the shapes and sizes of the rings on Fig Island argue for distinctly different functions within the (ceremonial?) system at that site.

The limited testing done at most sites with multiple rings does not indicate significant differences in the kinds of artifacts in the rings.[4] On the other hand, the two "simple" circular rings on St. Catherines Island, Georgia, have marked differences in artifact content that may indicate "differences in function, group identity, or spatial marking" (Sanger and Thomas 2010, 68). The bulk of construction at both rings

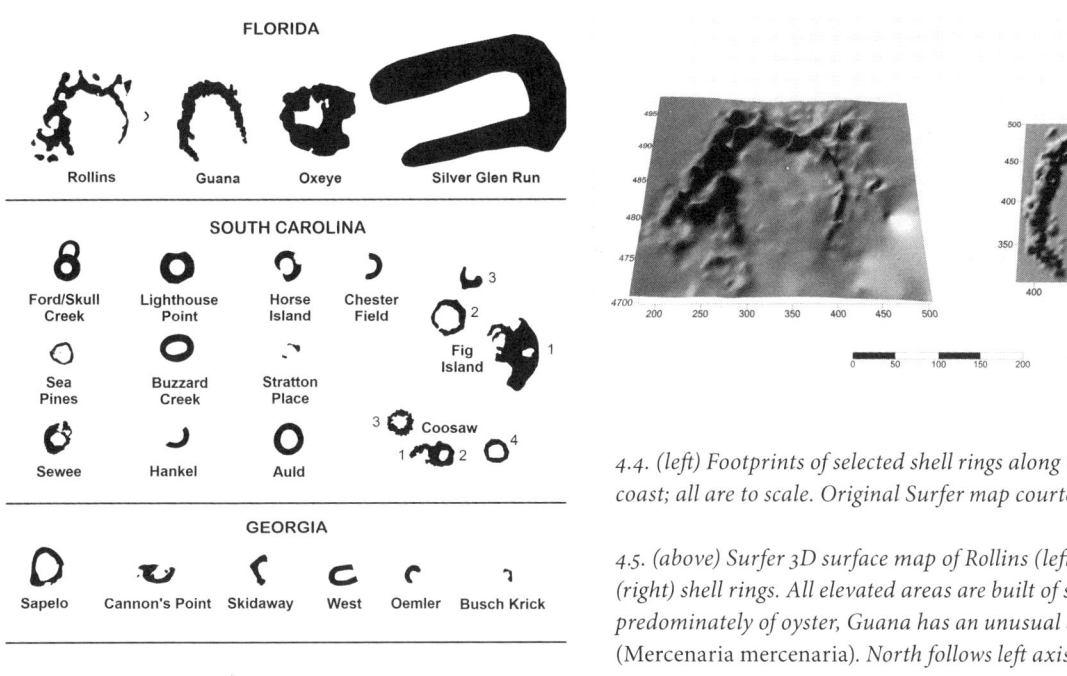

FLORIDA

Rollins Guana Oxeye Silver Glen Run

SOUTH CAROLINA

Ford/Skull
Creek Lighthouse
Point Horse
Island Chester
Field Fig
Island

Sea
Pines Buzzard
Creek Stratton
Place

Sewee Hankel Auld Coosaw

GEORGIA

Sapelo Cannon's Point Skidaway West Oemler Busch Krick

N   0   100m

4.4. (left) Footprints of selected shell rings along the lower Atlantic coast; all are to scale. Original Surfer map courtesy of Mike Russo.

4.5. (above) Surfer 3D surface map of Rollins (left) and Guana (right) shell rings. All elevated areas are built of shell. Rollins is built predominately of oyster, Guana has an unusual abundance of clam (Mercenaria mercenaria). North follows left axis.

was contemporaneous, between 4300 and 4000 cal BP (Sanger and Thomas 2010, 66), and the rings are similar in shape and size. At the western "St. Catherines" ring, only 1 percent of the recovered fiber-tempered pottery was decorated; at the eastern "McQueens" ring, 14 percent of the pottery was decorated. Baked clay objects were abundant at St. Catherines (n > 3000) and rare at McQueens (n=15). Both rings are unusual in having a relatively large amount of lithic material—all of which is exotic to the coast—but at St. Catherines the lithic assemblage is predominantly Coastal Plain chert, while McQueens has a more diverse assemblage including "gray chert, metavolcanic materials, quartz, and quartzite" (Sanger and Thomas 2010, 69). This situation recalls that of two U-shaped ring sites at the mouth of the Pearl River in extreme southwestern Mississippi, Cedarland and Claiborne. These poorly dated (ca. 4000 BP?), now-destroyed sites were separated by a 50-meter-wide swale and had, among other things, the following series of subsistence and material culture oppositions (respectively): oyster/rangia (*Rangia cuneata*); clay-lined hearths/baked clay objects; no pottery/pottery; no steatite/ steatite vessel caches; red jasper beads, no effigy forms/no jasper beads, effigy forms; bipolar reduction/no bipolar reduction; no Jaketown perforators/Jaketown perforators. The original researchers (Gagliano and Webb 1970) proposed that the occupations were sequential, with the Late

Archaic population of Cedarland building the Claiborne site after the introduction of Poverty Point culture traits. James E. Bruseth (1991), however, argued that the dramatic differences in layout, feature type, and artifacts between the two sites indicated that an intrusive population constructed Claiborne. Because they have been destroyed, there is little hope that the relationship between Cedarland and Claiborne can be determined. Additional research on St. Catherines Island, however, may provide some relevant information. At the very least, the diametrically opposed artifact assemblages at the St. Catherines rings indicate that something quite different was occurring at those sites than at rings, such as Rollins and Guana, in which the artifact assemblages, even the pottery design assemblages (Saunders and Wrenn 2011), are quite similar.

The two largest and most complex ring sites studied to date are the Rollins Shell Ring in northeast Florida and the Fig Island Ring Complex in South Carolina. These two sites contain the aforementioned "ringlets," smaller U- or circular-shaped constructions attached to the exterior main ring wall. It was originally hypothesized (Saunders 2002, 2004a) that the ringlets might be later than the main ring; perhaps ringlets emerged as ritual became more competitive and exclusive. Radiocarbon dates at Fig Island indicated that this was a feasible hypothesis—the top of Fig Island Ring 1 dated approximately 100 years earlier

Table 4.1. Radiocarbon dates from sites discussed in text[a]

Site Name & No. / Sample No.	Provenience	Type	Conv date	Err	1 sigma*	2 sigma*
SOUTH CAROLINA						
Sea Pines (38BU7)						
I-2848	20–26 inches	clam	3810	110	4094–3779	4254–3627
I-2847	0–6 inches	conch	3520	110	3695–3417	3859–3313
Coosaw River Ring 1 (38BU1866)						
GX-29192	EU1 base, 90–95 cmbs (base of shell)	oyster	3790	70	4020–3822	4119–3694
Coosaw River Ring 2 (38BU1866)						
GX-29193	EU2 base, 110–120 cmbs (base of shell)	oyster	3560	70	3703–3498	3818–3427
GX-29527	EU2 top, 25–30 cmbs (top of shell)	oyster	3610	70	3780–3574	3866–3470
Coosaw River Ring 3 (38BU1866)						
GX-29194	EU3 base, 25–30 cmbs	oyster	3810	70	4046–3836	4143–3714
Fig Island Ring 1 (38CH42)						
Wk-9746	TU2, 90 cmbs, base of ringlet shell	oyster	3861	50	4078–3920	4150–3840
Wk-10103	TU2, top of ringlet shell	oyster	3816	50	4030–3857	4128–3774
Wk-10105	TU1, top of shell	oyster	3953	50	4226–4054	4308–3958
Fig Island Ring 2 (38CH42)						
Wk-9762	ST 4, Feature 4b, base of shell	oyster	4112	50	4421–4259	4507–4176
Wk-10102	ST 4, 30 cmbs, top of shell	oyster	4009	60	4309–4116	4402–4036
Fig Island Ring 3 (38CH42)						
Wk-9763	TU5, Posthole test, base of shell, west arm	oyster	4030	50	4331–4152	4403–4079
Wk-9747	Trench, TU2, base of shell	oyster	3993	50	4272–4094	4374–4016
Wk-10104	Trench, TU 1, top of shell	oyster	4074	50	4389–4230	4446–4126
Sewee Shell Ring (38CH45)						
GX- 30186	EU1, 33–48 cmbd	oyster	4010	70	4331–4106	4410–3987
GX- 30187	EU1, 150 cmbd, ring base	oyster	4120	70	4448–4241	4564–4137
GEORGIA						
Cannons Point (9GN57)						
UM-521	Marsh shell ring, sq.18N, 3E, 13cmbs, level 3, dates final occupation	oyster	4085	90	442–4167	4574–4039
UM-520	Marsh shell ring, base of midden deposits 1.47 m bs, initial occupation of shell ring	oyster	4600	90	5088–4843	5271–4798
Cannons Point West Ring (9GN76)						
UM-523	West Shell Ring Test 1, 12–20 cmbs (level 2), dates final occupation of ring	oyster	4015	110	4385–4073	4513–3895
UM-522	West Shell Ring Test 1, 45–55 cmbs (level 4), dates initial occupation of ring	oyster	4270	90	4695–4427	4818–4331

Site Name & No. / Sample No.	Provenience	Type	Conv date	Err	1 sigma*	2 sigma*
Sapelo Ring 1 (9MC23-1)						
UGA-73	1-m depth in ring 50-m diam, 2–3 m high	oyster	3840	70	4073–3876	4185–3775
UGA-74	2-m depth in ring 50-m diam, 2–3 m high	oyster	3840	70	4077–3869	4206–3769
UGA-15084	Unit 1, Level 2, 10–20 cm, borrow area on south side of ring	sooted sherd	3610	50	3979–3852	4084–3826
UGA-15085	Unit 1, Level 2, 10–20 cm, borrow area on south side of ring	sooted sherd	3730	60	4154–3981	
Sapelo Is. Ring 2 (9MC23-2)						
UGA-75	2-m depth in remnant of ring neighboring one with UGA-73, 74 assays	oyster	3955	70	4238–4019	4354–3927
Sapelo Is. Ring 3 (9MC23-3)						
UGA-15082	Unit 9, Level 4, shell midden or pit in "pre-ring" surface	charcoal	3560	50	3925–3825 (0.75) 3791–3768 (0.13) 3746–3729 (0.09) 3957–3952 (0.03)	3977–3704
UGA-15083	Unit 9, Level 7, shell midden or pit in "pre-ring" surface	charcoal	3730	50	4150–4065 (0.58) 4047–3987 (0.42)	4237–3962
UGA-15086	Unit 11, Level 4, non-shell area in "pre-ring" surface	charcoal	3730	50	4150–4065 (0.58) 4047–3987 (0.42)	4237–3962
Sapelo Island (9MC23)						
RL-580	Refuse pit, 80–135-cm bs in unit approx. 30 m south of Shell Ring I	hickory nut	4120	200	4871–4382	5083–4087
UGA-15081	Unit 3, Lev 10, 90–100 cm	charcoal	4060	50	4588–4506 (0.52) 4486–4440 (0.27) 4614–4593 (0.10) 4784–4766 (0.10)	4653–4421 (0.82)
	4809–4757 (0.13) 4705–4669 (0.6)					
UGA-15087	Unit 2, Lev 9, 80–90 cm	charcoal	3070	50	3359–3241	3391–3144
St. Catherines Ring						
Beta 231334	Pre-ring W82 S2	shell	4040	50	4350–4170	4410–4090
Beta 231335	Pre-ring W82 S2	shell	4170	40	4510–4370	4570–4280
Beta 215824	Pre-ring N789 E801	oyster	4120	60	4440–4250	4528–4150
Beta 215821	Pre-ring N782 E801	oyster	4140	50	4480–4310	4550–4220
Beta 229423	Primary shell deposit W82 S2	shell	3970	50	4240–4070	4340–3980
Beta 229424	Primary shell deposit W82 S2	shell	3960	50	4240–4060	4330–3970
Beta 215823	Overlying shell N789 E801	oyster	3880	50	4120–3950	4200–3860
Beta 215822	Overlying shell N784 E801	oyster	3800	60	4010–3830	3720–4110
McQueen Ring						
Beta 238324	TPII Top	shell	4100	60	4420–4230	4510–4140
Beta 238325	TPII Base	shell	3780	50	3980–3820	4060–3720
Beta 238326	TPII Middle	shell	3990	50	4270–4090	4370–4010
FLORIDA						
Oxeye (8DU7478)						
Beta 119814	ST 1262, 200 cmbs (base of shell)	oyster	4580	80	5060–4829	5246–4794

Table 4.1. (continued)

Site Name & No. / Sample No.	Provenience	Type	Conv date	Err	1 sigma*	2 sigma*
WK7437	EU5, 10–15 cmbs (top of shell)	estuarine shell	4400	60	4820–4647	4865–4523
Beta 119815	EU5, 100 cmbs (base of shell)	oyster	4570	70	5030–4835	5214–4795
Rollins Bird Sanctuary (8DU7510)						
Beta 119816	Trench 1, Main ring, west side, base of shell	oyster	3670	70	3843–3644	3955–3555
Beta 119817	Unit 3197, Main ring, east side, base of shell	oyster	3710	70	3894–3690	4005–3588
Beta 50155	4850N,250E, 60–65 cmbs, center of shell	oyster	3760	60	3964–3773	4061–3685
WK 7438	Trench 1, Main ring, west side, top of shell	oyster	3600	60	3753–3568	3833–3476
GX 25750	Trench 1, Feature 11, base, earth midden below shell	bulk carbon	3730	80	4162–3973 (0.85) 4230–4198 (0.10) 4180–4168 (0.04) 3938–3934 (0.01)	4299–3864
GX-30737	TU 10, Ringlet F, base of shell	oyster	3930	80	4220–3972	4352–3866
GX-30379	TU 11, Ringlet D, base of shell	oyster	3630	70	3810–3609	3894–3491
GX-30340	TU 11, Feature 28 (below ringlet base)	oyster	3820	70	4058–3849	4153–3720
GX-30378	TU12, Feature 26, shell feature south of ring	oyster	3840	70	4077–3869	4206–3769
GX-29516	TU1097, Feature in plaza of Ringlet J	oyster	2460	70	2340–2154	2474–2061
Guana River Shell Ring (8SJ2554)						
GX-31906	Feature 1, top of feature inside main ring	oyster	2740	70	2730–2530	2780–2385
GX-31908	Feature 1, center of feature inside main ring	oyster	2880	70	2864–2714	2994–2647
GX-31909	Feature 5, feature inside main ring	clam	3620	70	3800–3597	3879–3479
GX-31907	Feature 2/4, top of feature inside main ring	oyster	3740	70	3940–3727	4057–3638
Beta 166869	340N, 440E, feature inside main ring	clam	3720	60	3897–3711	3993–3624
Beta 154816	340N, 540E, shell deposit just south of ring	oyster	3860	60	4087–3899	4201–3825
GX-29517	469N, 453E, top of shell, main ring (reverse sequence)	oyster	3820	70	4058–3849	4153–3720
Beta 154817	469N, 453E, base of shell, main ring (reverse sequence)	oyster	3600	50	3735–3572	3824–3503
Beta 165598	380N, 400E, base of shell, southwest arm	oyster	3490	60	3605–3440	3686–3365
Beta 165599	410N, 520E, base of shell, east arm	oyster	3590	70	3757–3549	3841–3449

[a]Additional dates may be available from these sites (Russo 2006; Sanger and Thomas 2010; Sanger 2010; Saunders 2010; Thompson 2007). Dates shown are top and bottom ring dates and pre- or post-ring feature dates. All dates were recalibrated using Calib 5.0. following Thomas (2008), Delta R = -134 ± 26.

* For calibrations that produce multiple age ranges, if the probability of one range is over 90 percent, only that range is shown.

Type = type of material dated; Conv date = corrected for isotopic fractionation; Err = 1 sigma range.

than the top and bottom dates of Ringlet C. Dates from Rollins, however, did not bear this hypothesis out. Ringlet shell dates at Rollins were either contemporaneous with the main ring (as in Ringlet D) or more than 200 years earlier (at Ringlet F). This might suggest that at Rollins, the society became more inclusive rather than exclusive through time. Indeed, one might hypothesize that U-shaped rings invite inclusion, as they can be expanded whereas closed circles cannot. Such expansion may be visible at the Guana Shell Ring (Figure 4.5), where the somewhat unconsolidated, southernmost deposits may date later than the main ring, indicating growth at the ends of the ring arms. In any event, results like these confirm what ring shapes indicate: shell rings have many attributes in common, but they are highly variable in other respects.

Indeed, nowhere is this variability more apparent than in ring plazas. As noted, the broad commonality among rings is that, by definition, they are all enclosures of one sort or another and that they embrace an area of *relatively* sterile coastal tan sand, a plaza in virtually all interpretations. While most shell-ring plazas do not contain anywhere near the density of artifacts and ecofacts present in the ring walls, this does not mean that artifacts and features are absent. At the St. Catherines ring, there are an estimated 500 large cylindrical features in two concentric circles within the plaza; the McQueens ring also has such features (Sanger and Thomas 2010, 59). However, these earth-filled features predate the ring wall. Indeed, at the St. Catherines ring, the 21 acceptable dates from the site indicate three successive spates of activity, concluding with the erection of the ring wall. Initial activity at the site occurred between 4540 and 4490 BP and is reflected in a series of small, shallow, semicircular features filled with burned and calcined shell. These features occur below the ring wall and nowhere else. The aforementioned cylindrical features in the ring interior were emplaced between 4410 and 4210 cal BP; as noted, the majority of the ring wall was deposited between 4230 and 4030 cal BP (Sanger and Thomas 2010).

The cylindrical features in the plaza, at least so far, are unique to the St. Catherines Island rings, but pre-ring features conforming in distribution to the footprint of the ring also occurred at Sapelo 1,[5] where, according to Antonio J. Waring Jr. and Lewis H. Larson (1968), small (2-foot-diameter [0.61-meter]), shallow (0.5-foot [0.15-meter]) pits were infilled by the first shell-ring deposits (cf. Thompson and Andrus 2011).[6] Subring features also occurred at Sapelo Ring 3 (Thompson 2007) and at Rollins (Saunders 2004a). At Sapelo 3, the subring pits were also shell-filled;

shell in subring features at Sapelo 1 and 3 was not burned like the St. Catherines Island subring shell. At Rollins, a nonshell, 25-centimeter-thick earth midden precisely underlay the nucleus of the ring wall (i.e., the initial deposits, not the extent of the final shell mantle). At the base of this earth midden, a series of overlapping circular pits became visible. These also were devoid of shell, and there was little bone or pottery. However, many of these features had a lens of particulate charcoal at the base, suggesting a cooking function. One sample of this particulate charcoal returned a date of 4160–3980 1 cal BP, approximately 300 years earlier than the shell at the ring base. Thus, while ring walls went up relatively quickly, at Rollins ring activity spanned hundreds of years. Curiously, during initial main ring activity (deposition of the earth midden) shellfish were deposited elsewhere. A date on a shell feature below the base of Ringlet D (4160–3970 1 cal BP) is almost identical to the charcoal date, and shell from the base of Ringlet F dates to this period (4050–3820 1 cal BP) (Saunders 2010).

SHELL-RING FUNCTION

The function of shell rings is debated. Early interpretations included functions ranging from dance grounds and torture chambers (McKinley 1873) to fish traps (Edwards 1965). In the compilation of his writings released in 1968, Waring considered rings to be ceremonial sites built of habitation debris, though that pronouncement is contradicted in another paper in the volume (Waring and Larson 1968) (see Saunders 2002; Russo 2006 for more thorough summaries of excavation and speculation). In an influential paper published in 1985, Michael B. Trinkley argued for a strictly secular function for rings, an interpretation echoed by William H. Marquardt (2010a, 2010b; see also DePratter 2010). Marquardt argued that the two St. Catherines rings could have been built as reservoirs.[7] The interior of the rings "may have been excavated to enhance access to fresh water from below and/or to collect rainwater" (Marquardt 2010b, 258), and the deep features uncovered by Matthew C. Sanger and David Hurst Thomas (2010) could represent wells. Most archaeologists, however, argue for a secular habitation function, a sacred function, or some combinations of these two. Russo (2008) argued that rings were village sites that also served a ceremonial function, while Thompson (2007) offered a kind of compromise. On the basis of analogies to shell-ring sites in Ecuador and Japan, Thompson proposed an "Evolution of Place" model, in which the function of southeastern shell rings changed

through time. Sites began as circular habitation settlements, perhaps occupied throughout the year, with houses
adjacent to large pits that were slowly filled with shell and
other household garbage. Once the pits were filled, garbage was allowed to accumulate in piles next to structures.
Over time, these piles formed a closed ring, and residences
shifted either to the inside or to the top of the shell ring. At
some point the village site was abandoned, after which the
site took on a purely ceremonial function and additional
shell was dumped on the ring in ritual deposits.

It is plausible that ring function changed through
time—certainly the Rollins data indicates major changes
in intrasite use through time—and I would be particularly
amenable to the idea that earlier rings *were* habitation sites
that provided the prototypes for larger, ceremonial rings.[8]
The idea of habitation on top of, or adjacent to, large piles
of garbage, however, does not conform to the expectations
derived from studies of disposal patterns for long-term
habitation sites. I will not cite olfactory arguments, as
medieval European cities, not to mention 19th-century
New York City neighborhoods, were probably more odor-
iferous than shell middens. Urban situations aside, most
long-term habitation sites have trash disposal away from
habitations. Susan Kent's (1992) study of disposal practices
among extant (in the Kalahari Desert) and archaeological
cultures (in the American Southwest) indicated that when
a habitation is expected to last several months or more,
garbage is disposed of in formal middens some distance
away from habitation areas, a finding confirmed by
Robert L. Kelly and colleagues (2005, 2006) in Madagascar, and by Morgan Schmidt (2010) in the Xingu basin.
Removal is especially desirable for bulky items (Hayden
and Cannon 1983) like shell, and for sharp items such as
shell, fish vertebrae, and spines. In the Xingu basin, manioc pulp (and other garbage) is deposited away from the
house because informants say the pulp rots and "raises
bugs" (Schmidt 2010, 289, 832, 897). And, while cultural
logic surely does intercede in practical decisions (Hutson
and Stanton 2007)—indeed I argue that it is cultural logic
that drove the piling of shell to create rings—it is difficult
to envision life on top of shell rings or inside them. If the
population lived on top of the rings, shell would be
crushed, not whole, and traversing the ring from top to
bottom by the population numerous times a day would
undoubtedly destroy the integrity of the walls and the
appearance of segmentation. If people lived inside, trash
disposal would become quite costly, as shell and bone
would have to be tossed or carried up slopes, which would
also be detrimental to the integrity of the ring walls. In

short, logistics and ring-wall integrity argue against casual
disposal and accretion from the top or bottom of the ring.

My idiosyncratic vision for the way that *some* shell rings
functioned in the Middle and Late Archaic landscape of
the lower Atlantic coast[9]—and I consider this a string of
hypotheses to be tested—is that shell rings were ceremonial sites that served an integrative function. Ring sites are
generally isolated from the other two characteristic site
types of the period, the aforementioned residential sheet
shell middens and nonshell sites, which are often interpreted as hunting camps. The isolation of rings provided
neutral ground for macro-bands or tribes to come together
at "integrative facilities" (Adler and Wilshusen 1990) for
mate selection, trade, information exchange, ceremony,
and perhaps for corporate work projects. Such separate
structures were and still are created for the Green Corn
Dance, one of the most important of the surviving seasonal celebrations of the Southeastern Indians (see below).

What I envision in terms of the function of rings is similar to what Willem de Boer (1997) and de Boer and
John H. Blitz (1991) described for the Chachi of coastal
Ecuador, and what Tom D. Dillehay (1990) has recorded for
the Mapuche of south-central Chile. Since the early 1900s,
the Chachi have lived in dispersed, single-house settlements but periodically aggregate in vacant ceremonial
centers such as Punta Venado during the major holidays of
Christmas and Easter, and also during more aperiodic
events such as weddings and funerals. These centers serve
not only for ceremony, but also as "capitol, court, cemetery, and territorial marker" (de Boer 1997, 225). "Test pits
excavated at Punta Venado exposed 80 cm of midden
chock-full of artefactual and culinary refuse" that had
been accumulating for two centuries (de Boer 1997, 225).
"In contrast, single house residential sites (where the Chachi actually live) are typically occupied for only a decade
or so and are associated with relatively shallow, even
superficial, middens" (de Boer 1997, 227). Punta Venado
has "a number of separate guest houses, each assignable to
a particular area within its territory. In essence, Punta
Venado resembles a village, much like the ancestral villages that the Chachi claim to have occupied before adopt-
ing the dispersed settlement pattern of recent times" (de
Boer 1997, 225). The houses at the ceremonial center are
"microcosmically arranged," suggesting that the ceremonial center, symbolically conceived, is a "big house." De
Boer cites such disparate Amerindian cultures and lin-
guistic groups as the Ohio Hopewell (100 BC–AD 400),
Mississippian (ca. AD 900–1400), and historic Cree, Yuchi,
Iroquoian Cherokee, the Souian Omaha, the Caddoan

Pawnee, and the Cheyenne as sharing the notion that "a domestic house can be expanded progressively to a 'big house,' a settlement layout, and, as an ultimate extension, the cosmos itself" (de Boer 1997, 229–30).

De Boer's descriptions and analogies are important in any number of ways, but several aspects of the Chachi ceremonial center deserve note here. First, the presence of an apparently domestic midden at a ceremonial center is to be expected. Second, the presence of domestic-looking structures is an expectable occurrence at ceremonial centers where rituals last for several days or even weeks. Third, feasting is an important part of this population amalgamation: "In addition to the religious observances, the celebrants engage in feasting" (de Boer and Blitz 1991, 57–58). Finally, these ceremonial centers emerged when the Chachi were forced out of their nucleated villages and into a dispersed settlement pattern around AD 1900.

The Mapuche, who live in dispersed villages in south-central Chile, also have a biannual (at planting and harvesting season), four- to six-day event that requires that they journey from scattered villages and converge on a semicircular or U-shaped ceremonial field—a field separate from habitation sites—for social and religious ceremony. These ceremonial fields are "permanently designated sacred spaces" (Dillehay 1990, 227) that play a role in the "social and territorial stability of local corporate ceremonial groups" (Dillehay 1990, 223). Each participating lineage returns to a designated section of the field, where each family occupies a permanent hut (*ruka*) (Dillehay 1990, 228). "This pattern is a contraction or microcosm of the actual domestic household settlement pattern of local lineages" (Dillehay 1990, 228). Fields may expand or contract "as a result of the gain or loss of membership due to demographic expansion or fragmentation, internal and external conflict, or political marriage" (Dillehay 1990, 230). "During the ceremonial period families perform such domestic chores as cooking, eating, weaving, and woodworking in their respective *rukas*" (Dillehay 1992, 414). In contrast to the Chachi, however, the ceremonial fields of the Mapuche are ritually cleaned before and after the ceremony. "Although foreign materials are carried to the ceremonial field by different groups for use *during* the ceremony, they are carried out *afterwards*. The only visible evidence of ceremonial activity in unused and abandoned fields is the presence of *rukas*, scraps of food, broken ceramic vessels, glass bottles, grinding stones, bones of sacrificial animals [which would be found in the center of the plaza], and ashy areas around hearths" (Dillehay 1992, 394; emphasis in original). Thus, while considerable

domestic activity occurs within the confines of both ceremonial centers, Chachi ceremonial sites have as much or more midden debris than domestic sites, and Mapuche fields have less. In both the Chachi and the Mapuche cases, festivities are accompanied by feasting. It is interesting to note in this respect that both the Chachi and the Mapuche prize shellfish; the Chachi "import" them for feasting at ceremonial centers and the Mapuche are careful to maintain trading relationships with peoples with access to shellfish (de Boer and Blitz 1991; Dillehay 1992, 390).

Returning to the southeastern United States, the southeastern ethnohistoric record is replete with references to Native American feasting in conjunction with ceremonial and social life (see, e.g., Swanton 1979 [1946]). It is probably significant that one of the major ceremonies that has survived to the present is the Green Corn Ceremony, which celebrates, with feasting, the major subsistence item of late prehistoric and early historic Southeastern Native Americans. For our Archaic folks, I envision that when they came together at ring sites, they also feasted, not with exotic or high-trophic-level foods but with dietary mainstays. Subsistence remains from rings indicate that small schooling fishes provided the bulk of the calories, with shellfish providing most of the rest (see note 1). Indeed, Brian Hayden (2001) noted that only certain kinds of feasts involve high-trophic-level or rare species. Feasting for integrative purposes is characterized by large quantities of the most important everyday foods, just what is seen at shell rings. I argue that shell rings are the tangible remains of those feasts, with the leavings piled high to demonstrate the success of the corporate groups. Rings are consumption made conspicuous.

The quotidian nature of the subsistence remains and material culture in ring deposits, however, has been the central conundrum for the assignment of function, for early researchers such as Waring and for modern researchers such as Trinkley and Marquardt. With reference to site formation processes at Chachi and Mapuche ceremonial sites, however, this result is expected.

How, then, is one to discriminate between a ceremonial site with debris (subsistence items and shelter) prepared during week- or month-long festivities and village sites that were occasionally used for ceremony? Drawing on the reports of previous and current research into shell rings, on the ethnographic literature, and on Hayden's (e.g., 2001) work on the archaeological manifestations of feasts, one can develop a set of characteristics that might be used to identify ceremonial shell midden sites on the lower Atlantic coast from domestic sites (see also Russo, chap. 3 in this volume; Widmer, chap. 2 in this volume). Presented below is a list of these criteria; most are presented "asked and answered." However, I would like to conclude this chapter with a short discussion of the difference in debris accumulation between shell rings and domestic sites that are often analogized to shell rings.

Criteria to consider in the assignment of function include:

Aspects of the settlement system: Shell-ring sites are quite distinct in character from the other two site types of the Late Archaic, and rings are isolated from these other site types.[10]

Intrasite organization and contemporaneity: Dated deposits should indicate that the site layout was present in the initial deposits. Because of the difficulty of reaching basal deposits at large ring sites, there are few good sets of dates demonstrating this presence. However, at Rollins Shell Ring, initial shell deposits on the east and west sides of the ring were contemporaneous (Saunders 2004a).

Maintenance of a relatively shell-free plaza and ring exterior, as well as the retention of segmentation in ring walls, occurred throughout the period of site use. Betty Meehan's (1982) description of accretional shell midden formation among Australian aborigines (see below), and especially Schmidt's (2010) description of earth-midden formation behind Xingu circular villages, emphasize how dynamic the habitation/disposal system is (e.g., Schmidt 2010, 822), with middens expanding haphazardly and area function changing through time. Ring sites, however, were rigorously maintained. In addition, although rings are strategically located with respect to resources, most show no signs of significant reoccupation after Archaic abandonment. This is not the case with sheet shell middens. It is as if later cultures recognized the sacredness of the ring space (Russo, chap. 3 of this volume, also makes this point).

Stratigraphy indicates purposeful and rapid mounding of large quantities of shellfish and other subsistence items. Oyster shell in the ring walls is jumbled, valves are whole and are often vertical (making it difficult to dig in small levels). Gradual accretion would result in soil accumulation and admixture in the midden; midden deposited within a village would also be subject to post-depositional crushing and other cultural and natural disturbances. Though some areas of crushing have been noted for some rings (Waring 1968, noted for Sapelo 1), neither of these characteristics (soils and crushing) is apparent in the walls of Fig Island, Rollins, Guana, Coosa, or Sewee—site excavations with which I am most familiar.

In principle, Marquardt's (2010a, 2010b) criticism of the assignment of ceremonial function to almost any large concentration of shell is correct. He argued that any formal midden away from habitation sites (and he insisted that these middens should be away from habitations) that is continuously used could result in a similar stratigraphy, and this is true. However, he failed to account for (among other things) the formal layout of ring sites and their stark differences in disposal practices at other contemporaneous sites of the period (or any other period for that matter). Ring deposition is different. On another note, none of the ring profiles with which I am familiar show a break in deposition—from gradual accumulation to mounding—that would be expected from the Evolution of Place model.

Size of the deposits: The smallest undisturbed ring is the Sea Pines ring, which is only 37 meters in interior diameter and 0.6 meters tall. This tiny ring appears almost as a scale model of other rings. At the opposite end of the scale is the Fig Island 1 ring, which towers six meters above the surrounding marsh; other rings are commonly from two to four meters high. As discussed in more detail below, this is much higher than middens at archaeologically or ethnographically described habitation sites. In the Xingu basin, ethnographically documented middens are rarely over 40 centimeters in depth (Schmidt 2010, 835) and these are intentionally built up for use as compost.[11]

Stratigraphy, artifacts, and ecofacts indicate that the sites are not solely shell-processing sites. They lack the "bedded stratigraphy" characteristic of large-scale shell-processing sites such as those reported by Barbara Voorhies (2004) in the Acapetahua Estuary of southern Mexico, or the Jomon sites briefly discussed below. Voorhies (2004) also reported archaeological and ethnographic instances of large shell dumps, but these do not contain other faunal material or artifacts.

Elaboration of artifact assemblage: The frequency of decorated ceramic wares is much higher in shell rings relative to contemporaneous sheet-midden or nonshell sites. This is true for all Orange Tradition sites studied (Saunders 2004b), and it is true for the Fig Island rings (Thoms Creek Tradition pottery; Saunders 2002b) and for the Daws Island rings (Stalling Tradition pottery; Saunders unpublished data).

Like Marquardt, Thompson (2006, 2007) has criticized one or another of these hypotheses as inconclusive and subject to the whims of equifinality. However, I have always insisted that individually, none of these traits (i.e., whole shell) is decisive, but when a number of them co-occur, there should be some consideration that the site is ceremonial and that ceremonial feasting can be considered a site activity. In arguing against a primarily ceremonial function for rings, Thompson (2006) has been particularly emphatic in pointing out that accretional shell midden sites—habitation sites—could accumulate rapidly and form complex patterns. He (2006, 45–46) specifically cites Meehan's (1982) work with Australian shellfish collectors as a good example of how large piles of shell can accumulate. However, Thompson (2006, 46) undermines his own argument by illustrating the irregularity of the Australian midden deposits and their low elevation ("up to 50 cm thick"; Meehan 1982, fig. 19), which is lower than the lowest of the known shell rings except Sea Pines.

COMPARISONS WITH ECUADOR, COLUMBIA, AND JAPAN

Many archaeologists who ascribed a domestic function to shell-ring sites did so on the basis of analogy to circular midden sites in other parts of the world. Indeed, this analogy dates back to James A. Ford's (1966, 1969) vision of the Formative Stage in the New World. I find many of those analogies flawed. Here, I would like to compare the stratigraphy of lower Atlantic shell-ring sites with other shell-ring sites from coastal locations around the world—with an emphasis on the stratigraphic and chronological characteristics that researchers used to assign site function.

Ecuador

Ford (1969, vii) cited the results of investigations in coastal Ecuador as the earliest evidence he could find of the "American Formative," his chain of maritime cultures stretching from the shores of Ecuador to the estuaries of the southeastern United States. Ford (1969) specifically cited the Sapelo Island Ring Complex in Georgia as similar to circular occupations in Ecuador. However, as indicated in the contemporary site reports by Betty Meggers and colleagues (1965), the analogy of coastal Ecuadoran sites to Atlantic coastal shell rings is weak. Only four of the ten Valdivia-phase sites discussed in their report were mapped; three of these four, including the Valdivia site itself, had oval or suboval midden accumulations. Only Punta Arenas had what appeared to be a central plaza.

Nor, with the exception of parts of the Valdivia site, were the site middens particularly deep. Most appear to be only 30–45 centimeters, in residential sites estimated to have been in use for up to 400 years. Midden material was described as consisting of "powdery soil containing large amounts of shell, sherds, and other kinds of natural and cultural refuse" (Meggers, Evans, and Estrada 1965, 15); in

other words, midden contents had been subject to exposure (evidenced in aeolian soil accumulation) throughout the life of the site.

In a more recent summary of the Early Formative in the western lowlands of Ecuador, however, J. Scott Raymond (2003) presented better evidence that many early Valdivian sites were U-shaped or elliptical villages, with plaza areas kept scrupulously clean. Still, these sites are not good analogs for shell rings because midden deposits are shallow—Valdivian people did not live on top of or against meters of garbage. Although Raymond did not directly discuss the depth of the middens, because midden debris does not alter the natural contours in the maps presented (Raymond 2003, figs. 7, 8), the middens do not appear to have been deep. Again, these sites were occupied for hundreds if not thousands of years.

Site function in the Valdivia period did change through time. As with the Chachi, more formal ceremonial centers appeared with population dispersal during the Middle and Late Valdivia (Raymond 2003). This congruence makes one wonder if something similar did not occur in our southeastern coastal sites. For the southeastern case, one might speculate that the population nucleation that may be represented by early shell-ring sites was unsustainable, due to either climatic and/or social disruptions (both climate and sea level were unstable during the Middle and Late Archaic), and integrative shell rings were created as populations dispersed. At present, there are not enough well-dated rings to thoroughly test this hypothesis, although Matthew C. Sanger (2010) hypothesized that there were in fact three waves of abandonment of shell-ring sites (or, alternatively, that there were three major periods of construction). The first set of rings were built, and abandoned, between ca. 4900 and 4100 cal BP, a second set arose around 4050 and was abandoned by 3800, and the final set occurred between 3800 and 3500.[12]

Columbia

Raymond and other researchers have noted the similarity of early Formative sites on the Guayas coast of Ecuador to the Caribbean coast of Columbia. In turn, in a discussion of shared characteristics between Columbian and Orange Period sites, Geraldo Reichel-Dolmatoff (1972) described the Puerta Hormiga site, which was occupied between 5100 and 3000 BP, and is characteristic of other Columbian ring sites:

> Like other early shellmounds in the area, Puerta Hormiga is a habitation site, as could be observed from

several living floors covered with trampled shells and containing hearths and ash layers . . . The principal mound is ring-shaped accumulation of clam shells, with a diameter of 80 metres, which encloses a flat circular area. Width of the ring varies little from an average of 20 metres and its height above ground level is hardly more than one metre . . . There are also indications that what eventually became a circle originally had a bracket-shaped ground-plan with diagonally opposed openings. This pattern, of *slow circular formation*, can also be observed at other shellmounds. [Reichel-Dolmatoff 1972, 2, emphasis added]

Referring only to stratigraphy, the important comparative points here are: the height of the Columbian rings, not over one meter, which accrued over an occupation span of some 2,000 years. In addition, living floors were "covered with trampled shells" and contained hearths and ash layers. This contrasts with southeastern shell rings, where heights can reach over six meters, accumulation is rapid, and trampling and features are present in only a few ring walls.

Japan

The massive shell rings in Jomon-period (14,500–300 BC) sites in Japan have also been compared to southeastern rings (Thompson 2007). The Jomon rings are associated with pit dwellings that often occur "beneath the shell layers" (Habu 2004, 73). However, only a few dwellings were ever occupied at the same time (Habu 2004). One of the largest of the Jomon shell rings, the horseshoe-shaped, 170-meter-diameter Kasori South shell midden, was occupied for ca. 1,000 years; Junko Habu described shell accumulation as "relatively slow" (Habu 2004, 75). Ultimately, the main elevation of the southeastern arm of the Kasori South ring was about a half-meter above ground surface, with the highest points at one meter (Habu 2004, 75).

Indeed, in a more general discussion of ring- "or horseshoe"-shaped sites, Tatsuo Kobayashi noted,

According to studies of the annual growth lines on shells by Koike Hiroko, approximately seventy percent of shells from the shell middens [shell rings] were harvested during a limited season from spring to summer. This fact indicates that the large scale of some of these shell middens was the result of intensive seasonal harvesting and processing of shellfish for preservation and export, rather than regular gathering for local consumption throughout the year. [Kobayashi 2004, 92]

Other Jomon-period shell midden sites, like the 4.5-meter-deep Nakazato midden, display lenses of burnt shell and charcoal that clearly indicate special-purpose shellfish processing sites like those documented by Voorhies (2004) in Mexico.

In sum, I think that the data, in the categories discussed above, indicates that Late Archaic shell rings on the lower Atlantic coast are distinct from sheet-midden habitation sites or special processing sites and that the suite of characteristics suggests large-scale feasting. As is typical of archaeological interpretations, other aspects of this discussion are more speculative. Ideas are offered as a string of hypotheses, some more susceptible to testing than others. I suggest that, in their isolation from habitation sites, rings were neutral territory where bands of fisher-gatherer-hunters congregated, probably when resources were most abundant, for ritual, feasting, information, and mate selection. The ring plaza was the focus of the events, and the ring wall provided an amphitheatric atmosphere, and possibly protection from external evil forces, as Jon L. Gibson (2001, 183–84) proposed for the rings of Poverty Point. Segments of the same lineages may have returned to the same segment of the ring for each festival, and, as the remains of the feasts were piled up, the success of the corporate group would be visible to all. The rituals, feasts, and construction activity all served an incorporative function. Individual lineages may have gotten bragging rights (as opposed to more formal prestige; see Russo 2004) if they produced the highest ring segment—they would have improved their "credit rating" (Hayden 2001, 32)—but these were not competitive, sumptuary feasts. In their splendid isolation, rings were all about inclusion.

AFTERWORD

The last section was dedicated to demonstrating that many sites/cultures that had been used in analogies to buttress a village interpretation for southeastern shell rings were, in fact, not that similar. That said, analogizing southeastern shell-ring sites to circular habitation sites is not wrong on all counts. As noted at the beginning of this chapter, Native Americans may have done the same thing. There is good ethnographic evidence, literally from around the world, that the layout of ceremonial sites often replicated broader community physical and social relationships. De Boer (1997), for instance, found that the common element in prehistoric ceremonial centers in the New World was that they could all be characterized as "big houses"; they are massively enlarged versions of domestic prototypes.

Raymond (2003, 52) noted that for both North and South America, among diverse ethnic groups, terms for *house* and *settlement* are used interchangeably, and villages and ceremonial centers are all considered big houses (for Europe, see Bradley 2005). Such layouts can also reflect a more expansive cosmology. Drawing on ethnographic work emanating from the Amazon, Raymond (2003) and Karen Stothert (2003) note the repetition of cosmological motifs in house, ceremonial structure, and village layout. For Stothert (2003, 344), the circular and oval-shaped plans of the Early Formative villages of the coast are "constructed sacred landscapes and cosmic metaphors." In short, Archaic ceremonial centers are supposed to look like village sites, only village sites on a grand scale; these sites are intermediaries between individual houses and villages, and the cosmos, which looks like a ceremonial center or a village or a house, only larger. This almost fractal, cosmological settlement pattern may be one reason why we have so much trouble accepting shell rings as shell monuments.

NOTES

1. Some rings have zooarchaeological assemblages that are more diverse (though equitability remains low). Both the early Canons Point rings in south Georgia and the two St. Catherines Island rings in north Georgia are examples.

2. The circular enclosures of the Old World Neolithic, too, have journeyed from the secular to the sacred (Bradley 1998).

3. In the Xingu basin (southeastern Amazonia), oval to circular Kuikuru village sites are moved (sometimes immediately adjacent to the former village) due to factional disputes/fissioning, catastrophic events like fires, and sorcery or other otherworldy concerns (Heckenberger 1996, 339, table 7).

4. Although there are some interesting differences in artifact frequency at Fig Island.

5. The Sapelo 1 ring is a massive, closed ring, reported as nine feet (2.74 meters) tall in 1873 (McKinley 1873).

6. Thompson and Andrus (2011) was published just as revisions for this article were due. There is much to discuss in that article; unfortunately that discussion is beyond the scope of this chapter.

7. There are a number of problems with the reservoir hypothesis, but the easiest argument against it is that all rings were built on well- to excessively drained sands that would not hold water.

8. Claassen (2010) argued that there were no villages in the southeastern Archaic.

9. Archaic shell rings in southwest Florida and elsewhere may have functioned differently.

10. Some shell rings are close (ca. one kilometer distant) to contemporaneous sheet-midden sites that might be considered associated villages, including Rollins, Guana, and the Daws Island rings.

11. What is going on with deep (up to two meters) earth-ring middens surrounding individual terrace areas (houses?) over an area some 200 meters in length in the Central Amazon remains to be seen (Schmidt 2010, 910ff).

12. Ultimately, between 3500 and 3000 cal BP (coincident with terminal Valdivia), Archaic shell-ring construction ceased. This time range marks the onset of a climatic disturbance that apparently caused the disruption and dispersion of a number of vigorous Late Archaic cultures across the Southeast (see papers in Thomas and Sanger 2010; Saunders 2009). The eventual societal reformulation, in the Early Woodland period, saw the rise of a different type of ceremonialism (Russo, chap. 3 in this volume).

CHAPTER FIVE

LATE HOLOCENE COASTAL ECONOMIES AND THE *ANADARA GRANOSA*–DOMINATED SHELL MOUNDS OF NORTHERN AUSTRALIA

Evidence from Blue Mud Bay, Northeast Arnhem Land

Patrick A. Faulkner

SUMMARY

Large shell mounds dominated by the sand/mudflat bivalve *Anadara granosa* are prominent features across much of the north Australian coast. There have been numerous explanations proposed for these mounds, ranging from purely economic to ceremonial, but all largely based on the direct use of ethnographic analogy. For the most part, Australian archaeologists have focused on the larger shell mounds without investigating the broader timing and nature of coastal occupation within a given region. As a result, we have not had an integrated view of the real significance of these sites in Australian prehistory, and no real way of evaluating the strength of prior interpretations. By investigating the structure and timing of the archaeological record in Blue Mud Bay, northeast Arnhem Land—specifically the timing, distribution, and morphology of shell deposits, coupled with a detailed investigation of longer-term *A. granosa* size change (Faulkner 2013)—this chapter explores patterns of economic change and the role of shell mounds in the north Australian coastal economy and presents alternative explanations for dynamic human behavior and resource use.

ANADARA GRANOSA SHELL MOUND INVESTIGATIONS IN NORTHERN AUSTRALIA

Large mounded deposits of shell, largely composed of the sand/mudflat bivalve *Anadara granosa*, are prominent archaeological features across much of the north Australian tropical coast. While not being the sole focus, much of the archaeological research conducted on the north Australian coastline has been centered on the investigation of

these shell mounds. This fascination with the "mound phenomenon" (Bailey 1999, 105) has arisen out of their high visibility and apparent dominance in many coastal areas. While it is not possible to provide definitive numbers of *A. granosa*–dominated middens recorded across northern Australia, large numbers of these sites occur across a vast geographic area (Figure 5.1). For example, within the Darwin region Patricia Bourke (2000) recorded 178 shell mounds; on Milingimbi Island Andrew Roberts (1991) recorded 118 mounds; and in the Weipa region of far north Queensland more than 300 mounds have been recorded (Bailey 1977; Morrison 2010). As a result of their prevalence, there has been a relatively long history of inquiry into the nature and significance of these shell mounds. The earliest observations occur in the ethnographic literature from approximately 1900 (Roth 1901), and initial excavations of the north Australian shell mounds were undertaken between the 1920s and the 1940s. These pioneering excavations by W. Lloyd Warner (1969, 462–63) and by Frederick D. McCarthy and Frank M. Setzler (1960, 232–33, 244, 250) on the large Milingimbi Island shell mounds in northeast Arnhem Land, followed by the work of Richard V. S. Wright (1971) in the early 1960s at Weipa, were undertaken primarily to determine the nature, origin, and antiquity of these deposits. The continuation of this work until the present, with more detailed research in a number of distinct and widely separated geographic regions, has provided us with a relatively broad-scale understanding of the morphology and content, spatial distribution, and temporal patterns of *A. granosa* shell mounds.

Although these sites occur across a considerable geographic area (from northern Western Australia to north

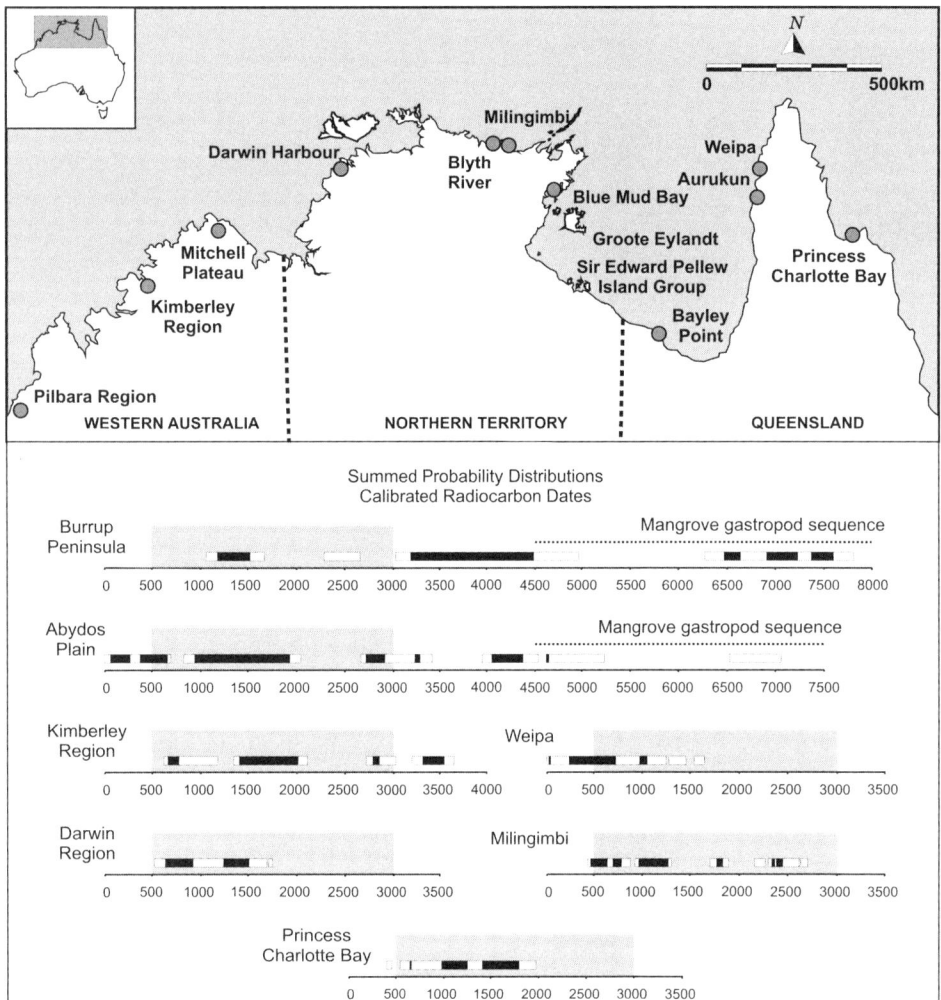

5.1. Regions investigated in detail containing Anadara granosa shell mounds (above). Regional summed probability 1σ (white bar) and 2σ (black bar) calibrated age range (BP) distributions (below).

Queensland), and there is a degree of regional variability in the timing and nature of these *A. granosa* mounds, there are a number of commonly occurring features (see also discussion in Hiscock 2008, 175–76; Hiscock and Faulkner 2006, 209). These sites are characteristically dense, tightly packed concentrations of shell, with minor amounts of sediment, stone artifacts, animal bone, and charcoal/ash. *A. granosa* dominates the molluskan assemblages of the majority of the mounds at 70 to 90 percent, while the subspecies components vary both spatially and temporally. Although the chronological patterns for the occurrence of *A. granosa* shell mounds vary by region, the most intensive period of mound formation appears to fall between approximately 3,500 and 500 cal BP (Figure 5.1). The sequences from Western Australia (the Burrup peninsula and Abydos Plain on the Pilbara coast, and the Kimberley region) are considerably longer; however this reflects the

transition within the same sites from mangrove gastropod-dominated assemblages (*Terebralia* or *Telescopium* spp.) of the early Holocene (8,000 to 6,000 BP) to overlying *A. granosa* mounded deposits of the mid- to late Holocene (after 4,500 BP) (Clune and Harrison 2009). The Weipa area presents a more anomalous pattern, with a major peak at 500 BP and a significant proportion of the calibrated age ranges extending into the last 500 years (Morrison 2010). Mounds often occur as clusters or linear distributions of up to 26 sites (e.g., Faulkner 2006; Morrison 2003), ranging in height from approximately 20 centimeters to greater than 10 meters above the land surface. In terms of their position, many sites are presently located away from the current shoreline (up to seven kilometers in some areas due to progradation and sedimentary infilling), and are situated variously on salt flats, chenier ridges, or lateritic slopes/platforms overlooking mangroves, often within or at the edge of the open eucalypt woodlands on the laterite surface. Sites are often positioned in relative proximity to current or infilled embayments, suggesting that these areas were focal points for economic activity, possibly related to the density of molluskan resources in these kinds of environments.

During the past 50 years Australian archaeologists have cycled through a number of analytical or interpretive frameworks attempting to explain the *A. granosa* shell mounds. Many of the interpretations of these shell mounds have been economic in nature, relying heavily on environmental and ecological data, often combined strongly with ethnographic information. For example, these sites have been seen to directly reflect past human diet and/or the purposeful construction of large mounded deposits as camping places or sites for the promotion of plant foods (Bailey 1977, 1983, 1994; Bourke 2000; Cribb 1996; Roberts 1991). These economic interpretations rely heavily on inferred regular, low-intensity subsistence foraging by small groups of hunter-gatherers, patterns of behavior that are derived from ethnographic and ethno-archaeological observations of seasonal mobility and resource exploitation (e.g., Meehan 1982; Roth 1901; Thomson 1949; Warner 1969). More recently, a number of researchers have proposed the argument that *A. granosa*–dominated mounded shell deposits are more related to past social and ceremonial structures (Bourke 2000; Clune and Harrison 2009; Harrison 2009; Morrison 2003; although see Klokler, chap. 11 in this volume; Okumura and Eggers, chap. 8 in this volume; Gaspar et al., chap. 7 in this volume). These explanations are largely based on higher exploitation levels, generally on a more irregular basis to support large groups participating in ceremonial activities. Again, these interpretations draw heavily on comparatively recent ethnographic or historical observations of Australian Aboriginal people, emphasizing those connections between the landscape and religious and political beliefs (Bourke 2000).

These interpretations are potentially problematic as they are based on ethnographic observation to interpret long-term behavioral patterns (Hiscock and Faulkner 2006). In many respects, these scales of observation are not easily correlated, and ethnographic sample points of short duration cannot be used to make direct inferences about long-term processes, their properties, or causes (for example Beaton 1990, 28–33; Erlandson 2001, 295; Faulkner 2013, 181; Moss and Erlandson 1995, 29; Peterson 1971, 241). Those interpretations outlined above often do not adequately consider changes in environmental and climatic conditions, and therefore the structure of the resource base, during and

beyond the period of mound formation. Additionally, these dominant interpretations reflect behaviors that would be continuous, but not excessive in terms of *A. granosa* exploitation. In fact, there have been very few studies aimed at investigating whether the intensity of *A. granosa* exploitation within the shell mounds matches or potentially exceeds that observed during the more recent past (for exceptions, see Bailey 1993, 10; Bourke 2000; Faulkner 2009, 2013). If shell mound sites reflect foraging behaviors different from those seen ethnographically (Meehan 1982, 168), then we may see differences in the intensity of use of the landscape and the available resources. To explore the possibility of continuities or discontinuities in human behavior relative to mounded *A. granosa* shell deposits, we need to assess possible changes in the foraging economy, landscape use, and intensity of resource exploitation.

BLUE MUD BAY, NORTHEAST ARNHEM LAND

Archaeological research on the Point Blane peninsula provides a case study for investigating issues of the formation and behavioral factors associated with *A. granosa* shell mounds. The study area is located within the northern coastal plains of Blue Mud Bay in northeast Arnhem Land (Figure 5.2). This is a low-relief landscape, with low-energy shorelines and extensive coastal swamps or wetlands (Haines et al. 1999, 1–2). The littoral zones within the study area are characterized by widely spread, fine estuarine and riverine alluvial deposits with some beach ridge development, the latter more prominent on the eastern side of the peninsula in Myaoola Bay (Haines et al. 1999, 77). Highly saline soils are located adjacent to the coast (salt flats), forming on intertidal and supratidal flats and in tidal channels, covering extensive areas near the coast and in the tidal reaches of major rivers, backed by extensive freshwater wetlands (Haines et al. 1999, 77; Isbell 1983, 192). These landscape zones are prominent within the more sheltered Grindall Bay area of the Point Blane peninsula. Active and recently active cheniers and sandy beach ridges occur as narrow ridges a few meters in height on the coastal fringes (Haines et al. 1999, 77). These landform characteristics have largely resulted from two main processes occurring throughout the Holocene, these being the effects of changes in sea levels during the marine transgression, followed by ongoing patterns of progradation and sedimentary infilling initiated during the mid-Holocene (Haines et al. 1999, 77).

Of the 141 archaeological sites recorded within this area, 34 shell middens are situated on the present-day coastline

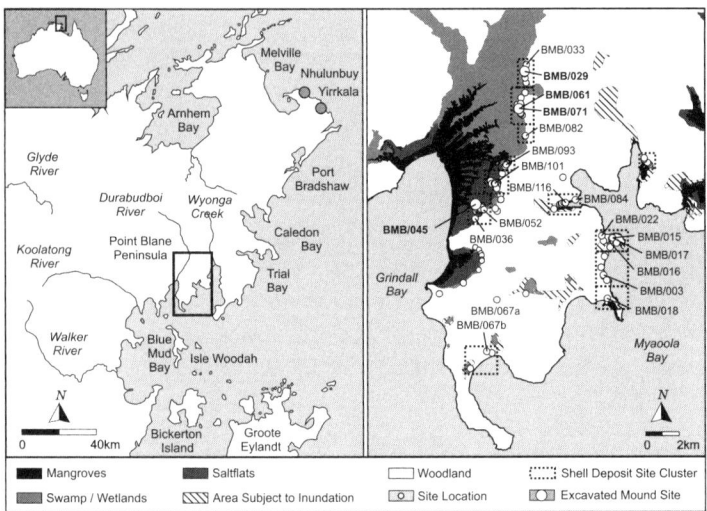

5.2. Location of the Point Blane Peninsula study area, Blue Mud Bay, northeast Arnhem Land (left), and the distribution of shell deposits across the study area, with radiocarbon-dated sites labeled (right). Also depicted are the site cluster boundaries and the location of the four Anadara granosa–*dominated shell mound sites excavated within the Grindall Bay area.*

within Myaoola Bay, and 85 shell midden and shell mound sites are located on the edges of the Dhuruputjpi freshwater wetland (an infilled former embayment) that feeds into Grindall Bay (Figure 5.2). The shell midden and mound deposits are composed primarily of molluskan remains, with minimal amounts of charcoal (1.3–22.6 grams), fish and reptile bone (2.3–46.1 grams), fragments of crab carapace (0.07–47.9 grams), and stone artifacts (0.9–64.4 grams) recovered from the excavated sites. The remaining 22 sites recorded across the peninsula are isolated or low-density scatters of stone artifacts (see Faulkner and Clarke 2009). Within Myaoola Bay, shell deposits are characteristically low, horizontally spread middens (morphologically similar to those recorded ethnographically), whereas larger shell mounds composed principally of *A. granosa* dominate the margins of Grindall Bay. Rather than being viewed in isolation, shell mounds are considered here as forming one aspect of the overall spectrum of the economic structure of the area, which includes smaller sites and surface scatters of shell (Bailey 1999, 105; Cribb 1996, 169; Faulkner 2013, 165). This is an important point, as across much of the north Australia coastline there appears to be significant variation in the type or nature of resources being exploited, and the size and processes/timing of the formation of shell deposits (e.g. Bailey 1993, 1999; Bourke 2000; Bourke et al. 2007; Brockwell et al. 2009;

Cribb 1996; Faulkner 2006, 2008; Hiscock 1999; Meehan 1982; Mowat 1995; O'Connor 1999; Roberts 1991; Veitch 1999). If shell mounds are analyzed as distinct or isolated site types, then their true significance cannot be adequately evaluated, as there is no clear point of comparison. Variability in site formation and the intensity of resource exploitation, as well as the overall chronological patterns of occupation, need to be taken into account to assess possible differences in site function and foraging behavior.

THE ENVIRONMENTAL CONTEXT

In the absence of detailed regional paleoclimatic data for northeast Arnhem Land (with the exception of Lees 1992; Lees et al. 1995; Shulmeister and Lees, 1992; see Bourke et al. 2007), this discussion draws on information from the broader north Australian and Indo-Pacific region (Figure 5.3). In broad terms, the coastal landforms of northern Australia result from changes in sea levels during the last marine transgression, followed by ongoing progradational processes and sedimentary infilling of shallow embayments during the mid-Holocene. Sea-level change is not spatially uniform, and significant regional differences in the timing and extent of sea-level rise have been attributed to variations in sedimentation regimes and isostatic and/ or tectonic activity along different parts of the coast (Yokoyama et al. 2001, 9). Within the Gulf of Carpentaria, sea-level data indicates a rapid rise of approximately 21 meters from 10,000 BP, reaching a high stand of one to three meters above present levels between 6,000 and 5,000 BP. Following this rise was a slow regression to present sea levels, including a series of minor oscillations in relative sea level in response to hydro-isostatic adjustment until approximately 600 years ago (Chappell et al. 1982; Rhodes 1980; Yokoyama et al. 2001, 14). These changes in sea level are strongly linked to long-term patterns of climatic change, particularly the intensity of the summer monsoon and cycling periods of aridity and increased precipitation during the mid- to late Holocene (Chivas et al. 2001, 20; Gagan and Chappell 2000, 35; Gagan et al. 2004).

During the mid- to late Holocene, many of the shallow embayments in northern Australia were gradually infilled to form freshwater wetlands and salt or mudflat areas. Marine incursion into prior valleys occurred between approximately 8,000 to 6,000 BP (Transgressive phase) when sea level was 10 to 12 meters below present levels. Between approximately 6,000 to 4,000 BP (Big Swamp phase), widespread mangrove forests established as sea-level rise decelerated and stabilized. These mangrove forests were eliminated between approximately 4,000 BP and the present (Sinuous and Cuspate phases), with tidal flows being confined to channels. This last phase saw the coastal embayments change to the current seasonally flooded freshwater wetland systems and extensive salt flats (e.g., Clark and Guppy 1988, 680–81; Woodroffe 1988; 1995, 80; Woodroffe et al. 1986). While these are significant environmental changes, and were particularly pronounced between 5,000 and 3,000 BP (Woodroffe and Mulrennan 1993), they were relatively gradual for much of the mid- to late Holocene, particularly in sheltered embayment areas with relatively slow input of fine-grained sediment (Chappell and Thom 1977, 284). Importantly, continuing processes of sedimentation leading into and during the last 500 years changed the gradient of coastal plains, eventually reducing tidal inundation and freshwater input (Woodroffe et al. 1986).

Climatic variability in the Australasian region also increased from approximately 2,000 BP to the present (Gagan and Chappell 2000, 44; Gagan, Chivas, and Isdale 1994; Kershaw 1995; Prebble et al. 2005, 367–69; Shulmeister 1999, 82; Wasson 1986). Most of these climate-change events are related to the El Niño/Southern Oscillation (ENSO) cycle and are characterized by polar cooling, tropical aridity, and major atmospheric circulation changes (Haberle and David 2004, 166–69; Mayewski et al. 2004, 243; Shulmeister and Lees 1992). Adjacent to the Gulf of Carpentaria is the Western Pacific Warm Pool, an area responsible for the greatest transfer of heat from the Pacific Ocean into the Indian Ocean, and that is implicated in the generation of El Niño/La Niña phases of the southern oscillation (Chivas et al. 2001, 20; Gagan and Chappell 2000, 35). Pollen and paleohydrological research conducted across several northern Australian regions suggests that observed changes in precipitation levels and climatic instability, linked strongly to the ENSO cycle, are synchronous, and as such represent coherent, broad-scale climatic signals (Kershaw 1995; Kershaw and Nix 1988; Lees et al. 1995; Prebble et al. 2005; Shulmeister 1999). Across northern Australia effective precipitation and temperature gradually increased from the beginning of the Holocene until approximately 5,000 BP. A period of higher effective precipitation occurs between 5,000 BP and approximately 3,700 BP, followed by a sharp decline. From approximately 2,000 BP to the present there is an increase in climatic variability, characterized by patterns of increasing aridity and seasonality across north Australia.

There are a number of phases of rapid climatic change identified throughout the Holocene within these

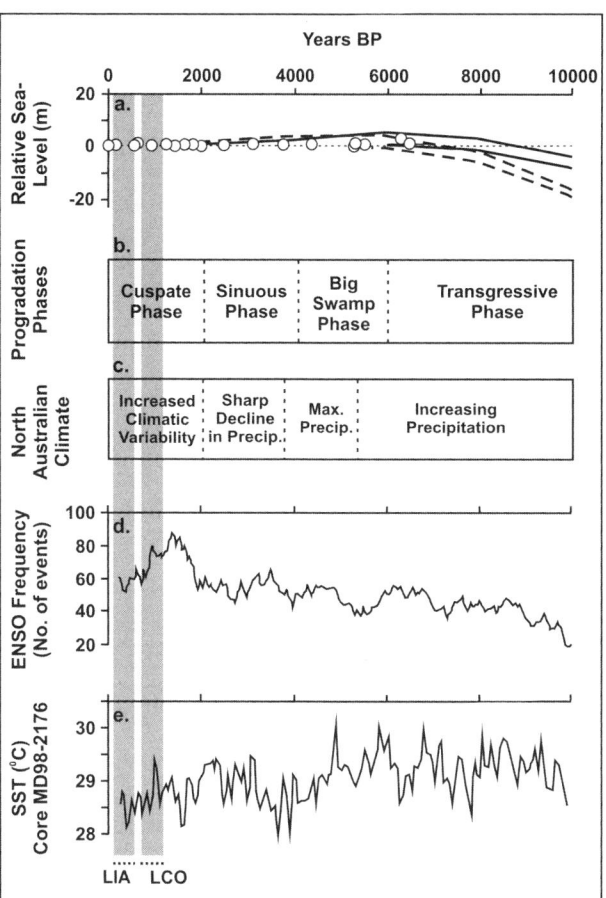

5.3. Holocene paleoenvironmental patterns for Australasia and the Indo-Pacific; data derived from: (a) Nakiboglu et al. 1983; (b) Woodroffe et al. 1986; (c) Shulmeister 1992, 1999; (d) Gagan et al. 2004; (e) Brijker et al. 2007; Faulkner 2013.

longer-term environmental patterns (Allen 2006; Gagan et al. 2004; Hendy et al. 2002, 1512). At 1,200 to 700 BP in low latitudes there is evidence for a warm and dry (relative to present) period referred to as the Little Climatic Optimum (or Medieval Warm Period). This was followed by the Little Ice Age, a cool, dry period occurring at about 600 to 100 BP (Nunn 2000, 716). Rapid cooling and two stages of sea-level fall mark the transition between the Little Climatic Optimum and the Little Ice Age throughout the Pacific Basin at 650 BP and 500 BP (Nunn 2000). Closely linked to those processes described above, sea-surface temperature (SST) and rainfall have varied over the mid- to late Holocene; however, there appears to be an estimated difference of only 1.5°C to 2.0°C or less in SST between 3,000 BP and the present in low-latitude regions (Shulmeister 1999, 86; Tudhope et al. 2001, 1515). Erica J. Hendy and colleagues (2002) have also suggested that conditions in the tropical southwest Pacific during the Little Ice Age were consistently more saline than present, although this change occurs largely between approximately 500 and 200 BP. While colder and/or more saline conditions in the western Pacific appear to occur between 6,000 and 4,500 years ago, sea-surface temperatures and salinity levels have been relatively stable between 3,000 years ago and 500–200 years ago, following which salinity levels dramatically increased (Brijker et al. 2007; Gagan et al. 2004, 132; Hendy et al. 2002).

Chronological Patterns

There are limitations in the interpretation of the available radiocarbon chronologies from any given area due to the degree of resolution in radiocarbon dates related to the timing, nature, and rates of site formation (e.g., Stein, Deo, and Phillips 2003). That said, long-term temporal trends in site and landscape use can be characterized through an analysis of an adequate sample of multiple determinations (Holdaway et al. 2002; Ulm 2006a). Thirty-nine radiocarbon age determinations have been obtained from 20 sites on the Point Blane peninsula, reflecting a cross-section of site types in varying environmental contexts (Faulkner 2008, 81–84). All dates were obtained from marine shell samples and all taxa that come from near-shore habitats. The conventional radiocarbon ages were converted to calendar years using the CALIB (v6.1.1) calibration program (Stuiver and Reimer 1993) with the marine04.14c calibration curve data set (Hughen et al. 2004) and a northeastern Australian ΔR correction value of 55 ± 98 (Reimer and Reimer 2000; Ulm 2006b). The calibrated radiocarbon age determinations indicate that the sites located in the study area fall predominantly between 2,953 calibrated years BP and the present, but there is a degree of variability in the chronologies for sites located in the two bay areas.

The 17 radiocarbon dates from the nine sites located on Myaoola Bay are graphed in chronological order in Figure 5.4A. Although three dates fall between 1,115 and 2,953 cal BP, there is a clustering of age determinations between approximately 1,000 years ago and the present. As Myaoola Bay is the more exposed area of the peninsula, this concentration of radiocarbon dates within the last 1,000 years relative to the three separate dates between 1,000 and 3,000 years ago may reflect taphonomic processes and coastline alteration over the mid- to late Holocene, particularly given the dynamic nature of beach ridge development (Haines et al. 1999). Alternatively, it can be argued that the relative scarcity of midden deposits older than 1,115 cal BP in Myaoola Bay could relate to decreased

archaeological visibility due to differential preservation in combination with low-intensity and/or infrequent occupation (e.g., Rowland 1983, 73). The 22 calibrated radiocarbon dates from the 11 Grindall Bay sites are also graphed in chronological order in Figure 5.4B. The radiocarbon dates available for these sites indicate that occupation in this area spanned an approximately 2,000-year period, with the phase of mound formation within the area falling between 2,287 cal BP and 526 cal BP. Within this sequence, there is a concentration in site deposition between approximately 2,287 and 1,009 years ago, and a second grouping of radiocarbon determinations between approximately 584 and 526 cal BP. This clustering of radiocarbon determinations into these two phases within Grindall Bay may be more firmly related to use of the area than differential destruction or sampling issues (Faulkner 2008). Although this area has been subjected to long-term seasonal inundation and sedimentary buildup that could potentially obscure some sites, Grindall Bay is an area that is comparatively well protected from extreme environmental conditions such as strong wind and wave action. Rather than a hiatus in occupation (as originally presented in Faulkner 2008, 2009), the clustering of radiocarbon dates in combination with differences in the location of sites between these two phases suggests that there was a shift in the intensity of landscape, resource utilization, and mound formation in this area (Faulkner 2013, 140–43).

Gaps or discontinuities occurring at various points throughout a chronological sequence may indicate different patterns of human behavior and variation in human-environmental interactions (Faulkner 2006, 2013; Holdaway et al. 2002, 362; Holdaway, Fanning, and Shiner 2005; Ulm 2006a). If these patterns do represent discontinuous use of the landscape and foraging behavior, then occupation of this coastline during the mid- to late Holocene may not reflect a stable, long-term adaptation to the environment leading into the more recent past (contra to what the use of ethnographic analogy to directly interpret the archaeological record suggests). It is therefore imperative that the degree of variability in the intensity of foraging behavior through time and space also be taken into consideration.

Site Characteristics and Distribution

Characterizing the overall pattern of molluskan exploitation on the Point Blane peninsula provides an indication of the level of variability through time and space relative to processes of environment/landscape alteration (e.g., Bailey and Craighead 2003, 176). Given their susceptibility to variations in environmental and climatic conditions, the range of species exploited across the peninsula should vary spatially and chronologically. Table 5.1 lists the 30 molluskan species identified on the surface of all sites across the peninsula. In comparison with the contemporary pattern of molluskan exploitation, where the harvesting of mollusks is limited to only six species (Barber 2005), the range of taxa identified from the archaeological sites in the area indicates that the intensity and diversity of molluskan exploitation was much greater in the past. In addition, the differential availability of resources across the study area reflects Holocene climatic and landscape alteration, the diversity of environmental conditions, and distribution of molluskan habitats. Therefore, some taxa may have been more abundant on the exposed coastal margins of Myaoola Bay, such as *Anadara antiquata, Gafrarium tumidum, Marcia hiantina, Polymesoda (Geloina) coaxans, Septifer bilocularis, Isognomon isognomon*, Ostreidae species, and *Terebralia palustris*. Other taxa, such as *A. granosa, Mactra abbreviata, Placuna placenta*, and *Telescopium telescopium*, by contrast, are more abundant in those sites concentrated on the margins of Grindall Bay.

There is also a significant difference in species richness between Grindall and Myaoola Bays (Table 5.2). The mean species richness of 7.25 in Myaoola Bay, compared with a mean of 5.06 for the Grindall Bay sites, suggests that there was a comparatively broader range of molluskan taxa

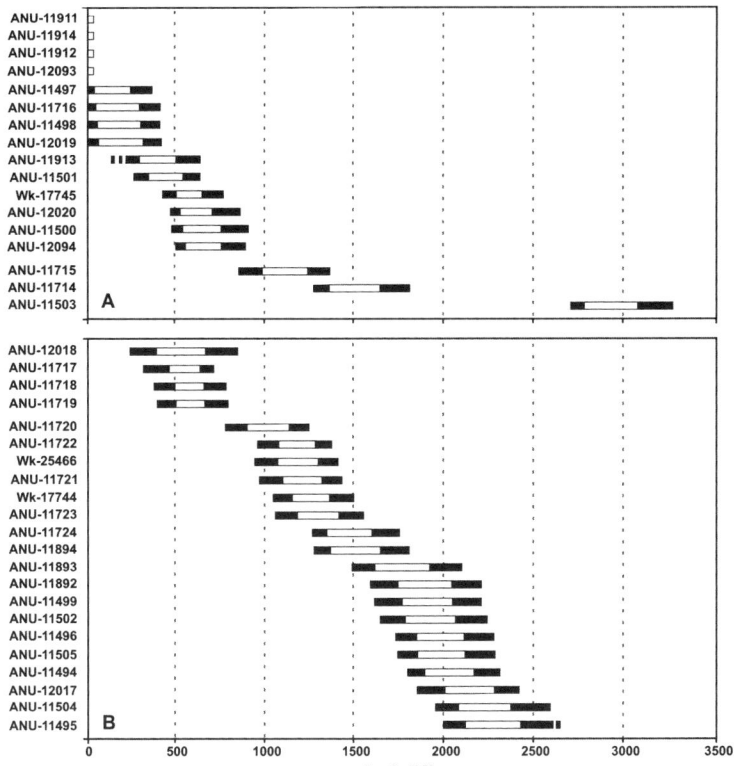

5.4. (A) Myaoola Bay 1σ (white bar) and 2σ (black bar) calibrated age ranges (BP) (above). (B) Grindall Bay 1σ (white bar) and 2σ (black bar) calibrated age ranges (BP) (below).

Table 5.1. *The number and percentage of sites containing molluskan species by broad locality*

Molluskan Species	Total (n=119)		Myaoola Bay (n=34)		Grindall Bay (n=85)	
	# Sites	%	# Sites	%	# Sites	%
Anadara granosa	96	80.67	15	44.12	81	95.29
Polymesoda (Geloina) coaxans	61	51.26	20	58.82	41	48.24
Marcia hiantina	61	51.26	31	91.18	30	35.29
Mactra abbreviata	56	47.06			56	65.88
Telescopium telescopium	51	42.86	9	26.47	42	49.41
Ostreidae f.	47	39.50	17	50.00	30	35.29
Placuna placenta	44	36.97			44	51.76
Terebralia spp.	33	27.73	25	73.53	8	9.41
Isognomon	27	22.69	23	67.65	4	4.71
Nerita spp.	22	18.49	14	41.18	8	9.41
Cerithidea spp.	21	17.65	10	29.41	11	12.94
Anadara antiquata	21	17.65	15	44.12	6	7.06
Septifer bilocularis	21	17.65	20	58.82	1	1.18
Gafrarium tumidum	19	15.97	17	50.00	2	2.35
Cassidula angulata	15	12.61			15	17.65
Dosinia mira	10	8.40	6	17.65	4	4.71

Table 5.1. (continued)

Molluskan Species	Total (n=119)		Myaoola Bay (n=34)		Grindall Bay (n=85)	
	# Sites	%	# Sites	%	# Sites	%
Pinctada spp.	10	8.40	8	23.53	2	2.35
Syrinx aruanus	9	7.56	7	20.59	2	2.35
Modiolus spp.	6	5.04	4	11.76	2	2.35
Volema cochlidium	5	4.20	3	8.82	2	2.35
Melo amphora	4	3.36	1	2.94	3	3.53
Monodonta labio	4	3.36	2	5.88	2	2.35
Tellina spp.	4	3.36	3	8.82	1	1.18
Barbatia spp.	3	2.52	3	8.82		
Pinna bicolor	3	2.52	3	8.82		
Tectus pyramis	3	2.52	3	8.82		
Turbo cinereus	3	2.52	3	8.82		
Chitonidae f.	2	1.68	2	5.88		
Placamen calophyllum	1	0.84			1	1.18
Chama spp.	1	0.84	1	2.94		

exploited in Myaoola Bay compared with a limited range of species available in Grindall Bay. A Mann-Whitney U test revealed a significant difference in species richness between these two areas ($U = 899.5$, $z = -3.463$, $p = 0.001$, $r = 0.32$), suggesting that different exploitation patterns were operating in the study area relative to the broad location. This difference may relate to availability as well as choice in the exploitation of resources. A degree of chronological variability across the peninsula in the exploitation of molluskan taxa from different habitats can also be identified, again reflecting longer-term patterns of coastline alteration (Bourke et al. 2007, 95–97; Faulkner 2006, 257; 2013, 58). Prior to approximately 2,500 BP, in conjunction with those taxa from the sand flats and mudflats, there was a greater emphasis on harvesting mollusks from the shallow-water, near-shore zone. Between 2,500 and 500 BP, a period associated with shell mound formation in the area,

there was an increase in the exploitation of species from the sand flats and mudflats, particularly *A. granosa* and *M. abbreviata*, with some variability in the use of mangrove species. After 526 cal BP, there was a decline by approximately 60 percent in the frequency of sand flat and mudflat bivalves and a corresponding increase of 25 percent in the abundance of mangrove species (Figure 5.5).

Given the variation apparent in the chronological patterns and the exploited molluskan taxa, it can be argued that variations in the size and density of shell deposits, plus an investigation of the size/age structure of the dominant species, are reasonable proxy measures of the distribution and intensity of human behavior (Bailey 1994, 108). There are constraints with this type of analysis due to possible variations in patterns of cultural discard through time and associated site accumulation rates (see Stein, Deo, and Phillips 2003), and where post-depositional

Table 5.2. Descriptive statistics for the number of molluskan taxa by broad peninsula locality

No. of Molluskan Taxa by Peninsula Locality	Myaoola Bay	Grindall Bay
Mean	7.25	5.06
Median	6.50	5.00
Standard deviation	4.17	3.01
Minimum	1	1
Maximum	23	23
Number of sites	34	85

processes alter site visibility or morphology. Combined with the number of radiocarbon ages available, the period of time over which a site forms can affect the resolution of accumulation rates, particularly where variable rates of formation and successive phases of occupation occurs (Stein, Deo, and Phillips 2003, 309–10). Investigations based on only two or three samples, the number generally available from the sites within Blue Mud Bay, will not provide accurate comparisons (Stein, Deo, and Phillips 2003, 310). Therefore, the density and distribution of shell mound and midden sites combined with analyses of site area and volume are used to investigate differences in the intensity of occupation and resource use. This approach is therefore adequately suited to identifying broad trends in human behavior within highly time-averaged contexts.

Site density estimates and site size comparisons are presented in Table 5.3 for Myaoola and Grindall Bays as a measure of landscape use. Within Myaoola Bay, 34 sites were recorded along 22 kilometers of coastline, with 85 sites recorded along 13 kilometers surveyed on the margins of Grindall Bay. The density of sites within Myaoola Bay is relatively low, with 1.54 sites recorded per kilometer of coastline surveyed, compared with 6.54 sites per kilometer in Grindall Bay. In the latter area of the Point Blane peninsula there are approximately four times more sites per kilometer of coastline surveyed (or former coastline), and by extension this suggests that there was a greater occupation intensity in Grindall Bay. In many coastal areas the distribution of resources is not homogenous, with variation in the abundance of resources relative to the structure of shoreline (Bailey 1975; 1983, 567; Rowland 1994, 155; Waselkov 1987, 133). The clustering of sites is therefore an important feature of site distribution patterns, and may be used as evidence for investigating the intensity of occupation (e.g., Bourke 2000, 107). As a further comparison, the number of sites per site cluster or grouping is compared between these two areas. Divisions between clusters are based on site distribution relative to prominent and relatively stable environmental or geographic features. For example, sites grouped around headland areas are distinguished from those distributed linearly along open beaches, or where sites are separated by natural features like rivers (see Figure 5.2). Referring to Table 5.3, the density of sites per cluster conforms well to the patterns identified for the number of sites per kilometer surveyed. The average number of sites per cluster in Grindall Bay is 14.17, more than twice as many as the average for Myaoola Bay at 5.67 sites per cluster. As the number of sites per cluster potentially reflects the density

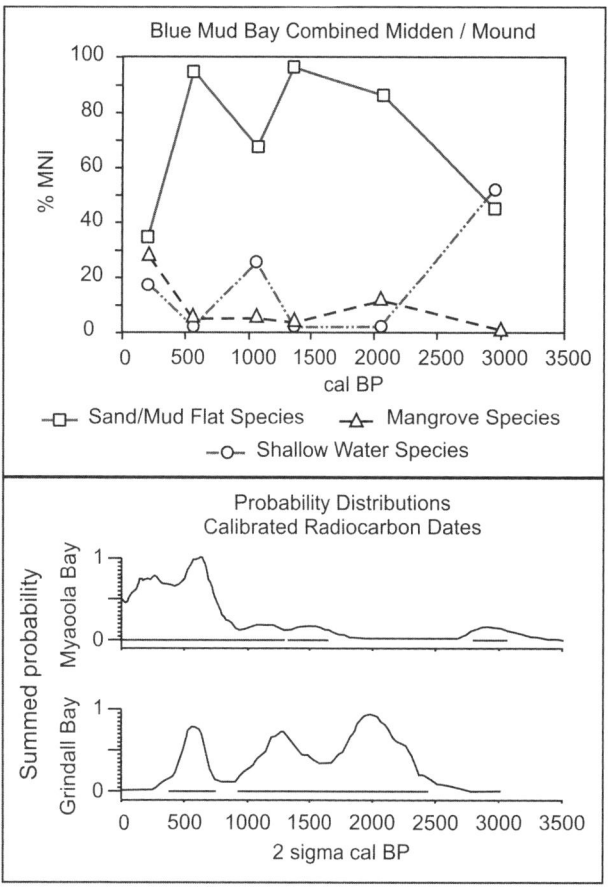

5.5. *Chronological variation in the exploitation of mollusk species by habitat, compared with calibrated radiocarbon-age-summed probability plots for Myaoola and Grindall Bays.*

of occupation relative to the focal points of resource exploitation within each area (i.e., sheltered embayments), perhaps more so than the number of sites per kilometer surveyed, there appears to have been a greater intensity of occupation and use of resources in the Grindall Bay area (Faulkner 2013, 144-46).

This interpretation is further supported by comparing site area and volume between the two margins of the peninsula (Table 5.3). Mann-Whitney U tests indicate that there are significant differences in site area (U = 998.5, z = -2.867, p = 0.004, r = 0.26) and site volume (U = 646.5, z = -4.903, p = 0.000, r = 0.45) between Myaoola and Grindall Bays. Comparing site morphology between these two areas (as noted above), within Myaoola Bay shell deposits generally conform to a pattern of low, horizontally spread out middens, with larger mounded shell deposits

Table 5.3. Site density estimates and site size comparisons by broad peninsula locality

	Myaoola Bay	Grindall Bay
Approx. Length of Coastline Surveyed (km)	22	13
Number of Sites Recorded	34	85
Number of Sites per Kilometer Surveyed	1.54	6.54
Number of Site Clusters	6	6
Average Number of Sites per Cluster	5.67	14.17
Descriptive Statistics—Site Area (m2)		
Mean	1085.02	490.46
Median	79.39	238.35
Standard Deviation	3282.40	1179.77
Minimum	0.50	22.44
Maximum	16000	10620
Descriptive Statistics—Site Volume (m3)		
Mean	111.76	461.26
Median	7.94	113.72
Standard Deviation	328.04	1023.02
Minimum	0.05	2.24
Maximum	1600	7327.80
Number of Sites	34	85

dominating the margins of Grindall Bay. While site area is generally larger within Myaoola Bay, in assessing variation in the potential intensity of resource use and site formation, the fact that there is a dramatic increase in the volume of material deposited within sites in Grindall Bay is of more importance. Based on the density of sites and the volume of material deposited within Grindall Bay, combined with the available radiocarbon age determinations, there appears to have been a greater intensity of occupation and exploitation of resources in that area relative to the patterns of occupation in Myaoola Bay. If this is indeed the case, then with a higher level of human predation, the size and structure of *A. granosa* populations in Grindall Bay may have been altered. To evaluate potential patterns of this type, however, the spawning, growth rates, and tolerated environmental and climatic ranges for this particular species need to be assessed.

SHELL MOUNDS AND *ANADARA GRANOSA* EXPLOITATION

The Biological and Ecological Characteristics of A. granosa

Much as they appear to have been in the past, marine bivalve mollusks of the family Arcidae (subfamily Anadarinae) are presently an important source of protein for coastal populations in many tropical, subtropical, and warm temperate areas (Broom 1985, 1). In the Indo-Pacific region, the molluskan bivalve genus *Anadara* is economically important, particularly in the Philippines, Thailand, Malaysia, and Borneo, and there is a long history of commercial culturing of *A. granosa* in several of these areas (Pathansali and Soong 1958, 26). Due to their commercial importance, there is a significant body of information to draw from relating to the optimal habitat conditions, tolerated environmental and climatic ranges, and breeding and growth rates for this species, allowing for relatively robust comparisons with known mid- to late Holocene paleoenvironmental sequences.

Three of the most important factors for the establishment and proliferation of *A. granosa* shell beds are the nature of the substrate, the slope of bed, and salinity levels. Naturally occurring in the soft substrate of large estuarine mudflats backed by mangrove forests (Broom 1985, 4; Pathansali 1966, 90), the optimal habitats for this species are situated outside the mouth of estuaries and tidal creeks and protected from strong wave action (Pathansali 1966, 91). The shell beds require a moderate seaward slope of 5–15 degrees, as growth rates will be affected if exposure is too prolonged between tides (Broom 1985, 4–7). The tolerated temperature ranges are relatively wide and will vary with geographical range; for example, the average annual water temperature in Malaysia is between 29 to 32°C, though within higher shore areas subpopulations are able to cope with minimal water movement and a temperature range of 25 to 40°C (Broom 1985, 7). *A. granosa* is able to function relatively efficiently at salinity levels of between 23 and 31 parts per thousand, although young individuals are able to continue normal feeding activity at a lower salinity than older specimens, down to 18 parts per thousand. This species has the ability to cope with short-term salinity fluctuations, but is characteristically stenohaline (Bayne 1973, 804; Broom 1985, 6; Healy and Wells 1998; Peterson and Wells 1998).

Although some spawning takes place throughout the year, *A. granosa* displays a definite seasonality pattern (Broom 1985, 24). Two spawning cues have been linked to seasonal salinity depression, where temperatures on intertidal mudflats are reduced during high rainfall periods of the summer monsoon (Broom 1982, 1985, 24). In shallow coastal areas, drainage patterns from seasonal rainfall causes considerable changes in salinity that directly (lowering of salinity) or indirectly (lower water temperature at low water levels compared to higher temperatures and salinity at high water) affect breeding and spawning (Pathansali 1966, 85, 90; Pathansali and Soong 1958, 26). As well as breeding cycles, environmental conditions are known to have an effect on growth rates, which can vary enormously between subpopulations subjected to a range

of different environmental conditions (Broom 1985, 16; Richardson 1987). Importantly though, *A. granosa* is characterized by rapid growth rates, attaining sexual maturity at about 25 millimeters in shell length (Broom 1983, 1985, 23; Pathansali 1966, 85; Pathansali and Soong 1958, 27). Commercial data reinforces this, where mean lengths of monthly samples indicate rapid growth of approximately 25.4 millimeters by 50 percent of a population within 6 months (Pathansali 1966, 89), and between 30–32 millimeters in 8 to 12 months (Broom 1985, 14; Pathansali and Soong 1958, 28). This data also indicates that there is a strong size-age relationship in this species (Figure 5.6). It has been suggested that maximum sizes larger than 53.5 millimeters would be a very rare occurrence in natural populations (Broom 1985, 15), although modern individuals collected from Indonesia, Bay of Bengal, Solomon Islands, and Papua New Guinea reaching sizes of 58–69 millimeters have been recorded in the Queensland Museum collection (Faulkner 2010).

While not resilient to long-term or sustained environmental changes, *A. granosa* will successfully cope with short-term environmental fluctuations (Davenport and Wong 1986; Nakamura and Shinotsuka 2007). Due to their high fecundity and rapid growth rates, populations of *A. granosa* also tend to be biomass dominant (Broom 1983, 395; 1985, 10). *A. granosa* is known to be successful in exploiting a niche typified by difficult trophic conditions for suspension feeders as well as widely fluctuating physical variables. At present, *A. granosa* only exists in very low densities along the north Australian coastline or has disappeared entirely from natural coastal habitats.

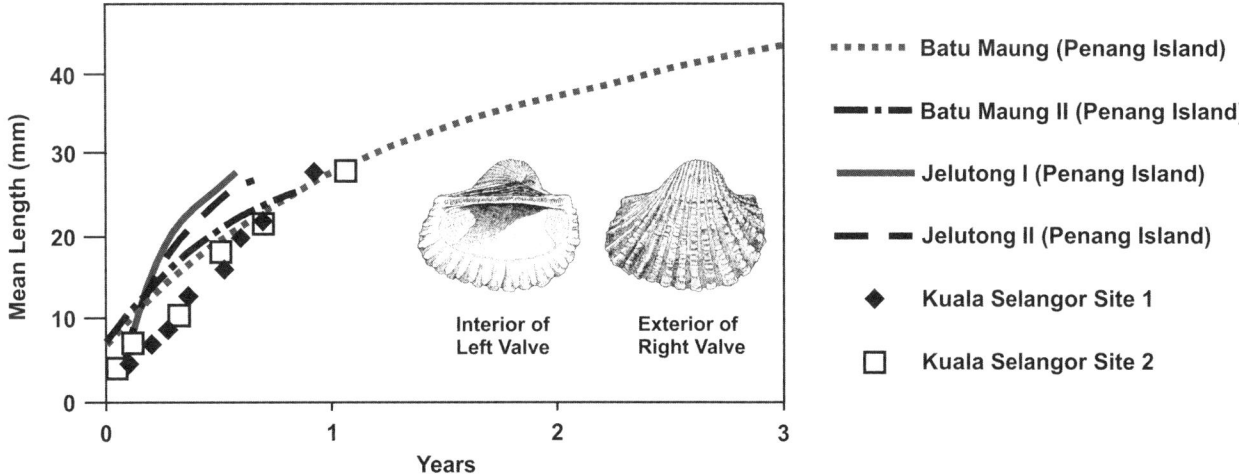

5.6. Growth rates of Anadara granosa *in Malaysian commercial culture beds (after Broom 1982, 73; Pathansali 1966, 98;* A. granosa *image redrawn from Poutiers 1998, 147).*

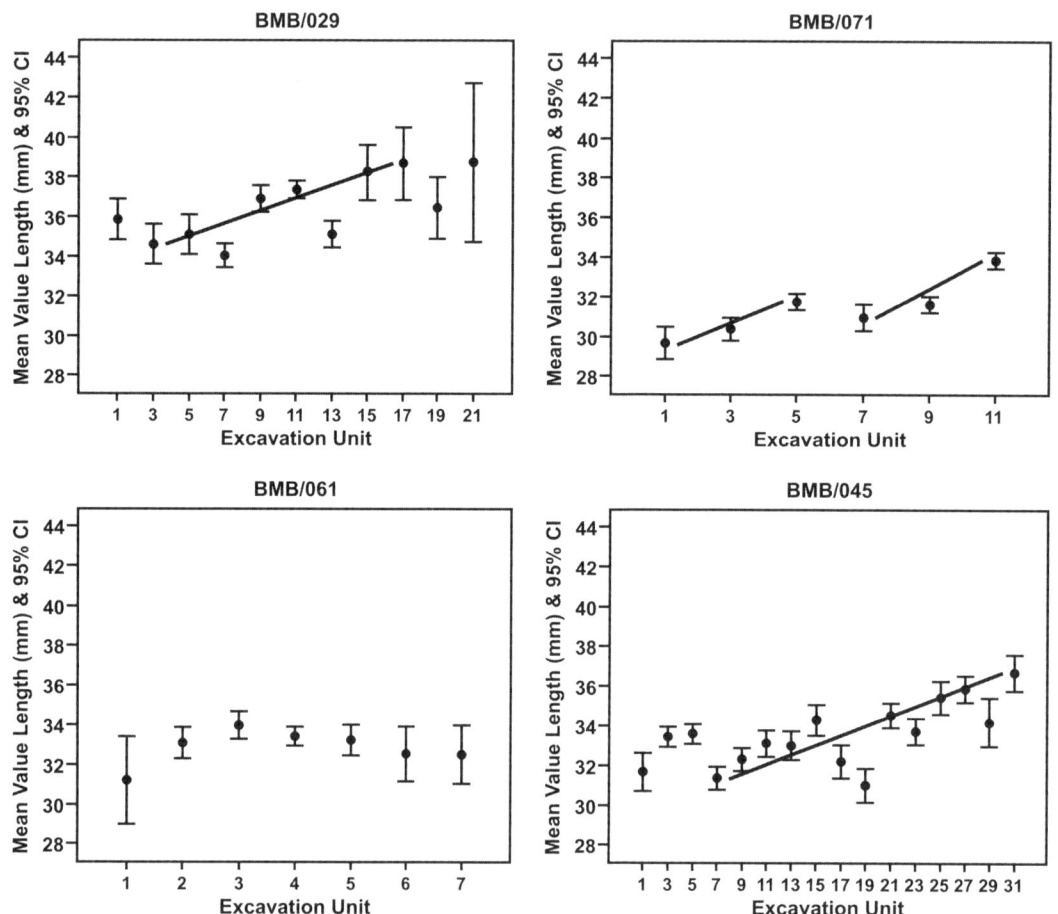

5.7. Mean Anadara granosa *valve length (mm) and 95 percent confidence interval by site and excavation unit. Solid black lines indicate significant difference at 0.05 level.*

Reasons for this may relate to the low occurrence or disappearance of suitable habitat and changes in environmental conditions by approximately 500 years ago beyond the range tolerated by this species (e.g., Bourke et al. 2007, 97; de Boer, Pereira, and Guissamulo 2000, 295; Faulkner 2009, 831; Hiscock 1997).

The Archaeological Evidence

Four sites, BMB/029, BMB/071, BMB/061, and BMB/045, were excavated to provide a spatial and temporal cross-section of occupation and phases of mound formation in Grindall Bay (Figure 5.2). Within these sites, *A. granosa* dominates the assemblages at between 70 and 90 percent by MNI (minimum number of individuals) (Faulkner 2006, 2009). A number of researchers investigating marine shellfish exploitation have viewed a reduction in mean shell size as indicating increased pressure via human predation or environmental factors (e.g., Botkin 1980; Braje et al. 2007; Jerardino 1997; Mannino and Thomas 2001; Milner, Barrett, and Welsh 2007; Spenneman 1987; Swadling 1976). While mean and/or modal size of a mollusk population is heavily influenced by recruitment levels and juvenile survivorship (Claassen 1998, 108), mean shell size can also vary significantly depending on whether a population has been subjected to human exploitation. M. J. Broom (1985, 15) used data published by D. Pathansali (1966) on modern *A. granosa* populations in Malaysia to determine mean asymptotic valve lengths of between 29.6 and 35.9 millimeters, where larger individuals were consistently removed by continuous harvesting. Broom (1985, 15) also presents data from two Malaysian study sites (Broom 1982, 1983; Pathansali 1966) that were not subjected to continuous exploitation and therefore unlikely to have been distorted by size-selective harvesting. In these areas, mean asymptotic shell lengths of 44.4 to 49.6 millimeters were recorded.

In order to investigate changes in size throughout the four shell mound deposits, measurements were taken on a total of 12,201 *A. granosa* complete and fragmented valves (BMB/029: 2,309; BMB/071: 4,300; BMB/061: 1,551; BMB/045: 4,041). For this analysis, the convention of measuring the greatest valve length of complete shells (maximum anterior-posterior measurement) (Bailey and Craighead 2003, 187; Claassen 1998, 108; Peacock 2000, 189; Spenneman 1987, 85–89) was used, as well as the application of morphometric equations to establish maximum size from fragmented valves (Faulkner 2010). *A. granosa* mean valve lengths by excavation unit for each of the four sites are presented in Figure 5.7, and descriptive statistics for *A. granosa* length are presented in Table 5.4. To provide a chronological context for these sites, the available calibrated radiocarbon ages are also shown for each site/excavation unit in Table 5.5.

Previously reported results for three of the four sites indicate that there is a high degree of variability in mean valve size (Analysis of Variance [ANOVA]—BMB/029: $F = 10.863$, $df = 10$, $p = 0.000$; BMB/071: $F = 27.996$, $df = 5$, $p = 0.000$; BMB/045: $F = 20.108$, $df = 15$, $p = 0.000$). Post-hoc comparisons using the Dunnett's *C* test indicates significant differences at the 0.05 level in mean valve size within each of these three sites, indicating an overall trend for size decrease throughout these deposits. In contrast, within BMB/061 the degree of variability is not significant (ANOVA: $F = 1.903$, $df = 6$, $p = 0.077$), nor is there a significant trend of size decrease through time. Chronologically, this site falls immediately before what is interpreted here as a period of decreased occupation intensity, resource exploitation, and mound formation in this area, the significance of which is explored further below. Viewing these sites on an individual basis may lead to the conclusion that

Table 5.4. Descriptive statistics for A. granosa *valve length (mm) by site and excavation unit*

Site	Excavation Unit	Mean	Median	Std. Dev.	Min.	Max.	No.
BMB/029	1	35.9	36.5	7.1	20.4	58.1	185
	3	34.6	35.2	7.8	16.7	55.9	229
	5	35.1	34.9	6.9	22.3	50.5	188
	7	34.0	34.1	6.6	19.4	55.2	493
	9	36.9	37.3	6.0	15.5	54.9	301
	11	37.4	37.8	4.5	19.4	51.6	382
	13	35.1	35.7	6.1	21.3	53.9	340
	15	38.2	38.9	7.2	23.1	55.2	102
	17	38.7	38.8	5.4	26.4	51.4	36
	19	36.4	36.6	5.0	25.8	47.0	43
	21	38.7	39.6	5.6	24.7	44.1	10
BMB/071	1	29.7	30.1	5.6	17.2	46.3	181
	3	30.4	30.3	6.3	15.6	51.8	442
	5	31.8	31.8	6.5	13.4	53.6	1408
	7	31.4	31.3	5.7	19.2	48.7	952
	9	31.6	31.5	6.0	17.3	49.2	1073
	11	33.8	34.1	6.4	16.5	50.8	244
BMB/061	1	31.2	31.0	6.4	19.1	51.7	35
	2	33.1	32.8	6.2	18.1	52.6	244
	3	33.9	33.9	6.6	18.5	53.5	356
	4	33.4	33.2	5.9	17.2	54.5	600
	5	33.2	33.2	5.1	21.1	49.4	164
	6	32.5	32.9	5.9	21.6	47.9	75
	7	32.5	32.5	6.5	20.3	52.5	77

Table 5.4. (continued)

Site	Excavation Unit	Mean	Median	Std. Dev.	Min.	Max.	No.
BMB/045	1	31.6	32.1	5.4	18.0	44.9	122
	3	33.4	33.6	4.4	20.7	45.4	283
	5	33.6	33.4	4.5	18.5	50.2	335
	7	31.3	31.3	5.4	20.9	47.6	355
	9	32.3	32.0	5.4	21.1	47.3	404
	11	33.1	33.3	5.5	20.5	48.0	272
	13	32.9	33.6	5.6	20.4	45.4	232
	15	34.3	35.4	5.6	19.8	48.5	200
	17	32.2	32.4	6.6	19.5	47.7	234
	19	30.9	31.3	7.6	18.6	51.2	306
	21	34.5	34.3	4.7	23.9	51.8	210
	23	33.7	33.6	4.4	10.7	48.3	176
	25	35.4	34.7	5.6	20.0	50.7	179
	27	35.8	36.9	6.8	19.6	51.9	410
	29	34.1	34.1	7.8	19.2	51.6	150
	31	36.7	36.8	6.1	22.8	47.6	173

these were mollusk populations subjected to continuous, but not overly excessive or intensive, levels of human predation (particularly for BMB/061) (see Bourke 2000; Bailey 1993). Mean valve size within the Blue Mud Bay samples fall within, or just above, the size range predicted by Broom (1985) for continuously exploited populations, and similar values have been reported in studies by both Bailey (1993) and Bourke (2000). However, given the nature of *A. granosa* to be biomass dominant, and to be able to cope with short-term fluctuating environmental variables, the data presented here is more significant when viewed in terms of the overall pattern within Grindall Bay. To examine long-term trends in *A. granosa* exploitation, mean valve length per excavation unit from each site is plotted chronologically. Due to the low chronological resolution and lack of internal stratigraphic differentiation within these sites, previous analyses grouped this data into broad analytical units according to chronological phases (e.g., Faulkner 2006, 2009), although recalibration of the radiocarbon ages here has effectively removed these groupings in the calibrated ages for each site. Therefore each excavation unit, as the principle unit of analysis, has been assigned an approximate age based on age depth curves to explore potentially finer-grained variability in valve size across the whole Grindall Bay sequence.

Across this sequence there is a high degree of variability in mean *A. granosa* valve size (ANOVA: F = 27.396,

df = 10656, p = 0.000); however, several trends can be identified (Figure 5.8). As *A. granosa* is a rapidly reproducing and fast-growing species, a low intensity of human exploitation would result in the size of collected mollusks remaining relatively stable. Comparative stability in the size of this species is seen between 2,287 and 2,140 cal BP, and conceivably between 1,310 and 1,009 cal BP. In contrast, if collection practices were intensified while the exploited species' reproduction and growth rates remained relatively constant, then there would be a significant decrease in the average size of the remaining shellfish within the population over time (Waselkov 1987, 134). Between approximately 2,140 and 1,310 cal BP, as well as 584 and 526 cal BP, there are significant reductions in the size of *A. granosa*, which may indicate increasing levels of human exploitation during these periods. Occurring between 1,009 and 584 cal BP, there is a phase of significant size increase within the overall Grindall Bay sequence. This may reflect a decrease in the intensity of exploitation, or alternatively and as noted above, a change in levels of occupation and site formation, allowing the shell beds to recover and stabilize. Variations in mean valve size between approximately 1,310 and 1,009 cal BP are not statistically significant, and as noted above, one interpretation may be of relative stability during this period. However, this could also reflect a period of rebound or recovery and subsequent decline (Rick et al. 2008). Given that there appears to be a decreased level of mound formation after 1,009 cal BP, this pattern could relate to variability or lowering of the intensity of harvesting during this period, changes in environmental processes such as sedimentation, or a combination of the two. After 526 cal BP, shell mounds ceased to be formed within Blue Mud Bay, and *A. granosa* is largely absent from the archaeological record of the area. Based on the statistically indistinguishable radiocarbon dates obtained from the base and surface of site BMB/045, combined with a significant decrease in shell size, this absence potentially represents rapid and intensive exploitation of *A. granosa* before its ultimate decline and/or disappearance from this area.

These patterns can potentially also be produced by shifts in environmental and climatic conditions. While there are a number of significant paleoenvironmental changes that occurred throughout the mid- to late Holocene (as noted above), this level of variability appears to fall within the environmental and climatic ranges tolerated by *A. granosa*. While there were changes in sea surface temperature during the mid- to late Holocene of 1.5°C to 2.0°C relative to present conditions (Gagan et al. 2004, 131–32), these changes do not appear to have been on a scale that would have

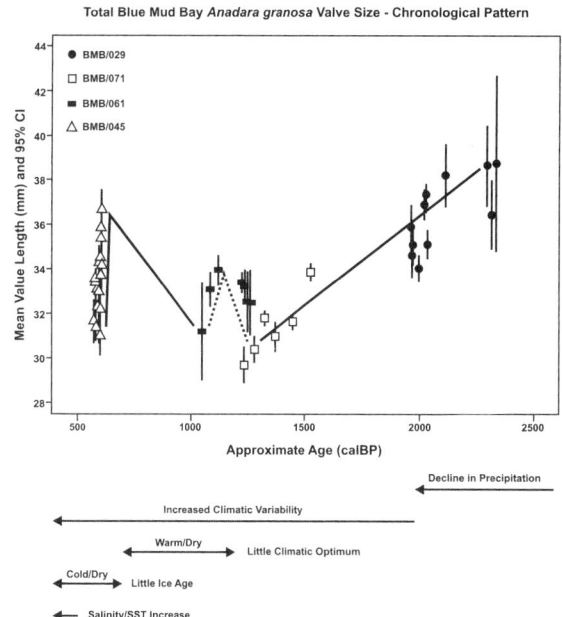

5.8. *Mean* Anadara granosa *valve length and 95 percent confidence interval by approximate calibrated radiocarbon age. Solid black line indicates significant difference at 0.05 level, with dashed black line indicating possible recovery and subsequent decline.*

Table 5.5. *Radiocarbon age estimate ranges for the four excavated sites on Grindall Bay*

Site Code	Excavation Unit	Depth (cm)	Lab Code	δ13C (*estimate)	14C Age	1σ Calibrated Age BP	2σ Calibrated Age BP
BMB/029	1	0–3	ANU-11496	-3.4 ± 0.1	2410 ± 50	1850–2120	1728–2279
	4	8–11	ANU-11499	-4.0 ± 0.1	2350 ± 60	1771–2058	1613–2207
	8	23–28	ANU-11502	0.0 ± 2.0 *	2360 ± 60	1788–2074	1646–2242
	12	41–45	ANU-11505	-2.8 ± 0.1	2420 ± 50	1858–2129	1742–2287
	14	49–53	ANU-11494	-2.6 ± 0.1	2460 ± 50	1892–2171	1795–2314
	16	58–62	ANU-11504	-3.1 ± 0.2	2630 ± 60	2085–2380	1952–2595
	20	75–81	ANU-11495	0.0 ± 2.0 *	2660 ± 60	2122–2435	1995–2648
BMB/045	1	0–2	ANU-11717	3.5 ± 0.2	990 ± 60	461–637	314–708
	16	43–46	ANU-11718	-3.7 ± 0.2	1040 ± 60	492–659	375–781
	31	91–95	ANU-11719	3.1 ± 0.2	1050 ± 60	496–664	387–791
BMB/061	1	0–4	ANU-11720	4.6 ± 0.2	1510 ± 50	900–1137	776–1243
	4	9–12	Wk-25466	-3.8 ± 0.2	1684 ± 35	1071–1280	951–1373
	7	17–22	ANU-11721	4.1 ± 0.2	1720 ± 50	1095–1320	962–1433
BMB/071	1	0–3	ANU-11722	2.9 ± 0.2	1700 ± 60	1067–1299	936–1412
	6	19–24	ANU-11723	-2.5 ± 0.2	1810 ± 60	1176–1419	1053–1551
	11	42–46	ANU-11724	3.1 ± 0.2	1980 ± 60	1343–1599	1259–1753

adversely affected *A. granosa* shell beds. Salinity levels appear to have peaked between approximately 500 and 200 BP, but this peak occurs at the end of the period of shell mound formation across much of northern Australia. When viewing the longer-term pattern of mean *A. granosa* valve size, the larger-scale peaks and troughs in this sequence also do not appear to correlate with any known climatic changes for the broader region. It must be acknowledged, however, that ongoing processes of progradation, combined with increasing aridity during the mid- to late Holocene, may have contributed to a certain degree. For example, continuing processes of sedimentation would have changed the gradient or slope of the coastal plain, eventually reducing freshwater input and tidal inundation in these areas (Woodroffe et al. 1986), a process that would have led to the gradual isolation of the shell beds (Macintosh 1982, 13). Combined with variations in the intensity of human exploitation, this may explain the degree of variability observed in mean valve size in three of the four sites within Grindall Bay. That said, the available data does not explain the period of *A. granosa* size recovery prior to cessation in mound formation at approximately 500 years. Due to the range of possible environmental causes for size change in mollusks, particularly those that may adversely affect *A. granosa* populations operating at scales that may not be easily identified archaeologically, the longer-term trend identified in the archaeological sample suggests that the patterns presented above are here attributed to human predation, but cautiously rather than definitively (i.e., Braje et al. 2007; Braje, Erlandson, and Rick, chap. 1 in this volume; Erlandson et al. 2008; Mannino and Thomas 2001). This interpretation is strengthened when the trends in *A. granosa* size variability are viewed in combination with the broader archaeological evidence for site chronology, distribution, and morphology detailed above.

DISCUSSION AND CONCLUSION

The archaeological patterns presented here directly reflect the dynamic and changing nature of the coastline throughout the mid- to late Holocene in north Australia. These patterns indicate flexibility in foraging behavior on the coastal margins to incorporate newly available or increasingly abundant species (Mowat 1995, 163). The evidence presented here suggests that shell mounds in the study area are not consistent with either continuous low-level or sporadic high-intensity harvesting. Neither form of behavior would have had a long-term impact on this species, particularly given the nature of the environmental and climatic

conditions between 2,287 and 526 cal BP and the high breeding and fast growth rates of *A. granosa*. Instead, the archaeological evidence is consistent with a more focused level of activity and intensive exploitation of the dominant species within the landscape. Based on this data, an alternative interpretation can be proposed, that coastal foragers operated within a distinctly different economic pattern during the period of *A. granosa* mound accumulation. The establishment and relatively long-term proliferation of *A. granosa* may have enabled a lowering of mobility levels and an increase in population size, although only a moderate increase as the data are more suggestive of an increase in the intensity of resource exploitation and site deposition.

The suggestion here is that the observable differences between shell mounds and low, horizontally spread middens relates to variability in settlement strategies and resource exploitation, patterns of mobility, and potentially population size through time. This interpretation is based on the inter- and intra-site chronological patterns, the observed differences in site density and morphology, and the focused and intensive exploitation of *A. granosa* over a long period. The systematic exploitation of coastal habitats and near-shore taxa, especially *A. granosa*, has been seen by several researchers to imply the beginnings of a new, specialized, and focused subsistence strategy between 2,000 to 1,600 BP (Haberle and David 2004, 172; Lourandos 1983; Veitch 1999). It has been argued that the archaeological record reflects a coherent pattern of population expansion accommodated by progressive environmental and economic adaptations, such as a broadening diet and intensive exploitation of secondary resources. Aspects of this model fit the archaeological evidence well, and what is seen between 2,287 and 526 cal BP with shell mound formation reflects a phase of economic intensification, but importantly, it is one that does not follow a progressive or linear pattern. The subsequent restructuring of the economy following the cessation of mound formation on the Point Blane peninsula, and in other areas of coastal northern Australia, relates to a general decrease in biomass of coastal resources extending into the more recent past. This pattern may well correspond with a decrease in population size or patterns of demographic reorganization (Hiscock 1999, 99–100; Faulkner 2013, 182-83).

During the period of mound formation, the exploitation of molluskan resources was far more focused and intensive than was observed during the historic period, contrary to the interpretations of a number of other researchers who have relied on the ethnographies to explain the role of mollusks within the diet (e.g., Bailey 1975; Bourke 2000). Distinct changes occurring at approximately 500 BP indicate a widespread period of economic reorganization following the build-out of suitable habitats and the disappearance of *A. granosa* from many areas across the north Australian coast. The archaeological evidence presented here indicates that foraging behavior on the coastal margins of the Point Blane peninsula was indeed flexible and dynamic. The *A. granosa* shell mounds from this area, and potentially from other regions of north Australia, indicate that through time people actively changed their foraging strategies to incorporate newly available or increasingly abundant species into their economic system.

ACKNOWLEDGMENTS

This research was conducted for my PhD dissertation as a part of the Australian Research Council–funded Blue Mud Bay Project. The fieldwork was undertaken in collaboration with Annie Clarke, as well as with Marcus Barber, Frances Morphy, Howard Morphy, and Nicolas Peterson. The radiocarbon determinations were awarded by the Centre for Archaeological Research and the Waikato Radiocarbon Dating Laboratory. Sarah Robertson, Annie Clarke, Peter Hiscock, Sally Brockwell, Trish Bourke, Robin Sim, Betty Meehan, and Brit Asmussen all contributed significantly to the development of many of the ideas presented here. Finally, thanks go to the Yolngu people of the Yilpara, Rurrangala, Gan-Gan, Djarrakpi, and Yirrkala communities for their support and assistance throughout the project.

CHAPTER SIX

Shell Middens in Western Algarve (Southern Portugal) during the Mesolithic and Early Neolithic

Functionality, Subsistence, and Material Culture

Maria João Valente, Rebecca Dean, and António Faustino Carvalho

SUMMARY

During the past decade, new research has been conducted on several shell midden sites in western Algarve (southern Portugal), dated from the Preboreal to the early Atlantic climatic periods (ca. 10,400–7400 cal BP or 9400–5400 cal BC). New sites (four shell middens at Barranco das Quebradas and one at Rocha das Gaivotas) provided new data on Mesolithic occupation patterns: geographic location, radiocarbon dates, size, archaeological context, and materials. This study uses these characteristics to infer the function and duration of the occupations. Data on shellfish, namely on the abundance of species and processing techniques, helps us define diet choices and their changes through time.

The Mesolithic shell middens in western Algarve are located either atop sea cliffs or in nearby small valleys. The overwhelming majority of shell remains—and the reduced number of any other kind of fauna or lithic materials—define these as specialized, temporary locations. From this we can conclude that these human groups had high mobility indexes and traveled to the coast in order to collect local marine resources and, later on, flint raw material. The preferred animals were mussels, limpets, common topshells, and, at a later period, gooseneck barnacles. There is no evidence of overexploitation of any species during the Mesolithic, and the change of relative abundances should indicate adaptation to local availability of resources.

We hypothesize that other Mesolithic sites, with residential features, may be located in more interior areas. Such camps were probably situated either northward along the coast, where more permanent settlements with broad-spectrum subsistence have been identified, or in the estuaries of the Algarvean rivers, where they are presently buried under alluvial sediments.

Early Neolithic sites still include important deposits of shell remains. However, most of these sites do not display the density of real shell middens, while others are reoccupations of old Mesolithic middens with thin and scattered shell deposits when compared to the previous periods. Non-faunal material, such as lithics and ceramics, are more abundant than in the Mesolithic times, and access to flint sources seem to be one of the main purposes of the occupations.

The middens cease formation altogether after ca. 6900 cal BP (5000 cal BC), during a younger stage of the Early Neolithic. At this time, there is growing evidence of agriculture and domestication of some animal species and a noticeable change in subsistence strategies.

INTRODUCTION

This study compares diet and landscape use across space and time in western Algarve, from 10,400 to 6400 cal BP (8500–5400 cal BC), a period that corresponds to the Mesolithic and Early Neolithic settlements in the area. All archaeological sites occupied within these dates have shell deposits, which range from thin scatterings to thick layers with a high density of specimens. Among these, the most significant are the shell middens of Praia do Castelejo (Silva and Soares 1997), Armação Nova (Soares and Silva 2003), and, the focus of this chapter, Barranco das Quebradas (a complex of four preserved archaeological sites) and Rocha das Gaivotas (Figure 6.1).

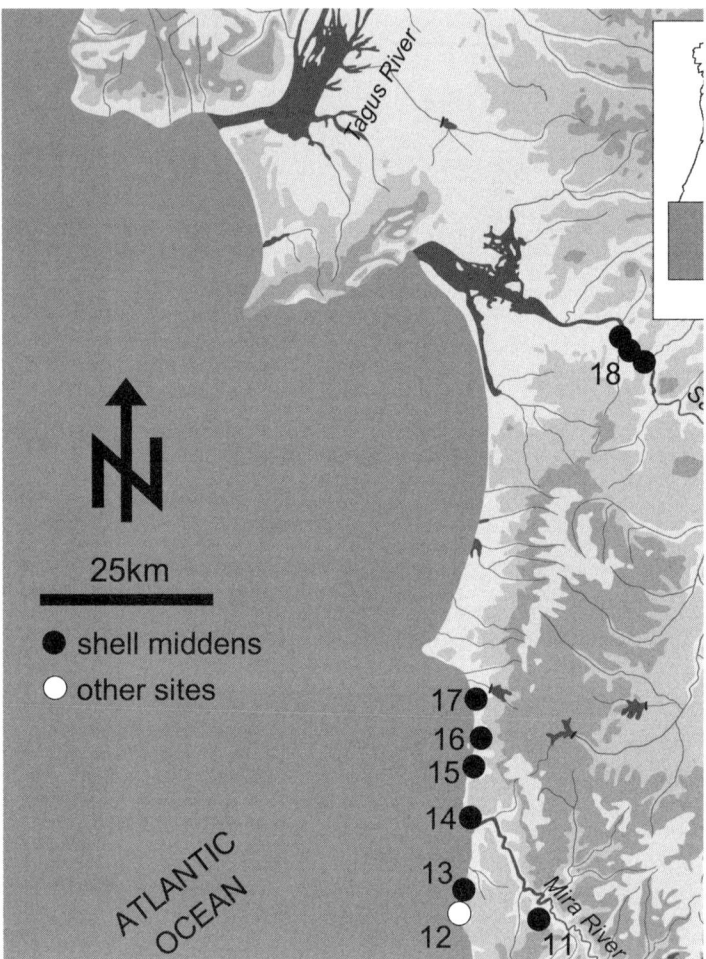

6.1. Map of southwestern Portugal with sites mentioned in text. Western Algarve inside rectangle. Legend: *(1) Barranco das Quebradas, Rocha das Gaivotas, and Armação Nova; (2) Vale Santo and Cabranosa; (3) Praia do Castelejo; (4) Padrão; (5) Vale Boi; (6) Alcalar 7; (7) Ibn-Amar Cave; (8) Ribeira de Alcantarilha; (9) Castelo Belinho; (10) Montes de Baixo; (11) Fiais; (12) Palheirões do Alegra; (13) Medo Tojeiro; (14) Pedra do Patacho; (15) Vidigal; (16) Samouqueira; (17) Oliveirinha; (18) Sado Valley (several sites).*

Shell midden research has a long tradition in Portugal, going back to the 19th-century discovery of the Late Mesolithic *concheiros* of Muge (Ribeiro 1884). These middens, which date from the early Atlantic period (ca. 8300–7250 cal BP or 6300–5300 cal BC), were recognized as analogous to the Danish *køkkenmødding*. They are located in central Portugal, at the bottom of a large estuary in the confluence of the Muge and Tagus Rivers, and occupied an ecotonal position, accessing aquatic and wetland resources (mollusks, crustaceans, fish, birds) as well as forest game (red

deer, wild boar, and auroch). Since their discovery, the best preserved sites have been widely researched, with a special focus on the more than 300 human skeletons found there. They have provided valuable data for physical anthropology, demography, funerary rituals, and diet reconstruction (Roksandic and Jackes, chap. 9 in this volume; Jackes et al., chap. 10 in this volume). Given the diversity of animal remains, human burials, dwelling structures, and lithic industry, Muge shell middens have been generally characterized as base camps with semipermanent occupation, where the residents engaged in intense collection of local resources (e.g., Arnaud 1987; Jackes and Meiklejohn 2004).

During the course of the last two decades, shell middens of a new type have been identified in the coast of central Portugal. They are much smaller and show specialization in shellfish collecting. Most date from previous climatic periods, the Preboreal and Boreal (11,500–8800 cal BP or 9600–6900 cal BC), and the generally accepted theory holds that during this period (Early Mesolithic), the human communities were highly mobile between the coast and the Estremadura limestone massif, where they would access raw flint and forest resources. Data shows that later on, during the early Atlantic period (ca. 8300 cal BP or 6300 cal BC; i.e., Late Mesolithic), these sites were mostly abandoned. There was a clear shift in the landscape use system, focusing on the occasional occupation of the limestone massif and the large Muge middens in the Tagus valley (e.g., Araújo 2003).

Until the early 1990s, published data regarding these periods in southwestern Iberia was almost nonexistent. The first studies focusing on Mesolithic sites in this area examined Vidigal and Pedra do Patacho, shell middens situated in western Alentejo (Soares and Silva 1993; Straus, Altuna, and Vierra 1990). Studies of additional sites followed, but none had extensive faunal analysis.

Despite the lack of detailed publications, there is sufficient data from the Mesolithic and Early Neolithic periods in western Alentejo to show differing settlement patterns from central Portugal. In Alentejo, coastal settlements specializing in shellfish have existed since the early Preboreal, and although middens were being formed in the Sado and Mira interior estuaries during the early Atlantic period (with residential features), the littoral area was not abandoned during the Late Mesolithic. As for western Algarve, until recently its shell middens had only been featured in very preliminary publications, limited to descriptions of the general stratigraphy and basic accounts of faunal species and other materials.

Table 6.1. Barranco das Quebradas: Radiometric dates

Provenience [a]	Material	Lab code	Date BP	ΔR [c]	cal BP 2Σ [d]	cal BC 2Σ [d]
B. das Quebradas 1						
Test 2, a.l. 40–50cm	*Monodonta l.*	Wk–8939	8960 ± 70	-116 ± 44	9552–10093	8144–7603
Test 2, a.l. 110–120cm	*Monodonta l.*	Wk–8950	9020 ± 70	-116 ± 44	9633–10155	8206–7684
M6, a.l. 7	*Monodonta l.*	Wk–16428	9473 ± 54	-116 ± 44	10264–10573	8624–8315
B. das Quebradas 3						
Test 1, a.l. 0–22	*Monodonta l.*	Wk–8940	8360 ± 80	-116 ± 44	8854–9379	7430–6905
F21, a.l. 2	*Monodonta l.*	Wk–12133	8374 ± 54	-116 ± 44	9013–9205	7373–7006
Sond.1, a.l. 60–70	*Monodonta l.*	Wk–8951	8780 ± 60	-116 ± 44	9415–9782	7833–7466
B. das Quebradas 4						
L18, a.l. 2	*Monodonta l.*	Wk–12134	8873 ± 57	-116 ± 44	9496–9902	7953–7547
B. das Quebradas 5						
M7, a.l. 15b [b]	*Thais h.*	Wk–13693	8415 ± 74	-116 ± 44	8977–9396	7447–7028
N9, a.l. 4	*Patella* spp.	Wk–16427	8449 ± 51	-116 ± 44	9023–9390	7441–7074

[a] Square (or Test) and artificial level.

[b] Corresponds to artificial level 2 from squares L-N/7-9.

[c] Marine reservoir correction (ΔR): -116 ± 44. Value calculated for Rocha das Gaivotas, the closest site, both geographically and chronologically (see Table 6.5 notes).

[d] Calibration curve and program used: Marine09 (Reimer et al. 2009); Calib v. 6.1.

In an effort to find new sites and establish a more complete database regarding Mesolithic and Neolithic settlements in the area, the University of Algarve developed several projects during the last 15 years.[1] These resulted in various site discoveries, including two sets of shell middens: Barranco das Quebradas and Rocha das Gaivotas, dated 10,400 to 7400 cal BP (8500–5400 cal BC; Tables 6.1 and 6.2).[2] Preliminary data was published (Bicho et al. 2000, 2003; Carvalho et al. 2005; Stiner 2003; Stiner et al. 2003), followed by more extensive excavations and full archaeological studies (Carvalho 2008; Carvalho and Valente 2005; Carvalho, Valente, and Dean 2010; Valente 2008, 2010). These studies established the age of the deposits, their density, and the type of archaeological materials. Full faunal analyses were conducted, including species identification, specimen size, and shell modification patterns.

The main purpose of this chapter is to interpret the data collected from shell middens in western Algarve. It will establish the context of their locations, their density and dimension, material and structures, shellfish species and abundance, and fauna processing strategies. We will then focus on the changes from the Early Mesolithic to Early Neolithic, especially regarding the exploitation of locally available aquatic resources and the shifting composition of species. We will also establish their relevance regarding human landscape use patterns.

As a final introductory note, during the excavations of Barranco das Quebradas and Rocha das Gaivotas, a grid of one x one meters was used and deposits were removed in five- or ten-centimeter artificial levels, depending on the density of materials. Changes in sediment color and matrix enabled the distinction of natural layers. All sediments were dry sieved with a three-millimeter screen size.

GEOGRAPHICAL CONTEXT

The main sites featured in this chapter are located on Algarve's western coast, near Europe's most southwestern cape, Cabo de São Vicente (Figures 6.1 and 6.2). Here the shore has been exposed to deep marine and aeolian abrasion, resulting in an irregular coast featuring very high cliffs, intercalated by small sandy beaches at the mouths of minor ravines. The geological substrate is largely sandy or sandy-clayish, with areas of schist and limestone that sometimes include a variety of siliceous bodies, making

Table 6.2. Barranco das Quebradas and Rocha das Gaivotas: List of identified species in each site

CLASS / Family	Taxonomic Name	Common Name	BQ1	BQ3	BQ4	BQ5	RGV
CIRRIPEDIA							
Pollicipedidae	*Pollicipes pollicipes*	Goose barnacle	x	x	x	x	x
Balanidae	*Balanus* sp. (cf. *perforatus*)	Barnacle	x	x	x	x	x
MALACOSTRACA							
Cancridae	not determined	crab (middle sized)	x	x	x	x	
GASTROPODA							
Helicidae	*Helix* sp.	land snail	x	x	x	x	x
Subulinidae	*Rumina decollata*	land snail				x	x
Neritidae	*Theodoxus fluviatilis*	River nerite	x				
Haliotidae	*Haliotis tuberculata*	Abalone or Green ormer		x			
Fissurellidae	*Diodora graeca*	Keyhole limpet				x	x
Patellidae	*Patella* spp.[a]	Limpet	x	x	x	x	x
Trochidae	*Gibbula umbilicalis*	Flat topshell				x	
	Monodonta lineata	Common or thick topshell	x	x	x	x	x
Turritellidae	*Turritella* sp.	—					x
Naticidae	*Natica* sp.	—	x			x	
Triviidae	*Trivia monacha*	European cowrie	x				
Ranellidae	*Charonia lampas*	Knobbed triton	x				
Muricidae	*Ocenebra erinaceus*	—		x			
	Ocenebrina edwardsii	—				x	
	Urosalpinx cinerea	Atlantic oyster drill					x
	Thais haemastoma	Southern oyster drill	x	x	x	x	x
Thaididae	*Nucella lapillus*	Dog whelk		x		x	x
Nassariidae	*Nassarius reticulatus*	Netted dog whelk			x	x	x
	Nassarius incrassatus	Thick lipped dog whelk			x	x	
Siphonariidae	*Siphonaria pectinata*	Striped false limpet	x		x	x	x
BIVALVIA							
Glycymerididae	*Glycymeris insubrica*	Dog cockle					x
Mytilidae	*Mytilus* sp.[b]	Mussel	x	x	x	x	x
	Musculus costulatus	Ribbed crenella				x	
Gryphaeidae	*Neopycnodonte cochlear*	Deepsea oyster				x	
Pectinidae	*Pecten maximus*	Great scallop			x		
	Chlamys sp.	Scallop		x			
Cardiidae	*Cerastoderma edule*	Common cockle					x
Veneridae	*Venus verrucosa*	Warty venus			x		
	Chamelea gallina	Striped venus clam					x
	Ruditapes decussata	Clam		x	x		

BQ – Barranco das Quebradas; RGV – Rocha das Gaivotas.

[a] Identified species: *P. vulgata*, *P. intermedia*, *P. aspera*, and *P. caerulea*.
[b] Either *M. edulis* or *M. galloprovincialis* (some authors consider them varieties of the same species).

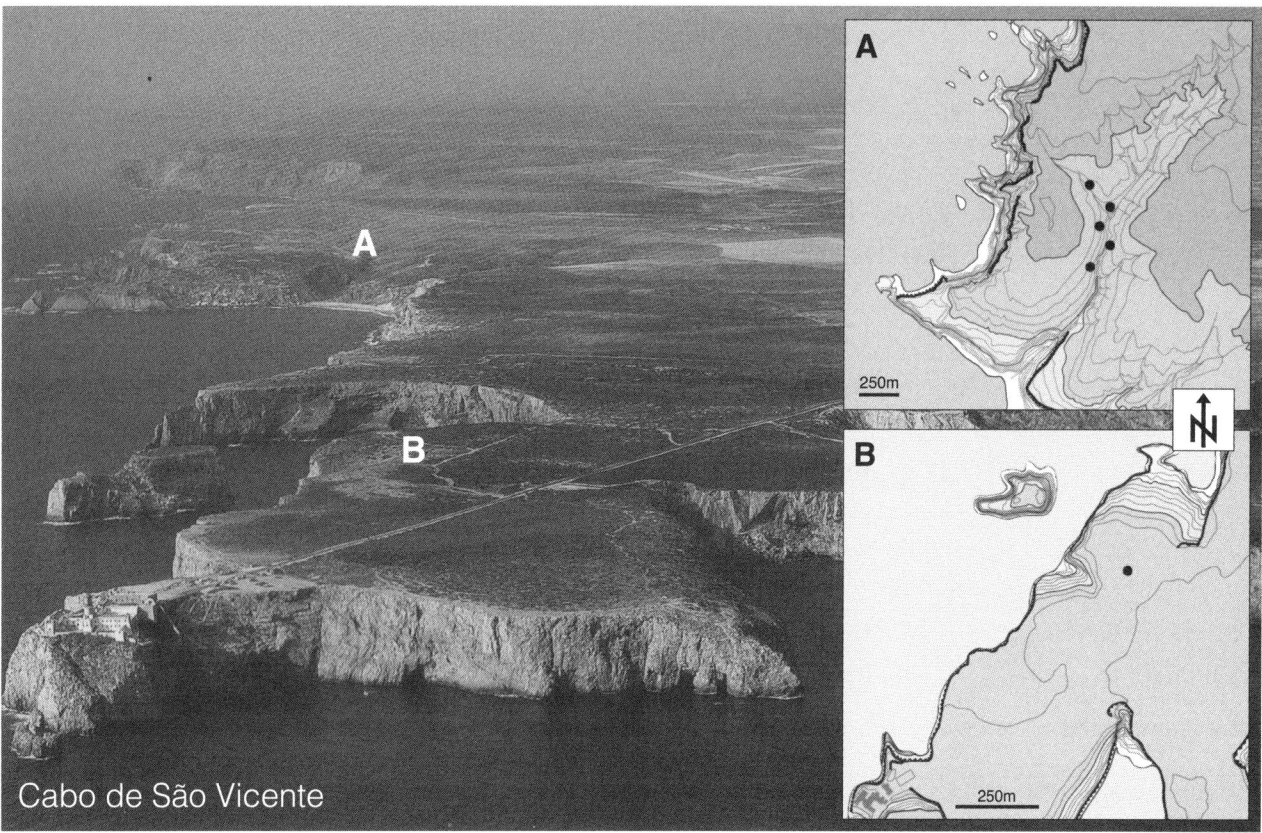

6.2. Coast of São Vicente (cape in foreground) with Barranco das Quebradas (A) and Rocha das Gaivotas (B).

them good sources of flint. On the cliff tops are several fossilized dunes, some with deposited archaeological materials. We can also find well-preserved sites on the slopes of the minor ravines.

Nowadays, as well as during the Early Holocene, the region is a harsh place to live. It is dominated by a thermo-Mediterranean, dry to subhumid environment, with vegetation reflecting the dryness of the soil and its direct exposure to salinity and strong Atlantic winds. The plants found here are mostly herbaceous trees and small shrubs.

This Atlantic coast territory is regarded as one of the richest areas in Portugal in terms of marine communities. It has a high concentration of fish and especially rock-dwelling mollusks or crustaceans such as limpets and gooseneck barnacles. The barnacles are still one of the most heavily consumed crustaceans in the area, and are considered a gourmet specialty.

The rest of western Algarve is marked by three latitude zones. From north to south, there are interior mountains composed largely of schist, a middle area called *barrocal*

with limestone and clay soil, and a southern littoral zone made of sandy soils, featuring several small estuaries (e.g., Alvor and Arade) and lagoons.

BARRANCO DAS QUEBRADAS

Located about 3.5 kilometers north of the Cape of São Vicente, Barranco das Quebradas (BQ) is a narrow, deep ravine caused by erosive draining. It ends directly on a sandy Atlantic beach (Praia do Telheiro) surrounded by rocky limestone cliffs (see Figure 6.2A). The area is ideal for human settlement; the ravine itself would provide protection from the winds that sweep the surrounding cliffs and high plains, access to the local seashore resources would be easy, and there are freshwater springs nearby.

The materials collected by 1996–2001 test works (BQ1 and BQ3 tests)[3] were mostly faunal and were analyzed and published by Nuno F. Bicho, Mary Stiner, and colleagues (Bicho et al. 2000, 2003; Stiner 2003; Stiner et al. 2003). Afterward (2002–2004), more surveys and extensive

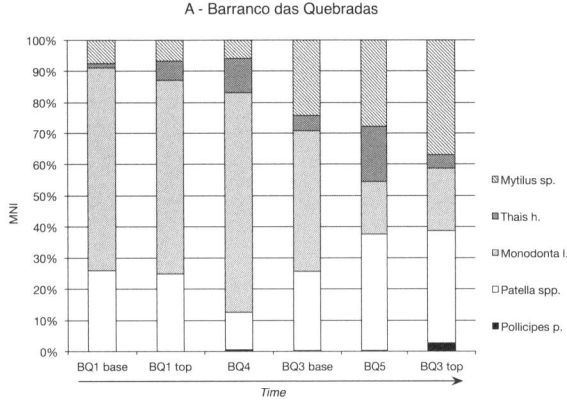

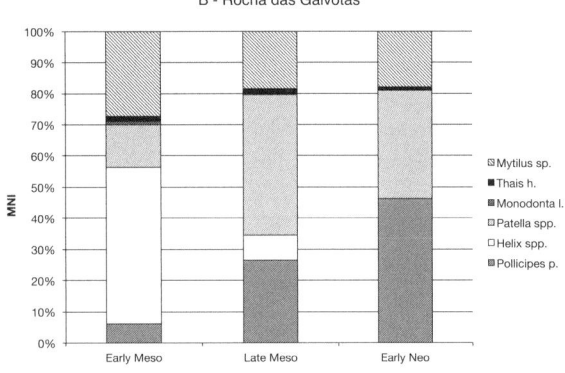

6.3. Main species relative abundance at (A) Barranco das Quebradas and (B) Rocha das Gaivotas through time.

excavations were pursued with the discovery of two other sites (BQ4 and BQ5; full results in Carvalho and Valente 2005; Valente 2008, 2010; Valente and Carvalho 2009).

All of the BQ sites are located below 75 meters above mean sea level and in general yield Early Mesolithic deposits, dating from the Preboreal and Boreal periods (ca. 10,400–8900 cal BP or 8500–6900 cal BC; Table 6.1). The most common species are common topshell (*Monodonta lineata*), mussels (*Mytilus* sp.), limpets (*Patella* spp.), and southern oyster drill (*Thais haemastoma*), all of which are still found on the rocky southern Portugal coast today (see Table 6.2 for all identified species).

The fauna presented in this chapter was completely analyzed, with the exception of the materials collected in the 1996–2001 test works (data in Stiner 2003; Stiner et al. 2003). Only a very small percentage of the materials (those less than 0.5 centimeter) was not identified. Taxonomic abundance is based on the minimum number of individuals (MNI).[4]

Barranco das Quebradas 1

BQ1 is a narrow, limited shell midden in a limestone rock shelter on the right slope of the ravine, with the archaeological materials located in the first meter of sandy-clayish sediments. This site encompasses at least two distinct periods of deposition, the younger dating from the Boreal period (ca. 9800 cal BP or 7900 cal BC at the middle of the sequence, corresponding to Layers 1 and 2; see Table 6.1), and the older dating from the Preboreal (ca. 10,400 cal BP or 8500 cal BC at the base of the sequence, corresponding to Layer 3), the latter being the most ancient occupation of all BQ sites. The estimated area of the midden is no more than 120 square meters.

Only two square meters were excavated (beside the 1999 tests), but within that excavation we identified more than 11,000 shell specimens. No significant changes are seen in taxa distribution between layers or occupations; the older occupation (BQ1 base) includes mainly topshells and limpets, while the younger one (BQ1 top) also includes a strong percentage of drills (Table 6.3, Figure 6.3A). The older deposits also yielded some unusual materials, including one small, perforated disc of dolomite, one European cowrie (*Trivia monacha*), and one river nerite (*Theodoxus fluviatilis*). The surface levels of one of the 1999 tests yielded a unique small ungulate tooth.

Shell breakage patterns seem to result from both human and post-depositional action, depending on the species. Topshells, which have a very thick exoskeleton, are well preserved with limited breakage (ca. 90 percent are intact). To extract their meat, human groups could apply a method still in use today, by insertion of a small pointed stick to pull the animal out.

Limpets and especially mussels show a higher degree of fragmentation, probably associated with sediment pressure and erosion. Limpets do not need to be broken to access their meat (most of the effort is made when detaching the animals from the rocky substratum) and in BQ1 their breakage is mostly limited to the external concentric growth lines. Mussels do not need to be fractured to be eaten; in fact, the easiest method to open these animals is by heating them over a fire or in water. On the other hand, they have very thin and delicate shells that are easily broken after deposition.

Drills show anthropic breakage patterns. Their shells are thick and not easily broken by sediment pressure or erosion, yet their degree of fragmentation is very high (only three intact specimens from a MNI of 173), which can be related to food processing. Their meat is more difficult

Table 6.3. Barranco das Quebradas: Fauna quantification

CLASS / Family	Taxon	BQ1 (bottom)		BQ1 (top)		BQ3 (bottom)[c]		BQ3 (top)[c]		BQ4		BQ5	
		MNI	%	MNI	%	MNI	%	MNI	%	MNI	%	MNI	%
MAMIFERA													
	non-identified									1	0.0		
AVES													
	Passariformes									1	0.0		
CIRRIPEDIA													
Pollicipedidae	Pollicipes p.	1	0.0			15	0.3	81	2.7	17	0.4	20	0.3
Balanidae	Balanus sp.	44	1.1	12	1.9	162	2.8	56	1.8	25	0.6	382	6.6
GASTROPODA													
Patellidae	Patella spp.	993	25.1	150	23.5	1406	24.6	1072	35.3	510	12.0	1960	33.9
Trochidae	Monodonta lineata	2497	63.2	373	58.6	2504	43.8	595	19.6	2966	70.0	893	15.4
Muricidae	Thais haemastoma	51	1.3	38	6.0	264	4.6	130	4.3	452	10.7	917	15.8
BIVALVIA													
Mytilidae	Mytilus sp.	292	7.4	40	6.3	1354	23.7	1099	36.2	252	5.9	1467	25.4
OTHERS													
	land snails[a]	67	1.7	24	3.8	d		d		6	0.1	75	1.3
	various[b]	8	0.2			11	0.2	4	0.1	10	0.2	72	1.2
	Total MNI	3953	—	637	—	5716	—	3037	—	4240	—	5786	—
	Total specimens	9068	—	2072	—	17072	—	10563	—	15160	—	52718	—

[a] Considered intrusive. The majority are from genus *Helix*, with some *Rumina decollata*.

[b] For taxonomic list, see Table 6.2.

[c] Only South area (North area test not included).

[d] Low number, not counted (considered intrusive).

to pull out than the meat from topshells, and its removal can be facilitated by shell breakage.

BQ1 also yielded some culturally atypical stone industry, mainly *expedient* tools in graywacke, but also in quartz and quartzite (macrolithics). In addition, a small number of flint artifacts were found, possibly representing occasional *curated strategies* (in the sense of Binford). Some of the larger artifacts could have been used as hammerstones for breaking shells. Several graywacke rocks showed fractures caused by fire, probably the result of fireplaces' being used to process the mollusks as food, although no actual fireplaces were identified.

Direct evidence of shellfish cooking is present in a very small amount of shell remains displaying color alteration (<1.2 percent; Table 6.4), predominantly gray and brown. The gray color may come from contact with burning coal or hot braziers (Chernorkian 1983), while the brown may

eventually be created by liquid boiling, particularly when mixing seaweed, which taints the shells (Dupont 2003). It is therefore likely that, besides eating raw meat, human groups were using food processing techniques such as heating by fire or boiling.

Barranco das Quebradas 3

BQ3 is also a spatially limited shell midden in a now destroyed limestone rock shelter on the right slope of the ravine. Well preserved, this site displays homogenous sandy-clayish sediments approximately 80 centimeters in depth. The extension of occupation should be around 150 square meters.

The data presented here comes from its south area, with four square meters excavated (further north, a test produced scarce materials). More than 17,000 identified specimens were collected. Changes in the density of materials along the

Table 6.4. Barranco das Quebradas and Rocha das Gaivotas: Percentage of color-modified specimens[a]

Site / Context	% Modified
Barranco das Quebradas—Early Mesolithic	
BQ1 top	0.8
BQ1 base	1.2
BQ1 top	0.6
BQ1 base	1.3
BQ4	1.6
BQ5	2.4
Rocha das Gaivotas—Early Mesolithic	
Sec I - general	26.0
Sec II - general	23.6
Sec III - 3a	7.1
Sec III - 3b	2.0
Sec III - 3c	8.4
Sec III - 3d	10.6
Sec III - F5	29.0
Sec IV - general	0.0
Sec V - general	0.0
Rocha das Gaivotas—Late Mesolithic	
Sec I - general	13.0
Sec I - F1	69.0
Sec II - general	7.1
Sec II - F3	32.0

[a] Color modification interpreted as result of cooking processes (development in the text.)

stratigraphy and variance in relative taxa abundance distinguish at least two different Mesolithic settlements. The oldest one (BQ3 base) contained shell remains with few lithic materials; the most superficial one (BQ3 top), besides mollusks and some lithics, also yielded one fragment of ungulate tooth and two pottery fragments stylistically attributable to the Early Neolithic. No other Neolithic materials were found, and both occupations date from the Boreal (ca. 9150 cal BP or 7200 cal BC for the top levels; ca. 9600 cal BP or 7650 cal BC for the inferior ones; see Table 6.1), making them consistent with Early Mesolithic establishments. Nonetheless, it is possible that after the *effective* Mesolithic occupations of the site, there were subsequent short-term occurrences of Neolithic communities in the area that did not result in an evident archaeological level, but merely in some scattered ceramics in the top deposits.

In the older deposits, topshell is the most common species, followed by limpets and mussels; in the younger

deposits, it is the inverse (Table 6.3 and Figure 6.3A). Other less frequent species are abalone (*Haliotis tuberculata*), knobbed triton (*Charonia lampas*, the largest European gastropod), clam (*Ruditapes decussata*), and warty venus (*Venus verrucosa*).

Fragmentation is more pronounced in this site than in BQ1. This is particularly noticeable in topshells, where the percentage of broken elements rises to 23.9 percent and 50.1 percent on the top and lower occupations, respectively. All drills are broken. In our opinion, these patterns are caused by humans, for the reasons previously explained.

As in BQ1, there are no preserved hearths. However, the same evidence in rocks (cracked by thermoclastis and/or calcinated) and modified faunal remains shows that they existed. Regarding shells, the lower deposits have more altered specimens than the top ones (0.6 percent and 1.3 percent, predominantly drills and then topshells; Table 6.4).

The lithic collection shows the same features as in BQ1: a small amount, mostly macrolithic, of simple and expedite characteristics.

Barranco das Quebradas 4

BQ4 is an open-air shell midden also found at the right slope of the valley, on a platform located at the confluence of the main ravine with a subsidiary branch. This site is wider than BQ1 and BQ3 (200 to 250 square meters), although with a thinner archaeological deposit that does not exceed 50 centimeters in depth. The faunal collection amounts to 15,160 identified shell specimens (Table 6.3). Dated at ca. 9700 cal BP (7700 cal BC; Table 6.1), this occupation is also from the Boreal period, again corresponding to the Early Mesolithic period.

The faunal collection is similar to the one already described for BQ1 and BQ3 base: common topshell is by far the most abundant species, followed by limpets, drills, and then mussels (Figure 6.3A). The assembled materials also include great scallop (*Pecten maximus*), one fragment of bone (probably from a mammal), and one passerine humerus.

Shell fragmentation and color modification show the same patterns as in BQ3: high fragmentation, including common topshells, and a low percentage of burned/boiled material (1.6 percent; Table 6.4), with the majority identified as southern oyster drill. Lithic materials are also similar to the ones described for BQ1 and BQ3.

Barranco das Quebradas 5

BQ5 is different from the other sites, in terms of both topography and sediments. The site, also dated from the

Boreal (around 9150 cal BP or 7200 cal BC; Table 6.1), was found 300 meters off the main ravine, in a subsidiary that intersects its right side. While materials can be found on the surface at the other sites, at BQ5 the archaeological materials occur about 130 centimeters deep, in a sequence that is approximately 30 centimeters thick. A little more than eight square meters were excavated, and presently we have no data to infer its extension. The number of identified shell specimens is more than 52,700.

Archaeologically, the site also shows several differences from the other three, starting with the distinction of multiple thin layers of overlapping shell deposits. Limpets, mussels, and drills are the most abundant taxa, while topshells, usually common in the other contexts, are rather scarce. Gooseneck barnacles (*Pollicipes pollicipes*) are present as well (Table 6.3; Figure 6.3A).

The percentage of specimens with color alteration is higher than in the other sites (2.4 percent, most displaying gray color; Table 6.4). Given the occurrence of charcoal and fire-broken stones, it is reasonable to assume that some fireplaces existed, even though none was revealed during the excavation (or perhaps their basic structure prevented preservation).

There is also a significant presence of graywacke and quartzite macrolithic industry, with flakes, choppers, and anvils. Marks on these last objects led us to surmise that they were mainly used to break drill shells, the only species visibly fractured by human action.

ROCHA DAS GAIVOTAS

Situated one kilometer north of Cabo de São Vicente, Rocha das Gaivotas is a wide shell midden located in a sand dune, around 60 meters above mean sea level (see Figures 6.1 and 6.2B). It was discovered in 1998, during a systematic survey after modern local mollusk collectors dug an earthen track to access the nearby rocky shores, and tests were conducted in 1999 (Tests I and II; Bicho et al. 2000; Stiner 2003; Stiner et al. 2003).

In 2003 and 2004, two more field campaigns were pursued, opening an extensive area (Carvalho 2008; Carvalho et al. 2005; Carvalho and Valente 2005; Carvalho, Valente, and Dean 2010; Dean and Carvalho 2011; Valente 2008; Valente and Carvalho 2009). These excavations spread across five different sectors (Figure 6.4) and resulted in the identification of three stratigraphic layers with several human settlements from the Early Mesolithic (9750 cal BP or 7800 cal BC) to Early Neolithic (7400 cal BP or 5400 cal BC; see Table 6.5). The archaeological deposits

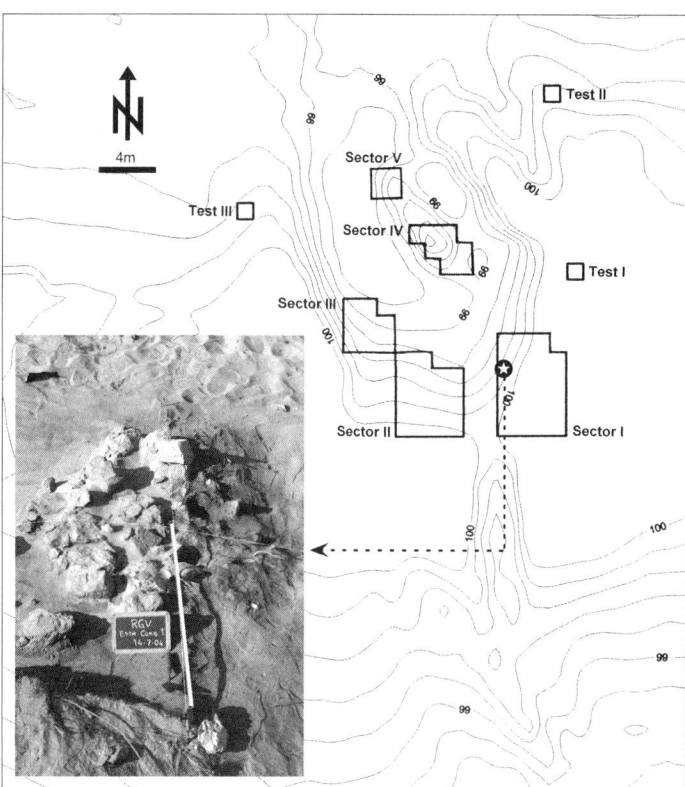

6.4. Rocha das Gaivotas: map with excavation areas (sectors). Note: Photo of Fireplace 1 (Late Mesolithic) with its location within Sector I.

were restricted to Layers 2c and 3, and only Sectors I and II included all the occupations; in the others, some of the deposits were either absent or eroded. As of now, the site is known to have at least 300 square meters, but it may be much wider.

All fauna from the Neolithic deposits were analyzed, but the large amount of material in the Mesolithic layers limited the analysis to half of the collected sample. The materials collected in 1998 are not included (data in Stiner 2003; Stiner et al. 2003).

Early Mesolithic

This period was identified in Layer 3, the thickest of the site, corresponding to the bottom of the sand dune. It consists of four different sublayers (3a to 3d), dated between approximately 9750 and 9150 cal BP (7800 to 7200 cal BC). All four are relatively thin and spatially circumscribed, with poorly preserved shells and fireplace areas, and rare lithic artifacts (n=4). There are two fireplaces of very simple typology (Fireplaces 4 and 5): only of burnt sand and shells, showing no stone structuring.

Table 6.5. Rocha das Gaivotas: Radiometric dates

Provenience[a]	Material	Lab code	Date BP	ΔR^c	cal BP $2\sigma^d$	cal BC $2\sigma^d$
Early Mesolithic						
I – Layer 3a	Mytilus sp.	Wk–16424	8420 ± 46	-116 ± 40	9003–9357	7408–7054
V – Layer 3a	Mytilus sp.	Wk–16426	8427 ± 51	-116 ± 40	9005–9370	7421–7056
III – Fireplace 5	marine shells[b]	Wk–16425	8673 ± 78	-116 ± 40	9245–9663	7714–7296
III – Layer 3b	Monodonta l.	Wk–13690	8674 ± 52	-116 ± 40	9291–9585	7636–7342
III – Fireplace 4	Patella spp.	Wk–13691	8965 ± 54	-116 ± 40	9579–10090	8141–7630
Late Mesolithic						
I – Fireplace 2	Patella spp.	Wk–14793	7117 ± 38	-116 ± 40	7580–7824	5875–5631
I – Fireplace 1	Patella spp.	Wk–13692	7092 ± 48	-116 ± 40	7558–7818	5869–5609
II – Fireplace 3	Pistacia sp.	Wk–14798	6820 ± 51	-116 ± 40	7577–7755	5806–5628
I – Layer 2c base	Patella spp.	Wk–14794	7201 ± 39	-116 ± 40	7660–7914	5965–5711
I – Fireplace 2	Juniperus sp.	Wk–14797	6862 ± 43	-116 ± 40	7612–7790	5841–5663
Test 1, Artif Lev 10	Patella spp.	Wk–6075	7270 ± 70	-116 ± 40	7668–8001	6052–5719
Early Neolithic						
I – Layer 2c top	Pollicipes p.	Wk–17029	6801 ± 39	-116 ± 40	7311–7545	5596–5362

[a] Sector and layer (or fireplace).

[b] Mix of *Thais haemastoma*, *Patella* spp., and *Mytilus* sp.

[c] Marine reservoir correction (ΔR): -116 ± 44. Value calculated by António Monge Soares (pers. communication) for the Fireplace 2 samples of limpet shells (Wk–14793) and charred wood of *Juniperus* sp. (Wk–14797). The procedure is similar to those done by Soares and Dias (2006) and the ΔR value is in agreement with the one obtained for Castelejo (-110 ± 40 in a sample with a conventional radiocarbon date of 8160 ± 40 BP).

[d] Calibration curves and program used: Marine09 (Reimer et al. 2009) and IntCal09 (Heaton, Blackwell, and Buck 2009); Calib v. 6.1.

Analyzed shells totaled more than 17,170 specimens, with the taxonomic composition mostly characterized by land snails (genus *Helix*), mussels, and limpets (Figure 6.3B; Table 6.6). Land snails were not considered intrusive (i.e., from a later period) given three factors: their high number, the sealing of the levels in which they occur by subsequent occupations, and the traces of burning often found on their shells. Nonetheless, given their small size (rarely exceeding 20 millimeters), these animals might not have been eaten by the human communities: they could have arrived to the site attached to wood gathered for fireplaces, for instance. On this point, David Lubell (2004, 82) mentions that he does not know of any Mesolithic or Neolithic Portuguese site with indubitable edible land-snail accumulations.

Individual examination of each sublayer reveals noticeable taxa changes between sectors and through time, as it can be seen in Table 6.7.

The assemblage generally showed a high degree of breakage, with some species displaying human-caused damage; for instance, all topshells and drills were broken. The amount of color-altered material (probably related to cooking) varied across the contexts, as shown in Table 6.4.

Late Mesolithic

Though found only on the lower part of Layer 2 in Sectors I and II, this is the most substantial human occupation, with thicker deposits and a higher density of materials. The faunal remains total more than 30,000 identified specimens, and there are more lithic artifacts than in any other layer. Radiocarbon dating points to settlements occurring between ca. 7850 and 7700 cal BP (5850 to 5700 cal BC).

Unlike the previous period, Late Mesolithic occupations include three fireplaces of complex typologies using stones of various sizes: one "in cuvette" (Fireplace 3), the others with flat base stones (Fireplaces 1 and 2; Figure 6.4). Numerous burned shells were found in their interiors, mostly from limpets and mussels, although Fireplace 3 yielded a very high percentage of land snails (Table 6.4). Vegetal charcoal

Table 6.6. Rocha das Gaivotas: Fauna quantification

CLASS / Family	Species	Early Mesolithic MNI	Early Mesolithic %	Late Mesolithic MNI	Late Mesolithic %	Early Neolithic MNI	Early Neolithic %
CIRRIPEDIA							
Pollicipedidae	*Pollicipes p.*	239	5.4	1728	25.0	1115	40.4
Balanidae	*Balanus* sp.	377	8.5	391	5.6	154	5.6
GASTROPODA							
Helicidae	*Helix* sp.	1915	43.1	512	7.4	b	b
Subulinidae	*Rumina decollata*	236	5.3	27	0.4	b	b
Patellidae	*Patella* spp.	517	11.6	2904	42.0	990	35.9
Trochidae	*Monodonta lineata*	42	0.9	24	0.3	4	0.1
Muricidae	*Thais haemastoma*	63	1.4	102	1.5	21	0.8
BIVALVIA							
Mytilidae	*Mytilus* sp.	1043	23.5	1206	17.4	437	15.8
OTHERS	various[a]	10	0.2	28	0.4	40	1.4
	Total MNI	4442	—	6922	—	2761	—
	Total specimens	17177	—	30051	—	8189	—

[a] For taxonomic list of identified species, see Table 6.2.

[b] Not counted, considered intrusive.

Table 6.7. Rocha das Gaivotas: Fauna abundance within the several contexts (in percentages)[a]

Context / Taxa	Pollicipes p.	Helix sp.	Patella spp.	Monodonta l.	Thais h.	Mytilus sp.
Early Mesolithic (n=4255)						
Sector I	25.5	12.7	24.5	—	2.9	**34.3**
Sector II	**48.4**	4.9	11.7	—	2.8	32.2
Sector III 3a	1.1	16.0	40.2	0.2	0.6	**42.0**
Sector III 3b	4.0	13.1	28.2	15.1	1.6	**38.1**
Sector III 3c	8.0	11.0	30.0	0.5	15.0	**35.5**
Sector III 3d	0.2	**63.4**	20.3	0.0	0.1	16.0
Sector III F5	13.0	15.4	26.8	—	1.6	**43.1**
Sector IV	10.3	**64.1**	9.4	0.4	3.0	12.8
Sector V	0.0	**53.2**	8.8	—	1.8	36.3
Later Mesolithic (n=8,380)						
Sector I	19.7	4.2	**61.2**	0.3	1.1	13.5
Sector I F1	24.0	0.0	**40.0**	0.0	4.0	32.0
Sector II	**34.1**	17.5	22.0	0.2	2.5	23.7
Sector II F3	14.6	**46.4**	19.8	0.0	2.1	17.2
Early Neolithic (n=2,417)						
Sector I	**46.9**	—	34.8	0.1	0.8	17.4
Sector IV	**34.9**	—	34.2	0.7	1.3	28.9

[a] In bold: the highest percentage for each context.

remains also found in their interiors were identified as juniper (*Juniperus* sp.), *Pistacia* sp., and wild olive tree (*Olea europaea* var. *sylvestris*) (Figueiral and Carvalho 2006), all plants that are still found in the area today.

The lithic industry (n=226) is made of local materials, mainly flint and dolomitic limestone. Most of the artifacts are unretouched flakes, some quite large. Bladelets are rare, and the retouched tools have a very simple typology. Only one geometric was found. There are no cores, perhaps because the lithic debitage area within the habitat was not identified.

The most common species are limpets, gooseneck barnacles, mussels, and land snails (Tables 6.6 and 6.7). In far fewer numbers were southern oyster drills, common topshells, and a scattering of other species, including a middle-sized crab, perhaps the velvet crab (*Necora puber*) or the European green crab (*Carcinus maenas*).

Fauna preservation and breakage are similar to the Early Mesolithic pattern, showing only a slight increase of fragmentation in common topshells and southern oyster drill. The percentage of altered material, however, is higher than in the previous period, especially in the fireplaces (Table 6.4).

Early Neolithic

Around 7400 cal BP (5400 cal BC), the Rocha das Gaivotas dune was occupied by Neolithic groups. This settlement was far less permanent than the previous ones, with no structures. The shell midden deposits, positioned on top of Layer 2c, are very thin and less coherent.

The biggest novelty of this occupation is its cultural material, with pottery being the most significant new artifact (Carvalho 2008). The pottery is composed of sherds of small-sized pots, most with no decoration (n=73). There is only one fragment with narrow incised grooves, and another with a horizontal incision beneath circular impressions. The lithics are heterogeneous with a predominance of flint (n=95). Debitage is very simple, mostly composed of flakes and a very small number of retouched tools. One hammerstone and one graywacke flat stone were found, with eroded patterns identified as *almofariz* (mortar). There were also two ornament pieces: a perforated shell of dog cockle (*Glycymeris insubrica*) and an oval pendant made of limestone, which has a shape resembling the red deer canine pendants typical of the Neolithic period.

The faunal remains are composed almost entirely of shells and three fragments of mammal bone. Analysis of the full collection identified 8,189 specimens, which corresponds to a MNI of 2,761. Twelve marine species are present, with a predominance of limpets and gooseneck barnacles, followed by mussels (Figure 6.3B; Tables 6.6 and 6.7). In far fewer numbers are common cockle, southern oyster drill, and other nonedible species. The land snails were considered an intrusive species.

Between the lower and top levels of the Neolithic occupation, the gooseneck barnacles gradually increase in number while the limpets decrease. The difference in abundances may indicate more than one Neolithic occupation de facto, or taphonomic movements of material with the lighter/smaller specimens (gooseneck barnacles) "fluctuating" into the surface sands. Some measurements indicate a diminishing mean size in both species from bottom to top levels, thus suggesting a more intensive exploration of both limpets and gooseneck barnacles. However, it has been shown (Claassen 1998, 47–48) that the average size of mollusks and crustaceans can vary between populations.

SITE FUNCTIONALITY

The main features of Barranco das Quebradas and Rocha das Gaivotas are summarized in Table 6.8.

Barranco das Quebradas sites are characterized by spatially limited human occupations (< 250 meters) dating from the Early Mesolithic, with dense shell deposits. Their analyses reveal an obvious specialization in processing marine invertebrates (by breaking the shells of some species, direct exposure to fire or coal, and eventually boiling), with rare vertebrate remains and expedient lithic technology. The harvested species do not suffer significant changes along the time frame of the occupations, but there is a noticeable preference for common topshell during the most ancient occupations (BQ1, BQ4, and BQ3 base), while the youngest show a majority of mussel and limpet remains (BQ5 and BQ3 top) (Figure 6.3A). There is no data supporting the overexploitation of taxa, and these proportions should correspond with cultural choices or with variations in local rocky seashore habitats and animal resource availability. The latter hypothesis is more consistent with an optimal foraging model; common topshells are much easier to gather than other mollusks, such as mussels or limpets, which are strongly attached to hard surfaces and need more effort to be collected. The change in its abundance can, therefore, be indicative of diminishing availability.

The size and specialization of these sites suggest short, timed Mesolithic occupations, probably seasonal. The collected shellfish (mollusks and crustaceans) and other

Table 6.8. Barranco das Quebradas and Rocha das Gaivotas: Summary of features

Site	Estimated area (m²)	Excavated area (m²)[a]	Deposit thickness (cm)	Climatic Period	Human Occupations (n=)	Fauna	Other materials / structures
Barranco das Quebradas 1	< 150	tests + 2	100	Preboreal Boreal	Early Mesolithic (2)	Mollusks: abundant. Mammals: one fragment of ungulate tooth.	Lithics: scarce, expedient; mostly macrolithic.
Barranco das Quebradas 3	< 150	tests + 4	80	Boreal	Early Mesolithic (2) (Early Neolithic?)	Mollusks: abundant. Mammals: one fragment of ungulate tooth.	Lithics: scarce, expedient; mostly macrolithic. Ceramics: two fragments (top occupation).
Barranco das Quebradas 4	200-250	tests + 5	50	Boreal	Early Mesolithic (1)	Mollusks: abundant. Mammals (?): two fragments of bone. Birds: one fragment of humerus (Passeriformes).	Lithics: scarce, expedient; mostly macrolithic.
Barranco das Quebradas 5	?	8	30	Boreal	Early Mesolithic (1)	Mollusks: abundant.	Lithics: scarce, expedient; mostly macrolithic; includes anvils and hammerstones.
Rocha das Gaivotas	> 300	tests + 72	< 80	Boreal Atlantic	Early Mesolithic (4) Later Mesolithic (2) Early Neolithic (1)	Mollusks: abundant.	Lithics: microlithic with some retouched tools (Later Mesolithic and Early Neolithic); includes hammerstone and mortar; Structures: fireplaces in the Mesolithic deposits, more structured in the Late Mesolithic.

[a] Fauna analyses did not include material for any of the tests.

possible marine resources (seaweed) would not supply the needed resources (calories, proteins, vitamins) for long-term residential settlements. In addition, the local environment, with its dry-soil vegetation and direct exposure to salinity and strong Atlantic winds, is not concomitant with a wide variety of terrestrial edible resources such as big game or fruit trees. The purpose of Mesolithic occupations must, therefore, be primarily related to shellfish collection.

Some later archaeological materials were also detected, possibly dating from the Neolithic (pottery sherds), but their vestiges do not include shell remains. These scarce materials do not indicate true reoccupations of the sites, but more likely the passage of human groups on their way to other sites, where a more permanent settlement would be pursued (e.g., Rocha das Gaivotas, Vale Santo, and Cabranosa, other nearby Early Neolithic sites; Figure 6.1).

Contrary to Barranco das Quebradas, Rocha das Gaivotas has a succession of occupational horizons ranging from the Early Mesolithic to Early Neolithic. The oldest comprises several contexts spread along a sand dune, where the

shell deposits are thin and there is a very limited amount of lithic industry. The human groups that carried out these occupations were probably small and remained on the dune for short periods, with the main purpose of collecting marine resources.

During the Late Mesolithic there is a change of pattern in the human occupations of Rocha das Gaivotas. They become more localized, with richer deposits and well-structured fireplaces. The human groups seem to be larger, or else they are extending their stay in the area over longer periods of time, collecting larger amounts of shellfish as well as flint.

The most recent occupations, dated from the Early Neolithic, are also localized in the dune but are of shorter duration than the Late Mesolithic ones. They left a limited number of remains (fauna, lithics, or ceramics) and no preserved fireplaces. These groups also focused on marine resources and flint collection as main activities.

As at Barranco das Quebradas, while the collected species remain largely the same, there is an obvious change in their relative abundance within the occupations: high numbers of land snails (human consumption is uncertain) and mussels during the oldest period, shifting to limpets and gooseneck barnacles in the Later Mesolithic and Early Neolithic.

REGIONAL INTEGRATION

Not far from Barranco das Quebradas and Rocha das Gaivotas are two additional Mesolithic shell middens: Armação Nova and Castelejo. Armação Nova is located near Rocha das Gaivotas and was excavated in the early 1990s by Joaquina Soares and Carlos Tavares Silva (2003, 2004; Figure 6.1).[5]

It contains two Mesolithic occupations, dating from about 8750 to 7900 cal BP (6800 to 5900 cal BC). Analysis indicates a mixed specialization, both in seafood gathering (mostly gooseneck barnacles, followed by mussels and limpets; no quantification available) and local flint exploration (a considerable amount of debitage materials was found). The site also yielded preserved fireplaces and/or ash deposits from fireplace cleaning.

Castelejo is situated farther north, on a beach with the same name, and was also excavated by Soares and Silva in the 1980s. Some general papers have presented its main traits (Silva and Soares 1997; Soares and Silva 2004), and it seems to be a wide settlement, estimated around 3,000 square meters, dating from the Boreal to the Atlantic period. The inferior layers were deposited from about 9500 cal BP (7600 cal BC) and are thus an Early Mesolithic occupation; the middle layers are dated around 8200 cal BP (6250 cal BC), corresponding to the Late Mesolithic; and the most recent ones, located on the top of the stratigraphy, are from the Early Neolithic, around 7400 cal BP (5400 cal BC). The Neolithic layers included ceramic materials with impressed decoration, while both of the Mesolithic assemblages yielded scarce lithics, of macrolithic character and mostly made of graywacke.

There is no quantitative zooarchaeological data for Castelejo, but information on the relative abundance of species indicates that during the Early Mesolithic the assemblage is dominated by limpets, common topshells, and mussels; these layers also included rare fragments of rabbit bones and probable fish remains. Late Mesolithic layers provided only shell remains, mostly limpets and mussels.

Summarizing all of the available data for the Mesolithic in the western Algarve leaves us with an incomplete archaeological picture. All known sites—Barranco das Quebradas, Rocha das Gaivotas, Armação Nova, and Castelejo—seem to be specialized locations for activities revolving around shellfish processing. Their residents were mainly dedicated to logistic activities: the gathering of local mollusks, with flint collecting (Armação Nova and Rocha das Gaivotas), fishing, and rabbit hunting (Castelejo's oldest occupations) taking a lesser role. We are still missing data regarding economically less specialized occupations during this period (residential camps), or locations where other activities and resources were the focus (e.g., big-game hunting).

However, if we enlarge our focus to all of southwestern Portugal and thus include western Alentejo, we can find additional data that allows us a more complete framework. This is especially valid for the Late Mesolithic (early Atlantic period, 8800–7400 cal BP or 6900–5400 cal BC), since the Early Mesolithic (Preboreal and Boreal, 11,500–8800 cal BP or 9600–6900 cal BC) sites are scarce and, in terms of functionality, seem to mirror those identified in Algarve.

In western Alentejo, for the Early Mesolithic there are three known sites: Pedra do Patacho and Oliveirinha, both shell middens, and Palheirões do Alegra. Located in sand dunes near the Mira River estuary, Pedra do Patacho is the oldest midden of the area, dating from at least 11,000 cal BP (9300 cal BC; Soares and Silva 1993). The taxonomic composition of the fauna reflects a mixture of rocky and muddy habitats, both of which are located nearby, with the majority consisting of common periwinkle (*Littorina littorea*), limpets, mussels, and peppery furrow shell (*Scrobicularia plana*). The number of lithic artifacts is very low, mostly comprising macrolithic facies (big flakes and choppers).

Farther north, Oliveirinha is situated on a low littoral slope between two beaches. Though it has not been fully studied, existing information shows that its fairly eroded Early Mesolithic deposits are composed of macrolithic industry and shell remains (mostly common cockle, *Cerastoderma edule*; Soares and Silva 2004).

There is one other Early Mesolithic occupation in Palheirões do Alegra (Raposo 1994). Located on sand dunes near the sea, this is a different kind of settlement since no faunal remains have been found. However, there are several fireplaces and thousands of stone artifacts. The lithic industry is mainly macrolithic, but there is also a small collection of microlithic facies done in local flint (Vierra 1995, 117–32). New research by A. C. Araújo and F. Almeida is focusing on the post-depositional processes of the site and has cast some doubts on the contemporaneity of all of the contexts. New data is to be expected in the future.

It is possible that these Alentejo settlements reflect a high mobility, of logistic nature, of small human groups. Unfortunately, just as for the western Algarve, we are lacking a more detailed regional site setting.

This picture of specialized shell middens changes in the beginning of the Atlantic period with the development of extensive sites in river valleys and estuaries, such as the shell middens in the Sado (eleven sites) or the Odemira River (Fiais and Vidigal). To some extent, the features of these sites mirror those of the Muge shell middens. Their zooarchaeological materials show the use of a wider set of faunal resources, including both large and small mammals, mollusks, crustaceans, fishes, and birds. The lithic component is also large and diversified. These characteristics are not indicative of logistic sites, but rather of residential camps, either temporary or of a more permanent character. Some of the Sado shell middens even include human burials similar to those seen in Muge, though showing different inhumation techniques (e.g., Arnaud 1989; Umbelino 2006). At the same time, we have the continuing existence of more specialized coastal shell middens such as Montes de Baixo and Medo Tojeiro.

Also on the coast is Samouqueira, a site with occupations ranging from the Later Mesolithic to the Early Neolithic. This shell midden includes a wide set of terrestrial and marine fauna (including fish and turtle), as well as a human burial. Unfortunately, the published data about the site is problematic in terms of chronological and cultural attribution (Silva and Soares 1997 versus Lubell et al. 2007).

Therefore, the Late Mesolithic gives rise to the development of a more complex set of sites in terms of location, size, and function. This complexity implies a more organized occupation of the territory, featuring residential camps that could be used during longer periods of time, as well as logistic smaller camps near the coast, specialized in the collection and processing of local resources (mollusks and flint).

In summary, it is probable that the Late Mesolithic human groups from southwestern Portugal had high mobility indexes, moving between logistic camps at the coast and residential camps in the interior. The latter have yet to be identified in the western Algarve, but were probably located either along the coast in northerly areas (as in western Alentejo, where settlements with broad-spectrum subsistence have been located), or in the wider estuaries of the rivers of the Algarve (Arade, Guadiana), presently buried under alluvial sediments.

What about the Early Neolithic? In the western Algarve, there are three known shell middens, Rocha das Gaivotas,

Castelejo, and Ribeira de Alcantarilha. The first two date from around 7400 cal BP (5400 cal BC) and are reoccupations of previously established Mesolithic middens, in which the Neolithic layers are much thinner than the older ones. Ribeira de Alcantarilha dates from approximately 6900 cal BP (5000 cal BC; Stiner 2003; Stiner et al. 2003), and its preliminary data shows a large dominance of clam, a species adapted to the local sandy coast and freshwater-saltwater transition in the estuary of Alcantarilha River. Other known sites have either limited or no shells (Cabranosa, Vale Boi, Castelo Belinho, and Ibn-Amar Cave), or do not form shell middens sensu stricto, though they do include important shellfish deposits (Vale Santo, Padrão, and Alcalar 7; Carvalho 2008).

It is therefore obvious that the Neolithic period in the western Algarve marks a shift of economical focus; mollusk collecting and processing, while present, are no longer central to subsistence and as a consequence shell middens are no longer the most featured type of site. While this shift may reflect an eventual decrease of available shellfish resources, it displays a more important change of behavior related to the establishment of a new socioeconomic system, probably initiated during the colonization of the land by new (Neolithic) populations (as proposed by Carvalho 2008; also see Dean 2010 and Dean, Valente, and Carvalho 2012). This change includes a lower degree of mobility across the land and the adoption of agriculture and domesticated animals (sheep, goats, and cattle) as main suppliers of food.

It must be observed, however, that the situation is different in the neighboring region of the western Alentejo. Here the Mesolithic lifestyle, with intense exploitation of marine resources, seems to last longer and the Neolithic lifestyle to have taken more time to be fully adopted (for full discussion see Carvalho 2008; Soares and Silva 2004; Zilhão 2000).

MAIN CONCLUSIONS

Although the database for the Mesolithic and Early Neolithic archaeological sites of the western Algarve is still lacking (in number and variety of sites, and in published data), we already have an interesting amount of knowledge that allows us an interpretative model regarding diet and settlement patterns during these periods. We consider that the five shell middens discussed here are an important contribution to this framework: Barranco das Quebradas with four small individualized settlements, all dating from the Early Mesolithic (Preboreal and Boreal periods), and Rocha das Gaivotas with a more extensive settlement, which dates from the Early Mesolithic (Boreal period) to the Early Neolithic (early Atlantic period). In all, the dates for these contexts go from 10,400 cal BP to 7400 years BP (8500 to 5400 cal BC).

Together with information from other known sites in the region, the assembled data shows that during the Early and Late Mesolithic, collecting and processing shellfish was a major subsistence activity in the western Algarve. During this time several shell middens were formed, most of them highly specialized in the gathering and processing of mollusks (with a very low proportion of other animal resources or lithic industry). A smaller number demonstrate mixed functions that include flint collecting and debitage. These shell middens are normally limited in size, situated very close to the coast, and containing animal species reflecting the rocky habitats in the area. The predominant species are common topshells (in Early Mesolithic occupations), limpets, mussels, or gooseneck barnacles (the latter mainly in Early Neolithic deposits), all of which are still abundant in the region today. No residential featured sites have been found.

However, other areas in southwestern Portugal (the western Alentejo) show a less specialized scenario, particularly during the Late Mesolithic, when some wider shell middens were assembled (e.g., Sado, Fiais, Vidigal). These demonstrate the local availability of mollusks and their importance to the subsistence of the human groups, but also integrate other animal resources, as well as complex lithic technologies and, sometimes, burial structures. The function of these sites seems to be residential (temporary or semipermanent), rather than simple locations for gathering and processing of resources. In the western Algarve, these types of sites could be situated in the valleys of local rivers and would therefore now be buried under thick layers of sediments.

Through the Early Neolithic, the number of shell middens in the western Algarve is greatly reduced, and the existing ones seem to be less extensive reoccupations of preexisting sites. In general, archaeological sites from this period may have a considerable amount of shellfish materials, yet do not compose true shell middens, thus reflecting a change in subsistence behavior probably related to a new (Neolithic) socioeconomic system.

ACKNOWLEDGMENTS

We thank the reviewers of this chapter for their valuable input, namely Mary Jackes. We also thank António Monge Soares for helping us to determine the ΔR value for the radiocarbon date samples here presented, and Carol DeLancey for editing the final version of the text. The data presented here has been obtained thanks to two projects ("A Importância dos Recursos Aquáticos no Paleolítico Médio e Superior do Algarve" and "O Processo de Neolitização do Algarve") under Projecto SAPIENS Proj, financed by Plano Nacional de Trabalhos Arqueológicos of Instituto Português de Arqueologia and by Fundação para a Ciência e a Tecnologia. The photograph used in Figure 6.2 is reprinted by permission of Filipe Jorge and we are grateful for his permission to reproduce it here (Jorge 2005).

NOTES

1. The University of Algarve projects were: "A Ocupação Humana Paleolítica do Algarve" (PRAXIS/PCSH/C/HAR/70/96, dir. N. F. Bicho), "A Importância dos Recursos Aquáticos no Paleolítico Médio e Superior do Algarve" (POCTI/HAR/37543/2001, dir. N. F. Bicho), and "O Processo de Neolitização do Algarve" (POCTI/HAR/39434/2001, dir. A. F. Carvalho).

2. The radiometric dates in text are given after applying the oceanic reservoir effect correction according to Soares and Dias 2006; for all data regarding these dates, see Tables 6.1 and 6.5.

3. In published works prior to 2004 (e.g., Stiner 2003; Stiner et al. 2003), BQ1 was regarded as Barranco das Quebradas I (BQI) and BQ3 was Barranco das Quebradas II (BQII). BQ2 is very eroded and only a very reduced amount of surface faunal remains was collected.

4. For the MNI, the following criteria were used: for Pollicipedidae, number of carina, or scuta and terga (divided by two); for Balanidae, specimens with presence of more than half the operculum; for Gastropoda, specimens with apex; for Bivalvia, specimens with umbo (divided by two); for Cancridae, it was counted by the number of dactyls (with awareness of their parity).

5. Rocha das Gaivotas and Armação Nova could be considered different loci of the same site (Carvalho 2008).

CHAPTER SEVEN

WERE *SAMBAQUI* PEOPLE BURIED IN THE TRASH?

Archaeology, Physical Anthropology, and the Evolution of the Interpretation of Brazilian Shell Mounds

Maria Dulce Gaspar, Daniela Klokler, and Paulo DeBlasis

SUMMARY

Human remains have repeatedly been described in the studies of shell mounds (or *sambaquis*) of the Brazilian coast since the first publications in the 19th century. However, they were rarely considered a decisive feature in understanding this type of site. This chapter examines the role of funerary structures in the evolution of archaeological thinking with regard to sambaqui studies in Brazil, exploring the (frequently disparate) relationships between physical anthropology and archaeology. Adequate understanding of the nature of sambaqui funerary contexts requires a complementary approach from both disciplines, rather than one-sided emphasis on particular issues. By studying burials in their archaeological context, amid the fascinating stratigraphy that quite often characterizes sambaquis, it is possible to grasp social constructs such as ritual, gender, and customs, as well as lifestyle and health.

INTRODUCTION

Sambaquis are mounded coastal archaeological structures composed of large quantities of fauna, especially shellfish and fish remains, sometimes reaching monumental dimensions. These sites occur all along the Brazilian coast, although studies have focused mostly on its southeastern portion (Figure 7.1). Radiocarbon dates indicate that the expansion of these coastal mound builders started at least 8,000 years ago, while the most recent sites were active by 1,000 years ago, thus confirming a very well-established cultural tradition (Gaspar 1998; Lima et al. 2004). Sambaquis are usually located near large bodies of brackish water and surrounding landscape, forming into organized settlement systems that include mounds of different dimensions and morphology. Although shells are the most prominent component, assemblages typically include a variety of other faunal remains, lithic and bone tools, and hearths, postmolds, and—notably—a large number of burials (Prous 1991; Gaspar 2000; Lima and Lopez Mazz 2000).

Indeed, since the first archaeological reports, whether from an archaeological or a physical anthropological perspective, burials and/or human bones have been conspicuous in the descriptions of these coastal structures. Curiously enough, burials have rarely been considered as a defining aspect of sambaquis, or as playing a significant role in understanding mound building as a process, or as addressing the mound builders' social organization. Both archaeologists and physical anthropologists who studied sambaquis shared broad evolutionist assumptions and perspectives, characteristic of early Brazilian archaeology, which played an important role in the development of large-scale, macro-regional models of cultural history such as the ones created by PRONAPA (National Program of Archaeological Research) during the 1960s. The goal of this chapter is to show that this neglect has had important implications for interpretative models, perpetuating a skewed perspective of these coastal groups that has endured in Brazilian academia.

With the recent revival of systematic research on sambaquis, it is interesting to examine the perspectives adopted by these two disciplines and to rearticulate their unique and specific points of view, drawing upon current understanding of site formation processes (Klokler 2001, 2008, chap. 11 in this volume), as well as of forms of social organization, in

7.1. Map of Brazil with approximate distribution of sambaquis (organized by Christina Leal Rodrigues) and indication of areas mentioned in the text.

space and time, among these societies. In this chapter, we examine a few notable authors of sambaqui archaeology and physical anthropology, and conclude that the integrative and multidisciplinary approach, as represented by recently conducted research in Brazil, is more appropriate for future research on these coastal populations.

BONES FOR THOUGHT

According to Giralda Seyferth (1985, 81–82), the first anthropological studies in Brazil date from the 1860s and are marked by the influence of French and German authors, especially diffused through publications of the Société d'Anthropologie, along with works by Broca, Topinard, Quatrefages, and Virchow. Today, their line of research would be called Physical or Biological Anthropology, and its main area of interest was craniology, strongly influenced by deterministic racial theories. The premises of social Darwinism and its French counterpart,

anthroposociology, were well known and accepted in Brazil, together with Gobineau's Aryan theses, published in 1853, which gained notoriety at the end of the 19th century.

Defined as a branch of natural history that focused on "man" and "human races," anthropology was constructed as a racial typology that sought to discover the permanent characteristics that distinguished biological "types," an approach adopted by many Brazilian scientists (Seyferth 1995, 179). A paraphernalia of measuring tools and indices, with special attention to craniometry, permeate this period. A short manual written by the director of the National Museum (Museu Nacional), Ladislao Netto, emphasized the need to acquire skulls and other human bones to form the collections of the museum. In the instructions about the preparation and shipment of collections, the beginning of the anthropology section refers to "skeletons or isolated bones, only aboriginal, and especially skulls" (Netto 1890, 10). This priority underscores the almost exclusive importance of skulls for that era's approach to anthropology, making clear the lack of attention given to the rest of skeleton, not to mention its archaeological and/or social context. A special room was prepared for the skulls in the Museu Nacional, the Lund Room, as seen in the *Guia da Exposição Antropológica Brasileira* (*Guide for the Brazilian Anthropological Exhibit*), published in 1882.

Until the first half of the 20th century, the goal of most of the archaeological excavations was to produce skeletons used to establish the human types considered representative of the past. It is in this context that the concepts of the "Lagoa Santa man" and the "Sambaqui man" appeared, so often compared to each other and to Botocudo skulls (Lacerda and Peixoto 1876). Human bones, particularly skulls from sambaquis, were analyzed apart from their original archaeological context. The sambaquis were considered merely as *jazidas* (or mines, a term used widely at the time) from which the bones—the sole focus of anthropological interest—were extracted. In a sense, it was mankind (and not a specific culture) that was considered from the perspective of cultural evolutionism, and this has been a long-lived paradigm in Brazil, still evident in the 1960s (Alvim and Mello Filho 1965, 1967/1968, among others).

Walter Neves (1984a, 1984b), reviewing these positions, proposed that physical anthropology should focus on the study of the biological aspects of society within the context of archaeological studies, unifying the fields' emphasis on the study of human behavior (Neves 1984a, 287). Examples of this new approach would include studies of lifeways, their transformations, and the organization of labor

(Machado 1983; Neves 1984b; Neves, Unger, and Scaramuzza 1984). Later, physical anthropology research focused on detailed studies about diet, stress, diseases, and habits, broadening the knowledge of scientists regarding the ways of life of coastal populations, while at the same time partnering with archaeologists in multidisciplinary projects (Boyadjian, Eggers, and Reinhard 2007; Carvalho 2004; Lessa and Coelho 2010; Souza 1995, 1999, chap. 12 in this volume; Okumura, Boyadjian, and Eggers 2007; Storto, Eggers, and Lahr 1999; Wesolowski 2000, 2007).

Changing theoretical perspectives on skeletal studies beginning in the 1980s did not immediately lead to the investigation of behavioral patterns regarding funerary activities or, more generally, the formation processes involved in sambaqui mound building. As a matter of fact, the relationships between the funerary activities performed on (and into) the mounds and the incremental layering nature of the building processes recorded therein remained elusive for decades.

SAMBAQUIS AND THE INFLUENCE OF EVOLUTIONISM

The presence of human remains called the attention of researchers since the first descriptions of sambaquis, but the role played by this evidence in understanding these sites varied deeply. The end of the 19th century was dominated by debates between researchers defending their natural origin (Ihering 1903; Calixto 1904) and authors who believed they were the result of human action (Lacerda and Peixoto 1876; Wiener 1876). Thus, the presence of human bones was sometimes seen as preserved remains disposed amid natural shell beds and sometimes as clear evidence of the anthropogenic nature of the whole shell structures.

As the idea of the natural formation of sambaquis was gradually dismissed, the debates turned to two dichotomical interpretations of the depositional sequences depicted by the rhythmically banded stratigraphy of the mounds. Some have considered them as food refuse middens, generated by successive camping or settlement episodes. Others have perceived them as intentionally built funerary monuments. These ideas appeared quite simultaneously. Carlos Wiener (1876) was among the first to suggest that some of these mounds would have funerary purposes, while those who considered sambaquis as the result of fortuitous accumulation of food refuse, like Guilherme Capanema (1876), José B. Lacerda and R. Peixoto (1876), Alberto Loefgren (1908), Luis Gualberto (1924), and Antonio T. Guerra (1950), remained more common (for a detailed review, see Gaspar 2000; Lima 1999/2000; and Barbosa-Guimarães 2003).

Typical of the studies developed in the first half of the 20th century is the frequently cited synthesis by Antonio Serrano (1946) that appeared in the well-known *Handbook of South American Indians*. The author writes about the shape, structure, and artifacts that characterize the "cultures and races" that occupied the Brazilian coast, also focusing on the distribution of sites and features, and their relationships with inland cultures. Serrano suggests regional and chronological divisions, linking the coastal "archaic culture" to the "Lagoa Santa man" cultural traits. In formulating the first classification of cultural and chronological variability of coastal sites, it is symptomatic that Serrano does not take into account the presence of human remains. This is the main point of our interest: though generally recognized, the ubiquitous presence of human remains, usually disposed in clearly layer-structured funerary features—quite frequently displaying considerably large areas with dozens of individuals—has never been taken as a reference for understanding the depositional structuring of the mounds and, for that matter, their functional and cultural nature.

After 1950, studies focused on the elaboration of site typologies and their organization in archaeological traditions, assumed to represent distinct cultural entities (Dias 1980). Even though Paulo Duarte (1967) reintroduced the idea of funerary mounding circa 90 years after it was first proposed, suggesting that they were similar to funerary structures frequently mentioned in archaeological literature from Mediterranean and southern Asian areas, burials were but a peripheral concern in archaeological interpretation. They were simply another trace, not an essential feature to be taken into account, and attention was mostly drawn to the abundant, outstanding faunal materials present at the sambaquis, usually taken as food remains (thus indicative of everyday activity), and studied mostly for dietary and economic purposes.

GATHERER-FISHERS OR GATHERERS, THEN FISHERS?

Elman R. Service's (1971) famous model of social evolution soon became a reference for Brazilian archaeologists, remaining influential to this day. The lack of easily recognizable features and the rather opaque lithic tools scattered into the layers led to the description of the sambaqui society, rather aprioristically, as bands, implying collecting-based subsistence, nomadic (in fact, highly mobile) lifestyles, and simple social organization. For example, Dorath P. Uchôa (2007 [1973], 190), referring to the sambaquis, affirms that "the absence of economic, political and religious organization, institutions inherent to other populations, gives to groups of the band level its character of simplicity."[1]

Anamaria Beck (1972a and b) studied the sambaquis of the coast of Santa Catarina, in southern Brazil, with the goal of establishing their "cultural content," following the premises of Service. She organized data obtained from archaeological excavations into the "phase and tradition scheme" broadly adopted by studies made from the 1960s through the 1980s in Brazil (Barreto 2000), proposing not only a chronological sequence but also cultural differences among mound builders, arguing that ceramic-producing groups were the last to colonize the coast, representing the final occupation of the sambaquis. Beck used environmental characteristics, especially the availability of shell resources, to explain the large dimension of the mounds in certain productive (particularly regarding shellfish) *lagunar* spots of the Santa Catarina coast, suggesting that continuous utilization of these abundant resources has led to their depletion. The scarcity of mollusks would have led to the increase of fishing and hunting activities toward the final period of the sambaqui occupational sequence, with corresponding shifts in technology. The introduction of ceramics (supposedly associated with horticulture) is seen as a radical change in the lifeway of these coastal groups (Beck 1972a, 265, 282).This cultural sequence and these interpretations have been reflected elsewhere on the Brazilian coast (see Rauth 1976; Dias 1980; Kneip 1980; Kneip et al. 1991).

There are two fundamental assumptions in this line of interpretation, both of them equivocal. The first is that faunal remains are direct indicators of subsistence activities and/or diet. By assuming that the sambaquis represent daily activity or habitation areas, faunal remains seem to provide a cultural sequence for analyzing economic and dietary shifts. Zooarchaeological studies (Figuti and Klokler 1996; Klokler 2001, 2008; Klokler et al. 2010; Nishida 2007) and more detailed stratigraphic and chronological contextualization (Fish et al. 2000) have demonstrated, however, that piling-up sequences were fast and frequently secondary (Villagrán 2008), and no apparent habitations were present.

The second is the supposed transition from a mollusk-gathering-based subsistence (associated with high mobility and very simple social organization), toward the adoption of a more productive fishing technology, the "gatherers-to-fishers" model (Lima 1991). This evident linear evolutionary perspective did not significantly impact the interpretation of the mound builders' social organization, variously identified as bands or macro-bands (i.e., Machado 2006). The premise that the sambaqui people were small nomadic bands in constant search for mollusks to fulfill their subsistence needs provided basic parameters for calculating population size and interpreting mound formation processes.

One particularly interesting corollary of these assumptions is that sambaqui people simply buried their dead in trash deposits. This unstated assumption precluded the possibility of seeing other ways to interpret the archaeological record, alternative perspectives on interpreting the complex interplay of tiny layering and discrete features typical of the sambaqui stratigraphy. Accustomed to viewing habitation sites as shallow horizontal deposits, this generation of archaeologists was not prepared to observe the complex sequence of layers within sambaqui sites as evidence of building, a mounding-up building process. In such a context, burials are no more exquisite features in the trash, but rather emerge as the very key for understanding mound-building processes and sambaqui construction.

In stark contradiction to understanding these sites as refuse heaps stands Beck's (1972a, 283–84) observation that funerary practices varied considerably among sites in coastal Santa Catarina. While she recognizes the presence of elaborate burials and graves lined with clay, large quantities of adornments and tools, and abundant red ochre, suggesting differential treatment of the dead as a reflection of differential social status, she does not consider the possibility that deposition of the dead could explain the very construction of these mounds.

Nevertheless, Beck (1972a, 286) reintroduced the question of site function: were sambaquis dwelling settlements or simple trash deposits located at some distance from habitation sites? The presence of elaborate burials seemed contrary to the notion that sambaquis were simple garbage heaps (Gaspar 1994/1995).

Current archaeological and ethnographic research on hunter-gatherer societies admits the existence of great variability between groups that defy generalizations regarding their size, degree of mobility, technology, and social organization. T. Douglas Price and James A. Brown (1985) advance the notion that these populations incorporated a wide range of behaviors, overlapping in many aspects with those usually attributed to agricultural societies.

SETTLEMENT SYSTEMS AND SITE FUNCTION:
HABITATION OR CEMETERIES?

The first regional studies of sambaquis were undertaken after 1980, focusing on settlement systems and the site diversity. Cristiana Barreto (1988) described freshwater, riverine sambaquis on the South Atlantic hinterlands, small mounds composed mostly of land snail shells (*Megalobulimus* sp.), terrestrial fauna, lithic assemblages, and human burials. Some sites yielded several early dates, approaching 11,000 BP (Collet 1976; Collet and Prous 1977; Figuti et al. 2004). Settlement patterns and a few maritime specimens led Barreto (1988) to suggest that the occupation of the hinterland valleys originated on the coast, implying Late Pleistocene origins, probably deriving from early submerged coastal sambaqui occupations (Calippo 2010). This hypothesis has also been considered by several bioarchaeological studies (Filippini and Eggers 2005; Neves 1984a; Neves and Okumura 2005; Neves et al. 2005; Figuti and Plens, chap. 16 in this volume), providing an important example of the benefits of a multidisciplinary approach.

Maria Dulce Gaspar's (1991) work in the Lagos region of Rio de Janeiro used resource catchment analysis to explore aspects of territoriality among sambaqui builders and demonstrates the need to examine groups of sites as the basic analytical units for inferring sociological significance (Gaspar 1998). Gaspar (1991, 1994/1995) also focused on an area centered on the very similar sambaquis Ilha da Boa Vista I, II, and III, evincing their contemporaneity and functional equivalence. These mounds exhibit habitation features over a built platform floor, and yet, a number of burials below it, resembling a graveyard. In another study, from available publications and reports, Gaspar (1994/1995) gathered a large amount of data regarding recurrent patterns in sites of the Brazilian coast. This survey enabled the identification of some basic common traits pointing to characteristic social patterns (rules) of the coastal fisher-gatherers. First, recurrent occupations occur along the margins of large bodies of water, usually productive mixohaline environments consisting of lagoons, bays, and islands, with diverse and abundant resources. Second, the typical large shell structures were usually built in a manner that resulted in great visibility across the landscape. Third, the presence of human burials is ubiquitous in these structures.

Extensive site surveys and chronological refinement at the Santa Marta lagoonal region in Santa Catarina demonstrate that the sites clustered in areas where one or more larger sites form the epicenter for groups of smaller sites, sometimes in areas of extensive production and use of stone tools (Assunção 2010; DeBlasis et al. 2007; Peixoto 2008). The presence of site clusters occupied simultaneously suggests higher demographic standards and more complex social organization. Parallel research centered on human remains also questioned the notion that sambaqui groups were small-sized (Souza [chap. 12] and Okumura, and Eggers [chap. 8] in this volume).

Thus the functional aspects of sambaquis are still under debate, and whether or not they include habitation areas has not yet reached a conclusive level. While some sites have been clearly identified as cemeteries, such as Jabuticabeira II (Fish et al. 2000) and Amourins (Gaspar and Klokler 2011), others might depict a more diversified functional nature (Gaspar 1994/1995). Also, the small shell sites—usually lacking burial features—were surely used for other purposes, perhaps as processing camps or other uses (Belém 2012; Klokler et al. 2010; Peixoto 2008).

Lina M. Kneip (1974), Kneip and Lilia M. C. Machado (1993), Eliana T. Carvalho (1984), and others contributed with detailed descriptions of burials and associated materials by means of meticulous, horizontal excavations influenced by the French-styled "paleoethnographic" approach (Duday 2006; Leroi-Gourhan 1981; Pallestrini and Morais 1980). Added to the deep-rooted idea that sambaquis represent dwelling areas, burials and their goods were usually seen as part of an occupational floor (Kneip and Machado 1993). Illustrations that accompany some publications (Figures 7.2A and B) make it clear how the horizontal approach privileges the idea of "single-plane" occupational floors rather than three-dimensional features that characterize the funerary structures in sambaquis. The focus on dwelling (horizontal) structures has been transferred to the burial features, thus missing the "architectural," vertical constructive features of sambaquis that, ultimately, allow the perception of essential characteristics of the funerary rituals therein recorded, and make it possible to link these funerary practices to other aspects of the lives of sambaqui mound builders.

While, at several sites, mound building related to burial ceremonies has become evident, the idea that sambaquis are habitation sites should not be discarded too easily. Kneip and Machado (1993), Carvalho (1984), Gaspar (1998), and Barbosa (1999) consider sets of postholes as indicators of huts and habitation areas. Postholes were also used as evidence of living areas in the southern coast (Hurt and Blasi 1960; Rauth 1968). Dark compacted layers were also considered indicative of living floors, and the co-occurrence of postholes and occupation floors reinforced the hypothesis that some sambaquis, or at least some areas within them, served as habitations.

MATERIAL REMAINS

Research focused on lithic, bone, and shell tool assemblages almost always treated these remains separately, as isolated phenomena (e.g., Rohr 1977), without interest in their possible relations with social organization of the

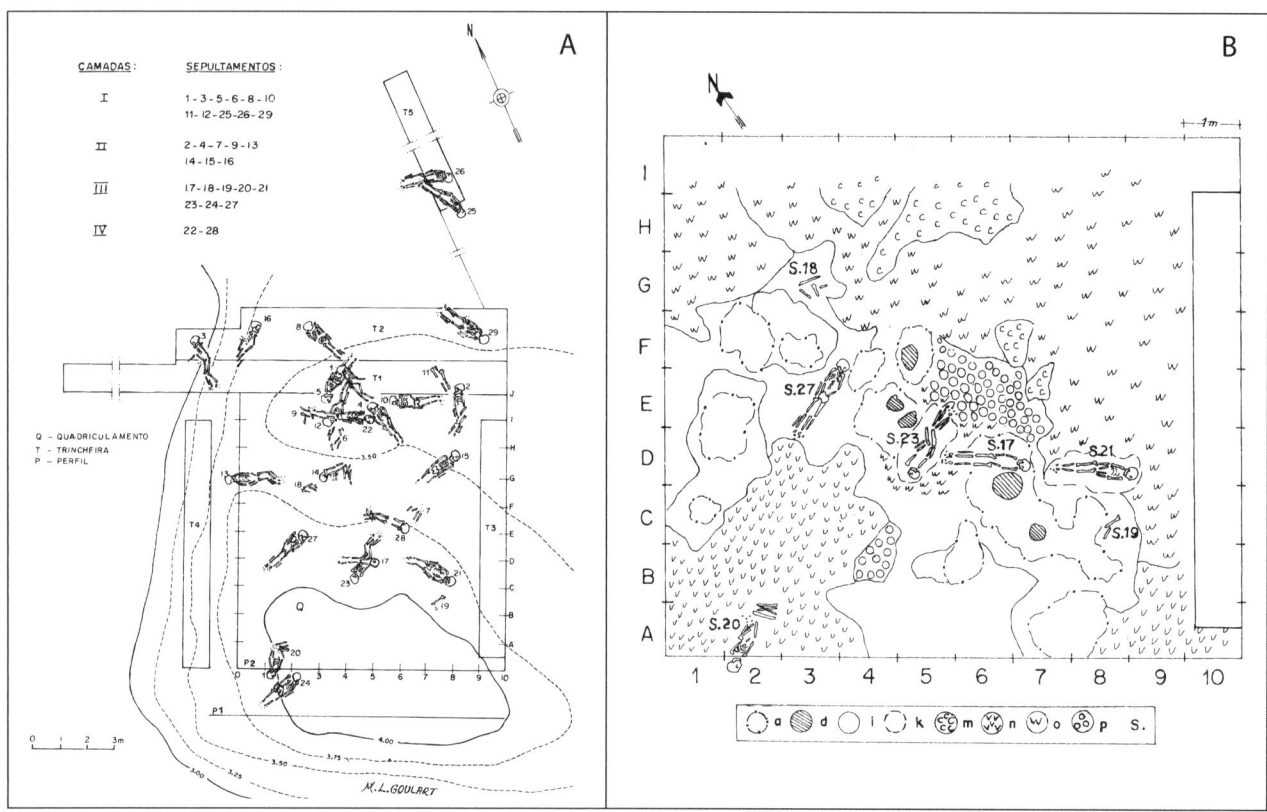

7.2. Representations of skeletons recovered in several sambaquis. (A) Kneip and Machado (1993, 43). (B) Kneip and colleagues (1991, 41). Notice how the drawings privilege a horizontal perspective of the remains.

groups that produced, used, and disposed of the artifacts. Faunal remains recovered from different layers were analyzed for their connection with technology and diet, without any concern about the depositional history and the events that formed the sites. In most publications, lists of identified species were added as appendices, without discussion of their depositional context and contextual significance. Former analyses of faunal remains by Maria Margarida Gomes Correia and colleagues (1984), Caio Garcia (1970, 1972), and Kneip and colleagues (1975) discussed aspects of the diet and changes in subsistence, following the paradigms of that period. Garcia (1970) suggested that the sambaqui builders were sedentary, but his subsequent research did not elaborate on this observation. Until the late 1980s, zooarchaeological research was characterized by a certain naiveté, not only in terms of simply equating faunal remains to food refuse, but also in relation to field methods that primarily relied upon selective sampling. Levy Figuti's (1989, 1992, 1995) work introduced systematic sampling procedures and detailed analysis of the matrix. He has demonstrated that fishing has always been the principal, reliable food procurement activity for coastal groups, instead of shellfish gathering, which was confirmed in further studies (Figuti and Klokler 1996; Klokler 2001; De Masi 1999), thus breaking down the deep-rooted notion that the sambaqui archaeological record would display an evolution from shellfish gathering toward a full fishing economy and subsistence.

Changes in the perception of the mound structuring were also on the way. More attentive stratigraphic studies led by Gaspar (1991) and Afonso and DeBlasis (1994) proposed not only that these sites were intentionally built, but that their construction was organized by a set of rules. Gaspar (1994/1995) argues that sambaquis are both sacred and mundane locations, where daily and ritual activities are performed, calling attention to the possibility of identifying and studying traces of ritual behavior. Archaeologists started to change their focus to the behavior behind the construction of sambaquis. Sites that were previously considered trash mounds are now recognized as resulting from specific and coordinated building episodes (Afonso and DeBlasis 1994; Figuti and Klokler 1996; Klokler 2001).

Daniela Klokler (2001) focused on formation processes from a zooarchaeological perspective to comprehend gathering, processing, use, and deposition of faunal remains that compose the complex sambaqui stratigraphy. At the sambaqui Espinheiros II, Figuti and Klokler (1996) describe two distinct phases in the site construction. In its initial stage, building was accomplished through fast depositional episodes of massive quantities of clams, abundantly available in the nearby bay. The scarcity of tools and lack of features attest that the site was initially built as a platform. In its second building stage, the site has clear evidence of funerary practices and other activities.

Studies of human burials focusing on mortuary rituals or attitudes toward the dead are rare, not only in Brazilian archaeology (Roksandic 2002; Roksandic and Jackes, chap. 9 of this volume); attention is usually focused upon the analysis of skeletal remains. Since archaeologists primarily characterized sambaquis as trash mounds with burials interspersed within the refuse, little attention was paid to the structural context of funerary depositional sequences. Mortuary activities were recognized only in the immediate vicinity of human remains. Contextual aspects such as the covering of graves and assorted paraphernalia (tomb structures, fences, celebratory fires, etc.) were not recorded.

Grave shape and grave goods were privileged elements used to characterize burials. Grave inclusions such as lithics, bone tools, and adornments were quantified, but usually no special attention was paid to unmodified animal bones or shell remains encountered within these deposits, unless the bones came from unusual, highly visible, or rare species such as whales, dolphins, and turtles. The significance of faunal remains in funerary rituals was rarely mentioned, despite their (sometimes spectacular) association with burials. Indeed, since many elements associated with funerary rituals, such as mollusk valves and animal bones, were similar to the abundant materials scattered all around the mound, it is not easy to perceive all of the paraphernalia associated with funerary rituals (Klokler 2008). Archaeologists did not investigate the associations of faunal remains with funerary contexts, even though commensalism related with death is a recurring custom among many peoples of South America (Vilaça 1996)[2] and elsewhere.

THE FIRST UNEQUIVOCAL SAMBAQUI CEMETERY: JABUTICABEIRA II

The Santa Marta lagoonal area in southern Santa Catarina contains more than 80 shell mound sites, one of which, Jabuticabeira II, has been subjected to in-depth

analysis. It is an average-sized sambaqui (400 meters long by 250 meters wide, with a maximum height of 8 meters). Shell mining left large vertical walls, allowing the examination of its stratigraphy all through the mound, in central and peripheral areas as well. Approximately 373 meters of profiles uncovered a complex series of deposits in a recurrent pattern of thick, shell-dominated layers and thin, dark, organic-rich lenses. Large quantities of postholes originate from these dark lenses, initially understood as habitation floors, interspersed within thick deposits composed mainly of shells. However, the absence of a pattern in the distribution of the posts coherent with what would be expected in a hut floor, as well as the scarcity of tools and the large number of burials in these lenses, showed that this first assumption was mistaken. Excavation of one of these dark lenses confirmed that they were funerary areas, with no indication of activities related to daily life. Three hundred and eighty-four postholes clearly surrounding graves or groups of graves were identified during the excavation of a single layer. Systematic studies of the profiles across the mound demonstrated that such a pattern can be generalized to the sambaqui as a whole (Bendazzoli 2007; Fish et al. 2000; Gaspar and Klokler 2004; Klokler 2008; Nishida 2007).

Jabuticabeira II was constructed through episodic events of collective internments (Klokler 2001). Several intercalated lenses of shell, fishbone, sand, and charcoal frequently cover the deceased and its accompaniments, either individual interments or clusters of burials disposed over a larger burial ground. This depositional behavior, repeated through time by means of recurrent revisiting of the burial areas, has a mounding-up incremental effect that, ultimately, displays up to two meters of successive layering over a unique burial. The concomitant or subsequent presence of a number of burial structures like this at the same place explains the overall mound-building process resulting in a present-day sambaqui. Massive shell layers were used to close specific graves and whole funerary areas where remains of ritual feasts were deposited. Over these built platforms, new funerary areas were opened, in a continuous and incremental process that, ultimately, has provided many a mound with rather monumental dimensions. Sambaqui builders were in no way burying their people in the trash. Rather, they were *building upon* them with carefully selected materials, full of significance.

Isotopic analysis demonstrated that mollusks seem not to have been intensively consumed, suggesting that they were used mainly during mound-building episodes (Klokler 2008). Choice of clam shells (*Anomalocardia*

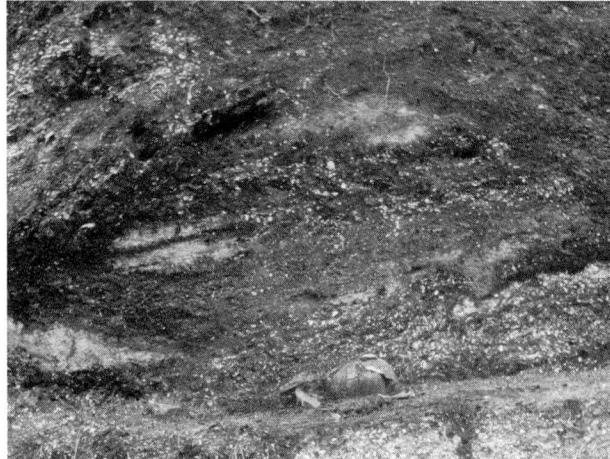

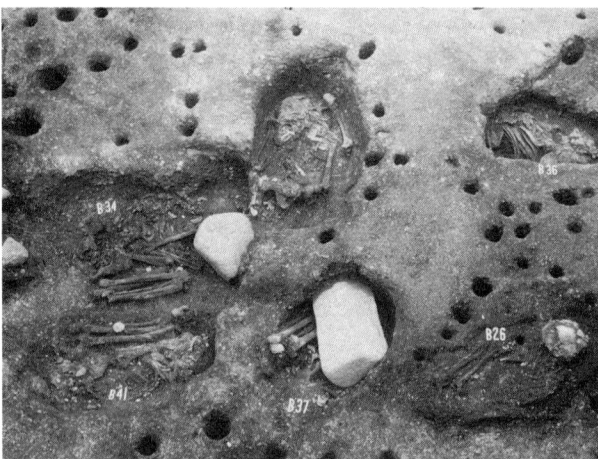

7.3. *View of a profile with burial mound, close-up of a funerary area, and 3D representation of burial in Jabuticabeira II (drawing by Henrique Vences).*

brasiliana) is believed to be related to their thickness, bulkiness, and color (Klokler 2008). The first two characteristics ensured the rapid elevation of a structure, while the last emphasized a distinction between interment and covering deposits (Figure 7.3). Gaspar (2004, 166) suggests that shell valves were also preferred for construction due to an interest in the preservation of the bones. Integrating information from the field excavations, ethnography, and physical anthropology allowed the reconstruction of a whole set of activities involved in the performance of the funerary rites, from the burying ceremonies to the recurrent (and incremental) instances of depositional episodes related to the memorialization of the dead that, ultimately, contributes to mound building (Klokler, Gaspar, and DeBlasis 2009; Klokler, chap. 11 in this volume). Okumura and Eggers (chap. 8 in this volume) offer a complementary interpretation of this same site based on a bioanthropological perspective.

Gaspar (1994/1995) has already claimed burials to be a defining feature of sambaquis, while attentive examination of the literature shows that dark lenses are common in sambaquis with human burials (Prous 1991; Schmitz and Bitencourt 1996; Wiener 1876). Association of dark layers with substantial numbers of human burials, animal bone caches or burials, large quantities of fish remains, and hearths show that similar activities to those at Jabuticabeira II can be postulated for other shell sites (Klokler 2008). The burial of several people in the same place seems to be associated with a strong affirmation of territorial rights and group affiliation (Parker Pearson 1999). The message would be continually reinforced and become more visually evident through repeated building activities that expanded the site horizontally and vertically (Fish et al. 2000; Klokler 2008, chap. 11 in this volume).

The multidisciplinary studies at Jabuticabeira II and other sites of the region have placed the ceremonial activities toward the dead as the principal rationale behind mound-building processes. These highly visible structures, built to honor the dead, represent territorial markers full of symbolic value and domesticate the lagoonal landscape where several communities of fisher-gatherers pursued their living (DeBlasis et al. 2007; Klokler 2008). Instead of elusive and casual features, the burials in the mounds became direct archaeological evidence of a sedentary society, with dense demography (Okumura and Eggers 2005; Storto, Eggers, and Lahr 1999), displaying many traces of economic intensification, including evidence for use of plant resources and for food consumption, among others (Bianchini, Scheel-Ybert, and Gaspar 2007; Scheel-Ybert et al. 2009; Scheel-Ybert, chap. 22 in this volume). All of these aspects are indicative of a society largely different from the nomadic bands of mollusk gatherers portrayed in earlier research. Changes in this early portrayal were severely hindered by—among other things—the lack of effective integration between archaeologists and physical anthropologists, thus delaying the attainment of a comprehensive picture of these coastal societies.

SAMBAQUI BUILDERS: A NEW PARADIGM

Recent studies performed in lowland riverine shell sites of the Ribeira river valley confirm statements made for coastal sambaquis that the building processes were directly related to funerary activities, as no evidence of habitation areas inside or near the mounds could be identified. At these small mounds, crosscut profiles show a recurrent stratigraphic succession of layers with plenty of food remains (mostly terrestrial game) containing dozens of ceremonially disposed burials. Like their coastal counterparts, these riverine mound shell clusters (composed mostly of terrestrial gastropods) over burials do not seem to represent an important dietary component (Constantino 2009; Plens 2007), but, rather, offerings embodied with symbolic meaning disposed over the burial ground. Also similar to coastal shell mounds, some of these small freshwater mounds appear to have been regularly (re)visited for many millennia, with an overall chronology spanning from the Pleistocene/Holocene transition to the arrival of ceramic groups into the area, around a thousand years ago (Figuti et al. 2004; Figuti and Plens, chap. 16 in this volume; Plens 2007).

Funerary ritual was an extremely important social form of expression for sambaqui mound builders, and participation in the festivities was vital for the enhancement of community cohesion and social solidarity in a situation where signals of incipient inequality seem to be evident (Klokler 2008, chap. 11 in this volume). The excavation of some funerary areas and careful analysis of context have shown the deposition of animal remains (fish, bird, and mammal bones) as offerings within and close to graves (Klokler 2008). An indisputable example of animal offerings is the presence of articulated partial fish skeletons and fish bones inside thick lucine (*Lucina pectinata*) clams, associated with burials in the Amourins site (Rio de Janeiro State). Differences regarding the types and quantities of animals might be indicating some differentiation between individuals in Jabuticabeira II (Klokler 2008). Some groups might have symbolic connections with specific groups of animals, such as fish and birds in Jabuticabeira II.

Episodic feasting celebrations were carried out along generations of communities living in integrated regional networks; in fact, some shell mounds have been uninterruptedly built upon for thousands of years, showing that the sambaquis imparted a deep symbolic significance, far beyond the memories of a few generations. The resources used for mound building and the manner of capture demonstrate that feasting events had prominent cooperative characteristics instead of indicating competitiveness between groups. Evidence of large mortuary feasts indicates that these communal gatherings worked to preserve cooperative solidarity among communities (Klokler 2001, 2008, chap. 11 in this volume).

The last 20 years of archaeological research have demonstrated that the fisher-gatherer groups that built the sambaquis are characterized by territorial stability and broad circulation of people along the coast, based both on archaeological (Gaspar 1991; Prous 1991) and bioanthropological premises (Neves and Okumura 2005; Okumura and Eggers 2005; Okumura, chap. 13 in this volume). Their social network involved a significant number of people, given the large number of burials and sites, and evidence of contemporaneous groups of sambaquis (DeBlasis et al. 2007; Gaspar 2000). Subsistence seems to be diversified; fishing had a central place, but there was also hunting and gathering of mollusks and plant foods (Figuti 1995, 1993; Klokler 2001, 2008; Nishida 2007; Scheel-Ybert et al. 2003). Economic intensification in lagoonal environments (probably including plant management) was efficient enough to generate surpluses (Tenório 1991) that were shared during funerary rituals (Fish et al. 2000; Gaspar 2004; Klokler 2001, 2008; Nishida 2007; Scheel-Ybert et al. 2003).

Sambaqui societies from the southern Brazilian shores had a rich and elaborate symbolic world, permeated in the mounds themselves by the funerary rituals that mobilized these fisher-gatherers for the construction of social, impressive, often quite monumental structures. The very mound building associated with the funerary ritual suggests, besides intense feasting, preoccupation with the preservation of human remains (Fish et al. 2000; Gaspar 2004; Klokler 2008, chap. 11 in this volume; Okumura and Eggers, chap. 8 in this volume). Lithic sculptures (zooliths), occasionally found within elaborate burials, display refined aesthetic sense in depicting a variety of different species of fish, bird, and mammals (Prous 1991). Long and permanent occupation places and coeval chronology provide strong evidence for sedentism and control over a broad and integrated (mostly aquatic) territory, a perception enhanced by the mounds' visibility across the coastal plains (Andreas Kneip 2004). Moreover, the circum-lagoonal settlement distribution indicates an integrated, face-to-face social network, facilitated by canoe-based communication across the lagoon, allowing for not just economic intensification, but also for intense social circulation and mobilization of large amounts of resources for feasting and other purposes (DeBlasis et al. 2007; Gaspar 2000; Klokler 2008, 2001; Souza, chap. 12 in this volume; Scheel-Ybert et al. 2009; Wesolowski 2007).

BUILDING A BETTER APPROACH

To conclude this chapter, a few considerations are in order. A paradigm shift in sambaqui research is represented by the adoption of the premise that funerary rituals stand at the very heart of the symbolic life of these coastal groups, and were, therefore, also central to the construction of the mounds. Currently, researchers have all but abandoned studies about environmental changes based on shell mound location or layer composition. The visual impact of huge accumulations of mollusk remains, which once led to inferences about diet based on quantifications of shell and fish bones, now guide interpretations about the symbolic realm of these coastal societies. Although not all mounds are associated with funerary events, these last are no doubt the raison d'être of most of them, particularly the larger, more obtrusive and monumental mounds.

If in the past human skeletons were the major/only source of information about burial behavior, health, demography, and so forth, they are at present studied as part of funerary features that include multiple sets of behaviors/activities, including the preparation of the ground, treatment and deposition of the bodies, provision of grave offerings, performance of celebratory events honoring the dead, and closure of burial pits and funerary areas. Contrary to the traditional "horizontal plan approach," privileging a flat reading of the events, modern studies focus on the complex arrangement of mounding-up elements emanating from the burial ceremony and how the afterlife occupied an important place in sambaqui people's daily concerns.

From this perspective, the articulation of the often-so-distinctive approaches of archaeology and physical anthropology is, simply put, essential to achieve a full understanding of these populations' ways of life, establishing research proposals that unify settlement patterns with paleodemography studies, as well as behavior toward the dead with paleopathology and gender, among other questions. It is only through the integration of multiple approaches that a full picture of these fascinating, complex coastal Archaic societies will emerge.

ACKNOWLEDGMENTS

We would like to extend our thanks to Christina Leal Rodrigues and Henrique Vences for helping us with the illustrations, the reviewers for their comments and suggestions, and Mirjana Roksandic and all coeditors for the invitation to join the book. Funding for our research came from CNPq (grant 151457/2009-3), CAPES (process 1501-02-0), NSF (doctoral dissertation improvement grant), FAPESP (grants 97/04094-5 and 04/11038-0), and FAPERJ (project Sambaquis médios, grandes e monumentais: estudo sobre as dimensões dos sítios arqueológicos e seu significado social—Pronex- Edital FAPERJ N.º 17/2009).

NOTES

1. It is important to note that this perspective has been attributed not only to prehistoric groups, but also to contemporary Brazilian native societies, seen as people without religion, justice, or state (Fausto 2000, 10).

2. It is important to note the lack of academic and intellectual connection between archaeology and sociocultural anthropology in Brazil, especially ethnography, which hindered the studies of both disciplines by that time.

PART II: PEOPLE AND BURIALS

Cultural Formation Processes of the Bioarchaeological Record of a Brazilian Shell Mound

Mercedes Okumura and Sabine Eggers

SUMMARY

Formation processes are the natural and cultural processes that make up the archaeological record. Whereas natural formation processes are the environmental factors that influence the survival of the archaeological evidence, cultural formation processes include the accidental or deliberate human activities that can affect the archaeological record in a positive or negative way. In this chapter, we identify and discuss the cultural processes influencing the burial features and the later interpretation of burial patterns in a prehistoric Brazilian shell mound, named Jabuticabeira II, dated between 2890 ± 55 and 2186 ± 60 BP. This work argues in favor of true multidisciplinary research, where specialists such as bioarchaeologists participate in the decision processes of the exact location and strategy of excavation, coordinate sample collection of burials and the associated documentation, and, as usual, carry out their specialized work in the laboratory. The ideas put forth here represent an updated version of a previous work on formation processes (Okumura and Eggers 2008), where now a greater emphasis has been put on the cultural aspects of the formation processes of this particular site.

INTRODUCTION

What Are the Formation Processes of Archaeological Sites?

Formation processes are the natural and cultural processes that make up the archaeological record. Natural formation processes are the environmental processes that influence the survival of the archaeological record, while cultural formation processes include the accidental or deliberate human activities that can help preserve or aid in the destruction of the (bio-)archaeological record (Schiffer 1987). "By closely defining site formation processes, one can frame and test hypotheses concerning areas of knowledge which at present remain hazy" (Gifford 1980, 105). The archaeological contexts associated with human skeletal remains deserve special attention, since they might be the only source of information about the way of life of past populations. Here we focus on the cultural formation processes and how they impact the preservation and interpretation of skeletal remains, using the Jabuticabeira II shell mound as an example.

Bioarchaeology Is Paramount to Reconstructing Mortuary Ritual

Burial grounds provide the basis from which past funerary behaviors are inferred. The social position (inferred through the burial structure, the features of grave goods, and the position of the deceased, among others) and the ritual (what happens before, during, and after burial according to tradition) make up the funerary customs of a human group. These customs, together with bioarchaeological data (sex, age, health, and so forth) are the basis for estimating sociodemographic parameters of the past. Ethnographic accounts can be used to suggest what might have happened, but taphonomy (the study of processes through which organic remains pass from biosphere to lithosphere) must always be considered, especially because its effects can be confounded with cultural formation processes. Based on ethnographic studies, some authors claim that burial practices were part of the intangible domain of religious belief (Piggott 1973). Nonetheless, there has been a shift "from a referential focus to a focus on the practices" to "*what people did with their dead*" (Nilsson Stutz 2003, 320). Mortuary practices involve elements that leave no material trace (speech, song, dancing, crying, and so forth), but some material remains, and the body itself, are available, so archaeologists can reconstruct a significant part of the mortuary ritual (Nilsson Stutz 2003, 231).

Also based on ethnography, Peter J. Ucko (1969) believed there is no correlation between social structure and burial rites, but for Vere Gordon Childe (1945), burial pattern and social functioning were associated: the greater the material progress, the less social energy is invested in the burial rituals. In contrast, the Archaeology of Death of the 1970s postulated that mortuary practices express social reality, where social identity is equivalent to social status (Goodenough 1965; but see Gilman 1983 for a different view). For Lewis R. Binford (1971), counterbalancing Childe, form and structure of mortuary practices were conditioned by the society's form and complexity, so the more complex the social structure, the more complex the burial ritual. Despite these opposing views, for Diane P. Gifford (1980), ethnoarchaeological studies provide an actualistic arena for framing, testing, and refitting general models of human behavior and its material effects, allowing researchers to go beyond the limits of strict analogy as an explanatory tool.

Marxist approaches interpret burial sites as deposits of social labor. Since funerary rituals indirectly reflect the society's material conditions (homage, payment of tributes, or covering up of inequalities), ethnography is mandatory for reconstructing their meaning (Lull 2000). According to materialistic views, the basic information necessary to reconstruct and understand past funerary rituals include (Alekshin 1983): conceptions of death and the other world; the development and succession of cultures; sex and age differences regarding wealth of grave offerings; social stratification based on number, type, material, and rarity of grave offerings; form of marriage and family structure, better understood through ancient DNA and other biodistance studies; and finally, demographic and epidemiologic patterns. Additional information includes detailed skeletal analyses (Bartel 1983), using microscopy, tomography, 3D reconstructions, and detection of pathogen DNA. Crucial for studying funerary practices in the past are also the materials and technologies used to construct the burial containers (Lull 2000).

Ethnography can be important to interpret funerary contexts. However, ethnographic information does not necessarily parallel archaeological evidences drawn from burial studies (Binford 1971; Brown 1971a, 1971b; O'Shea 1984; Shennan 1975). In fact, ethnographers focus on social phenomena that may or may not incorporate material culture, whereas material culture is the only evidence the archaeologist can rely upon to reconstruct social structure in the past (Alekshin 1983). Additionally, post-depositional processes may distort inferences from simplistic observation (Chapman and Randsborg 1981), and sometimes counterintuitive ritual behavior can influence archaeological interpretation (Hodder 1982). Therefore, an integrative approach based on bioarchaeology may provide a more complete picture.

Integrative Approaches to Studying Cultural Formation Processes

Bioarchaeology is a key element in the integrative study of cultural formation processes and funerary analyses, since it bridges the gap between social and biological approaches, innovating research methods. In the first two decades of its existence, Sciencedirect retrieved only 22 papers and books focusing on bioarchaeology. The following five-year periods, however, witnessed 14 (1996–2000), 68 (2001–2005), and 189 (2006–2010) publications. Bioarchaeology is an integrative research strategy and requires close collaboration between bioanthropologists, zooarchaeologists, palaeobotanists, and archaeologists right from the start of research design of an excavation project, and is totally different from the tradition of relegating osteology to the appendix of archaeological papers (Gamble, Walker, and Russell 2001, 139; Nilsson Stutz 2003).

Bioarchaeological work in the laboratory and at the excavation allows for obtaining enough data to reconstruct formation processes, based not only on skeletal material but also on the archaeological context involved and the features associated with the burial. The new information on Paleoindian funerary patterns revealed by recent results from Lagoa Santa (Central Brazil) is a great example. Until recently, these Paleoindian funerary patterns were thought to be simple and homogeneous. However, painstaking excavations and meticulous analyses (Strauss 2010) revealed that the highly variable mortuary rituals among these Paleoindians focused directly on the bodies of the deceased. There were disarticulated burials (happening shortly after death), bones with cut and fire marks, skulls with extracted teeth, and the presence of ochre. Extraordinary was the case of an amputated male skull (with the cervical vertebrae preserved) found in upright position, with its face covered with postmortem amputated hands, so that the fingertips of the right hand looked up and covered the left side of the face, whereas the left hand covered the right side of the face, with the fingertips pointing downward (Strauss 2010). Without a skilled and experienced bioarchaeologist, much of the information on this unusual funerary ritual could not have survived.

Cultural Processes Influencing Burials and Bones

Cultural as well as natural formation processes may damage bone preservation and conservation and act on bone position at the time of excavation. However, some of these processes can actually favor preservation.

Natural factors, such as the chemical nature of the material and the type of burial environment, can deteriorate buried material (Cronyn 1990), but cultural rules determine who will be buried, when, where, and how it will happen. Furthermore, the location and the way the individual is disposed of will influence the position in the grave and the preservation of the burial and its contents (Roksandic 2002).

Burial Arrangement: Primary and Secondary Burials

Basically, the arrangement of a burial can be classified as primary or secondary. The primary arrangement refers to the situation in which the initial place where the corpse is left shortly after death is the same as the final one. Although secondary burials commonly refer to corpses processed before final interment, the formal definition of secondary burial simply states that the remains were removed from their initial place, being later left either in the same place or somewhere else. Common examples of secondary burial include corpses buried, exhumed, and then buried again (usually in non-anatomical position) and corpses buried only after partial or total (either natural or anthropogenic) skeletonization occurring sometimes in charnels (rooms used to accumulate the remains of the dead; O'Shea 1984, 37).

A secondary burial can be easily identified when the reburial includes just the largest bones (Duday 1978), but also when the small bones were lost between the primary and the final disposal. However, small bones may also be "lost" due to bad preservation in a primary context, and distinguishing between primary and secondary burials is not always straightforward. Even when all bones are present and in anatomical position, the corpse could have been removed from an initial to a final place of burial before decomposition and disarticulation, thus characterizing a secondary burial (Roksandic 2002). Moreover, corpses wrapped in textiles or bound together with ropes and in baskets can be removed from their initial places without loss of bones. Consequently, no indication regarding this displacement would be left over for the bioarchaeologist to identify, except the possible movement of bones due to the decomposition of soft tissues or the wrap's arrangement.

Position of the Skeleton, Dismemberment, and Bone Conservation

Even in an undisturbed primary burial, there will always be a difference between the original in vivo position of the skeleton and what archaeologists discover during exhumation. This difference is due to the decomposition of soft tissues, which causes movement of the bones due to lack of articulation and presence of empty spaces left after decomposition (Nilsson Stutz 2003, 150–51). Although decomposition and subsequent bone movement is a natural process, it is influenced by cultural factors (for example, grave structure and size, position of the corpse). Acute angles of arms and legs indicate manipulation of the body before burial, as they are impossible to attain while the soft tissue is still intact. Depending on the stage of decomposition, dismemberment may or may not leave cut marks (Marshall 1989).

Bone conservation can provide clues about cultural processes acting during the funerary ritual, where bleached and friable bones, presenting longitudinal cracking, can suggest that they were exposed to weathering (Nelson, Darling, and Kice 1992).

Although the physical characteristics of the burial place (or natural processes) influence corpse preservation, the place where and the manner by which someone is buried are determined by a cultural choice. Therefore, although pH and humidity, among others, are key natural factors for the preservation or decomposition of the body, they are influenced and often manipulated by people. This manipulation accelerates decomposition (cremation or watering; Ramos 1951, 181–82) or reduces decomposition odors and aids bone preservation (lime spread; Edwards et al. 2001).

Secondary burials are common in groups where death is perceived as a drawn-out process and where the dead are considered part of society. For the Dayak in Borneo, for example, the second interment ensures the soul access to the land of the dead, and frees the living from the obligations of mourning (Hertz 2006).

AIMS

The aim of this chapter is to discuss cultural formation processes influencing the interpretation of burial patterns using the shell mound Jabuticabeira II (southern Brazil) as a case study.

8.1. Map with indication of shell-site concentrations and study area.

MATERIAL AND METHODS
The Jabuticabeira II Shell Mound

Among more than 1,000 shell mounds (5000–1000 BP) catalogued in Brazil, Jabuticabeira II, built between 2880 and 1400 BP and measuring 400 by 250 by 9 meters, is one of 68 sites surrounding the Garopaba do Sul lagoon in the Santa Catarina State (DeBlasis et al. 1998; Giannini et al. 2010; Figure 8.1).

The osteological material from Jabuticabeira II derives from profiles and horizontal excavations from different loci, showing a long and continuous depositional history of recurrent burial activities, as well as a lack of obvious habitation structures (DeBlasis et al. 1998, 2004; Fish et al. 2000; Klokler, chap. 11 in this volume). Primary and secondary

burials are distributed over most of the excavated locations, presenting hearths and postholes, as well as stone tool artifacts, beads, fish remains (interpreted as offerings for the dead and food for the living), and red pigment (DeBlasis et al. 1998; Edwards et al. 2001; Klokler 2001; Klokler, chap. 11 in this volume). The material described herein consists of the remains of a minimum number of 89 individuals (using the criteria established by White and Folkens 1991)[1] excavated from 1997 to 1999. Although relevant information on skeletal material (sometimes in a bad state of conservation) derived from many areas of the site will be included in our discussion, a greater emphasis will be given on material exhumed in Locus 2. A very detailed description of Locus 2 is given by Gaspar and colleagues:

A horizontal excavation of 36 m² within a funerary area confirmed that the corresponding dark layers are successive occupation surfaces, sometimes with localized shell pavements and always with numerous postholes in the vicinity of the burials. Posts encircled some burial pits and similarly demarcated whole funerary areas. Additional posts may have supported miniature structures over graves (as in ethnographic practices), suspended offerings, marked the graves, or served still other purposes. [Gaspar et al. 2008, 325]

Locus 2 has been considered as the cemetery of an "affinity group": a group of individuals who were buried close to each other in a delimited area within a relatively short period (2340 ± 50 and 2320 ± 50BP; DeBlasis et al. 2004; Gaspar et al. 2008).

Excavation, Curation, and Analyses

During the first field campaigns, a 120-meter profile was cleaned. Burials were recorded and excavated at all levels and across the whole length of the profile. The trenches and horizontal decoupages in other areas of the site revealed numerous burials, which were carefully inspected, recorded, and photographed. The human remains were cleaned while still in the ground so as to reveal traces of pigment. Many of the burials recorded were exhumed and transported to the Laboratory of Biological Anthropology at the University of São Paulo for curation and further analyses.

Age at death was estimated based on tooth formation and eruption, long bone size, and degree of epiphyseal and cranial suture closures, while sex was based on pelvic and cranial morphology (Johnston 1962; Ubelaker 1989; Buikstra and Ubelaker 1994). For details on paleodemography and paleopathology, see Okumura and Eggers (2005).

The analysis of natural and cultural processes acting on bone was carried out macroscopically, and, where necessary, with a magnifying glass. Features considered relevant for the understanding of natural or cultural processes were recorded, described, and photographed. Burial forms, descriptions, croquis, and photographs taken in the field were also used to access information for the analysis.

RESULTS

The analysis of the human remains from the Jabuticabeira II shell mound, in the field as well as in the laboratory, revealed the following types of cultural formation processes.

Due to the great concentration of shells, the soil pH of shell mounds is usually higher than that found in other tropical soils, neutralizing their typical acidic destructivity and allowing the conservation of human remains. The fact that the majority of Brazilian skeletal remains were exhumed from shell mounds (Okumura, Boyadjian, and Eggers 2007) supports the idea that the soil alkalinization in these sites is a natural formation process that allows the preservation of human remains. However, the accumulation of shells in shell mounds is a cultural phenomenon, since these were accumulated on purpose by the dwellers during site construction (Fish et al. 2000; Gaspar 1998; Gaspar and DeBlasis 1992).

The human remains stemming from profile cleaning and horizontal decoupage at Jabuticabeira II reveal that approximately one-third of the individuals died before 21 years of age (Okumura and Eggers 2005). This high proportion of juveniles agrees with the percentage observed in other prehistoric cemeteries (Waldron 1994), and means that, a priori, the natural and cultural processes affecting bone preservation did not distort the original (and expected) demographic composition of these groups. Since similar numbers of males and females and all age classes are represented in the osteological collection (Okumura and Eggers 2005), no strong selection processes (either cultural or natural) acted on the people buried. The exhumed individuals also reflect recent selection processes (such as the decision of which part of the site to excavate and which of the individuals recorded to exhume).

During excavation red pigment was recorded on bones impregnated with diffuse reddish stains; bones with delimited red lines; and bones covered with thick layers of pigment. Most of the individuals with ochre marks presented diffuse ochre stains on long bones and sometimes also on the skull. The majority of children excavated were stained with this red pigment. In these cases, there was no loose ochre or ochre crusts left near the skeleton, and most were secondary burials. The pigment must have been distributed relatively evenly on top of the decomposing or already decomposed corpse after final interment. Percolation of water could have washed the excess away.

In rare cases, ochre marks were narrow, longish, clearly delimited lines of about 3 by 30 millimeters, probably deliberately drawn by the shell mound people on the bones of their dead, thus representing a cultural process. Finally, Raman spectroscopy revealed pure hematite on a humerus with a thick pigment crust (Figure 8.2) (Edwards et al. 2001).

Between the red pigment and the bone there was a layer of lime wash (Edwards et al. 2001), possibly the product of

8.2. Massive layer of red pigment on humerus.

heating shells. If mollusk shells are heated to high temperatures, calcium oxide is released; this reacts with sodium bicarbonate solutions to form powdered calcium carbonate that precipitates on the shells (Waselkov 1987). Whether this procedure was intentional, in order to avoid putrefaction smells and attraction of flies and scavengers,

is not known. Therefore, whereas soil alkalinization is a natural process related to a cultural habit, the consequences of the spread of lime on the corpses is a natural process that could be linked to a cultural one.

Horizontal excavations at Locus 2 presented numerous burials with complex features. These include extremely flexed individuals of all age categories and both sexes, covered with shells and hearths containing fish as offering and feast remains (Klokler, chap. 11 in this volume), and, in some cases, mortars and shell beads (Gaspar et al., chap. 7 in this volume; Okumura and Eggers 2005). Vestiges of postholes surrounding the burials could be observed (Bianchini, Scheel-Ybert, and Gaspar 2007; Scheel-Ybert, chap. 22 in this volume) (Figure 8.3). It has been proposed that the function of these posts would be to prevent the access of scavengers (no clear gnawing marks present), and to hold offerings or the deceased themselves before final interment (Bianchini, Scheel-Ybert, and Gaspar 2007; Gaspar et al., chap. 7 in this volume; Klokler, chap. 11 in this volume). However, it is possible to observe other postholes that do not seem to be directly associated to burials. Obviously, each time a corpse was buried, any previously

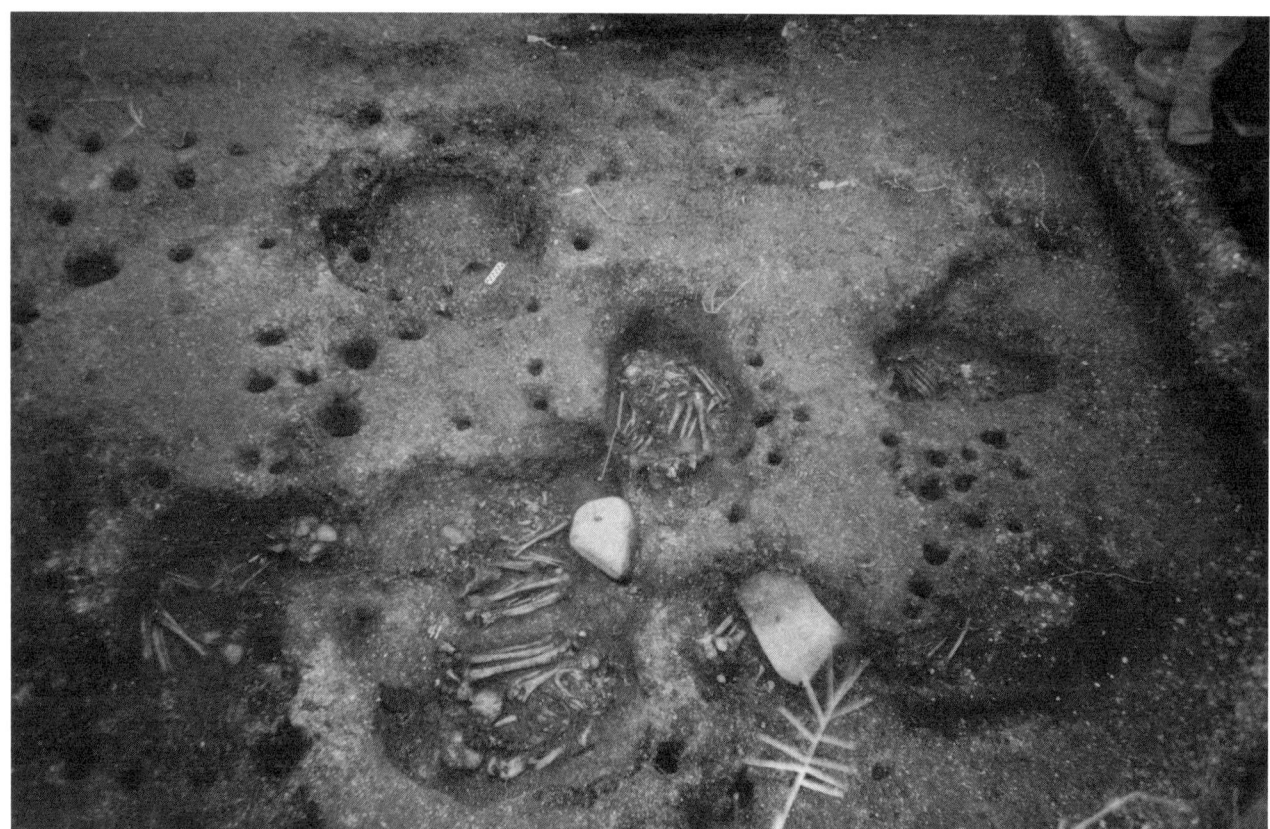

8.3. Locus 2. The tightly flexed skeletons were deposited in small, non-intruding burials surrounded by postholes.

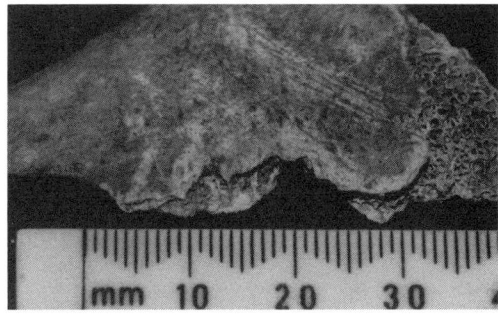

8.4. (left) General aspect of Burial 26B. The very acute angles of the lower limbs suggest a period between death and burial long enough for the soft tissue to deteriorate.

8.5. (above) Possible defleshment marks left on the pelvis of a young individual.

present postholes (if there were any present) would have been eliminated; postholes surrounding burial pits would be more represented than postholes not associated with burial pits. Moreover, only a small area of Locus 2 has been excavated, and the location of all postholes has not been mapped in a systematic way. Therefore, it is not possible to rule out any other functions for the postholes, including holes related to habitation structures (although no clear evidence of habitation floors have been observed), besides the ideas discussed previously.

The majority of Locus 2 burials in Jabuticabeira II contained complete or nearly complete skeletons. The state of conservation was very good, since most of the bones were not bleached, not friable, and exhibited no longitudinal cracking, suggesting that they were not exposed to the elements for a very long time (Nelson, Darling, and Kice 1992). However, the very acute angles on lower limbs (probably held tightly with ropes, strings, or bundles) could not be obtained while the soft tissues were still on the corpse (Figure 8.4). Therefore, if the corpses were being exposed until natural decomposition of most soft tissue occurred, it must have been in a place protected from weather elements. An alternative explanation for these very acute angles would be intentional defleshment carried out by members of the group (Fish et al. 2000). However, only one among 89 analyzed presents cut marks (Figure 8.5), rendering defleshment extremely rare. Consequently, the deceased must have been left to deteriorate naturally before secondary interment in an environment protected from weathering, which would also explain the lack of bleached and friable bones. Considering that decomposition is mainly attributed to temperature, for a 68-kilogram human cadaver, with an average

summer daily temperature of 25°C, the onset of "advanced decay" would occur after 16 days, while an average daily winter temperature of 5°C would result in the onset of the same stage after 80 days (Carter, Yellowlees, and Tibbett 2007; Vass et al. 1992).

Most of the skeletons exhumed from Jabuticabeira II are fairly complete (exhibiting hand and foot bones), suggesting that the transport from the place where the corpse was left to decompose to the final burial place must have been done carefully and/or in wraps (Gaspar et al. 2008). Whereas all tiny bones preserved were found in perfect anatomical position (ligaments still intact during transport), only very rarely were long bones found in wrong anatomical position (upside down), suggesting that people repositioned bones (wrongly) whose ligaments had breached before final interment.

However, some secondary burials miss some bones, leading to incompleteness of the skeleton. These bones could have been deliberately ignored (when the burial includes just the largest bones) or accidentally lost (Duday 1978), which is more common in the secondary burial of juveniles, such as in a secondary double burial, where a three-year-old child presented more than 50 percent of the bones, while a six-month-old infant presented just a few long bones (Okumura and Eggers 2005).

Clear evidence of cultural marks left on bones from the Jabuticabeira II site includes small star-shaped marks (Figure 8.6). Since they are tiny and localized, with no hard implement found associated to them in the burial, and considering that these marks certainly do not resemble rodent gnawing or defleshment marks, we hypothesize that they represent marks carved (accidentally or deliberately) onto

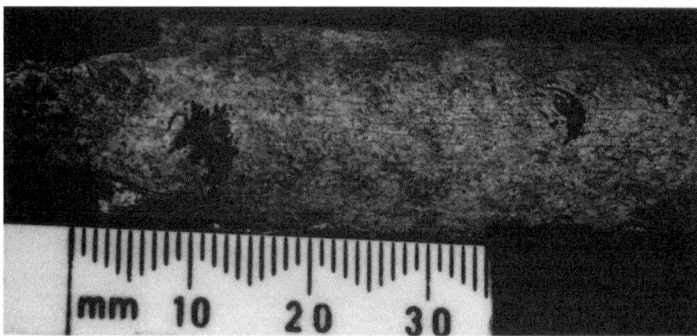

8.6. Star-shaped carved mark found on a few long bones (Photo: Wagner Sousa e Silva).

the bones during preparation of the deceased for secondary burial.

Bioarchaeological analysis also helped to further explore the possibility that the individuals buried in Locus 2 could represent a unity where "these funerary areas are interpreted as the designated burial locations for specific affinity groups, whose membership was based on kinship, territorial affiliation, or other social principles" (Gaspar et al. 2008, 324–25).However, a comparison between individuals buried in Locus 2 with other samples from the same site revealed no differences regarding dental and cranial metric and non-metric data, or in osteoarthrosis frequencies and patterns (Okumura and Eggers 2011).

In summary, at Jabuticabeira II, we found 12 types of cultural processes that in some way changed the features of the human remains and contributed to the formation process of this huge site. They allowed some important inferences to be made regarding the funerary ritual (Table 8.1).

DISCUSSION

Cultural formation processes are often interrelated with natural formation processes, because cultural choices in mortuary rituals strongly affect natural formation processes. This influence can be clearly observed in many examples. Distinguishing cultural from natural formation processes is crucial, and it is treated in detail elsewhere (Okumura and Eggers 2008).

Clearly, the same mortuary context can be representative of different funerary behaviors. For example, tightly flexed individuals can, a priori, be indicative of active defleshment, after which the individual was put in bundles and only then buried; manipulation of a primary inhumation in the same place, moving long bones to a different position; or a temporally extended funerary ritual where

the body, partially decomposed, is interred in a secondary burial. It may be difficult and sometimes impossible to distinguish among these possibilities, although some features can indicate which possibility is more likely.

The hyperflexed burials of Locus 2 were possibly not the result of active defleshment, since defleshment marks are rare. The manipulation of a primary inhumation in the same place can also be excluded, since they are nonintruding and very small (measuring about 70 by 50 centimeters—just enough to contain a hyperflexed skeleton). The most parsimonious explanation is that the corpse was left in a place protected from scavengers and weathering, since it explains the extreme rarity of defleshing and gnawing marks, and is in accordance with the small size of the pits.

Although there are no extant Brazilian groups that can be culturally associated with the shell mound groups, some ethnographic accounts inspire models about the mortuary ritual (Klokler 2001). The burial pattern at Locus 2 is of secondary burials with hyperflexed individuals, on top of whom little individual mounds of shells were put after final interment. Later, groups of burials were covered by a bigger mound, contributing to the construction of the main mound (Gaspar et al. [chap. 7] and Klokler [chap. 11] in this volume).

Individual mounds on top of burials were described in ethnographic accounts of the Brazilian Kaingang (Lozano 1974 [1873], 423), although the mounds were built with sediment rather than with shells. Protecting and delimitating burials were also reported among contemporaneous Brazilian Indians including the Kaingang, who delimited cemeteries with wooden posts (Baldus 1979, 20); the Botocudo and Guayaki, who erected sheds above burials (Manizer 1919; Métraux 1946b; Métraux and Baldus 1946; Saint-Hilaire 1838); the Mbaya, who buried their dead in mortuary huts where each family owed a piece of ground demarked by posts (Métraux 1948); the Kamayura, who surrounded the burial place with a low fence (Métraux 1948); and the Tupinamba, who sometimes suspended the corpses in hammocks over a pit lined out with posts and covered with branches (Métraux 1948). These widespread cultural practices can help to propose and test new models about the funerary practices of ancient shell mound groups.

Integrating the abovementioned ethnography and the results of this and other works (see Gaspar et al. 2008; Gaspar et al. [chap. 7] and Klokler [chap. 11] in this volume) suggests that the funerary practices in Jabuticabeira II probably lasted for several weeks and involved many people. The deceased was placed to naturally decompose in a place protected from scavengers and weathering, while

Table 8.1. Types of cultural formation processes acting on human remains excavated at Jabuticabeira II

Observed Feature	Suggested Cultural Behavior	Impact on Human Remains
Burial in shell-rich sediment	Shells used to prepare pit and cover burial	Increase of pH and better preservation of bones
High proportion of juveniles	No selection of age-specific cemetery area	Individuals of all ages represented
Sex ratio between males and females ~1	No selection of sex-specific cemetery areas	Female and male skeletons represented in similar proportion
Red pigment evidence	Use of hematite as part of the funerary ritual	Staining of bones
Lime wash between bone and red pigment	To accelerate decomposition or reduce decomposition smell?	Better preservation of bones
Posts surrounding burials	Individualization, protection, and demarcation of burials?	Individualization of burials, little gnawing marks?
Hyperflexed individuals	Possible manipulation of the corpse	Manipulation marks left?
Defleshment marks	Use of techniques to mechanically loosen soft tissue from bones for secondary burial	Marks on bones
Wrong anatomical position of bones	Manipulation of corpse after decomposition of corresponding ligaments	Eventual lack of bones not attached to each other by ligaments
Absence of bones in secondary burials	Certain parts of the body or skeleton are being discarded	Incomplete skeletons
Star-shaped marks on bones	Manipulation of the corpse before burial	Marks on bones
Archaeological unity (like Locus 2)	Individuals buried in the same area in a relatively short time	Individuals from this group may have been linked by some kind of affinity

some people prepared the pit and collected shells. Other persons prepared offerings (mortars, shell-bead strings), whereas still others traveled to collect hematite and to select, collect, and transport the wood to the site and prepare the posts (Scheel-Ybert, chap. 22 in this volume). Shortly before the final interment, fish for offering and feast were caught (Klokler 2001, 2008, chap. 11 in this volume). Finally, mourning people participated, perhaps in the presence of other people of the community, in the final burial ritual (Klokler, chap. 11 in this volume). At this occasion, the skeletonized body (in most cases, with some of the strongest ligaments still intact) was transported to the final burial place, laid down carefully, and covered with heaps of shell. On top of this little shell mound, a ceremonial fire, possibly using scented wood, was lit (Bianchini, Scheel-Ybert, and Gaspar 2007; Scheel-Ybert et al. 2003; Gaspar et al., Klokler, Scheel-Ybert, chaps. 7, 11, and 22 in this volume). Judging from the burnt fish bones, however, this fire also was used to prepare a meal (Klokler 2008, chap. 11 in this volume). Only after this complex

funerary ritual were the mourning people released to resume their normal life, if the ethnographic accounts on secondary burials can be applied to this archaeological context. Every time somebody of this group died, the postholes of those dead in the past indicated if there was enough space for another burial. Some years after the initial burials in a certain area, it was time to cover it with more shells and begin a new cycle of funerary rituals. This funerary scenario emerges from the integration of results from different fields. The recurrent covering of the deceased and their offerings with charcoal, fish, shell, and sand over many generations grew an almost flat structure into what is now known as a sambaqui. Thus, in the case of Jabuticabeira II, the funerary ritual, with all its complexity, plays a fundamental role in the formation process of this shell mound (Gaspar et al. and Klokler, chaps. 7 and 11 in this volume). This reconstruction of the funerary ritual, although compelling, needs to be confirmed through various other interdisciplinary analyses in the field and in the laboratory.

CONCLUSION

The understanding of cultural formation processes is essential to the studies on human skeletal remains. This understanding demands an intense participation of bioarchaeologists in the field, and integration with zooarchaeologists, palaeobotanists, and geoarchaeologists, among others. This chapter is limited to cultural processes affecting human remains from Jabuticabeira II; however, each context must be analyzed in its own particularity.

ACKNOWLEDGMENTS

We are very grateful to the editors for inviting us to write this book chapter. We would like to thank P. DeBlasis, M. Gaspar, P. Fish, S. Fish, F. Silva, C. Frochtengarten, I. Fazzio, C. Petronilho, A. Araujo, and two anonymous reviewers. Financial support was received from the Wenner Gren Foundation, FAPESP (98/8114-3; 03/02059-0; 04/11039-0), USP, CEPID/ FAPESP (98/14254-2), and CNPq ("bolsa de produtividade" for SE).

NOTE

1. The MNI is calculated by counting all the left and right long-bone epiphyses separately, as well as other larger skeletal elements. The largest number of these is then taken as the MNI. The MNI is likely to be lower than the actual number of skeletons, but represents the minimum number of individuals that can be safely estimated to be present.

CHAPTER NINE

THE SKELETAL ASSEMBLAGE AND BURIAL RITUAL AT THE SITE OF CABEÇO DA AMOREIRA

The 1960s Excavations by Veiga Ferreira and Roche

Mirjana Roksandic and Mary Jackes

SUMMARY

Skeletal remains from the valley of Muge figure prominently in recent discussions on the Mesolithic/Neolithic transition in Europe and the role Mesolithic substrate populations played in the process of Neolithisation. The largest, relatively flood-free shell middens of the Muge valley served as burial grounds for the Mesolithic population that occupied the valley, elevating their status from refuse dumps to places of uncontested ritual significance. Yet little is known or published systematically about the symbolic value of the skeletons buried in the shell middens, and precious little has been published about the burial position and the distribution of the burials within the sites. Our ability to reconstruct burial ritual depends on the quality of documentation concerning the disposition of individual bones and bone fragments. Given that these shell middens were excavated in the late 19th to mid-20th century, affecting the quality of documentation, burial reconstruction would be at best limited. However, bones encased in the breccia of the Muge shell middens retained a number of original spatial associations. This crucial, although partial, information represents the main focus of present research. In this chapter we compare the Cabeço da Amoreira skeletal material, currently housed in the Museu Geológico, Serviços Geológicos de Portugal, Lisbon (MSG), with the field journals of Octávio da Veiga Ferreira and previously unpublished photos and drawings compiled recently by J. L. Cardoso and Jose M. Rolão (1999/2000) in order to reconstruct—to the extent possible—ritual activities associated with the burials excavated in the 1960s by Abbé Jean Roche and Veiga Ferreira. Observation of the skeletal material in the MSG was undertaken in 2006 by the first

author (MR) and her assistants, the skeletal elements being recorded photographically and on graphic inventory forms developed by Roksandic (2003).

Our purpose is to provide information on the unpublished 1960s material, to illustrate the reconstruction process, and to provide interpretations and arguments to facilitate discussion about the Muge sites and the population that used them through the analysis of burial ritual. Reconstruction of the excavations from the 1930s, following the same general principles, is forthcoming (Jackes, Alvim, and Cunha, in press).

THE SITE

Together with the other shell middens of the Muge valley (see Figure 9.1, adapted from Van der Schriek et al. 2007), Cabeço da Amoreira (CAM) was discovered by C. Ribeiro in 1863 and was first described by F. A. Pereira da Costa (1865). While Pereira da Costa discussed in great detail the possible scenarios for the formation of the Muge shell middens, especially as they pertain to the skeletal remains from the Cabeço da Arruda (CA), he notes that the evidence of human occupation on the Cabeço da Amoreira midden is sparse—charcoal, broken mammal bone, flints, and pebbles, often broken. The Portuguese text states clearly that no human remains were found (Pereira da Costa 1865, 11). The site is described as follows: "on the left bank of the Paul do Duque approximately 30 m southeast, and about 1 km across from the Cabeço da Arruda but at a higher elevation, there is a small hill formed on the Pleistocene sands" (Pereira da Costa 1865, 11). It is interesting that Pereira da Costa says that the hill is three meters high,

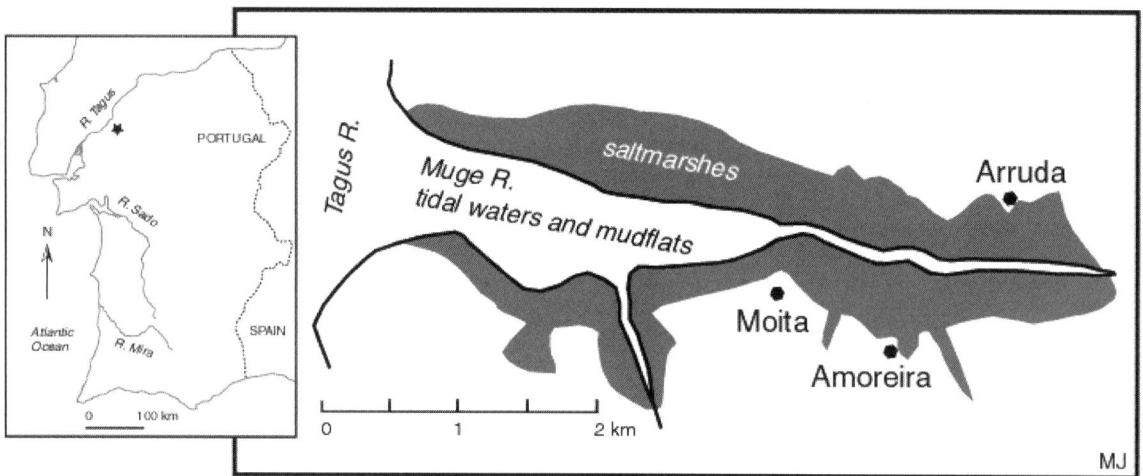

9.1. Map of the Muge valley in the Mesolithic.

since this would indicate that he knew the archaeological deposits were around three meters deep, the hill itself rising to considerably more than three meters above the Muge River. After limited *sondages* by Pereira da Costa, and again by Paula e Oliveira in the 1880s, Cabeço da Amoreira was first excavated in the 1930s by Mendes Corrêa (1930–1933) with Santos Junior and Serpa Pinto, and later, from 1961 to 1967, by Abbé Roche and Veiga Ferreira. New excavations commenced in 2000 (Roksandic 2006; Rolão and Roksandic 2007) and are ongoing (new dates are provided in Bicho et al. 2010).

Muge middens are relatively large structures that are easily visible on the landscape of this Tagus tributary. The high shell content of the middens, together with the conditions of humidity, resulted in an environment conducive to the formation of the breccia. Skeletons were often buried in direct association with shells, promoting breccia formation around the bones. The meaning of the term *breccia* for the Muge sites is not fully defined and varies within and between sites. Breccia is most extensively developed at Moita do Sebastião (see, for example, Jackes and Alvim 2006; Roche 1972a, 81), and a study of its varying characteristics is ongoing. Sometimes the agglomerated shells are visible among the bones buried in the same context, and while excavated in several different campaigns over one and one-half centuries, this breccia allows a detailed—albeit partial—reconstruction of burial position on the basis of preserved anatomical connections. As stated, the recently published field drawings, field journal entries, and photos add further information.

Skeletal material from the site of Cabeço da Amoreira is housed in three different locations: material from the 1930s went to the Museu de Antropologia e Pré-História Mendes Corrêa and to the Museu de História Natural in Porto, and from the 1960s to the Museu Geológico (MSG) in Lisbon. The material from the new excavations is housed in the Institute of Anthropology in Coimbra. The first attempt at systematic publication of the material by Cunha and Cardoso (2001, 2002/2003) reported 21 individuals from both the Porto Museum and the MSG in Lisbon. No publications discuss the ritual as evidenced by Cabeço da Amoreira burials (but see Jackes, Alvim, and Cunha, in press).

Further complicating the picture, Muge material in the MSG was subject to post-excavation mixing (Jackes and Meiklejohn 2004, 2008 provide detail on Moita do Sebastião and Cabeço da Arruda). The Mesolithic skeletons in the museum display room were stored in wooden drawers under display cases. Each storage cabinet had two sets of double doors, and each set of doors opened onto three banks of drawers. A maximum of 14 shallow drawers could be held within each of the three banks, but the arrangement of drawers depended on the size of the bones contained in them. The bones were not individually marked, but were loose in the drawers, accompanied (in principle, but not in practice) by one loose paper label per drawer. The cabinet drawers were locked, but for many years Veiga Ferreira frequently led tours around the museum, opening the cabinets and passing bones around among the visitors. After the early 1980s, the Mesolithic bones were transferred to heavy cardboard core boxes and removed from the display room. While the Moita and Arruda bones were studied and inventoried before removal, the Amoreira bones were boxed and marked without being studied.

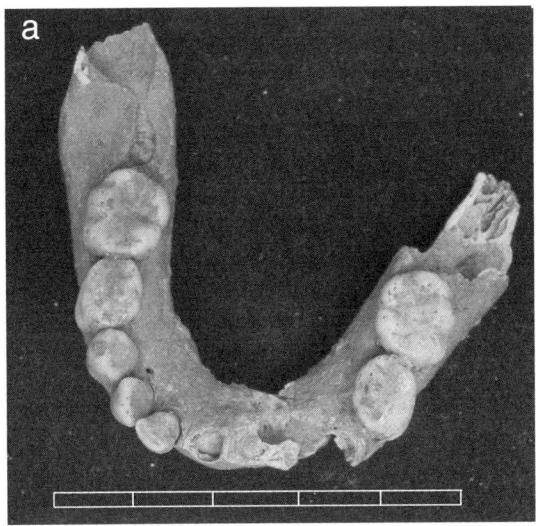

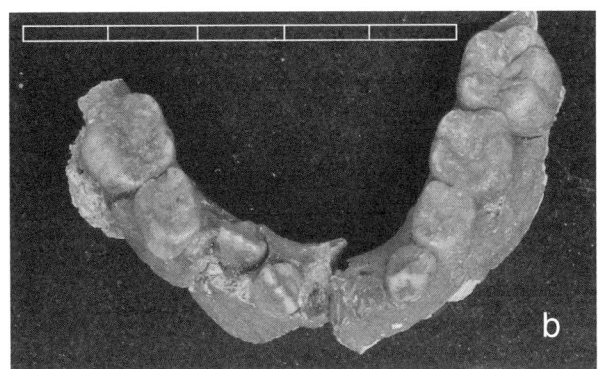

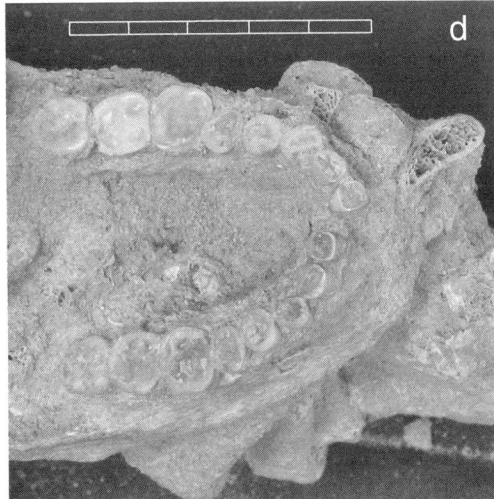

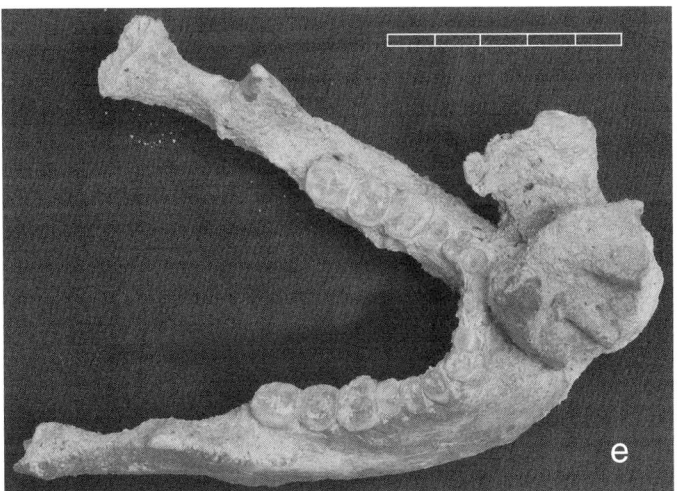

9.2. *(a): Child with deciduous molars only, mistaken by the excavators as deciduous and adult molars. This individual is likely to be Amoreira 2. (b) Child with erupted first adult molars. This individual is likely to be Amoreira 3. (c) Detail from photograph of Amoreira 7, taken by D. Lubell in 1989. The attrition indicates that this is the youngest of the three adults for which we have photographed mandibles. (d) Amoreira 8, photographed in 2002 by Lubell. The dentition is heavily worn, but note that the first molars still have complete enamel rings. (e) Amoreira 6, photographed in 2002 by Lubell. The dental attrition is advanced, with root canals exposed on the premolars and canines and first molars without complete enamels rings. Note the incisor wear.*

The extent of bone loss can be suggested by the following examples. On Veiga Ferreira's plan of Amoreira, 12 adult right humeri are illustrated. The 2006 inventory shows that only three adult right humeri can be counted toward the minimum number of individuals (MNI) present. And yet distal humeri are normally a good control for the number of individuals. Equally, we might expect 14 adult frontal bones with supraorbital regions preserved; in fact, no more than four supraorbital regions can be counted. Even more surprising is the lack of mandibles (Jackes and Meiklejohn 2004, 2008) and of mandibular dentitions (Jackes 2009). By way of comparison, it can be estimated that close to 100 skeletons were found at Moita do Sebastião, of which probably 84 were actually removed from the site between the 1860s and the 1950s, and of these around 80 can still be recorded by the use of mandibular MNI and infant bone counting (Jackes and Alvim 2006). The situation for the Amoreira material excavated in the 1960s is much worse. Three children are represented by mandibles with dentition, unexpectedly, since it is much more likely that adult dentitions will be found, whereas three adults are represented by relatively complete mandibles, one by a small mandibular fragment, and two more by loose mandibular teeth. Such a highly unusual pattern of loss can be considered evidence of "museum taphonomy" (Jackes 2011; Stodder 2008).

Amoreira was unfortunately not included in the inventories of Muge material in the MSG undertaken by Denise Ferembach and Christopher Meiklejohn in the 1960s (Newell, Constandse-Westermann, and Meiklejohn 1979) and by Meiklejohn and Mary Jackes in 1984–1986. A descriptive guide produced under the direction of Veiga Ferreira in 1977 and again in 1982 (Museu dos Serviços Geológicos de Portugal 1982) made no mention of Amoreira, while Moita material took up display cabinets 9–12 and Arruda completely occupied the cabinets numbered 13–16 in the MSG. On a plan of storage drawers under the cabinets made by Meiklejohn in 1984, including faunal material, Arruda actually filled eight or more sets of drawers, and Moita five, while Amoreira filled only two sets of drawers. Veiga Ferreira made no mention of further material, although in the 1980s there was extensive searching for archival and other relevant Muge documentation. After Veiga Ferreira's death in 1997, the owner of a nearby storage facility approached museum personnel requesting unpaid back rent and proved to have Muge material stored on his property. The material was reported to Jackes as 51 individuals from Arruda.[1] David Lubell photographed the dentitions in 2002 in an interim museum storage facility,

and we were able to confirm that the material comprised the 13 Arruda individuals excavated in 1964–1965 (Jackes and Meiklejohn 2004, 98). Included were a number of Amoreira materials, also photographed by Lubell in 2002 (Figure 9.2 a–e), recorded as being numbered Skeletons 2, 3, 6, and 8. While this suggested that those individuals had avoided the mixing sustained by bones in the museum display room drawers, there proved to have been other problems; the material stored outside the museum had undergone flooding and much was discarded in 1999. Extensive searching in October 2010 provided no information on material originally stored in the museum display room, and it seems that only bones that had been in the interim storage area outside the museum are now available for study. Given this information on 35 years of curatorial conditions, it is obvious that some rather tedious details have to be provided in order to move beyond establishing what constitutes each burial to informed discussions. Table 9.1 lists information to assist the reader with the details for each of the skeletons from Amoreira currently housed in the MSG.

BURIALS FROM THE EXCAVATIONS BY VEIGA FERREIRA AND ABBÉ ROCHE

The composite plan of the 1960s excavations (Cardoso and Rolão 1999/2000, 209, fig. 45—this will be cited below as "the composite plan" without reference details) shows Skeletons 1 to 16. Another skeleton, number 17, was recovered after the composite plan was made. In this chapter, we will provide the descriptions as they appear in the diary of O. da Veiga Ferreira and refer to the drawings and published photos (Cardoso and Rolão 1999/2000). They represent the only published documentation of these burials and, while partial, provide some contextual information. For each burial mentioned, we will present the best possible match based on the bones observed in the MSG, referring to the inventories of the bones drawn up by MR and her students in 2006. Identifications will be based on the match between the reconstructed burial position (from bones still embedded in breccia), demographic parameters, and specific traits mentioned by O. da Veiga Ferreira.

Skeleton 1. The excavation of Cabeço da Amoreira by O. da Veiga Ferreira and Abbé J. Roche began in January 1962 after cleaning of the 1930 trench walls in 1961. Veiga Ferreira mentions that there had previously been "cleaning of the site and the profile for the Archaeological Congress in 1958," and that "in profile C we had already noted an incomplete skeleton in 1958 encased in breccia and above

Table 9.1. Amoreira numbered material now in the MSG[a]

Burial No.	Name Given by Veiga Ferreira	Box Number in MSG	Age	Sex	Position
1			Adult		
2		80.04 bag 2/3	Child		
3		80.04 bag 2/3	Child		
4		80.04	Young adult		
5		80.05	Adult		
6	Zé Sequeira	80.06 + Esqueleto 6 + 80.08	Fully to older adult	Female	Knees flexed
7	Igino	Missing (present in 1989 in a tray)			Knees flexed
8	Patrôa	80.08	Fully to older adult	Female	Knees flexed
9					
10					
11			Child		
12	Domingo	80.221	Young adult	Female	Knees flexed
13	Antonio	80.162.79	Older adult	Female	Possibly extended
14		80.180.2	Adult	Male	
15	Santos Junior	80.187?	Adult		
16	Maria Jose Bexiga	80.187?	Adult		
17		80.39.9?	Adult		
		80.221 (2)	Adult	Male	
		80.221 (3) + 80.169.79 (3)	Child associated with adult bones		
		80.221 (4)	Infant		
		80.41	Isolated teeth and foot bones		
		80.42	Isolated teeth and foot bones		
		80.47	Fragment of maxilla and a clavicle		

[a] Boxes were marked by the number ascribed to the site (80 for Amoreira) and a burial number (e.g., 80.04 for burial 4) where it was known, or a tray number (e.g., 80.41). Trays 41, 42, and 47 contained fragmentary unassociated dental and postcranial material.

the shells as in Moita de Sebastião" (Cardoso and Rolão 1999/2000, 208). He further compares it with the burials found on January 18, 1962, which were "closer to the surface." There is no other mention of Burial 1.

The skeleton is drawn on the composite site plan in square H24 with the note "breccia without shells" (*sem conchas*). The "*ponto cotado*," or depth below surface recorded for most individuals on the composite plan, is given for Skeleton 1 as -1.50 meters. The stratigraphic position of this skeleton is most likely to have been in bed 27 (Roche 1967, 249), a sandy layer within the lower level described as mostly yellow sand with some gray sand lenses, in some areas mixed with a few crushed shells. The yellowish sand lay above a bed of crushed shell, in accordance with Veiga

Ferreira's description of the burial location. The skeleton clearly lay well below a disconformity evident in much of the trench, and already recognized in the 1930s as dividing the Amoreira deposits into dark upper and light lower levels (Jackes, Alvim, and Cunha, in press).

On the composite plan, the skeleton is represented by the skull, rib cage, and both humeri. There is no indication of the age, leading us to believe that it was an adult, since remains of children were recognized systematically. Among the remains housed in the MSG, there is no immediate candidate for this burial, and if the drawing is correct and we assume that bones in the museum trays represented—at least to an extent—individual burials, there is no skeleton that corresponds to this burial.

BURIALS IN THE *TERRA PRETA*

Skeletons 2, 3, 4, and **5** were excavated from "*terra negra*" (as recorded on the composite plan) or "*terra preta*" (as recorded on the original MSG labels). Both terms mean "black earth." This is what was called "the middle level" in the 1930s, found just below the superficial deposits in those areas of the trench that were undisturbed.

In discussing the stratigraphic position of skeletons and the meaning of descriptive terms used by Veiga Ferreira in his field notes, we refer to two publications on Amoreira stratigraphy: Roche (1964/1965) provides a profile for the south wall of the excavation trench (Veiga Ferreira referred to this wall as "corte A," as distinct from the north wall or "corte B"), and Roche (1967) provides information on the west profile of the trench (sometimes, but not on the composite plan, referred to by Veiga Ferreira as "corte C"). The description of the black beds is detailed by Roche (as levels 2 to 7 in the south profile: 1964/1965, 199–200; 1967, 243–44) as follows: beds immediately below the surface level and overlying the disconformity. The levels are mostly black and contain much organic matter, charcoal, and many hearths. While corresponding beds of the west profile are numbered differently (6 to 18; Roche 1967, 250), there is no contradiction, simply a different numbering system (see Roche 1965, 150, fig. 3), and the beds are again described as a mixture of hearths, black earth, and lenses of crushed shells. Roche's (1964/1965) stratigraphic profile key simply refers to the great mass of the deposits above the disconformity as "black earth."

The first mention of the burials from black deposits is early on in the excavation, in the notes for January 18, 1962: "Today along profile B in the black earth 3 skeletons appeared approximately 40 cm below the surface. . . . Those found today are more superficial [i.e., than the one from 1958] and they are the first two in the same interment [—] two children of approximately 7–8 years" (Cardoso and Rolão 1999/2000, 208). The drawing mentioned is reproduced as figure 49 in Cardoso and Rolão (1999/2000, 213). This set of burials is relatively easy to recognize, as the bone surfaces do not have a covering of breccia, but rather of dusty gray-black soil.

The box labeled 80.05 in MSG contained three bags. One bag was labeled "burials 2+3" and contained remains of sub-adults, in addition to several teeth and a mastoid process of an adult. The most complete individual was a 7–8-year-old child (Figure 9.2b), represented by elements of the skull including the mandible and maxilla, and the postcranial skeleton. The right transverse distal humerus diaphysis measurement was estimated as close to 360 millimeters.

The second individual is represented by both arms and some fragments of femora, vertebrae, and cranial base, and can be assigned an age of around 4–5 years based on the size; the right distal humerus width was about 280 millimeters. It can be associated with a mandible for which the age was established as 4–5 years based on tooth formation and eruption (Figure 9.2a). Also preserved were several small cranial fragments and a maxillary fragment lacking teeth.

Another right distal humerus with a broken margin has an estimated width of about 300 millimeters, indicating a further individual of roughly the same age. A fourth sub-adult individual in this assemblage is an infant represented by a complete right humerus with a transverse distal diaphysis measurement of about 160 millimeters.

The presence of material from extra skeletons of children could result from the inclusion of bones from a disturbed previous burial, or more likely, from the addition of isolated material from the dark earth or surface layers. Roche recorded both layers as being disturbed, particularly in the lower slopes of the mound, and in the 1930s stray human bone had been discovered in these levels. At this point, the 1962 excavation was going extremely fast, without full notes being taken, so that there is no proof that the composite plan provides accurate placement of any of the black earth skeletons from 1962. Veiga Ferreira's sketch of January 18, 1962, showed the two skeleton numbers clearly, with Skeleton 2 to the northwest of Skeleton 3, and reverse numbering on the composite plan (cf. Jackes et al., chap. 10 in this volume).

The composite plan drawing representing burials 2 and 3 indicates relatively good preservation and a discernible semiflexed position of the body. On the basis of the figure 49 sketch (Cardoso and Rolão 1999/2000, 213), we see Skeleton 3 as more complete than Skeleton 2. Thus, we could suggest that the more complete and older individual would be the juvenile burial 3, while the younger individual would be Skeleton 2, in which lower limb and axial elements are few and fragmentary.

Skeleton 4, as well as being recorded on the composite plan and in a small sketch from January 18, 1962, is also mentioned in the notes. It was excavated at the same time as the previously discussed burials (from the bag 2+3). This could explain why the burials were eventually stored in the same box, and could also explain the presence of some adult remains among the juveniles, as well as juvenile fragment remains in the bag containing burial number 4 (not duplicated by the skeletal elements of the nonadults in the bag labeled 2+3). Since there is no duplication in the adult fragments mixed with the juveniles and the adult in the bag labeled "4," we can safely conclude that the adult fragments stored with the juvenile burials 2 and 3 in fact are part of Skeleton 4.

Skeleton 4 was a young adult based on the preserved teeth and open cranial sutures. The individual is drawn as a nearly complete skeleton (the left forearm appears to be missing on the composite plan), extended on the back with the right leg crossed over the left at the ankles. Despite the apparent completeness of the skeleton on the composite plan, the preserved remains are extremely fragmentary. Skeleton 4 was found close to the northern wall of the trench. While there is no record of the stratigraphy, a sketch from the 1931 excavation (Gonçalves 1986, doc. II-b) indicates that the uppermost archaeological layers are likely to have been trending toward the surface in this area, so that the overburden was thin. The skeletons must have lain very close to the upper limit of the midden since they were discovered at around 40 centimeters below the site surface.

Skeleton 5 from the terra preta was stored with the other material from that context in a bag labeled "terra preta: esqueleto 5." Except for the lateral end of the left clavicle and several unsided phalanges of the hands, all other bones belong to lower extremities. The burial is not mentioned in the notes from the field, nor is it shown on the small sketch drawn on January 18, 1962. However, it figures on the composite plan as lying beside burial 4, with the same orientation and similar, but not identical, burial posture, at the same level (lying on a surface at 50-centimeter depth).

According to the composite plan, Skeletons 2 and 3 were found together in P20 and P21, and Skeletons 4 and 5 were found in P13 and P15, with five one-meter squares separating the two groups. All were lying on a surface one-half meter down and within the upper "black earth" section of the deposits in an area where the mound surface lay between 19 and 19.5 meters above sea level. They were thus all buried at a height of roughly 18.75 meters above sea level. These skeletons were found and boxed together during the same excavation period, from January 11 to January 23, during which work was directed toward clearing away deposits of lesser interest not removed during the 1930s. In fact, excavation of most or all of the area was excluded from the site plans in some publications (Roche 1972b, 79, abb. 20; Roche and Veiga Ferreira 1967, 25). This lack of focus no doubt explains the poor documentation for these finds. Despite the uncertainties, the dusty, ashy gray covering of the bones contributes to the identification of this material.

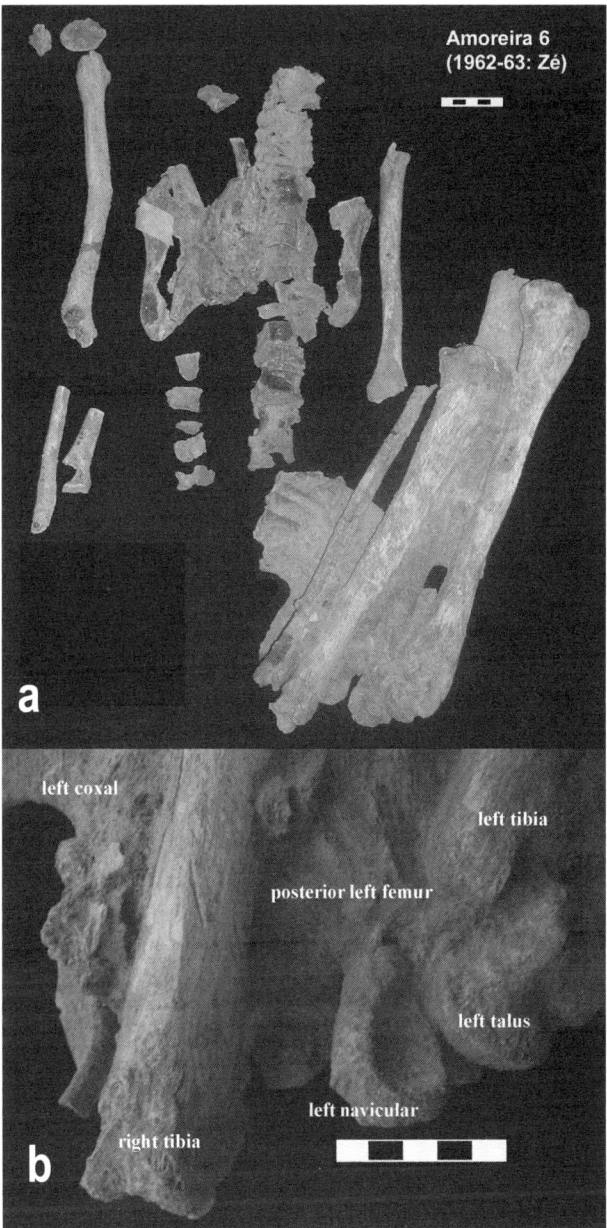

9.3. *(a) Reconstruction of Amoreira 6 in the MSG laboratory: the position of the arms and the spine were not established during reconstruction but on the original field photo. All other elements are interconnected by breccia; highlighted are the elements reproduced in detail in figure 9.3b. Note the position of metacarpals on the ilium. (b) A detail of the same skeleton showing the relationship of the left talus/navicular with the tibiae. The feet could have been oriented toward the sagittal plane—a strong indication of cranio-caudal restriction.*

9.4. Reconstruction of the position of Amoreira 6 based on bones preserved in breccia and the drawing and photo by Veiga Ferreira (Cardoso and Rolão 1999/2000). The cranio-caudal restriction could have acted to move the feet toward the body. Note that we have no information regarding the position of the left forearm and hand. The right hand was on the abdomen.

BURIALS IN BRECCIA

Skeleton 6. Zé Sequeira (Veiga Ferreira gave names to many of the skeletons he excavated). Box 80.06 contained the remains of only one individual. In addition, bones labeled 80.6.1 and 80.6.2 were found in two additional boxes, a box marked "Skeleton 6" and a box marked "80.08." Since the scapular body from the "Skeleton 6" box can be associated with the glenoid portion of the left scapula of the individual in the "80.08" box, and each had a small mammal bone fragment attached by breccia, we can assume the material represents the same individual. The skull and the mandible and maxilla were stored separately in the second and third boxes respectively; the facial portion and dentition found in box 80.08, marked as 80.6.2, match the missing portion of Skeleton 6.

By reconstructing the elements in breccia (Figure 9.3), we could discern the burial position (Figure 9.4) and match Skeleton 6 to the drawing and photo from the Veiga Ferreira archives (Cardoso and Rolão 1999/2000, 218–19, figs. 51, 53). Based on the greater sciatic notch morphology and the extended area between the notch and the auricular surface, the individual was a female, contradicting the excavator's naming of the individual as Zé Sequeira. The preserved postcranial elements indicate a fully adult individual. The wear on both maxillary and mandibular dentition is advanced, with the very strong anterior attrition characteristic of Mesolithic Muge sites (Jackes, Silva, and Irish 2001, 103; Lefèvre 1973, 323). The field drawing (Cardoso and Rolão 1999/2000, 218, fig. 51) and the photo show the skull, thorax, and lower extremities with the partially preserved pelvis. There are discrepancies between the material in box 80.06 and the description of the skeleton

given by Veiga Ferreira (Cardoso and Rolão 1999/2000, 216), "cranium deformed but fairly complete [—] ribs and vertebrae in reasonable condition, no hands, lower limb bones in reasonable condition at least one of the tibia is complete." For example, this material includes a hand on the ilium (Figure 9.3), shown in the field sketch (Cardoso and Rolão 1999/2000, 218, fig. 51), confirming the identification of this material as part of Skeleton 6.

The location of the skeleton provided the excavators with difficulties. On February 9, 1962, they were cleaning the western section of square I25 and were in the basal sand, when they came across part of a skeleton and left it in a pedestal until the skull was found within the profile. Indeed, Veiga Ferreira reported another skeleton appearing in the same area, and specifically at the base, at noon the next day. It can only be that this was another portion of Skeleton 6. We have one clear photograph of the skull (Cardoso and Rolão 1999/2000, 219, fig. 53). The skull can also just be seen in the profile in figure 52 on the same page above the remnant of deposit, which must have been left until excavation was possible.

An interesting feature of the skull is a very specific hole in the upper frontal region. Rounded above and square below, the hole exactly matches the hand-held picks used by Roche's excavators (see Jackes et al., chap. 10 in this volume). The hole has breccia within it, explained by the fact that the skull was left exposed for a fortnight, during which time there was rain. Furthermore, Skeleton 6 was one of the skeletons in the off-site storage facility referred to above, which was subject to periodic flooding over many years.

Skeleton 6 is very well recorded in terms of stratigraphic location since it was found while cleaning the basal sands and was clearly photographed (Cardoso and Rolão 1999/2000, 219, figs. 52 and 53) within a section that was fully published (Roche 1967). The skeleton lay just above the basal sands, below the lowest layer of crushed shells and in association with some river pebbles.

Insofar as burial position could be reconstructed (Figure 9.4), it is dorsal decubitus, with knees drawn tightly toward the chest and to the left of the body. The slumping of the knees to the left side of the body indicates that there was a space lateral to the body. The drawing, the photo, and the reconstruction of the thoracic cage, with constricted ribs on the scapula and the migration of the sternum toward the lower portions of the abdomen, indicate substantial constriction of the upper body. The extremely contracted hip and knee, together with the feet at the level of the ischium, indicate cranio-caudal constriction as well. The effect of a pit wall can be deduced for the right side of the body, with some free space to the left of the body allowing left lateral slumping. The observations would be consistent with an oval burial pit.

Skeleton 7. Igino. Since Skeleton 7 appears to have been complete when excavated, we attempted to identify which elements from other boxes could be associated with this skeleton, taking into account two photographs of a partially en bloc individual (Figure 9.5 shows the overall view). The material had been in the MSG in the cabinet that contained other Amoreira materials, labeled Amoreira 7, from at least 1984, and accords exactly with the documentation (Cardoso and Rolão 1999/2000, 213, 215, figs. 49 and 50).

No material labeled Amoreira 7 was found in the MSG in 2006 and no material recorded in 2006 matched this skeleton. The mandibular dentition was photographed in detail in 1989 (Jackes and Lubell 1996, 469; Figure 9.2) and shows the individual to have been younger than both Skeleton 6 and Skeleton 8 (compare Figure 9.2c with Figure 9.2d and e). Veiga Ferreira inventoried the bones of Skeleton 7 as follows: cranium in bad shape, right humerus, radius, ulna completely broken, vertebral column quite rotten, sacrum complete, right side of the pelvic basin broken, femur in reasonable state, tibia and fibula broken, arms complete and hands quasi complete, under the legs (Cardoso and Rolão 1999/2000, 216).

The burial position and location for Skeleton 7 will be discussed below with that of Skeleton 8.

Skeleton 8. Patrôa. The main individual from box 80.08 is fully adult with fused epiphyses. The worn dentition with exposed dentin (Figure 9.2d) marks this as an older adult, though with a greater mandibular molar crown height than Skeleton 6. Based on the sciatic notch morphology and the gracility of the humerus, the sex can be determined as female, although the cranium is robust. There has been no post-excavation mixing, since the robusticity of the skull is seen in the excavation photograph (Cardoso and Rolão 1999/2000, 215, fig. 50). Despite the skull's robusticity, Veiga Ferreira gave Skeleton 8 a female name; we can assume that he recognized some ambiguity since the name Patrôa has the meaning of "the boss's wife" or perhaps more tellingly for a 1960s designation: "the lady boss."

Many elements of the skeleton could be reconstructed by refitting breccia fragments and broken bone pieces. There are several important observations. All vertebrae are held in place by breccia along with the sacrum. The skull, mandible, left scapula, left clavicle, phalanges, and upper ribs are encased in breccia and articulate with the humerus. The skull is depressed medio-laterally (Veiga

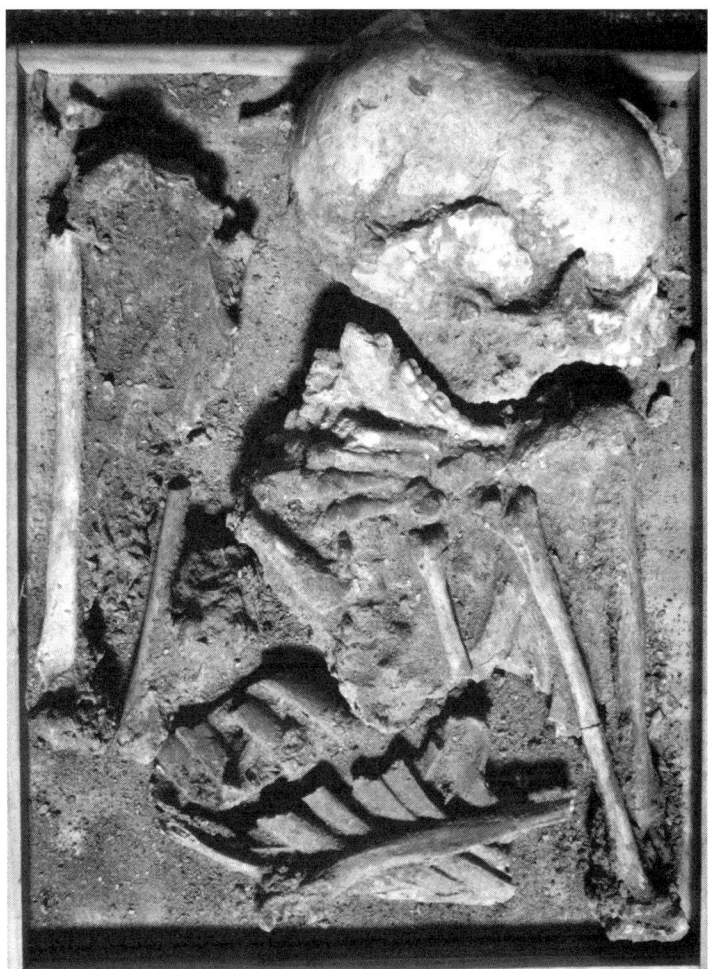

9.5. Overall view of Amoreira 7 photographed in the MGS in 1989 by Lubell. Note that ulna was already displaced in comparison to the original photo made in the field.

Ferreira describes it as "*muito escangalhado*" (very broken up); Cardoso and Rolão 1999/2000, 216). The skull, left first rib, left scapula, and left humerus are in anatomical position in such a way as to suggest dorsal decubitus. Two hand phalanges are attached to the mandible, which has fallen onto the left shoulder. The skull is crushed and the prominent right mastoid process of the temporal bone is almost on top of the mandible. The manubrium and corpus sterni are attached to a rib. Several of the right ribs are held together by the breccia.

Burial Position for Skeletons 7 and 8. Skeletons 7 and 8 represent two apparently synchronously buried individuals. When Veiga Ferreira mentioned their discovery on February 13, 1962, he spoke of two skeletons, male and female in the same *cova*, which can be translated here as "a

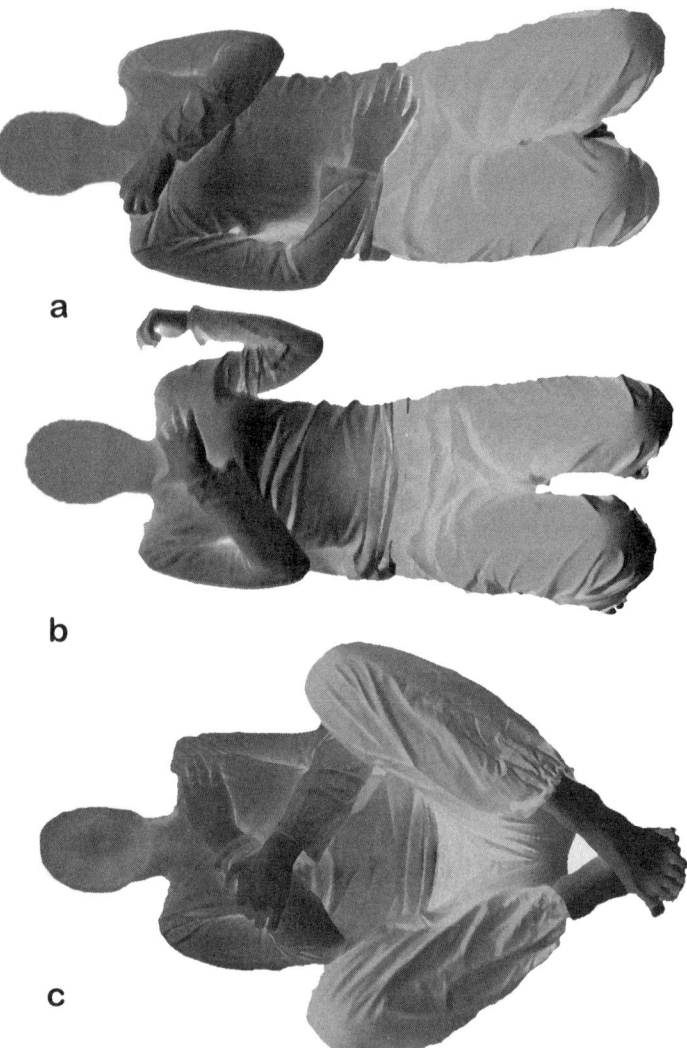

a

b

c

9.6. (a) Reconstruction of the position of Amoreira 7 based on the photo by Lubell taken in 1989 and the drawing and photo by Veiga Ferreira (Cardoso and Rolão 1999/2000). The legs were drawn toward the pelvis, knees flexed and perpendicular to the body. Position of the arms is different from the burial 8. (b) Reconstruction of the position of Amoreira 8 based on bones preserved in breccia and the drawing and photo by Veiga Ferreira (Cardoso and Rolão 1999/2000). The position is similar to the skeleton 7 for the legs; arms are positioned differently. (c) Reconstruction of the position of Amoreira 12 based on bones preserved in breccia and the drawing and photo by Veiga Ferreira (Cardoso and Rolão 1999/2000). The cranio-caudal constriction is evident, but more space is allowed laterally. Arms are positioned differently than in other burials.

hollow." The photograph and the drawing in the Veiga Ferreira archives show two individuals in the same pit, positioned in dorsal decubitus, with legs drawn toward the chest and with post-depositional movement that caused the legs of both individuals, but especially 7, to collapse toward the left side of the body (Figure 9.6a). While preservation issues (neither of the skeletons has tibiae, and only 7 has the right femur) prevent a thorough reconstruction of the position, the photo by Veiga Ferreira (Cardoso and Rolão 1999/2000, 215, fig. 50) shows that the long bones of Skeleton 8 were upright or oblique to the ground, which is consistent with feet drawn toward the pelvis and knees up and flexed (Figure 9.6b). In fact, the photograph and sketch both show that the Skeleton 8 knee region must have been sheared away, exactly as occurred at Moita do Sebastião (Jackes et al., chap. 10 in this volume), suggesting that excavation was too hurried.

It is likely that the position of Skeleton 7 was the same, with strongly flexed knees. However, after decomposition there was displacement of the Skeleton 7 right knee toward the left and the right knee toward the ground, so that the femur came to lie over the tibia and the fibula. From the position of the right femur, with the tibia and fibula showing hyperflexion, we can conclude that the foot was drawn very close in to the pelvis. This position is noted by Veiga Ferreira as *"pés debaixo das pernas"* (feet underneath the legs) (Cardoso and Rolão 1999/2000, 216). The way the humeri are positioned indicates that the bodies were placed next to each other; the right humerus of Skeleton 7 is parallel and in close proximity to the left humerus of Skeleton 8. While the complete lack of space between the humeri might suggest that the burials were not synchronous (since even a very thin arm would have created some empty spaces after the decomposition of the soft tissue), complete lack of space between the two could also have resulted from a post-decompositional movement with a slight rolling over of the humerus of Skeleton 7. However, this is not evidenced by the bones. Rather, the shoulder girdles of both skeletons show constriction. Very limited depositional space and "effect of the wall" (Duday 2006) are evident in the thoracic cage of Skeleton 7. Ribs are slumped downward and slightly more to the left part of the body, and the arms line the thorax with no post-decompositional rotation. An abrupt change in the orientation of the lower vertebrae is consistent with this interpretation, as the abdominal cavity would have created more empty space for the movement of the bones. The photograph (Cardoso and Rolão 1999/2000, 215, fig. 50) also shows that there is no splaying of the pelvic girdle, even though hyperflexed legs would induce splaying if any movement were possible. Overall, there is a strong indication of a very restrictive burial space at the level of the thorax and of the pelvis. While the two individuals are in close proximity, there is no intermixing of the bones.

The space allocated to the upper body of Skeleton 8 was slightly more generous, especially on the left side of the body, allowing for more significant movement of the left side of the thorax, splaying of the coxal bones, and more substantial dislocation of the thoracic spine. The curvature of the spine, the slumping of the ribs, and general constriction of the thoracic cage of Skeleton 7 all suggest that Skeleton 8 was deposited first in dorsal decubitus, with more constricted space on the right side of the body. While synchronous burial is possible, we cannot rule out a diachronous burial, in which case a good indicator for the mourners of the exact position of the previous burial would have been needed. In the case of a diachronous burial of Skeleton 7, we can suggest that it happened relatively shortly after the death of individual 8, and that the Skeleton 8 burial pit could have been extended to include the body of individual 7. The same position was practiced in both interments.

Skeletons 7 and 8 are recorded on the composite plan as lying on deposits 2.30 meters below the surface. The two burials lay at a location where the original surface was around 19.5 meters above sea level (Jackes, Alvim, and Cunha, in press), and were therefore lying at a height of just over 17 meters above sea level. There can be little doubt that the two skeletons lay well below the disconformity in association with either the yellow sands or the lenses of crushed shells. The description of Skeleton 8 above suggests that the matrix was well consolidated and rich in carbonates.

Skeletons 9 and 10. These two skeletons are not identified as such within the MSG collections. Burials 9 and 10 lay 1.8 meters deep in P24–P25 and N22–N23 according to the composite plan, in which they are both illustrated as lying on their backs. Skeleton 9 appears to have the arms lying alongside the body and the legs slightly flexed at the knees. Skeleton 10 has the right arm lying by the side of the body and the left forearm resting across the thorax. The legs are flexed, but not tightly, and they have fallen to the left.

Site reconstruction allows us to specify that Skeleton 9, and no doubt 10 as well, lay below the black earth in the lower level (22/30), described as gray deposits, with charcoal and river pebbles in places; in the region of Skeleton 9, true breccia ("true" meaning cemented and white) had occasionally developed (Roche 1967, 245, 248). It is presumed that the

skeletons were excavated at the end of the 1962 field season since the 1963 excavations appear to have started in the next line of squares to the west (N26, P26). The pattern of digging at the end of the 1962 season appears to have been slightly unsystematic since there is a mention of finishing OP, which is where Skeleton 9 would have been, on February 16, whereas the excavation of the deposits containing Skeleton 10 should have been completed long before. Nevertheless, it is recorded that the work in MN 22–23 began on February 17. The record for February 20, 1962, is incomplete since there is—without context—a note "hand in reasonable condition, feet under the legs." This was at the end of the season and at that time Veiga Ferreira (Cardoso and Rolão 1999/2000, 216) was concentrating on screening, cleaning the deposits containing shells, and making sure that the profiles were ready (no doubt for plotting). The work at this time was complicated by the need to remove Skeleton 6 from the profile before the end of the excavation season.

Skeleton 11. A child. In the field journal, Veiga Ferreira mentions that a very fragmented child's skeleton was found in square O27 on October 24, 1963: "*encontramos um esqueleto de creanca muito esmagado*" (we encountered a very crushed skeleton of a child) (Cardoso and Rolão 1999/2000, 220). We have already dealt with Skeletons 2 and 3, the subadults in the terra preta. Apart from those remains, additional children were present in the Amoreira collection at the MSG in 2006. They were contained in boxes marked 80.162.79 and 80.221, mixed with the adult remains.

Child 1. In box 80.162.79, we recorded an extra calvarium of an adult and, adhering to it by breccia, three postcranial fragments of a child, including a distal right humerus for which we can estimate an age of 2–4 years. In box 80.221 there were also subadult fragments, brecciated and adhering to adult bones; one set of them can be given an age of around three years, based on mandibular and maxillary bones and dentition. A few additional postcranial remains are also included. We may assume, then, that these bones together represent remains of one child.

Child 2. Box 80.221 contained a further child represented only by a broken mandible. Although clearly from a brecciated level, the mandible is clean enough for us to identify the dentition of a child of about 18 months of age. The adult remains associated with these subadult fragments would have certainly been recognized by excavators, making it very unlikely that these bones represent Skeleton 11.

We will discuss and identify the associated adult bones below.

We are left with no subadult candidates for Skeleton 11 within the MSG collections seen in 2006.

No depth below surface is given for Skeleton 11, but as it was found before the adjacent skeletons (Skeletons 15 and 16), it is obvious that it lay at a slightly higher level than others in the area. Indeed, Veiga Ferreira speaks of it as being found in "the breccia which we are calling the upper layer" (*camada superior*; Cardoso and Rolão 1999/2000, 220). Square O27 at this level is described as having compact, light-colored deposits that were quite hard but contained little in the way of artifacts.

Although using the same terms as those from the 1930s, when the terms *superior*, *middle*, and *lower* beds were used, Veiga Ferreira's similar terms (e.g., Cardoso and Rolão 1999/2000, 222, *camada superior*, *camada intérmedia*, and *camada inferior* or *camada de base*) did not have the same referents. It is clear that the "upper level" did not refer to the superficial layer; in the context of Skeleton 11, Veiga Ferreira speaks of "the breccia which we are calling the upper layer" (Cardoso and Rolão 1999/2000, 220) and then continues on to describe the next level down as being the base of the midden sitting directly on the terrace sands. However, at one point Veiga Ferreira discussed finishing the *camada de terra negra* and starting on the camada intermédia (Cardoso and Rolão 1999/2000, 222), so his use of terms was not completely consistent. What is particularly interesting is that he described the "upper level" (camada superior) as having beds of *Scrobicularia plana* in close proximity to Skeleton 11 (Cardoso and Rolão 1999/2000, 220). The presence of numerous *Scrobicularia plana* in the lower level was also recorded by the excavators during the 1931 field season (Cardoso and Rolão 1999/2000, 161); however, they are present in the upper levels as well. In the excavations in 2001–2003, they were recovered in concentrations starting at 50 centimeters below the present-day surface.

Skeletons 12 (Domingo) and 13 (Antonio). We have just discussed subadult material stored in two boxes marked 80.162.79 and 80.221. We will now move on to the adult material contained in these two boxes. The more complete of the two adults in box 80.221 could be identified as Skeleton 12 based on the position of its femora. The second individual does not match either individual 12 or 13 and will be discussed later. Box 80.162.79 also contained two adult individuals. The more complete individual is easily identified as Skeleton 13 on the basis of the reconstructed position, and a skull from the box with associated dentition can be matched to the photograph of Skeleton 13. The additional adult is represented by a calotte associated with the

remains of the youngest child described above under the heading "Skeleton 11." This skull cap does not match Skeleton 12 and will be discussed later.

Skeletons 12 and 13 were found in the same area in squares KL26–27. The drawing and the photos taken by Veiga Ferreira (Cardoso and Rolão 1999/2000, 220, 223, figs. 54 and 55) suggest that the burial of Skeleton 12 disturbed the earlier burial of Skeleton 13 below the pelvic girdle.

Skeleton 12. The individual is relatively gracile, probably an adult female who was fairly young, in that the broken femoral head shows no signs of trabecular bone loss and still exhibits a faint epiphyseal line. The left clavicle, in association with a scapular fragment, is compatible with a dorsal decubitus burial posture. The femoral head in the acetabulum, with the distal end of the femur oriented cranially, is in accordance with knees hyperflexed toward the chest in dorsal decubitus, and might have splayed out toward the left and right sides of the body in accordance with the images available to us from Veiga Ferreira's records. The right proximal ulna and radius are cemented in breccia with three proximal and two intermediate phalanges, indicating placement of the left hand on the right forearm. This is observable in the field drawing by Veiga Ferreira, supporting our identification of the burial (Figure 9.6c).

The additional individual in the same box shows substantial duplication of elements with both Skeletons 12 and 13 and is generally more robust. Elements present include the right scapula, left humerus, right proximal radius and ulna fragments, femoral heads, metatarsals, metacarpals and phalanges, and a small fragment of coxal in association with sacrum. Post-excavation mixing seems the only explanation for these additional bones.

Skeleton 13. The individual consists of an almost complete thorax, skull, and upper limbs, and an incomplete pelvis; no elements of the lower limbs are present. A very broad sciatic notch and the presence of a preauricular sulcus (Bruzek 2002), a small mastoid process, and a relatively sharp supra-orbital margin (Ascadi and Nemeskeri 1970) indicate a female. Based on available elements for age estimation, the individual was mature, but not senile; the epiphyseal union is complete; the individual displayed very extensive occlusal wear, especially on the anterior teeth. On the auricular surface, all billowing was obliterated and a degree of lipping was visible, indicating a mature adult individual (Buckberry and Chamberlain 2002). Other aspects of the auricular surface, such as micro- and macro-porosity, were obscured by breccia. The

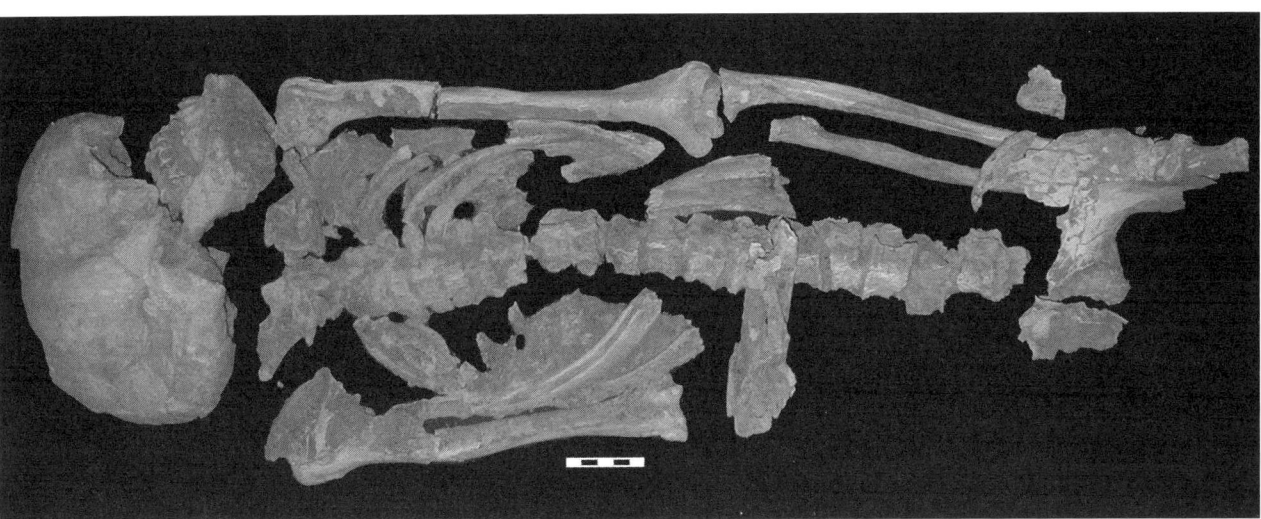

9.7. Reconstruction of the position of Amoreira 13 from bones preserved in MSG. Except for the position of the left forearm, all other bones perfectly match the photo by Veiga Ferreira taken during the excavations (Cardoso and Rolão 1999/2000).

individual showed a rare condition known as "split atlas," the non-fusion of both anterior and posterior arches (Bonneville et al. 2004). Close inspection of the unfused edges showed no evidence of fracture, healing, lesions, or discoloration, and since the neural canal and edges of the unfused lamina appeared normal, the indication is of a rare congenital abnormality in the Skeleton 13 atlas.

The position of the rib cage and the spine is consistent with dorsal decubitus (Figure 9.7). The left ribs are brecciated to the endo-thoracic portion of the scapula. Both right and left ribs are slumped inferiorly within the body cavity with no splaying, indicating the constriction of the thorax, more noticeable on the left side of the body. The right humerus is in anatomical connection with the right scapula, with the humeral head moved toward the acromion, indicating constriction at the level of the right shoulder. The right forearm is slightly raised above the level of the rest of the burial in supination and slight flexion, and the second metacarpal lies below the radius. The axis is attached to the superior portion of the scapular spine; unexpectedly, the dens is facing caudally and anteriorly, indicating movement of the head. The head is smashed and its original position was impossible to reconstruct, except for the white residue that indicates that the right side was visible during excavation. Veiga Ferreira notes that "Today there was a horrible storm / and we could not work in the field / The skeletons were protected by / an oil cloth (*oleado*)" (Cardoso and Rolão 1999/2000, 222). The right side of the pelvis is not preserved, and the splaying of the pelvis on the left side is substantial. There are no lower limb elements, in

contrast to other Amoreira burials that seem to be interred on their backs with strongly flexed legs. If this individual was interred in a similar way, one would expect that at least some elements of the leg/foot would be found pasted to the rest of the body.

It is possible to establish the stratigraphic position of Skeletons 12 and 13 (on the basis of Cardoso and Rolão 1999/2000, 215, 223, figs. 50 and 55). Both skeletons lay on the basal sands at just less than 2.5 meters below the surface; we know that the skeletons were discovered when the excavators were at the level of the midden base. The burials are described as being in a small pit above the sand (Cardoso and Rolão 1999/2000, 222). The fact that there are no elements of Skeleton 13 preserved below the pelvis, and that the bones in the putative burial 12, as preserved in the MSG, did not include any additional remains that could be associated with the burial 13, strongly suggests that the burials were diachronous and that the burial 12 was dug into burial 13.

With regard to the lack of lower limb elements for Skeleton 13, we note that in 2002 several fragmented human bones were unearthed while clearing eroded deposits within Roche's trench in the vicinity of K24. These bones, both left and right sides, clearly brecciated, included femoral fragments, metatarsals, and pedal phalanges (Laboratório de Paleodemografia e Paleopatologia 2003). Other material consisted only of long bone fragments. While we cannot ascertain this, it is possible that lower limb elements of Skeleton 13 had been displaced deeper into the deposits when Skeleton 12 was interred and had eroded downslope after Roche's team missed finding them at the very end of an excavation season made extremely difficult by torrential rains (Cardoso and Rolão 1999/2000, 224).

Skeleton 14. There is no mention of burial 14 in the Veiga Ferreira field notes, and no drawing and no photos were provided. We know that the weather was extremely bad at the time when the skeleton was most likely found, which must have been about November 8, 1963. On the composite plan, the burial is noted at the margin of the excavated trench in the southwest corner of square J28. There is no depth below surface noted and no remains are visible on the photo of that corner that depicts Skeletons 12 and 13 and shows the trench profiles (Cardoso and Rolão 1999/2000, 223, fig. 55). The photograph shows deposits in that corner that would have had to be removed in order to expose the skull. This suggests that Skeleton 14 must have lain at about the same depth as Skeletons 12 and 13. The skull may well have been covered over again because of the weather and because the excavation season was coming to an end. There is no record that it was excavated at the beginning of the next season (though Skeletons 15 and 16 were). The composite plan provides proof that a skull and possibly some elements of the brachial complex were discovered. The skull without dentition and with two cervical vertebrae cemented to it in breccia from box 180.2 could have belonged to this individual. It was tentatively identified as male based on a strong mastoid process and general robusticity. It is compressed laterally. No other indication of burial position was available.

While there is no evidence that the skull of Skeleton 14 was removed, it is reasonable to identify an isolated skull in the MSG collection as that of individual 14. The skull is drawn on the composite plan facing away from the excavated trench, toward the southwest. The postcranial bones must have lain beyond the trench wall, and the decision not to extend the excavation into this corner during what were the last few days of the full-scale Amoreira excavation campaign is understandable.

The 2000 excavation in that corner would have exposed the remnants of the Roche profile (Jackes, Alvim, and Cunha, in press) from around 70 centimeters west to about 30 centimeters east of the location of Skeleton 14. The 2000 excavation extended well down into the sterile sands, probably to within a short distance of the location of Skeleton 14, if not as far east as that point. Since no postcranial elements were found in the area, any extant bones of Skeleton 14 remain unexcavated (a visit by MJ to the site has confirmed that it is very likely that part of Skeleton 14 remains in situ).

Skeletons 15 (Santos Junior) and 16 (Maria Jose Bexiga). Two skeletons in a very bad state were found on October 25, 1963, at the bottom of the excavations in O27 and O28 (Cardoso and Rolão 1999/2000, 220). The excavators were moving south across the trench, and no doubt because the skeletons were in the trench walls, the bones were left in the ground at the northern edge of the trench. The two skeletons were covered in oilcloth because of wet weather on November 9, 1963, and on November 11 the excavators went back and began working in O28 and P28 again, excavating down through the black deposits by the next day. It seems likely that they in fact left the skeletons, because of torrential rain, until the next excavation season. They were working at Arruda that next year, but on November 2, 1964, Veiga Ferreira returned to Amoreira and drew and described the two burials (Cardoso and Rolão 1999/2000, 224). While the drawing is not reproduced, a partial description under the drawing is recorded that seems to refer to one of the two individuals: "the left leg has a tibia and the fibula broken and then fused. It is a very rare find." Veiga Ferreira goes on to say, "the poor fellow would have had one leg shorter than the other and limped, because the fusion was not aligned properly" (Cardoso and Rolão 1999/2000, 226). Among the material housed in the MSG there is one individual that might conform to this description. These bones were found in box 80.187. The box contained the remains of two individuals mostly represented by the bones of the lower extremities. Only some fragments of the ribs and the left tibia and fibula were cemented by breccia, and they do not give us sufficient information to attempt reconstruction of the burial.

The skeletons lay within squares O28 and P28 according to the composite plan. It is obvious that they were found against the trench wall, just as Skeleton 14 had been. However, the trench was extended to the west for a short distance. In the case of Skeleton 15, it extended through the trench wall and was probably excavated out in the same way as for Skeleton 6. We are told (Cardoso and Rolão 1999/2000, 220) that the skeletons were found the day after Skeleton 11 was found. They were encountered on the day when breccia was being removed to the midden base level and the day before Roche drew a profile of the squares. We can assume that they lay at the very bottom of the midden.

All indications are, then, that these skeletons were found almost as deep as Skeletons 6, 14, 12, and 13. In the case of Skeletons 12 and 13, the photography (Cardoso and Rolão 1999/2000, 223, fig. 55) allows us to recreate the depth below surface as just less than 2.5 meters. No doubt this is also true of Skeletons 15 and 16. Since the height above sea level is recorded on a contour map (Roche 1951,[2] consistent with IGP 1960, which shows the Mendes Corrêa trench, and with IGeoE 2007), it is possible to specify that the mound surface above those skeletons would have been at about 19.5 meters above sea level. Thus, again, the skeletons lay at close to 17 meters above sea level.

Skeleton 17 is mentioned briefly on November 10, 1964, as having been removed together with Skeleton 16. The next page of the journal also contained the drawing of the individual, which was unfortunately not reproduced (Cardoso and Rolão 1999/2000, 228). Skeleton 17 seems to have been of an adult female, lying in dorsal decubitus. The cranium was three-quarters complete, with the maxilla fragmented. Veiga Ferreira continues with his description by saying that the legs were strongly flexed and the arms were extended with the hands over the ilia. The clavicle, scapulae, and ribs were in position, and the vertebral column was complete. There is also a mention of ochre that was packed up with the bones when they were readied for transport to Lisbon. Evidence of ochre staining was found only on an isolated fragment of frontal that was packed with relatively worn teeth in box 80.39.9.

The skeleton was lower than the base of the midden, about 30 centimeters into the layer of yellow sand; its position was thus comparable with those previously found in the 27 and 28 lines of squares. According to Roche and Veiga Ferreira (1967, 25, fig. 3), the 1964 work was in the area of O28 and P28. We know from the field notes that N26–27 and O26–27 had been completed in 1963; therefore it follows that P26 and P27 must have been completed in 1964. This would help us date the composite plan to the end of the 1963 season because P26, 27, and 28 are shown as unexcavated; the later plot (Roche and Veiga Ferreira 1967, 25, fig. 3) shows them as excavated. The suggestion is that Skeleton 17 extended into P28 and could not be drawn in 1963.

Our dating of the composite plan (Cardoso and Rolão 1999/2000, 209, fig. 45) to the end of the 1963 excavation season accords perfectly with our re-creation of the 1964 work, including the resolution of the inconsistency between the composite plan and the published site plan of Roche and Veiga Ferreira (1967). Further work was undertaken at Amoreira in 1966 (Cardoso and Rolão 1999/2000, 237). There is a note that between L and P in the profile there was a surface that was particularly rich in lithics and fauna. Since it appears from the composite plan and from Roche and Veiga Ferreira (1967) that about 75 centimeters of J28 to N28 were already dug by 1963, we can assume that in the first week of November 1966, the only work that was done was the plotting of that profile by Jean Roche. However, a visit to Amoreira by MJ in October 2010 showed that an unrecorded excavation of a 5- by 7.5-meter area of a parallel, southern Amoreira trench had been undertaken; this excavation must date from the 1960s since that area was left unexcavated in the 1930s (Roche 1951).

BURIAL RECONSTRUCTION

Burial reconstruction can only be partial for this site. Skeletons in the black earth lack any burial information, as no breccia has preserved their depositional connections. Of the skeletons we could identify, sufficient information can be gathered for burials 6, 7, 8, 12, and 13.

Skeletons 6, 7, and 8 were buried in what seems to be a common position for the three Muge Mesolithic sites: the individuals are in dorsal decubitus with feet drawn toward the pelvis, with knees flexed. The space accorded, however, differs substantially among the three burials. Since we do not have precise spatial information, it is hard to say whether this was guided by reasons other than burial ritual itself. For example, specific conditions of the soil may have been a limiting factor, but the homogeneity of the deposits makes this an unlikely explanation.

Individual 6 was buried in dorsal decubitus with knees drawn up toward the chest. Subsequent to the decomposition of the soft tissues, the knees collapsed on the left side of the body very close to each other (Figure 9.3a). The position of the shoulder girdle, the slumping of the ribs downward, and the slight rotation of the right humerus all indicate constricted space, very likely a restricted oval structure with evidence of the "effect of the wall" (Duday 1985, 2006; Duday et al. 1990; Roksandic 2002) on the right side of the body and at the level of the shoulder girdle. Cranio-caudal constriction is evident in the position of the skull, which had slumped slightly onto the chest and was rotated to the left (Cardoso and Rolão 1999/2000, 218–19, figs. 51 and 53). Similarly, both distal tibiae were aligned with the ischium, as were the talus and navicular of the left leg (Figure 9.3a). A substantial cranio-caudal constriction would have been necessary to account for the feet located very close to the pelvis (Figure 9.3b). This is difficult in the case of an in-flesh primary burial with all of the soft tissue still present, as seen in the reconstruction (Figure 9.4), where the feet are suspended in the air because of the presence of soft tissue. Furthermore, it is likely that the pit was covered by some architectural element that provided additional constriction and prevented immediate infilling; a perishable material such as hides, cloth, or bark could have been used.

Burials 7 and 8 suggest substantially lesser cranio-caudal constriction than burial 6, with a relatively commodious oval pit for burial 8 (Figure 9.6). For Skeleton 8, there is no evidence that the feet were drawn toward the pelvis. Indeed, there is strong evidence that the legs more or less stayed in their original position upon interment. The knees were not drawn toward the chest but they were perpendicular to the body (which resulted in their breakage during excavations). That they did not slump indicates that they were immediately covered with sediment.

As discussed above, the burial of Skeleton 7 seems to be an afterthought. It could be that the individual died relatively shortly after individual 8 and, the site of the first burial still being visible, that it was extended to accommodate the other individual. Such a conclusion is based on the lack of overlap between any of the bones, on the much more substantial constriction of the thoracic cage of Skeleton 7, and on the fact that the thoracic vertebrae have been substantially dislocated in relation to the lumbars. This could be explained by the somewhat laterally inclined thorax of Skeleton 7 that filled in a much smaller but still oval initial space. The limited burial pit for Skeleton 7 is evidenced by the constriction of the shoulders and slumping of the right thorax toward the left side of the body and downward slumping of the left ribs. It seems that the right side had been slightly elevated, while the left side followed an outline of a preexisting oval construction. The inclination of the head toward the thorax supports this conclusion.

In Skeleton 7, the feet were drawn toward the pelvic basin as in Skeleton 8, with little cranio-caudal constriction but a substantial right lateral constriction and no immediate infilling. This resulted in the left femur's collapsing onto the tibia and fibula, and the right leg's collapsing across the left. The dislocation of the spine just below the thoraco-lumbar transition also suggests postmortem movement of the body into a small, deeper pocket within the burial pit.

The position of Skeleton 13 is unusual, but not unprecedented in the Muge series (Figure 9.6c). The position of the shoulder girdle, the arms, and the ribs indicate a very laterally constricted space, accentuated by the inclination of the head toward the left shoulder clearly visible in the photo of the burial (Cardoso and Rolão 1999/2000, 221, fig. 54). The burial is disturbed below the pelvis and no elements of legs were encountered. If the knees were drawn toward the chest or feet drawn toward the pelvis, we should have encountered some of these elements in the MSG collection for the burial. We can envisage a narrow and elongated pit, with a substantial effect of the wall on both the left and

the right sides; wrapping is not excluded as a possible explanation, although rotation of the humeri is missing.

Skeleton 12 appears to have been buried over Skeleton 13. Burial 12 presents a variation on the theme of an oval burial pit; here there is substantial cranio-caudal constriction and little lateral constriction, the bones slumped to both sides of the body. It is likely that the knees were initially slightly apart (Figure 9.6c), unlike burial 6. The burial position is unusual for other Muge sites in having both hands high on the thorax and the legs splayed out, having fallen back onto either side of the body. However, this position is perfectly matching the burial position of the child excavated in 2000 at the bottom of the sequence, the child no doubt lying within a meter of the original location of Skeleton 12. This splaying of the legs is also seen in one of the Amoreira skeletons retrieved in the 1930s, lying perhaps nine meters away from Skeleton 12 (Jackes, Alvim, and Cunha, in press).

The few burials that could be reconstructed show both uniformity and variation; constricted oval burial pits are encountered in four out of five analyzed burials as well as in the burials recovered during 2000 and 2001. Wrapping into hides, bark, or some other perishable material is likely in burials 6 and 13.

Apart from the later burials in the black earth, above the disconformity, all the burials discussed here were at much the same level, both absolutely, in relation to sea level, and relatively, in relation to the bottom of the midden at the juncture with the sterile sands of the original mound. The situation is very similar to other Muge sites (Jackes and Alvim 2006; Jackes and Meiklejohn 2004). While general similarities and differences among sites have been examined (Jackes, in press), further work is required, especially in relation to burial modes.

The excavators noted indications of shallow grave pits dug into the basal sands, but there is no mention of deep excavations into the deposits for interment of the dead. This can be confirmed in relation to Skeleton 6 for which we have photographs and a detailed profile at the level of the skull. Skeleton 6 is associated with a few pebbles and a slight indication in the stratigraphic section of infill in an extremely shallow pit.

We also have some indications of covering of graves with perishable items such as wood or hide, and can imagine that the graves would then be further covered—and marked—by a mounding of sand, fine sediment, shells, or a combination of these. The sand would have eroded away over time, leaving no archaeological indication of grave structure.

That carbonates were included in the grave fillings is clear from the development of light breccia on skeletons, for example Skeleton 6. And yet, this breccia is not of the extremely hard white breccia type noted by Roche (1964/1965, 1967), but described as occurring in the form of "ribbons" or "nodules." In Roche's profiles of the trench, we see no "true" breccia (hard, white ribbons or nodules) in the vicinity of Skeleton 6. It can be observed only in M25 and N25, western walls in an area where no burials were found. In Amoreira then, we do not have evidence of close association of "true" breccia with burials, but we have clear indications that consolidated matrix formed on skeletons lying on, or in, the basal sands. It is that consolidated matrix that has facilitated recognition of some of the individuals excavated in the 1960s by Roche and Veiga Ferreira.

We are separated in time by almost half a century from the excavations of Roche and Veiga Ferreira at Amoreira. And yet we were able to reconstruct several of the burials from that site on the basis of material preserved in the MSG and the recently published field notebooks maintained by Veiga Ferreira. While he noted a number of important observations on the burials, there was not a recognition of the full potential of human skeletons in the reconstruction of past behavior. Curatorial issues with the osteological materials arose immediately after excavation; the loss and mixing of bones and our lack of access to the full excavation records require us to undertake a tedious and detailed recording of each individual fragment. Breccia is often considered to be a nuisance obstructing anthropological analysis, but here it has helped with identification and has allowed us to verify some details of burial ritual. Although our information is partial, it is of great help in the interpretation of the Muge burial sites. Together with a forthcoming analysis of the burials from the 1930s excavations at Amoreira, and continuing study of Arruda and Moita, our examination of the 1960s Amoreira material will shed light on the ritual behavior of the Mesolithic inhabitants of the Muge valley.

ACKNOWLEDGMENTS

Both MR and MJ are very grateful to Dr. Miguel Magalhães Ramalho and Sr. José António Anacleto at the Museu Geológico, Laboratório Nacional de Energia e Geologia, Lisbon, for access to and assistance with the Muge collections over the years. MJ wishes to thank Pedro Alvim for his involvement with her work on Amoreira and David Lubell for invaluable continuing assistance. Thanks to Cleia Detry for a visit to Amoreira in October 2010. MR is grateful to students who participated in the University of Toronto Experiential Study Abroad program and acknowledges the University of Toronto Connaught Foundation, the University of Winnipeg, and the SSHRC for financial support.

NOTES

1. In a message dated January 2001, subsequently published as Cunha and Cardoso (2002/2003).

2. Cardoso and Rolão 1999/2000, 207, fig. 44, is also consistent but shows the top of the mound at an erroneous height. The correct figure was published in Roche (1951) as 22.2 meters above sea level.

CHAPTER TEN

NEW PHOTOGRAPHIC EVIDENCE ON THE 1954 EXCAVATIONS AT MOITA DO SEBASTIÃO, MUGE, PORTUGAL

Mary Jackes, Pedro Alvim, José Antonio Anacleto, and Mirjana Roksandic

SUMMARY

Four enlargements of previously unpublished photographs provide a great deal of additional information on a Muge Mesolithic site. We show that these images are of Moita do Sebastião and were taken during the 1954 field season. The four skeletons in the photographs are identified using details from contemporary field notes and inventories of bones made during excavation and in the 1960s. Additional information comes from examination of the skeletons themselves. Our limited prior knowledge of these four skeletons means that the photographs are of great importance.

The newly discovered photographs are used in conjunction with published materials to provide background for a discussion of the nature of the Moita sediments and mortuary ritual. We propose that the majority of the individuals excavated in the 1950s were buried with knees flexed up within cranio-caudally constricted shallow pits. Fill must have been placed immediately within the graves and built up into mounds, so that the flexed position of the legs was to some extent maintained, despite movements resulting from decomposition.

INTRODUCTION

In 2004 several photographic enlargements were discovered in the Museu Geológico of the Laboratório Nacional de Energia e Geologia, Lisbon. They had been set aside to be discarded since they were unlabeled and the image surfaces had been damaged by insects.

Four images were found, each measuring 23.5 by 17.5 centimeters and showing the excavation of an archaeological site containing human skeletons. One of the images showed the skeletons indistinctly in the background. An archaeological trench was in the foreground and a building, agricultural machinery, and a car could be seen beyond the skeletons.

Although these images have never been published before, and there is no published photograph of any of the skeletons shown, we can identify the photographs to site, to year of excavation, and to the identity of the skeletons. The images provide us with new knowledge of the site, of the skeletons, and of the history and circumstances of the excavation. Since the site is significant to European archaeology of the late Mesolithic, it is important that these images not be lost if we are to accurately reconstruct burial rituals at the Muge sites (see Roksandic and Jackes [chap. 9] and Valente, Dean, and Carvalho [chap. 6] in this volume).

THE PHOTOGRAPHS

We assume that the photographs were prepared for use in a display at the Museu Geológico on burials from a Muge Mesolithic site by O. Veiga Ferreira (1917–1997), who was working for the Serviços Geológicos de Portugal in the 1950s and 1960s. During this period, in association with Abbé Jean Roche, he excavated at three Mesolithic sites: Moita do Sebastião, Cabeço da Arruda, and Cabeço da Amoreira. A general discussion of Muge dating, stable isotope analyses, site location and formation, and burial distribution and mortuary detail will be found in Jackes and Lubell (2012).

Figure 10.1 provides evidence that the site must be Moita do Sebastião, because there is no other Portuguese

10.1. Photograph 1 shows two burials in the background, close to a shed storing agricultural machinery.

Mesolithic site with skeletons upon which agricultural structures had been built. The other two Muge Mesolithic sites excavated during this period are quite different. The top of the mound at Moita had been bulldozed for construction of these buildings during the winter of 1951–1952, providing a plane surface for the excavations of 1952–1954. The present situation at the Muge sites still shows the clear contrast between the flat, denuded surface and now-ruined building at Moita, and the deep excavations into the vegetation-covered mounds at Amoreira and Arruda.

The building at Moita was under construction at the same time as the excavation there, that is, from 1952 to 1954. We have evidence from published photographs and from sketch maps (see, e.g., Cardoso and Rolão 1999/2000, figs. 25, 31, 32; Roche 1972a, plate 7.2) that the excavations had to be undertaken in close proximity to the buildings. The machine shown under the shelter of the building is some sort of combine harvester/thresher. This was not a fixed machine; it had large wheels at each end. Since the

adjacent Muge valley fields had been developed for rice cultivation, and the building was intended to serve as a rice processing plant, we conclude that the combine was used in rice cultivation. Veiga Ferreira wrote on May 13, 1954, of features beside the *debulhadora* (thresher) (Cardoso and Rolão 1999/2000, 192).

The date of the photograph can be tied down by reference to the car, which is an Opel Olympia Rekord, first released in March 1953. The photograph thus dates to the 1953 or the 1954 excavations—there were no excavations at Moita after June 1954. The car also gives us a rough estimate of scale, since the width of an Opel Olympia Rekord was 1.63 meters. From diagrams, aerial photographs, and a survey of the ruins undertaken by Alvim, we know that the width of the building shown here was close to seven meters to the far side of the pillar.

These four new images date to 1954, when excavations around the already-erected pillars took place in the northern part of the Moita site (Roche 1972a, 30, fig. 5). The footprint of the building (Jackes and Alvim 2006, 25, fig. 7B) transected only one trench of any depth and that was along the northern face of the excavation, where the 1880s archaeological trench was re-excavated in 1954. We know from the north-south section of the excavation (Roche 1972a, 32, fig. 6) that the deepest excavation in that portion of the site was the reopening of the 1880s trench, and that it was at least 30 centimeters deep. Photographs from June 1954 (Cardoso and Rolão 1999/2000, figs. 31 and 32) show that both the re-excavation and the new excavation extended under the northern wing of the new building. In May and June 1954, Veiga Ferreira expressed irritation that the pillars of the building damaged archaeological features and stated that they were excavating beside the pillars (e.g., May 14, 1954, and June 10, 1954) (Cardoso and Rolão 1999/2000, 194–95).

The combination of a trench and a building indicates that we see the northern part of the Moita site in 1954. The view is from a trench over an excavated area that is flat and featureless, and the camera records two skulls lying close together (a further shape, apparently a third skull, can just be discerned beyond these to the left when the image is enlarged). From these clues, we know that our viewpoint is neither from the west toward the building, nor from the south. We can only be looking from the north toward the western wing of the building. In the background, an excavator leaning on his shovel appears at the extreme upper right of Figure 10.1. He must be beside the consistently plotted hole number 66 (Roche 1972a, 98, fig. 25), which is also shown in a photograph (Roche 1972a, plate 8.2), beside the pillar on the right. Further evidence for the identity of the photograph is the pit, which had previously been dug into the trench wall on the left side of the image; a test pit (*sondage*) was dug at that point in 1953 (Roche 1972a, 30, fig. 5).

Figure 10.1 can provide us with more information. The size of the pick can be estimated from the fact that an identical tool was photographed (Cardoso and Rolão 1999/2000, fig. 39; note that the labels for this figure are reversed). The pick in that photograph lies beside Skeleton 12 and at the same angle as MT V. We have an idea of the mean size of Moita MT V in the Lisbon collection— the rounded mean physiological length is 58 millimeters (sd 2.9, n=12 adults). Denise Ferembach (1974, 121), who considered Moita 12 to be female, gives the mean overall length of female MT V as 56.3 millimeters. Based on these figures, the picks used at Moita were 30–40 centimeters long. Similar picks used in an excavation in western central Spain in 2010 consistently measured

33 centimeters. The 1885 trench shown here (see Jackes and Alvim 2006) was probably re-dug to slightly more than 40 centimeters.

Note that one skeleton—to the left—is oriented generally west to east. The other skeleton appears to have the back of the skull pointing straight to the north toward the camera position in Figure 10.1. Two skeletons lying in close proximity to each other and adjacent to an already erected building can only be those given the identifying numbers 30 and 32 (Roche 1972a, fig. 29). A further skeleton in close proximity would be Skeleton 33, a supposition supported by the fact that the skulls of 33 and 32 both lay directly toward magnetic north (Roche 1972a, fig. 30).

Figure 10.2 is a close-up of the two skeletons shown in the background in Figure 10.1. Photographs of these have never been published before, and the only information we have on them comes from sketches by Veiga Ferreira (Cardoso and Rolão 1999/2000) and inventories published by Roche (1972a) and Ferembach (1974). There is a problem, however; the numbers have been reversed in some sources.

It appears that on May 15, 1954, and May 18, 1954, Veiga Ferreira mistakenly changed 30 to 32 and 32 to 30 in his notebook (Cardoso and Rolão 1999/2000, 205, fig. 43). The evidence presented below confirms that the numbers used by Roche (1972a, 116, fig. 29) are also reversed.

Roche (1972a, 126, referring to *Sépulture* XXX) recorded notes on the skeleton identified in the caption for Figure 10.2 as 30, and we summarize his observations as follows:

Orientation north-west—south-east. The frontal is staved in, the nasal and orbital region crushed. Maxilla is complete. Complete vertebral column with remarkably well-preserved lumbars. Both arms lying straight by body, left hand missing, the bones of the right hand are slightly turned in. Innominates in good condition, the pubes are absent. No long bone shafts. The proximal femora are retained. The feet are almost intact.

Ferembach's (1974, 30) description of Skeleton 30 seems to agree, for example, vertebrae present, all forearm bones present in reasonable shape, right and left tarsals present. The discrepancy is only regarding Skeleton 30, where Roche notes that the sternum is absent, while Ferembach describes it as being present. Thus, the information from Roche and Ferembach correctly describes the skeleton on the right identified in the caption to Figure 10.2 as 30.

Skeleton 32 (in accordance with the caption for Figure 10.2) was recorded (Roche 1972a, 127–28, referring to *Sépulture* XXXII) in the following summarized notes:

10.2. Photograph 2 shows a close-up of the two skeletons that lay close to the agricultural machinery storage shed. Skeleton 30 is on the right and Skeleton 32 is on the left.

Skeleton has north-south orientation. The incisors lost, the clavicles displaced. The forearms are folded in slightly, with the hands on the pubis. The vertebral column is incomplete, with no lumbars. The innominates are badly damaged. A few fragments of feet only.

Roche is clearly describing the skeleton identified as 32 in Figure 10.2, as is Ferembach (1974, 30), although her inventory provides less detail. Nevertheless, she says that only the right fibula is present and that both forearms exist but are badly damaged. She makes no mention of vertebrae and describes only the left calcaneus. Thus, the information from both Roche and Ferembach is consistent with the photograph of the skeleton identified as 32 in the Figure 10.2 caption.

In 1984, Jackes visited the Museu de Antropologia e Pré-História Mendes Corrêa in Porto, where A. Huet Bacelar Gonçalves helped in an attempt to relocate Muge material that had been dispersed because of a fire ten years

previously. In 2010, Jackes revisited the museum and was able to see further material relocated since 1984. In 1984, it was recorded that lumbar vertebrae were complete only in Porto Moita Skeletons 3, 4, 10, 12, 13, and 30 and in an unnumbered specimen en bloc that had no skull and the hands crossed over L-5. Jackes suggested that this was Skeleton 5 (whose skull is kept in Lisbon). Therefore, what was labeled 30 in 1984 (but mixed up with 31, as described below) had complete lumbar vertebrae and both forearms present. The arms were complete enough to allow description of a traumatic abnormality of the right elbow. The skeleton with the complete vertebrae was 30 for Roche, and also for Ferembach, and was still labeled 30 in Porto in 1984. As we shall see later, Skeleton 33 also has lumbar vertebrae, but these are fragmented.

Veiga Ferreira's original sketch of 30 (with the number wrongly changed to 32), when compared with the new photograph, accords perfectly with the description by Roche (1972a) and with the skeleton present in Porto in

1984. Additional confirmation of the identity of 30 comes from Ferembach's (1974, 99) description of the mandible of 30 as possibly having an abscess and caries of the left first molar and perhaps of the left P4. Jackes, in 1984, described the left M1 as having two huge interproximal lesions, and the left P4 as reduced to the roots by a large carious lesion accompanied by an abscess. The dentition of Skeleton 30 can still be clearly identified, and the unusual flattening across the anterior maxillary teeth, seen in Figure 10.2, is evident.

What was the reason for this confusion? On May 13, 1954, Veiga Ferreira recorded the discovery of two skeletons that were said to be virtually destroyed. They would have been the first numbered skeletons of the 1954 season, Veiga Ferreira having recorded that 27 skeletons were found up to the end of the 1953 excavation period (Cardoso and Rolão 1999/2000, 192). However, no numbers were originally assigned to them and they were later described only as being indeterminable bone debris by Ferembach (1974, 30). Roche (1972b, 99, fig. 24) labeled them only with question marks, although in a publication of the same year (Roche 1972a, 116, fig. 29), he had noted them as 28 and 29.

On May 15, 1954, Veiga Ferreira wrote that new skeletons were found belonging to group 1, that is, the group of skeletons from previous excavations in the area, which, by 1954, was underneath the harvester in photograph 1 (see Figure 10.3). On the same day, when he drew the two skeletons whose numbers he changed between 30 and 32, he actually called them 28 and 30. On May 17, 1954, he again referred to 28 and 30 and the next day (May 18, 1954), he recorded finding a new skeleton near the "first two of this year" as though no other skeletons had been found. He thus ignored the "bone debris" skeletons. He sketched this new skeleton (33) together with the other in closest proximity to it (actually 30), and he labeled them 33 and 30 altered to 32 (actually, of course, 33 and 30). On May 19, 1954, he drew a skeleton that he labeled 31, but—in writing of it—he called it skeleton 29. It is clearly identifiable since he mentioned damage to the skull from a spade and he noted that it was found at the extreme end of the 1952 trench. It is the skeleton that came to be called 31.

Thus, the material called 28 and 29 was not originally given those numbers; it seems they were just indeterminate bones and there is no evidence that they were human.

10.3. Aerial photograph (Jackes and Alvim 2006, 25, fig. 7) showing the angle of sight for figure 10.1. The camera angle is indicated by the dashed white lines. The position of the "bone debris" is marked by X. Approximate cartographic north is indicated.

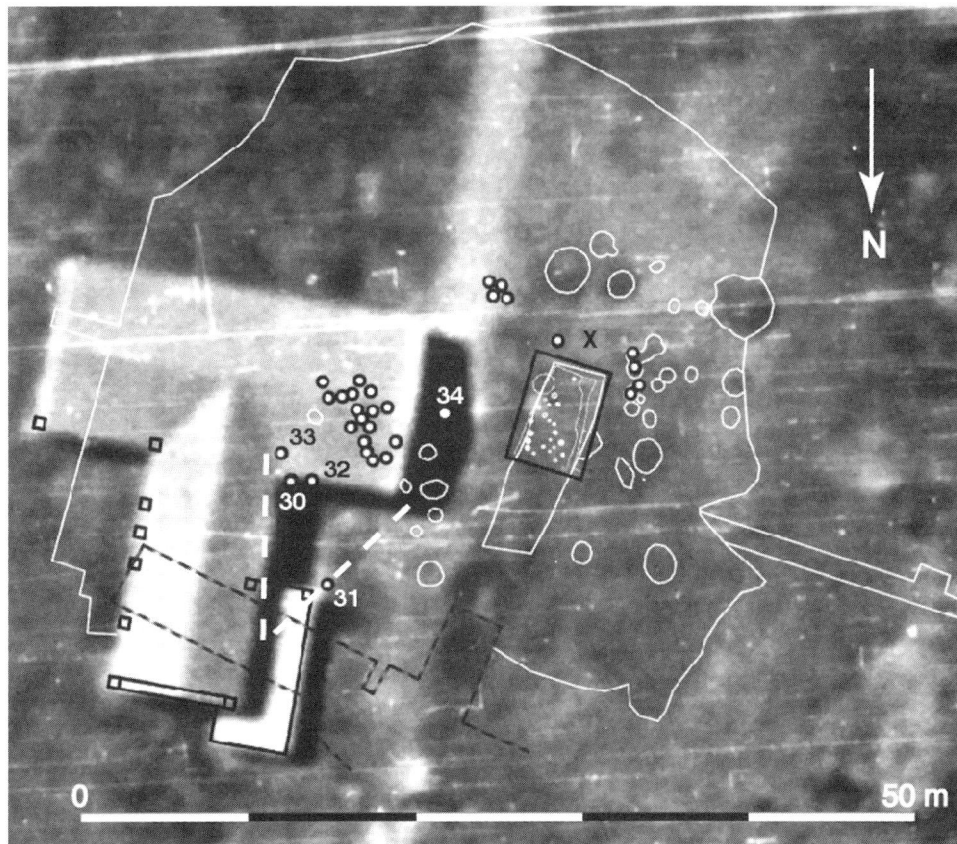

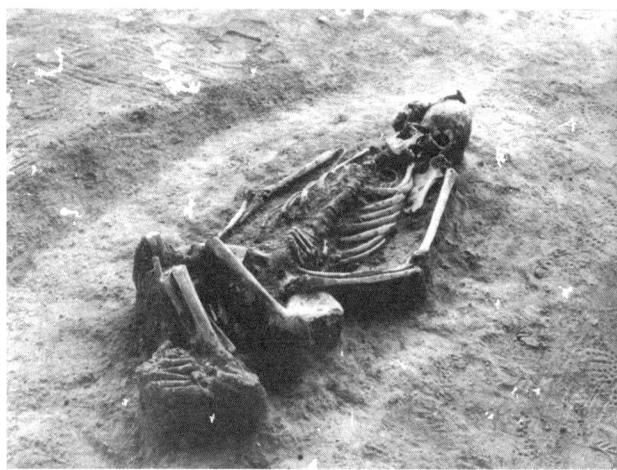

10.4. Photograph 3, Moita Skeleton 31.

10.5. Photograph 4, Moita Skeleton 33.

There was no material with those numbers in the Porto Museu de Antropologia e Pré-História Mendes Corrêa in 1984 and there is none now. The number 28 was originally given to Skeleton 32 and the number 29 was given to Skeleton 31. Apparently there was continuing doubt over whether 28 and 29 were human skeletons, and the sketches were given numbers that were altered and/or different from the numbers recorded in notes.

Comparison of the skeletons in photographs 1 and 2 is difficult, but Skeleton 30 as seen in Figure 10.1 can be reversed and enlarged to compare details, such as the flattened innominates and the missing left hand. Moreover, the unusual configuration of the metatarsal/tarsal region and the absence of femora and tibiae appear to confirm the identity of the skeleton seen in Figure 10.1. The 1984 Jackes inventory of Skeleton 30 records that the femora were represented by proximal fragments only, with "no sign of shafts," and the tibiae only by a left distal fragment. There can be little doubt of the identity of the skeletons shown in Figures 10.1 and 10.2.

Figure 10.3 shows the relationship of Skeletons 30 and 32 to Skeleton 33 and to the overall situation at the site. Skeletons are here represented by black circles filled with white. The location of Skeletons 28 and 29, the "bone debris," is indicated by an X in the upper center of the image. The angle of sight of the camera (the heavy dashed white lines) for photograph 1 (Figure 10.1) is estimated on an unrectified 1:10 000 aerial photograph (Figure 10.3) taken in 1956, with the building on the left and Skeleton 31 just beyond the photograph 1 right frame.

Photograph 3 (Figure 10.4) shows a skeleton with very specific characteristics, namely a skull in which the left

side has been sheared off and with legs that have collapsed to the right side. On May 19, 1954, Veiga Ferreira described Skeleton 31 (which he called 29) as having the skull cut in half. He illustrated it (Cardoso and Rolão 1999/2000, 205, fig. 43) with the skull cross-hatched, indicating breakage. Roche (1972a, 127) clearly described the curve formed by the cervical vertebrae—there can be no doubt that this is Skeleton 31. Roche noted that the face was missing, and his further observations can be summarized:

> The right arm is along the body and the humeral head is missing. The forearm is placed across the stomach, with the hand over the left forearm. The left hand is disturbed but lies over the pubic area. The legs are strongly flexed and lie to the right side. The feet are crossed.

All such details, and more, confirm that Figure 10.4 shows Skeleton 31 from the 1954 Moita excavations. However, once again there is a discrepancy between Roche and Ferembach over whether or not there is a sternum.

The individual who seemed to be Skeleton 31 in 1984 is still recorded as Skeleton 31, with the crown of the right second mandibular molar lost to caries and the first molar on the left lost premortem. The mandible recorded by Ferembach in the 1960s is clearly the same as the Skeleton 31 mandible described by Jackes in 1984; Ferembach's (1974, 100) description of the mandibular pathology of Skeleton 31 (right M_2 reduced to the roots, left M_1 lost premortem and alveolus resorbed) is entirely consistent.

Roche (1972a, 128) said that the mandible of Skeleton 33 lay over the maxilla, the damaged skull turned to the left. His notes can be summarized by the following:

The left shoulder region complete but the right very fragmentary. The left arm complete and slightly away from the side of the body. The hand is open over the lumbar vertebrae with the thumb separated from the fingers. The right ulna is crossed over the radius. Upper femora and distal tibiae and fibulae only (knees gone) leaning slightly to the left with the right leg raised slightly. The fibula is displaced behind. Feet are crossed, with the left over the right.

There can be no doubt that Figure 10.5 represents Skeleton 33 from the 1954 Moita excavation, although in 1984, label 33 was associated with no more than a few ribs in the museum. In 2010, however, Skeleton 33 was represented by bones as shown in Figure 10.5. It is to be noted that the femoral and tibial breaks are fresh, confirming that the knees were probably damaged by the bulldozer before excavation. The surviving skull is without doubt that shown in Figure 10.5.

Unfortunately, there is no photographic image of Moita Skeleton 34 from 1954, although we do have a reasonable idea of it from Veiga Ferreira's sketch (Cardoso and Rolão 1999/2000, 205, fig. 43). This was quite an old individual who was extremely large, larger than the others. The transverse width of the right humeral head (53 millimeters) is 4 millimeters broader than in the next largest male, Moita 17, described in 1984 as "extremely large." Veiga Ferreira (Cardoso and Rolão 1999/2000, 195) recorded that his legs were forced into hyperflexion and had become dislocated. The sketch indicates that the left leg was strongly flexed, while the right femur had fallen to one side and the tibia and fibula had separated from the femur, falling straight down distal to the pelvis. Roche (1972a, 129) confirmed that the right knee was tightly flexed and that the left femur had fallen to one side. The feet appear to have been placed very close to the trunk. The skull was partially burned and the individual was crushed. Skeletal elements labeled 34 survive in the Porto collection, where they show extreme brecciation with a rather unusual coarse sand encrustation, and with medullary canals that are completely filled with white sediment. The sketch and the descriptions provided by Veiga Ferreira and by Roche (1972a, 129) make it very clear that 34 could not be confused with Skeletons 30, 31, 32, and 33. For this reason, we can be absolutely sure of our identifications of the skeletons in the four photographs as 30, 31, 32, and 33.

WHAT THE PHOTOGRAPHS TELL US ABOUT BURIAL PATTERNS AND GRAVE FILL

The new photographs provide us with information on burial details. In the absence of extremely detailed plotting and description of burials at the time of excavation, it is essential to have good photographs (Nilsson 1998, 6) taken from as many angles as possible in order to carry out what is called *anthropologie de terrain* (Duday et al. 1990) or, more recently, archaeothanatology (Duday 2009), that is, a study of the burial characteristics. The structure of the grave and the nature of the surrounding sediments interact with the processes of decomposition, and the final outcome may lead us to a greater understanding of burial practices. For this, the new photographs are vital. The photographs make it clear that the burials were in hollows dug into the sterile sands underlying the midden deposits. Analyses have shown that Moita breccia, adherent matrix on bone and deposits within the medullary canal of a femur,[1] contains sand. We therefore have to take into account the particular qualities of sand as grave fill, considering also that the sand would have been intermittently humid. Roche (1989, 613, ftn 1) noted that the Moita sands had a higher clay content than the other Muge sites, perhaps explaining the development of broad areas of brecciated material at Moita in contrast to the isolated nodules typical of Arruda and Amoreira. Our analyses show the presence of aluminum silicates at Moita (but also at Arruda). From still adherent matrix, we know that the grave fill also contained comminuted shells, ash, and charcoal. The area of the burials excavated at Moita during the 1950s was, however, specified by the excavators (e.g., Cardoso and Rolão 1999/2000, 183, fig. 25) as having breccia directly overlying sand. Nevertheless, it is unlikely that the bodies were surrounded by sand alone. Since sand is very fine-grained sediment, it would infiltrate body cavities coincident with soft tissue decomposition. As the soft tissues decomposed, progressive (Duday 2009, 54; Roksandic 2002) and continuous infilling by fine-grained sediments into the body cavities would lead to the maintenance of the original form of the thoracic cage and pelvic girdle, and this has not happened with the Moita skeletons. Rather, as we shall see, the ribs have been depressed downward (slumped), and the pelves were splayed. Both suggest the sudden collapse of structures no longer supported by the soft tissues. If sand were indeed the main (or exclusive) sediment covering the body, one possible explanation is that the body was covered with a hide, preventing continuous infilling as decomposition progressed. Alternatively, the sand could have been mixed

10.6. (a) The breccia within the cranial vault of Skull 17 exhibits small pebbles and shell fragments within the grave fill. Photo: D. Lubell. (b) Despite the exigencies of nearly 60 years post-excavation, the area beneath the left femur head of Moita 5 indicates that grave fill (the upper darker sediment) contained pebbles and shell fragments. Photo: D. Lubell.

with crushed shell, ash, and charcoal in such quantity as to reduce its capacity to flow. This would limit erosion from a mound built above the burial and reduce the capacity of the sand for continuous infilling of the body cavities. Our interpretation is that the grave fill was in fact firm and stable, and this is supported by the evidence that sediments were securely in place immediately surrounding the cadavers, maintaining limbs in their original burial postures, to some extent. It is clear that the sands around the bodies did not simply erode away, exposing the skeletons to the risk of disarticulation and dispersal, despite what appear to be very shallow graves (Roche 1972a, 118, 121–22, 127, 131, mentions shallow cavities hollowed out of the sand in relation to burials 3, 5, 12, 14, and 31; he also states that the children were buried in small holes in the sand). In addition, there must have been strong downward pressure on cadavers, leading to common, if partial, crushing and deformation of the skulls; we can therefore envisage immediate infilling, with mounds built over the burials, compacting the sediments and adding to the weight of the deposits (especially when wet) over the skeletons. Henri Duday (2009, 54) distinguished progressive and "staggered" filling of spaces, and it is clear that the Moita skeletons were subject to staggered, discontinuous collapse

and filling of voids created by the decreased volume of the cadaver. Several unknown factors mediate the final outcome, leading to variability: the possible use of some covering (perhaps hides) over the cadavers, the purity of the sand, and the season of the year determining the water content of the sediments. Examination of Moita 1 from the 1950s excavation showed that the matrix was particularly hard, and since the skulls of both Moita 1 and 20 were varnished without being fully cleaned, it can be seen that both were surrounded by sand that contained a good deal of fragmented shell. The facial orifices are likely to have retained such fragments differentially, no doubt skewing our idea of the nature of the sediments.

Figure 10.6a suggests that fine-grained deposits may have been washed away from those skeletal elements that could have caught and retained moisture filtering through the deposits, while Figure 10.6b makes it clear that fill generally contained a variety of constituents—shell, charcoal, and small pebbles—which would indeed be selectively deposited in skeletal cavities. The lack of a clearly defined lower margin of the fill is to be expected as a result of liquid filtering through deposits and the activities of, for example, earthworms (Duday 2009, 54–55), as well as the circumstances of excavation and curation.

Other examples, maintained en bloc in the museum in Porto, give us a very clear indication that fill could be heavily charged with charcoal, small pebbles, and shell, to such an extent that it seems likely that anthropogenic fill was packed around the skeletons and in some cases served to keep selected skeletal elements in place, despite the tendency of joints to slide apart after the disintegration of ligaments. We will discuss Skeleton 19 below, providing a particularly clear indication that compacted grave fill, rather than the shallow hollows within the sterile sands, provided support, allowing some joints to remain in articulation.

Further evidence that there was preparation of the grave surface, before the body was laid down, comes from Roche's (1972a, 118) description of Skeleton 3 as lying on a bed of unopened *Tapes decussates* and surrounded by charcoal and some ochre. Skeleton 33 had crushed *Scrobicularia plana* to a thickness of five centimeters beside it, particularly around the skull and left shoulder. Skeleton 12 was buried with a large number of *Helix pisana* (land snails are recognized as a common accompaniment of burials in the circum-Mediterranean Mesolithic, Lubell 2004 specifically referring to nonintrusive shells). Other skeletons were buried with pierced *Theodoxus fluviatilis* shells, most dramatically Skeleton 25, a child mislabeled already in the early 1960s as 27 (Ferembach 1974, 30).

Moita 30 was no doubt buried with the knees flexed so that the femora were perpendicular to the body axis. Although the leg bones have disappeared, it is clear from the fixed position of the feet, flat on the ground and undisturbed, that the leg bones also remained in place. The now broken left femoral diaphysis must have been retained in an upright position, but Figure 10.2 allows us to see that the broken right femoral shaft had collapsed outward. The skull is slightly inclined toward the thorax, indicating that the head was placed on a downward slope, and there seems to have been some shoulder constriction in that the right humerus is slightly rotated medially, while the radius, ulna, and hand lie flat on the ground surface. It is likely that the left side of the body followed the same pattern. Because there is no lateral splaying of the ribs, but rather slumping of the ribs in a caudal direction, along with the clavicles, there is further evidence of restricted space around the thorax. In general, the evidence is of downward compacting, but not continuously in-filling grave deposits. The mandible has stayed pressed against the chest and the face has been compressed inward. The evidence indicates that a mound was built over the body, while Figure 10.2 shows that the body was buried on a flat bed of anthropogenic sediment,

dark with ashes and charcoal. The position of the cranium and the legs indicates a cranio-caudally constricted oval grave. As indicated by the fully splayed iliac blades, there was no lateral constriction and the bottom there was flat, although it is likely that compacted fill held the head slightly raised, the shoulders pushed in to some extent, and the left leg flexed up.

Moita 31 lay in dorsal decubitus (lying on the back) with the arms crossed over the abdomen. In this case, it is obvious that the knees were not upright, since the position of the feet indicates that the individual was buried with his legs folded tightly and lying to the right. The skull was apparently not held firmly in position, since it has fallen away from the cervical vertebrae, perhaps from the third cervical vertebra, toward the right shoulder. The photograph (Figure 10.4) appears to indicate sand, rather than anthropogenic grave fill, to the left of the skull. Since fill did not constrict movement of the head and shoulder, it is unlikely to have been closely pressed against the upper body. The ribs have slumped rather than splayed, except at the level of the left shoulder. The left clavicle is displaced, with its medial end moved cranially, indicating that the cranium and shoulder probably moved at the same time, the head movement pulling the clavicle. This medial to cranial clavicular movement is not replicated among the other 1954 Moita skeletons. The iliac blades are splayed, but fill can clearly be seen under the left ilium and the lack of complete splaying suggests that the grave floor was most likely concave. Once again, a cranio-caudally restricted grave is indicated, but with evidence of lateral space and less compacted fill; however, the right knee, especially, was held in place, presumably by fill. There is no indication of large spaces left, as would be the case if the body was loosely covered with a perishable material such as hides; immediate infilling of the grave with no barrier between the sediment and the body is suggested.

It is noteworthy that Skeleton 31 was buried away from the main areas of overlying breccia recorded by the excavators. The medullary canals of the bones broken since excavation do not contain sediment, and although there was breccia conserved on the mandible, it was apparently less heavily encrusted and difficult to clean than others from the site. In fact, the bones in general seem less brecciated and damaged by the cleaning that Mendes Correa requested be done in Porto (Roche 1972a, 115).

Moita 32 had been extensively disturbed. Nevertheless, it is possible to gain some impression of the burial position as dorsal decubitus with hands on the pelvis and knees flexed up. The burial must have been partially constricted on the right side at the level of the shoulder, but the lower ribs are laterally splayed, indicating less constraint around the trunk. The medial end of the right clavicle has moved caudally and the right humerus has rotated in. The "effect of the wall" (Duday et al. 1990; Roksandic 2002) explains the features of the right shoulder; here we refer to support from compacted grave fill rather than to any specific constraining feature or structure. The "verticalization of the clavicle" (Nilsson Stutz 2006), together with the right first rib and the extreme inward rotation of the humerus, is indicative of constriction; Duday (2009, 46) notes that clavicular verticalization can take place only when the shoulders are pushed up and forward. We do not argue for a tight wrapping of the body because of a number of features, particularly on the left side on the body. The skull has moved to the right and has fallen forward onto the mandible, which is slightly dislocated to the left. While the left arm could have been disturbed during excavation, Figure 10.2 in fact indicates that the left humerus and clavicle are less constricted than those on the right. The position of the scapulae, maintaining a curve, suggests a concave grave floor in the region of the thorax, and it is possible that the ilia were also able to resist complete splaying. Again the feet seem to have been drawn in toward the body, so that the knees must originally have been flexed and it is evident that the broken left femoral shaft was positioned up and medially. Ferembach (1974) noted that it is the right fibula that is present, although the fibula now with Skeleton 32 is a left; the surviving talus and calcaneus are also left.

We therefore have an indication of a grave with sediments pressed against the back of the skull and the upper body, but less so in the lower body region. Empty spaces certainly allowed movement during the process of decomposition. Pressure from above, for example the settling of the sediment of a mound sometime after decomposition was well under way, could account for the downward movement of the head and the collapse of the legs. The skeletal elements now in the museum collection show evidence of heavy brecciation with ash, sand, charcoal, and shell adhering so closely to the surfaces that the breccia defied effective cleaning. Both excavation and cleaning damage, together with abandonment of attempts at development from the matrix, are present, as well as medullary canal infill with very hard material.

We have no explanation for the state of Skeleton 32 overall, but it must have been an ancient disturbance. While we cannot forget that the site had been worked over with heavy machinery before excavation, Roche's description of the crushed face, the damaged incisor area, and the disturbance to the lower abdominal, pelvic, and leg regions would surely have included a comment if he considered the damage to have been modern. Certainly Veiga Ferreira was so angered by the damage to the site (e.g., Cardoso and Rolão 1999/2000, 194, where he calls the building work "a truly monstrous thing") that he would have stated it very clearly had he felt the damage had been perpetrated by contemporary building activities.

Moita 33 is again lying in dorsal decubitus with knees flexed and no doubt originally perpendicular to the body. Figure 10.5 shows us that the body is thickly underlain by anthropogenic grave fill, particularly around the legs, which are held partially upright by sediment. The material in the museum collection is heavily brecciated and the sediment, with ash, sand, pebbles, charcoal, and shell, has resisted cleaning, or has unfortunately led to damage, for example to the mandibular dentition. The skull is completely filled with matrix.

The left humerus does not appear to have rotated away from its original position, suggesting that it had lateral support, and in fact the completely vertical clavicles indicate that the shoulders had originally been tightly constricted. The left hand lies over the abdomen; it seems that the forearm had rotated away from the wrist and fallen caudally, explained by the space created as a consequence of the decomposition of the abdomen. We can see from the left scapula that the grave floor is unlikely to have been flat. The skull was slightly inclined toward the thorax and had been elevated (Roche 1972a, 123). There was obviously post-depositional movement and fracturing of the cranial vault relative to the upper facial bones. The ribs have slumped caudally and there is complete splaying of the pelvis, so at that level there was space provided by decomposition and less compact fill. The feet were parallel and flat on the ground close to the pelvis. Immediate infilling with compaction in some areas is indicated by the relative lack of movement of the legs to the side. In general, we have again an oval, cranio-caudally constricted grave, restriction in the area of the shoulder girdle, with a mound covering the body.

The skeletons excavated in 1954 suggest that the modal burial position for Moita is for the body to be placed in a shallow oval pit with the knees flexed up and the feet close to the pelvis; based on Veiga Ferreira's description (Cardoso and Rolão 1999/2000, 195), Moita 34 was probably consistent with this. Only Moita 31, with the knees and feet to the right, contradicts this pattern.

The importance of these new images becomes evident

when we understand that photographs of only eight Moita skeletons have been previously published in sufficient detail to indicate burial posture; these eight are broadly distributed through the main concentration of burials and should provide a representative sample (Figure 10.7).

Although in a glass case (now with Skull 18—the correct skull is in Lisbon), it is possible to see that Moita 3 (Figure 10.8) has the right arm across the chest, the left hand across the fifth lumbar vertebra, and the right leg tightly flexed at the knee, with the left foot crossed over the right foot. The individual is in dorsal decubitus and, according to the published photographs, the skull and mandible were in connection (Roche and Ferreira 1967, 35, have Moita 12, which has open jaws inaccurately identified as Moita 3; Ferembach 1974, plate 1, is correctly labeled Moita 3). The indication of the grave shape or fill is provided by contrasting the completely flat left ilium with the scapulae (their lateral margins are identifiable), which tightly embrace the rib cage. The shoulders are hunched with the clavicles still in place (Roche 1972a, plate 4.2), articulated with the manubrium and oriented medio-caudally. The rib cage shows minimal distortion and only caudal slumping. It would seem that the grave bottom curved up underneath the skull and was also tight against the shoulders and the rib cage, thus keeping everything in good alignment. In fact, Roche (1972a, 117) states that the head lay on a little mound of sand. The arms and the hands support this interpretation of constriction. Complete splaying of the left ilium can occur because of the large volume of the soft tissue decomposing in the area; this can create sufficient space for outward movement in the pelvic girdle, but there must be a flat bottom to the grave in the pelvic area for such splaying to occur. The knees have been positioned perpendicular to the body with the feet relatively close to the pelvis. While the knees are still upright, there was some collapse, especially of the left leg, associated with the splaying of the left ilium. We see a cranio-caudally constricted oval grave with a slight upward curvature at the skull and feet. The lateral constriction in the thorax area is more relaxed around the hip and the knees, but with sufficient pressure from surrounding sediments to hold the right leg up and the vertebral column in aligned articulation. The details all suggest a shallow pit—as noted by Roche—with immediate infilling and the creation of a mound. The sediment retained en bloc and in the nasal aperture suggests that the sand was accompanied by fragmented shell.

The skeleton of Moita 5 had apparently lost its label already by 1969 (Meiklejohn inventory) and was without a

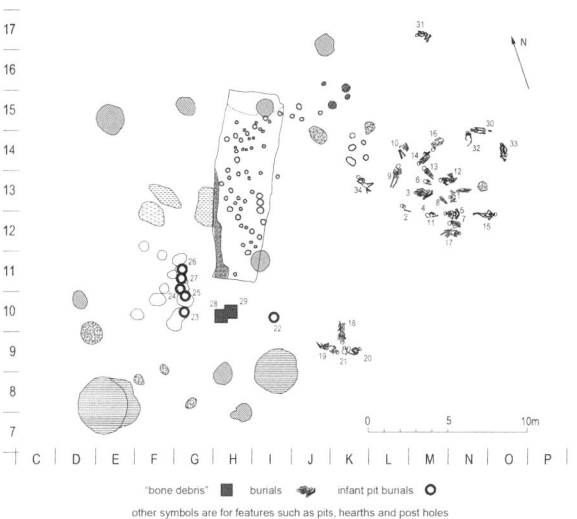

10.7. Reworking by Pedro Alvim of the available evidence on Moita features exposed by the 1950s excavations. Burials are numbered and other features are shown in order to provide context.

10.8. Moita 3 shows vertical orientation of the clavicles resulting from hunched shoulders (especially on the left side of the body), slumping of ribs, differential movement of right and left scapulae (the left is tighter), and left forearm and hand separation. Photo: P. Alvim.

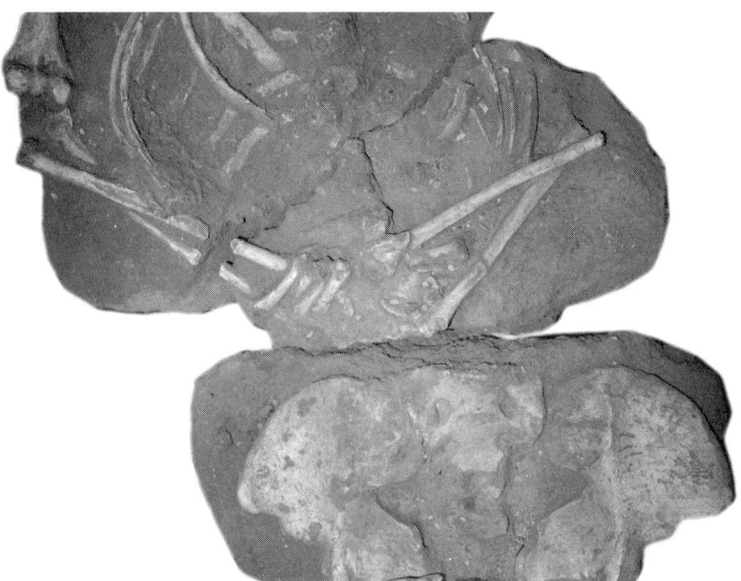

10.9. Surviving elements of the torso of Moita 5 illustrate that the iliac blades fell laterally, the left ulna slipped caudally away from the hand, and the right proximal radius moved from the immediate area of the elbow. Photo: D. Lubell.

10.10. The right shoulder of Moita 5 shows that the scapula has fallen laterally and the humerus has rotated outward relative to the forearm, despite the fact that the clavicle is relatively vertical. The shoulder was hunched up, but clearly not constricted against the ribs. Photo: D. Lubell.

label en bloc on the floor of the Museu de Antropologia e Pré-História Mendes Corrêa in 1984 when it was tentatively identified on the basis of previous publications. Confirmatory details were listed: the right and left hands were both on the fifth lumbar, the right over the left; the feet were crossed and the knees raised. The skull has fallen inward very slightly with reference to the mandible and was obviously placed on a sloped surface with a slight inclination to the right, possibly as a result of decompositional movement. There is constriction around the shoulders, with some verticalization of the right clavicle clearly seen in the photographs (especially Cardoso and Rolão 1999/2000, 201, fig. 39, top). The left humerus was completely rotated in, according to the excavation photographs. The forearm was pronated across the body, but the ulna had fallen away, perhaps in association with postburial movement of the humerus. Only the lower ribs slumped caudally and laterally, indicating that the constriction was tighter in the head and shoulder region. One photograph (Roche 1952, plate 1, fig. 1; not identified as Skeleton 5) suggests that the head and shoulders were in fact lifted. Published photographs show that while the pelvic bones are splayed flat, the knees remained completely upright, with very little lateral inclination (Cardoso and Rolão 1999/2000, 201, fig. 39, top, fig. 40, top; Ferembach

1974, plate 3; Roche 1952, plates 1.1 and 1.2; 1972a, plates 3.2 and 4.1). The broadly splayed ilia (Figure 10.9) indicate a flat bottom to the grave in that area. We again have cranial and caudal curvature of the grave, with constriction around the uppermost body and immediate infilling. The facial orifices do not indicate that the sediment was heavily charged with shell.

In 2010, it was possible to confirm the identity of Moita 5, now separated into four sections (Figures 10.6b, 10.9, and 10.10). The upright femora evident in the field photographs (Roche 1972a, plates ii.2, iii.2, iv.1), with the right femur already fallen soon after exposure (Roche 1952, plate i.1), have now been mislaid, as have the left clavicle and humerus. The skull and mandible are in Lisbon. An interesting observation can now be made regarding the right shoulder region (Figure 10.10). The clavicle suggests only that the right shoulder region was raised proximally, while the scapula has fallen away from the ribs. The right humerus has rotated slightly outward, with the proximal radius moving away from the distal humerus. In other words, extreme verticalization suggested by the multiple photographs of the right clavicle (with the important exception of Cardoso and Rolão 1999/2000, 201, fig. 39, top) may give a misleading impression of constriction at the shoulder. Photographs taken from an angle should be treated with caution.

Examination of the preserved en bloc sediments with Moita 5, in locations where the gray fill was clearly separate from the light-colored basal sands, shows that fill lay unevenly below the bones (Table 10.1). From this we can suggest that the hollow in the sands was generally flat, but that the upper body was slightly lifted with grave fill before a mound was built over the corpse. This suggestion was initially derived from photographs and was found to be valid when the actual specimen was examined.

Moita 9 was the only fully extended burial, in dorsal decubitus (Cardoso and Rolão 1999/2000, fig. 38, top and middle photos, though note that this is wrongly labeled Moita 5; Roche 1952, fig. 2; 1972a, plates 2.2, 3.1, and 5.2). This is a most unusual burial, since the others appear to have curved graves, with the head and feet on slightly rising surfaces. Yet it is possible to discern an "effect of the wall," meaning that there was indeed support, obvious from the continued alignment of all the bones. For example, the knees have rotated outward and yet the patellae are still in place, a clear indication that they were maintained in that position in some way (Duday 2009, 35). The pelvic bones are not completely splayed, but have fallen away at the sacro-iliac joints. There was a slight forward movement of the mandible and, as noted by Roche (1972a, 119), the right radius and ulna, which lie across the upper chest, have moved out of anatomical connection. In general, we can deduce a narrow grave holding the skeleton together, but with a slight concavity at the bottom. The mound covering this grave, being long and narrow, might have provided a slightly different environment from the other graves, for it was probably less high and less effective in providing firmly compacted grave fill. And yet we have the indication, especially from the patellae, of a grave covering that allowed movement (there was thus not continuous infilling with very fine sediment), but which limited slipping as articulations relaxed. One possibility is wrapping of the corpse. Since the skull and dentition are very well preserved with apparently little brecciation—there is even a hyoid, and the sacrum and vertebrae are in good condition—we could suggest less sediment pressure. Medullary canals are filled with fine white sediment that has apparently swollen and burst the humeral diaphysis with spiral fracturing, perhaps because of rain during the excavation (Cardoso and Rolão 1999/2000, 184) or because of cleaning methods (there are other indications that the breccia dissolved and rehardened, but no notes on cleaning methods survive). Moita 9 is therefore unusual in several ways.

For Moita 10, there is one published photograph, lacking clarity (Roche 1972a, plate 3.1), and the brief description by

Table 10.1. Depths of gray fill below specific observable skeletal elements in Moita 5, preserved partly en bloc

Skeletal Element	Depth of Fill Below Skeletal Element
Right ala and left ala	4 cm
Right ischium and left ischium	2 cm
Right anterior iliac crest	1 cm
Left anterior iliac crest	6 cm
Right talus	5 cm
Left metacarpals	6 cm
Left distal ulna	4 cm
Right acromion	7 cm
Right humerus head	10 cm
Right distal humerus	11 cm
Ribs on the left at T.4 level	4 cm

Veiga Ferreira (Cardoso and Rolão 1999/2000, 184), which states that the body lay on its side in a disarticulated state. In fact, Roche (1972a, 120) says that the skeleton gave the impression of a burial that had been disturbed after inhumation. However, the positions of the ribs make it very improbable that this body lay in dorsal decubitus. It is likely, then, that this is one skeleton in which the pit was wider than usual to accommodate the lateral posture, with flexed legs folded to the right. The skull appears to have been crushed.

With Moita 12 we return to burials with good published photographs (Cardoso and Rolão 1999/2000, 200, fig. 38, top; 201, fig. 39—the lower photo is, in fact, Moita 12; Roche 1952, plate 1.2; 1972a, plates 2.2, 3.2, 6.1). Again we observe dorsal decubitus and indications of a shallow oval pit. Nevertheless, there are differences from the burials previously described since the grave was of more generous proportions than usual, especially on the upper right side. While the left hand lies in the pelvis, the right arm is in an unusual position, removed from the side of the body, flexed and with the hand on the right shoulder. Although the skull shows more substantial movement and is now positioned on its left side with the mandible fallen open, it seems likely that the left shoulder was maintained in position by a support that also served to keep the left leg flexed upright even though the right leg fell against it. Maintenance of the right arm in tight flexion and the perpendicular left femur indicate immediate infilling that must have pressed tightly against the right lower body. Skeleton 12 is maintained partially en bloc in the museum, and we can see that the left innominate had fallen flat but that the right innominate has almost maintained its in vivo orientation (visible in Cardoso and Rolão 1999/2000, 201, fig. 39, bottom). The orbits and nasal aperture are remarkably free from shell, suggesting fine-grained sediments in the immediate grave fill, and this is supported by the fact that the retained en bloc material is not heavily charged with charcoal, shell, and pebbles. It is not possible, of course, to specify what went into the construction of a mound, but it is clear that a mound was built and helped to maintain the legs in their flexed position, despite the caudal slipping indicated by Roche (1972a, 121) for the right lower leg and also for the left hand bones, and slight movement of the lumbar vertebrae to the right during the process of decomposition.

Moita 14 appears to have lost the skull. The skeleton was sketched by Veiga Ferreira on April 30, 1953 (Cardoso and Rolão 1999/2000, 202, fig. 40) with a skull, but the photograph (Roche 1972a, plate 3.1) shows no skull and Roche (1972a, 122) says that there was no skull. Roche was of the opinion that the body had been buried with the legs tightly flexed on the trunk (and indeed the feet, which are crossed, with the left over the right, do not appear to have been placed flat). He states (1972a, 122) that the legs had then slid to the right. Roche's opinion was that the burial was placed within a small cavity excavated out of the sand, and the photograph (Roche 1972a, plate 3.1) certainly shows that the excavators had outlined a pit.

With regard to Moita 14, we can say only that there is no evidence that the legs had ever been upright and that Roche may well have been wrong in his assessment. There are two possibilities that need to be considered. In the first scenario, the individual was in dorsal decubitus, legs flexed so that the knees were drawn up. The legs collapsed, after the decomposition, to one side. In this case, the grave could not have been immediately covered by sediment, contradicting the evidence from the other Moita burials. In fact, it is likely that the body was quite tightly constrained around the shoulders, which seem hunched. In the second scenario, the individual was laid with legs flexed and knees placed to the left side of the body. In this instance, the sediment would have been pushed in immediately after the body was put into the grave. The position of the feet and the fact that the bones are neatly aligned

argues strongly against the first scenario, and Skeleton 14 should be considered as a deviation from the modal burial position.

Roche's interpretation, the legs drawn up onto the trunk, is improbable given the position of the feet, which are below the pelvis to the left side and apparently in good anatomical position. It is likely that the right tibia and fibula and the knees are also well placed anatomically. Such good positioning would be an unlikely outcome if a large amount of empty space had been created by the decomposition of the cadaver.

Several photographs are available for Moita 15 (Roche 1952, plate 1.2; 1972a, plate 6.2), showing that the burial was in dorsal decubitus, almost extended but with the legs slightly flexed. There was immediate infilling, evident because the right knee stayed upright and the left knee leans against it. Furthermore, since the feet and legs have maintained their position, it is likely that a mound was also present. The pelvic bones have splayed out and the arms are akimbo with the hand on the hips. The right radius has fallen out of articulation and the skull has moved slightly downward and to the right so that the maxilla is no longer in contact with the mandible. Any type of shallow pit must have been more generous than usual since no lateral constriction is evident. The skull is on display in a glass case in Porto, and this is one of the very few examples of more or less complete skulls from the site, and the only one kept in Porto. As with Moita 9, which has the facial region preserved, it appears that an extended burial allowed for a mound that exerted less weight on the skeleton.

From the photograph of Moita 17 (Roche 1972a, plate 4.1), we can see that the individual lay in dorsal decubitus. There was a marked constriction of the shoulders, with the left elbow placed on the thorax and the left arm across the abdomen. The skull is drawn toward the chest, indicating strong cranio-caudal constriction. The slumping of the thoracic cage and the caudal movement of the medial clavicle confirm this interpretation. The alignment of the bones on the left side of the body suggests that the body filled a very narrow and restricted grave with the underlying fill thicker in the area of the skull and thorax. Splaying of the pelvis is complete and the left leg collapsed across the body. The position of the femur—seen from the posterior view—in relation to the tibia and the fibula, both with the lateral aspect visible, is significant in this respect. Their normal anatomical connection was fairly closely preserved in this burial. Therefore Roche's (1972a, 123) interpretation that the legs were initially flexed and drawn up onto the trunk seems justified. Given immediate covering of the body with sediment, the initial volume of the legs and the abdomen would create sufficient space to allow the observed movement of the tibia and fibula. Furthermore, there is nothing to suggest that the feet were on the ground. Rather, while the photograph does not provide clear evidence of the position of the feet, the one bone that can be cautiously identified as a left calcaneus, in medio-plantar aspect, suggests that at least one foot fell close to the pelvis after the decomposition of the soft tissue. This is consistent with the feet not touching the ground; if the knees were on the chest, the feet would not reach the ground. Roche's statement that the body was disrupted by nearby later burials (i.e., Moita 5 and 7) is not supported. The photograph (Roche 1972a, plate 4.1), which also shows Moita 5, gives us no reason to think that the burial was disturbed by Moita 5.

Roche (1972a, plate vii.1) published a photograph of Moita 19 that matches the sketch of the burial (Cardoso and Rolão 1999/2000, 204, fig. 42) and the skeleton now displayed in Porto. The skeleton is partly en bloc although the right tibia and the feet are no longer present. The published photograph shows that the body is in dorsal decubitus with the feet drawn to the pelvis, firmly on the ground and slightly caudal to the pelvis, as would be expected given the muscle volume of the thighs and calves. The right shoulder, ribs, and ilium do not display the splaying to be expected if there was space created by decomposition. The right iliac blade was surrounded by sediment heavily charged with charcoal and shell (Figure 10.11), and this fill continued under the right ischium and femur. The right arm is extended, the humerus perfectly aligned with the ribs, and the clavicle was apparently more or less verticalized. The scapula cannot be seen, but the humerus does not show any rotation and the hand was placed over the lower abdomen. There was no post-depositional movement of the radius and ulna, but the hand must have separated from the forearm prior to the decomposition of the radio-ulnar joint; otherwise it would probably have caused some dislocation of the radius. An immediate infill between the right arm and the thorax is obvious as there was no movement of the ribs.

Roche (1972a, 124) described the left arm as folded up upon itself, and the position of a fragment of an ulna and the left hand on the shoulder confirm this. The left clavicle is only semi-vertical, although the shoulder is constricted. In contrast with the constricted right side of the body, without splaying of the ribs, the position of the left arm and scapula flat on the ground indicates that additional space would have been available on the left for the slight

10.11. The lateral surface of the right ilium of Moita 19 remains oriented almost as in vivo. It is evident that fill containing comminuted shell and a good deal of charcoal was closely packed against it. Photo: P. Alvim.

splaying of the ribs. While the left radius and ulna are not preserved, the alignment of their remaining proximal fragments with the hand bones indicates the outline of the fill on the left side of the body.

The left femur is fully upright, with the knee region broken off. The right femur, with the femoral head in the acetabulum, was also initially in an upright position, as indicated by the upright right tibia and fibula in the available photograph (Roche 1972a, plate vii.1). However, the right femur slid down the posterior surface of the left femur during decomposition and must have pushed the left tibia and fibula away. If the body was placed with the right hip firmly against compacted sediment—as indicated by the position of the ilium—this would be a logical consequence of decomposition as soon as the knee joints loosened (relatively early in the sequence). The upright position of the right tibia and fibula, the position of the left femur, and the position of the foot imply that the body was immediately covered by a mound that prevented extensive movement of many of the bones. The coarse fill—a mixture of crushed shell, sediment, and charcoal—would not have flowed progressively; instead, it allowed the creation of empty space during decomposition, and the movement of the right femur into that space.

Table 10.2. Summary of burial disposition with regard to legs

Moita Skeleton	Position	Knees	Direction of Movement
3	modal	Knees upright	Partial collapse to left
5	modal	Knees upright	
9	extended	Knees straight	
10	lateral	Knees folded to the left	
12	modal	Knees upright	Slight collapse to left
14	dorsal	Knees folded to right	
15	extended	Knees slightly raised	
17	dorsal	Knees hyperflexed on trunk	Collapse to right
19	modal	Knees upright	Partial collapse to left
30	modal	Knees upright	(Legs removed)
31	dorsal	Knees folded to right	
32	modal	Knees upright	(Legs partially removed)
33	modal	Knees upright	Slight collapse to right

In sum, the burial is best described as dorsal decubitus in a shallow, restrictive grave with feet on the ground drawn toward pelvis and knees upright, surrounded by grave fill, and covered with a mound of sediment mixed with crushed shell and charcoal.

We have then eight skeletons for which we have clear enough previously published photographs to gain some idea of the burial disposition and the nature of the graves. To this we can add knowledge gained from the materials retained en bloc in the museum in Porto: elements of Moita 3, 12, and 19 and some skeletal parts identified as Moita 5.

Beyond the actual specimens, there are details from the field notes (now available thanks to Cardoso and Rolão 1999/2000) and descriptions by Roche (1972a), but it is obvious that Roche did not take decompositional movement of bones into full consideration when describing the skeletons. Added to this, the field sketches are rough, and published photographic evidence is limited and often of poor quality. The new photographs, representing four individuals, therefore add considerably to our knowledge of Moita mortuary practices and allow us to make firmer statements about the Moita burial posture as defined by the 1950s skeletons (Table 10.2). The evidence available, prior to the discovery of these new photographs, was that Moita 3, 5, 12, and 19 probably illustrated the modal posture for burial, with the knees perpendicular to the body axis, that is, flexed upright. But there was heterogeneity since

Moita 9 was buried fully extended and Moita 10 was a lateral burial, while Moita 15 had the legs only very slightly bent at the knees. In contrast, Roche saw Moita 17 as having the knees flexed onto the trunk.[2] This is an interpretation that we support and, in fact, Moita 17 perhaps echoed Amoreira burials with legs hyperflexed on the trunk (Roksandic and Jackes, chap. 9 in this volume), but with a different outcome. On the other hand, our interpretation is that Roche was probably wrong in thinking that the thighs of Moita 14 lay on the trunk; we interpret the position as knees initially flexed and placed to the right.

Thus, previously, "modal" applied to no more than 56 percent (5/9) of burials, i.e., 3, 5, 12, and 19 and perhaps, 17. Adding Moita 30, 32, and 33 now gives us eight modal burials (if Moita 17 should be regarded as simply an extreme form of the modal practice) and five deviant burials. We can say with a great deal more confidence now that the burials from the 1950s excavations were generally flexed up within cranio-caudally constricted shallow pits and must have had fill placed immediately on and around them, built up in the form of mounds, such that the flexure of the knees was to some extent maintained despite decompositional movement. This description now holds for 62 percent (8/13) of individuals.

A wrapping with hides might have permitted some unstable elements, especially patellae, to remain in place, but this suggestion is convincing for only one individual (Moita 9). A possible explanation for bone stability would

10.12. The skull of Moita 18 provides an example of downward sediment pressures collapsing and moving skeletal elements. Here the skull vault has collapsed and the face has slid so that the anterior dentition is at the level of the upper thoracic vertebrae. The mandible must have fallen away to the right, since it is complete and less heavily brecciated. Photo: M. J. Cunha.

be that the grave fill, heavy with ash and taking up all available humidity, would have fallen immediately into the decompositional voids and maintained joints in their place. Skeleton 19, just described, shows that heavy grave fill did not keep all bones in position. Perhaps we should propose that the bodies were covered with material like hides that would have kept bones in articulation in some areas of the body, but would have allowed the development of empty spaces in others, because the hides decomposed more slowly than human soft tissues and inhibited infilling with sediment.

However, we can argue against the use of hides; empty spaces created by decomposition are sufficient explanation for the bone movement we observe, and we can cite evidence (e.g., Figure 10.12) for the sudden collapse of bones, as well as sliding of elements because of putrefaction (Duday 2009, 34). These effects would result from the direct weight of the mound. The sliding effect would probably have been impeded by a closely adhering covering that might mold itself to the underlying form of the face. The best, and most parsimonious, argument therefore seems to be that no coverings were placed over the bodies, and that the grave fill and subsiding mounds filled the voids slowly and at intervals, depending on particular circumstances, the season of the year, drainage, and slight variations in the fill and mound construction.

IMPORTANCE OF THE FOUR NEW PHOTOGRAPHS

The importance of these new images lies in several facts:

1. The curatorial history at the Museu de Antropologia e Pré-História Mendes Corrêa in Porto has meant that the 1954 skeletons have at times been mixed or could no longer be identified with absolute certainty because of loss of labels and dispersal of skeletal material. Any collateral information is of great importance to further study of these skeletons. These photographs enable anthropologists to verify many details.

2. There was uncertainty over "skeletons" 28 and 29. In some of Roche's publications, these are referred to and in others they are ignored or questioned. Veiga Ferreira's changes in his notes and on his diagrams make it clear that the cause of all the problems was what to do about "skeletons" 28 and 29. Since Ferembach eventually described them as no more than indeterminable debris, our new knowledge of the 1954 excavations has a bearing on our attempts to arrive at the number of individuals, a basic question in paleodemographic studies (Jackes and Alvim 2006; Jackes and Meiklejohn 2004, 2008).

3. The constant changing of the numbering during the period of excavation resulted in contradictions between Veiga Ferreira's field notes and Roche's (1972a) and Ferembach's (1974) publications. The resolution of this

problem is an important clarification of the contradiction and provides an interesting historical note on the excavations.

4. Since there is some question about the scaling of the diagrams in Roche's publications (Alvim and Jackes, in prep), and since Veiga Ferreira's diagram (Cardoso and Rolão 1999/2000, 183, fig. 25) does not pinpoint the locations of skeletons 30, 31, 32, and 33, the new photographs provide important evidence of their exact locations.

5. The new photographs provide important additional evidence on mortuary archaeology. Published photographs on the more complete skeletons excavated in 1952 and 1953 give us detailed information on only eight individuals; the observations that can be made on four further skeletons is of great interest. We can now summarize what we know on body posture at burial at Moita.

6. Evidence from the new photographs gives us information not only of the disposition of bodies at the time of burial, but of subsequent movement of bones. This evidence provides an important clue as to the nature of the grave fill.

The Moita skeletons excavated from the central part of the mound, after the top had been bulldozed away, lay on a plane surface in what were apparently shallow constricted pits. The graves were prepared with fill derived from anthropogenic sediment, charged with ash, charcoal, and comminuted shell. The constricted grave space allowed for mounds to be built up over the dead, which maintained the bodies in a general cranio-caudally constrained posture during and after decomposition. This allows us to think of Moita as a gathering place, with shallow graves at the same level as a series of posts that seem to form some type of "monument." A rough U-shape of posts, with the graves in a broader U in front of them (as proposed by Jackes and Alvim 2006), marked by mounds, can be envisaged. In general, the grave mounds allowed burials to be located, but in some cases the mounds must have eroded down—especially since basically sandy sediments must have been used—explaining why in some cases one burial disturbed another. Nevertheless, the general location of graves was obviously known. The mounding of deposits over the shallow graves would have been necessary in order to protect the cadavers and to make the area available for activities such as ceremonial memorials and feasting, without

discomfort. Whether or not a covering of hides helped to reduce the discomfort cannot be stated with certainty, but it appears to be generally unlikely.

Discussion of Muge burials has moved beyond our initial interpretation of the simple placing of the dead among other elements of debris and rubbish (cf. Gaspar et al., chap. 7 in this volume: "people as trash"). Since it is unlikely that large numbers of corpses would be buried in shallow graves in close association with habitation areas, interpretation of the structure as a living site can be queried. There is the additional possibility that food debris may be kept at a distance from habitation sites (Saunders, chap. 4 in this volume) to discourage nocturnal scavengers. We suggest then that the considerable quantities of food debris, both bone and estuarine shell, close to burials in the Muge site deposits will not represent normal meals, but rather specific occasions. We can postulate memorial feasting and special structures (cf. Klokler, chap. 11 in this volume) in the context of the mound-covered burials laid out, not randomly, but around the hearths and pits associated with the postholes. This interpretation is supported by the fact that the Moita burials described here clearly demonstrate systematically patterned placement of human cadavers.

Note added in proof: The exceptional burial, Moita 9, has now been dated and is the earliest Muge burial so far known (Rita Peyroteo Stjerna, pers. comm. September 18, 2013).

ACKNOWLEDGMENTS

We are grateful to Dr. Miguel Magalhães Ramalho, Coordenador, Museu Geológico, Laboratório Nacional de Energia e Geologia, Lisbon, for permission to publish the photographs found there. Thanks to Eugénia Cunha for providing the opportunity to present the first version of this chapter at a symposium at the UISPP Congress in Lisbon, September 2006. A. H. Bacelar Gonçalves, Museu de Antropologia e Pré-História Mendes Corrêa, Porto, provided essential help to Jackes in 1984 in Porto, and his successor, Maria José Cunha of the Museu de História Natural, Faculdade de Ciências do Porto, has become a valued collaborator in our work. We are grateful to Christopher Meiklejohn for continuing access to information derived from his work in Portugal in the 1960s and 1980s and to David Lubell, whose help and encouragement go far beyond his assistance in Porto in 1984 and 2010.

NOTES

1. The dominant features within this deposit were shown to have up to 93 percent normalized weight Si (S-2700 Hitachi PGT IMIX EDX) according to analyses conducted in association with Christina Barker, Chemical and Materials Engineering, University of Alberta, Canada. Goodness of fit for the two specific 1-micron-point analyses with 93 percent Si: 1.32 and 1.15. The bone analyzed is labeled "diverse burials" from the 19th-century excavations, not from those under discussion here.

2. Roche's suggestion of a ligature seems unwarranted. Indeed, his opinion obviously wavered between suggesting that it was unlikely (1972a, 131) and saying that it is a reasonable assumption (1972b, 100).

CHAPTER ELEVEN

A RITUALLY CONSTRUCTED SHELL MOUND

Feasting at the Jabuticabeira II Site

Daniela Klokler

SUMMARY

New research has articulated the interpretation of large shell mounds as the result of centuries of repetitive rituals involving death and social memory. Zooarchaeological analysis of samples from a Brazilian shell mound site indicates that the fauna are the remains of feasts deposited in conjunction with funerary rituals. Jabuticabeira II served as a special locale for ritual feasting in honor of deceased members of the communities that inhabited the surrounding area. The site's construction occurred simultaneously with, and as a result of, the mortuary ritual.

INTRODUCTION

In the indigenous Tupi language (spoken by horticulturalist groups that occupied the Brazilian coast at the time of contact with Europeans), shell sites are called *sambaquis*. This term is commonly translated as "hill of shells." Shell mounding groups occupied most of the Brazilian coast (Figure 11.1), but they also inhabited inland areas and built mounds and middens with freshwater mollusks and land snails (Barreto 1988; Figuti et al. 2004; Figuti and Plens, chap. 16 in this volume; Plens 2007; Roosevelt et al. 1991). The oldest shell-bearing sites located in coastal Brazil date to approximately 8000 BP, but between 5000 and 2000 BP there is a boom in sambaqui construction (Gaspar 1998, 2000; Lima et al. 2004). Large shell mounds only began to be built at around 4000 BP and are located solely in southern coastal areas.

Shell sites can have many different functions, such as long- or short-term habitations, seasonal camps, specialized stations, dinnertime camps, and cemeteries. Sambaquis were historically defined mainly as habitation sites (see Gaspar et al., chap. 7 in this volume). Since the early 1990s, the multifunctional nature of large sambaquis, in which domestic, funerary, and refuse activities were performed, has become widely accepted, while smaller sites are usually considered seasonal or short-term camps. Development of research centered on the analysis of settlement systems and formation processes brought attention to the determination of site functions.

The focus of this chapter is the formation of Jabuticabeira II, located in a lagoonal area where approximately 80 additional shell mounds and middens have been identified. Faunal analyses of samples from Jabuticabeira II focused on site construction processes and ritual activities. Analysis of its stratigraphy and faunal remains revealed that it was built over an extended interval through an intricate sequence of ritual activities. The results suggest that Jabuticabeira II is a testament to the effort of the living to honor and remember the dead.

GATHERING, FISHING, ACCUMULATING, FEASTING: CHANGING PERSPECTIVES

Shell-bearing sites are a great source of information on animal-human relationships (see chapters in this volume by Burchell et al.; Braje et al.; Orchard and Clark; Daniels; Faulkner; Pickard and Bonsall; and Valente et al.) since the accumulation of shells also allows the preservation of bones due to pH levels. In Brazil, early work by Charles F. Hartt (1885) and Sylvio Fróes Abreu (1932) focused on the hardships imposed on the coastal populations by the lack of valuable resources in their environment. According to

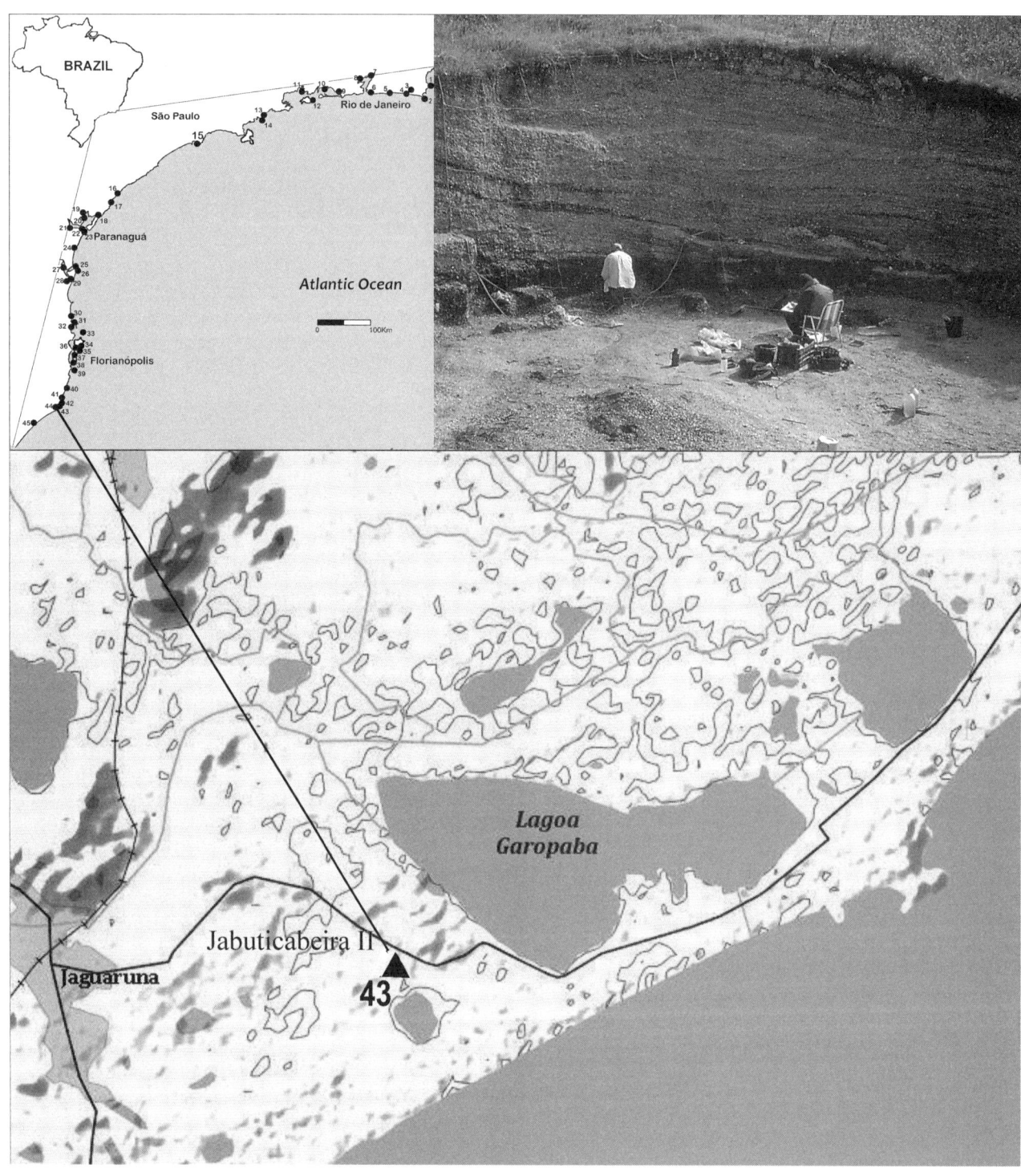

11.1. Map with indication of shell-site concentrations and study area.

this view, sambaqui populations had to rely on shellfish as their main staple and would roam the shores looking for food. The massive amounts of shell valves found in the sites were explained by the quantity necessary to satisfy a group's subsistence requirements.

Later sambaqui research on diet was greatly influenced by cultural ecology theory, directly linking the differences in the composition of archaeological remains with environmental alterations that forced shifts in the diet of these coastal populations (Beck 1972b; Dias 1972; Kneip 1980; Piazza 1966; Prous 1991; Schmitz 1987). Some researchers (Beck 1972b; Lima 1991; Lima et al. 2004) proposed that overexploitation led to the collapse of mollusk beds due to an increase in population, leading the groups to focus their attention on fishing. Nevertheless, no clear evidence of overexploitation was provided to support these assumptions and so far no studies have found signs of shellfish overexploitation.

Levy Figuti's (1992, 1993, 1995) work changed the perspective on the diet of sambaqui builders. His innovative approach treated the site's matrix as an artifact and demonstrated that the high quantity of shellfish found in most sambaquis, in fact, corresponds to roughly only 15 percent of available meat, whereas vertebrates (mostly fish) account for 80 percent of edible meat. Figuti showed that these populations always relied heavily on fishing, in clear contrast to previous assumptions.

New perspectives in shell mound research view the sites as intentionally built structures, inspiring researchers to focus on the sambaquis' formation processes (Afonso and DeBlasis 1994; Gaspar and DeBlasis 1992) and consequently leading to discussions of site functions and possible changes through time. In 1996, work at the Espinheiros II site (located approximately 300 kilometers north of the study area) marked the first attempt to study the formation processes of a shell site in Brazil with the use of zooarchaeological analysis (Figuti and Klokler 1996). The authors demonstrated that the lower portions of the site, with layers composed almost exclusively of shellfish remains, were a product of the initial phases of construction of a shell platform above nearby mangroves (Figuti and Klokler 1996). The subsequent accumulation of materials at Espinheiros II, on the other hand, resulted from a complex set of activities corresponding to what would be expected at a habitation site. The study demonstrated the use of shell valves as construction material in sambaquis (check Gaspar et al., chap. 7 in this volume, for a more in-depth exploration of this topic).

The collection and deposition of shellfish in sambaquis could result from activities not directly related to their consumption as a staple or daily food. In fact, mollusk valves can be an excellent and accessible construction material. The small clam most commonly deposited in large shell sites in southern Brazil, *Anomalocardia brasiliana*, has a sturdy shell and is easily collected in beds. Research at Jabuticabeira II demonstrates that the importance of shellfish and fish far exceeded fulfilling caloric requirements, and that the selection and accumulation of shell valves to form mounds was not fortuitous but part of the funerary ritual (Klokler 2001, 2008; Nishida 2007).

THE DECIPHERMENT OF JABUTICABEIRA II

Jabuticabeira II is located in the vicinity of the Garopaba do Sul Lagoon, a large body of water fed by nearby rivers that is connected to the Atlantic Ocean by coastal outlets. The region has several interconnected lagoons where modern fishing communities thrive. Similarly, in the past, the area attracted populations whose lives were deeply connected to aquatic resources by at least 5,300 years ago (DeBlasis et al. 2007). At the time of the site's occupation, the area was dominated by a large paleolagoon, and several shell sites were located along its margins (Kneip 2004). Jabuticabeira II has been extensively dated (39 radiocarbon dates), and its occupation dates between 2880 ± 75 and 1400 ± 40 BP (DeBlasis et al. 1999; DeBlasis et al. 2004).

Jabuticabeira II is an average-sized mound, measuring approximately 400 meters long by 250 meters wide (DeBlasis et al. 1999). At its highest point, the site currently reaches nine meters, but its mean height is five meters. Based on available site dimension data from the Santa Catarina State, approximately 70 percent of shell sites are between one and nine meters in height (Gaspar et al. 2009). On the other hand, at least three shell mounds in the Jabuticabeira II region (Garopaba do Sul, Carniça, and Cabeçuda) were estimated at more than 30 meters in height and are thus regarded as monumental sites.

In several areas of the site, long-term shell extraction left deep scars in the form of vertical faces. Examination and mapping of more than 300 meters of these cross-sections and 18 trenches provided an exceptional opportunity to access the stratigraphy in the center and periphery of the mound. The stratigraphy at Jabuticabeira II is characterized by a pervasive combination of: thick, mostly clean, light-colored shell layers; thin, dark (black to dark gray) layers (see Figure 11.1 top corner); and a massive,

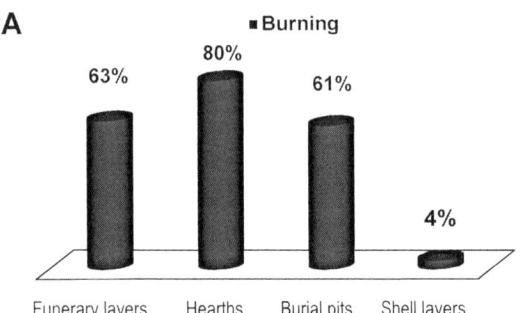

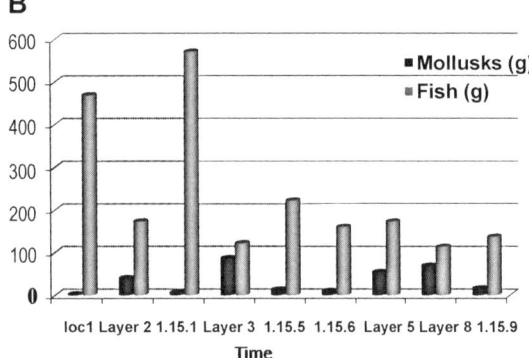

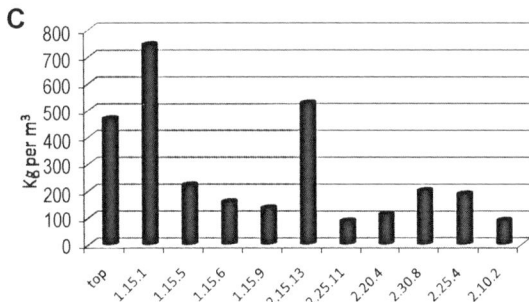

11.2. (A) Percentage of burned faunal materials in funerary features (based on NISP [number of identified specimens]) and shell layers (based on weight). (B) Average shell and bone weight and meat yields of mollusks and fish in grams (per liter) from shell layers (identified as layers) and funerary areas from Jabuticabeira II. Darker bars in the chart indicate shell layers. (C) Edible meat quantities available in different funerary areas (in kilograms per cubic meter). Conversions made using generic multipliers presented by Figuti (1992, 1993).

dark-colored fish-dominant deposit, also referred to as a fish mound (Villagrán et al. 2010; Villagrán et al. 2011b). The fish mound covers the top of almost the entire site. The thick, light-colored shell layers are devoid of features and often enclose very thin, dark lenses composed mostly of charcoal fragments and fish bones interspersed within the primary shell matrix. Thin, dark layers occur repeatedly along the profiles, both horizontally and vertically. They

are of finite extent, horizontally oriented, have variable thickness (usually not exceeding 20 centimeters), and consistently include features such as hearths, postholes, and burials in different quantities. Their composition is distinct from the large shell layers; the frequencies of mollusk remains decrease sharply from an average of 80 percent of the total components to 15 percent in the latter. Their darkened color can be explained by a combination of decomposition of organic materials along with great quantities of burned remains and charcoal fragments. The dark layers enclose all features identified in the site.

Conical features are prominent in the dark layers and seem to be postholes marking habitation structures. This led to the belief that these layers were areas where daily activities were concentrated. Profile documentation identified 390 of these features in a span of approximately 150 meters. The depths vary between 6 and 82 centimeters, while diameters range between 2 and 22 centimeters, with most postholes having a depth between 6 and 8 centimeters. Hearths were very distinguishable in profiles due to their distinct color plus the presence of burned materials and ash. Most hearths were 40 to 60 centimeters in diameter, but range between 3 and 137 centimeters in diameter and vary in depth from 3 to 20 centimeters. Some hearths contained large amounts of ash, indicating not only that they were lit for an extended period of time but also that they were quickly covered. In some cases, hearths were superimposed, and sets of three to six hearths can be seen in profiles and excavated areas (Karl 2000).

Burial pits were just large enough to accommodate the body (or bodies), were relatively shallow, and were usually dug into the preceding shell layer. Similarities in the fish contents from burial pits and surrounding areas (thin dark layer), and the slightly higher frequency of shells in burial pits, indicate that graves were filled with a mix of materials from the shell layer removed to create the pit, plus the faunal materials from the dark layer. Burial pits were always located under or to the side of hearths. Notwithstanding their most apparent use for cooking, the small size and location of hearths at Jabuticabeira II indicate they could have been used for other purposes.

The few artifacts recovered from the site appear exclusively in association with burials, either as grave goods or in the immediate surroundings (Klokler 2008). Grave goods were found in most burials and include personal adornments made of faunal and stone materials. According to Alexandre Hering (2005), 73 percent or 197 non-lithic objects are associated with burials; 68 percent (183) are shell beads and pierced teeth. Most lithic artifacts at

Jabuticabeira II also seem to be associated with burials. Flakes and debitage materials have similar frequencies: approximately 72 percent were recovered from funerary contexts and their immediate surroundings.

The horizontal excavation of the dark thin layer identified as 2.13.15 indicated that postholes are in close proximity to graves and hearths as observed in the vertical profiles, and they often surround or mark these features in a fashion that contradicts the team's initial interpretation of postholes as evidence of houses. The spatial and temporal relationships among 28 hearths, 12 graves (21 individuals), and 384 postholes identified in an excavation of 32 cubic meters within 2.13.15 indicated that the features are evidence of a sequence of mortuary activities and that dark layers are funerary areas.

Despite multiple test pits, extensive excavations, and profile analyses throughout the site's structure, researchers found no indication of daily domestic activities in either the shell or the dark layers. Jabuticabeira II lacks domestic artifact assemblages and manufacturing debris, habitation floors, processing areas, and other features that would indicate its use as a habitation.

BUILDING WITH SHELLS AND BONES

The study of Jabuticabeira II's formation processes was approached using faunal analyses, deemed suitable since the site matrix was composed of faunal remains and since the processes of accumulation of shell valves and fish bones were regarded as indicative of the relationship between these coastal groups and aquatic resources. The zooarchaeological research included column, profile, and excavation samples. Column sampling was selected for the initial work as a collection strategy because it allows the verification of vertical changes in layer composition. Columns of samples from three different loci of the site were collected for an initial assessment of the site's construction process. The concurrent investigation of the site's core and margin facilitated the study of the site's construction in a more comprehensive way. Most of the samples are from the shell-dominant component of Jabuticabeira II, where research efforts were concentrated until 2003. After this date, focus was directed to the fish-rich deposit (for detailed information, see Nishida 2007; Villagrán 2008; Villagrán et al. 2010).

Both types of layers identified in the profiles had significant differences in their composition. The light-colored, thick, and loose layers, composed of clam-shell valves, dominated most of the site's stratigraphy and were mostly composed of whole loose shells (many still articulated) of the small West Indian pointed Venus clam (*Anomalocardia brasiliana*), a common small bivalve that occurs in the region's estuaries and can be easily collected in great quantities (Gaspar, Klokler, and DeBlasis 2011; Klokler 2001). By weight, this species made up approximately 60 percent of the total components (including animal bones, charcoal, lithics, other mollusks, etc.) of the layers, far surpassing any other element. Additional shellfish, such as gastropods and different clam species, were present in lower volumes, not exceeding 15 percent of the sample. Within shell layers closer to the site's surface, frequencies of mussels increased slightly, while basal layers had the lowest amounts of this type of shellfish. However, it is unlikely that these differences were related to shifts in subsistence or collection strategies, since the same pattern occurs within some of the site's internal mounds (Klokler 2001).

The lenticular aspect of the layers suggests that they were not formed by a single dumping episode, but by several depositions. The mollusk valves did not show signs of intentional breakage and have low fragmentation rates, and just a small percentage (2 percent) show signs of burning. The fish remains recovered from shell layers include mostly estuarine species (Table 11.1).

The second basic type of layer in Jabuticabeira II consisted of thin, dark-colored compacted lenses. They were deemed funerary areas since more than 90 percent of the site's burials are located within these layers. In clear contrast to the shell layers, few mollusk remains are recovered in these lenses. *A. brasiliana* and mussels, on average, account for 15 percent of the samples by weight, and most valves exhibit signs of weathering marked by the presence of a brownish-reddish pellicle present on the surface, along with evidence of different degrees of calcium carbonate dissolution (Klokler 2008). Weathering affected other materials recovered from the dark deposit, and the process seems to have been associated with higher organic matter content. Fish bone quantities increased within funerary areas, greatly surpassing amounts recovered from shell layers by weight (Figure 11.2b). Most of the components in the funerary areas show signs of burning, indicating differential processing of the remains (Figure 11.2a).

The composition of the materials in features such as hearths, burial pits, and postholes closely resembled the characteristics of the funerary area matrix. However, there were minor differences. For example, there was a higher presence of mammal and bird remains in graves (Table 11.2) and increased degrees of burned materials recovered from hearths (Figure 11.2a). Some graves

Table 11.1. Percentage of fish species (based on MNI), and diversity and equitability values

Common Names	Scientific Names	Shell Layers	Funerary Layers + Features
Catfish	*Genidens barbus, G. genidens*	28.6	30.9
Sheepshead seabream	*Archosargus probatocephalus*	13	6.8
Atlantic spadefish	*Chaetodipterus faber*	-	0.5
	Haemulidae	5.8	1.8
Smooth puffer	*Lagocephalus laevigatus*	1.3	0.2
Mullet	*Mugil* sp.	2.6	6.3
Leatherjacket	*Oligoplites* sp.	-	1.4
Weakfish	*Cynoscion* sp.	1.3	3.4
Whitemouth croaker	*Micropogonias furnieri*	31.8	42.9
Black drum	*Pogonias chromis*	11	4.2
Bluefish	*Pomatomus saltatrix*	0.6	0.1
Snook	*Centropomus* sp.	-	0.1
Shorthead drum	*Larimus breviceps*	0.6	-
Ray	*Rhinoptera bonasus*	2.6	1.1
Shark	*Selachimorpha* sp.	0.6	0.3
N		12	14
H'		1.809	1.587
V'		.728	.601

Note: N is the number of fish taxa or richness; H' is diversity (calculated using Shannon-Weaver formula); and V' is equitability (Sheldon formula).

contained astounding amounts of fish (four burial pits have remains of more than 100 fish), suggesting that they might also have been used as grave goods deposited to surround the dead (Klokler 2003, 2008).

Fragmentation analysis reveals no clear distinction in fragmentation rates in different areas of the site. However, dissimilarity was found between the shell and the funerary layers, with the first showing very low degrees of broken valves and the latter containing more fragmented components and a more compacted matrix.

Analysis demonstrated that members of the community were buried among great quantities of fish bones, suggesting that the funerary areas' matrix corresponds to remains of consumption of communal meals or feasts (Klokler 2001). Funerary areas have an average of 275 kilograms of available fish meat per cubic meter, clearly an amount that could have been used to feed large gatherings (Figure 11.2c). The shell layers dominated by *A. brasiliana* represent repeated episodes of collection and transportation of

massive amounts of mollusks, used for covering the funerary areas or particular graves within funerary layers, adding volume to the mound.

The collection of one particular species forming large shell deposits is similar to the lower levels of Espinheiros II that appear to have been built for the purpose of constructing a platform. Domestic activities could be discerned in the upper portion of Espinheiros II, and faunal analysis identified relatively similar percentages of clams, mussels, and oysters (15 percent, 25 percent, and 32 percent, respectively), indicating a diverse collection made by gathering mussels and oysters in the mangrove and clams in mud banks.

The recurrence of circumscribed burial areas throughout the complex vertical and horizontal accumulation of the shell mound at Jabuticabeira II suggests that multiple funerary areas were actively used at the same time. This fact inspired the idea that each area corresponds to the mortuary domain of a sociological unit, called an "affinity group" by Dr. Maria Dulce Gaspar. The concept refers to the social units associated with these clusters of burials. Affinity groups, based on kinship, neighborhood membership, or other social principles, shared each funerary area and participated in rituals at these areas (Klokler 2008). Since it is difficult for archaeologists to know for certain whether the individuals buried in a particular funerary area are blood relatives (unless DNA analysis can be performed), we prefer to use a sociologically neutral term that includes other forms of relationship such as political, economic, or other connections of place and cooperation that commonly unite fishing communities. The identification of bounded deposits that can be assigned to specific affinity groups allows studies of the potential nature of social relationships.

Faunal evidence provides an important avenue to explore the ritual activities performed at shell mounds and the social implications of feasting practices. The identification of differences in rituals that are particular to specific affinity groups could provide evidence of differential resource access by these groups based on the animals used in feasts or as grave goods. These patterns could also indicate differences in the scale of feasts. Assessment of any changes that occurred in the use of faunal remains through time, especially regarding the massive fish mound that covers the site, is also an important avenue of research.

Examination of distinct funerary areas at Jabuticabeira II, spanning from 2345 ± 105 to 1975 ± 95 BP, focused on the set of behaviors involved in the funerary ritual. By comparing the types and quantities of items served during the banquets, we could infer whether the groups had unequal access to resources and/or food preferences for the rituals performed in the site (Klokler 2008). Differences regarding the scale of feasting events could indicate more investment in the communal meals due to status or number of participants. Bulky samples from 11 funerary areas (9 of them recovered from profiles) were analyzed along with materials from graves, postholes, and hearths.

Whitemouth croaker and catfish accounted for approximately 70 percent of the fish identified in Jabuticabeira II. Measurements of croaker and catfish otoliths indicated that most specimens were juveniles. Fishing with nets in the estuaries was confirmed in all samples. Identification of the same fish species in similar frequencies in funerary areas indicates that the groups analyzed had access to similar fishing grounds (Klokler 2008). Similar fishing patterns and species preference were recorded for the final fish-mound deposit, suggesting continuity in the performance of rituals by sambaqui people over the 1,500 years of construction of Jabuticabeira II. If we consider the area that contains the lowest value of biomass per cubic meter, area 2.25.11, with an estimated size of 13.5 cubic meters, and calculate the total volume of fish refuse, more than one metric ton of fish meat would be available for the gathering. Three areas show outstanding amounts of fish remains, which could correspond to affinity groups with richer feasts, since more fish meat was available for guests, or with more guests, indicating groups that could assemble more participants.

The massive black deposit or fish mound overlying the site signifies a major change in the depositional regime (Fish et al. 2000) or "site engineering" (Klokler 2001). Instead of shell valves, this final deposit is primarily composed of fish bones. The deposited materials also include rocks, charcoal, and sand. This change in the shell mound's matrix begins roughly at 1700 BP and continues until the end of the site's occupation at approximately 1300 BP (Nishida 2007; Villagrán et al. 2010, 2011b). The construction pattern that produced the massive black fish deposit represents continuity in relation to patterns identified within the earlier, shell-dominated portions of the site

Table 11.2. NISP (number of identified specimens) of bird and mammal remains distribution

	Birds				Mammals			
Locus	Funerary Layer	Grave	Hearth	Shell Layer	Funerary Layer	Grave	Hearth	Shell Layer
1	15	67	24	6	73	241	16	1
2	61	26	2	4	62	85	6	19
3		2			1			
5					1			
6	13	17	32		36	763	75	
Total	89	112	58	10	173	1089	97	20

(Gaspar and Klokler 2004; Nishida 2007). Faunal studies and analysis of the profiles further confirmed that this continuity in mound building is closely associated with burials (Nishida 2007). Paula Nishida (2007) verified that fish components in this deposit occur in similar frequencies as in the shell-dominated area of the site, and Ximena Villagrán (2008) notes that the characteristics shared by both the main and the terminal matrices include archaeosedimentary units with mounding characteristics, hearths, fish-bone concentrations, and ash.

RITUAL CONSUMPTION

Based on projections from burials encountered in extensive profiles, test excavations throughout the mound, and comparison with data from several sites, Suzanne Fish and colleagues (2000) calculated that approximately 43,000 individuals are buried in Jabuticabeira II. The presence of recurring mortuary features along with the lack of domestic activities confirms the ritual nature of the site. The ceremonial function of this shell mound facilitates the identification of ritual deposits, but some of the fauna could represent either grave goods or food refuse. In other words, the site contains different types of ritual fauna that probably served different functions. For example, articulated fish were reported in several different areas of the site in association with burial pits, and they could either be part of the feasts, food offerings for the dead, or both.

Ritual plays a vital role in society, and because of its fundamental importance in the study of social change, it should be studied more closely by archaeologists. The widespread normative thinking that associates all faunal remains solely with subsistence practices has obstructed the study of their ritual significance. Animals were used for consumption, companionship, beasts of burden, and transport, but their relationships with humans also involve the ritual realm of life. Unfortunately, researchers repeatedly examine animal remains found in ritual contexts without assessing their ritual functions (J. D. Hill 1996; Erica Hill 2000; Klokler 2003). The general apprehension about discussing animal remains in ritual deposits stems from difficulties in identifying such deposits. In the case of Jabuticabeira II, consumption and ritual use are interconnected. The juxtaposition of these activities demonstrates that they are not mutually exclusive, which complicates the interpretation of some attributes that are commonly used to distinguish ritual fauna.

Ritual deposition can be defined as being distinct from the vestiges of daily activities, but the events are not necessarily rare. Ritual consists of "formalised, repeated actions" (Bell 1997; Hill 1996), and the repetition of specific patterns is paramount in defining a ritual deposit. J. D. Hill (1996) suggests that researchers should not try to define a model with general patterns that would pertain to any ritual deposit. On the contrary, close attention to formation processes of deposits helps archaeologists recognize their nature. Formation processes and life histories of materials included in the deposits are better indicators of ritual function. According to William H. Walker (1995), ritual objects will follow specific pathways throughout their life history, and understanding these pathways can lead archaeologists to the identification of ritual behavior. In Jabuticabeira II, the steps through which faunal remains cycled during the course of the site's formation are indicative of their ritual status. The contents and locations of deposits are the most common characteristics used to define ritual function, but archaeologists need to devote careful attention to spatial context. Clear ritual contexts such as human interments facilitate the identification of faunal remains as ritual deposits, such as food offerings for the dead, as sacrificial gifts, or as refuse from funerary feasts (Horwitz 2001).

In the case of Jabuticabeira II, the several groupings of burials, the substantial quantities of faunal remains, and the architectural and behavioral implications of the arrangement of the deposits are all indicative of communal meals consumed during funerary rituals. Feasting episodes at Jabuticabeira II offer a unique opportunity for analysis. In this case, researchers have some control over the temporal aspect of the deposits because each funerary area represents a very limited number of feasting events, in contrast with other instances where deposits can become a palimpsest of many events. Typically, archaeologists are faced with feasting deposits that correspond to several episodes, sometimes spanning generations or even hundreds of years (Rosenswig 2007).

The growing realization that feasting corresponds with social phenomena of great importance in most societies has attracted the attention of many researchers toward hunter-gatherer feasting behavior (Hayden 2001). The characteristics of feasts performed by complex hunter-gatherers and other types of complex societies might have differences regarding scale, location, and foods used. These traits contribute to the difficulties of identifying the material manifestations of feasts. Nevertheless, recent research from the southeastern United States uncovered clear evidence of the performance of feasts in shell-bearing sites (see chapters by Russo and by Saunders, chaps. 3 and 4 in this volume; Claassen 2010).

A MODEL OF THE FORMATION
OF JABUTICABEIRA II

Jabuticabeira II is a cemetery that was created through the sustained enactment of feasts organized around a complex series of mortuary activities. These behaviors probably communicated solidarity, territoriality, and other values in a ritual context. The groups that used Jabuticabeira II chose to settle in an area that encompassed diverse habitats: a coastal plain with rivers, lagoons, and the ocean, plus nearby higher elevations with forest vegetation. The more interior areas of the continent appear to have been rarely explored, confirming the strong attachment that shell mound populations had with the coast. The estuarine area of the lagoon also attracted animals other than those that lived in its waters, such as birds and mammals, facilitating their capture. Proximity to the paleolagoon and its interconnections with drainages could have also made the funerary events more accessible, given the possibility of travel by boat. The large size of Santa Catarina's shell mounds enhances their visibility against the flatness of the coastal plain.

Mortuary rituals at Jabuticabeira II may have been initiated during a specific season or time of the year. Archaeological observations suggest that when a person died, the body was kept at habitations or other as yet unidentified sites for a period of time prior to interment (Klokler 2008). The funerary rituals were organized and scheduled over a lengthy period of time prior to their occurrence, since the planning and arrangements for the interments and feasts involved a level of organized effort to coordinate fishing, mollusk collection, wood procurement (see chap. 22 in this volume for more details), and other activities that contributed to the ceremonies. The area for interment was established by an individual's affinity group and was prepared on top of a mound of shells that covered earlier funerary areas. Once established, funerary areas always encompassed multiple individuals, and graves were prepared by opening shallow pits within shell layers. While the exact length of this stage of the ritual celebration cannot be stated, there are strong indications that bodies in shallow pits, ash in hearths, and offerings of whole animals were not exposed over an extensive amount of time (see Okumura and Eggers, chap. 8 in this volume, for more information regarding Jabuticabeira II burials based on analyses of human remains).

Fishing for ceremonial interment feasts occurred in the lagoon and did not employ special techniques that targeted large specimens. Most of the fish procured for the feasts were small, weighing less than 200 grams with an average length of 200 millimeters, indicating the use of nets for their capture. It appears that no specific fish species was selected for the funerary banquets because no significant differences were detected between species from funerary feasts and the shell layers (see Table 11.1).

The fish were not intensively processed, and they seem to have been roasted or smoked whole since proportions of cranial and postcranial bones are similar. Cooking activities either occurred at habitation sites or near Jabuticabeira II. Since abundant charcoal is found in the funerary areas, the feast was probably cooked near the site. Due to the completeness of shell valves in the shell layers underneath and overlying funerary areas, trampling appears to have been minimal, contrasting with expectations for an area where groups of people were holding banquets. Intensive foot traffic would be expected during these events that would have led to increased fragmentation of shell and bone materials; the presence of whole mussel valves of *Brachidontes* sp., a species that has very fragile shells, and low fragmentation of materials point to most activities related to the banquets being carried out off-mound.

Recent analysis of the matrix of the fish mound that covers Jabuticabeira II demonstrated that materials were burned before being deposited at the site (Villagrán 2008; Villagrán, Giannini, and DeBlasis 2009). The same behavior seems to be represented by the high frequency of burned bones of all taxa present in the funerary samples. The thermal alteration of feast refuse and the large quantity of organic material have darkened the appearance of interment areas. The differential processing of feasting remains seems to reinforce their ritual characteristic, as argued by William Walker (1995).

The graves were covered with remains from the feast, and hearths were lit on top of or near the graves. Posts or stakes were positioned surrounding the burial pit or a group of burials. The use of posts and some associated structure could guarantee the protection of graves and/or whole areas until the ritual was finalized and the area was closed. The hearths and post structures would also increase the visibility of mourning activities. The use of an aromatic wood (Bianchini, Scheel-Ybert, and Gaspar 2007) would have added to the sensory experience of the ritual.

The choice of fish as the main food item assured that huge quantities of animals could be captured, providing a reliable source of protein for the banquets. Fishing cooperatively would have increased the productivity of the activity (Gaspar et al. 2011). The spreading of feasting remains and the inclusion of whole fish on top of the funerary ritual area reinforced the connection of the group with the lagoon.

The four most common species (whitemouth croaker, catfish, sheepshead, and mullet) appear in all sampled funerary layers, although in varying quantities. Two of the three funerary layers with unusual quantities of fish coincide with a later period of the site's use, which could indicate an increase in the importance of fish in the end of the site's occupation, although it could also suggest adoption of more intensive fishing strategies or other changes in social organization or mortuary ritual. Analysis of the components of the funerary areas suggests that groups had equal access to the resources and that, in some sense, they are socially equivalent.

Eventually, the use of a particular funerary area ceased and vast quantities of shells were deposited on top of it in multiple episodes. Groups could have separately stored the by-products of the daily consumption of mollusks, along with fish and other food remains, for some time at habitation sites. This debris could then be brought to Jabuticabeira II at the time of the termination of funerary rites at that place.

Alternatively, shells could have been gathered exclusively for use as covering material, with the dark facies representing refuse from meals held during the episodes of shell deposition. The groups responsible for the shell accumulations may have prepared special meals and deposited them among the shells. These meals could represent the end of the mourning period or episodes of memorializing the dead.

The monumentality of the mound is no accident, but rather results from massive, repetitive construction episodes. The gathering of mollusks occurred around the site, requiring minimal transport since Jabuticabeira II was located at the margins of the lagoon. The use of *A. brasiliana* to build the mound can be explained by their ease of collection and some of their properties. *A. brasiliana* shells are thick and light colored, making them good materials for mounding, since they can add volume and retain some of the shape of the structure. The shells also provide good drainage and reflect light, making the mound even more visually distinctive within the surrounding landscape. Very low degrees of burning indicate that food refuse in the shell layers was not burned after consumption, indicating differences regarding refuse management.

Around 1700 BP, groups stopped using shell valves as the primary raw materials for mounding. From that point on, the site's expansion primarily consisted of soil and fish bones, which led to the formation of a fish-dominant matrix at the end of the occupation. However, the change in mounding materials does not appear to have been accompanied by changes in the other activities related to the funerary rituals.

Isotopic analysis of human remains from different areas of Jabuticabeira II demonstrates that people had a marine-based diet during the entire occupation (Klokler 2008). The individuals belong to five different funerary areas, with radiocarbon dates ranging from approximately 2320 ± 50 to 1400 ± 40 BP. Mean carbon (-10.92) and nitrogen (17.98) isotope values from 14 individuals show reliance upon high-trophic-level fish or marine mammals as staples (Table 11.3). On the other hand, plant elements were also an important part of the diet and of feasts performed at Jabuticabeira II, as demonstrated by Célia H. Boyadjian and Sabine Eggers and by Rita Scheel-Ybert (chaps. 21 and 22 in this volume). The site's assemblage is dominated by fish in mid-trophic and low nitrogen levels, with rare occurrences of marine mammals (Klokler 2008). Differential processing of high-trophic-level fish, such as sharks, could limit their representation in the zooarchaeological record, leading to their underrepresentation in analyses. A similar situation could explain the very rare evidence of marine mammals. It is possible that these animals were processed and their bones were deposited away from the site, resulting in the absence of their elements at Jabuticabeira II.

Focus on the identification and sampling of residential shell sites in the vicinity of Jabuticabeira II would provide important data not only for understanding the isotopic results but also for comparison with the data generated by a myriad of studies. Intensive surveys located two sites whose diverse and rich lithic assemblage are suggestive of habitation locales (Belém 2012; Belém and Penin 2011; Peixoto 2008).

Isotopic results also show that the lack of shells in the fish mound at the site is solely related to a change in construction methods (Nishida 2007) due to a decrease in importance of shellfish in the ritual. At the same time, a shift between the two most common fish species is apparent, with catfish becoming predominant. These changes could be related to the contraction of the lagoon, which would have made the transportation of large quantities of shell valves to the site cumbersome, or it could be due to changes in the mortuary ritual. Further excavations of burial groups in the fish mound can help us understand these changes.

Jabuticabeira II can be envisioned as a monumental site that emitted strong messages to the populations that inhabited the margins of the paleolagoon. The recurring funerary activities that took place within the site, and the site itself, served as testimonies of the shell mound people's ties to the environment and their ancestors. The exact message conveyed by Jabuticabeira II and other shell

Table 11.3. Carbon and nitrogen values from individuals from Jabuticabeira II

Individual	Location	δ 13C	δ15N	Lab ID
B 121, male, adult	Locus 6	-10.6	20.9	CR114538
B 2a, indet, adult	Locus 6	-11.9	17.9	AA77105
B 114, indet, adult	Locus 6	-11.6	18.5	AA77106
B 115, male, old adult	Locus 6	-11.9	21.5	CR114540
B 131, indet, adult	Locus 3	-11.7	15.1	BETA 234201
B 15, male, mid adult,	profile 1.05	-11.17	16.39	S-EVA 4173
B 17, male, mid adult	profile 1.05	-10.95	16.99	S-EVA 4174
B 10b, female, mid adult	1.15.9	-10.01	17.71	S-EVA 4172
B 43, male, mid adult	profile 1.77	-10.02	17.47	S-EVA 4176
B 37, male, old adult	2.15.13	-10.9	18.9	CR114539
B 34, female, young adult	2.15.13	-10.41	17.77	S-EVA 4177
B 36, male, young adult	2.15.13	-10.54	17.58	S-EVA 4178
B 40, female, adult	2.15.13	-11.01	17.22	S-EVA 4179
B 41, male, adult	2.15.13	-10.19	17.85	S-EVA 4171

mounds was lost with the passage of time, but they can be seen as representing earlier successful and sustainable use of the area, as well as constructions indicating the reverence and memorialization of ancestors (Klokler, Gaspar, and DeBlasis 2009).

Jabuticabeira II demarcates three important moments of the ritual lives of sambaqui people. The first is linked with the activities performed for the deposition of the dead: preparation of the funerary area, treatment of the body, interment, placement of offerings, use of hearths, demarcation with palisades, and feasting. Paulo DeBlasis and colleagues (2004) define this as the first level of memory. The second level is related to the maintenance of the ancestral cult through the closing of the funerary area, covering with mounded shell, and possible seasonal performances of feasts that culminated over time in the formation of the final mound. Finally, the mound itself becomes an element of the landscape, representing a third level of social memory (DeBlasis et al. 2004).

Brazilian ethnography offers interesting examples of the performance of feasts and construction of mounds within funerary activities. I (2001, 2008) found similar characteristics between Kaingang funerary rituals and feasting, and the evidence uncovered in sambaqui sites, such as ritual fires, palisades around graves, and mound building (Becker 1995; Manizer 2006). Kaingang groups inhabited the southern coast during colonial times, and

archaeologists commonly identify evidence of their camps at the top of sambaquis. Ethnohistoric research by Ítala Irene Basile Becker (1999) describes three different sets of rituals for the dead. The first was performed right after death and is called *Kiki*; a second set of rituals was organized after eight days; and a final ritual was performed a year after interment, called *Veingréinyã*. This last festival included feasting, reconstruction of mounds, and lighting of ritual fires (Becker 1995; Manizer 2006).

In other regions of South America, ethnographic studies report similar associations of mortuary features and festivals involving food that are performed by several groups in Brazil (Becher 1956; Lowie 1946; Métraux 1946b, 1949; Steward 1949). Descriptions of feasts were found among the Kaingang, Bororo, Tukano, Guaicuru, and Shipaya, among other groups. During the events, food and drink offerings were reserved for deceased group members. These examples highlight the potential time depth of some mortuary practices and are not intended to infer any type of direct continuity between the sambaqui people and these groups.

CONCLUSIONS

In 1875, Carlos Rath offered a translation of the word *sambaqui* as "house of the spirit" (1968 [1875]), more in keeping with the current demonstration that these sites have acted as burial mounds (DeBlasis et al. 1999; DeBlasis et al. 2004; DeBlasis et al. 2007; Fish et al. 1998, 2000; Gaspar 2000; Gaspar et al. 2008; Klokler 2001, 2006, 2008). The realization that Jabuticabeira II was a cemetery has changed the perception of the nature of activities involved in its construction and influenced further research in this area (Gaspar et al., chap. 7 in this volume). The excavation and reanalysis of the small sambaqui of Amourins (in Rio de Janeiro) has confirmed that it too had mortuary character (Gaspar and Klokler 2011). Claudia R. Plens (2007) has identified an example of a freshwater mound that served as a graveyard in Moraes, and we expect that the renewed interest in shell-site studies in Brazil (e.g., Figuti and Plens [chap. 16], Gaspar et al. [chap. 7], Mendonça de Souza [chap. 12], Okumura and Eggers [chap. 8], Scheel-Ybert [chap. 22], all in this volume) can further define the functions of sites within their settlement. Also, detailed studies of habitation sites will provide data that can be compared and contrasted with evidence recovered from funerary sambaquis.

The presence of spatially distinct interment areas at Jabuticabeira II provides archaeologists with a key opportunity to study socially meaningful units. This situation permitted the development of a sampling strategy that targeted shell mounds' social units, a breakthrough approach. The concurrent use of several interment areas in different locations across the site suggests that multiple affinity groups were burying their dead, celebrating their ancestors, performing feasts, and depositing shells and other faunal remains. The enduring nature of these activities ultimately increased the volume and height of the site.

Focus upon the site's most ubiquitous materials, aquatic resources, offers a promising alternative approach to address the existence of variations in ritual behavior, resource access, social status, and changes in resource use. Aquatic resources pervasively structured the lifeways of these societies, and a more nuanced understanding of their significance obviates the notion that faunal assemblages from shell mounds only offer information regarding subsistence and diet. A refinement of the characteristics that identify ritual fauna in archaeological sites can generate new avenues for study and expand our understanding of the past.

ACKNOWLEDGMENTS

I would like to thank all the participants of the "Sambaquis e Paisagem" research project, and the financial support of CAPES (process 1501-02-0), FAPESP (process 97/04094-5), NSF doctoral dissertation grant (SBR-0652177), and CNPq (process 151457/2009-3). I also thank the reviewers, editors, Paulo DeBlasis, and David Mehalic for their comments and suggestions.

CHAPTER TWELVE

Sambaqui People, the Shell Mound Builders of Brazil

A Challenge for Paleodemographers

Sheila Mendonça de Souza

SUMMARY

Paleodemographic analysis of the prehistoric inhabitants of coastal Brazil is challenging as only a small proportion of their sites have been excavated. Based on archaeological evidence, Brazilian shell mounds were generally thought to represent a demographic transition that followed the expansion of the fisher-gatherer populations along the coast after the middle of the Holocene, moving to a more sedentary preagricultural subsistence. Alternatively, this could be regarded as a result of both increased visibility provided by this kind of mound burial and increased preservation afforded by the shell matrix. Here, I discuss existing interpretations concerning the chronology, the density, and the size of the shell mounds along the south-southeastern coast of Brazil, taking into account the variable number of burials in different mounds, especially the small number of immature individuals, and the notion that some of them were built especially for burials. Paleodemographic projects that use up-to-date bioarchaeological approaches and modern laboratory methods for the determination of skeletal age and sex must review these prehistoric burial mounds before it is possible to properly count the dead and face the challenge of explaining what the large number of Brazilian shell mounds represent, and whether they signify a period of increased population growth in prehistory.

INTRODUCTION

Brazil is a tropical country where the preservation of biological remains in archaeological sites is generally poor. For this reason, skeletal series are generally small, with incomplete or poorly preserved skeletons, explaining a dearth of paleodemographic contributions to Brazilian prehistory. In addition, despite the fact that some of these archaeological sites are among the largest prehistoric cemeteries in South America (Alvim, Uchôa, and Gomes 1989; Gaspar 1995; Machado 1983, 1992, 2006; Souza and Souza 1981/1982; Souza 1992/1993), few sambaquis were subject to extensive archaeological excavations, preventing any serious paleodemographic study.

The sambaquis represent a successful prehistoric cultural tradition of the southeastern Brazilian coast that lasted for millennia. The practice of burying the dead among shell remains and ashes aided the preservation of hundreds of human skeletons (Gaspar 1994/1995; Lima 1999/2000; Prous 1991). The large number of sites, as well as the monumental nature of the Brazilian sambaquis, has resulted in paleodemographic hypotheses of relative or increased sedentism. Sambaquis have been compared to the Mesolithic sites of Europe, and may represent a prehistoric social and economic marker of the transition to more sedentary settlements. Improving the paleodemographic research of sambaquis skeletal series will certainly help to elucidate the characteristics of that cultural period of prehistory, as well as the social changes involved, helping to explain the collective projects that built the monumental Brazilian shell mounds.

Brazil has one of the world's most important concentrations of shell mounds, including the biggest sites in the world, harboring several hundred skeletons. Such a heritage has an enormous scientific potential for paleodemography. To perform successful investigations about population size, age composition, sex composition, population growth, and other demographic functions for sambaqui people, it is necessary, of course, to face some methodological challenges (Bocquet-Appel and Masset 1996; Bocquet-Appel and Naji 2006; Buikstra and Königsberg 1985; Chamberlain 2006). Population attributes such as mortality by age and sex, size of groups and populations, number of individuals inhabiting a territorial unit (or population density), life expectancy at birth, mean number of children per childbearing woman, and temporal and spatial variation of populations are extremely relevant to the understanding of sambaqui prehistory. But it is also necessary to understand the relationship of these attributes to the processes that may have added or removed individuals from the groups, to the economic changes that occurred over time, and to the emergence of increased social complexity and other social and cultural changes that accompanied land occupation strategies. Morbidity associated with the mortality profile is also a helpful indicator of the paleodemographic changes of the past populations, and paleopathology must be included in the paleodemographic studies, even while considering the limits imposed by the osteological paradox (Goodman et al. 1988; Larsen 1997; Roksandic and Armstrong 2011; Souza, Carvalho, and Lessa 2003; Wood et al. 1992).

Paleodemography is most often based on the study of skeletal remains, although indirect evidence such as the composition of dwellings, the number of settlements, the area of the sites, and other cultural data have been used for the same purpose. Problems arising from skeletal material are substantial because of the inherent bias, since funeral practices and post-depositional changes act to reduce or distort information. Cultural practices such as the selective burials of the deceased by age, sex, social status, cause of death, and so on may affect the representativeness of the series (for an excellent method in detecting bias, see Jackes 2011).

Since death is a bioculturally selective process, the funeral series from sambaquis, as from other cemeteries, never reproduce the age, sex, and social structure of the original groups, and different individuals have different probabilities of death (Chamberlain 2006; Hassan 1981; Waldron 1994; Wood et al. 1992). In spite of the large number of individuals in some sambaqui collections, they generally do not represent what would be expected of a "natural population." Furthermore, a population cohort, representing a short occupation with a well-known context and good chronology, is extremely rare. As in other skeletal series, the loss of frail skeletons because of differential preservation, and the underestimation of the

number of older adults and females, are some of the biases expected in sambaqui paleodemographic studies (Bass 1995; Buikstra and Ubelaker 1994; Nagaoka and Hirata 2007; Ubelaker 1978; Weiss 1972). Methodological approaches have been attempting to address these problems for a long time (Bocquet-Appel 2002; Bocquet-Appel and Masset 1996; Greene, Van Gerven, and Armelagos 1986; Owsley and Bass 1979).

Our inability to directly assess archeological fertility is another limiting factor in paleodemography. Fertility has to be estimated through indirect formulae such as the juvenility index or juvenile/adult ratio (Bocquet-Appel and Masset 1996): the ratio of juveniles between 5 to 14 years old, to adults more than 20 years old—and the mean childhood mortality (MCM): mean mortality for ages 5–10, 10–15, and 15–20 (Jackes 2011). These two are biologically correlated, and where these two estimates differ they provide information on the direction of bias in the archaeological assemblage. Based on modern mortality models, these methods help to discuss funeral series representing populations whose age structure is unknown. With the help of the juvenility index, the demographic transition accompanying sedentary lifestyles and crop domestication has been studied in different parts of the world (Bocquet-Appel 2002; Bocquet-Appel and Naji 2006), and its application to the study of the sambaqui series would be welcome.

The present chapter discusses some paleodemographic challenges of the study of Brazilian sambaquis and the possibilities offered by paleodemography to understand the prehistory of those groups who lived along the southern coast of Brazil for 6,000 years. The information presented here is based on past publications, but also on current questions, hypotheses, and speculations emerging from the invisible schools of the Brazilian academy. This exercise aims to raise ideas, concerns, and new challenges in order to contribute to future investigations, with the expectation that substantial information on this subject will further our knowledge of Brazilian prehistory in the next years.

SAMBAQUIS OF THE BRAZILIAN COAST: ARCHAEOLOGICAL CONTEXT AND PALEODEMOGRAPHY

Sambaqui people belong to the waves of prehistoric people coming from Asia to America, displaying certain levels of biological diversity. Multivariate analyses (Neves 1988; Neves and Blum 1998; Neves, Bernardo, and Okumura 2007) confirmed Marilia C. de M. Alvim and colleagues' (1975) conclusion that sambaquis varied considerably in time and space and suggest that different groups might have built this type of sites. Genetic distances based on skull epigenetic traits support the hypothesis that sambaqui populations were part of the same population system, probably sharing genes along their wide coastal territories, but keeping their differences (Alvim and Souza 1990; Alvim, Vieira, and Machado 1975).

Cultural variability was also present among the sambaquis across time and space, probably expressing cultural as well as adaptive differences (Souza and Souza 1980). Lina M. Kneip (1998), among others, noticed differences in the composition and cultural content of sites built from 4500 to 1700 BP in Saquarema, Rio de Janeiro. Confirming what was proposed by Paulo Duarte (1968), recent archaeologists agree that in spite of their cultural unity these sites show substantial cultural variability.

Archaeological evidence also indicates changes in the social system of sambaqui builders over time. The emergence of complexity in some areas is suggested, for instance, by the ability to organize cooperative efforts to build monuments, and to keep communal burial mounds for hundreds of years. This new condition would certainly impact grouping and mobility, the frequency of contacts between people, the demographic structure, and the risk of transmissible diseases, among other aspects of their lives. The presence of prestige objects and differential burials in some sites reinforces the hypothesis of social changes (DeBlasis et al. 1998; Lima 1999/2000). Very special artifacts associated with some burials, such as stone and bone sculptures, most of them representing the coastal fauna, suggest an artisan specialization and a possible incipient hierarchy.

Mounds that contain hundreds of burials in complex stratigraphy are highly suggestive of social complexity and large populations. But the very archeological visibility of sambaquis has a considerable impact on our perception of their paleodemography, as their substrate, rich in calcium carbonates and other salts, helped to preserve human bones much better than any other sites in a wet tropical environment. It is even possible that one of the purposes of building sambaquis was to preserve human remains for subsequent worship (Gaspar et al. 2007; Plens 2007). Used for hundreds of years, the sambaquis could have been built by fewer people than expected. Based on the assumption that the substrate of a sambaqui was basically food refuse, José W. Rauth (1968) conducted an exercise estimating how much food per capita would be necessary to build one cubic meter of a typical mound. He concluded that considering dietary needs, a few people eating and building for a

continuous period could easily build a sambaqui. Although we could disagree with Rauth about the function of these sites, it is obvious that an accurate chronology is necessary before we can estimate population size.

Finally, some other types of prehistoric coastal sites were contemporaneous with the sambaquis. Fishermen cultures of the Itaipu Tradition settled on the sand dunes and lagoons near Rio de Janeiro (Dias 1992; Machado 1983; Souza 1977; Souza and Souza 1981/1982). Other kinds of mounds containing more or fewer shells have been described in different regions of the Brazilian coast, making the paleodemographic scenario still more complex.

PALEODEMOGRAPHY OF THE SAMBAQUIS: SOME PREVIOUS ATTEMPTS

Most of the skeletal collections from sambaquis are precarious witnesses. The heterogeneity of the archaeological substrate; the swampy, compressed archaeological layers; and the intense process of diagenesis make the bone and teeth very fragile. In addition, most of the burials are difficult to excavate because of the heterogeneous nature of the archaeological matrix. At the first moment of exposition from the soil, the bones are usually brittle and the cancellous portions are easily shattered or lost.

The literature review for Brazilian sambaquis offers no more than one specialized paper on their paleodemography (Uchôa and Alvim 1989), even though monographs, dissertations, or papers describing burials offer general information concerning sex and age determination. However, paleodemographic considerations are prominent in discussions of sambaquis as they are an important part of the speculations about the peopling of the coast.

SEX AND AGE DISTRIBUTIONS

The sex and age of prehistoric skeletons from sambaquis have been estimated since the 19th century. High sexual dimorphism is a characteristic of the well-nourished sambaqui groups, making sex estimation easier when compared to other prehistoric groups in Brazil. Dimorphism inconsistencies and discrepancies in sex estimation are common in the literature (Sheila M. F. M. de Souza 1991), making bioarchaeological studies of the museum collections difficult.

On the other hand, age estimation is still a major problem for adults and subadults, and most of the papers address this by using broad age intervals (infant, child or immature, and adult). The histology of long bones was first used by Machado (1983) for a coastal site of the Itaipu Tradition, but a second test for sambaquis of Rio de Janeiro was frustrated by differential preservation of bones at the microscopic level. Cultural practices could explain part of the differential preservation, as in the case of the Moa sambaqui, when the intentional use of red clay in the grave seems to have helped to preserve the microscopic structure of bones and DNA integrity (Carter and Tibbett 2008; Marinho et al. 2006). A similar condition seems to be present in the Cubatão I sambaqui (Fischer, Wesolowski, and Souza 2009), where the tiny brittle bones of the newborns and babies found in clay are in a good state of preservation. Transverse cement annulation lines (TCA) (Blondiaux et al. 2006) have also been tested in adult skeletons from the Cabeçuda sambaqui, Santa Catarina State. Teeth roots of premolars provided age for 60 different adult skeletons, and age estimation was obtained in 10 different microscopic fields for each individual. The mortality distribution was reported by Jöel Blondiaux and colleagues (2009), and compared to previous studies (Sheila M. F. M. de Souza 1991, 1995) pointed to underestimation of age.

Few series of sambaquis are equivalent to natural populations (Souza and Ferraz 1974; Souza, Wesolowski, and Rodrigues-Carvalho 2009). Underrepresentation of children and infants, often explained by differential taphonomy (Guy, Masset, and Baud 1997), makes it difficult to estimate juvenility index, life expectancy, or any other life-table parameter for most of these series. Recent fieldwork revisiting sambaquis in the Guapimirin area, Rio de Janeiro State, increased the number of human skeletons documented in the area fourfold and improved knowledge about funeral practices. The total absence of immature individuals of any age is remarkable and confirms the descriptions from the seventies and eighties for the same area where mounds seem to be graves for adults. On the other hand, in other areas, where reported, sambaquis yielded crushed, heavily damaged juvenile skeletons that could not be identified, described, or recovered (Rauth 1962). Field notes and reports provide information on individuals that archaeologists estimated were infants. Dozens of meters of heavy shell layers, a lack of protective encasement, disturbance by animals, the growth of tree roots, and the continuous anthropogenic intervention at the burial grounds, of course, all contributed to the destruction of the evidence.

Where estimates were possible, Souza and Ferraz (1974) and Souza and colleagues (2009) indicated that in São Paulo State 34.7 percent of the skeletons in 11 sambaquis belonged to children. In Paraná State and Santa Catarina State, respectively, 7.2 percent of the skeletons from six sites, and 24.6 percent of the skeletons from eight sites were juveniles. These figures suggest that the mortality profiles of the sambaqui are biased, rendering unreliable any more precise mortality estimates based on currently available collections. Some exceptions, however, point to the possibility of recovering infant burials. In the sambaqui Piaçaguera, São Paulo State, and Cubatão I, Santa Catarina State, infants are found in the expected proportions, suggesting high and early mortality among those prehistoric human groups. In both cases, it is interesting to notice that young children seem to have had a special social meaning, because they were buried with special grave goods made of nonperishable materials like beads, pendants, and big shells (Fischer, Wesolowski, and Souza 2009; Uchôa 2007 [1973]; Wesolowski, Souza, and Fischer 2009). The lowest ratio of infant skeletons is reported for some sambaquis from Rio de Janeiro State, where only 3.5 percent of the skeletons belong to infants. Such large discrepancies point to different archaeological biases. While the absence of children could represent taphonomic effects, differential funeral practices for infants and smaller children should always be considered. In the sites of Rio de Janeiro State, Maria Dulce Gaspar (2003) noticed an elevated number of immature individuals associated with adult graves. Different burial rites for infants and children, or burying them in the reopened graves of adults, are well-described practices for different Brazilian native people (Métraux 1947; Souza 2010). Those practices could have existed in prehistoric times as well.

COLLECTIVE BURIALS? COLLECTIVE DEATHS?

Groups (2 to 12) of primary burials in close contact representing different ages and sexes were found in some sambaquis (Faria 1952; Garcia and Uchôa 1980; Gaspar 1998; Machado 1983). In Piaçaguera, one-third of the burials represented an association of individuals (Uchôa 2007 [1973]). Although the intricate building of the sambaquis hinders individual identification of the funerary structures, the contact between the bones of undisturbed skeletons is strong evidence of their contemporaneity. In the absence of indicators of interpersonal violence in the sambaqui series (Lessa 2009; Lessa and Coelho 2010), the paleoepidemiological hypothesis of collective risk of death caused by toxic red tides, or bursts by coastal salt water *Vibrio*, was proposed (Souza 1995, 1999). The exposure to periodic collective risks of death could cause major demographic oscillations.

In recent excavations, improved taphonomic approach

(Duday 2009; Roksandic 2002) and well-trained teams allow a more detailed examination of burial context. The grouping of burials often suggests that families used the same burial place, and there is evidence of the process of removing shells from the sambaqui for covering of a subsequently deposited corpse, a practice that could explain accidental contacts between the bones. This should be especially true if layers of more fragile shell like the *Mytillus* were crunched or solubilized between two skeletons. Although collective deaths are always a real paleoepidemiologic possibility, close associations between skeletons must also be considered in the cultural context of mound building and funeral practices before any final interpretation about mortality can be proposed.

ESTIMATING THE SIZE OF THE GROUP: AMOUNT OF FOOD? AREA/VOLUME? NUMBER OF BURIALS?

For decades, the sambaquis were thought to have been built on trash. The relationship between what was supposed to be food refuse and the group size was considered logical: counting the shells was counting people. José Wilson Rauth (1962) reported that Kröne was the first to calculate the daily consumption of shells per capita in a sambaqui. Estimating the consumption of mollusks by their remaining shells, Kröne hypothesized that such sites could have been built by a few individuals, in a relatively short time, just using inedible parts of their diet. Other attempts were made to estimate the size of the groups based on the total area of the sites, or in dwelling areas eventually identified on the sambaquis (Barbosa 1999; Hurt and Blasi 1960; Orsich 1977; Rauth 1968).

In *Parâmetros demográficos para a ocupação pré-histórica dos pescadores, coletores e caçadores (Demographic Parameters of the Prehistoric Occupation by Fishers, Gatherers, and Hunters)*, Gaspar (1995) revisited this discussion, recognizing that ethnographic models were insufficient for the interpretation of archaeological sites. Trying to reduce the limitations of the available model, she applied a *log* formula (Wiessner 1974) to the total area of some sambaquis from Rio de Janeiro State. Assuming that they could have had an intermediate social system between hunter-gatherers and horticulturalists (Service 1971), she used 0.68—an intermediate between hunter-gatherers ($\alpha = 0.91$) and horticulturalists ($\alpha = 0.45$)—as a value of the constant α, and applied the formula to 19 sambaquis or similar sites (Gaspar 1995). The results pointed to a group size variation from 36 to 165 individuals. Based on ethnographic data, she further assumed that only 78 percent of

these individuals usually remained in the dwellings, proposing that the groups should actually have between 28 to 127 individuals. She considered that the results were consistent with the prehistoric models for the Brazilian coastal groups without ceramics. Rio de Janeiro State sambaquis are small- and medium-sized, and the sites include some cultural and biological peculiarities (Prous 1991), so Gaspar's results cannot be generalized to sites in other states of Brazil.

It is possible that local populations explored communal areas of coastal resources, living and burying their deceased in neighborhoods (Gaspar 1995, 1998; Gaspar, Barbosa, and Barbosa 1994). The chronology obtained by authors such as Lina M. Kneip (1998), Dione R. Bandeira (2004), and Levy Figuti (2010) confirms that many sambaquis were contemporaneous, probably sharing a common social interactive system at a local/regional level. Adding the size of the groups using the same geographical area, Gaspar (1995) proposed that in Rio de Janeiro, the biggest community of sites could have had up to 180 individuals.

An interesting example is the sambaqui Jabuticabeira II, in Santa Catarina State (8 meters high, 84,000 square meters), which is considered to have been used mostly for burials. The interpretation of 373 meters of profiles, 20 pits, and 3 systematic excavation areas with dozens of human skeletons (DeBlasis et al. 1998; DeBlasis et al. 2007; Fish et al. 2000; Klokler 2008, chap. 11 in this volume) produced an estimate of 0.137 burials per cubic meter of sambaqui. Assuming that the entire site contained mainly funeral structures, more than 43,000 individuals could have been buried along 700 years of continuous occupation. If the estimate is correct, the sambaqui groups, at least in that area, could have reached more than 1,000 individuals, supporting the notion that sambaqui people lived in big groups and that their population could experience fast growth.

Accepting here the Jabuticabeira numbers, we could also estimate that the average deaths per year would be 70. And assuming that the interval between births was four years (as for other non-horticulturalists), the population would have an average number of 280 childbearing-age women, and an equivalent number of adult men (since the male-to-female ratio was in balance). Approximately 840 immature individuals (an average of three infant/children/young per mother) should also be expected. Based on such figures, the mean size of the group using Jabuticabeira II each year would be around 1,050 people. That is 10 to 30 times what was estimated by Gaspar for the Rio de Janeiro sambaquis, which is more than commonly expected for a hunter-gatherer group. Does this express the true conditions for sambaqui groups at Jabuticabeira II? The variable pattern of sambaqui funerary areas in different regions, including the density of burials, suggests that we should consider Jabuticabeira to be a very special example. Based on the 191 burials reported during the excavation of the Cabeçuda sambaqui, another monumental site in Santa Catarina State, Fish and colleagues (2000) calculated a slightly higher burial rate of about 0.160 individuals per cubic meter, reinforcing the conclusion based on Jabuticabeira II that groups on the southern coast of Santa Catarina were large, contrary to what has been described for the northern coast of the same state.

Paleodemographic studies based on life tables were rarely performed for sambaquis. Uchôa and Alvim (1989) tried to estimate parameters for Piaçaguera in São Paulo State. This sambaqui (Uchôa 2007 [1973]) was almost completely excavated, providing 80 burials dated between 4890 ± 110 and 4930 ± 110 BP (noncalibrated). The short, well-defined cohort is represented by an initial period of intensive use, and a gradual reduction of burials, until the complete abandonment of the cemetery in the upper levels. The paleodemographic analysis was based on 77 skeletons: 24 infants, 5 children, 7 adolescents, 4 subadults (18 to 21 years of age), 18 young adults, 15 mature adults, and 4 old adults (over 50 years of age). Proportional mortality was 18.18 percent up to one year of age, increasing to 31.17 percent when the second year of life was also considered. Life expectancy at birth was estimated at 20.87 years, while life expectancy at 15 years was estimated at 17.50 years. The mortality suggested by the figures was considered elevated by Uchôa and Alvim (1989), even sparking discussions as to the possibility of infanticide. But, as Hervé Guy and colleagues (1997) remind us, the mortality up to one year of age in pre-Jennerian populations is high, so the results for Piaçaguera are not really surprising. This may be especially true when data from historical demography in different Asian and European countries is considered. Reported infant mortality rates range from 22 percent to 32 percent of living births, and the figures became even more striking during the Industrial Period (19th century). At that period, the deterioration of sanitary and health conditions associated with the increased population density in the cities resulted in an infant mortality as high as 40 percent in London and 60 percent in Paris. Assuming that some of the youngest Piaçaguera skeletons were probably lost because of taphonomic factors, the infant mortality could be even higher before the number could be unexpected.

Other interpretations of the paleodemographic profile of Piaçaguera are subject to discussion. In Piaçaguera, a higher proportion of male skeletons was suggestive of an unbalanced male-to-female ratio in the original population. Here, the bias in the determination of sex from skeletons may partially explain the results. Another result was the apparent high mortality of young adult women (15.2 percent) compared to young adult men (2.17 percent), which was explained by the natural risks of childbearing. On the other hand, the higher proportion of medium-aged adult men (21.74 percent), compared to women in the same age class (8.7 percent), was attributed to intergroup conflicts. The recent paleopathological studies of the same series, and other series from sambaquis, did not find signs of violence from the bones, so other explanations must be searched for. Assuming a mean interval of four years between living births, it was also possible to estimate the total fertility rate for Piaçaguera, calculated to be 4.4 children per childbearing woman, indicating a positive population growth of 15/1,000 per year. Based on the same numbers, the authors estimated the size of the group building the Piaçaguera to be 40 individuals, close to what was proposed by Gaspar (1995) for some Rio de Janeiro sambaquis.

ADDITIONAL COMMENTS ON SAMBAQUIS PALEODEMOGRAPHY

The notion of groups' using affluent coastal resources and living/burying in the same sambaqui for centuries suggests stability and a demographic transition. Gathering plants, fishing, and hunting for centuries, some of these groups transitioned from small to bigger populations. It is evident that more sambaquis were built and used during certain periods, suggesting that the land occupation was denser, but it is necessary to confirm whether fertility and mortality rates were increasing.

The development of a successful, stable social system, integrating more people from different settlements into an emerging complexity, seems to be expressed in some artifacts and burials, and especially in the competence to build and maintain the monumental mounds for centuries. All that would have affected paleodemographic profiles. It is necessary to investigate the paleodemographic patterns associated with the first sambaqui occupations, as well as with their last occupations; associated with the monumental sites and with the small ones; with the "pure" tradition and with the period of contact and new cultural influences of ceramists. A variety of different paleodemographic conditions would likely emerge from comparative studies along time and space, confirming the transitions associated with a prehistoric Brazilian lifestyle.

At present, the scarce attempts to estimate the size of the groups related to the sambaquis have not overcome the most important methodological challenges of paleodemography, and the use of ethnographic models is especially difficult because there is nothing comparable to sambaquis. In *Um Modelo Etnográfico para Estimativas Paleodemográficas* (*An Ethnographic Model for Paleodemographic Estimates*), Alfredo Souza (1981/1982) tested the Wiessner (1974) formula for some modern Brazilian Indian groups, with moderate success, proposing to validate that the larger the occupation, the less grouped people would be in the settlement. Otherwise Gaspar (1995), in spite of her use of the Wiessner formula to estimate group size at sambaquis, points to the variability of size of groups/settlement areas (Costa and Malhano 1986).

Ethnographic descriptions of the Kayapó, a Brazilian group of horticulturalists speaking a Macro-Jê language, describe the constant movement of extended families (Turner 1992) and consequent low density in their main dwelling sites through the year. Moving from one temporary dwelling to another, one or two kilometers from the previous one, they stay approximately two days in each one. Meanwhile, they return frequently to their permanent crops, complementing their hunting and gathering. In the case of the Kayapó, as with other Macro-Jê groups, mobility does not result from the need for food, but is an important mechanism for maintaining social order. Based also on records prior to contact with the Brazilian national society, Terence Turner (1992) reports that the group even changes its main village site every two to five years, and that a community can have up to a dozen settlements that it occupies alternately over the course of decades. Would such a model fit sambaqui areas? Models of regional mobility have been proposed, and the chronology of synchronic occupation of sites may express a mobility pattern rather than a bigger social grouping. Permanent groups with sedentary lifestyles are generally associated with an increased risk of transmissible diseases (Cohen and Armelagos 1984). Contamination of the inhabited lands, exposure to infected vectors, and contagion by interpersonal contacts tend to increase in relation to the size of the group, and inversely with human mobility (Cockburn 1967; Martín 2005). Thus, mortality in hunter-fisher-gatherer groups is frequently lower than in horticultural groups (Hassan 1981). Meanwhile, sedentary or semisedentary conditions, especially in the presence of high-calorie diets, help to increase fertility and accelerate the population growth. Are the morbidity, mortality, and birth rates in sambaqui groups suggestive of mobile or sedentary groups? More precise and consistent age estimations in good and representative cohorts are needed before we can discuss mortality and fertility in sambaquis.

The prevalence of nonspecific stress indicators such as linear enamel hypoplasia, growth-arrested lines (Parker-Harris lines), porotic hyperostosis/*cribra orbitalia*, and also periostitis, is high for some sambaquis, which suggests increasing infectious or nutritional stress among those groups (Alvim, Uchôa, and Gomes 1989; Neves and Wesolowski 2002; Souza 1995, 1999; Storto, Eggers, and Lahr 2001; Wesolowski 2000). Such findings support low mobility and elevated population density in some areas. The interpretation of various health indices (Neves and Wesolowski 2002) suggests that the sambaqui groups were healthier than other prehistoric groups, in spite of the high frequencies of infection and stress indicators (Souza 1999; Souza, Wesolowski, and Rodrigues-Carvalho 2009). Were the sambaqui groups really the most successful hunter-fisher-gatherers of Brazil's prehistory? Can we use this as a general assumption? The first epidemiological surveys are being conducted through detailed analysis of existing collections; more information about health will be available in coming years to support discussions on paleodemography.

The Babitonga Bay and the Palmital channel, north of Santa Catarina State, are good examples of an area where an increasing number of sambaquis were built during a certain period. Bandeira (2004) reports 136 sambaquis, most of which are concentrated within the modern city limits of Joinville and the surrounding area, suggesting a significant expansion of the prehistoric population in the area between 2,000 and 4,000 years ago. Within that period, the site of Cubatão I in the heart of the coastal marshes was used continuously for about 800 years (Figuti 2010). Occupying new ecotones with a high carrying capacity, and developing an efficient and socially successful lifestyle, would certainly be advantageous to both increasing fertility and concentrating the population. Some sambaquis show discontinuous occupation or very slow increase in the archeological deposits (Kneip et al. 1991), while sites like Piaçaguera in São Paulo (Uchôa 2007 [1973]) were used for only a few decades. The long and short occupation periods, the continuity or lack thereof, seem to be related not only to economy but to social and cultural determinants, and funerary strata with large numbers of burials can be followed by others where burials are scarce (Faria 1952; Gaspar 1995). These fluctuations were interpreted as use/abandonment cycles, but they could have represented an intentional building strategy such as expansion of the mound for a residence, or a cemetery (DeBlasis et al. 2007; Lima 1999/2000; Prous 1991). These different interpretations will obviously affect paleodemographic analyses and call for better dating framework for all of these sites.

Fission-fusion patterns (Neel and Salzano 1967) explain the separation and aggregation of groups of families among many of the South American indigenous peoples; they are not necessarily defined by economic or ecological determinants. In areas where the sambaquis were used for no more than a few decades, it is possible that the cycles of use express similar processes. In the cemeteries, fission could be expressed by a decrease in the number of burials; fusion, on the other side, may be expressed by an increase in burials. This is a hypothesis to be verified in future bioarchaeological studies.

The presence of small family units seems to be visible in the spatial arrangement of burials, as in Cubatão I. Migrations, contacts, depopulation, fusion of groups, and other mechanisms leading to demographic changes should be searched for considering general archaeological data but also for funeral structures and other aspects of material culture, for the set of gestures and processes inferred from field taphonomy, and finally for counting the dead.

As in the Neolithic transition discussed for the Northern Hemisphere (Bocquet-Appel and Naji 2006), the management of affluent food resources can support population growth. It is possible that the incremental events for sambaquis occurred over a few hundred years, before the groups reached a higher threshold of food supply-demand equilibrium. The increase in energy intake provided by a diet strongly supplemented by carbohydrates seems to be present only in some sambaqui areas such as the Babitonga Bay, for instance. This special condition could have had a demographic impact by anticipating menarche, reducing postpartum amenorrhea, reducing interbirth intervals, and increasing fertility (Stearns and Koella 2008). Until new data is compiled and interpreted, the classic model proposing the sambaqui peoples as "large" groups still awaits proof. The biological and cultural diversity of the sambaqui groups, the specificities of the sites' funeral and dwelling uses, and other characteristics should orient such paleodemographic studies, since different sites can express different mortality and birth profiles. Meanwhile, the existence of prehistoric models proposing that the sambaqui groups underwent transitions over time and across space not only forces one to think of different demographic

moments, but highlights the importance of investigating such diversity in the context of Brazil's prehistoric coastal settlement.

The coastal sambaquis in Brazil were used for longer periods than the villages of ceramists and horticulturalists along the coast. This longer use is probably a consequence of a social pattern, but it was not the same in all coastal regions. Other prehistoric cultures also built mounds in Brazil. In Teso dos Bichos, on Marajó Island, 20 floors excavated in one occupation allowed an estimate of 50 people per dwelling, which would give a total of 1,000 individuals living on that site over the course of 900 years of occupation. Those figures are close to what was estimated for a large burial site like Jabuticabeira II on the basis of the hypothetical number of burials. The size of occupation in the first case, and the number of burials in the second case, suggest an approximate number of individuals using the site, as well as sedentary patterns. Here we can have an idea of what "large" means in terms of prehistoric sites in Brazil, even though this concept is not defined demographically. In both cases, the concentration of people was likely to be sustained by a social structure acting on abundant renewable resources.

Conservative demographic estimates, obtained when Europeans first arrived in Brazil, indicated an indigenous population of more than one million individuals. Recent estimates based on archeological evidence point to more than six million individuals in the Amazon alone. According to the ethnographic record for the Pau-d'Arco Kayapó, conducted in the late 19th century, there were some 1,500 individuals distributed in four neighboring villages (Cunha 1992; Turner 1992). According to Carlos Fausto (1992), the Tupinambá could have numbered between 500 and 3,000 individuals in a single village. These examples highlight that local populations of more than a thousand individuals are not unknown for horticulturalists; unfortunately, except for the Amazonian *cacicados*, even such references are scarce.

Although the sambaqui groups, like some other non-horticulturalist groups, may have reached a thousand individuals in certain areas, the absence of village floors compatible with such a group size suggests that the sambaqui people were probably distributed in different settlements, even when using the same burial mound. The emergence of a social system allowing the groups to share areas of economic exploitation, keeping them in close contact along bays, lagoons, and mangroves, is a model under discussion (Gaspar 2003; Lima 1999/2000). Possibilities including large groups, concentrations of smaller groups in nearby areas, or increasing population growth need to be verified, considering distinct elements to be tested with more adequate data and paleodemographic methods.

The demographic transition that followed sedentarization, confirmed in Europe and North America, probably also occurred on other continents. The paleodemographic investigation of sambaquis could be the key to understanding this process on the southern coast of Brazil. The juvenility index, used for current populations such as the Xavante (Flowers 1994), has proven to be sensitive, helping to discern situations where, for example, the censuses based on oral reports are very imprecise. Such tools are already available for paleodemography and should be applied to more detailed knowledge of the sambaqui peoples. Another transition, arising from the cultural and biological occupation of the coast by the pottery-bearing groups and other horticulturalists, brought about another important demographic transformation. It occurred along this immense frontier of prehistoric, interethnic friction, whether or not followed by the physical demise of the sambaqui groups. We should recall that recent ethnographic examples have yielded surprises due to the demographic resilience of populations pressured by contact (Pagliaro, Azevedo, and Santos 2005). Paleodemographic studies of the more recent coastal sites can help tell their past history of successes, changes, or disappearances.

Most of the sambaqui skeletal collections come from past excavations. Taphonomic factors have biased the series (Souza and Ferraz 1974; Souza, Wesolowski, and Rodrigues-Carvalho 2009), and a wide variation in the representativeness of excavated areas, besides the average number of 30 skeletons per site, makes most of the material of low interest or value for paleodemography. In some areas, the sites have been extensively destroyed. The few well-preserved areas are the focus of new bioarchaeological projects centered on funerary interpretation. Paleodemography of the sambaqui groups, or shell mound builders, is essential for understanding their cultural and economic cycle, with great adaptive significance for Brazil's prehistory. Saved and preserved inside those immense secret boxes built by the human hand are their cemeteries, resisting the wet tropical climate. Their skeletons are in sufficiently good conditions to be deciphered, as long as we are capable of investing more in recovering and analyzing them.

CHAPTER THIRTEEN

Do Cultural Markers Reflect Biological Affinities?

A Test Using Prehistoric Ceramist and Non-Ceramist Groups from Coastal Brazil

Mercedes Okumura

SUMMARY

Archaeologists have been proposing models about the prehistoric settlement of the Brazilian coast based on cultural differences and/or innovations observed in the archaeological record. However, are cultural changes associated with distinct biological groups?

In order to establish a better understanding of the potential affinities among series originating from different archaeological sites, we took into account the presence of possible cultural variables, focusing on the presence or absence of pottery. Pottery is the most important cultural variable observed in these sites, and most of the models about the occupation of the Brazilian coast are based on its presence or absence. Moreover, the occurrence of pottery along the Brazilian coast is one of the few well-established archaeological markers in terms of chronology.

In this chapter, we discuss the biological affinities among individuals exhumed from archaeological sites that do or do not present pottery, focusing on the region of Santa Catarina, using multivariate statistical tests applied to metric and non-metric cranial data. These analyses can provide valuable information to discuss whether biological differences can be paralleled with cultural changes observed among groups. The ideas put forth here represent an updated version of a previous work (Okumura 2007, 2008).

INTRODUCTION

Shell mounds are archaeological sites associated with populations that intensely colonized the southern Brazilian coast (Lima 1999/2000). These sites present an elevation showing layers formed by shells associated with faunal remains, charcoal, artifacts, and burials (Duarte 1968; Prous and Piazza, 1977). Currently, there is a consensus that these sites spanned 6500 and 800 years BP, and most of them are dated from between 5000 to 3000 years BP. Traditionally, the temporal boundary of 6000 BP was linked to the idea of changes in sea level, which rose after this date. Therefore, if shell mounds were built before 6000 BP, the sea-level change would have resulted in submerged sites and consequent destruction (Lima 1999/2000).

A very important feature of these sites in terms of material culture is the presence of pottery in some sites. Although this is not the only significant cultural variable observed in these sites, it is surely the one upon which most of the models about the occupation of the Brazilian coast were based. In fact, while the appearance of pottery in the Brazilian coast is one of the few well-established chronological archaeological markers (Lima 1999/2000), pottery seems to be associated with important lifestyle changes of these prehistoric coastal groups (Lima 1999/2000; Prous 1991; Schmitz 1984). It has been suggested that the appearance of pottery in the most recent layers of shell mounds is probably related to the migration of a new, biologically distinct group into this region (Neves 1988; Neves and Cocilovo 1984).

Around 1000 years BP, the first evidence of pottery can be seen on the coast of Brazil. In the Rio de Janeiro and Espírito Santo states, the first occurrence of pottery is associated with the Una Tradition[1] (Dias 1967/1977), while in the northern coast of Santa Catarina and Paraná, with the Itararé Tradition[2] (Chmyz 1976). Certainly both traditions originated inland and later dispersed to the coast.

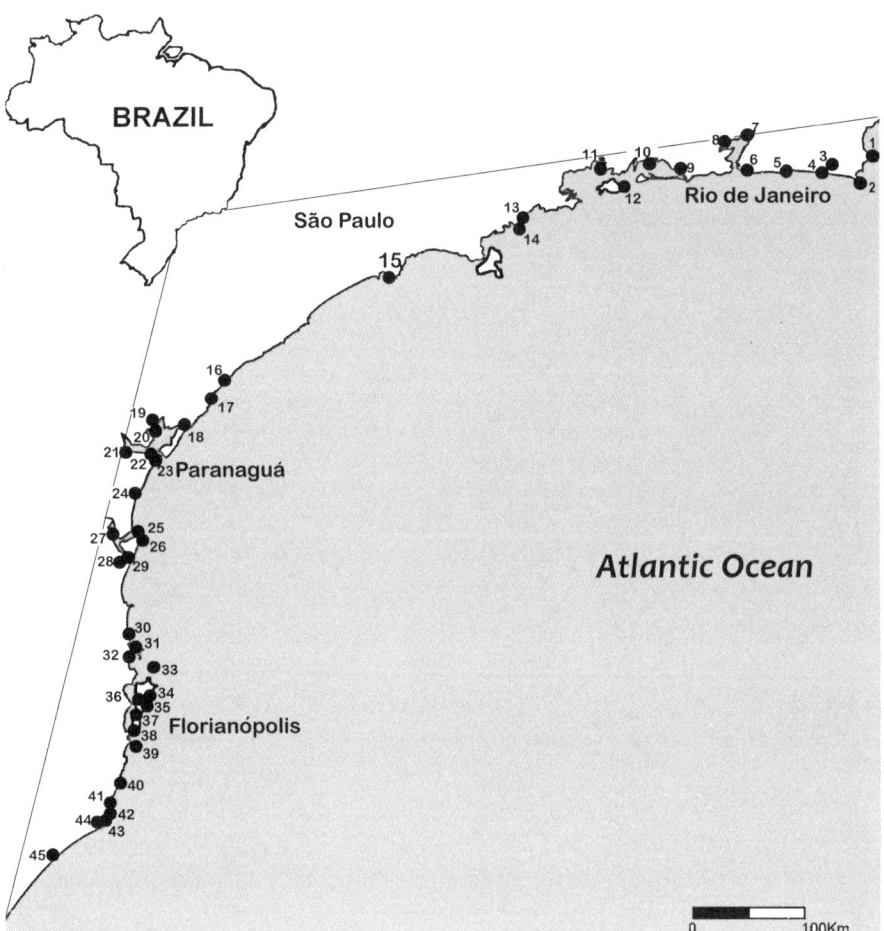

Evidence of contact between Una pottery makers and shell mound groups in Rio de Janeiro can be observed, in some cases, in terms of a change in the material cultural and funerary practices (Barbosa-Guimarães 2007). The supposed arrival of horticultural groups with pottery from the inland to the coast would have accelerated the end of the shell mound societies, potentially through extinction or absorption. The presence of pottery-producing horticulturalists by around 1000 BP was a widespread phenomenon observed all over the Atlantic coast, being at least partially responsible for the drastic decrease, in some cases, or the total paralysis, in other cases, of the shell mound-building activity (Beck 1972a; Chmyz 1976; Neves 1988).

The presence of pottery in the coastal areas of Santa Catarina and Paraná is still an issue under discussion. Some researchers argue that the fisher-gatherer groups living there acquired the knowledge of making pottery through contact with ceramist groups coming from the inland, or that pottery was being traded to the coast and that the coastal subsistence system remained constant (Bryan 1977).

However, Anamaria Beck (1974) defends the idea that, at least in Santa Catarina, the changes in material culture could only be explained by the replacement of the coastal cultural tradition by an inland ceramist tradition. The presence of a new biological group (defined in terms of cranial morphology) on the coast of Santa Catarina has been supported by Walter A. Neves (1988), who described important differences between groups associated or not with pottery on the northern coast of Santa Catarina. Therefore, it seems that at least in the northern region of that state, the presence of ceramics would be associated with the arrival of a new biological group, distinct from the one that built the shell mounds. Following the same idea (that pottery played no part in the shell mound culture), Igor Chmyz (1976, 12) describes the pottery found on the top layers of shell mounds at the coast of Paraná as "not belonging to the shell mounds themselves." In São Paulo, this question also remains unsolved, mainly because there is a paucity of studies about the presence of pottery in shell mounds. It is known that there are some shallow sites associated with the

Itararé Tradition, as in the Ilhabela region (Cali 2004), but there are no descriptions about the presence of pottery on the surface of shell mounds, as observed in Santa Catarina and Paraná.

MATERIAL AND METHODS

In this study, we present the results of a morphological comparative analysis involving human skeletons recovered from coastal shell mounds in southern Brazil, with emphasis on the Santa Catarina region (Figure 13.1). This choice is justified due to the greater amount of information regarding the presence of pottery in sites from this region (Santa Catarina) in comparison with the others (Rio de Janeiro, São Paulo, and Paraná). Only adult skeletons from both sexes were included in this analysis. Table 13.1 presents the male and female samples utilized in the first general analyses, including the maximum number of 939 individuals from the southern Brazilian coast. Table 13.2 presents the samples used in the second set of analyses, focusing on the coast of the Santa Catarina State (390 individuals from 32 groups), and Tables 13.3 to 13.5 present the series included

in the analysis of the northern coast (114 individuals from 19 sites), the central coast (50 individuals from 4 sites), and the Island of Santa Catarina (123 individuals from 9 sites), respectively.

For craniometric data, the use of average values for each series, instead of individual values, had to be adopted in the case of Principal Component Analyses (PCA) (Table 13.6). The biological affinities were explored through cluster analyses applied to the Euclidian distance using the Ward method (Ward 1963).

In the analysis based on non-metric data, male and female samples were grouped together because we could not find any significant difference between the frequencies of traits between sexes. Only the left side of the skull was considered (in the case of lateral traits), and 32 non-metric traits were recorded according to Gertrud Hauser and Gian F. De Stefano (1989). Non-metric traits were analyzed using the Sanghvi Distance (Sanghvi 1953) and the Mean Measure of Divergence (MMD), and the morphological affinities among groups were explored through multidimensional scaling and cluster analysis (Ward method, Ward 1963).

Table 13.1. Series included in the general analysis of the Southern Brazilian coast[a]

Series	Description	Number on Map	N male	N female	N (both sexes)
NRJ	Northern coast of Rio de Janeiro state	1–5	30	31	84
CRJ	Central coast of Rio de Janeiro state	6–8	2	-	-
SRJ	Southern coast of Rio de Janeiro state	9–12	16	18	47
NSP	Northern coast of São Paulo state	13–14	5	7	18
CSP	Central coast of São Paulo state	15	27	15	68
SSP	Southern coast of São Paulo state	16–17	5	10	22
NPR	Northern coast of Paraná state	18–23	19	28	62
SPR	Southern coast of Paraná state	24	10	16	37
NSCC	Northern coast of Santa Catarina state	25–29	24	20	58
NSC	Northern coast of Santa Catarina state (with pottery)	25–29	38	51	153
CSCC	Central coast of Santa Catarina state	30–32	28	20	66
CSC	Central coast of Santa Catarina state (with pottery)	30–32	5	4	9
ISC	Island of Santa Catarina	33–39	52	57	129
ISCC	Island of Santa Catarina (with pottery)	33–39	10	16	30
SSC	Southern coast of Santa Catarina state	40–45	53	54	156
Total			324	347	939

[a] Skulls for which sex could be determined were used for craniometric analysis ("N male" and "N female" columns). The column "N (both sexes)" refers to the individuals used for the analyses of non-metric traits.

Table 13.2. Series included in the Santa Catarina coast analysis (craniometric data) a

Series	Number on Map	N male	N female
Areias Pequenas	29	3	-
Armação do Sul	38	4	5
Balsinha I	40	8	4
Base Aérea	37	18	17
Cabeçuda	42	25	26
Cabeçudas	30	8	8
Caieira	41	2	-
Carniça I	42	1	-
Congonhas I	44	2	4
Enseada I	26	11	8
Forte Marechal Luz (without pottery)	25	5	3
Forte Marechal Luz C (with pottery)	25	3	-
Içara	45	7	7
Ilha de Espinheiros II	29	2	5
Itacoara	28	10	11
Jabuticabeira II	43	4	3
Jaguaruna 32	43	1	-
Laguna (region)	42	-	2
Laranjeiras I	31	5	4
Laranjeiras II	31	19	11
Linguado (region)	29	1	-
Linguado Estadual	29	1	-
Magalhães	43	1	3
Morro do Ouro	29	12	18
Pântano do Sul I	38	1	6
Passagem do Rio D'Una I	40	2	-
Ponta das Almas	35	3	4
Porto do Rio Vermelho 2	34	3	5
Rio Lessa	36	1	-
Rio Pinheiros (region)	29	3	-
Rio Pinheiros 8	29	3	3
Tapera	37	30	34
Total		199	191

a Only skulls where sex could be determined were used.

Table 13.3. Series included in the Northern Santa Catarina coast analysis (craniometric data)

Series	Number on Map	N male	N female
Areias Pequenas	29	3	2
Conquista	29	2	3
Costeira	29	1	-
Cubatãozinho	27	1	-
Enseada I	26	11	7
Estrada de Ferro	29	-	1
Forte Marechal Luz (without pottery)	25	5	1
Forte Marechal Luz C (with pottery)	25	3	1
Gamboa	29	1	-
Ilha de Espinheiros II	29	2	3
Itacoara	28	10	11
Linguado (region)	29	1	1
Linguado Estadual	29	1	1
Morretinha	29	1	1
Morro do Ouro	29	12	9
Rio Comprido	29	2	1
Rio Pinheiros (region)	29	3	1
Rio Pinheiros 8	29	3	3
São Francisco do Sul (region)	29	-	1
Total		62	52

Table 13.4. Series included in the Central Santa Catarina coast analysis (craniometric data)

Series	Number on Map	N male	N female
Cabeçudas	30	8	5
Laranjeiras I	31	5	1
Laranjeiras II	31	19	10
Praia do Embrulho	32	1	1
Total		33	17

Table 13.5. Series included in the Island of Santa Catarina analysis (craniometric data)

Series	Number on map	N male	N female
Armação do Sul	38	4	3
Base Aérea	37	17	13
Ilha do Arvoredo	33	1	1
Pântano do Sul I	38	1	4
Ponta das Almas	35	3	2
Porto do Rio Vermelho 02	34	3	4
Praia Grande	34	1	1
Rio Lessa	36	1	-
Tapera	37	31	33
Total		**62**	**61**

RESULTS

Biological Affinities Among Groups from the Southern Brazilian Coast

Table 13.7 shows the Eigenvalues and percentages of original variation expressed by each Principal Component (PC) for the male series.

Figure 13.2a shows the cluster generated from the first nine PCs (98.1 percent) for the male sample. As verified in previous analyses (Okumura 2007, 2008), the skeletal series of the southern coast cluster into two main groups: one formed by the Santa Catarina series (except the Island of Santa Catarina group without pottery) and those excavated at the northern coast of Paraná, and another formed by the São Paulo and Rio de Janeiro series. The groups associated with pottery from the northern and central coasts of Santa Catarina are grouped together; however, the ceramist group from the Island of Santa Catarina presents more affinities with the non-pottery group from the northern region of this state.

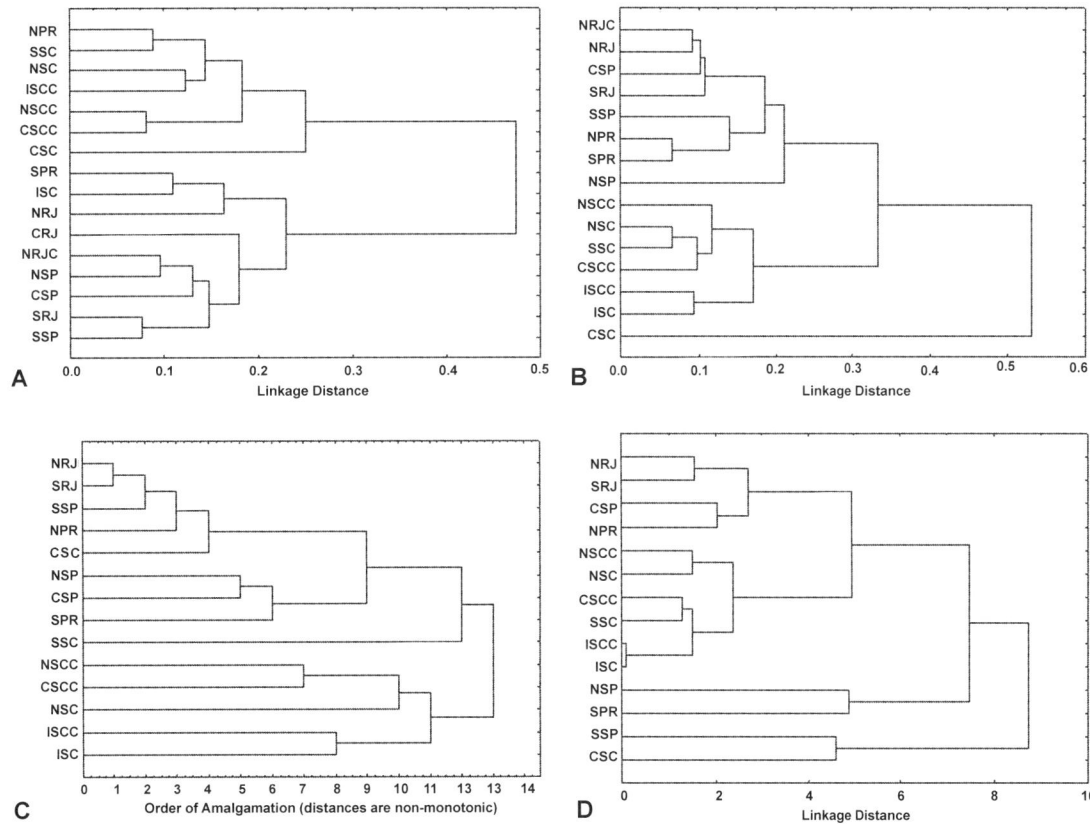

13.2. *Southern Brazilian coast samples. (A) Cluster analysis generated from the first nine PCs (male sample). (B) Cluster analysis generated from the first nine PCs (female sample). (C) Representation of the matrix of MMD based on the cluster analysis through unweighted pair-group centroid method. Both sexes. (D) Representation of the matrix of Sanghvi Distance based on the cluster analysis through Ward method.*

Table 13.6. Variables utilized in the Principal Component analysis of craniometric data[a]

Variable	Description	Southern Brazilian Coast		SC Coast		Northern SC		Central SC		Island of SC	
		Male	Female	Male	Female	Male	Female	Male	Female	Male	Female
GOL	Glabella-occipital length	+	+	+	+	+	+	+	+	+	+
XCB	Maximum cranial breadth	+	+	+	+	+	+	+	+	+	+
STB	Bistephanic breadth	+	+	+	+	+	+	-	+	+	+
AUB	Biauricular breadth	+	+	+	+	+	+	+	+	+	+
NLB	Nasal breadth	-	-	+	+	-	-	-	+	-	+
MAB	Palate breadth	-	-	+	+	-	-	-	+	-	+
ASB	Biasterionic breadth	+	+	+	+	+	+	+	+	+	+
NLH	Nasal height	-	-	-	-	+	-	-	-	-	-
OBH	Orbit height	-	-	-	+	-	-	+	-	+	-
OBB	Orbit breadth	-	-	-	+	-	-	+	-	+	-
ZMB	Bimaxillary breadth	-	-	-	+	-	-	-	-	-	-
FMB	Bifrontal breadth	+	+	+	+	+	+	+	-	+	+
NAS	Nasio-frontal subtense	+	+	+	-	+	+	+	+	+	+
DKB	Interorbital breadth	+	+	+	+	+	+	+	+	+	+
WMH	Cheek height	+	-	+	+	-	+	+	+	+	+
FRC	Frontal chord	+	+	+	+	+	+	+	+	+	+
FRS	Frontal subtense	+	-	+	-	+	+	+	+	+	+
PAC	Parietal chord	+	+	+	+	+	+	+	+	+	+
PAS	Parietal subtense	+	+	+	+	+	+	+	+	+	+
OCC	Occipital chord	+	+	-	+	-	+	-	+	+	+
OCS	Occipital subtense	+	+	-	+	-	+	-	+	+	+
VRR	Vertex radius	+	+	+	+	+	+	+	+	+	+
BRR	Bregma radius	+	+	+	+	+	+	+	+	+	+
NAR	Nasion radius	+	+	+	+	+	+	+	+	+	+
LAR	Lambda radius	+	+	+	+	+	-	+	-	+	-
OSR	Opisthion radius	+	+	-	+	-	-	-	-	+	-

[a] +: metric values available; -: metric values not available.

Table 13.8 shows the Eigenvalues and percentages of original variation expressed by each PC for the female series.

Figure 13.2b presents the cluster analysis generated by the first nine PCs (98.8 percent) concerning the female sample. Again, the southern Brazilian coast presents a separation into two main branches: a branch formed by groups from Santa Catarina, and another one formed by groups from the rest of the coast. The pottery groups from north and central Santa Catarina are in the same branch, which also includes series without pottery. The groups from Santa Catarina Island show affinities to the rest of the Santa Catarina groups, regardless of the presence or absence of pottery. The group from the central coast of Santa Catarina is an outlier.

Table 13.9 presents the matrix of significance obtained through the distances given by MMD for both sexes together. It is possible to observe that most of the series from Santa Catarina are significantly different from those of the northern coast of Rio de Janeiro. Strangely, the series from the north and south coasts of Santa Catarina

without pottery are different from the pottery and non-pottery series from the Island of Santa Catarina. Moreover, the northern coast of this state is also significantly different from the southern coast of the same state.

In the cluster analysis shown in Figure 13.2c, there are again two main branches formed by Santa Catarina in opposition to the other regions (except the central coast of Santa Catarina, which groups with São Paulo, Rio de

Table 13.7. *Eigenvalues and percentages of original variation expressed by each PC (male series), Southern Brazilian coast analysis (craniometric data)*

PC	Eigenvalue	Total %	Cumulative Eigenvalue	Cumulative %
1	0.007281	51.14591	0.007281	51.1459
2	0.002176	15.28459	0.009456	66.4305
3	0.001158	8.13509	0.010615	74.5656
4	0.001037	7.28522	0.011652	81.8508
5	0.000942	6.61810	0.012594	88.4689
6	0.000657	4.61335	0.013250	93.0823
7	0.000315	2.21202	0.013565	95.2943
8	0.000226	1.59075	0.013792	96.8850
9	0.000168	1.17980	0.013960	98.0649
10	0.000127	0.89564	0.014087	98.9605
11	0.000088	0.62095	0.014176	99.5814
12	0.000038	0.26623	0.014213	99.8477
13	0.000013	0.09066	0.014226	99.9383
14	0.000009	0.06167	0.014235	100.0000

Table 13.8: *Eigenvalues and percentages of original variation expressed by each PC (female series), Southern Brazilian coast*

PC	Eigenvalue	Total %	Cumulative Eigenvalue	Cumulative %
1	0.008869	51.50460	0.008869	51.5046
2	0.003161	18.35834	0.012031	69.8629
3	0.001969	11.43432	0.014000	81.2973
4	0.000905	5.25514	0.014905	86.5524
5	0.000660	3.83159	0.015565	90.3840
6	0.000528	3.06581	0.016092	93.4498
7	0.000446	2.59032	0.016539	96.0401
8	0.000288	1.67035	0.016826	97.7105
9	0.000180	1.04286	0.017006	98.7533
10	0.000124	0.72007	0.017130	99.4734
11	0.000079	0.45917	0.017209	99.9326
12	0.000010	0.05733	0.017219	99.9899
13	0.000002	0.01011	0.017220	100.0000

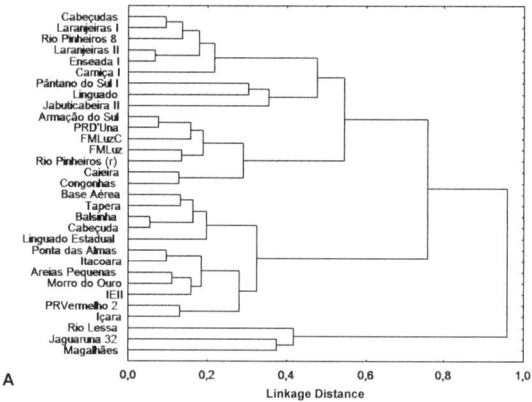

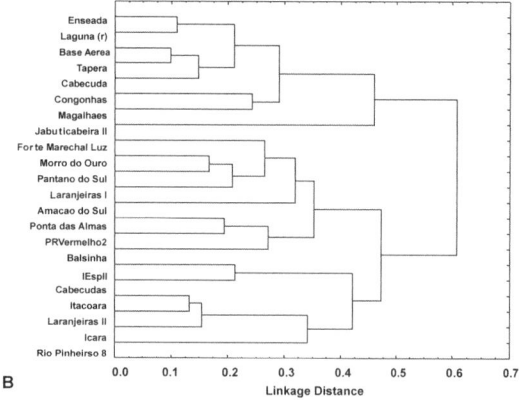

13.3. *Santa Catarina coast samples. (A) Cluster analysis generated from the first ten PCs (male sample). (B) Cluster analysis generated from the first 13 PCs (female sample).*

Janeiro, and Paraná). Again, the pottery series from the north and center of Santa Catarina cluster into one group, whereas the pottery series from the Island of Santa Catarina presents similarities to the island series without pottery.

Figure 13.2d presents the cluster analysis based on the Sanghvi distance for males and females together. The series from Santa Catarina can be observed in an exclusive branch (except for the central coast without pottery), and the pottery series from the Island and the northern coast show affinities with their own regions, independently of the cultural affiliation (with or without pottery). The pottery group from the central coast of Santa Catarina is associated with the southern coast of the same state.

Biological Affinities Among Groups from the Coast of Santa Catarina

Table 13.10 shows the Eigenvalues and percentages of original variation expressed by each PC for the male series.

Figure 13.3a presents the cluster analysis generated by the first ten PCs (97.5 percent). There are some interesting associations, particularly the association of Base Aérea and Tapera (groups from the Island of Santa Catarina presenting pottery associated to Itararé Tradition). This is also the case with Laranjeiras II and Enseada I, both associated with pottery groups. On the other hand, there are pottery series that show more affinities with series from the same geographic location, rather than cultural association. This

Table 13.9. *Significance matrix obtained through MMD (mean measure of divergence)*[a]

	NRJ	SRJ	NSP	CSP	SSP	NPR	SPR	NSCC	NSC	CSCC	CSC	ISCC	ISC
SRJ	0												
NSP	0	0											
CSP	0	0	0										
SSP	0	0	0	0									
NPR	0	0	0	0	0								
SPR	0	0	0	0	0	0							
NSCC	1	0	0	0	0	0	0						
NSC	1	1	0	0	0	0	0	0					
CSCC	1	0	0	0	0	0	0	0	0				
CSC	0	0	0	0	0	0	0	0	0	0			
ISCC	1	1	0	0	0	0	0	0	1	0	0		
ISC	1	1	0	0	0	0	0	0	1	0	0	0	
SSC	1	0	0	0	0	0	0	0	1	0	0	1	1

[a] Males and females together. Significant distances are signaled by number one. Non-significant distances are referred to as zero.

Table 13.10. Eigenvalues and percentages of original variation expressed by each PC (male series), coast of Santa Catarina

PC	Eigenvalue	Total %	Cumulative Eigenvalue	Cumulative %
1	0.012312	31.29023	0.012312	31.2902
2	0.007995	20.31950	0.020306	51.6097
3	0.005021	12.76108	0.025327	64.3708
4	0.004123	10.47770	0.029450	74.8485
5	0.002895	7.35791	0.032345	82.2064
6	0.001898	4.82377	0.034243	87.0302
7	0.001184	3.00861	0.035427	90.0388
8	0.000996	2.53093	0.036423	92.5697
9	0.000922	2.34228	0.037344	94.9120
10	0.000702	1.78425	0.038046	96.6963
11	0.000381	0.96859	0.038427	97.6649
12	0.000267	0.67917	0.038695	98.3440
13	0.000244	0.61903	0.038938	98.9631
14	0.000182	0.46298	0.039120	99.4260
15	0.000111	0.28108	0.039231	99.7071
16	0.000078	0.19768	0.039309	99.9048
17	0.000023	0.05847	0.039332	99.9633
18	0.000012	0.02994	0.039343	99.9932
19	0.000003	0.00680	0.039346	100.0000

is the case of Cabeçudas, a pottery site from the central coast that is found associated with Laranjeiras I, a site without pottery from the same region. The same was observed with the series without pottery from Forte Marechal Luz and Rio Pinheiros (region).

Table 13.11 shows the Eigenvalues and percentages of original variation expressed by each PC for the female series.

Figure 13.3b presents the cluster analysis generated from the first 13 PCs (98.1 percent). There is no exclusive branch formed by a unique region of Santa Catarina. Base Aérea and Tapera are again associated. The formation of a branch presenting Cabeçudas, Itacoara, and Laranjeiras II shows that there is a certain degree of affinity between pottery groups.

Biological Affinities Among Subgroups
from the Coast of Santa Catarina
Northern Coast of Santa Catarina: Babitonga Bay Region

Table 13.12 shows the Eigenvalues and percentages of original variation expressed by each PC for the male series.

Figure 13.4a presents the cluster analysis generated by the first ten PCs (98.4 percent). One group is formed by Costeira, Rio Pinheiros 8, and Linguado, while another

group is formed by Gamboa, Cubatãozinho, Linguado Estadual, Areias Pequenas, and Ilha de Espinheiros II. The third group observed is formed by Morretinha, Morro do Ouro, Conquista, Enseada I, Itacoara, Rio Pinheiros (region), Forte Marechal Luz, Rio Comprido, and Forte Marechal Luz C (with pottery). Enseada I and Itacoara, both associated with pottery, are found together. However, Forte Marechal Luz C (with pottery), presents affinities with Rio Comprido (without pottery).

Table 13.13 shows the Eigenvalues and percentages of original variation expressed by each PC for the female series.

Figure 13.4b presents the cluster analysis generated from the first 12 PCs (99.07 percent). It is possible to verify the formation of two main groups. Ilha de Espinheiros II, Linguado, Linguado Estadual, Estrada de Ferro, Forte Marechal Luz, and Morretinha form a very well-defined group in opposition to the other series.

Central Coast of Santa Catarina: From Itajaí to Bombinhas

Table 13.14 shows the Eigenvalues and percentages of original variation expressed by each PC for the male series.

Figure 13.5a presents the cluster analysis generated from

Table 13.11. Eigenvalues and percentages of original variation expressed by each PC (female series), coast of Santa Catarina

PC	Eigenvalue	Total %	Cumulative Eigenvalue	Cumulative %
1	0.009993	24.82150	0.009993	24.8215
2	0.007648	18.99817	0.017641	43.8197
3	0.006099	15.14868	0.023740	58.9683
4	0.004168	10.35291	0.027908	69.3213
5	0.002928	7.27369	0.030836	76.5949
6	0.002119	5.26234	0.032955	81.8573
7	0.001702	4.22665	0.034657	86.0839
8	0.001218	3.02458	0.035874	89.1085
9	0.001015	2.52082	0.036889	91.6293
10	0.000895	2.22425	0.037785	93.8536
11	0.000724	1.79816	0.038508	95.6517
12	0.000556	1.38200	0.039065	97.0337
13	0.000422	1.04786	0.039487	98.0816
14	0.000375	0.93193	0.039862	99.0135
15	0.000147	0.36483	0.040009	99.3784
16	0.000087	0.21605	0.040096	99.5944
17	0.000074	0.18277	0.040169	99.7772
18	0.000036	0.08943	0.040205	99.8666
19	0.000034	0.08343	0.040239	99.9501
20	0.000016	0.04020	0.040255	99.9903
21	0.000004	0.00974	0.040259	100.0000

Table 13.12. Eigenvalues and percentages of original variation expressed by each PC (male series), Babitonga Bay region

PC	Eigenvalue	Total %	Cumulative Eigenvalue	Cumulative %
1	0.007408	34.91536	0.007408	34.9154
2	0.003994	18.82448	0.011401	53.7398
3	0.002731	12.87223	0.014132	66.6121
4	0.002293	10.80754	0.016425	77.4196
5	0.001355	6.38816	0.017781	83.8078
6	0.001173	5.52978	0.018954	89.3375
7	0.000796	3.74964	0.019749	93.0872
8	0.000564	2.65610	0.020313	95.7433
9	0.000300	1.41627	0.020613	97.1596
10	0.000268	1.26501	0.020882	98.4246
11	0.000211	0.99330	0.021093	99.4179
12	0.000065	0.30460	0.021157	99.7225
13	0.000047	0.22026	0.021204	99.9427
14	0.000011	0.05175	0.021215	99.9945
15	0.000001	0.00529	0.021216	99.9998
16	0.000000	0.00023	0.021216	100.0000

Table 13.13. Eigenvalues and percentages of original variation expressed by each PC (female series), Babitonga Bay region

PC	Eigenvalue	Total %	Cumulative Eigenvalue	Cumulative %
1	0.011288	37.43623	0.011288	37.4362
2	0.004697	15.57706	0.015985	53.0133
3	0.003553	11.78225	0.019538	64.7955
4	0.002561	8.49183	0.022098	73.2874
5	0.001911	6.33646	0.024009	79.6238
6	0.001553	5.15064	0.025562	84.7745
7	0.001374	4.55564	0.026936	89.3301
8	0.001126	3.73521	0.028062	93.0653
9	0.000613	2.03324	0.028675	95.0986
10	0.000449	1.48746	0.029123	96.5860
11	0.000396	1.31459	0.029520	97.9006
12	0.000353	1.17016	0.029873	99.0708
13	0.000188	0.62387	0.030061	99.6946
14	0.000060	0.20010	0.030121	99.8947
15	0.000025	0.08333	0.030146	99.9781
16	0.000005	0.01792	0.030152	99.9960
17	0.000001	0.00399	0.030153	100.0000
18	0.000000	0.00002	0.030153	100.0000

Table 13.14. Eigenvalues and percentages of original variation expressed by each PC (male series), Itajai to Bombinhas region

PC	Eigenvalue	Total %	Cumulative Eigenvalue	Cumulative %
1	0.017073	86.05815	0.017073	86.0581
2	0.001626	8.19498	0.018699	94.2531
3	0.001140	5.74687	0.019839	100.0000

Table 13.15. Eigenvalues and percentages of original variation expressed by each PC (female series), Itajai to Bombinhas region

PC	Eigenvalue	Total %	Cumulative Eigenvalue	Cumulative %
1	0.020908	74.93720	0.020908	74.9372
2	0.005436	19.48291	0.026344	94.4201
3	0.001557	5.57989	0.027901	100.0000

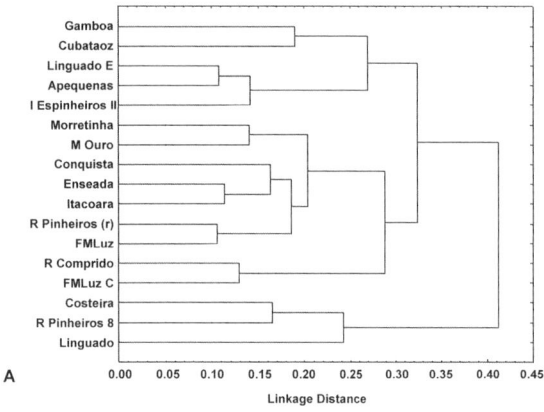

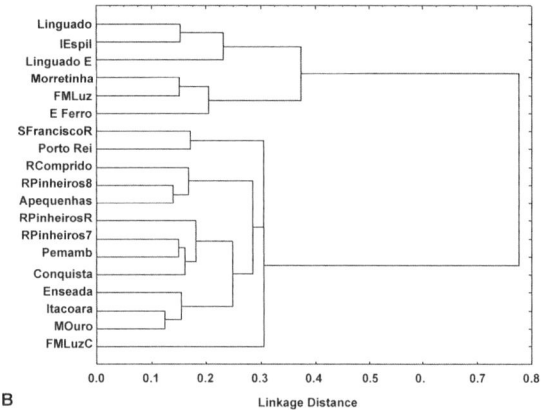

13.4. Babitonga Bay region samples. (A) Cluster analysis generated from the first ten PCs (male sample). (B) Cluster analysis generated from the first 12 PCs (female sample).

the three PCs (100 percent). Again it is possible to verify that the pottery series Cabeçudas and Laranjeiras II are closely related. However, Praia do Embrulho, also associated with the ceramic tradition Itararé, is far from Cabeçudas and Laranjeiras II.

Table 13.15 shows the Eigenvalues and percentages of original variation expressed by each PC for the female series.

Figure 13.5b presents the cluster analysis generated from the three PCs. It shows Laranjeiras I, the only non-ceramic site, as an outlier in relation to the other ceramic sites. Laranjeiras II and Cabeçudas present a great similarity, whereas Praia do Embrulho, also a ceramist site, is not so closely related.

The Island of Santa Catarina: Island of Santa Catarina, Island of Arvoredo, and Island of Corais

Table 13.16 shows the Eigenvalues and percentages of original variation expressed by each PC for the male series.

Figure 13.5c presents the cluster analysis created from the first eight PCs (100 percent) showing that the ceramic sites Base Aérea and Tapera are closely related, although Tapera is found more strongly associated with the non-ceramic site Armação do Sul.

Table 13.17 shows the Eigenvalues and percentages of original variation expressed by each PC for the female series.

Figure 13.5d presents the cluster analysis generated from the first six PCs (99.6 percent). Armação do Sul and Praia Grande are outliers, and there is the formation of two main branches, subdivided in two groups. The first group is formed by Ponta das Almas and Porto do Rio

Table 13.16. Eigenvalues and percentages of original variation expressed by each PC (male series), Island of Santa Catarina

PC	Eigenvalue	Total %	Cumulative Eigenvalue	Cumulative %
1	0.043532	62.54756	0.043532	62.5476
2	0.011933	17.14557	0.055465	79.6931
3	0.004946	7.10691	0.060412	86.8000
4	0.003884	5.58077	0.064296	92.3808
5	0.002813	4.04156	0.067109	96.4224
6	0.000972	1.39666	0.068081	97.8190
7	0.000802	1.15299	0.068883	98.9720
8	0.000715	1.02799	0.069599	100.0000

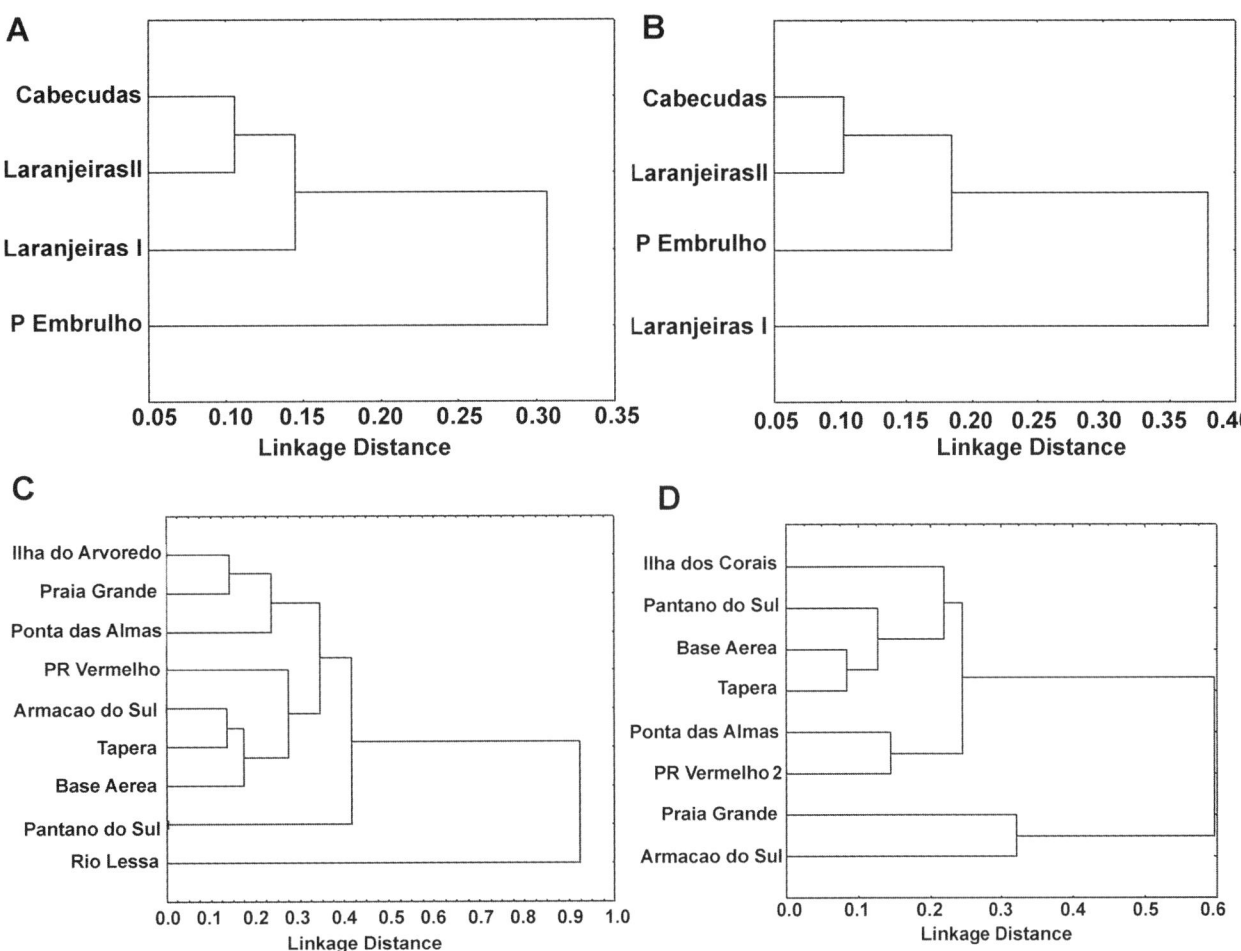

13.5. *Itajai to Bombinhas samples. (A) Cluster analysis generated from the first three PCs (male sample). (B) Cluster analysis generated from the first three PCs (female sample). Island of Santa Catarina samples. (C) Cluster analysis generated from the first eight PCs (male sample). (D) Cluster analysis generated from the first six PCs (female sample).*

Vermelho 02, and the second one is formed by ceramic sites: Ilha dos Corais, Base Aérea, and Tapera (Pântano do Sul would be an exception in this branch).

DISCUSSION

Some models based on cultural similarities (represented by the presence of pottery) could be tested in this work. Although the sample size is far from ideal, the results obtained here allow us to infer that the relations among groups from the Brazilian coast, culturally different or not, are quite complex.

The analysis that takes into account the entire south Brazilian coast shows that the relations between ceramist and non-ceramist sites are not always obvious or easy to interpret.

As observed in previous studies (Okumura 2007, 2008), the skeletal groups of the southern coast generally segregate into two main groups: one formed by Santa Catarina and another formed by São Paulo and Rio de Janeiro. The lack of similarity between Santa Catarina and the rest of the coast has also been observed in ancient DNA studies, where the haplogroups of a small sample from Rio de Janeiro and Santa Catarina were different from each other (Fabio P. N. Leite, pers. comm.).

There is considerable variation in the degree of affinity found in ceramic sites from the coast of Santa Catarina. Therefore, there is no clear pattern of affinities of these ceramic sites among each other. In general, it is possible to see that the northern and central ceramic series from Santa Catarina present a strong and frequent affinity among them, although in some cases these series have

Table 13.17. Eigenvalues and percentages of original variation expressed by each PC (female series), Island of Santa Catarina

PC	Eigenvalue	Total %	Cumulative Eigenvalue	Cumulative %
1	0.023642	63.71414	0.023642	63.7141
2	0.006033	16.25876	0.029675	79.9729
3	0.002659	7.16543	0.032334	87.1383
4	0.002281	6.14654	0.034614	93.2849
5	0.001387	3.73664	0.036001	97.0215
6	0.000958	2.58217	0.036959	99.6037
7	0.000147	0.39633	0.037106	100.0000

shown more proximity to non-ceramic series from their own region (for example, the ceramic series from the northern coast presenting more affinity with the non-ceramic series from the same region). In the case of the Island of Santa Catarina, it was often possible to verify affinities with the non-ceramic series from the island (and sometimes with the non-ceramic series from the northern and the southern coast of Santa Catarina[3]). Nonetheless, the ceramic series do not present significant differences among themselves when analyzing non-metric traits in the MMD.

Regional (focusing on the Santa Catarina State) and microregional analyses (focusing on specific regions of Santa Catarina) show associations of some culturally related groups. Usually this association carries a geographical meaning as well. The best example is the strong and persistent association between Base Aérea and Tapera, both from the Island of Santa Catarina and associated with the Itararé ceramic tradition. Itacoara and Enseada I, as well as Cabeçudas and Laranjeiras II, are also nice examples of ceramic sites from the same region that show affinities in both regional and microregional analyses.

If we focus on the results of the microregional analyses, the picture is not very simple either. However, a strong tendency of association of the ceramic sites does appear. On the northern coast, Enseada I and Itacoara present strong affinities among themselves, although these affinities are not exclusive. On the central coast of Santa Catarina, the ceramic site Cabeçudas is close to Laranjeiras II (also a ceramist site) in several analyses. The other ceramist site of this region, Praia do Embrulho, is sometimes associated with Cabeçudas and Laranjeiras II, but sometimes it is not.[4] On the Island of Santa Catarina, the ceramic sites of Base Aérea and Tapera are always found in association.[5] In one case, there is a division of the coast between ceramic

and non-ceramic sites, in which Ponta das Almas and Porto do Rio Vermelho 02 (non-ceramic sites) cluster apart from Ilha dos Corais, Base Aérea, Tapera, and Pântano do Sul I (ceramic sites, except Pântano do Sul I).

Although these results do not point in an unmistakable way to an exclusive identity of the ceramic sites, the tendency for ceramic series to cluster apart from non-ceramic groups is quite consistent. Several models have been proposed to explain the origins of this technological innovation in the archaeological record of the coastal sites of Brazil. Different models proposed different levels of contact among coastal fisher-gatherer groups with inland ceramist groups, including the transfer of technological knowledge from the ceramists to the fisher-gatherers, or the acquisition of pottery made by the ceramists without any other modification of the subsistence system of the fisher-gatherers (Bryan 1977; Rohr 1977a). Other models, however, assume that the origin of pottery in the material culture of the coastal groups could only be explained by the arrival of ceramist groups from the inland (Beck 1974), who completely absorbed or eliminated the shell mound people. This model was supported by Neves (1988), who found important differences of cranial morphology in groups with and without pottery on the northern coast of Santa Catarina.

On the central coast of Santa Catarina, before the arrival of pottery, there are classic shell mounds and others called pre-ceramic shell camps (Prous and Piazza 1977). Neves (1988) observed the separation between Armação do Sul (classified as a pre-ceramic shell camp) and the classic shell mounds of the central coast of Santa Catarina.[6] This result led him to propose the presence of two biologically distinct groups in this region of the coast before the arrival of pottery. The results presented here show that the individuals from Armação do Sul cluster together with the other series from the coast of Santa Catarina, and it is only in the microregional analysis of the female sample that they appear as an outlier in relation to the other groups of the coast of Santa Catarina.[7] Therefore, it was not possible to support the model that proposes the presence of two biologically different groups on the central coast of Santa Catarina before the introduction of pottery.

Finally, it is important to bear in mind that the differences observed between analyses of male and female samples might be related to a myriad of factors, including differences in the sample size, differences in the archaeological sites that were included in the analyses, and differences in the micropopulation dynamics between the two sexes.

CONCLUSIONS

Our study supports the hypothesis that, in the case of the coastal Brazilian groups addressed here, cultural changes in the archaeological record were accompanied by distinct biological groups. Here, the cultural change is represented by the presence or absence of pottery, and the biological affinities were tested through multivariate statistical analysis of cranial metric and non-metric data of hundreds of skeletons. The case of Santa Catarina, where the richness of archaeological information and material allowed us to test such a hypothesis, should call attention to the importance of having good contextual information, together with well-preserved material.

We hope that this study will raise more awareness of the diversity within what archaeologists call "Brazilian shell mounds." Clearly, these coastal groups shared some similarities, while also having, obviously, some idiosyncratic aspects varying from group to group. The diversity among these groups has been observed independently through the analysis of cranial morphology (Okumura 2008). We anticipate that our study will inspire future investigation guided by the test of the hypothesis about the diversity using many other factors, from biology to material culture

and faunal remains that can be observed in these coastal groups.

ACKNOWLEDGMENTS

I would like to thank the editors for the invitation to write this chapter, Walter Neves of the IB (USP) for his guidance, and the staff of the following institutions: MNRJ (UFRJ), IAB, MAE (USP), Museu de Anatomia "Professor Alfonso Bovero" (USP), CEPA (UFPR), Museu Paranaense, MAE (UFPR), Museu Universitário "Professor Oswaldo Rodrigues Cabral" (UFSC), MASJ (SC), Museu do Homem do Sambaqui "Padre João Alfredo Rohr," Instituto Anchietano de Pesquisas (UNISINOS), and Marsul. This research was supported by FAPESP (grant 02/13441–0).

NOTES

1. The Una Tradition is associated with pottery-making groups that expanded from inland to the coast around 1000 BP. This tradition has been identified in inland Espírito Santo, Rio de Janeiro, São Paulo, Minas Gerais, and part of central and western Brazil. It also has been identified on the coast of Rio de Janeiro and Espírito Santo.

2. According to Astolfo G. M. Araujo (2001), the similarities between Itararé and Una pottery (Dias 1969; Brochado 1984) suggest a possible cultural continuity. The Itararé Tradition (also known as Itararé-Taquara) can be observed in southern Brazil (São Paulo, Paraná, Santa Catarina, and Rio Grande do Sul). These pottery-making groups expanded from inland and reached the coast by approximately 1200 BP.

3. See Neves 1988.

4. It is important to mention that Praia do Embrulho is represented by just one individual.

5. However, this association sometimes includes non-ceramist sites.

6. In this case, the central coast of Santa Catarina is formed by Ponta das Almas and Pântano do Sul (Island of Santa Catarina) and Laranjeiras I (in the region of Balneário de Camboriú).

7. Praia Grande also appears as an outlier in these results.

CHAPTER FOURTEEN

General Considerations about the Bioarchaeological Contexts in Patagonian Coast Shell Middens

Jorge A. Suby and Ricardo A. Guichón

SUMMARY

One of the most relevant indicators of maritime resource consumption by past human populations in Southern Patagonia is the formation of shell middens of anthropogenic origin. Their composition and relationship with subsistence strategies have motivated extensive investigations, particularly at the Beagle Channel. Moreover, shell middens constitute contexts from which human remains are frequently recovered in Southern Patagonia. Taking this into consideration, this chapter evaluates the proportion of human remains recovered from shell middens on the coast of Southern Patagonia, discussing their general conditions, diet, and associated information. We included only those sites with human remains for which contextual information is available (n=78). Twenty-nine sites associated with shell middens resulted in the recovery of human remains. The results show that shell middens with buried human remains appear as a frequent practice along the coast of Tierra del Fuego, and are unusual, although not absent, in the continental coasts of Southern Patagonia. Moreover, the buried individuals in sites associated with shell middens do not seem to have had an exclusively maritime diet, while individuals with this type of diet were also buried in other mortuary contexts, such as rock-shelters. This information is useful for further interpretations about the exploitation of maritime resources and their relationship with mortuary practices.

INTRODUCTION

The bioarchaeological record in Southern Patagonia, considered to include the provinces of Santa Cruz and Tierra del Fuego (Argentina), and Magallanes (Chile), has been the object of a wide variety of studies in the last few years (Guichón, Barberena, and Borrero 2001; Guichón, Muñoz, and Borrero 2000; Martin 2004; Martin, Barberena, and Guichón 2004; Suby and Guichón 2010; Suby, Guichón, and Zangrando 2009). These studies have allowed, among other things, the recognition of archaeological variability observed in the human skeletal record. This research has suggested, through different lines of evidences, a strong relationship of past human populations with maritime resources in some regions of Southern Patagonia, in part due to the elevated oceanity of these continental and insular territories.

One of the most relevant indicators of maritime resource consumption by past human populations in Southern Patagonia is the formation of shell middens of anthropic origin. Their composition and relationship with subsistence strategies have motivated extensive investigations, particularly at the Beagle Channel (Estévez and Vila 1996; Estévez et al. 2001; Legoupil 1993/1994; Ocampo and Rivas 2000; Orquera 2005; Orquera and Piana 1999a, 2001; Villagrán et al. 2011a), and more recently in the continental coast of Southern Patagonia (e.g., Muñoz, Caracotche, and Cruz 2009). In addition to the representation of zooarchaeological remains (mainly birds, pinnipeds, and cetaceans), shell middens constitute contexts in Southern Patagonia from which human remains are frequently recovered. During the last few years, the studies about the frequency of human remains associated with coastal sites provided an important volume of information. Therefore, this chapter seeks to evaluate the proportion of human remains recovered from shell middens in the coast of

Southern Patagonia and to discuss their general conditions and associated information. From a review of the literature, the specific objectives are: (a) to evaluate the frequency of human bone remains associated with shell middens in Southern Patagonia in relation to other archaeological contexts; (b) to recognize their spatial and temporal distribution; and (c) to critically examine the hypothesis that individuals buried in shell middens could be associated exclusively with maritime diets. Overall, the available information corresponds with approximately 600 individuals, the total number of human skeletons recovered from Southern Patagonia to date (Guichón et al. 2006), 13 percent of which have some associated contextual information. The chapter describes bioarchaological record recovered in shell middens, and general tendencies observed for the different environments and temporal periods of occupation.

HUMAN SKELETAL REMAINS FROM THE COAST OF SOUTHERN PATAGONIA

The taphonomic research carried out in Southern Patagonia has shown a spatially and temporally heterogeneous distribution of human remains, with some differences between the coast and the inland territories. The results indicate that the potential for the preservation of human bone remains, without intentional mortuary practices, is very low in inland areas (Guichón, Barberena, and Borrero 2001). Difficulties of archaeological visibility in some areas, like in the Patagonian woods (Borrero and Muñoz 1999), and biases in archaeological explorations, could contribute to this heterogeneity. Therefore, heterogeneous patterns of differential preservation and visibility mediate the recovery of human bones in the interior of Southern Patagonia, and could be possible explanations for the absence of discovered human remains from some temporal periods, such as the late Pleistocene and the early Holocene (Dillehay 1997; Guichón, Barberena, and Borrero 2001).

In contrast with inland areas, at the coasts a high percentage of human bones lies on the surface, partially or completely exposed, mainly due to the high coastal erosion processes that affect the archaeological sites (Guichón, Suby, and Fugassa 2008; Muñoz, Caracotche, and Cruz 2009). Across coastal sites, shell middens are frequently encountered examples of buried bioarchaeological remains, together with other burial contexts including *chenques* (structures with rocks covering the corpse), cremations, and natural burials. In the Beagle Channel, shell middens had a

ring shape, often characterized by circular depressions of variable height, which enhance the growth of vegetation (Ocampo and Rivas 2000; Orquera 2005; Orquera and Piana 2001). An extensive review of these structures was recently presented by Luis A. Orquera, Dominique Leogoupil, and Ernesto L. Piana (2011). In contrast with the large shell mounds described in southern North America and Brazil (see Braje, Erlandson, and Rick [chap. 1]; Widmer [chap. 2]; Souza, chap. 12] in this volume) and the shell rings of North America (see Russo [chap. 3]; Saunders, chap. 4] in this volume), ring-shaped shell middens of Southern Patagonia are usually three–four meters in diameter and one meter in height (Orquera, Leogoupil, and Piana 2011). On the contrary, in the north of Tierra del Fuego and on the continental coasts of Santa Cruz, the shell middens appear as dome-shaped structures of variable heights. In both cases, they represent indicators of archaeological visibility for systematic excavations and archaeological rescue projects for sites at risk of destruction.

The taphonomic results presented by Ricardo Guichón and colleagues (2001) for San Sebastian Bay and by Fabiana Martin and colleagues (2004) for Los Chorrillos, both on the Atlantic coast of Tierra del Fuego, and by Martin (2004) for Bahía Inutil and Primera Angostura, both in the Strait of Magellan, showed the fast erosion and dispersion of surface human bone remains, including those in shell middens. This fast erosion on the surface, as well as the moment when they are detected by researchers, affects and partially determines the recovery of human remains. Additionally, differential preservation of human bones on the coast seems to be mediated by bone mineral density, where denser bones are better preserved in superficial sites (Martin 2004; Suby 2007). Therefore, at coastal sites human remains on the surface are rapidly disarticulated and dispersed (Caracotche and Ladrón de Guevara 2008; Guichón, Suby, and Fugassa 2008). Moreover, current industrial activities, including the increased exploitation of mine resources, constitute a recognized significant conservation risk for archaeological sites (Caracotche and Ladrón de Guevara 2008). Associated with fast erosion, human activity, and the enhanced archaeological activity in the area, the number of human remains found in Southern Patagonia has increased in the last few years (Caracotche and Ladrón de Guevara 2008; Guichón, Suby, and Fugassa 2008).

At the same time, past and current environmental and geological factors seem to be important to the availability of human bones in shell middens and on the coast in general. The environmental changes that occurred during the Holocene in the southern extreme of America, including the opening of the Strait of Magellan; climatic changes such as the Antarctic cold reversal, the little Ice Age, and the Climatic Medieval Anomaly (Rabassa et al. 2000; Stine 1994); and catastrophic events such as volcanic eruptions (Borrero 2001) could have favored or made the relationship of human communities with the coast and their marine resources more difficult. In addition, the movement of coastal lines could have affected the current availability and visibility of archaeological sites, many of which are probably now under the sea (Guichón, Barberena, and Borrero 2001; Rabassa et al. 2000).

In this context, the Patagonian coasts demonstrate a great environmental, cultural, and biological variability through space and time that could imply, on the one hand, changing factors of access to the maritime resources by past human populations, and on the other hand, scenarios that heterogeneously affect the archaeological visibility and availability of human skeletal remains.

HUMAN SKELETAL REMAINS RECOVERED FROM SHELL MIDDENS IN SOUTHERN PATAGONIA

In order to evaluate the proportion of shell middens with human skeletal remains on the Southern Patagonian coast, we studied the number and percentage of archaeological sites associated with this kind of biological record in relation to other mortuary contexts, based on bibliographical information. We included only those sites with human remains for which contextual information is available (n=78), considering that only approximately 60 percent of human remains recovered from Southern Patagonia have spatial information regarding their origin (Guichón et al. 2006). According to the obtained results, 29 sites associated with shell middens resulted in the recovery of human remains, which represents 37 percent of the total number of sites with this kind of record found on the coast of Southern Patagonia (Table 14.1). Moreover, a high proportion of shell middens with human remains are located along the shore of Tierra del Fuego, represented by 24 archaeological sites (82.7 percent) (Figure 14.1). Among them, 11 sites (37.9 percent) are along the Beagle Channel, 4 (13.8 percent) are on the north of the Atlantic coast of Tierra del Fuego, 6 (20.7 percent) are on the insular coast of the Strait of Magellan, and 3 (10.3 percent) are on the southeast of the Atlantic coast of Tierra del Fuego. In contrast, shell middens with human skeletal remains are less frequent in the continental territories of Southern Patagonia, including only 5 sites (17.3 percent), two of them on the continental coast of the Strait of Magellan (San Gregorio 13 and Punta Santa Ana), while there are three sites on the Atlantic coast of Santa Cruz (Punta Entrada 1, 2, and 3).

With regard to paleodietary and chronological information, human remains from 41.3 percent of the sites associated with shell middens (12 individuals) have stable isotope analyses, 31 percent (9 individuals) have radiocarbon dates, and only 7.7 percent (2 individuals) have haplotype information (Table 14.2). From these results, the most frequently represented temporal period is the middle and late Holocene, specifically from the last 2,000 years. In addition, it is interesting that some of the earlier human bones found in Southern Patagonia have been recovered in shell middens (Punta Santa Ana, La Arcillosa 2, and Imiwaia 1).

From the few shell middens for which there is stable isotopic data from human remains, the $\delta^{13}C$ and $\delta^{15}N$ values of bone collagen show considerable variability. A similar range of variation was observed in continental and insular sites from all kinds of mortuary contexts, with $\delta^{13}C$ values between approximately -11 and -22 percent. Only Bahia Inútil 13 and Maria Luisa 5 showed higher $\delta^{13}C$ values (-6.1 and -9.1 percent, respectively), compatible with a higher proportion of maritime resources in their diets (Figure 14.2). However, groups from different geographic regions showed distinct isotopic signatures. The results from the north of the Atlantic coast of Tierra del Fuego showed low $\delta^{13}C$ values, which imply a higher consumption of terrestrial resources than of maritime resources (San Genaro 2, La Arcillosa 2, Punta Maria, and Margen Sur), a pattern also observed among human remains from shell middens from the coast of Santa Cruz (Punta Entrada 2 and 3 sites). In contrast, human skeletal remains from the Beagle Channel and the southeast Atlantic coast of Tierra del Fuego presented higher $\delta^{13}C$ values, compatible with higher intake of maritime resources (Figure 14.2). The human skeletal remains of the Strait of Magellan (Bahia Inútil 13 and Punta Santa Ana) fall out of the patterns observed, although the first is from Tierra del Fuego, with more maritime consumption, and the second is from the continent, with more terrestrial consumed resources. Similar results were found in remains with both $\delta^{13}C$ and $\delta^{15}N$ values, which showed diets with a higher proportion of maritime resources and a higher trophic level in southern Tierra del Fuego than in the sites from the north Atlantic coast (Figure 14.3). All of these results agree, in general, with those previously presented from human skeletal

Table 14.1. Sites with human skeletal remains in shell middens and other contexts from the coast of Southern Patagonia

Sites in Shell Middens	Sites in Other Contexts	Sites in Shell Middens	Sites in Other Contexts
Punta Baxa 7	Bahía Azul 22	Aleph 3	Bahia Santiago
La Arcillosa 2	Bahía Azul 24	Punta Entrada 1	Punta Delgada
María Luisa 5	Bahía Laredo 5	Punta Entrada 2	Dungeness 5
Bahía inútil 13	Concentración 1	Punta Entrada 3	Punta Daniel 1
Bahía inútil 17	Concentración 2		Punta Daniel 2
Imiwaia 1	Englefield		C. Johnny 1
Margen sur	Fuerte Ultima Esperanza		C. Johnny 2
San Genaro 2	Mandíbulas 1		Las Horquetas
Caleta Virginia	Mandíbulas 2		Cueva Trinidad
Bayly 1	Marazzi		P. Natales
Acatushun	Marazzi 8		L. Sofia
Ajej 1	Mischiwen III		Cerro Guido
Punta María	Olimpia 1		Cabo Vírgenes 17
Sitio 130	Olimpia 2		Estancia la Verde
Punta baxa 4	Pahiashauaia 1		Fortaleza
Punta Santa Ana	Punta Anegada 33		Canal Abra
Lauta 2	Punta Dungeness 5		Estancia la Costa
Marazzi 38	Rincón del Buque		Imiwaia 2
Marazzi 34	San Genaro 3		Orejas de burro
Harberton cementerio	San Genaro 4		Punta Entrada 4
Caleta Falsa	San Gregorio 11		Puerto Santa Cruz
Shamakush 1	San Gregorio 12		Cañadón Misionero
Shamakush 10	San Gregorio 4		Bajo Nuevo
San Gregorio 13	Shamakush entierro		Estancia San Julio
Wollaston 9	Palermo Aike	Percentage: 37%	Percentage: 63%

Ref: Piana, Tessone, and Zangrando 2006; Guichón, Barberena, and Borrero 2001; Martin 2004; Suby, Guichón, and Zangrando 2009; Salemme et al. 2007; Barberena 2004.

remains for the regions of Tierra del Fuego and Santa Cruz (Barberena 2002, 2004; Borrero et al. 2001; Tessone et al. 2003; Yesner et al. 2003; Zangrando et al. 2004).

DISCUSSION

The relationship of past human populations with the coast of Patagonia has been the motive of extensive research, the results of which have suggested to some authors some specialization and adaptation to the exploitation of maritime resources, particularly in the Beagle Channel (Orquera 2005). However, as pointed out previously (Guichón et al.

2006), the bioarchaeological record of Patagonia is scarce, particularly in terms of its contextual information. Consequently, the study of the distribution, availability, and differential preservation of human skeletal remains is a key aspect for other bioarchaeological and paleopathological research, including those concerned with mobility patterns, health, and economic strategies of past populations.

A high frequency of human skeletal remains was found in shell middens in comparison to other archaeological contexts in Southern Patagonia. This high frequency could be explained as a result of: (a) the elevated visibility of shell middens as archaeological biases in comparison to other

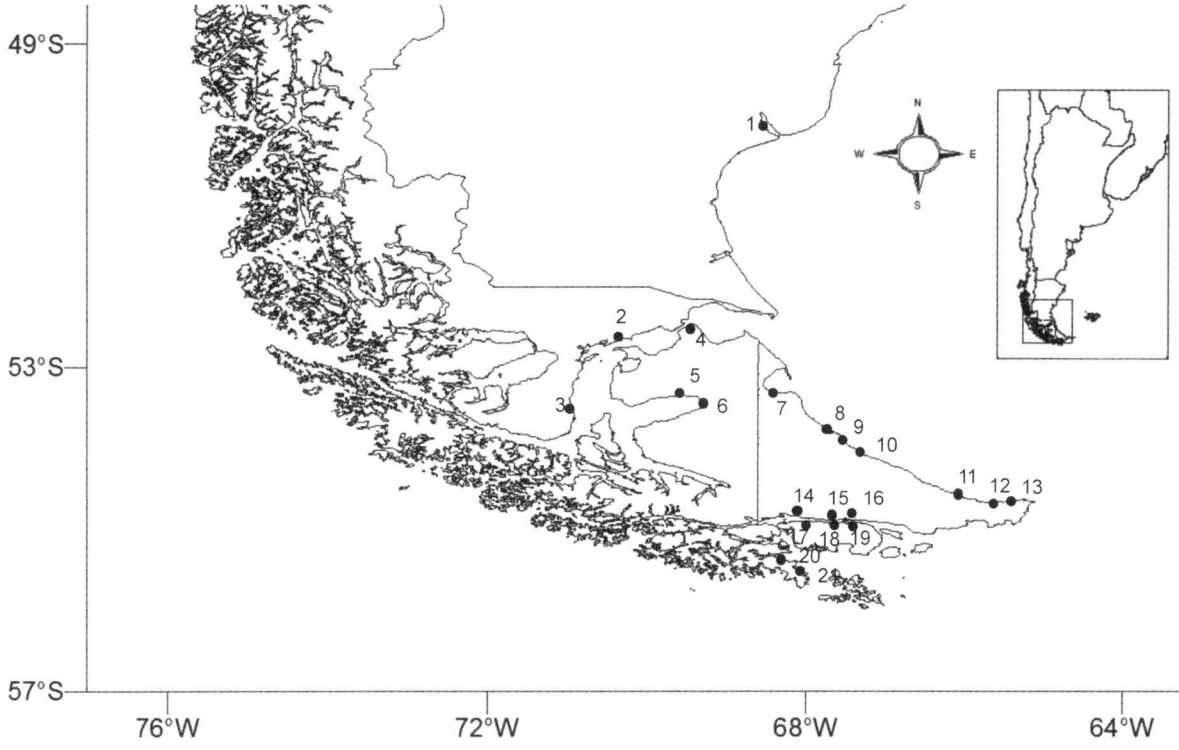

14.1. *Map with the spatial location of shell middens with human skeletal remains of Southern Patagonia.* Legend: *(1) Punta Entrada 1, 2, and 3; (2) San Gregorio 13; (3) Punta Santa Ana; (4) Punta Baxa 4 and 7; (5) Bahia Inútil 13 and 17; (6) Marazzi 34 and 38; (7) San Genaro 2; (8) La Arcillosa 2; (9) Punta Maria; (10) Margen Sur; (11) Maria Luisa; (12) Caleta Falsa; (13) Aleph 3; (14) Shamakush 1 and 10; (15) Harberton Cementerio; (16) Acatushun and Imiwaia; (17) Caleta Virginia; (18) Lauta 2; (19) sitio 130; (20) Bayly 1; (21) Wollaston 9.*

14.2. *$\delta^{13}C$ values of human skeletal remains recovered from continental and insular territories of Southern Patagonia. Filled circles and legends represent shell middens.*

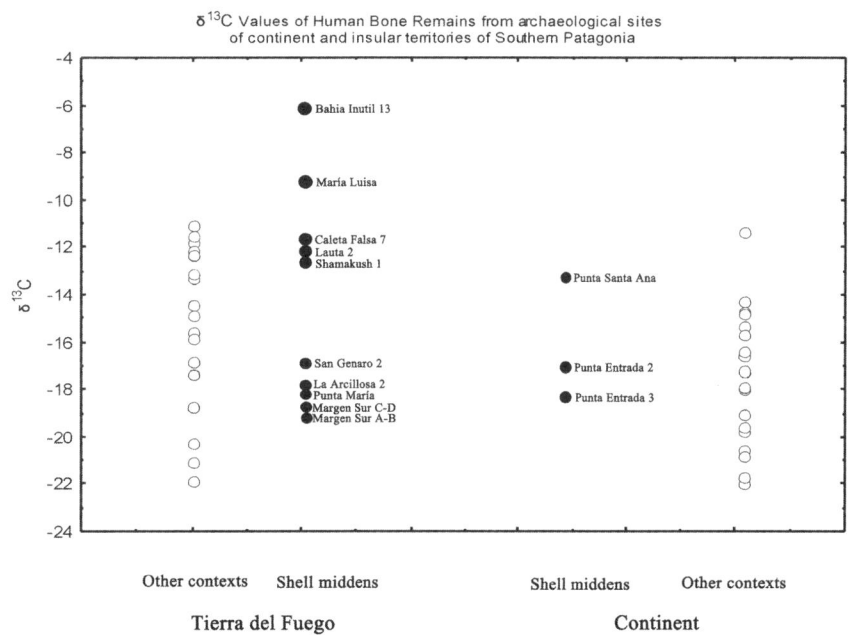

Table 14.2. Location, chronological data, and isotopic information of human skeletal remains recovered from shell middens of Southern Patagonia

Site	Location[a]	Chronology[b]	δ13Ccol	δ15N	Haplotype	Reference
Punta Entrada 1	Cacsp	-	-	-	-	Suby, Guichón, and Zangrando 2009
Punta Entrada 2	Cacsp	1748 ± 45	-16.6	-	-	Suby, Guichón, and Zangrando 2009
Punta Entrada 3	Cacsp	400 ± 30	-18.4	-	-	Suby, Guichón, and Zangrando 2009
Punta Santa Ana	Ccsm	6330 ± 50	-13.24	20.02	-	San Román 2010
San Gregorio 13	Ccsm	-	-	-	-	Prieto 1993/1994
Bahía Inútil 17	Ism	-	-	-	-	Martin 2004
Marazzi 34	Ism	-	-	-	-	Martin 2004
Marazzi 38	Ism	-	-	-	-	Martin 2004
Punta Baxa 4	Ism	-	-	-	-	Martin 2004
Punta Baxa 7	Ism	-	-	-	-	Martin 2004
Bahía Inútil 13	Ism	-	-6.1	16.3	-	Martin 2004
La Arcillosa 2	Nactdf	5205 ± 58	-17.9	-		Santiago et al. 2011
Margen Sur A	Nactdf	897 ± 38	-19.41	10.67	-	Santiago et al. 2011
Margen Sur B	Nactdf	897 ± 38	-19.90	10.97	-	Santiago et al. 2011
Margen Sur C	Nactdf	897 ± 38	-18.35	13.04	-	Santiago et al. 2011
Margen Sur D	Nactdf	897 ± 38	-18.29	13.60	-	Santiago et al. 2011
Punta María	Nactdf	-	-18.6	10.8	-	Borrero 1986, 1993
San Genaro 2	Nactdf	-	-16.9	13.9	-	Martin, Barberena, and Guichón 2004
Aleph 3	Sactdf	450 ± 60	-	-	-	Guichón, Barberena, and Borrero 2001
Caleta Falsa	Sactdf	820 ± 40	-11.8	18.5	-	Guichón and Suby 2011
Maria Luisa 5	Sactdf	360 ± 50	-9.1	18		Guichón, Barberena, and Borrero 2001
Acatushun	Bc	Postcontact	-	-	-	Piana, Tessone, and Zangrando 2006
Ajej 1	Bc	1400 ± 90	-	-	-	Piana, Tessone, and Zangrando 2006;
Bayly 1	Bc	1410 ± 50	-	-	-	Piana, Tessone, and Zangrando 2006
Caleta Virginia	Bc	-	-	-	D	Aspillaga, Ocampo, and Rivas 1999
Harberton Cem.	Bc	Postcontact	-	-	-	Piana, Tessone, and Zangrando 2006;
Imiwaia 1	Bc	5870 ± 145	-	-	-	Macciarelli et al. 2006
Lauta 2	Bc	-	-12.3	17.3	C	Piana, Tessone, and Zangrando 2006
Shamakush 1	Bc	940 ± 100	-12.8	-	-	Piana, Tessone, and Zangrando 2006;
Shamkush 10	Bc	500 ± 100	-	-	-	Piana, Tessone, and Zangrando 2006;
Sitio 130	Bc	490 ± 30	-	-	-	Piana, Tessone, and Zangrando 2006;
Wollaston 9	Bc	-	-	-	-	Piana, Tessone, and Zangrando 2006

[a] Cacsp: Continental Atlantic coast of Southern Patagonia; Ccsm: Continental coast of Strait of Magellan; Ism: Insular Strait of Magellan; Nactdf: Northern Atlantic Coast of Tierra del Fuego; Sactdf: Southeast Atlantic Coast of Tierra del Fuego; Bc: Beagle Channel.

[b] Radiocarbon dates are not calibrated.

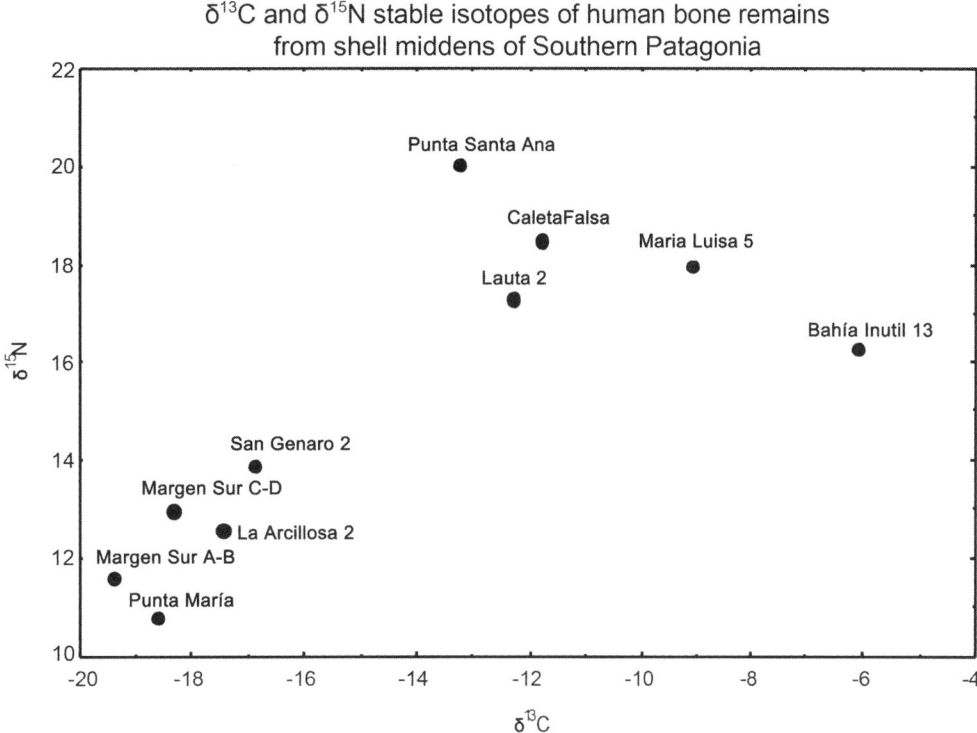

14.3. *$\delta^{13}C$ and $\delta^{15}N$ values of human skeletal remains associated with shell middens in Southern Patagonia; n=6*

buried contexts; and (b) the higher differential preservation of human bone remains in shell middens compared to other sediment matrices. As reported by Martin (2004), Orquera and Piana (1999), and Suby (2007), the human skeletal remains below the surface in shell middens are, in general, well preserved in Southern Patagonia. This preservation could be explained by the neutral pH observed in shell middens (Orquera and Piana 2001; Okumura and Eggers, chap. 8 in this volume). These results are in accordance with the expectations generated for these contexts as supported in pH studies and with the disposition of the shells that protect the bones from the action of some post-depositional processes (Lyman 1994; Reitz and Wing 1999).

The results presented in this chapter have shown that the human remains recovered in shell middens are frequently distributed along the coast of Tierra del Fuego, at the Atlantic coast, the Strait of Magellan, and the Beagle Channel, and are less represented on the continental coast, although not absent. However, the Atlantic coast of Santa Cruz presents only few instances of uncovered human

remains, even though current research has been oriented to explore that area. Recently, we have been working to evaluate the bioarchaeological record from this region, which has already yielded the recovery of human remains of at least nine individuals (Suby and Guichón 2007; Suby, Guichón, and Zangrando 2009).

In terms of dietary patterns, the human remains in shell middens demonstrate a high variability, with consumption of maritime and terrestrial resources in different proportions. In general, the human skeletal remains from the Beagle Channel and the southeast of the Atlantic coast of Tierra del Fuego showed isotopic values compatible with the high proportion of maritime resources in their diets. In contrast, the values of individuals recovered in the north of the Atlantic coast of Tierra del Fuego were lower, which indicates the consumption of proportionally higher amounts of terrestrial resources. Finally, the individuals near the Strait of Magellan showed variable results, with the distance from the coast being a factor in the proportion of consumed maritime resources (e.g., Borrero and Barberena 2006). In this sense, the individuals buried in shell middens are not limited to the Beagle Channel, where the diets were based mainly on maritime resources. On the contrary, they are present in other areas, such as the north of Tierra del Fuego and Santa Cruz, where the diets were compatible with the consumption of terrestrial resources in different proportions. Moreover, even in southern Tierra del Fuego, skeletal remains with maritime diets were not exclusively buried in shell middens, but also in rock-shelters and bogs, as has been demonstrated previously (e.g., Piana, Tessone, and Zangrando 2006).

Only two samples from shell middens have been analyzed for aDNA, one representing haplogroup C and the other haplogroup D, the same haplogroups recognized from other sites of Southern Patagonia. However, aDNA analyses were only conducted in 48 individuals from the occidental coast (Guichón et al. 2006; Lalueza-Fox 1995), while there have been no molecular analyses of human remains from the Atlantic coast. Analyses of biological distance by cranial morphology suggests two biological groups involved in the peopling of Tierra del Fuego, one on the Pacific and one on the Atlantic coast (Cocilovo and Guichón 1985/1986; Guichón et al. 1989/1990). Given the dearth of evidence so far, it is possible to suggest the existence of other haplogroups for these last regions, which require future aDNA analyses to confirm or reject that idea.

CONCLUSION

The results exposed in this work involve an evaluation of buried human remains in the particular mortuary context of shell middens, which appear as a frequent practice along the coast of Tierra del Fuego and an unusual, although not absent, practice along the continental coasts of Southern Patagonia. Therefore, these burials are distributed along the coasts of Southern Patagonia and are not limited only to the southern extreme of Tierra del Fuego. From the bibliographic references consulted, we suggest that shell middens and spaces near them have been used as burial places from at least 6000 BP to recent times. Finally, the buried individuals in sites associated with shell middens do not seem to have an exclusively maritime diet. In synthesis, the use of shell middens as burial sites is complex in Southern Patagonia. Comprehension of this complexity will help us understand the use of the coast and its resources, important for further interpretations of mobility patterns, health and disease, and other bioarchaeological and paleopathological investigations about past human populations in Southern Patagonia.

ACKNOWLEDGMENTS

We would like to express our gratitude to Drs. Mirjana Roksandic and Sheila M. F. Mendonça de Souza for inviting us to participate in this volume; to Luciano Valenzuela for suggestions about the interpretation of stable isotope values; and to the editors and two anonymous reviewers for their comments and suggestions. This work was supported by the grant *Ecología Evolutiva Humana en Patagonia*, FONCYT-PICT 01520, PIP 5576, PICT 0385, UBACyT F447 and UNPA 29/A260-1.

PART III: SUBSISTENCE AND ECOLOGY

CHAPTER FIFTEEN

Shell Middens, Vertebrate Fauna, and Northwest Coast Subsistence

Intensification and Generalization of Prehistoric Northwest Coast Economies

Trevor J. Orchard and Terence N. Clark

SUMMARY

Recent use of multidimensional scaling (MDS) has demonstrated the applicability of the technique to the analysis and interpretation of zooarchaeological faunal assemblages. Building on these previous results, we apply MDS to the analysis of 63 faunal assemblages from 39 shell midden sites that span the geographic and chronological range of human occupations on the Northwest Coast of North America. This analysis provides insight into geographic and temporal trends in prehistoric First Nations economies across the culture area. Specifically, temporal patterns suggest that the earliest known economies in most parts of the coast are characterized by moderately generalized adaptations. Later patterns point to a variable shift to even more generalized adaptations in some parts of the coast while other regions became more highly specialized. The results of this analysis provide new insight into pan-coastal patterns in economic development, and highlight the high degree of variability that existed in Northwest Coast economies in relatively recent times.

SHELL MIDDENS, ZOOARCHAEOLOGY, AND ECONOMIC DEVELOPMENT ON THE NORTHWEST COAST

First Nations of the Northwest Coast (NWC) of North America are perhaps the world's best known examples of complex hunter-gatherers (Ames and Maschner 1999; Arnold 1996; Matson and Coupland 1995; Price 2003; Sassaman 2004). While traditional NWC aboriginal groups relied primarily on hunting, fishing, and gathering to meet their subsistence needs, they ultimately developed ranked societies with clear class distinctions (Ames and Maschner

1999; Donald 2003; Matson and Coupland 1995; Owens and Hayden 1997). This complex sociocultural organization has typically been argued to arise from the local presence of abundant, storable resources that could form the basis for surplus production, most notably salmon (*Oncorhynchus* spp.) (Hayden 1981; Johnson and Earle 1987; Matson 1983; Matson and Coupland 1995; also see Monks 1987; Moss 1993). Unfortunately, the long-term development of these characteristics is relatively poorly understood and likely varies across the culture area.

Building on these common ethnographic patterns, archaeological reconstructions have tended toward culture area-wide evolutionary models of cultural development. Aubrey Cannon (2001; cf. Ames 1994) has summarized two models that have traditionally dominated discussions of NWC economic development. The first assumes an early development of intensive salmon harvesting after ca. 6000 BP, largely independent of later cultural and social developments (Cannon 2001; Cannon and Yang 2006; Carlson 1996), most notably associated with evidence for very early salmon intensification at the site of Namu on the central coast of British Columbia. The second model ascribes a more direct link between the late (ca. 3500 to 3000 BP) intensification of salmon harvesting, the development of storage, and other factors such as population increase and social differentiation (Ames 1998, 2003; Coupland 1988, 1998; Croes and Hackenberg 1988; Matson 1983, 1992; Matson and Coupland 1995), a pattern more consistent with faunal data from Prince Rupert Harbour and the Gulf of Georgia. It is increasingly evident, however, that these models speak to locally variable subsistence trajectories (cf. Ames 2003; Cannon and Yang 2006), and that they do not account for the variability now evident on the coast (Acheson 1998; Maschner 1991; McMillan et al. 2008; Monks 2006; Orchard 2007, 2009; Orchard and Clark 2005). Regardless, a commonality among virtually all discussions of NWC cultural development is an assumption that a more focused and intensive use of salmon must ultimately occur at some point in the precontact cultural historical sequence for all regions of the coast.

Ultimately, a more refined understanding of long-term economic development on the NWC can only be attained through the analysis of archaeological evidence for long-term trends in subsistence patterns. Shell middens are the dominant archaeological site type along the coastal margins of the NWC and have thus been the primary focus of most archaeological research in the region. Furthermore, the naturally acidic forest soils in the area provide very poor conditions for faunal preservation (Cannon, Burchell, and Bathurst 2008; Stein 1992). The abundant shell middens on the NWC, which speak to the importance of invertebrate resources, provide a more basic environment through the neutralization of acidic soils by the calcium carbonate matrix of the shells themselves (Ham 1982; Stein 1992; also see Klokler, chap. 11 in this volume). NWC shell middens thus provide a necessary context for the preservation, and thus archaeological recovery, of vertebrate and invertebrate faunal remains.

While economic development is central to discussions of NWC cultures, systematic analysis of faunal assemblages from the region's shell middens are only recently playing a prominent role in archaeological studies (e.g., Butler and Campbell 2004). Furthermore, the majority of published faunal analyses have been conducted at the scale of a single site, and while larger, comparative analyses are becoming increasingly common, these are typically limited to comparisons across local regions (Cannon 2000; Clark 2010; Hanson 1991; Orchard 2009; Orchard and Clark 2005; see Butler and Campbell 2004 for a more extensive study). The current study represents one of the first attempts to systematically incorporate a large body of faunal data from shell midden sites into a broad overview of NWC economic trends. A regional sampling strategy will not only provide considerable insight into trends across the culture area, but this approach should also help limit the effects of taphonomic and sampling variability that can greatly skew the results of site-based or even small regional studies.

One of the difficulties in meaningfully comparing a large sample of faunal data is the ability to visualize and interpret trends across these complex data sets. Multivariate statistics, such as multidimensional scaling (MDS; also known as principal coordinates analysis), principal components analysis (PCA), and correspondence analysis (CA), provide tools to simplify such comparisons, and these are increasingly being applied to the analysis of faunal data (e.g. Bar-Oz and Dayan 2003; Betts 2005, 2008; Betts and Friesen 2004; Clark 2010; Orchard and Clark 2005). These procedures reduce the dimensionality of the data set by compressing the overall variation into more interpretable dimensions or factors (Baxter 1994; James and McCulloch 1990; Legendre and Legendre 1998; Manly 1994). Variation within data sets is expressed as dimensions, or factors, of variability that can be represented graphically through dimensional plots. These procedures have been successfully applied to the analysis of artifact assemblages on the NWC, aiding in the interpretation of temporal and regional patterning (Burley 1980; Clark 2000, 2010; Grier 2003; Matson 1974; Monks 1976; Thom 1992). Zooarchaeological assemblages are analogous to artifact assemblages in several important ways: they contain abundant items that can be meaningfully quantified (number of identified specimens [NISP] for this study); the taxonomic sorting of fauna is similar to artifact classifications; and faunal assemblages reflect differing cultural activities and adaptations.

In the current chapter we further test the utility of MDS as a simple means of analyzing large, complex sets of zooarchaeological data. We also examine the potential for such large-scale regional analyses to limit the local-scale effects of taphonomic and sampling variability. Through our specific NWC case study of these methodologies we aim to move beyond the locally dominated discussions of NWC economic development to identify whether any pan-culture area trends or patterns exist.

CONSTRUCTING A NORTHWEST COAST FAUNAL DATABASE

This project began with the creation of a NWC faunal database. In the current analysis, only village sites and large shell midden sites have been included. Villages are defined as shell middens that have visible evidence of the presence of houses. Large shell middens are those having a surface area greater than 1,000 square meters (Acheson 1998, 33), and are often assumed to represent the remains of villages, or at least substantial camps. Villages and large shell middens are typically understood to represent general activity locations (e.g., Mackie 2003, 262), major settlements from which economic activities are directly conducted and to which resources obtained through logistical forays to smaller, temporary camps are returned. In other words, these sites represent palimpsests of multiple activities over a relatively long time period (cf. Braje, Erlandson and Rick, chap. 1 in this volume). Furthermore, the size of shell middens on the NWC has been argued to roughly correlate with the intensity of cultural activity (Maschner and Stein 1995, 62; Mackie 2003, 262). Villages and large middens, then, should contain remains of many of the faunal-related economic activities undertaken in each region. Smaller middens, in contrast, more likely represent locations of more specialized or limited activities. By removing small middens from the current analysis, site function is largely removed as a possible contributor to assemblage variability. The removal of small sites should not heavily impact the overall results, while potentially simplifying our ability to identify and interpret regional and local trends, or the lack thereof, across the culture area. In addition to eliminating small midden sites, other sites were excluded due to very small total faunal sample sizes, while others were simplified to combine site components that had temporal, cultural, or depositional similarities.

Ultimately, these exclusions and simplifications resulted in a final sample of 63 assemblages from 39 shell midden sites (Table 15.1; the complete data set is available from the authors). Other assemblages have not yet been added as the raw data are not easily available, because inconsistent sampling or analysis has been conducted across vertebrate taxonomic classes, or because they have become available, or we have become aware of them, subsequent to the initiation of this project. To facilitate visual representations, each assemblage was assigned a two- or three-figure code, prefaced by a single-letter code representing broad geographic regions commonly employed in discussions of NWC culture history (Table 15.1; Figure 15.1). Assemblages were also labeled according to wide, arbitrary time periods to facilitate examination of possible temporal trends (Figure 15.1). These geographic and temporal categories are used purely to aid in visually representing and organizing the assemblages for interpretive purposes. *These categories in no way represent manipulation of the data, nor do they influence the results of MDS or other statistical analyses described below.*

The initial faunal data sets for these assemblages included more than 350 taxonomic faunal categories below the class level, many of which were non-mutually-exclusive categories. As such, these initial data were compressed into a set of mutually exclusive categories that encompassed all of the varying levels of faunal identification. The majority of taxa were lumped into family-level

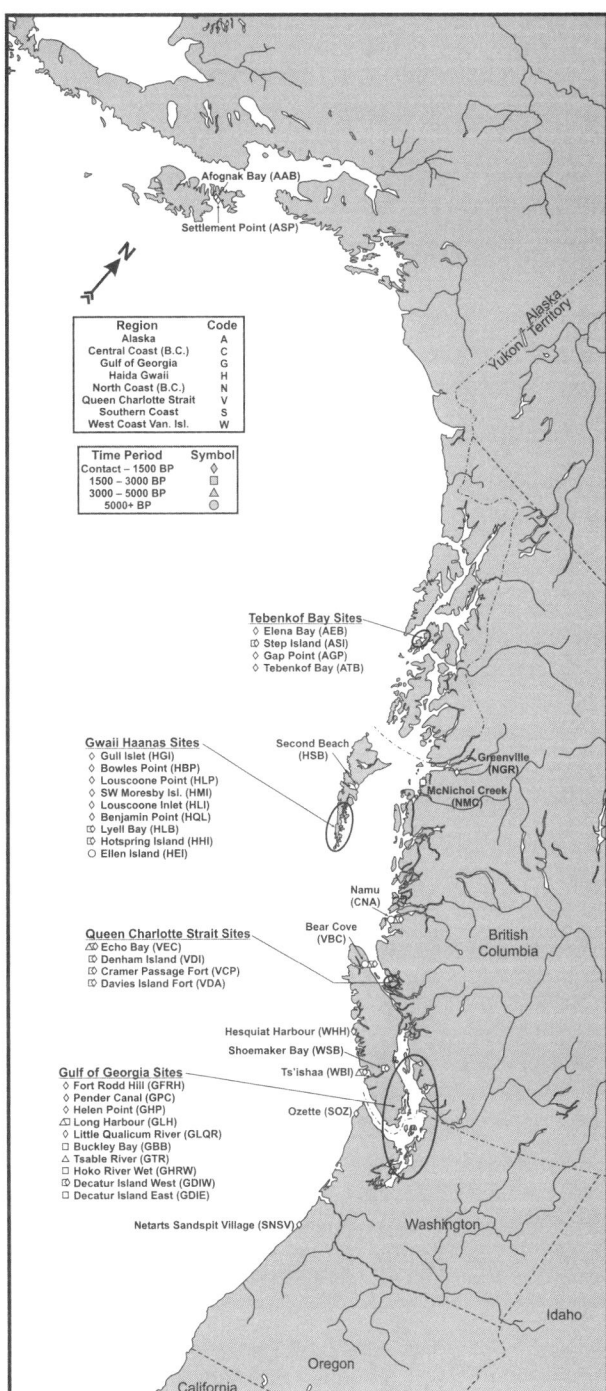

15.1. Map of the Northwest Coast of North America showing the locations and approximate ages of all assemblages included in this study.

Table 15.1. Summary of Northwest Coast faunal assemblages included in the analysis

Code	Site	Name/Location	Component	Dates	Source(s)
			ALASKA (A)		
AAB	49-AFG-012	Afognak Bay	n/a	ca. AD 1400–1650	Partlow 2000
ASP	49-AFG-015	Settlement Point	n/a	ca. AD 1300–1650	Partlow 2000
AEB1	49-XPA-29	Elena Bay	Early	1550–1250 BP	Maschner 1992
AEB2	49-XPA-29	Elena Bay	Late	300 BP–early 20th c	Maschner 1992
ASI2	49-XPA-39	Step Island	Comp. II	2900– 2600 BP	Maschner 1992
ASI3	49-XPA-39	Step Island	Comp. III	1950–1550 BP	Maschner 1992
ASI4	49-XPA-39	Step Island	Comp. IV	1200–800 BP	Maschner 1992
AGP	49-XPA-106	Gap Point	n/a	750–550 BP	Maschner 1992
ATB	49-XPA-112	Tebenkof Bay	n/a	750–550 BP	Maschner 1992
			HAIDA GWAII (H)		
HGI2	FaTr-3	Gull Islet	Comp. 2	800 BP–contact	Acheson 1998; Wigen 1990
HGI1	FaTr-3	Gull Islet	Comp. 1	1470–800 BP	Acheson 1998; Wigen 1990
HBP	FaTs-3	Bowles Point	n/a	745 BP (< >)	Acheson 1998; Wigen 1990
HLP	FaTt-9	Louscoone Point	n/a	935–300 BP	Acheson 1998; Wigen 1990
HMI3	FaTt-16	SW Moresby Isl.	EU1	< 800 BP (approx.)	Acheson 1998; Wigen 1990
HMI2	FaTt-16	SW Moresby Isl.	Comp. 2	< 800 BP (approx.)	Acheson 1998; Wigen 1990
HMI1	FaTt-16	SW Moresby Isl.	Comp. 1	1431–1170 BP	Acheson 1998; Wigen 1990
HLI3	FaTt-28	Louscoone Inlet	EU2	1040 – ?? BP	Acheson 1998; Wigen 1990
HLI2	FaTt-28	Louscoone Inlet	Comp. 2	590–300 BP	Acheson 1998; Wigen 1990
HLI1	FaTt-28	Louscoone Inlet	Comp. 1	1120–995 BP	Acheson 1998; Wigen 1990
HQL	FbTs-4	Benjamin Point (*Qai'dju Inaga'-i*)	n/a	1375 BP–contact	Acheson 1998; Wigen 1990
HSB	FhTx-19	Second Beach	EU2	ca. 1200 BP–contact	Christensen et al. 1999
HLB	785T	Lyell Bay	n/a	1810 BP–contact	Orchard 2007, 2009
HHI	922T	Hotspring Island	n/a	1880–1100 BP	Sumpter 1999; Wigen 1999
HEI	1325T	Ellen Island	n/a	9500–9400 BP	Fedje et al. 2001
			NORTH COAST (N)		
NMC	GcTo-6[a]	McNichol Creek	n/a	2500–1500 BP	Coupland, Bissel, and King 1993; Coupland, Colten, and Case 2003
NGR	GgTj-6	Greenville	n/a	AD 566–1290	Balkwill and Cybulski 1992; Cybulski 1992
			CENTRAL COAST (C)		
CNA6	ElSx-1	Namu	Period 6	2000 cal. BP–contact	Cannon 1991
CNA5	ElSx-1	Namu	Period 5	4000–2000 cal. BP	Cannon 1991
CNA4	ElSx-1	Namu	Period 4	5000–4000 cal. BP	Cannon 1991
CNA3	ElSx-1	Namu	Period 3	6000–5000 cal. BP	Cannon 1991
CNA2	ElSx-1	Namu	Period 2	7000–6000 cal. BP	Cannon 1991

Code	Site	Name/Location	Component	Dates	Source(s)
NORTHERN VANCOUVER ISLAND/QUEEN CHARLOTTE STRAIT (V)					
VEC1	EeSo-1	Echo Bay	Comp. 1	ca. 3000–500 BC	Hogg 1985; Mitchell 1981b, 1988
VEC2	EeSo-1	Echo Bay	Comp. 2	ca. AD 300–1800	Hogg 1985; Mitchell 1981b, 1988
VDI	EeSo-19	Denham Island	n/a	ca. AD 300–1800	Hogg 1985; Mitchell 1981b, 1988
VCP	EeSp-12	Cramer Passage Fort	n/a	ca. AD 300–1800	Hogg 1985; Mitchell 1981b, 1988
VDA	EeSp-95	Davies Island Fort	n/a	ca. AD 300–1800	Hogg 1985; Mitchell 1981b, 1988
VBC1	EeSu-8	Bear Cove	Comp. I	8020–4470 BP	C. Carlson 2003
VBC2	EeSu-8	Bear Cove	Comp. II & III	4360–1035 BP	C. Carlson 2003
WEST COAST VANCOUVER ISLAND (W)					
WBI6	DfSi-16	*Ts'ishaa* (Benson Island)	2000 A/B	500 BP–contact	Frederick and Crockford 2005; McMillan and St. Claire 2005
WBI5	DfSi-16	*Ts'ishaa* (Benson Island)	2000 C	900–500 BP	Frederick and Crockford 2005; McMillan and St. Claire 2005
WBI4	DfSi-16	*Ts'ishaa* (Benson Island)	2000 D/D*	1230–900 BP	Frederick and Crockford 2005; McMillan and St. Claire 2005
WBI3	DfSi-16	*Ts'ishaa* (Benson Island)	1999 A-C	< 1490 BP	Frederick and Crockford 2005; McMillan and St. Claire 2005
WBI2	DfSi-16	*Ts'ishaa* (Benson Island)	1999 D-G	1800–1490 BP	Frederick and Crockford 2005; McMillan and St. Claire 2005
WBI1	DfSi-16	*Ts'ishaa* (Benson Island)	Back Terrace	4470–3000 BP	Frederick and Crockford 2005; McMillan and St. Claire 2005
WSB1	DhSe-2[b]	Shoemaker Bay	I	> 2860 – > 1450 BP	Calvert and Crockford 1982; McMillan and St. Claire 1982
WSB2	DhSe-2[b]	Shoemaker Bay	II	1450 BP & 1180 BP	Calvert and Crockford 1982; McMillan and St. Claire 1982
WHH2	DiSo-1	Hesquiat Harbour	II	520 BP	Calvert 1980
WHH3	DiSo-1	Hesquiat Harbour	III	540–520 BP	Calvert 1980
WHH4	DiSo-1	Hesquiat Harbour	IV	1200–700 BP	Calvert 1980
GULF OF GEORGIA (G)					
GFRH	DcRu-78	Fort Rodd Hill	n/a	ca. AD 500–1800	Mitchell 1981a
GPC	DeRt-1	Pender Canal	Unit 18	1200–500 BP	Hanson 1991
GHP	DfRu-8	Helen Point	Comp. III	AD 1200–contact	R. Carlson 1970; Hanson 1991
GLH1	DfRu-44	Long Harbour	Stratum 4, Layer 4	mid-Locarno Beach	Johnstone 1991
GLH2	DfRu-44	Long Harbour	Stratum 4, Layers 5&7	2310–2220 BP (mid-Marpole)	Johnstone 1991
GLQR	DiSc-1	Little Qualicum River	n/a	AD 800–1300	Bernick 1983; Bernick and Wigen 1990
GBB	DjSf-13	Buckley Bay	n/a	2770 BP (shell); 2640 BP	Wigen 1980
GTR2	DjSf-14	Tsable River	II	3220 BP; 3060 BP	Wigen 1980
GTR1	DjSf-14	Tsable River	I	4090 BP; 3310 BP	Wigen 1980
GHRW	45-CA-213	Hoko River Wet	n/a	3000–2500 BP	Croes 1995
GDIW	45-SJ-165	Decatur Island West	n/a	2700–1200 BP	Lyman 2003; Ives and Walker 2003; Wigen 2003

Table 15.1. (continued)

Code	Site	Name/Location	Component	Dates	Source(s)
GDIE	45-SJ-169[c]	Decatur Island East	AU2, AU3, & AU5	2600–2060 BP	Lyman 2003; Walker 2003; Wigen 2003
SOUTHERN NWC (S)					
SOZ	45-CA-24	Ozette	Unit V	440 BP–historic	Butler and Campbell 2004
SNSV	35-TI-1	Netarts Sandspit Village	Pits 5, 12, & 13	AD 1300–1800	Losey 2002

[a] Fauna from the McNichol Creek Site (GcTo-6) represents combined data for house depression D and midden deposits reported in Coupland, Bissell, and King (1993). Other data from McNichol Creek have not been reported in sufficient detail for inclusion in this analysis. Coupland, Colten, and Case (2003) is used as a source of radiocarbon dates not reported in Coupland, Bissell, and King (1993).

[b] Only the "Unmixed Sample" from 1973 presented by Calvert and Crockford (1982) is included in the sample presented here for Shoemaker Bay (DhSe-2). Other samples from 1973 and 1974 collections are not comparable across the mammal, bird, and fish classes, as mammals and birds contain only the 1973 assemblages and the fish category contains both 1973 and 1974 assemblages. Though the unmixed 1973 sample presented here is a subset of the total site assemblage, it shows the same basic patterns as the total site assemblage and is entirely comparable across faunal classes.

[c] Samples from Decatur Island East (45-SJ-169) are not entirely comparable, as mammals and birds are based on level-bag samples, and fish remains are based on subsampled column samples.

categories, though single-species families were left as species-level categories and some universally identified taxa were also left at the specific level (i.e., sea otter [*Enhydra lutris*], northern river otter [*Lontra canadensis*]). Other categories were necessarily at higher taxonomic levels (Subclass, Order, Suborder), reflecting the difficulty of distinguishing species within these groups. Rare domestic animals (cow, sheep, pig, horse, cat, turkey), were removed from consideration. Small rodents and small insectivores were also excluded as they likely represent intrusive, non-economic taxa. Finally, very rare taxonomic categories, those identified in three or fewer assemblages, were removed from the analysis to simplify the database and limit the number of zero-frequency cases (see Orchard and Clark 2005). All of these exclusions involved taxa that held little power over the general trends in the data. The final database includes 48 taxonomic categories (Table 15.2; the complete data set is available from the authors).

As an additional interpretive tool, a measure of equitability was calculated for each of the assemblages. Equitability (V'), following Reitz and Wing (1999), represents the degree to which taxa are represented evenly (V' = 1) or unevenly (V' = 0) across an assemblage. This calculation provides a measure of the degree to which an assemblage is generalized (i.e., contains numerous equally abundant taxa; V' closer to 1) or specialized (i.e., dominated by one or a few taxa; V' closer to 0).

STATISTICAL ANALYSES OF FAUNAL ASSEMBLAGES

The final database consists of NISP values (Grayson 1984; Lyman 2008) for 48 taxonomic categories (Table 15.2) from 63 faunal assemblages from shell midden sites across the NWC (Table 15.1). This database was analyzed statistically using MDS, with all statistical analyses conducted using NCSS 2007 (Hintze 2007). MDS was selected over PCA and CA for two main reasons. First, MDS has seen widespread usage on the NWC (Burley 1980; Clark 2000, 2010; Matson 1974; Matson, Ludowicz, and Boyd 1980; Monks 1976, 1977; Thom 1992) and is generally understood by NWC archaeologists. Second, MDS does not require internal distance transformation, which occurs in PCA (Legendre and Legendre 1998). While in most cases this has no discernible effect, certain distance measures can be significantly altered using PCA. In the current study, where data are metric and distances are Euclidean, PCA results should closely mirror MDS results (Flury 2006; James and McCulloch 1990; Legendre and Legendre 1998).

MDS analysis begins with a pair-wise comparison of each site assemblage to all others, resulting in a distance matrix that indicates the relationship between each pair of site assemblages in multivariate space (Kruskal and Wish 1978). Components with a greater degree of difference in the composition of their faunal assemblages have a higher distance; similar ones have a lower distance. MDS then offers a series of best-fit explanations, expressed as

Table 15.2. Taxonomic categories utilized in the MDS (multidimensional scaling) analysis

Code	Common Name	Taxonomic Name
Sharks	Sharks, Skates, and Rays	Subclass Elasmobranchii
Ratfish	Ratfish	*Hydrolagus colliei*
Clupeids	Herring, Sardines, and Shad	Family Clupeidae
Anchovy	Northern Anchovy	*Engraulis mordax mordax*
Salmonids	Salmon and Trout	Family Salmonidae
Smelt	Smelt	Family Osmeridae
Midshipman	Plainfin Midshipman	*Porichthys notatus*
Clingfish	Northern Clingfish	*Gobiesox maeandricus*
Codfishes	Codfishes	Family Gadidae
Surfperch	Surfperch	Family Embiotocidae
Prickleback	Prickleback	Family Stichaeidae
Wolf-Eel	Wolf-eel	*Anarrhichthys ocellatus*
Sand Lance	Pacific Sand Lance	*Ammodytes hexapterus*
Scombridae	Mackerels and Tunas	Family Scombridae
Rockfish	Rockfish	Family Scorpaenidae
Sablefish	Sablefish	*Anoplopoma fimbria*
Greenling	Greenling	Family Hexagrammidae
Sculpins	Sculpins	Family Cottidae
Flatfish	Flatfish	Order Pleuronectiformes
Goat	Mountain Goat	*Oreamnos americanus*
Deer	Deer	Family Cervidae
Odontoceti	Toothed Whales	Suborder Odontoceti
Cetacea	Other Whales	Order Cetacea
Canids	Canids	Family Canidae
Sea Otter	Sea Otter	*Enhydra lutris*
River Otter	Northern River Otter	*Lontra canadensis*
Mustelids	Other Mustelids	Family Mustelidae
Raccoons	Raccoons	Family Procyonidae
Bears	Bears	Family Ursidae
Pinnipeds	Pinnipeds	Order Pinnipedia
Porcupine	Porcupines	Family Erethizontidae
Beaver	Beavers	Family Castoridae
Sciuridae	Squirrels and Marmots	Family Sciuridae
Loons/Grebes	Loons and Grebes	Family Gaviidae/Podicipedidae
Albatross	Albatrosses	Family Diomedeidae
Procellariidae	Fulmars and Shearwaters	Family Procellariidae
Cormorants	Cormorants	Family Phalacrocoracidae
Anatidae	Ducks, Geese, and Swans	Family Anatidae
Falconiformes	Eagles, Hawks, and Relatives	Order Falconiformes
Phasianidae	Grouse and Ptarmigan	Family Phasianidae

Table 15.2. (continued)

Code	Common Name	Taxonomic Name
Herons	Herons	Family Ardeidae
Shorebirds	Sandpipers and Phalaropes	Family Scolopacidae
Gulls	Gulls and Related Birds	Family Laridae
Alcids	Alcids	Family Alcidae
Owls	Owls	Order Strigiformes
Picidae	Woodpeckers and Relatives	Family Picidae
Corvids	Crows, Ravens, and Jays	Family Corvidae
Passeriformes	Other Perching Birds	Order Passeriformes

dimensions of variability, for the overall patterning within the distance matrix (Kruskal and Wish 1978). The first dimension explains the greatest amount of variation, with subsequent dimensions explaining relatively less. Dimensions may be plotted individually, in pairs, or in groups of three. In archaeological contexts, where variability is often a product of temporal, geographic, and/or stylistic difference, MDS aids in isolating and quantifying the contribution of the multiple influences that may be structuring variability within the data.

Dimensional scores were also subject to Ward's cluster analysis (Anderberg 1973), providing a visual representation of data objects that may be clearer than patterns seen in the MDS plots alone. PCA was also used to validate the robusticity of the patterning and to provide factor loading scores for each variable, in this case faunal taxa, which represent their influence in each dimension and greatly aid in interpreting the MDS patterning. In all statistical runs, PCA results were comparable to MDS results.

RESULTS OF MDS ANALYSIS

Analysis of the Complete Northwest Coast Faunal Sample

Initial MDS analysis identified five significant dimensions, accounting for 43.08 percent, 23.29 percent, 7.84 percent, 5.22 percent, and 4.42 percent of the variability in the data, respectively. These dimensions provide a stress of 0.022, considered to be an excellent depiction of compressed variation (Kruskal 1964). Dimensions 1 and 2, accounting for the majority of the variability within the data, formed three rough clusters of sites (Figures 15.2 and 15.3). Dimension 1 balances salmon (PCA loading of -0.90) against rockfish (0.36), and to a lesser extent herring (0.19), while

dimension 2 balances rockfish (-0.62) and greenling (-0.11) against herring (0.75) and gadids (0.14) (Figure 15.2).

Based on these trends, and on examination of the assemblage contents, it is possible to identify commonalities among assemblages in each cluster. Cluster I is characterized by general adaptations (mean V' = 0.544), with assemblages typically containing abundant rockfish and greenling, and also showing substantial quantities of pinnipeds and flatfish. Subclusters Ia and Ib are distinguished by greater quantities of herring, salmon, sculpins, and pinnipeds in the latter. Cluster I is dominated by sites from the west coast of Vancouver Island, includes several sites from southern Haida Gwaii, and contains isolated sites from other regions.

Assemblages in cluster II contain large quantities of herring and gadids and low quantities of salmon and rockfish, and are moderately generalized (mean V' = 0.477). This trend is most prominent in subcluster IIa (mean V' = 0.436), with assemblages completely dominated by herring and gadids, whereas subcluster IIb (mean V' = 0.538) has relatively greater numbers of surfperch, rockfish, greenling, sculpins, and flatfish. Geographically, cluster II is dominated by sites from the Gulf of Georgia and from Tebenkof Bay in southeast Alaska, and also contains the Second Beach site from northern Haida Gwaii and the Netarts site from the south coast.

Finally, cluster III contains relatively specialized assemblages (mean V' = 0.354) characterized by the highest relative proportions of salmon among the entire sample. Assemblages in subcluster IIIb (mean V' = 0.395) contain 42 to 85 percent salmon and show significant numbers of rockfish, greenling, and flatfish. Assemblages in subcluster IIIc (mean V' = 0.440) contain 26 to 80 percent salmon, and variably contain significant numbers of herring and gadids. Subcluster IIIa demonstrates the epitome of this salmon specialization (mean V' = 0.255), with assemblages that contain 62 to 95 percent salmon and have relatively minor contributions from other taxa. Geographically, cluster III is diverse, containing assemblages from all parts of the coast except the south coast.

Analysis of a Revised Northwest Coast Faunal Sample

Based on the initial results, it was evident that herring abundance had a significant impact on the MDS analysis. While herring is certainly a major contributor to human diets across the coast (e.g., Cannon 2000; Kopperl 2001; McMillan et al. 2008; Monks 1987; Orchard 2009), herring abundance in zooarchaeological assemblages is highly impacted by sampling strategy. The recovery of herring and other small fish is largely dependent on the mesh size of screens used for recovery, and these small-bodied taxa are often highly underrepresented in projects that do not systematically employ fine screening (Orchard 2009; Partlow 2006; Zohar and Belmarker 2005). In the current sample, a range of excavation strategies was employed, and many of the assemblages did not result from systematic fine screening. As such, the influence of herring in the

initial MDS analysis may represent either a meaningful cultural pattern or an impact of variable sampling strategies. To minimize this bias, a second analysis was conducted on a revised data set, in which small taxa, whose relative abundance was likely impacted by variable sampling, were removed from all of the assemblages (e.g., Orchard and Clark 2005). Eight taxonomic categories were eliminated from the revised analysis: herring and related fish, northern anchovy, smelt, plainfin midshipman, northern clingfish, surfperches, pricklebacks, and Pacific sand lance (taxonomic names in Table 15.2).

MDS analysis of this revised sample identified five dimensions that accounted for 51.01 percent, 16.67 percent, 8.88 percent, 5.85 percent, and 5.46 percent of the variability, respectively. These dimensions have a stress of 0.013, which is considered excellent (Kruskal 1964). Only dimensions 1 and 2, accounting for the majority of the variability in the data, are discussed here. Dimensions 1 and 2 of this revised analysis produced very similar clusters (Figures 15.4 and 15.5) to those identified in the initial analysis. Dimension 1 again relates largely to salmon abundance; salmon (PCA loading of -0.874) is balanced against rockfish (0.466), and to a lesser extent greenling (0.096).

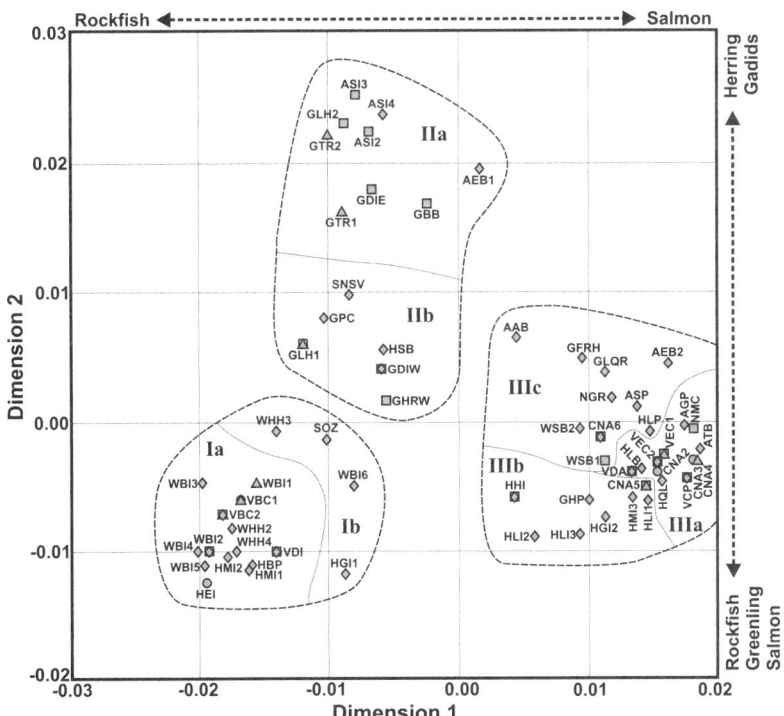

15.2. *Plot of dimensions 1 and 2 of the MDS analysis of the complete Northwest Coast faunal sample.*

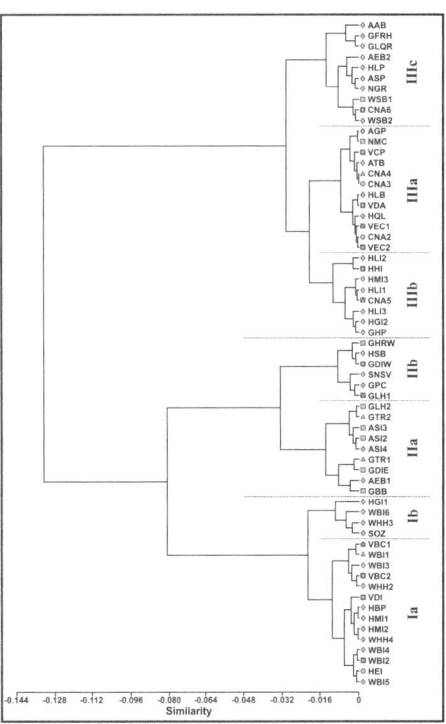

15.3. *Ward's cluster analysis of the eigenvectors from dimensions 1 and 2 of the MDS analysis of the complete Northwest Coast faunal sample.*

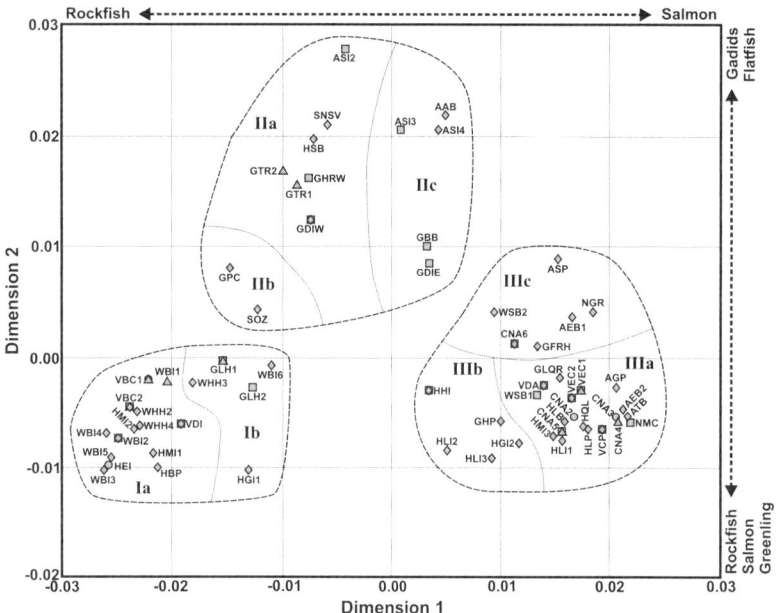

15.4. *Plot of dimensions 1 and 2 of the MDS analysis of the revised Northwest Coast faunal sample with small taxa excluded.*

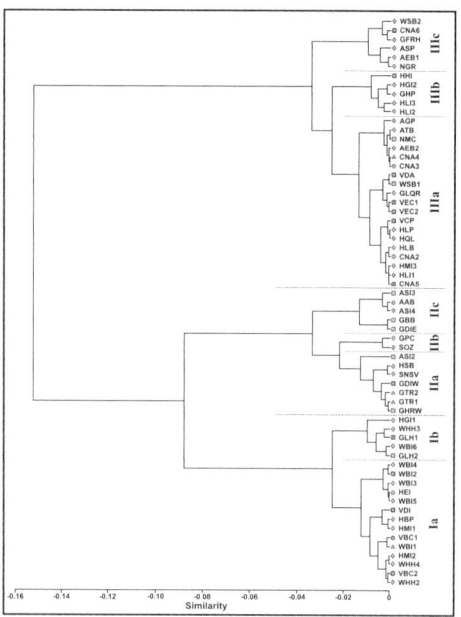

15.5. *Ward's cluster analysis of the eigenvectors from dimensions 1 and 2 of the MDS analysis of the revised Northwest Coast faunal sample with small taxa excluded.*

Despite the removal of herring, dimension 2 also remains similar, balancing gadids (-0.720) and flatfish (-0.125) against rockfish (0.608), salmon (0.281), and greenling (0.081).

Cluster I is characterized by general adaptations (mean V' = 0.541), with abundant rockfish, low proportions of salmon, and significant proportions of greening. Subcluster Ia (mean V' = 0.519) contains the greatest proportions of rockfish and greenling, while subcluster Ib is more generalized (mean V' = 0.601) and contains relatively greater proportions of salmon. Geographically, cluster I continues to be dominated by assemblages from the western and northern coasts of Vancouver Island and from southern Haida Gwaii.

Cluster II is also generalized (mean V' = 0.540), and is characterized by low proportions of both salmon and rockfish, and by relatively high proportions of gadids and/ or flatfish. Subcluster IIa (mean V' = 0.530) epitomizes this pattern, with assemblages typically dominated by gadids, flatfish, or in a few cases sculpins or deer. Subcluster IIb (mean V' = 0.562) trends toward cluster I and contains relatively greater quantities of rockfish or greenling. Subcluster IIc (mean V' = 0.545) trends toward cluster III and contains relatively greater quantities of salmon. The revised cluster II contains assemblages from Alaska and the Gulf

of Georgia, as well as the two south-coast assemblages and the single assemblage from northern Haida Gwaii.

The final cluster (III) is characterized by more specialized economies (mean V' = 0.331) focused primarily on salmon. This is particularly evident in subcluster IIIa, which contains highly specialized assemblages (mean V' = 0.262) that are completely dominated by salmon. Subclusters b and c are more generalized (mean V' = 0.432 and 0.463, respectively), and are distinguished by higher proportions of rockfish and greenling in the former, and gadids, deer, and "ducks, swans, and geese" in the latter. Cluster III continues to show a wide range of assemblages from many regions of the coast.

RECONSIDERING NORTHWEST
COAST ECONOMIES

The similarity between the results of analysis of the full and revised samples suggests that the patterning in the data is robust, and does not entirely depend on only one or two specific taxa, though likely this would not apply to salmon, and possibly rockfish, which show considerable influence on the results of both analyses. This consistency suggests that we can meaningfully identify three prominent subsistence adaptations that dominated human occupation of the NWC throughout the mid- to late Holocene. First (I) is a moderately generalized adaptation focused on near-shore fishes such as rockfish and greenling, which is prominent on the western and northern coasts of Vancouver Island, in southern Haida Gwaii, and in the relatively early assemblages from the Long Harbour site in the Gulf of Georgia. Second (II) is a generalized adaptation with a focus on deep-water fish (gadids) and bottom-dwelling fish (flatfish), though this cluster may be better defined by the relative absence of either salmon or rockfish. This adaptation is most common in Alaska and the Gulf of Georgia, and also includes the two sites from the south coast and the one site from northern Haida Gwaii. The final adaptation (III) is more specialized, with a dominant focus on salmon, and is widely represented on the coast.

While these primary foci structure the formation of these three adaptations, considerable variation remains within the peripheral subclusters b and c, and a wide range of other taxa make sometimes significant contributions to some assemblages. Admittedly, our sample is far from exhaustive, and these patterns may change with the addition of more assemblages, particularly from underrepresented regions. In addition, these patterns are not entirely mutually exclusive, with the identified subclusters representing various combinations of these particular subsistence foci. Overall, however, we argue that the patterns identified through this analysis are robust and reflect true variability in economic orientations across the NWC.

A more detailed consideration of these trends and of possible temporal patterns is best done on a more regional level. The very small samples from the north coast, the central coast, and the south coast preclude major interpretations about these regions as a whole, though some preliminary statements are warranted. On the north and central coasts, the assemblages from McNichol Creek, Greenville, and Namu all fall within the salmon-dominated cluster, supporting Gary Coupland's (Coupland and Stewart 2005; Coupland, Stewart, and Patton 2010) suggestion of extreme salmon intensification in the Prince Rupert Harbour area and Cannon's (2001; Cannon and Yang 2006) arguments for the long-term prominence of salmon at Namu. These results also suggest that salmon were of considerable importance for at least the past several thousand years in "inner-coast" locations near large, productive salmon-spawning rivers (e.g., Monks 2006; Orchard 2009). The two south-coast assemblages, both located in cluster II, show divergent faunal patterns. Their clustering has more to do with a common lack of salmon or rockfish than with any shared subsistence focus,

supporting our suggestion that cluster II may be defined by its lack of salmon or rockfish, rather than by a coherent focus on an alternate resource.

The remaining regions have larger samples, facilitating greater consideration of regional and temporal patterns. Assemblages from Alaska are split between clusters II and III. The two Kodiak Island sites are roughly contemporaneous (Table 15.1), but show somewhat different adaptations. Afognak Bay (AAB; subcluster IIc) is dominated by gadids (65.7 percent) followed distantly by salmon (25.9 percent), whereas Settlement Point (ASP; subcluster IIIc) is dominated by salmon (56.8 percent), followed by gadids (34.2 percent). This may reflect local, seasonal, or depositional differences in an overall subsistence pattern that is focused on both salmon and Pacific cod, as suggested by Megan Partlow (2000). The Tebenkof Bay assemblages show a clear temporal pattern. Assemblages from Step Island (ASI), all predating 800 BP, are dominated by gadids (cluster II). The early component from Elena Bay (AEB1; subcluster IIIc), also predating 800 BP, shows moderate salmon abundance (68.6 percent), though also containing significant gadid remains (18.0 percent). The remaining southeast Alaska assemblages (AEB2, AGP, ATB; subcluster IIIa) all postdate 800 BP, and all show a dominance of salmon (89 to 96 percent). These data point to a strong increase in the importance of salmon in this region after 800 BP (Maschner 1991, 1997), while also highlighting the local importance of gadids (Bowers and Moss 2001; Moss 2004).

Assemblages from southern Haida Gwaii are split between clusters I and III, showing variable importance of rockfish and salmon. Ellen Island (HEI), the oldest site in the database, is moderately generalized (V' = 0.531), with significant numbers of rockfish (63.0 percent) and a range of other taxa. The late Holocene assemblages from southern Haida Gwaii include: moderately generalized assemblages (mean V' = 0.481; cluster I) with a slight focus on rockfish (49–70 percent); slightly more specialized assemblages (mean V' = 0.428; cluster IIIb) with a focus on salmon (48–68 percent); and highly specialized assemblages (mean V' = 0.270; cluster IIIa) with a dominance of salmon (71–88 percent). A slight temporal trend is evident, with salmon-focused assemblages (IIIa) all dating to less than 1120 BP, generalized, rockfish-oriented assemblages (I) all older than 745 BP, and intermediate (IIIb) assemblages showing intermediate dates. These data support a late Holocene trend toward increasing use of salmon after ca. 1200 BP (Acheson 1998; Orchard 2007, 2009; Orchard and Clark 2005). The single site from northern Haida

Gwaii, Second Beach (HSB; cluster IIa), shows a moderately generalized assemblage (V' = 0.472) with a focus on flatfish (61 percent). While additional data from northern Haida Gwaii are needed to clarify this patterning, this site is likely analogous to rockfish-focused sites in southern Haida Gwaii, but is located in an environmental context more suitable for flatfish than for rockfish (Orchard 2009).

Sites from northern Vancouver Island and the Queen Charlotte Strait region fall discretely into clusters I and III. Bear Cove, on the northern end of Vancouver Island, consists of two moderately generalized assemblages (VBC1, V' = 0.562; VBC2, V' = 0.484) with abundant rockfish (55–59 percent). These assemblages cluster (Ia) with sites from the west coast of Vancouver Island, in areas ethnographically associated with the Wakashan language family. This patterning may reflect a common Wakashan economic adaptation through the precontact period. Denham Island (VDI) in Queen Charlotte Strait also falls within subcluster Ia, and is a generalized assemblage (V' = 0.742) with abundant rockfish (41.8 percent) and moderate numbers of salmon. This site differs from all other Queen Charlotte Strait sites (VDA, VEC, VCP; subcluster IIIa), which are more specialized (mean V' = 0.351) and focused on salmon (62–86 percent).

Notably, these northern Vancouver Island and Queen Charlotte Strait assemblages fall within the extreme expressions of clusters I and III (i.e., Ia and IIIa). These sites show a clear distinction between a focus on either salmon or rockfish, with no clear temporal patterns accounting for this variation. Most Queen Charlotte Strait assemblages cluster with the assemblages from Namu, further north, raising the suggestion that this represents a Northern Wakashan pattern (e.g., Mitchell 1988, 283). However, the early dates on many of the Namu assemblages (Table 15.1) predate the suggested migration of Wakashan speakers into the area, which Mitchell (1988, 282) dates to between 500 BC and AD 300. Furthermore, the possible pre-Wakashan assemblage from Queen Charlotte Strait (VEC1; Mitchell 1988) is also salmon-dominated. Notably, the Bear Cove assemblages cluster with assemblages from the west coast of Vancouver Island. Following Donald Mitchell (1988), these should represent both northern and southern Wakashan regions. Rather than representing Wakashan economic patterns, these likely represent adaptations to inner-coast locations characterized by large rivers with abundant salmon populations (Queen Charlotte Strait; Namu) and outer-coast locations characterized by abundant near-shore and off-shore marine resources (north and west Vancouver Island).

The Denham Island site is an exception, clustering with the Vancouver Island assemblages due to a predominance of rockfish and pinnipeds. This site has been associated with the Queen Charlotte Strait Culture Type (AD 300 to European contact; Mitchell 1988) based on artifact and faunal patterns and not on radiocarbon dates. This site may, then, date to the transitional period between 500 BC and AD 300, in which Wakashan speakers may have first migrated into the region (Mitchell 1988). The outer-coast pattern at this site may reflect a holdover from adaptations in the Wakashan homeland on the northern end of Vancouver Island, prior to a reorientation to the conditions of the Queen Charlotte Strait region. This is purely speculative at this point, however, and Denham Island may alternately represent a seasonally occupied location or special activity site in a wider economy focused largely on salmon (Mitchell 1988, 1981b).

Similar issues exist in assemblages from the west coast of Vancouver Island. At the Benson Island site (WBI; cluster I), the earliest five assemblages (4470 BP to 500 BP; Table 15.1) show increasing specialization (V' = 0.669 to 0.307), reflecting increasing relative quantities of rockfish (25 percent to 78 percent) and decreasing quantities of greenling (36 percent to 7 percent). The most recent assemblage from Benson Island (WBI6) is again generalized (V' = 0.683), relating to elevated quantities of salmon (18.7 percent). This late increase in salmon use has been noted elsewhere on western Vancouver Island (Monks 2006). Hesquiat Harbour assemblages are also generalized (mean V' = 0.601; cluster I), containing moderate to abundant rockfish (29.9 percent to 50 percent). All of these west coast Vancouver Island assemblages cluster with sites from northern Vancouver Island and Queen Charlotte Strait. The very different assemblages from Shoemaker Bay (WSB; cluster III) are a notable exception, containing abundant salmon (63.6 percent and 43.5 percent). This pattern is distinct from all other analyzed west coast Vancouver Island sites, and may support the suggestion that Shoemaker Bay is associated with pre-Wakashan, Salishan occupations (McMillan 1999; McMillan and St. Claire 1982). Alternately, these patterns may simply reflect the very different local ecology at the head of Alberni Inlet (McMillan and St. Claire 1982).

Finally, the Gulf of Georgia is the most diverse of the examined regions, with assemblages associated with all identified subclusters except Ib. Much, though not all, of this variation appears to reflect temporal trends. The pre-1500 BP period, for example, is represented by generalized assemblages with varied economic orientations aligning with clusters I and II. In contrast, the post-1500 BP period is represented by both specialized and generalized assemblages aligned with subcluster IIb and the three subclusters of cluster III. Pender Canal (GPC; subcluster IIb) is very generalized (V' = 0.715), with moderate numbers of rockfish, gadids, salmon, deer, sharks, sculpins, and greenling. The remaining post-1500 BP assemblages all show significant increases in the quantities of salmon (GFRH, 61.5 percent; GHP, 64.8 percent; GLQR, 70.2 percent). Overall, the Gulf of Georgia is characterized by relatively general assemblages. Most recent sites show some increase in salmon, but not the dominance of salmon evident elsewhere on the NWC. Only three of the Gulf of Georgia sites fall within the salmon-focused cluster (III), and only a single assemblage within the subcluster of complete salmon dominance (IIIa). In contrast, many Gulf of Georgia assemblages show economic orientations including abundant rockfish (cluster I) or a relative absence of both rockfish and salmon (cluster II). While site seasonality *may* explain some of this variability, we would not expect to see the temporal trends that we do if seasonality was the major factor. It is interesting that the Gulf of Georgia, a region often argued to exemplify salmon intensification (Matson 1992; Matson and Coupland 1995), is *typically* characterized by general adaptations, and with few exceptions shows little focus on salmon.

Returning to a consideration of pan-NWC patterns, several trends are notable. Early adaptations in many areas are moderately generalized (Figures 15.2 and 15.4, Table 15.1), while later, derivative adaptations *do not* show a consistent shift toward salmon-focused economies. Rather, some assemblages record a shift to salmon dominance, others show a shift toward more generalized economies, and others remain moderately generalized. Salmon specialization is most prevalent in southern Haida Gwaii, southeast Alaska, and the northern coast of British Columbia, and among some sites from Queen Charlotte Strait and the Gulf of Georgia. The most generalized assemblages tend to contain large proportions of rockfish, flatfish, herring, and gadids.

CONCLUSIONS AND FUTURE PROSPECTS

This analysis of NWC faunal assemblages from shell midden sites has provided insight into pan-culture area economic patterns, or lack thereof. Attempts to homogenize NWC cultural development into simple, coherent models (e.g., Ames and Maschner 1999; Matson and Coupland 1995) seem doomed to fail given the diverse economic adaptations and developmental trajectories highlighted

by the current study. Such models must explicitly consider the range of zooarchaeological data now available across the NWC, and need to account for the range of economic patterns and divergent temporal trends evident in these data. Likewise, attempts to generalize about the timing and nature of salmon intensification on the NWC will necessarily fail to capture the variability that exists in these developments. If salmon intensification is, in fact, a necessary component of the cultural complexity widely documented for ethnographic cultures of the NWC, then the variable faunal data summarized here suggest a range of developmental trajectories. Salmon intensification does not appear to be a NWC universal, at least not for much of the past 1,500 years. The ethnographic dominance of salmon in NWC subsistence (Drucker 1965; Jorgensen 1980) may represent an ethnographic-period or a late-precontact-period phenomenon for much of the coast.

Interestingly, several previous discussions of NWC economic development characterize pre-intensification economies as based on a range of locally abundant resources. R. G. Matson (1992, 381), for example, indicates that such a generalist adaptation would result in "differences in faunal remains between contemporary sites," a pattern well represented in data presented here. Culture area-wide differences in economic development may thus relate to the specifics of such early broad-scale economies and subsequently to the variable presence or timing of a shift to a more focal economy. Regardless, it is increasingly clear that long-term patterns of economic and cultural development are highly variable, both temporally and geographically, across the culture area (e.g., Ames and Maschner 1999; Cannon and Yang 2006; Monks 2006; Orchard 2009; also see Daniels, chap. 17 in this volume).

Clearly it is difficult, if not impossible, to identify a pan-NWC subsistence pattern. Rather, a number of macro-patterns, represented by the three dominant clusters discussed above, are identified here. Importantly, the majority of these patterns cross-cut local regions of the NWC. Madonna Moss (2008) has similarly commented on the difficulty of identifying a distinctively Haida subsistence pattern from faunal data. The central coast and the north coast are the only regions included here that fall entirely within a single cluster identified in the MDS analysis. These regions are poorly represented, however, consisting of only a single central-coast site, Namu, and two northern-coast sites, McNichol Creek and Greenville, which are all dominated by salmon. An expanded sample from these regions may reveal further variability. Notably, all of these central- and northern-coast sites are "inner-coast" localities (Monks 2006; Orchard 2009) near large salmon rivers, which may account for their narrow economic foci.

This chapter also has important implications for the analysis of NWC shell midden assemblages and more generally for zooarchaeological methodologies. The remarkable similarity of the results of MDS analyses of the full and revised samples is striking. While small taxa, particularly herring and surfperches, were prominent in many assemblages, removal of these taxa did not change the basic results of this analysis, a stability that highlights the robustness of the methodology. The use of large samples from multiple sites across a large geographic region inherently minimizes the impact of potential biases in the data from sampling and other sources. In the current case, this stability suggests that the patterning in the data is very robust and does not entirely depend on only one or two specific taxa.

Finally, this chapter provides further support for the use of MDS and similar techniques (cf. Betts and Friesen 2004) for meaningfully examining patterning across large samples of faunal data. As demonstrated here, MDS facilitates the identification of patterns in complex data sets that are not apparent through more qualitative approaches. We look forward to expanding such applications through both enlarging our NWC sample to better represent all areas and time periods, and through integrating faunal and artifact samples into a broader MDS analysis, work that has already been considerably advanced through parallel research (Clark 2010).

ACKNOWLEDGMENTS

We would like to thank Steve Acheson, R. G. Matson, Don Mitchell, and Becky Wigen for contributing data and ideas to the current chapter. Financial support for both authors during the preparation of this chapter was provided by the Social Science and Humanities Research Council of Canada. This chapter has benefited greatly from comments provided by two anonymous reviewers. Finally, we thank the editors of this volume for encouraging us to contribute this research and for facilitating the publication of the volume.

CHAPTER SIXTEEN

The Riverine *Sambaqui*

Zooarchaeological Studies of Inland Brazilian Shell Mounds

Levy Figuti and Claudia Plens

SUMMARY

Between 8000 to 1000 BP, Archaic fisher-gatherers inhabited large areas of the Brazilian coast and built numerous shell mounds, the sambaquis. Those mounds can be more than 100 meters in length and 5 meters in height, and are made of bivalve marine shells. In the highland rainforest (Mata Atlantica), less than 50 kilometers from the contemporary coastline, some shell mounds of land-snail shells, called riverine sambaquis (sambaquis fluviais), have been recently studied. These sites are morphologically very similar to the coastal ones, but tend to be smaller. They were made by groups of hunter-gatherers from 9250 to 1200 BP, and burials are the most important (and only) archaeological features, while faunal remains are the most numerous elements in the sites' compositions. Excavations of four different sites, Caraça, Estreito, Capelinha, and Moraes, indicate a high diversity in the ratios of species that may be linked to the exploitation of different micro-environments or to the development of different activity areas. Attempting to understand this issue, this study will discuss the analysis of the faunal remains from each site, seeking to comprehend how these groups managed the rainforest to obtain their resources.

INTRODUCTION

Some outstanding archaeological features are found in the Brazilian lowlands due to extensive earthwork, such as the earth mounds at Marajó Island (tesos) and in the southern plains (cerritos), the shell mounds on the northern and south-southeast coast (sambaquis), and the riverine shell mounds at the Pantanal (aterros), Amazon, and Ribeira de Iguape Rivers (riverine sambaquis).

Sambaqui is the Brazilian designation for shell mounds, derived from the Tupi words tamba (shell) and ki (mound). The coastal sambaquis present round or oval mound shapes, a large variation of dimensions (diameter: 25 to 500 meters; height 1 to 30 meters), and a sediment content of more than 80 percent shells, with a wide range of mollusk species; frequently these shell mounds have more than a few burials. The coastal sambaquis encompass two major clusters of sites: the northern sambaquis are present near the equatorial coast or the Amazonian seashore, in the states of Pará and Maranhão. The few studies of these sites indicate ages between 7000 to 900 BP, but they also present some of the earliest evidence of pottery in Brazil, the Mina ceramics tradition (Roosevelt et al. 1991). The second cluster includes the south-southeastern sambaquis, consisting of more than 300 sites. They are located in the tropical and subtropical latitudes. Extensive research has shown that they are pre-ceramic fisher-gatherer sites, built between 8500 to 1000 BP.

The sambaquis are the most studied sites in Brazilian archaeology, according to Maria Dulce Gaspar (1998), with 91 published studies and 231 radiocarbon dates. These studies show their cultural patterns: the construction of the shell mounds; the presence of burials; the great amount and variety of crafted shells, bones and teeth; and also the elaborate polished lithic industry composed mostly of axes, grinders, polishers, and sculptures. These sculptures are called zoolitos in Brazil, and they appear at the coastal sites from Uruguay to São Paulo State (Prous 1977).

It initially seemed that these sites were characterized by the spatial association of three important domains of daily life: it was the place for the accumulation/disposal of food remains, the place of the dead, and the space of habitation. However, in recent studies (Fish et al. 2000; Klokler 2001) there is some compelling evidence of mound building or sambaqui construction exclusively associated with funerary events.

The earliest sites have dates near 8000 BP; Cambriu Grande (Ilha do Cardoso, Cananéia, São Paulo State) dates to 7870 ± 80 BP (Calippo 2004), and Algodão (Ilha do Algodão, Angra dos Reis, Rio de Janeiro State) dates to 7860 ± 80 BP (Lima et al. 2002), while the most recent date to approximately 1000 BP.

Studies indicate that those sites did not acquire their form and volume in one event; in the largest sambaquis, the dates show a difference of a thousand years (or more) between the bottom and the top layers, so they were probably built in several episodes of occupation/construction.

Meanwhile, Upriver...

In the middle upper Ribeira de Iguape Valley (southeast São Paulo State), there are artificial accumulations of land-snail shells and earth, known as the riverine sambaquis. These sites are also named concheiro, or shell deposits, but their morphology and composition are undeniably those of a shell mound, or sambaqui, and that is the reason to adopt this terminology. As described previously, the term sambaqui is found in the archaeological literature to designate shell mounds that share food remains, burials, and settlement. Evidence of differences in economy, chronology, burial patterns, artifacts, and biological characteristics of their builders, among other archaeological aspects, challenges archaeologists to investigate their relationship to the more abundant coastal sambaquis.

The riverine sambaquis seem to concentrate specifically in three cluster areas (Figure 16.1) of the Ribeira de Iguape Valley (southeast São Paulo State): Itaoca (middle-upper valley); Rio Jacupiranguinha (southern effluent); and Rio Juquiá (northern tributary).

According to Cristiana N. G. B. Barreto (1988), the specificity of these areas would suggest an integrated system of settlement. Because of their proximity to large rivers and their recent age, this author hypothesized a coastal migration to the inland. There is other evidence to support this migration, namely the presence of marine faunal remains at the riverine sambaquis. Based on that hypothesis, Barreto (1988) tried to distinguish similarities between the riverine and coastal sambaquis, such as the manner of mound construction, albeit on a different scale. Results of the recent investigations are adding more data to the discussion, especially evidence of the antiquity of the riverine sites, some of which are, in fact, older than the coastal ones.

The riverine sambaquis have thick layers composed of land-snail shell, disposed in circular-convex shapes over the ground. They can vary in size from 500 to 1,900 square meters (Figuti et al. 2004). The faunal remains found in the riverine sambaquis are mostly composed of land-snail shells of Megalobulimus sp. and bones of terrestrial mammals; fish, amphibians, birds, and reptiles appear with variable and minor frequencies. It has been suggested that this assemblage could reflect the main diet of that population.

The riverine sambaquis present an abundant industry of faunal material (bones, teeth, antler, and shell), mostly arrowheads and adornments, and a few marine faunal artifacts (shark teeth beads, ray spine tips, and seashells). The lithic industry remains are also abundant and are characterized by knapped tools and polished artifacts including arrowheads, mortars, and axes, which show significant techno-typological and quantitative intersite variations.

The project entitled Archaeological and Geophysical Investigations on Riverine Sambaquis of São Paulo (IAGSFL) was developed from 1999 until 2004 and carried on by professors from the University of São Paulo Archaeological and Ethnological Museum, and the Biology and Geology Institutes. This project aimed to investigate the São Paulo riverine sambaquis using different geophysical, archaeological, and bioarchaeological methodologies (Figuti et al. 2004). The project uncovered the preference of these groups for settling the construction of these sites on plains or lowlands, with some few exceptions such as sites located on mountains or otherwise far from water resources. This project has also generated a series of radiocarbon dates for 18 sites, with samples obtained from the top and bottom of each site.

Figure 16.2 and Table 16.1 indicate three chronological clusters for the riverine sambaquis. The first includes the earliest riverine sambaquis (9250 to 8500 BP); these sites are concentrated in the Jacupiranguinha area. The second seems to represent the riverine sambaquis expansion (7000 to 3500 BP), since it includes nine sites dispersed in the three cluster areas. The third temporal cluster is the late period of riverine sambaquis (1700 to 1200 BP), including seven sites located in the Itaoca area, the most western and inland zone.

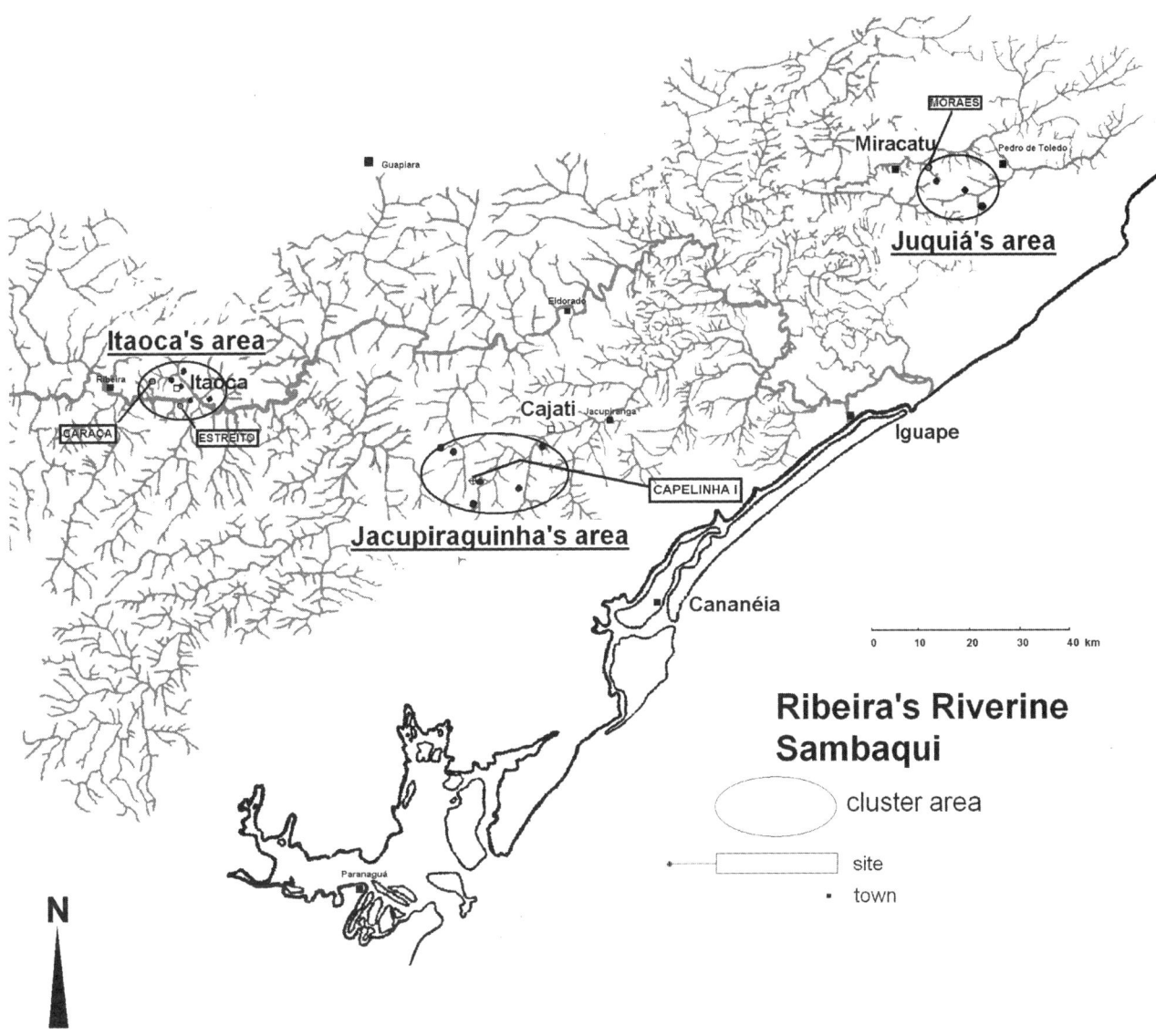

16.1. *Ribeira de Iguape river basin, location of the major riverine sambaqui concentration areas and some major sites (adapted from Barreto 1988).*

The obtained dates indicate that the riverine sambaqui inhabitants in this area are among the earliest already known from the entire Brazilian area, and burial 2 from Capelinha (8860 ± 60 BP) site is the earliest in São Paulo State.

In a preliminary study of the earliest skeletal remains from the riverine shell mound, burial 2 of the Capelinha site, Claudia R. Plens and colleagues (2001) uncovered the differentiated genetic morphology of the human bones, comparing riverine with coastal remains. The riverine sambaquis present a much more gracile human bone structure in comparison with coastal ones. The entire collection from Capelinha as well as from the Moraes site confirms this difference. Similarly, José Filippini (2004) undertook a non-metric analysis on cranial and postcranial samples from riverine and coastal sambaquis, an analysis that indicated a significant morphological difference between those populations.

Table 16.1. Riverine sambaquis' radiocarbon dates

Cluster Área	Site	Depth (cm)	Conventional Age (BP)	Calibrated Age (BP)	Material Dated	Sample
Jacupiranguinha	Capelinha I	10–20	9250 ± 50	10560–10250	shell	Beta 189331
Jacupiranguinha	Batatal I	50–60	9050 ± 100	10415–9915	shell	Beta 189329
Jacupiranguinha	Capelinha I	0–30	8860 ± 60	10180–9710	bone	Beta 153988
Jacupiranguinha	Capelinha I	90–100	8795 ± 105	9544–9293	coal	A 11239
Jacupiranguinha	Capelinha I	80–90	8500 ± 70	9963–9539	shell	A 11236
Juquiá	Laranjal	40–50	6980 ± 90	7965–7645	shell	Beta 189337
Jacupiranguinha	Capelinha I	10–20	6090 ± 40	7020–6850	bone	Beta 184619
Juquiá	Moraes	130	5895 ± 45	6777–6665	bone	KIA 15561
Jacupiranguinha	Timbuva	20–30	5740 ± 50	6660–6410	shell	Beta 189339
Juquiá	Moraes	35	5420 ± 30	6289–6174	bone	KIA 20843
Juquiá	Alecrim I	10–20	5310 ± 50	6250–5940	shell	Beta 189330
Jacupiranguinha	Capelinha II	30–40	5000 ± 70	5910–5600	shell	Beta 189332
Juquiá	Moraes	100	4985 ± 35	5745–5658	bone	KIA 15562
Jacupiranguinha	Capelinha III	90–100	4530 ± 50	5320–4990	shell	Beta 189333
Juquiá	Moraes	25	4511 ± 32	5200–5048	bone	KIA 20844
Jacupiranguinha	Capelinha III	90–100	4500 ± 40	5310–4980	coal	Beta 189334
Itaoca	Estreito	130	4124 ± 27	4658–4567	bone	KIA 20846
Itaoca	Tatupeva	10–20	3990 ± 70	4800–4770	shell	Beta-184623
Itaoca	Estreito	25	3655 ± 26	4011–3893	bone	KIA 20845
Itaoca	Pavão II	10–20	3530 ± 70	3980–3640	shell	Beta 178127
Itaoca	Itaoca I	50–60	1730 ± 40	1720–1540	coal	Beta 189336
Itaoca	Gurutuba IV	50–60	1650 ± 40	1620–1430	coal	Beta 189335
Itaoca	Caraça	70–80	1607 ± 24	1434–1416	coal	KIA 20839
Itaoca	Pavão XVI	30	1571 ± 24	1525–1408	bone	KIA 20842
Itaoca	Itaoca I	20–30	1460 ± 60	1500–1280	shell	Beta 178126
Itaoca	Lageado IV	10–20	1460 ± 60	1500–1280	shell	Beta 178128
Itaoca	Caraça	10–20	1300 ± 60	1310–1070	shell	Beta 178125
Itaoca	Guaracuí	10–20	1270 ± 70	1300–1050	coal	Beta-184621
Itaoca	Pavão III	20	1219 ± 24	1182–1062	bone	KIA 20840

THE SITES

The Capelinha 1 Site

The riverine shell mound Capelinha is situated at Cajati, in São Paulo State (SP) (UTM 22J 0778967 / 7249040). This site is located in the high valley (elevation of 310–320 meters) at the upper portion of the Capelinha River basin, a southern tributary of the Ribeira River basin. In a mountainous landscape, the site is settled in a small terrace with a low slope to the east and an abrupt one to a stream. According to the testimony of elder inhabitants of the area, the site was a conspicuous mound in the past but was partially razed for farming. Today, the remaining shell deposits have filled the depressions and irregularities of the slope, and its presence is only perceptible due to the occasional exposure of shell fragments on the surface.

Geophysical and archaeological studies revealed that the site is composed of two shell deposits: the bigger primary deposit occupies the southern area, spanning 30 meters (east-west) by 10 meters (north-south) and reaching 1.5 meters deep; the secondary deposit is 15 meters northeast from the primary, spans 10 meters (north-south) by 8 meters (east-west), and is less than 70 centimeters deep. Around the shell deposits, there is a thin, dark organic soil with small pockets of shells soil (less than 20 centimeters). The excavation (40 square meters) indicated that three different groups occupied this site in different periods, the riverine sambaquis, the Umbu Tradition (hunter-gatherer), and the Itarare Tradition (agriculturalists with ceramics).

The samples for radiocarbon dating were obtained from the following excavation areas:

• Southeast section of the primary deposit, top layer, shell sample, 9250 ± 50 BP

• Western portion of the primary deposit, basal layer, shell sample, 8795 ± 100 BP

• Secondary deposit, human bone—burial 2, 8860 ± 60 BP

• Dark organic soil, human bone—burial 5, 6090 ± 40 BP

These dates were all associated with the riverine sambaqui occupation, which exhibits a large time span in that site. The other occupation levels did not offer samples for dating analysis, but they are known as much more recent cultures (less than 2000 BP).

Two different kinds of artifacts are predominant at this site, namely the faunistic and the lithic assemblages. While lithic arrowheads have been largely related to the Umbu Tradition (Barreto 1988; DeBlasis 1988; Dias 2004), the massive presence of them is not exclusively in the

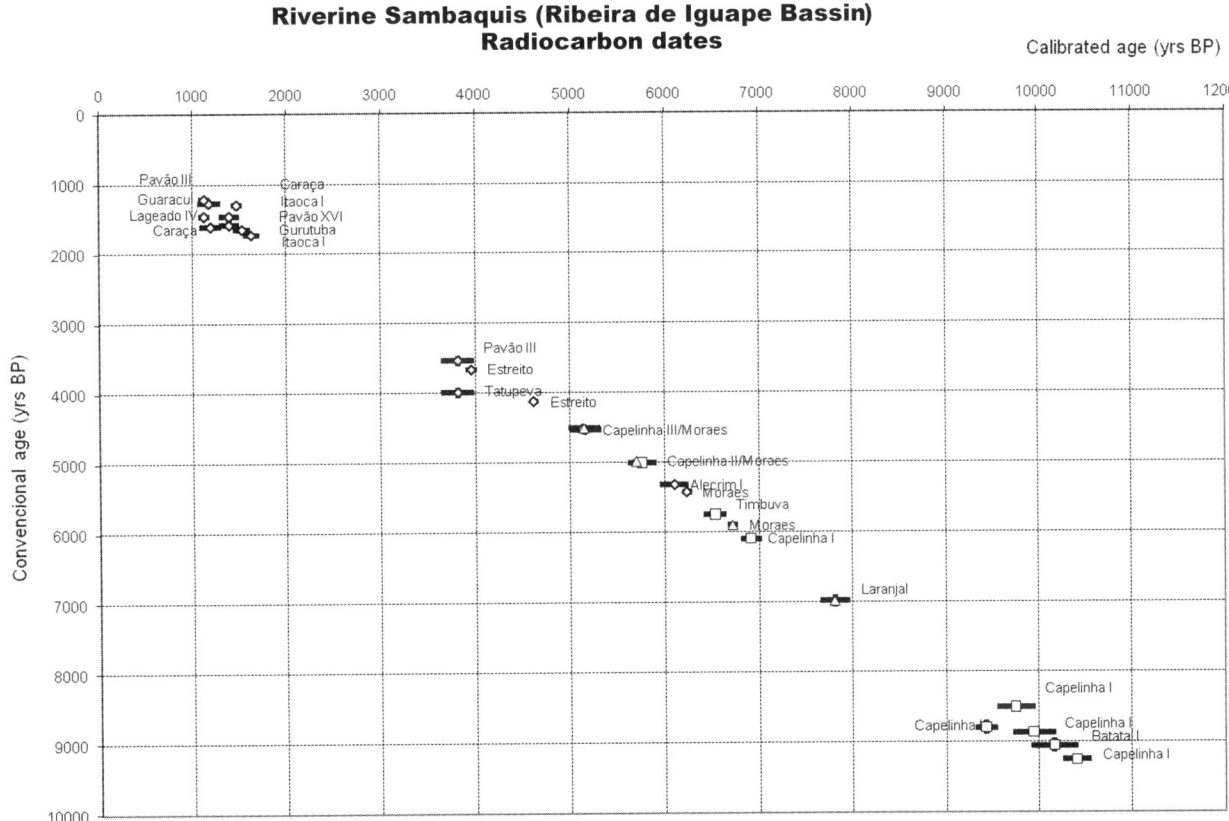

16.2. *Ribeira de Iguape riverine sambaquis radiocarbon ages. Sites from the cluster Itaoca area; r Sites from the cluster Juquiá area, o Sites from the cluster Jacupiranguinha area.*

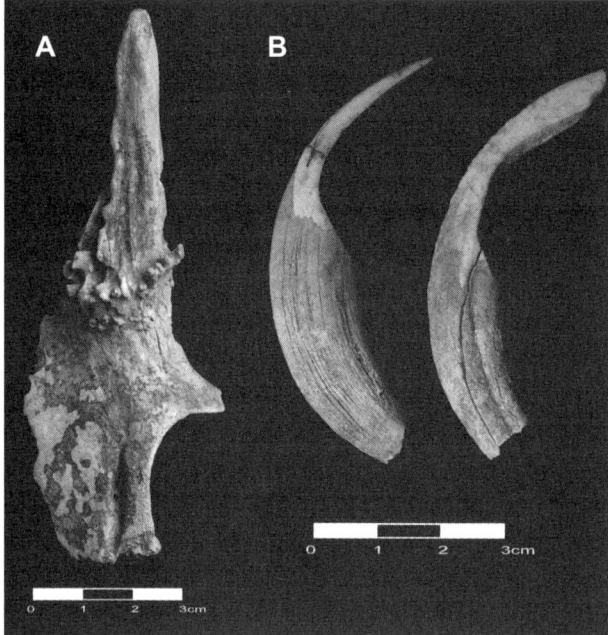

16.3. Capelinha artifacts. (A) perçoir. (B) retouched tool, awl (Photo courtesy of Wagner Souza e Silva).

Umbu Tradition layer, but also in the sambaqui layer at the Capelinha site. The mix of what has been called a fossil artifact of the Umbu Tradition to the sambaqui layer has led researchers to think about the possibility of a taphonomic process that pushed the lithic remains among the land-snails shell deposits. Trying to work on this issue, André Penin (2005) studied the lithic remains from this site. He concluded that a complex set of taphonomic process (bioturbations, erosion events, and the very permeable nature of the shell layers) pushed a massive number of Umbu fossil artifacts into the land-snail layer. He also differentiate the lithic sambaqui assemblage from the Umbu artifacts, concluding that the lithic artifacts related to the sambaqui layer kept some similarity to the coastal sambaquis, which were much less sophisticated than the Umbu specimens.

The faunistic industry (Borges 2006) is much less numerous (103 specimens) and has a very peculiar composition: bone projectiles (20 percent), retouched tools (14 percent), and "perçoirs" (50 percent). Beads are rare (4 percent) and include a pierced shark tooth. The bone projectiles are small bipoints (± 5 centimeters) made from mammal-bone fragments; the antler billet (Figure 16.3) are antlers of brocket deer (Mazama sp.), which only

present working traces and abrasions on the tip; the "perçoirs," or the awls, are made on peccary (Tayassu sp.) canines, which are deeply rasped and polished on the lingual surface of the crown until they become a thin, curved, needlelike point.

Despite the relatively large area excavated, only a modest amount of human skeletal remains was found. Five recognizable burials and a few dispersed human bones survived at the Capelinha site, but they have a great potential, as sites with human remains from the Early Holocene are rare.

The Caraça Site

This riverine sambaqui is located at Itaoca, SP (UTM 22J 0715161 / 7272520) in a small valley situated two kilometers from the Ribeira River, in a flat terrain near a meandering stream. The surrounding area is covered by rainforest and marsh. According to the local inhabitants, the site had a mound morphology a few decades ago. However, nowadays it is a flat landscape and a house was built above a portion of the site.

According to estimates made through gamma-spectrometry analysis, the shell midden reaches an area of approximately 40 by 40 meters with major concentration on the northeast and another, more discrete concentration in the southwest area. Later, several test pits and trenches confirmed those measures. In the smallest concentration, the test pits showed two occupation soils in sandy-silty, dark layers with dispersed fragments of land-snail shells, and with some concentrations of entire land-snail shells that reached up to 50 centimeters in depth. From those layers, two charcoal samples were submitted for radiocarbon dating: top soil, 1607 ± 24 BP; bottom soil, 1300 ± 60 BP.

The geophysical electromagnetic survey detected some other anomalies in the southwest and northeast areas of the site, portions of the site that were verified by some test pits. After that, it was clear that there was a correlation between the anomalies and the presence of dark, sandy soils, with medium granulometry and a high content of organic matter. The posterior analysis of these soils indicated their exposures to high temperatures (70000C), which might be associated with fireplace areas.

The lithic assemblage presents great quantities of burned, chipped artifacts. These are relatively unsophisticated but exhibit significant traces of use and recycling, despite the relative abundance of raw material, such as flint and quartzite, in the region. The industry of faunal material was rare and limited to a few bone tips.

The Estreito Site

Located at the Adrianópolis, in Paraná State (PR) (UTM 22J 0716887 / 7269427), this site is situated in the floodplain of the Ribeira River and presents a rounded morphology, with a width of 20 meters and a thickness of 2 meters, easily visible in the landscape. A road cut the mound in the east-west axis, so the profile opened by the road shows a deposit of dark sediment with sparse land-snail shell fragments and a few human skeletal remains.

The analysis of this profile indicates four layers: on the top, there is a 10- to 40-centimeter brown sandy layer. The second and third layers are located at a depth of 40 to 50 centimeters, and their colors vary between dark brown and black tones. These layers present some land-snail shell fragments dispersed in the sediment and some thin land-snail shell lenses. The bottom layer is sand-silt sediment, with a dark yellow-orange color. Faunal remains, mostly mammals and fish bones, are scarce and very fragmented in the first layer, are abundant and less fragmented in the second and third layers, and are scarce in the bottom layer.

The geophysical surveys of the site showed higher and distinctive magnetic readings than the surrounding area, and the radiometric measurement indicated higher measures compared to other sambaquis. Two test pits were opened in the mound to observe the susceptibility anomalies on the geophysical maps. The only thing that could be associated to the anomalies was some burned remains of a lithic and a shell concretion located at a depth of 70 centimeters.

During the cleaning of the profile, eight concentrations of human bone fragments were observed, of which six could be rescued. Three of these showed relatively intact burial structures: there were two primary burials with the presence of large pebbles, and one secondary cremated burial. Burial 6, in the bottom layer, was dated to 4124 ± 27 BP; burial 1, in the top layer, was dated to 3655 ± 26 BP.

The lithic assemblage shows a predominance of quartz, but flint flakes are rare. Most lithics are fragments and big flakes, and the majority presented some kind of burnt surface. The faunistic material industry is composed of some bone tips. However, there is an abundance of lithic remains surrounding the site that is similar to those found in the sambaqui, indicating the presence of activity areas outside the site.

The Moraes Site

The Moraes site is located in the Moraes stream basin, a tributary of the São Lourenço River, Miracatu, São Paulo (23 J 0256908 / 7313340). The surrounding area is a small marsh plain around the small, sinuous watercourse in the middle of a banana plantation, while forest covers the hills around the valley. The site is a small mound, an anthropogenic accumulation of shells, bones, charcoal, and rubble, with a height and depth of approximately 2 meters and a diameter of 30 meters, which was exposed and cut in the middle by a road on its north-south axis. Today it is covered by shrub vegetation, but according to oral information, banana, manioc, and beans were cultivated above the site some years ago.

The geophysical research in the Moraes site demonstrated magnetic and radiometric readings that indicate a high correlation between the high-susceptibility area (organic material/burnt lithics) and the low-radiation area (shell deposits). High-radiation areas indicate the presence of granitic rocks. This high-radiation zone in the top of the site matches a thick deposit of soil without any land snail.

The excavation area of the site was 70 square meters and the resulting profile was 20 meters long; analysis of this profile indicates four major stratigraphic features. On the surface, there is one layer with 10 to 30 centimeters of sandy-clay dark layer. The second feature is 50 to 100 centimeters thick, consisting of a complex grayish-brownish assemblage of lenses and pockets of shell fragments, clay, ashes, and burials, subdivided in four subunits. The third feature is 30 to 50 centimeters thick, a gray sandy layer. The bottom layer is sterile yellow clay originating from the decomposition of matrix rock (granite and gneiss).

The archaeological remains are not homogeneously distributed in the three features. The first feature-layer presents very fragmented and burned faunal remains, sparse and few burials, some historical elements (glass and metal), and indisputable traces of recent disturbance (plastic bags, cans, etc.). The second feature has a higher density of burials and better preserved archaeological remains. In the third feature, the burials are less numerous than in the higher layer but are very well preserved; they are also the only archaeological evidence present in this layer, as the sediment between the skeletons is nearly archaeologically sterile.

At the end of the excavation it was possible to verify a high density of burials, with 41 burials and some dispersed human bones. Most of these were located in the superior half of the shell layer, but the better-defined burial structures were found in the inferior layers of the site, probably due to the better conservation of these layers.

A particular characteristic for these burials was the presence of big stones and pigments (ochre) above the

Table 16.2. Radiocarbon-dated burials from Moraes

Burial	Location	Conventional Age
13	middle of the site, in the third layer	5895 ± 45 years BP
35	north periphery at the junction between the second and third layers	5420 ± 30 years BP
5	middle of the site, in the second layer	4985 ± 35 years BP
25	middle of the site between the first and second layers	4511 ± 32 years BP

skull. Generally, it can be said that there are differences in the burial position, mainly whether the individual is crouched or extended, although one is seated.

With the goal of understanding the chronology of the site, four burials were selected for dating (Table 16.2).

Since the only archaeological structure detected was the burials, the site is understood as a funerary place. If further studies confirm this assumption, the chronology of the site (around 6000–4000 BP) indicates the use of this site for mortuary practices during 2,000 years.

RESULTS AND DISCUSSION

To examine how the riverine sambaqui inhabitants used to manage the rainforest to obtain their resources, we used four data sets, one from each site (Table 16.3).

The Moraes data set is the complete sample from the excavation of 70 square meters, the Capelinha data set is a sample from two excavation areas (20 square meters), and the Caraça and Estreito data sets were collected by sampling pit-tests and trenches. The total assemblage identified for this study is 25,142 bone fragments from all sizes and all vertebrate classes.

In this research, the faunal analysis of each data set included anatomical and taxonomic identification, kind and degree of preservation state (fracture, burning, and other traces of human activities) of each specimen, and spatial data (trench and level). In Figure 16.4, one can

Table 16.3. Riverine sambaquis' number of indentified specimens (NISP)

Site	NISP
Estreito	643
Caraça	296
Moraes	20,553
Capelinha	3,650

observe the predominance of mammals in three sites (Capelinha, Caraça, and Moraes), with an NISP of more than 70 percent of the total sample. Considering that they are tropical rainforest hunter-gatherers, the dominance of small mammals is not unexpected; however, the important numbers of amphibious remains in the Moraes and Caraça sites are an unusual pattern. Meanwhile, the Estreito site's faunal assemblage is very distinctive from the others because fish are the dominant category, more than 50 percent.

In general, the mammals with higher abundance ratios are the peccary (Tayassu sp.), the howler monkey (Allouatta sp.), the aperea (Cavia sp.), the paca (Agouti paca), the brocket deer (Mazama sp.), and the armadillo (Dasypodidae). The fish remains are mostly from freshwater catfish (Pimelodidae) and suckermouth armored catfish (Locariidae), with a few remains of Characidae. The Amphibia remains indicate the frequent capture of toads/frogs (Anura order). Among the identified reptiles were turtles and tegu lizard (Tupinambis teguixin), and a few alligator remains. The avian vestiges are few and were not identified beyond the anatomical level.

The species range in these sites strongly suggests that these groups were well adapted to the exploitation of the terrestrial and aquatic resources of the Mata Atlantica, but the incidence of the species seems to vary according to the distance and the importance of the nearest hydric system. Whenever the site is near important water systems, there is a higher incidence of small-size mammals (howler monkeys, apereas, pacas) and higher frequencies of fish. Inversely, when the site is farther or the water system is smaller, the site seems to present more medium-size mammals such as peccary and deer, fish become rare, but amphibians become more frequent, a trend that might be explained by geographic factors and an expedient marshland economy of these inhabitants.

In summary, the results indicate that hunting and fishing activities reflected the environmental conditions of the surrounded area of each site, specifically:

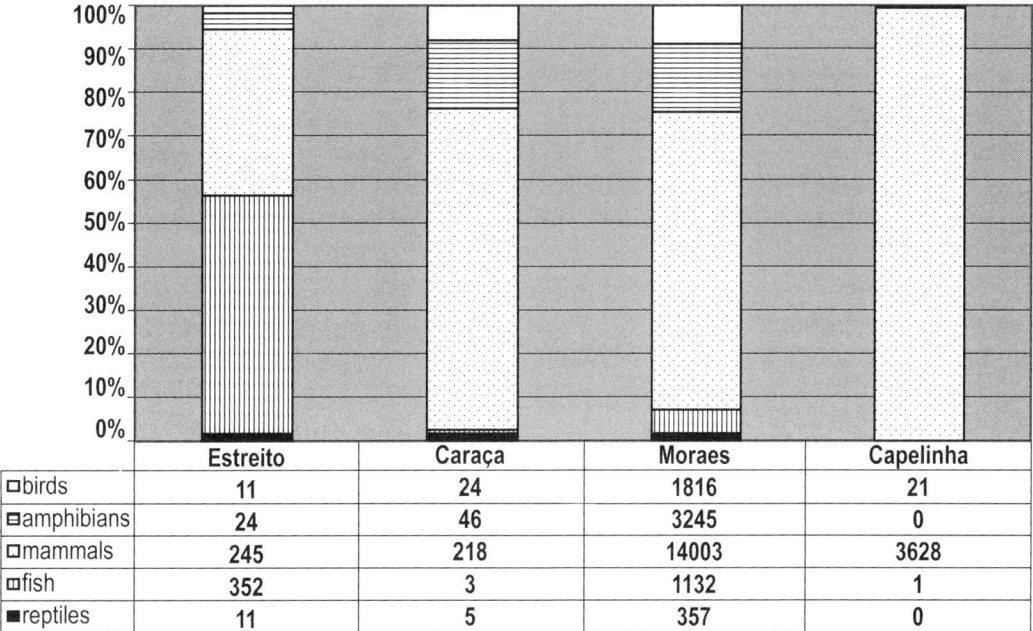

16.4. Riverine sambaquis: Sites, NISP by vertebrate class

	Estreito	Caraça	Moraes	Capelinha
◻birds	11	24	1816	21
▤amphibians	24	46	3245	0
◻mammals	245	218	14003	3628
▥fish	352	3	1132	1
∎reptiles	11	5	357	0

• The Estreito site is the only one next to a big river (Ribeira de Iguape) and has a higher percentage of fish.

• The Caraça and the Moraes sites are located next to small meandering streams, marshlands areas, and forested slopes. Hence, we found a predominance of small mammals and the relatively important presence of amphibian bones.

• The Capelinha site is located next to a small headwater stream in the midst of the mountain ridge of the "Serra do Mar" formation. Therefore, the ancient inhabitants of Capelinha had the montane rainforest at their disposal, which is poor in aquatic resources but rich in small- and medium-sized mammals.

The diversity of species found in these sites indicates that these groups exploited all kinds of faunal resources available in close range of each site, without any indication of hunting specialization, long-range procurement of resources, or any kind of activity that requires a larger time investment. This behavior seems to suggest that each occupation episode had a short time duration.

The only trace of long-range procurement is some occasional vestiges of marine animals: oyster (Ostrea sp.) and clam (Lucina pectinata) shells; snook (Centropomus undecimalis) and croaker (Micropogonias furnierii) bones; a perforated shark tooth (Carcharhinus plumbeus, Carcharodon carcharias), and a spearhead of ray spine.

The presence of marine remains obviously indicates some kind of liaison with the coastal environment and/or with coastal cultures, but the nature of that connection remains debatable. The rise of the coastal sambaquis does not seem to be a reason for this presence, because those sites appear after the earliest riverine ones, and these early riverine sites already have marine organism remains. Therefore, the distance from the sea seems to be a more important element; the Moraes site is the closest (40 kilometers) to the sea and presents many more marine remains than the other sites of Capelinha (60 kilometers) and Caraça and Estreito (100 kilometers each).

The bone preservation in these sites is mostly good; bones from small fauna like amphibians and micro-rodents are well preserved in large amounts, due to the neutral/alkaline geochemical features associated with the shells. Whether the micro-rodents were eaten by humans or were merely post-depositional inclusions is still a matter of study, but the contextual data from the sites shows that none of these bone assemblages of medium-sized animals or micro-rodents were found in anatomical connection.

A first overview of the burn traces on bones from all sites indicates that most of the marks are post-depositional and not from cooking activities. It is very rare to find a preserved fire structure, though we often observe thin lenses of charcoal and ash, and analysis has shown great quantities of charcoal fragments and burned/carbonized faunal elements dispersed in the sediments (Plens 2007).

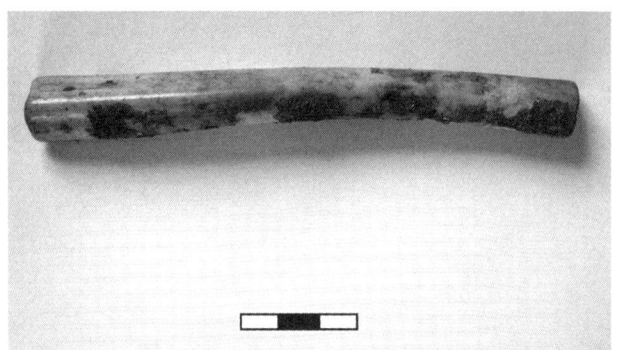

16.5. Capelinha I. Polished bone, burial 2 (Photo courtesy of Wagner Souza e Silva).

Thus the different degrees of burning seem to be more related to the position of each specimen to the concentrations of burnt bone/soil or the past fire.

Another complementary aspect of the zooarchaeological remains is the study of the artifacts of faunal material (Borges 2006), which are still in the process of analysis. It is already possible to identify six general categories: bone tips, beads, awls, antler billets, hooks, and polished bones (Figure 16.5).

In the riverine sambaqui collection, the bone tips (arrowheads/spear points) are a common feature, relatively abundant, and present a diverse morphology, including single points, bi-points, leaf-points, needle-points, and so on. Most of these artifacts are made of mammal bones, except for a few ray spine points. Nevertheless, this collection is quite similar in morphology to the bone tips from the coastal sambaquis. Among the sites of this study, the tips are the most abundant artifact in the Moraes site (47 percent), but they are less numerous at Capelinha (21 percent), while in the other sites the samples are numerically insignificant.

The second most abundant artifacts are the beads made of perforated teeth from mammals. Among these teeth, howler monkey (Allouatta sp.) canines are predominant, besides some isolated specimens (two necklaces were found, amounting to nearly a hundred teeth, at the Moraes site). After the mammal teeth, perforated shark teeth (nearly a dozen specimens) are the most abundant beads in the riverine sambaqui collection.

The artifacts identified as awls are from peccary (Tayassu sp.) tusks with cusps that were thinned to make a very sharp point. These artifacts seem to be abundant only at the Capelinha site, where we found nearly 50 specimens; otherwise they are very rare. In the same fashion, antler billets (Mazama sp.) are frequent only at the Capelinha site (15 specimens) and extremely rare in the other sites. These two categories are not found at the coastal sambaquis.

Hooks are very rare, and in the entire collection, fewer than a dozen specimens were found, most of these fragmented and made from mammal bones. This artifact type was found only in two sites (Moraes and Lageado IV), which are both near shallow streams. The last artifact type includes two long bones (femur), with sectioned epiphyses and polished surfaces; these artifacts were found as grave goods of burial 2 from the Capelinha site.

CONCLUDING REMARKS

The term sambaqui can give a first inaccurate notion about the population of the riverine sambaquis. Although they show the same basic pattern of mound building as the coastal sambaquis, the riverine population remains exhibit a characteristic behavior of tropical rainforest hunter-gatherers: diversified faunal acquisition, low specialization, low investment in big-game hunting, predominance of small-medium prey, and little to no evidence of cooperative hunting.

Otherwise, the shells observed at Capelinha and Moraes are inarguably the remains of the only collective acquisitive activity positively identified, namely intensive land-snail gathering. This activity resulted in a pile-up of shells and earth that is the basis of the mound building.

Furthermore, these patterns of hunter-gatherer consumption seem to reflect a strict opportunistic behavior, conditioned by the degree of access to aquatic resources and the (short) time they spend during each mound-building/burial episode. Hence the hunting pattern observed indicates a similar variety of species, but the diversity of species is peculiar to each site, or the frequency of species reflects the nearest environments of each site.

NOTE

1. The Umbu Tradition, a hunter-gatherer archaeological group from southern Brazil, is defined by a lithic industry of flaked small bifacial artifacts, mostly triangular points.

CHAPTER SEVENTEEN

Shellfish and Resource Sustainability on the Central Northwest Coast of North America

Phoebe Daniels

SUMMARY

The intensification of subsistence resources is critical to many explanations of the development of semi-sedentary complex cultures on the Northwest Coast of North America. In order to support increasingly sedentary populations, some resources would have had to be sustainably harvested, naturally resilient to resource depression, or both. Taxonomic and size analyses of archaeological shell remains from two large winter villages in the San Juan Islands, USA, indicate that shellfish populations were stable over time, but size profiles show no evidence of active management in the form of selective harvesting of senile clams. These results suggest that shellfish were an important, stable resource for people in this area but do not indicate that the shellfish habitat was actively managed, though it remains possible that management strategies not tested for in this study may have been in place.

INTRODUCTION

The intensification of subsistence resources is critical to many explanations of the development of semi-sedentary complex cultures on the Northwest Coast of North America. It was once thought that this intensification occurred simply because of an inexhaustible resource base (e.g., Fladmark 1975). Subsequently, the recognition that oscillating resource availability presented challenges to semi-sedentary foragers (Fitzhugh 2003; Suttles 1987) made it clear that resource abundance and stability could not be assumed. Recent zooarchaeological studies have shown that in many locations important faunal resources remained stable over time despite foraging pressure from human populations (Butler and Campbell 2004; Campbell and Butler 2010; Moss 2012).

Shellfish are relatively unique among Northwest Coast resources in that they are available year-round and have some natural resilience to resource depression. This likely made them an increasingly valuable resource as people became more sedentary and populations increased. The importance of shellfish in Northwest Coast economies is exemplified by the profusion of dense shell middens. Recently, analysis of shells recovered from auger samples suggests that alongside winter villages, shell fishing may not only have been sustainable but actively managed (Cannon and Burchell 2009; Cannon, Burchell, and Bathurst 2008). The English Camp (45SJ24) and Watmough Bay (45SJ280) village sites in the San Juan Islands, Washington (Figure 17.1), provide robust samples to further evaluate the sustainability of shellfish exploitation. Taxonomic and size analyses are used to test for evidence of resource depression and active management in the form of selective harvesting. The results indicate that the most common taxon at each site increasingly dominates the assemblages over time, that their average sizes remain stable over time, and that adult clams in their reproductive prime were the most common age class. These results indicate that shellfish harvesting at English Camp and Watmough Bay was sustainable but not actively managed by selective harvesting.

SHELLFISH BIOLOGY

Shellfish biology suggests that they might be particularly resistant to resource depression as they are relatively

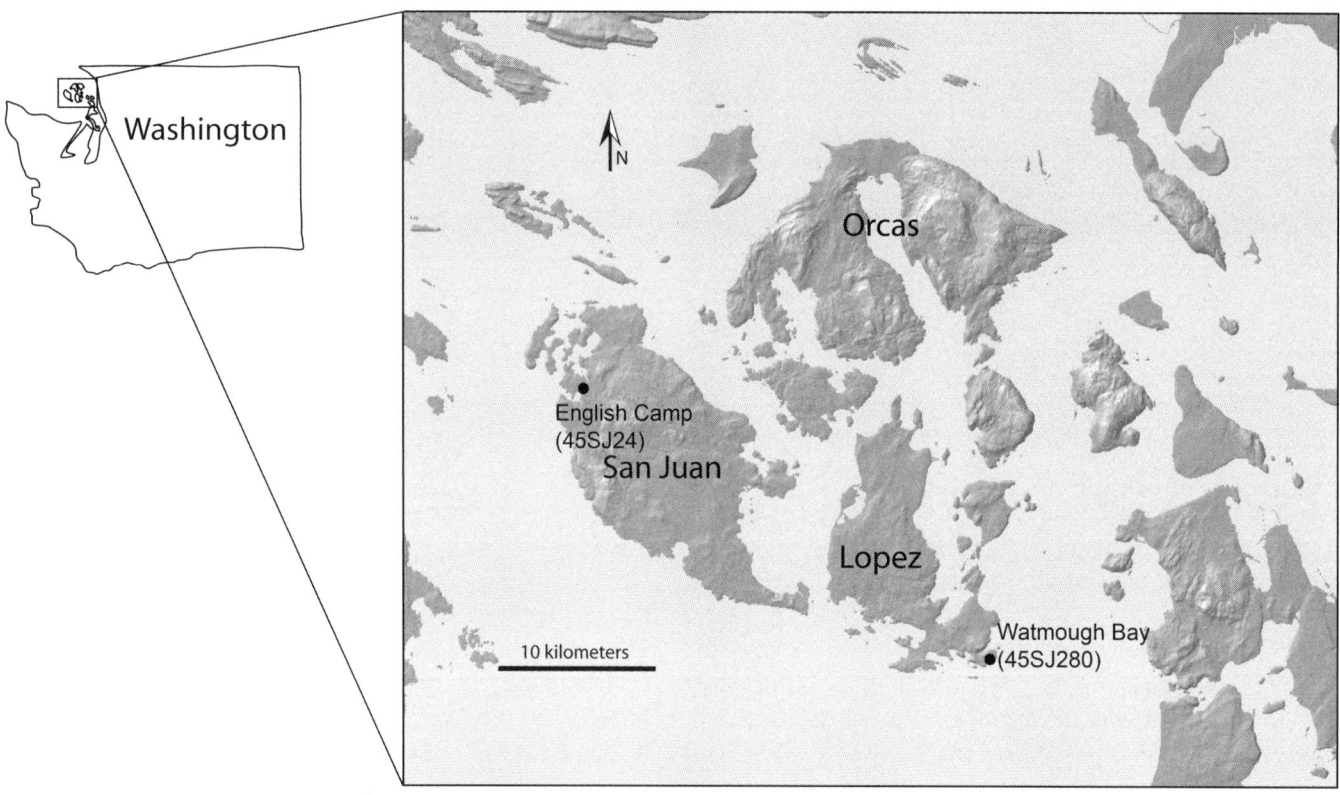

17.1. Location of the English Camp site (45SJ24) and Watmough Bay site (45SJ280) in the San Juan Islands.

short-lived, have high fecundity, and follow an open-water reproductive strategy, which facilitates fast growth rates, high recruitment, and greater survival rates (Kozloff 1990, 1993). The sensitivity of individual shellfish species to human exploitation can be gauged by considering life history, habitat, and proximity to refugia (Catterall and Poiner 1987; de Boer and Prins 2002; Jamieson 1993; Lasiak 1992). Species that reach sexual maturity at a small size, for example, are more likely to maintain higher reproducing populations since small individuals are more often ignored by human predators. Species that dwell in cryptic habitats or are relatively mobile may also escape predation more often than easily seen and captured species. In addition, species with high fecundity and open-water fertilization are better equipped to maintain high densities because of greater opportunities for recruitment from refugia. Similarly, populations with wide geographic distribution and proximity to refugia will also have greater opportunities for recruitment. In sum, the potential for people to cause resource depression in shellfish populations is likely to vary across species and populations within species.

SHELLFISH RESOURCE DEPRESSION STUDIES

The size and relative abundance data used to test past resource depression of shellfish assumes that a decrease in the relative abundance or size/age of higher-ranked taxa indicates a decrease in their availability due to resource depression (e.g., Anderson 1981; Koike and Okamura 1994; Lightfoot and Cerrato 1988; Raab 1992; Swadling 1976). L. Mark Raab (1992) argued that the decline in large, easily processed abalone in favor of the small, hard-to-process *Tegula* in California resulted from declines in the former as a result of human foraging. Similarly, in New Zealand, Atholl Anderson (1981) attributed the shift in foraging strategy, from one focused on a few larger species to one that included a wide variety of smaller species, to resource depression of the larger species. In Japan, H. Koike and M. Okamura (1994) showed that during the Jomon period the mean age of the dominant species, *Meretrix lusoria*, was three years, while in the later Kofun period, the mean age increased to five years, which they argue reflects a reduction in exploitation intensity. Most recently, Kenneth D. Thomas and Marcello A. Mannino (2001) determined that, in southern Britain, the main species declined through time and that one of these species, *Monodonta lineata*, decreased in mean age as well.

Resource depression may not be the only explanatory mechanism, as environmental changes (Claassen 1998, 47; Jerardino 1997; Keegan, Portell, and Slapcinsky 2003) and human behavioral changes (Bird and Bliege Bird 2000, 2002) can also account for these patterns. Since each species has optimal environmental parameters, changes in environmental variables can result in decreased recruitment and growth rates, and can negatively influence the timing of spawning, thus creating assemblages that mimic resource depression. For example, Antonieta Jerardino (1997) showed that the decrease in size and abundance of black mussels in the Western Cape coast of South Africa was caused by a combination of exploitation by people and increased water turbidity. William F. Keegan and colleagues (2003) determined that the change in relative abundance at Jamaican sites was caused by sea-level rise and increased precipitation.

Since the environment affects growth rates, it can affect average size, but should have no influence on average age; we can therefore control for environmental change by analyzing mean age rather than mean shell size (Claassen 1998, 130; Mannino and Thomas 2002). Decreases in the average age over time would exclusively reflect resource depression. Alternatively, vertebrate faunal analysts routinely control for environmental change by comparing faunal records with independent environmental data (e.g., Bovy 2007; Broughton 1994a, 1994b; Butler 2000, 2001; Nagaoka 2002). If faunal changes coincide with environmental change, environment cannot be ruled out.

Recent ethnoarchaeological shellfish studies conducted among the Meriam of Torres Straits, Australia, indicate that children's foraging and field processing can create patterns in shell assemblages that mimic resource depression through slower foraging rates and processing ability limited by strength and coordination, resulting in a wider diet breadth and an increase in smaller taxa that are easier to process (Bird and Bliege Bird 2000). While it is possible that children's foraging routinely accounts for the small percentage of smaller species and individuals in an assemblage, it will create patterns that mimic resource depression only if children's foraging increases over time relative to adult foraging. This increase is only likely to occur if birth rates steadily increase, child mortality decreases, or there is a major cultural shift in child-care strategies. If smaller taxa and individuals increase over time, the possibility that children's foraging is increasing must be examined. Douglas W. Bird and Rebecca Bliege Bird (2002) also

observed that foragers increasingly processed shellfish in the field as a function of distance from the home base, meat to shell ratio, and processing time. If larger species have a higher meat to shell ratio and are easier to process, their presence in an assemblage may decline if foragers are increasingly exploiting more distant shellfish beds. Of course, increased traveling is often associated with decreased local availability, and so travel and overexploitation may be interrelated and difficult to separate. Thus, it is unlikely that field processing will produce assemblages that mimic resource depression in its absence.

NORTHWEST COAST SHELLFISH STUDIES

The Northwest Coast environment supports highly productive shellfish communities and makes them less susceptible to resource depression. Multiple river outlets and upwelling of deep ocean water produce nutrient-rich waters that foster high marine productivity (Kozloff 1993; Ricketts, Calvin, and Hedgpeth 1968). In addition, the many bends and folds of the irregular coastline bring distinct populations in close proximity to each other, which allows for greater recruitment from refugia (Ricketts, Calvin, and Hedgpeth 1968). As a result, areas that are highly exploited may continue to have high recruitment rates because they can be repopulated from adjacent areas that are less intensely exploited.

Regional shellfish studies were recently and thoroughly reviewed by Aubrey Cannon and colleagues (2008), and I will only briefly summarize those that pertain to tests of shellfish sustainability. At Ozette, Washington, Gary C. Wessen (1988, 201–2) identified a shift from *Mytilus californicus* (California mussel) to *Protothaca staminea* (common littleneck clam) without any concurrent decrease in the size of mussels or in any of the major clam species. He concluded that the shift was likely due to broader economic changes associated with European contact. Dale R. Croes (1992) used size profiles of *M. californicus* and relative abundance data to argue for resource management of mussels at the Hoko River Rockshelter, Washington. The increase in alternative, smaller shellfish taxa at a time when mussels were depleted is used to further argue that mussel beds were managed by intentionally decreasing the pressure when their populations were depressed (Croes 1992). Alternatively, without implying active management and based on foraging theory (Smith and Winterhalder 1992), when higher-ranked resources decline, the diet breadth expands to include more lower-ranked resources to optimize return-rates; if the higher-ranked resources rebound, the optimal strategy would be to narrow the diet breadth again.

Gary Coupland and colleagues (2003) argued that the decrease in size and abundance of *P. staminea* across the upper and lower portions of one unit at the McNichol Creek site, British Columbia, is evidence of resource depression. Alternatively, greater exposure to taphonomic processes in lower levels may have differentially broken down smaller shells relative to larger ones (Cannon, Burchell, and Bathurst 2008). Since only one date was obtained for the unit from which the shell originated, and given that different areas within shell middens can accumulate at different rates and at different times (Stein, Deo, and Phillips 2003), without additional dates for that unit, it cannot be ascertained whether the upper and lower portions of the unit represent different time periods or can be compared against environmental data to rule out environmental change.

Most recently, Cannon and colleagues calculated relative shellfish abundances and *Saxidomous giganteus* (butter clam) age profiles from multiple sites in the Namu region, British Columbia (Cannon and Burchell 2009; Cannon, Burchell, and Bathurst 2008). They found that each site was dominated by the taxon most abundant in the local environment and that relative abundances remained stable through time. Age profiling produced high ratios of senile clams at residential sites, whereas multipurpose sites had relatively equal proportions of mature and senile clams. From this they conclude that sustainability was maintained at residential sites by a resource management strategy that limited exploitation to clams beyond reproduction age.

The research presented here adds to this body of work, providing new insights into the long-term relationship between foragers and shellfish communities by using theoretically informed hypotheses and considering shellfish data from the San Juan Islands against local environmental records.

THE SAN JUAN ISLANDS

The San Juan Islands are part of an archipelago of more than 400 islands in the Salish Sea, located between the southwestern corner of British Columbia, Canada, and the northwest corner of Washington State, USA. The Northwest Coast region is characterized by a mild maritime climate with cool summers and wet and mild winters, but the San Juan Islands lie within the rain shadow of the Olympic Mountains, making their summers drier than is typical of

the region. Mixed coniferous forests, open prairies, and rock and sandy beaches cover the islands, while the mixing of cold ocean water with warmer, brackish water from the Strait of Georgia supports productive intertidal and marine environments.

The San Juan Islands lie within the Gulf of Georgia culture area and the traditional territories of Coast Salish language groups (Stein 2000; Suttles 1990). Human occupation of the islands dates back at least 4,000 years, though inundation and erosion may have destroyed evidence of earlier occupations (Taylor, Stein, and Jolivette 2011). Extensive radiocarbon dating of 41 sites across the islands indicates that the number of sites increased substantially during the periods between 1000–500 BP and 500–0 BP, peaking between 650 and 300 BP (Taylor, Stein, and Jolivette 2011). Prehistorically, people were seasonally mobile, relying upon a diversity of terrestrial and marine mammals, birds, fish, shellfish, and plants as they became available, supplementing with stored food during the leaner winter months (Stein 2000; Suttles 1990).

PATCH CHOICE AT ENGLISH CAMP AND WATMOUGH BAY

Intertidal resources common in the English Camp and Watmough Bay archaeological deposits are patchily distributed across the Garrison Bay and Watmough Bay intertidal environments. The English Camp faunas originate from two distinct patches in Garrison Bay. The intertidal environment is primarily composed of a soft substrate, with small hard-substrate patches intermixed. The soft substrate grades from silt/clay in the south to coarse and compact sand in the north, with mixed sediments between (Gallucci and Gallucci 1982). The variety of soft-substrate sediments includes the preferred habitat of *S. giganteus*, *Tresus* spp. (horse clam), *Macoma nasuta* (bent-nose clam), *P. staminea*, and *Clinocardium nuttallii* (heart cockle). Boulders, cobbles, and small bedrock exposures create patches of hard-substrate environments throughout the bay. The hard substrate provides habitat for *M. edulis* and *Balanus glandula* (acorn barnacle).

The Watmough Bay intertidal region contains three distinct patches. Again, the soft-substrate environment dominates, though at Watmough Bay it is composed of homogeneous coarse sand. It also provides habitats for the bivalves *S. giganteus*, *Tresus* spp., *M. nasuta*, *P. staminea*, and *C. nuttallii*. The hard substrate is limited to a few large boulders at the north end of the beach. It provides habitats for *M. edulis*, *Balanus glandula*, and *Katharina tunacata* (black katy chiton) common in the archaeological deposits, as well as other gastropods that are less common or absent in the deposits. In addition, the Watmough Bay infralittoral fringe, the portion of the intertidal zone only exposed during low-low tides (Kozloff 1993), provides habitats for *Strongylocentrotus droebachiensis* (green sea urchin), *Strongylocentrotus purpuratus* (purple sea urchin), and *Cryptochiton stelleri* (gumboot chiton) that also occur in the site.

Optimal foraging theory can be used to determine if the shellfish assemblages at English Camp and Watmough Bay reflect resource depression or resource stability through time. When resources are patchily distributed, as they are here, foraging theory predicts foragers to rank resource patches based on their net return-rates (calories per unit handling time; Kaplan and Hill 1992). The patch choice model assumes that foragers encounter patches randomly and predicts that upon encounter they will exploit only those patches that increase their long-term returns; the marginal value theorem predicts that foragers will switch patches only when foraging causes the net return-rate in the exploited patch to drop below that of the next highest patch plus travel time (Charnov, Orians, and Hyatt 1976; Kaplan and Hill 1992).

These models need to be adjusted slightly to apply to the English Camp and Watmough Bay settings, where patches are not encountered randomly but located immediately in front of the sites. Therefore, it can be assumed that the foragers decided before they began foraging which patch to exploit. Given that distances to and between the patches are negligible, it follows that foragers will exploit the highest-ranked patch first, switching only when return-rates within that patch decline below that of the next highest-ranked patch.

Patch rank order can be derived from estimates of average resource return-rates of all taxa available within the patch and their density. Neither variable can be directly measured in archaeological contexts. However, the body size proxy, adjusted for likely pursuit costs (i.e., digging), can be used to estimate return-rates. Density can be estimated from modern abundances throughout the region and the relative size of each patch (Table 17.1).

The soft substrate is ranked highest, the infralittoral fringe second (at Watmough Bay), and the hard substrate the lowest. Although the average size of taxa within the infralittoral fringe, 12 centimeters, is slightly larger than the average bivalve size within the soft substrate, 11 centimeters, and both patch areas are relatively large, differences in resource density suggest that the soft substrate is higher-ranked. All of the commonly identified bivalves are

very abundant throughout the calm saltwater bays of the San Juan Islands (Kozloff 1993; Rudy and Rudy 1983). In contrast, the greater average size of the infralittoral fringe is due to the long length, 22 centimeters, of *C. stelleri*, which is very rare in the San Juan Islands and only available during extremely low tides (Kozloff 1993). When the infralittoral fringe average size is based only on *S. droebachiensis* and *S. purpuratus*, which are abundant in the area (Kozloff 1993), the average size drops to 8 centimeters, 3 centimeters less than the soft-substrate patch. Finally, the average size within the hard substrate, 3.75 centimeters, is significantly less than either of the other patches, and abundances are fairly low due to limited habitat in quiet saltwater bays.

When smaller resources are mass-collected, the body size proxy may fail to accurately rank prey types or patches (e.g., Madsen and Schmitt 1998; Schmitt, Madsen, and Lupo 2004). While all shellfish are relatively easy to collect, mussels and barnacles can occur as beds or mats that can be removed en masse. However, in the San Juan Islands they rarely occur in such density and are more commonly found adhering in small numbers to cobbles and the rare bedrock outcrop. There is no reason to think that the situation differed significantly in the past. To fully assess changes in foraging efficiency, within-patch relative abundances must also be measured. Intertidal zonation makes the distribution of resources within patches predictable. All organisms within the intertidal zone have an upper and lower limit to their distribution due to each species' unique physical and biological tolerances (Carefoot 1977). This limit creates a series of parallel patches between the high and low tides, with each taxon being most abundant within a single parallel patch, becoming decreasingly abundant with increasing distance from that patch. As a result, patches within the soft substrate can be ranked using the density of available taxa as proxies for ranking patches, where the most abundant taxon is the highest-ranked and the remaining taxa are lower-ranked.

The soft-substrate intertidal zones can be ranked by comparing the substrate composition of the bays with the known preferences of the common bivalves. At Watmough Bay the substrate is homogeneous coarse sand. Of the bivalves that occur in the site, only *P. staminea* prefers coarse sand, the others preferring muddier substrates (Rudy and Rudy 1983), making *P. staminea* the most common bivalve at Watmough Bay. And, in turn, the zone in which *P. staminea* is the most common has the greatest overall bivalve density, and thus is the highest-ranked patch within the soft substrate.

Table 17.1. Summary of the size, abundance, and habitat preferences of the common taxa occurring in the English Camp and Watmough Bay sites by patch

Taxon	Common Name	Max. Length (cm)	Depth (cm)	Primary Inter-tidal Zone	Regional Abundance	Habitat
Soft-substrate Patch						
Clinocardium nuttallii	Heart cockle	10	1–2	High	Common	Muddy fine sand
Tresus spp.	Horse clam	20	25–60	Low	Common	muddy sand
Macoma nasuta	Bent-nose clam	5	10–15	Mid	Common	muddy sand
Prototheca staminea	Littleneck clam	6	3–8	Mid	Common	Coarse sand
Saxidomus giganteus	Butter clam	14	20–30	Low	Common	Sandy or gravelly mud
Average		11				
Hard-substrate Patch						
Katharina tunacata	Black Katy chiton	7	Surface	Low	Common	Rocky
Mytilus edulis	Bay mussel	6	Surface	Low	Common	Rocky
Balanus cf. *glandula*	Acorn barnacle	1.5	Surface	High-mid	Common	Rocky
Average		3.75				
Subtidal Patch						
Cryptochiton stelleri	Gumboot chiton	20	Surface	Infralittorial	Rare	Rocky
Strongylocentrotus droebachiensis	Green sea urchin	8	Surface	Infralittorial	Common	Rocky
Strongylocentrotus purpuratus	Purple sea urchin	8	Surface	Infralittorial	Common	Rocky
Average		12				

When the substrate is heterogeneous, no one taxon can be expected to be naturally more abundant than any of the others. When this is the case, as at English Camp, then the zone in which the highest-ranked taxon is most common should also be the highest-ranked patch. Due to its relatively large size and position immediately below the surface, *C. nuttallii* is the highest-ranked bivalve. Modern shellfish surveys at English Camp suggest that *C. nuttallii* is currently less common than other bivalves (Dethier and Berry 2008), but people living in the area recall it being more abundant in the recent past (Megan N. Dethier, pers. comm. 2009). Dethier suggests that the low abundance of *C. nuttallii* today could be reflecting regional resource depression of these easily harvested bivalves but notes that this has yet to be tested. If recent observations are correct, the low abundance at Garrison Bay today is a modern phenomenon and cannot be used to predict past natural abundances. When quantifying the long-term exploitation effects within the soft substrate, *C. nuttallii* is the proxy for

the highest-ranked patch despite its lower abundance today.

The hard substrate is a homogeneous environment and all taxa that dwell within it are confined to the available bedrock and boulders. At English Camp, the hard substrate is primarily composed of large cobbles that are scattered throughout the intertidal zone and form long horizontal zones perpendicular to the shoreline. Since there are no differences in hard-substrate composition, the zone in which the highest-ranked taxon is most common should also be the highest-ranked patch. Due to its larger size, *M. edulis* is the highest-ranked hard-substrate taxon at English Camp; thus the zone in which it is most common is the highest-ranked patch.

At Watmough Bay, the hard substrate is confined to large boulders and bedrock outcrops at the north end of the bay, which encompass small horizontal areas but have great vertical relief. As a result, the different zones are available to the forager at different heights within a single location. With all zones equally available in a single location, the Watmough Bay hard substrate is best characterized as a series of heterogeneous patches that include all hard-substrate taxa. Following from the prey-choice model (MacArthur and Pianka 1966) and applying the body-size proxy (Broughton 1994a, 1994b), *K. tunacata* is the highest-ranked hard-substrate taxon at Watmough Bay.

The infralittoral fringe is itself defined by zonation, as the area of the intertidal zone that is only exposed during low-low tides (Kozloff 1993). Within the infralittoral fringe all taxa by definition have the same zone distribution. For the purposes of the model, distribution of resources should be considered random. By applying the prey-choice model and body-size proxy, *C. stelleri* is the highest-ranked infralittoral taxon at Watmough Bay.

Following from these rank orders, resource depression should result in a decline in the relative abundance of the taxa within the highest-ranked patch, the soft substrate. In addition, the relative abundance of the higher-ranked taxon within each patch should also decline. Alternatively, resource sustainability is predicted to result in either stability or an increase in the relative abundance of the higher-ranked patch and higher-ranked taxon within each patch.

Simple quantitative indices can be constructed using rank orders to identify changes in relative abundances of higher- to lower-ranked patches and prey in the diet (e.g., Bayham 1979; Broughton 1994a, 1994b; Butler 2000; Kennedy 2003; Nagaoka 2002). The indices give a simple value of 0 to 1, where a value of 1 indicates the sample is composed entirely of individuals from the higher-ranked patch and a value of 0 indicates the sample is composed entirely of individuals from the lower-ranked patches. The ranking discussion above was used to create both intertidal patch indices and intra-patch indices at both sites (Table 17.2).

Mean prey age provides an independent measure of resource depression because intense exploitation can lead to a decrease in the mean size or age of targeted species (e.g., Dye, Lasiak, and Gabula 1997; Keough, Quinn, and King 1993; Koike and Okamura 1994; Thomas and Mannino 2001). If shellfish resource depression occurred at English Camp or Watmough Bay, then the mean size of the highest-ranked taxa, *C. nuttallii* and *P. staminea*, is expected to decline. A decrease in mean size in the absence of relative abundance evidence for resource depression could indicate an increase in resource abundance since competition for space can result in decreases in size. However, size profiles that skew toward senile individuals could imply that foragers are managing shellfish communities by rejecting younger individuals (Cannon and Burchell 2009; Cannon, Burchell, and Bathurst 2008).

SITES

English Camp Site

The English Camp site is a large shell midden in Garrison Bay that stretches from a grassy field to a wooded area to the north. Lummi elders remember it as the location of a winter village, which is independently confirmed by British records (Stein 2000). Excavations at the site recovered marine and terrestrial fauna, shell, charcoal, and bone and stone artifacts (Stein 2000). The faunal and flora remains indicate that, consistent with the regional pattern, people at English Camp subsisted on a wide variety of marine and terrestrial mammals, fish, birds, plants, and shellfish. Extensive radiocarbon dates (Daniels 2009; Deo, Stone, and Stein 2004; Stein 1992; Stein, Deo, and Phillips 2003) show that the site was occupied from 1715 BP until 270 BP. Shell was sampled from four one x one-meter units (105365, 123347, 310300, and 310304; see Daniels 2009 for a detailed discussion of the sampling methods).

The stratigraphy of large shell middens on the Northwest Coast is often complex and defining natural strata is challenging, and efforts to correlate strata observed in

Table 17.2. Relative abundance quantitative indices for the English Camp and Watmough Bay sites

Index	English Camp site	Watmough Bay site
Intertidal Patch	ΣSoft-substrate/Σ Soft-substrate + Hard-substrate	ΣSoft-substrate/Σ Soft-substrate + Hard-substrate + Infralittoral
Soft-substrate	Σ*C. nuttallii*/ ΣAll bivalves	Σ*P. staminea*/ ΣAll bivalves
Hard-substrate	Σ*M. edulis*/ Σ*M. edulis + B.* cf. *glandula.*	Σ*K. tunacata*/ Σ*K. tunicata + M. edulis + B.* cf. *glandula.*
Infralittoral	NA	Σ *C. stelleri*/ Σ *C. stelleri + Strongylocentrotus* spp.

Table 17.3. English Camp: NISP (number of identified specimens) and percent of common taxa by chronological level

Level	Natural Strata	Ave. ^{14}C Date	M. edulis	C. nuttallii	P. staminea	Large bivalve	Small bivalve	B. cf. glandula	Total
1	310304 A-B	159	181	2,787	2,250	438	638	831	7,125
2	310304 D-F	398	472	7,539	1,909	637	870	773	12,200
3	310300 B	560	60	1,017	249	114	54	286	1,780
4	123347 A-G	738	56	3,970	1,731	446	1,311	242	7,756
5	310300 C-M, 310304 L	956	1,422	1,402	1,544	505	417	2,405	7,695
6	310300 P, 310304 M-2M	1075	3,041	10,555	2,306	991	344	5,727	22,964
7	123347 I	1285	84	121	128	27	173	458	991
8	105305 A-W	1393	1,464	10,716	6,854	714	8,272	5,082	33,102
9	310300 R	1475	98	154	1,296	154	98	660	2,460
Total			6,878	38,261	18,267	4,026	12,177	16,464	96,073
Percent			7	40	19	4	13	17	

profiles with those seen in units often fail (Stein, Kornbacher, and Tyler 1992). Instead, radiocarbon dates were used to organize the natural levels of all four units into a single, site-wide chronological sequence to evaluate changes in the shellfish patterns over time (Table 17.3). This strategy provides a single chronological sequence but does not control for horizontal differences in site use since each unit is not equally represented in every chronological level.

Watmough Bay Site

The Watmough Bay site was first excavated in the late 1960s by David Munsell and more recently by the Bureau of Land Management (BLM) (Bovy, Phillips, and Stein 2007). The site consists of a shell-rich layer overlying a dark, relatively shell-free layer (Bovy 2005). As at English Camp, terrestrial and marine mammal, fish, bird, and shellfish remains recovered from the site attest to a broad diet. The BLM excavation was limited to two adjoining one x one-meter units, EXU 1 and EXU 2, excavated by 10-centimeter arbitrary levels. The shell remains sampled from these units were used in this analysis.

Radiocarbon dates obtained from the shell-rich portion of the BLM excavation indicate that deposition occurred simultaneously in units EXU 1 and 2 (550–1000 BP), and slightly later than the shell midden in the main excavation area (1250–1650 BP; Bovy 2005). Since the lowest shell-rich levels of EXU 1 and 2 were not dated, the date range represents the minimum occupancy of the area. Given that

the radiocarbon dates are equivalent across adjacent levels of units EXU 1 and 2, they were combined and analyzed together.

METHODS

The shell material from the two sites was identified to the finest taxonomic and quantified using the number of identified specimen (NISP) counts and weights (see Daniels 2009 for details). The size of the two highest-ranked and abundant species, *P. staminea* and *C. nuttallii*, was measured using calipers. To increase the total sample size, *P. staminea* teeth length and *C. nuttallii* teeth height were used as proxy measures of overall size. Regression analysis shows that there is a significant positive relationship between *P. stamina* valve length and teeth length (R = 0.819, p <0.01; Figure 17.2A), and between *C. nuttallii* valve length and teeth height (R = 0.698, p <0.01; Figure 17.2B). The archaeological *P. staminea* teeth lengths and *C. nuttallii* teeth heights were converted into shell lengths using the regression equations shown in Figures 17.2A and 17.2B to estimate actual size.

RESULTS

A total of 147,007 shell fragments representing more than 20 different taxa were identified from the English Camp and Watmough Bay sites. However, 97 percent of the shell identified to the genus or species level at English Camp is accounted for by six taxa, and 98 percent by ten taxa at Watmough Bay (Daniels 2009). These common taxa are used exclusively to compare relative abundances across and within patches at each site (Tables 17.3 and 17.4).

RELATIVE ABUNDANCE

Differential Fragmentation

Shellfish are differentially sensitive to fragmentation due to variability in shell chemistry and morphology across taxa (Bowdler 2006; Claassen 1998). Since the relative abundance measures are derived from NISP, taphonomic processes that can cause differential fragmentation of taxa across levels could explain the relative abundance results. To maintain intra-site comparability while avoiding problems of fragmentation in patch analysis, the intertidal patch index is calculated using both NISP and weight for each site. Within-patch relative abundance analyses rely exclusively on the NISP-derived indices.

Intertidal Patch Relative Abundance

At English Camp, the NISP and weight intertidal patch indices indicate that the highest-ranked patch, soft substrate, increases in relative abundance over time (Figure 17.3A). The NISP intertidal patch index increases from approximately 0.7 to 0.8. Cochran's test of linear trends (Cannon 2001) shows that the trend is both linear and significant (χTREND = 875.13, p <0.05). Alternatively, the weight intertidal patch index appears fairly stable over time, with all levels except Level 7 ranging between 0.88 and 0.99. The apparent stability is due to the near complete dominance of the soft-substrate taxa shell remains, which are significantly

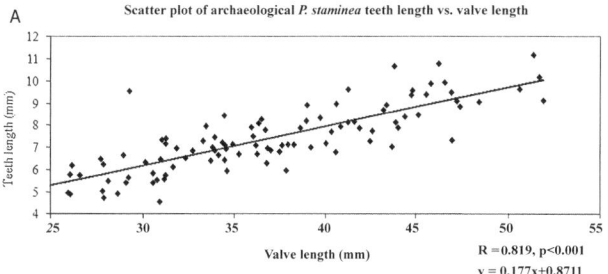

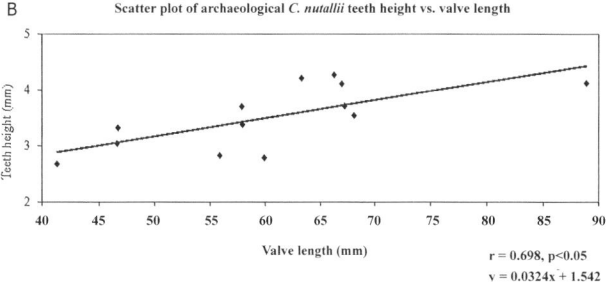

17.2. (A) Scatter plot of archaeological P. staminea *teeth length vs. valve length. (B) Scatter plot of archaeological* C. nuttallii *teeth height vs. valve length.*

larger and heavier than those of hard-substrate taxa. Despite the relative stability, the patch index does increase significantly over time (χTREND = 125.95, p <0.05).

At Watmough Bay, the NISP and weight patch relative abundance indices also increase over time (Figure 17.3B). The NISP index steadily increases from 0.2 to 0.8, and the trend is significant (χTREND = 173.14, p <0.05). The weight index increases significantly from approximately 0.6 to 0.9

Table 17.4. Watmough Bay: NISP (number of identified specimens) of most common taxa by level

Level	P. stam-inea	Large bivalve	Small bivalve	C. nut-tallii	B. cf. glandula	M. edulis	K. tuna-cata	C. stelleri	S. droeba-chiensis	S. purpu-ratus	Total
A	480	77	39	4	13	17	44	3	94	10	781
B	1,242	357	64	165	133	121	383	235	52	3	2,755
C	1,452	283	73	169	498	436	337	121	217	24	3,610
E/D	2,489	603	87	634	421	676	301	144	1,274	123	6,752
F/E	499	232	102	326	42	220	330	236	2,329	1,233	5,549
G/F	355	243	84	179	72	285	456	117	1,284	766	3,841
Total	6,517	1,795	449	1,477	1,179	1,755	1,851	856	5,250	2,159	23,288

A

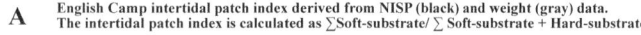

English Camp intertidal patch index derived from NISP (black) and weight (gray) data.
The intertidal patch index is calculated as ∑Soft-substrate/ ∑ Soft-substrate + Hard-substrate.

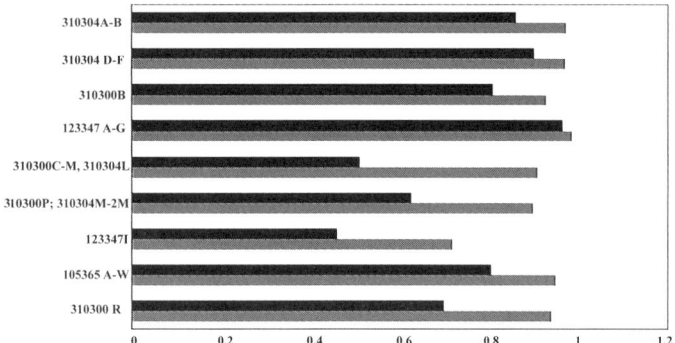

B

Watmough Bay intertidal patch index derived from NISP(black) and weight (gray) data.
The intertidal patch index is calculated as
∑Soft-substrate/ ∑ Soft-substrate + Hard-substrate + Infralittoral fringe.

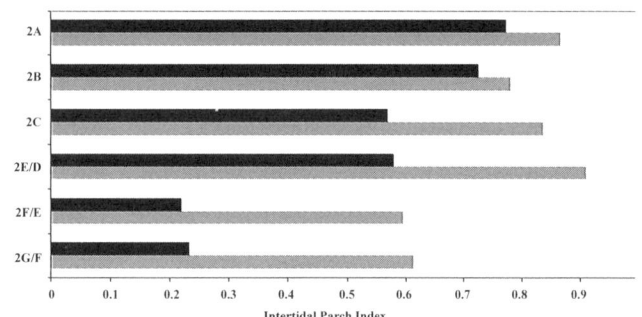

C   Scatter plot of the relationship between the Watmough Bay NISP and weight intertidal patch

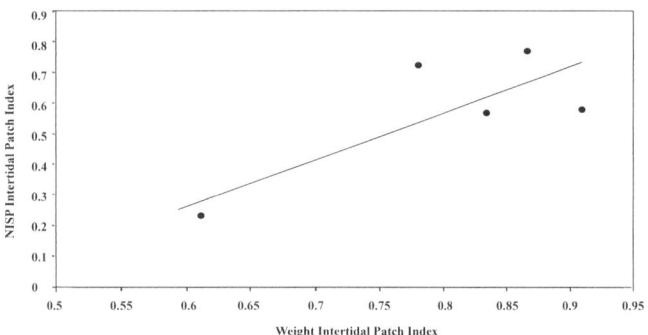

17.3. (A) English Camp intertidal patch index derived from NISP (black) and weight (gray) data. The intertidal patch index is calculated as ∑Soft-substrate /∑Soft-substrate + Hard-substrate. (B) Watmough Bay intertidal patch index derived from NISP (black) and weight (gray) data. The intertidal patch index is calculated as ∑Soft-substrate/∑Soft-substrate + Hard-substrate + Infralittoral fringe. (C) Scatter plot showing the relationship between the Watmough Bay NISP and weight intertidal patch indices.

(χTREND = 52.36, p <0.05). They differ in that the NISP index increases in two jumps, first in level E/D and again in level B, whereas the weight index increases dramatically only in level E/D.

This difference could be reflecting the effects of fragmentation on the NISP measure. Linear regression comparison of the relationship between NISP and weight values verifies that the relationship between the NISP and weight patch index values is significant (r = 0.90, p <0.05; Figure 17.3C), suggesting that the effect of differential fragmentation on NISP is small enough that it is not significantly altering the relative abundance trend.

Within-Patch Relative Abundance

At English Camp, the soft-substrate index increases significantly through time (χTREND = 1664.72, p <0.05; Figure 17.4A). This is reflecting a steady increase in *C. nuttallii*. The hard-substrate index ranges between 0.12 and 0.38, indicating that the lower-ranked *B.* cf. *glandula* is always more abundant than the higher-ranked *M. edulis* (Figure 17.4A). However, the index increases through time, reflecting an increase in the relative abundance of higher-ranked *M. edulis* (χTREND = 91.18, p <0.05). Therefore, the within-patch analyses at English Camp both indicate an increased reliance on the higher-ranked patch and taxon through time.

At Watmough Bay, the within-patch indices produced differing results. The soft-substrate index increases significantly over time from 0.21 to 0.80 (χTREND = 403.00, p <0.05) (Figure 17.4B). *P. staminea* increases in abundance from 41 percent in the lowest level to 80 percent in the uppermost. The hard-substrate index peaks twice, first in the lower levels (~0.50) and then again in the upper levels (~0.60) (Figure 17.4B). This peak is caused by a temporary increase in the abundance of both *M. edulis* and *B.* cf. *glandula* relative to *K. tunicata*. Chi-square analysis shows that the observed differences across these levels are significant (χ_2 = 566.17, p <0.05). Cochran's test of linear trends is also significant (χTREND = 24.54, p <0.05). Therefore, despite the decrease in *K. tunicata* in the middle levels, the hard-substrate index still increases significantly over time. The infralittoral index is below 0.1 in all but two levels (Level B = 0.81, Level C = 0.33; Figure 17.4B). The raw counts suggest that the spike is best explained by fluctuations in the lower-ranked *Strongylocentrotus* spp. rather than by changes in *C. stelleri*. *S. droebachiensis* and *S. purpuratus* are initially extremely abundant but decline rapidly and remain low thereafter, while *C. stelleri* remains stable over time except in level A, where it declines as well. In sum, at Watmough Bay the soft-substrate index

17.4. (A) English Camp soft-substrate index (black) and hard-substrate index (gray) by level. The soft-substrate index is calculated as ∑ C. nuttallii / ∑ All bivalves. The hard-substrate index is calculated as ∑ M. edulis / ∑ M. edulis + B. cf. glandula. (B) Watmough Bay soft-substrate index (black), hard-substrate index (gray), and infralittoral index (white) by level. The soft-substrate index is calculated as ∑ P. staminea / ∑ All bivalves. The hard-substrate index is calculated as ∑ K. tunacata / ∑ K. tunacata + M. edulis + B. cf. glandula. The infralittoral index is calculated as ∑ C. stelleri / ∑ C. stelleri + Stronglyocentrotus spp.

A

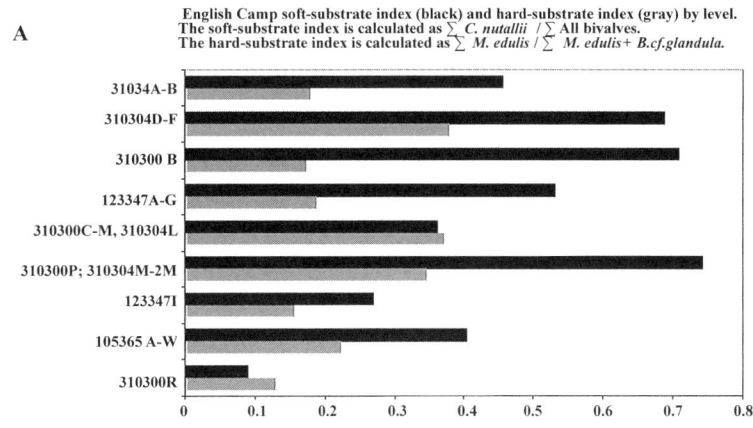

English Camp soft-substrate index (black) and hard-substrate index (gray) by level. The soft-substrate index is calculated as ∑ C. nutallii / ∑ All bivalves. The hard-substrate index is calculated as ∑ M. edulis / ∑ M. edulis+ B.cf.glandula.

B

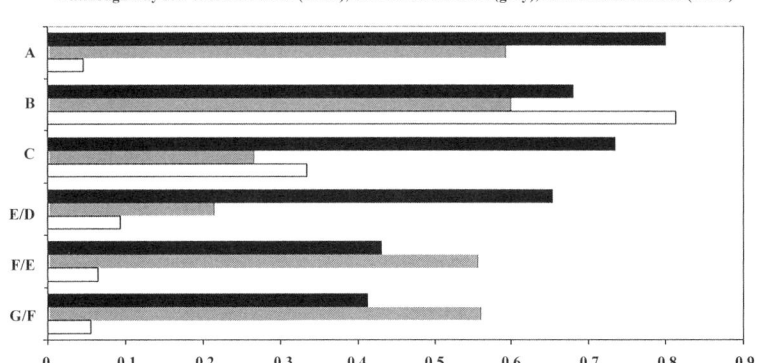

Watmough Bay soft-substrate index (black), hard-substrate index (gray), and infralittral index (white)

increases over time, the hard-substrate index is bimodal but increases slightly over time, and the infralittoral index increases over time but the increase is better explained by the decline in the lower-ranked taxa than by an increase in the higher-ranked taxon.

SIZE

Archaeological *P. staminea* size data can be compared to modern data collected from the closed beach at Garrison Bay. The beach was closed for clamming by the National Park Service in 1977. Modern measurements from 1983, 1993, and 2007 show that *P. staminea* size has remained stable over recent decades (Dethier 1993; Dethier and Berry 2008). The mean length is approximately 4.2 centimeters ± 1.3 (Dethier 1993) and the distribution is skewed toward larger size classes (Dethier and Berry 2008, fig. 9). Within the Northwest, the mean length of *C. nuttallii* today is between 6 and 7 centimeters (Liu, Alabi, and Pearce 2008; Rudy and Rudy 1983) and the maximum length is between 10 and 12 centimeters (McCrae 1994).

At English Camp, the measured mean teeth length of *P. staminea* shells is 7.10 millimeters. The calculated mean valve length is 3.5 centimeters, 0.8 centimeters less than the mean length measured in 1993. The distribution across size ranges is normal, peaking in the 4.0-centimeter size. The archaeological and modern size-class distributions differ significantly from one another ($\chi 2 = 134.06$, $p < 0.001$; Figure 17.5A), with the archaeological specimens under-represented in the smaller and larger size classes and over-represented in the middle size classes relative to the modern ones. Assuming the modern assemblage reflects past size distributions as well, these results suggest that foragers exploited smaller individuals at levels lower than their natural availability. Following from foraging theory, these results suggest that resource depression of large individuals led to an increased reliance on smaller ones.

Spearman's rho was used to analyze *P. staminea* size through time by comparing the size-class rank orders of contiguous levels. With one exception, adjacent levels are statistically the same (Table 17.5; Figure 17.5B). The one exception, between levels 7 and 8, may be due to the small

Table 17.5. English Camp: Spearman's rho Rank Order comparison of P. staminea *size in adjacent levels (significant results are in bold)*

Levels	(rs)0.05, 10 = 0.648
1–2	**0.7622**
2–3	**0.9600**
3–4	**0.8092**
4–5	**0.9847**
5–6	**0.9605**
6-7	**0.6738**
7–8	0.3284
8–9	**0.8457**
6–8	0.6383

sample size of level 7 (n=11). Spearman's rho was recalculated for levels 6 and 8 to avoid the sample size problem, and again the levels are statistically different. An examination of the level 6 and level 8 rank orders shows that size peaked in a smaller size class in level 8 (25–30 centimeters) than in level 6 (35–40 centimeters), indicating an increase in the size across this time period. The chronological data indicates that *P. staminea* initially increased in size and then remained stable during the course of the site occupation.

The measured mean teeth height of *C. nuttallii* is 3.017 millimeters. The calculated mean length is 4.55 centimeters,

about 1.5–2.5 centimeters below the modern mean adult length (Liu, Alabi, and Pearce 2008; Rudy and Rudy 1983). The distribution peaks in the 4-centimeter size class, and 48 percent of *C. nuttallii* measures between 3 and 5 centimeters (Figure 17.5C). The inclusion of smaller and larger individuals suggests that *C. nuttallii* was harvested as it occurred naturally without selectively harvesting the older, post-reproduction individuals. However, without a modern distribution to compare, it is not possible to test if this is in fact the case. In all but one case, Spearman's rho analysis of the size-class rank order of contiguous levels shows that the rank orders are statistically the same at the 0.05 level (Table 17.6; Figure 17.5D). Assuming growth rates have been stable over time, size analysis indicates that *C. nuttallii* was harvested before it reached modern mean adult size but that the size at the time of harvest was stable over time.

At Watmough Bay, the measured mean teeth length of *P. staminea* is 7.56 millimeters, which corresponds to a total length of 3.78 centimeters. The mean length of the archaeological shells is about 0.04 centimeter less than the modern mean size at Garrison Bay (Dethier and Berry 2008). The archaeological size distribution is similar to the natural distribution observed at Garrison Bay (Figure 17.6A), except the archaeological curve is normal and the modern one is slightly skewed toward the larger size classes. Chi-square analysis confirms that the two distributions are statistically different ($\chi2 = 100.41$, $p < 0.001$). As at English Camp, the archaeological specimens at Watmough Bay are underrepresented in the smaller and larger size classes and overrepresented in the middle size classes

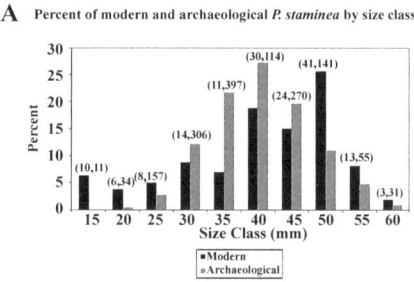

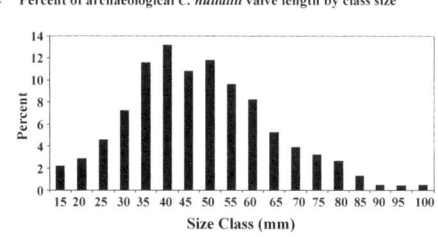

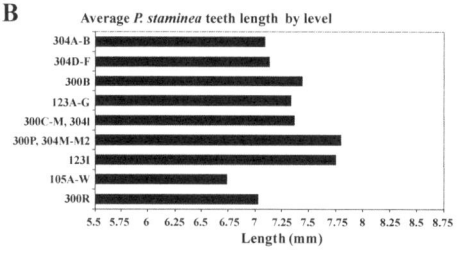

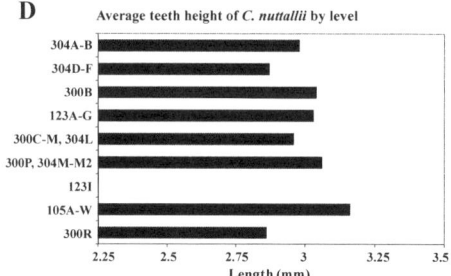

17.5. *(A) Percent of modern and archaeological* P. staminea *by size class at English Camp (modern data from Diether, pers. comm. 2009). Modern and archaeological counts are in parentheses. (B) Average* P. staminea *teeth length at English Camp by level. (C) Percent of archaeological* C. nuttallii *valve length by class size at English Camp. (D) Percent teeth height of* C. nuttallii *by level at English Camp.*

relative to the modern distribution. Assuming growth rates have not changed over time and are similar between site locations, this suggests that foragers ignored smaller individuals to some degree and that larger individuals were less available. Spearman's rho analysis of size-class rank order across contiguous levels shows that, with the exception of E/F-F/G, they are statistically the same at the 0.05 level (Table 17.7, Figure 17.6B). A comparison of the rank orders of levels E/F and F/G indicate that level E/F peaks in size-class 40 centimeters while level F/G peaked in size classes 35 centimeters and 45 centimeters. In general, the data suggests that *P. staminea* was taken before reaching full size but that the size at the time of harvest did not change over time.

The number of measurable *C. nuttallii* teeth from Watmough Bay is relatively small (n=78), and therefore the results are less compelling. The average teeth height is 3.211 millimeters, which corresponds to a mean length of 5.15 centimeters. The average size of the archaeological shells is about 2 centimeters smaller than the maximum adult size of 7 centimeters (Rudy and Rudy 1983), and the distribution across the size classes is skewed to the right. The curve peaks in the 4- to 5-centimeter range, one size class larger than the peak in the English Camp *C. nuttallii* data (Figure 17.6C). The average *C. nuttallii* teeth height appears to decrease through time (Figure 17.6D). Due to a high number of ties in the level rank orders, one-way ANOVA was used to compare the means of all levels except level G, which has a count of two. There is no statistical difference between the means across levels, $F_{3, 76} = 1.19$,

Table 17.6. *English Camp: Spearman's rho Rank Order comparison of* C. nuttallii *size in adjacent levels (significant results are in bold)*

Levels	(rs)0.05, 9 = 0.7000
1–2	**0.842**
2–3	**0.828**
3–4	**0.946**
4–5	0.662
5–6	**0.997**
6–8	**0.866**
8–9	**0.829**

Table 17.7. *Watmough Bay: Spearman's rho Rank Order comparison of* P. staminea *size in adjacent levels (significant results are in bold)*

Level	(rs)0.05, 9 = 0.7
B–C	**0.9830**
C–D/E	**0.9748**
D/E–F/E	**0.9283**
F/E–G/E	0.6481

17.6. *(A) Percent of modern* P. staminea *by size class at Garrison Bay (data from Diether, pers. comm. 2009) and archaeological* P. staminea *from Watmough Bay. Modern and archaeological counts are in parentheses. (B) Average length of* P. staminea *teeth length by level at Watmough Bay. (C) Percent of* C. nuttallii *by size class at Watmough Bay. (D) Average* C. nuttallii *teeth length at Watmough Bay by level.*

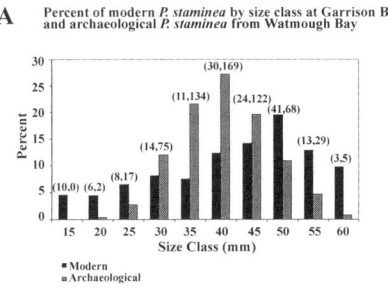

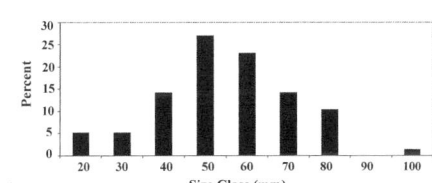

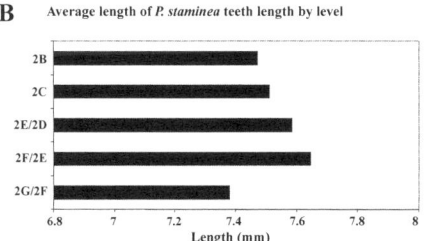

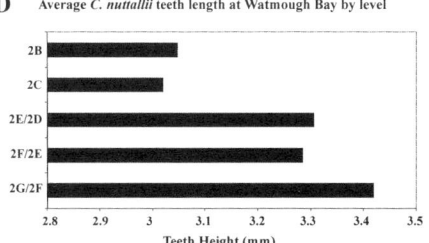

p >0.05. Assuming stable growth rates over time, it appears *C. nuttallii* was harvested before it reached modern adult size and was stable over time.

ENVIRONMENT

As discussed above, environmental change can influence shellfish relative abundances and mean size (Claassen 1998; Jerardino 1997; Keegan, Portell, and Slapcinsky 2003). Environmental parameters with the greatest potential to mimic resource depression are substrate composition, sea surface temperature (SST), and upwelling. I know of no studies examining substrate composition history at either site location. However, occupation at both sites postdates sea-level stabilization at 2000 BP (Booth 1987; Clague et al. 1982) and neither site is adjacent to a river outlet, suggesting at least that sea-level change and river runoff did not cause a major substrate change during the occupation of the sites. Alternatively, SST and upwelling are known to have fluctuated during the late Holocene (Barron et al. 2003; Daniels 2009; Deo, Stone, and Stein 2004; Hay et al. 2007). Therefore, the potential effect of SST or upwelling change on English Camp and Watmough Bay shellfish abundances and mean size values must be evaluated.

Local SST reconstructed from $\delta^{18}O$ values derived from archaeological shells from the English Camp site identified temperature fluctuations in Garrison Bay within the last 2,000 years that are generally in agreement with reconstructions from other regional climate studies (Daniels 2009). The SST cooled by approximately 1.5°C between 1400 and 1000 BP. Warmer SST returned around 1000 BP, which coincides with the globally identified Medieval Warm Period (MWP) (Crowley and Lowery 2000; Moberg et al. 2005). However, the $\delta^{18}O$ values suggest that warmer SST continued until 150 BP and thus into the Little Ice Age (300–100 BP), identified primarily through glacial moraines (e.g., Heikkinen 1984; Koch et al. 2004; Koch, Osborn, and Clague 2007; Ryder 1987, 1989; Wiles, Barclay, and Calkin 1999; Wiles et al. 2008).

Local upwelling history derived from paired charcoal-shell radiocarbon dates and stable isotope analysis identified a period of reduced upwelling between 1000 and 600 BP within an otherwise intense upwelling 3,000-year record (Daniels 2009). Since upwelling brings deep ocean water to the surface that is deplete of ^{14}C relative to the atmosphere (Broecker and Peng 1982), given certain assumptions, increases in the offset between marine shell and terrestrial radiocarbon dates are interpreted as evidence of more intense upwelling and decreases as declining intensity (Deo, Stone, and Stein 2004; Kennett et al. 1997). From 3000 BP until 1000 BP, a regional marine reservoir correction (ΔR) value of 400 years indicates upwelling was intense, which is consistent with peaks in fish productivity (Hay et al. 2007; Wright et al. 2005) but at odds

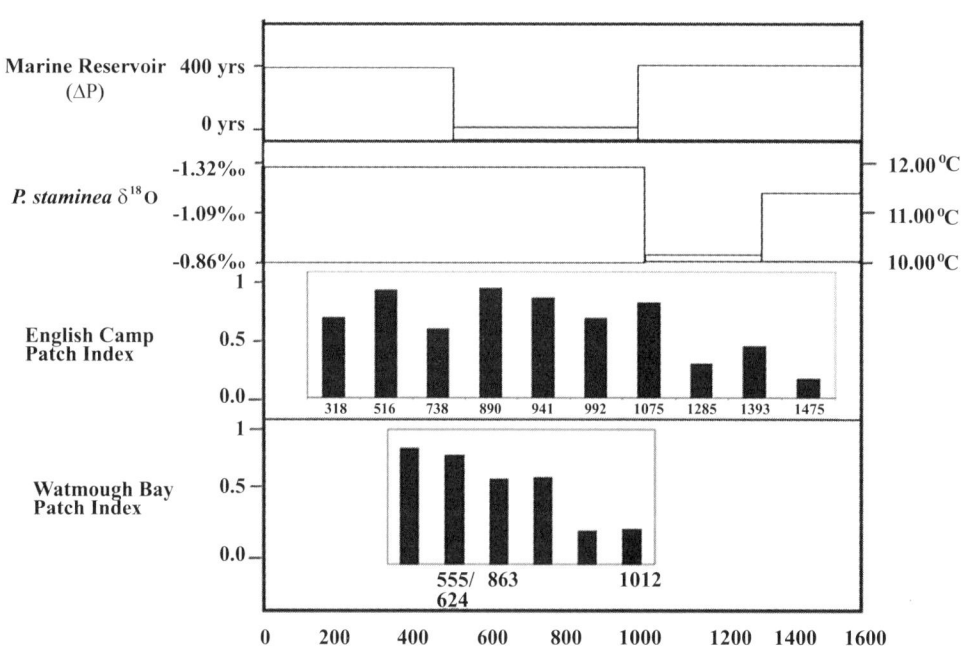

17.7. Comparison of English Camp and Watmough Bay patch relative abundances and Northwest coast sea-surface temperature and upwelling chronologies. From the top: ΔR values from the San Juan Islands and Puget Sound (Deo, Stone, and Stein 2004; Daniels 2009). $\delta^{18}O$ and calculated Celsius from English Camp, 45SJ24 (Daniels 2009). English Camp patch index values by level. Watmough Bay patch index values by level.

with decreases in diatom production (Hay et al. 2007) and varve thickness (Dallimore, Thomson, and Bertram. 2005) observed off Vancouver Island, British Columbia. From 1000 to 600 BP, the ΔR value drops to zero, suggesting a decrease in upwelling. This decrease is consistent with declines in fish productivity (Tunnicliffe, O'Connell, and McQuoid 2001; Wright et al. 2005) and increased diatom production off Vancouver Island. After 600 BP, the ΔR returns to 400 years, consistent with the modern ΔR value (Robinson and Thompson 1981).

In sum, the available marine climate data suggests that regional SST and upwelling were both bimodal during the latter half of the late Holocene. SST was relatively warm and stable, except for a short period of cooler temperatures between 1000 and 1400 BP, and upwelling was intense except between 600 and 1000 BP, when it appears to have been significantly reduced. These bimodal environmental trends are not correlated with the linear relative abundance trends identified at English Camp and Watmough Bay (Figure 17.7), suggesting the relative abundance patterns cannot be explained by fluctuating SST or upwelling.

DISCUSSION

The increasing relative abundance of the higher-ranked soft-substrate patch at both English Camp and Watmough Bay indicates that resource depression did not occur. If anything, it suggests that shellfish communities improved, with taxa in the higher-ranked intertidal patches becoming more available and thus allowing the lower-ranked patch or patches to be utilized less intensely. Sustainability cannot be concluded from the patch analysis alone, since the intertidal patch index could remain stable or increase while the individual patches of which it is composed decline.

At English Camp, the soft-substrate index increases through time. *C. nuttallii*, proxy for the highest-ranked patch within the soft substrate, also increases relative to all other bivalves, eventually accounting for more than 80 percent of all bivalves. At the same time, size analysis shows no decrease in the mean size of *P. staminea* or *C. nuttallii*. This shows that foraging pressure was not sufficiently intense to negatively impact the size of these higher-ranked taxa over time despite the increased utilization of the soft substrate and *C. nuttallii* within it. When combined with the patch analysis, these data suggest that shellfish foraging conditions actually improved over time.

The soft-substrate index also increased through time at Watmough Bay. *P. staminea*, proxy for the highest-ranked patch, is always the most abundant bivalve. This is not surprising given its preference for settling in coarse sand. Furthermore, it increases in relative abundance through time until it accounts for 80 percent of all bivalves. In addition, size analysis shows no decrease in the mean size of *P. staminea* or *C. nuttallii* over time. These data suggest that shellfish foraging conditions also improved at Watmough Bay.

There are several possible explanations for why shellfish harvesting remained stable at the English Camp and Watmough Bay sites over time. First, it is possible that human use of the islands was not intense enough to negatively impact shellfish abundances given their natural resilience. Saltwater bays in the San Juan Islands are highly productive (Dethier 1993), and exploitation may have always remained below the shellfish communities' natural abilities to replenish themselves. The biology of the higher-ranking taxa, *P. staminea* and *C. nuttallii*, may have allowed them to sustain populations despite prolonged harvesting. Both species fertilize in the open water, reach sexual maturation at a relatively small size, and are common throughout the San Juan Islands (Rudy and Rudy 1983).

People may have consciously limited the frequency at which they visited the site to allow shellfish, and other resources, to replenish. However, the English Camp and Watmough Bay occupations date to the period when site abundances peaked on the islands. The English Camp site was occupied from 1715 to 270 BP and the Watmough Bay site from 1000 to 500 BP (Daniels 2009; Taylor, Stein, and Jolivette 2011), within the period of time with the greatest density of sites on the islands (Taylor, Stein, and Jolivette 2011). Although the number of sites is not a direct measure of population, it does suggest that use of the islands was increasing at this time. It is unlikely that people would have harvested shellfish less intensively at a time when island occupation appears the densest.

Although the overall use of the San Juan Islands was at its highest when the sites were deposited, it is possible that other factors, not measured here, continued to limit the length of individual visits such that shellfish exploitation rates remained sustainable. The San Juan Islands lie in the rain shadow of the Olympic Mountains, and have low annual rainfall and limited access to permanent freshwater that could have been a limiting factor for human use of the islands (Taylor, Stein, and Jolivette 2011). Amanda K. Taylor, Julie K. Stein, and Stephanie A. E. Jolivette (2011) evaluated this hypothesis by comparing the distance between archaeological sites and sources of freshwater in drier and wetter climates. They found no significant differences in distance to freshwater between the periods.

An alternative explanation for shellfish sustainability is that populations were actively managed. One way that foragers could have managed the intertidal region is by selectively harvesting older individuals near the end of their reproductive time (Cannon and Burchell 2009). If this form of management was used at English Camp and Watmough Bay, then long-term age profiles should favor larger, older individuals (Cannon and Burchell 2009). Instead, young adults in their reproductive prime accounted for the majority of both *P. staminea* and *C. nuttallii* and were overrepresented relative to the modern natural distributions. This is likely due to the reduced abundance of larger individuals, either because of reduced growth rates or resource depression, and preferential avoidance of very small individuals with associated lower return-rates. In any case, there is no evidence of active management of either *P. staminea* or *C. nuttallii* by selective harvesting.

It remains possible that management strategies undetectable by age profiling were implemented. Resource ownership and environment enhancement are two practices observed ethnographically that may have been implemented to improve shellfish habitat. Productive shellfish habitats were owned by individual families or groups who controlled access to the resource (Suttles 1987). Owners may have consciously limited the number of people harvesting their area to ensure healthy shellfish populations.

Environment enhancement is another method that may have been implemented in the past to maintain shellfish populations. It is now generally accepted that people routinely enhanced the habitats of culturally important plant resources by burning, pruning, weeding, and other activities (Duer and Turner 2005). If people were enhancing plant habitats, then it is likely that they were enhancing the habitats of other resources as well. Ethnographic reports of people's clearing logs and other debris from beaches that would have negatively impacted shellfish communities provide some evidence of habitat enhancement (Suttles 1987). This type of groundskeeping is unlikely to have improved shellfish habitat significantly. However, the archaeological community has recently been made aware of the presence of another habitat enhancement strategy that would have significantly increased shellfish returns. Hundreds of clam garden remains have now been documented along the Northwest Coast in Canada (Williams 2007; Woods and Woods 2005). Clam gardens are enhanced shellfish habitats made by expanding sand flats

seaward by constructing stone walls. Clam-garden walls would have required a significant investment of time and labor, which signifies both the importance of shellfish as a resource and the need, at least in some places, of intensifying shellfish harvesting. No clam-garden feature remains have been reported adjacent to either English Camp or Watmough Bay but, then again, nobody has looked.

The rapid decline of *S. droebachiensis* and *S. purpuratus* in the infralittoral patch at Watmough Bay requires explanation. Sea urchins are relatively large and easily located, and ethnographic observation indicates that they were collected by spear and dip nets (Drucker 1950, 35). With human foraging of sea urchins uninterrupted by incoming tides, one explanation of their rapid decline is resource depression. Alternatively, the dramatic decrease in *Strongylocentrotus* spp. may have resulted from an intentional effort to keep sea urchin populations from negatively impacting kelp forest ecosystems. Kelp forests, common along the North Pacific coastline, support a diverse suite of plants and animals, including sea urchins (Erlandson et al. 2007; see Braje, Erlandson, and Rick, chap. 1 in this volume). However, when sea urchin populations are able to grow unchecked, their grazing is destructive to kelp forests (Harrold and Pearse 1987). By prohibiting the formation of kelp forests, sea urchin barrens reduce primary and secondary production, reducing the biomass throughout the food chain (Graham 2004; Harrold and Pearse 1987). The early occupants at Watmough Bay might have intensively foraged for sea urchins, and then repressed their populations from rebounding, not only because of their value as a food but also to manage and protect the kelp forest ecosystems and the rich intertidal and near-shore life that they support.

Finally, the relative abundance of *Balanus* cf. *glandula* at English Camp is surprisingly high. *Balanus* sp. is very small and contains little edible meat. In my experience, individuals are difficult to pry off rocks, and even when successful, the result is a mass of broken shell and tissue that needs to be separated. Ethnographic data often includes "barnacle" in lists of exploited shellfish. However, when the barnacles are identified more finely, the larger taxa are almost exclusively involved (e.g., Ellis and Swan 1981; Fournier and Dewhirst 1980; Norton 1985; but see Sepez 2001). If the abundance of *B. glandula* is representative of its role as a subsistence resource, then it implies severe resource depression. This is inconsistent with all the other shellfish abundance and size data. The alternative is that it is entering the site in some other capacity. English Camp has many cobbles that provide a hard surface to which barnacles adhere. It is fully possible that people were using those cobbles as boiling or roasting stones and that the barnacles are accidentals, or that stones laden with barnacles were intentionally selected for the extra nutrition and/or flavor they may provide. Evidence supporting this hypothesis is limited. Ethnographic data indicates that heated stones were commonly used in cooking (e.g., Drucker 1955, 40; Gunther 1927, 209), and small barnacle-scarred cobbles were identified during the initial shell sorting.

CONCLUSION

The availability of abundant resources has long been associated with the development of social complexity on the Northwest Coast. To support increasing populations with decreasing mobility, these resources would need to have been reliable and abundant over time despite increasing foraging pressure. It is becoming increasingly clear that shellfish were one of these resources (e.g., Cannon, Burchell, and Bathhurst 2008; Moss 1993, 2012). The shellfish patterns at English Camp and Watmough Bay further indicate that shellfish communities are sustainable even when alongside large winter villages. However, they differ from other Northwest Coast shellfish studies in that there is no clear evidence that the shellfish communities were actively managed. It remains possible that management strategies were used at the sites that are undetectable by the methods used in this study. For now, the abundance and size data suggest that the shellfish sustainability is best explained simply as exploitation intensity remaining below recruitment and growth rates.

ACKNOWLEDGMENTS

I would like to thank the editors for inviting me to contribute to this volume, especially Mirjana Roksandic, who gave generously of her time to format the tables and figures. I would like to thank Joni Howard for her assistance in measuring clam shells. I greatly appreciate everybody who commented on earlier drafts, from my dissertation committee to the editors and the anonymous reviewers. Thanks to the Burke Museum and National Park Service for allowing me to analyze the collections. This research was supported by the Burke Museum's Summer Research Fellowship and National Science Foundation Dissertation Improvement Grant #BCS-07297663.

CHAPTER EIGHTEEN

BIOGEOCHEMICAL SIGNATURES OF MARINE AND ESTUARINE BIVALVES

Implications for Interpreting Seasonality at Shell Midden Sites Using High-Resolution Stable Isotope Sclerochronology

Meghan Burchell, Nadine Hallmann, Bernd R. Schöne, Aubrey Cannon, and Henry P. Schwarcz

SUMMARY

The chemical and biological analyses of archaeological shells from shell midden sites can reveal important information regarding local ecology, environmental and climatic changes, seasonality, and the intensity of shellfish gathering. Most archaeological studies that seek to identify shellfish seasonality use low-resolution methods such as the presence or absence of "winter lines." Studies that apply stable isotope analysis may present a higher seasonal resolution; however, a critical examination of these studies demonstrates the lack of precise sampling and sufficient analysis of modern species that reduces the overall precision of the seasonal estimate. This chapter discusses the history of seasonality research in shellfish, and presents a case study comparing low- versus high-resolution analyses of modern shellfish from the coast of British Columbia. While this chapter does not provide any archaeological data, it does illustrate the importance of fully understanding the biology and chemistry of the shellfish species in question through isotope-sclerochronology, prior to attempting to identify seasonality through light stable oxygen isotopes or growth lines and/or increments.

IINTRODUCTION

The question of seasonality is often cited as central in understanding subsistence strategies in prehistoric economies (Andrus and Crowe 2000; Coutts and Higham 1971; Harrison 1988; Kennett and Voorhies 1996; Killingley 1981; Lieberman 1993). Although these studies state that seasonality is an important factor, some tend to neglect to explain *why* it is important. Gregory G. Monks (1981, 177) notes that there is "no overall rationale that is widely accepted in practices as to why seasonality studies should play a key role in archaeological research," nor is there a "framework within which the results of individual methods of seasonality estimates can be integrated." More than two decades have passed since this problem was noted, and yet very few archaeological studies have integrated what seasonal activities mean to the overall structure of a society, with some exceptions (including Atalay and Hastorf [2006]; Cannon [2002]; Lieberman [1993]; and Milner [2005]).

This chapter examines the current evidence for understanding the purpose of shellfish harvest and consumption in relation to the importance of seasonality. It will also review methods of examining seasonality based on the biological and chemical characteristics of mollusks. Understanding the seasonality of shellfish harvest and shellfish procurement strategies requires a multidisciplinary approach that can account for all of the variables influencing shellfish gathering (Cipriani, Antczak, and Antczak 2008, 248).

One of the most significant issues with seasonality estimates is defining a season and understanding the length of time within a year that a seasonal activity occurs. Contemporary concepts of seasons are broad periods of time, and identifying a season, such as "winter," may be an inflation of the length of time over which the actual events took place (Milner 2005, 58). If the analytical resolution is not sufficient, the presence of a very precise seasonal indicator may result in exaggerating the duration of an activity. Seasonality interpretations based on mollusks are frequently based on sequential estimates, presented as spring, summer, winter, or fall (Monks 1981, 178), or as "cold" or

18.1. Example of Saxidomus gigantea *with a disturbance line caused by an interruption in its spring/summer growth. Although this specimen was collected in July, there appears to be an "annual growth band" that typically forms in the winter in close proximity to the ventral margin. If this were an archaeological sample, analyzed using only the formation of growth lines, the season of collection would likely be incorrectly interpreted as "spring."*

"warm" based on periods of fast and slow growth (Claassen 1986). These interpretations may be too general since "cold" is not a season, nor does it take into account the fact that an activity may have occurred for only a short period of time, or even span between two seasons, such as late fall to early winter. Although assigning a month to the activity would be more precise, finding a chronological indicator that can yield such an estimate is unlikely—but not impossible.

Growth increment, growth line analysis, or growth coloration of the internal structure of an individual shell has been used frequently to identify seasonal patterns of shellfish harvest. Patterns of annual growth lines and colors were used to infer season of death, but this method can produce ambiguous results since different shells may be difficult to "read," and also because of the formation of "false annuli" caused by interruptions in growth.

Such disturbance lines may be caused by storm events or predation (Clark 1974), or they may result from spawning breaks (Rhoads and Pannella 1970). Growth can be randomly interrupted for variable periods of time, and in some species growth lines can form in the summer and winter (Kirby, Sonait, and Spero 1998), which can be species-specific based on their upper and lower temperature threshold; however, these limits differ among species.

Therefore, it is difficult to distinguish the true meaning of growth lines in some individuals, but in many cases, this difficulty can be resolved with high-resolution stable isotope data and sclerochronology. Sclerochronology is analogous to dendrochronology, and is defined as the study of the physical and chemical variations in the accretionary tissues of invertebrates (Buddemeir, Maragos, and Knutson 1974), such as bivalves and gastropods. The focus of sclerochronology is to understand the timing of different temporal scales (i.e., daily, lunar, weekly, monthly, and/or annually) to understand the organism's life-history traits as it relates to local environmental conditions, with the goal of interpreting the chemical and physical variations in relation to past and contemporary environmental conditions.

When high-resolution analyses are applied, a larger sample size is usually sacrificed to obtain fewer precise measurements of individual specimens. This happens commonly in increment studies of teeth and in stable isotope analysis of mollusks, but also in fish otolith studies (Van Neer et al. 2004). For example, a high-resolution study of increment structures in deer teeth may yield a more precise estimate for the season of death, but the study is meaningless if the sample size is small, and if the results do not consider the relationship of the resource in question within the broader context of the subsistence economy (i.e., Carter 2001). In some cases, it is possible to refine a seasonality estimate to within a few months, but the entire seasonal spectrum of resource use may not be observed if the sample is not sufficiently large. If a more accurate picture of seasonal resource use is to emerge, then samples of all periods of the occupational history of the site should be analyzed (Monks 1981, 223).

STABLE ISOTOPES AND SEASONALITY STUDIES

In aquatic mollusks, shells grow when submerged in water, thereby incorporating oxygen and carbon isotope signatures of the local water at variable growth rates. When the stable carbon and oxygen isotope ratios of the shell are analyzed sequentially throughout the history of shell growth, it is possible to produce an environmental record of the animal's life. Samples obtained from the last phase of growth indicate season of death and can therefore be used to interpret seasonal patterns of shellfish collection.

In marine carbonates, the ratios of carbon isotopes, specifically $^{13}C/^{12}C$, mainly reflect that of inorganic carbon dissolved in seawater (DIC), but may also reflect the animal's respired CO_2 and therefore the productivity (food supply) of the immediate area. Carbon isotopes in shell carbonate are also controlled by equilibrium fractionation between various forms of carbon, which varies only slightly with temperature (Tan 1989, 173) and kinetic effects leading to non-equilibrium fractionation during carbonate formation. However, some mollusks seldom show strong kinetic isotope effects (McConnaughey and Gillikin 2008, 289). In marine mollusks, relatively little carbon in shells is incorporated from the animal's respired carbon dioxide (McConnaughey et al. 1997). Salinity can also affect carbon isotopes, and in areas with lower salinity, carbon values will be lower (Tan 1989, 186). This is because river DIC is often isotopically lighter (lower $^{13}C/^{12}C$) than ocean DIC due to the input of CO_2 from the decomposition of terrestrial plants. Mollusks that live in estuarine environments will incorporate a combination of marine and fluvial DIC into their shell calcium carbonate (Gillikin et al. 2006). However, due to the number of variables associated with carbon fractionation, it may be difficult, if not impossible with some species, to understand the meaning of the carbon isotope values (Andrus and Crowe 2000, 39), since the carbon incorporated during shell precipitation can either be derived from ambient DIC or from respired metabolic CO_2 that would obscure environmental signals.

Stable oxygen isotope ratios ($\delta^{18}O$) in marine carbonates are influenced by water temperature during shell growth and by isotopic variation in source water; the latter co-varies with the salinity (Andrus and Crowe 2000, 39; Epstein et al. 1953; Wefer and Berger 1991). In some cases, salinity may correlate with oxygen isotope variation due to the freshwater mixing line, seasonal changes in precipitation, or increase in freshwater runoff from local rivers. Evaporation, which causes water to become more saline, also preferentially enriches the water in ^{18}O, resulting in values shifting toward the positive end. Water from precipitation (i.e., rain, snow) is depleted in ^{18}O and can locally lower the salinity (Andrus and Crowe 2000, 39). Seasonal patterns in salinity can be observed in areas with distinct wet and dry seasons (Andrus and Crowe 2000, 39; Kennett and Voorhies 1996).

If all the possible factors that influence $\delta^{18}O_{shell}$ are not considered, specifically the counter-effects of temperature and freshwater influxes, the interpretations may not be accurate. In a pure marine setting, the oxygen isotopes are directly correlated with changes in temperature; however, in estuarine settings, apparent temperature patterns based on oxygen isotope data can be the result of a combination of both changes in temperature and changes in local

salinity due to increases or decreases in freshwater influx. John S. Killingley's (1981) [mis]interpretation of the precision of stable isotope data did not take into account the factors that affect isotope results (Bailey, Deith, and Shackelton 1983). Killingley (1981) proposed that the results could be treated statistically to identify the month of collection based on the end values of the isotope profile. This has been criticized as being unrealistic because of known oxygen isotope differences between species and regional climate variation through time (Bailey, Deith, and Shackelton 1983). Therefore, it is the pattern of isotope variation and not the absolute end ratio that must be considered when attempting to identify season of capture.

ISSUES WITH USING STABLE ISOTOPES TO IDENTIFY SEASONALITY

Before a program of research using stable isotopes to resolve seasonality is started, four areas need to be considered: (1) the biological controls of the organism; (2) the environment in which it lived; (3) post-depositional alterations to shell calcium carbonate (diagenesis); and (4) the recognition that environmental conditions may have changed through time. The recrystallization of fossil/archaeological shells is associated with isotopic exchange with porewater, and therefore the isotope values (both $^{13}C/^{12}C$ and $^{18}O/^{16}O$) tend to shift toward negative values (Shackleton 1973, 139). Prior to using shells for analysis, compositional analysis such as X-ray diffraction should be completed to ensure that the shells are in their original mineralogical state.

The methods that have been used to obtain seasonality estimates via stable isotopes have changed dramatically since the 1980s, and this improvement in methodology has led to an overall increase in precision. Margaret R. Deith's (1983) study had a coarse sampling strategy, drilling 2-millimeter-diameter samples with 0.5-millimeter spaces between isotope samples. While Deith was able to conclude that shells were collected during multiple times of the year, it was impossible to refine the estimate to a month. Sampling strategies using milling techniques increase the resolution and improve precision because they incorporate fewer daily increments than coarse-resolution samples, and can therefore be used to reconstruct a fuller range of recorded environmental conditions (Goodwin, Schöne, and Dettman 2003, 125). For example, high-resolution sampling identified shellfish collection during the late autumn, winter, and early spring at the Mesolithic site of Culverwell (Mannino, Spiro, and Thomas 2003), though the sample size was sacrificed in this case to obtain a more precise measurement of seasonality for a handful of archaeological shells.

BIOLOGICAL CONTROLS

The biology of the species under question needs to be considered when deciding how to sample the shell and how to interpret results. The appropriateness of the species needs to be considered, since long-lived species can provide more consecutive years for detecting seasonal changes in growth rates and isotope ratios with increasing ontogenetic age; however, short-lived species can provide a higher temporal resolution (intra-annual). Vital effects and life history traits such as growth rates, growing season, the timing of spawning, and senescent growth are factors that can influence isotopic ratios and the accuracy of seasonality interpretations.

Vital effects are metabolic processes that modify the chemical composition of carbonate-secreting fluid and biogenic hard tissues (McConnaughey 1989). With increasing age, shells will incorporate either decreasing or increasing amounts of carbon and oxygen isotopes into their shells (Schöne 2008, 280). Other biological stressors, such as spawning, can also lower the rate of mollusk metabolism, thereby reducing the rate of shell production (Andrus and Crowe 2000, 37). Carbon isotopes can also be strongly influenced by metabolic signals, and cannot be used for understanding environmental conditions or seasonality in all species.

The length of time a shell grows throughout its life, as well as during an annual cycle, varies and should be evaluated prior to deriving any conclusions regarding seasonality from isotope data. Growth retardation through ontogeny periodically slows and/or stops recording environmental conditions, and therefore the data derived from shells is somewhat incomplete (Schöne 2008, 269). The duration of the growing season can decrease with increasing age, which results in a successive shortening of the physical distance in the shell between "summer" and "winter" peaks (Schöne 2008, 280). Older animals grow more slowly, which can create a "lag effect" in isotopic profiles (Deith 1986, 71). To account for this lag effect, a detailed understanding of the timing, duration, and formation of daily and annual growing periods/growth lines is required to quantify the potential bias introduced by growth cessation (Schöne 2008, 276). This understanding will allow the researcher to assess how much time is represented in each shell sample.

ENVIRONMENTAL CONTROLS

Abrupt changes in the environment, especially events where there are periods of extreme heat, salinity, or precipitation, can make interpreting seasonality difficult. Short-term temperature increases can lead to "heat shock," which can cause an abrupt cessation of growth, even during the ideal growing season (Andrus and Crowe 2000). In this situation, the shell would stop growing and recording environmental conditions. Another similar environmental effect arises from unusually high precipitation, leading to a "freshening" of the marine environment, which could also cause a shutdown in shell growth. These events can also drastically change the oxygen values of seawater; however, this change is likely only to occur for short periods of time during a year (Schöne et al. 2004, 228). When using a paleotemperature equation that assumes constant $^{18}O/^{16}O$ of seawater, extreme variations in salinity values can translate into large errors in temperature estimates (Schöne et al. 2004).

In regards to intertidal species, the animal's position in the intertidal zone can also influence the ratio of oxygen isotope values, since the direction and magnitude of tides affect both salinity and temperature (Andrus and Crowe 2000, 37). Furthermore, the growing period of shells from different heights in the intertidal zone will differ according to the amount of time a shell is exposed to air (Schöne 2008, 272); the longer a shell is exposed, the less it grows, which reduces the potential for environmental monitoring. This can create problems in some cases for reconstructing paleotemperature and seasonality when unexpected variation is observed in what is believed to be a relatively homogenous sample of shells.

MODERN AND ARCHAEOLOGICAL SAMPLING OF MOLLUSKS FOR SEASONALITY

Studies of modern species and the environment in which they live can be used to delineate some of the issues associated with variations in salinity and local environments. It is impossible to know the exact environment from which archaeological shells came; therefore, modern analogues may not always be able to produce the fidelity required to interpret seasonal patterns of shellfish harvesting for a specific location (Andrus and Crowe 2000, 40). Uncertainty in the oxygen isotope values of ancient seawater (Schöne et al. 2004, 228) will present problems for paleotemperature reconstructions, but most likely does not mask seasonal trends, though they may not be as pronounced.

Furthermore, not all shellfish populations will record annual temperature changes equally in their oxygen isotope values (Mannino, Spiro, and Thomas 2003, 673). Geoffrey N. Bailey and colleagues (1983) observed that the terminal growth value of the shells collected on the same day, at the same time, gave different $\delta^{18}O_{shell}$ values.

Additional factors that can affect the successful application of stable isotope analysis to the study of seasonality relate to the cost of analyses, the availability of modern control samples, and the expertise required to generate and interpret the data. The cost of isotope analyses is higher than more conventional methods for obtaining a seasonality estimate (Mannino, Spiro, and Thomas 2003, 668). Multiple samples must be taken from a shell, and this will depend on the age of the animal and the species in question. In order for a sufficient sample size to be obtained, many shells also need to be analyzed, but the size of the sample will depend on the nature of the site and the patterns observed in the isotope results. Many archaeological studies sacrifice sample size for a more precise seasonality estimate, and this sacrifice may reduce the overall accuracy of interpreting seasonal patterns. Marcello A. Mannino and colleagues (2003) propose using only three samples from a single shell to produce a seasonality estimate. This number is insufficient because small numbers of samples from an individual animal do not account for variation in marine climate from year to year (Bailey, Deith, and Shackelton 1983, 391). An isolated analysis of the most recent growth in a shell is inadequate as a proxy for seasonal temperature variation since the amplitude of seasonal oscillations may vary between individuals (Andrus and Crowe 2000, 41), and shells of different ages may have more (or less) time actually represented in a discrete sample.

In addition to archaeological shells, isotope studies require the analysis of environmental parameters and monthly-collected modern control samples, which are not always easily obtained (Schöne 2008). They also require a detailed sclerochronological and geochemical analysis of monthly-collected modern specimens (Schöne 2008, 273). An understanding of modern shell growth patterns, with regards to variability in both annual and seasonal growth rates, is necessary to temporally align the geochemical data. The data from the archaeological shells needs to be analyzed in relation to the data derived from modern shells in order to detect environmental and climatic changes, as well as season of death. A local calibration study is also needed for each geographic region since growth rates can vary as a result of latitudinal gradients in light cycle and water temperature.

IMPROVING THE PRECISION OF SEASONALITY ESTIMATES: A CASE STUDY FROM BRITISH COLUMBIA

The butter clam, *Saxidomus gigantea*, is one of the most commonly recovered bivalve species in shell midden sites in coastal British Columbia, and it has been the focus of several studies that have tried to determine seasonal patterns of shellfish gathering based on the formation of growth lines and coloration (e.g., Coupland, Bissell, and King 1993; Keen 1979; Maxwell 2003). Granted, many of these studies were conducted before micro-analytical techniques were integrated into archaeology, and when $\delta^{18}O$ analysis was a relatively rare application. Nonetheless, they provide valuable examples of the problems associated with low-resolution seasonality estimates.

Identifying the season of site occupation and/or resource acquisition has been a subject of much interest in coastal British Columbia because of the seasonal nature of many staple resources such as salmon and herring. In order to identify some of the problems associated with traditional seasonality estimates, we analyzed modern shells from Pender Island in southern British Columbia and Ormidale Harbour near the central coast of British Columbia, and examined variation in growth rates and different methods to obtain $\delta^{18}O_{shell}$ to examine how these factors influence seasonality interpretations.

Seasonality estimates using growth increment data from British Columbia are generally calculated by comparing growth increments (periods of rapid growth) to growth lines (periods of growth retardation or cessation), and then dividing the width of the pre-death increment by the width of the last complete increment (Monks and Johnston 1993). The end result is a seasonality estimate that can distinguish between "warm" or "cold" times of the year, and sometimes the season of collection is also inferred. However, this is an oversimplification of a season, and as a consequence, the length of an activity, such as site occupation or shellfish gathering, is likely exaggerated.

One of the most basic problems with seasonality estimates using growth coloration or line formation is the presence of senile or older shells in the archaeological assemblage. Senile growth occurs as the shell ages and its growth rate decreases. The size of the growth increments decreases, making an accurate seasonality estimate based on the formation of growth lines or increments impossible.

At sites with less intensive shellfish gathering, intermittent gathering, a preference for larger shells, or active resource management practices in place, the archaeological assemblage is likely to be dominated by older, senile

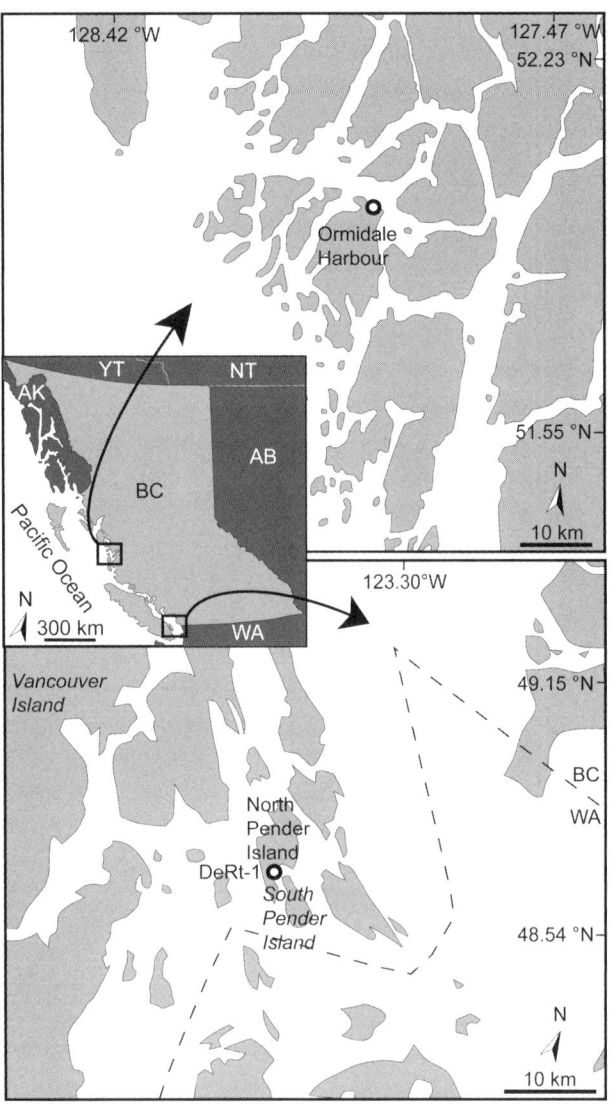

18.2. *Shellfish sampling sites used in this study.*

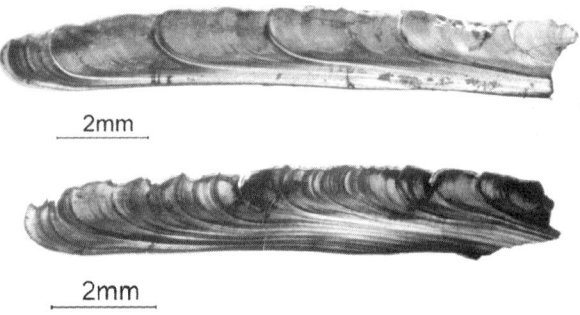

18.3. *Thin sections of* Saxidomus gigantea *showing mature (top) and senile (bottom). Note the compaction of growth lines leading up to the ventral margin in the senile specimen.*

shells (Cannon and Burchell 2009). In many instances, individual shells need to be discarded because their growth patterns cannot be "read," as in the case at the McNichol Creek site in northern British Columbia. For example, of the total sample of 1,128 shell specimens collected from McNichol Creek for seasonality analysis, the sample was reduced to only 127, or 11 percent that could be used for this purpose (Coupland, Bissell, and King 1993, 69). In cases where the archaeological sample is dominated by older shells, micro-milling samples for $\delta^{18}O$ may present a solution to this problem.

Another consideration regarding previous seasonality studies is that the relationship between time and growth is not linear, since shells grow at different rates during different seasons while the overall growth rate decreases with ontogeny (Hallmann et al. 2009). This presents a fundamental problem for the basic method of using only growth lines and increments, since the real amount of time represented in the increment cannot be equally divided between three (or four) seasons. In previous studies, it was assumed that shells grow quickly in warmer months and stop growing in the winter; however, rates of shell growth are more complex because shells grow at different rates depending on the temperature of the water, age, food, and salinity. This multitude of variables presents significant complications when attempting to identify seasonality based on the timing of increment and line formation.

David Maxwell (2003) analyzed a sample of monthly-collected butter clams from the Pender Canal site in the Gulf of Georgia on the south coast of British Columbia in order to evaluate the applicability of seasonality estimates based on growth line and increment formation. Unfortunately, his results were inconclusive and demonstrated how this method can produce ambiguous seasonality results, likely due to two main factors. The first was the fact that only a small portion of the last phase of growth was analyzed, without considering the life history and overall growth rates; and the second is that the magnification (30x) used to visualize the shells was insufficient. In our reexamination of Maxwell's shells, the shells were immersed in Mutvei's solution, which simultaneously etches the shell, preserves organic matrices, and stains the intercrystalline organic envelopes blue (Schöne et al. 2005), and were visualized under 40x magnification. With this preparation, micro-increment (i.e., daily/tidal) formations were visible and could be counted and measured in specimens with a known date of collection. It was therefore possible to understand how much "seasonal time" is present in a shell portion. When high-resolution sclerochronological measurements and $\delta^{18}O$ analyses were conducted, they showed that butter clams collected from Pender Island grow quickly in the spring, reach their peak growth in the summer, then begin to slow in the autumn months before growth rate reaches a minimum in the winter (Hallmann et al. 2009, 2359). The previous assumption that the growth increment can be divided into roughly three seasons (spring, summer, fall) is no longer valid since the largest portion of growth occurs in the summer; therefore, what macroscopically looks like "spring" or "fall" growth, can in fact be "summer."

As with visualizing shell growth using a higher resolution and improved techniques, isotope sampling strategies will also affect the interpretation of seasonality results. If the resolution is not sufficient, the season of death is more likely to be misinterpreted. To test the effects of isotope sampling, we analyzed two specimens collected from Ormidale Harbour on the central coast of British Columbia. Both were collected on June 6, 2008. Isotopic analysis for sample A was conducted on a VG OPTIMA gas-source mass spectrometer using a common 100 percent phosphoric-acid bath at 90°C (McMaster University), and sample B was conducted on a MAT 253 isotope ratio mass spectrometer coupled with a Gas Bench II (University of Frankfurt). Results of the analysis of both shells are reported in the usual δ notation, and samples were calibrated against a NBS-19 calibrated Carrara marble standard ($\delta^{18}O = -1.74‰$) with a precision error of 0.06–0.10‰. The $\delta^{18}O_{shell}$ values were calculated against the Vienna Pee Dee Belemnite standard and are given as parts per mil.

Figure 18.5 shows that the shell with the coarse sampling resolution (Shell A) produces a seasonal profile that shows the season of death as "winter," whereas the shell with the

higher resolution (Shell B) shows a seasonal curve with the time of collection in the predicted spot: directly between the most negative (summer) and most positive (winter) $\delta^{18}O_{shell}$ values. The difference in sampling resolution clearly shows how a lower resolution will provide an inaccurate season of death, and therefore an inaccurate seasonality interpretation.

CONCLUSIONS

Growth coloration or growth increment analysis of shellfish does not produce a precise season of collection. These methods can only identify warm or cold seasons, or at best, spring, summer, and fall with some degree of uncertainty. Identifying winter seasonality based on growth increments is impossible, since the period of shell growth is minimal in comparison to other seasons, such that the "winter" growth stoppage could actually be in the late fall and not resume until the spring; therefore, if a shell was collected in the winter, it would not be possible to identify the season based on growth banding or coloration alone. Furthermore, shells that are in senescent stages of growth cannot be used because of their irregular growth rates, since distances between growth lines become narrower, increment width decreases, and precise measurement is not possible. Geochemical analysis combined with sclerochronology can refine these interpretations, and provide greater precision and accuracy in seasonal estimates. Although environmental factors such as extreme salinity, temperature, and precipitation, and biological factors can decrease the precision required for a paleoclimate study, they do not present the same problems for identifying seasonality, because the seasonality estimate only requires the

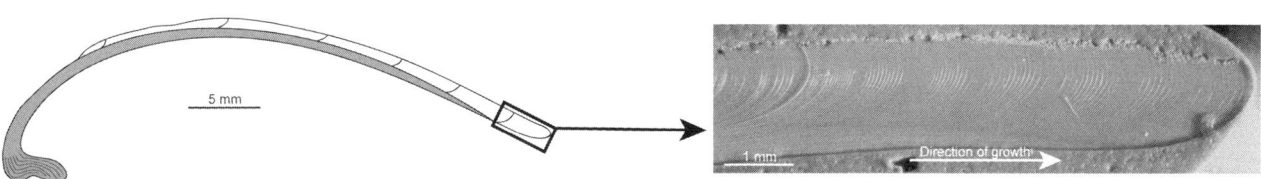

18.4. Ventral margin of Saxidomus gigantea *showing micro-increment formations that correspond to daily tidal lines (Hallmann et al. 2009). These lines can be counted from the known date of collection in modern specimens to understand the relationship between growth and time. To improve the resolution of growth-line visualization, the shell cross-section was immersed in Mutvei's solution (following the methods of Schöne et al. 2005) prior to analysis. As shells age, their rate of growth decreases, and less "time" is represented in each annual section (i.e., fast growth and slow growth). If the rate of growth is not calculated using high-resolution sclerochronology, it is impossible to use older specimens for seasonality using growth increment analysis because the amount of time represented between periods of perceived annual lines is unknown.*

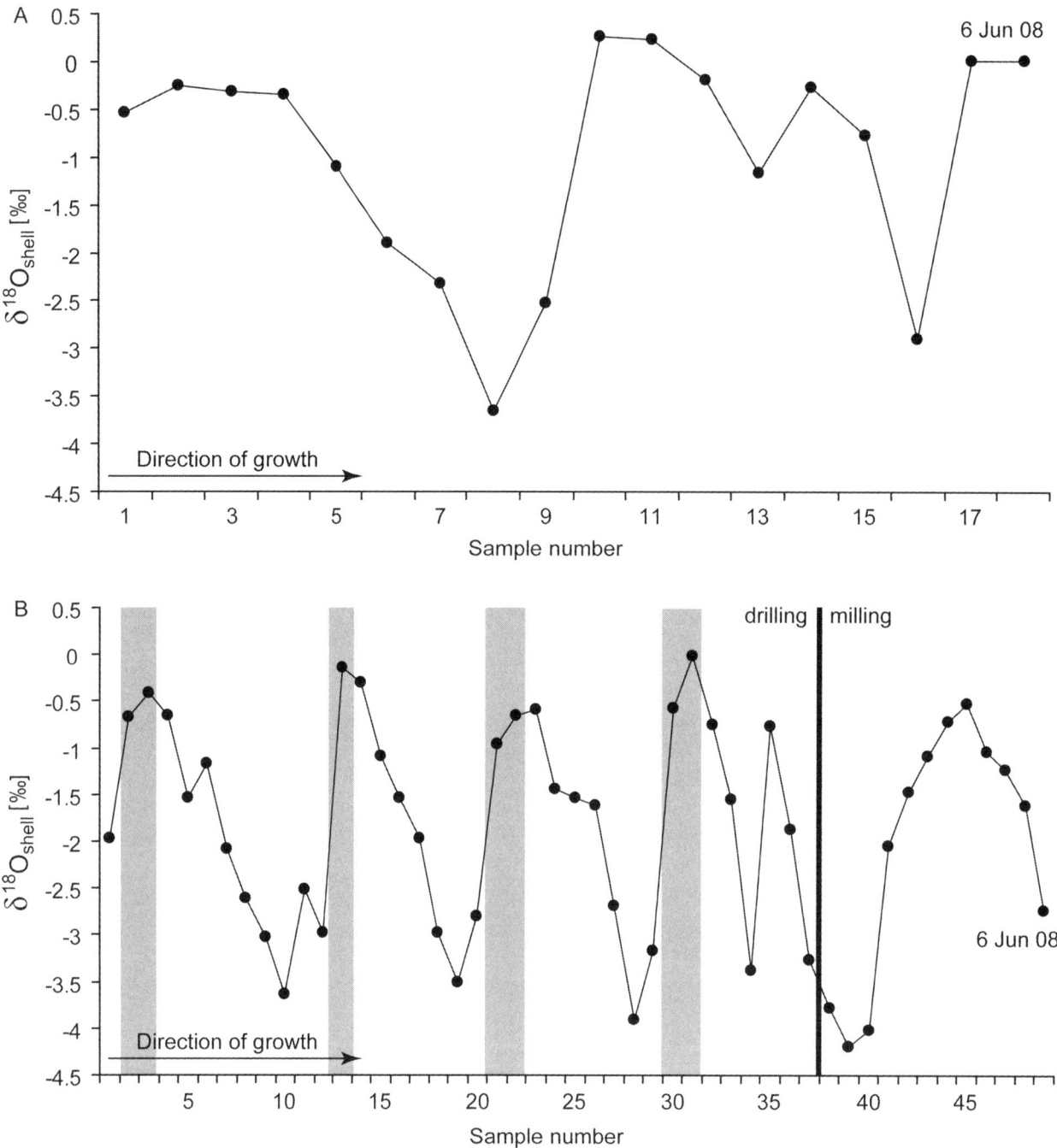

18.5. $\delta^{18}O$ profiles of modern Saxidomus gigantea *shells collected on June 6, 2008. The upper plot has a coarse sampling resolution that used a 0.5-millimeter-diameter dental drill bit with samples spaced ~one millimeter apart. Data from the lower plot was obtained by micro-drilling holes with a 300-micrometer drill bit, with spaces between samples ranging from 200 to 500 micrometers. Micro-milling yields a spatial resolution of 100 micrometers or less, and an uninterrupted shell record can be obtained. Gray bars indicate where distinct winter growth lines were observed.*

pattern of isotope variation, not the absolute isotopic ratios that are required to identify paleotemperature.

If stable $\delta^{18}O_{shell}$ is applied to determine the seasonality of archaeological shells, the following steps should be taken to minimize error and improve accuracy. First, a study of modern specimens and environmental parameters should be conducted to determine if the shells are secreted in isotopic equilibrium with ambient water. Second, a sclerochronological analysis should be applied to evaluate the timing and formation of growth lines (Andrus and Rich 2008). The growth rates of both modern and archaeological shells can be confirmed using stable isotope analysis, and this analysis will help to understand the amount of time represented in each individual isotope data point since the time represented by each sample can be identified by daily increment counts (Schöne 2008, 277). Finally, specimens should be analyzed at an appropriate resolution using micro-milling techniques to eliminate space between samples, thereby providing an uninterrupted record. This will ensure a more "even" record of shell growth, provide a more precise profile of the environmental conditions in which the shellfish lived, and ultimately produce a refined measure of the season of shellfish collection. In addition, drilling samples does not provide a sufficient resolution when working with specimens in the senile stages of growth; however, micro-milling is an effective method to obtain a seasonality estimate.

A precise seasonality estimate requires multi-site analysis and the monitoring of changes over time to account for variation in seasonal patterns. Seasonality estimates require a method that can produce a resolution high enough to refine seasonality interpretations to a more focused time frame such as "early winter" as opposed to "cold." According to Daniel E. Lieberman (1993, 605), it is necessary to understand past climatic conditions before reconstructing seasonality, and the application of stable isotope data can both help answer questions of past environments and improve seasonality estimates. The application of $\delta^{18}O$ analysis to mollusks has the potential to improve the precision of seasonality estimates, and to make it possible to understand more clearly the variability in seasons of shellfish harvest at shell midden sites.

ACKNOWLEDGMENTS

This chapter has been modified from the first author's comprehensive exams as part of the PhD requirement at McMaster University. We would like to thank Dr. Kostalena Michelaki, Natalie Brewster, and Nadia Densmore for providing helpful comments on earlier versions of this chapter, and Neil Bourne at the Department of Fisheries and Oceans Canada for providing shellfish samples from Ormidale Harbour. Dave Maxwell provided samples of modern collected bivalves from Pender Island, and Shannon Wood at Simon Fraser University provided laboratory facilities. Michael Maus and Martin Knyf are kindly acknowledged for their assistance with the operation of the mass spectrometers. Support for this research was provided by the Canadian Foundation for Innovation, the Social Science Humanities Research Council of Canada, and the German Research Foundation.

CHAPTER NINETEEN

MESOLITHIC AND NEOLITHIC SHELL MIDDENS IN WESTERN SCOTLAND

A Comparative Analysis of Shellfish Exploitation Patterns

Catriona Pickard and Clive Bonsall

SUMMARY

Shell midden sites are a common feature of the west Scottish Mesolithic and Neolithic and are distributed along mainland coasts and several of the Inner Hebridean Islands. This chapter provides an overview of the shellfishing practices of coastal foragers in the region. A comparative analysis of the shellfish exploitation practices at four midden sites, An Corran, Carding Mill Bay II, Raschoille Cave, and Ulva Cave, is presented. More than 30 species of shellfish were represented in the middens. However, only two genera were common: limpet (*Patella* spp.) and periwinkle (*Littorina* spp.). Both species have been widely used as food or as fish bait in recent times in this region. Variation in species representation between the middens is observed. This variation can be attributed in part to distinct sampling and/or recovery strategies, but also to local differences in shore substrate, topography, and exposure. Certain species (e.g., European cowrie [*Trivia* spp.], edible oyster [*Ostrea edulis*], and king scallop [*Pecten maximus*]) were specifically collected for use as raw material in the manufacture of utensils and adornments. The consistent occurrence of incidental species provides insight into a diverse range of economic activities conducted at the sites.

INTRODUCTION

The Early to Middle Holocene shell middens of Scotland have been the subject of archaeological enquiry since the mid-19th century. By the beginning of the 20th century middens of potentially Early to Middle Holocene age had been investigated at sites in almost all the coastal regions of Scotland (e.g., Curle 1908; Dalrymple 1866; Grieve 1872;

Tait 1868). Designated the "Scottish kitchen-middens" by J. Brodie (1970 [1869], 181), the shell mounds were described as "refuse heaps" (Anderson 1895); their function was assumed and their wider cultural meaning remained largely unexplored. During the past 40 years an upsurge in research into the Scottish Mesolithic and the transition from foraging to farming has led to renewed interest in the shell middens of western Scotland in particular. Many coastal midden sites on the west Scottish mainland and on the islands of the Inner Hebrides have been systematically excavated and recorded (e.g., Bonsall, Sutherland, and Lawson 1989, 1991; Bonsall et al. 1992, 1994; Connock, Finlayson, and Mills 1993; Hardy and Wickham-Jones 2003; Mellars 1987; Russell, Bonsall, and Sutherland 1995). Excavations of the Oronsay shell middens were designed to maximize recovery of economic and environmental remains (Mellars 1987). More recently the wider cultural significance of these sites has been discussed (e.g., Bonsall 1996; Cobb 2005; Cummings 2003; Johnson and Bonsall 1999; Mellars 2004).

Faunal and floral remains recovered from the Scottish middens reflect significant dietary diversity (Pickard and Bonsall 2012a). Remains of aquatic species—shellfish, echinoderms, brachyurans, fish, and sea mammals—invariably form the major components of the middens, but carbonized plant remains, such as burdock seeds (*Arctium lappa*) and hazelnut shells (*Corylus avellana*) and bones of terrestrial mammals, most commonly red deer (*Cervus elaphus*) and wild boar (*Sus scrofa*), are not infrequent.

This chapter presents a comparative analysis of the shell assemblages from four midden sites to provide an overview of the shell-harvesting strategies practiced in western

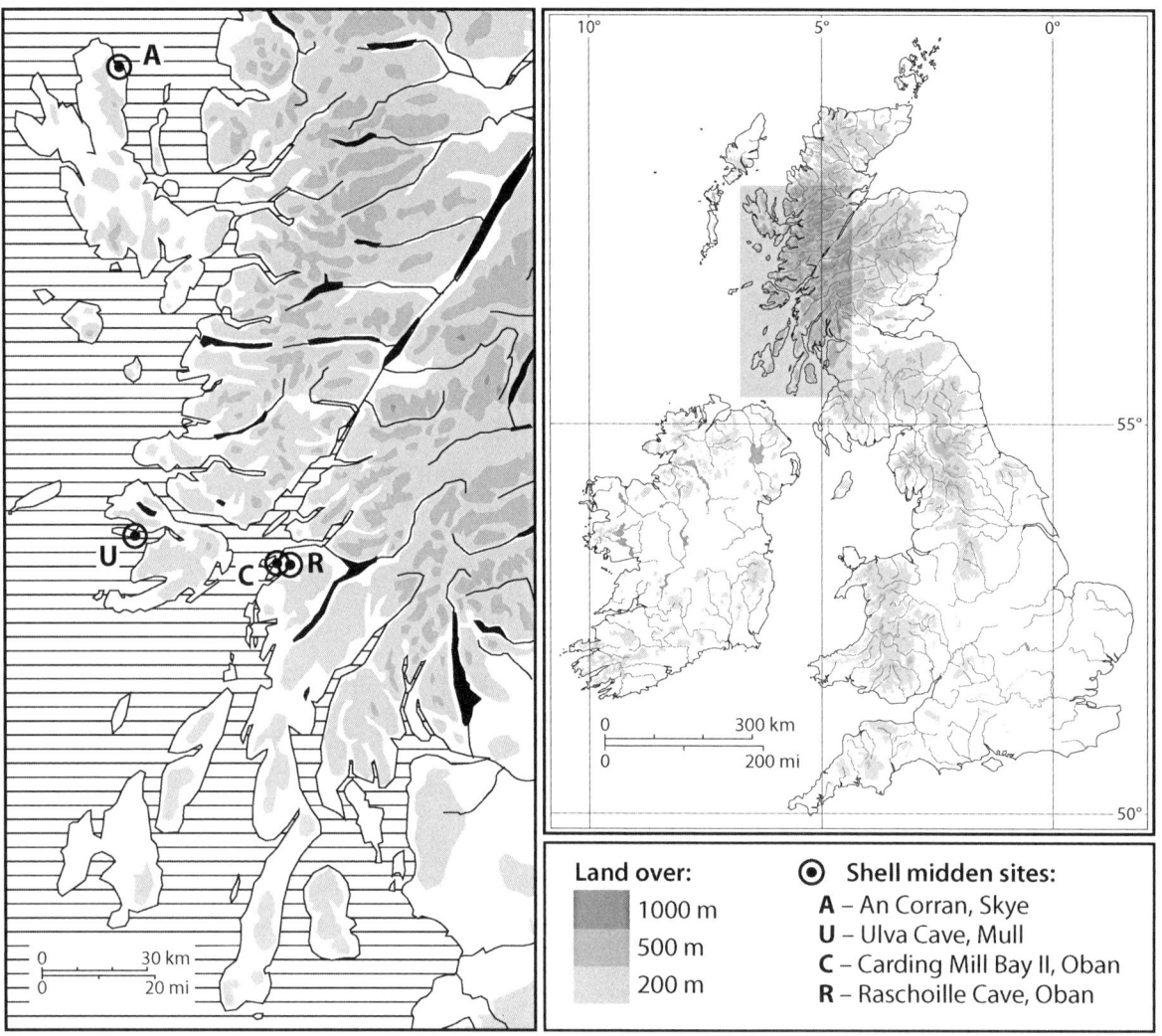

19.1. Site location map.

Scotland during the Early to Middle Holocene ca. 9500–3000 cal BC. Understanding the strategies employed can provide information on the economic and cultural significance of shellfish for foragers and early farmers. Species representation in the middens is compared in order to determine whether specific shellfish species were targeted. The harvesting strategies are reconstructed based on the ecology and behavior of the shellfish species represented in the midden, and based on ethnographic analogies with recent and historic shellfishing practices.

THE SHELL MIDDEN SITES

Of the four principal sites discussed in this chapter, An Corran and Ulva Cave are situated on islands of the Inner

Hebrides, while Carding Mill Bay II and Raschoille Cave are on the mainland coast. All four sites lie within caves or rock-shelters (Figure 19.1).

The An Corran rock-shelter is situated on the northeast coast of the Isle of Skye, at 57°38'14"N, 6°12'20"W. A salvage excavation in advance of road widening (Miket and Saville 1994) revealed a complex sequence of deposits, which included distinct layers or lenses of shell midden material. The present authors studied the shellfish remains and offered a provisional interpretation of the site chronology (Pickard and Bonsall 2012b). Radiocarbon and stratigraphic evidence was interpreted to indicate that the midden deposits belong to several different periods in the use of the site between ca. 7600 BP/6450 cal BC (Mesolithic) and ca. 3700 BP/2080 cal BC (Bronze Age) or even later.

Ulva Cave (56°28'04"N, 6°10'18"W) is an ancient sea cave on the south side of the small island of Ulva, which lies just off the west coast of the much larger island of Mull. The site has been under investigation by the present authors since 1987 (Bonsall, Sutherland, and Lawson 1989, 1991; Bonsall et al. 1992, 1994; Russell, Bonsall, and Sutherland 1995; Pickard and Bonsall 2009). A shell midden occupies the entrance area of the cave. Radiocarbon dates on marine shells, mammalian bone, and carbonized plant material from the midden range between ca. 7950 and 2420 BP (ca. 6900–470 cal BC; Bonsall et al. 1994, and unpublished data), although the vast majority of the ¹⁴C dates are older than 5200 BP (4000 cal BC), suggesting that the midden is very largely of Mesolithic age. A large subsample of the shell assemblage from Ulva Cave was analyzed by Nancy J. Russell, Clive Bonsall, and Donald G. Sutherland (1995), and we make use of their data in our consideration of the Ulva Cave shell assemblage.

The two mainland sites, Carding Mill Bay II and Raschoille Cave, lie within the town of Oban. They are situated on opposite sides of a NE–SW–trending ridge, which in the Middle Holocene (with a higher relative sea level) was a rocky peninsula separating the ancient Oban embayment from the Sound of Kerrera.

At Carding Mill Bay II (56°24'30"N, 5°29'31"W), archaeological deposits infilled a narrow cleft at the base of a former sea cliff backing the Main Rock Platform, an ancient shoreline that is extensively developed in central-west Scotland. The site, which faces northwest toward the island of Kerrera, was excavated by Clive Bonsall between 1991 and 1993. Two well-defined shell midden layers were recorded, separated by a thin layer of talus. No ¹⁴C dates are available for Carding Mill Bay II, but the presence of characteristic pottery and bones of domestic livestock indicate a Late Neolithic date for the upper midden layer; the age of the lower midden layer is uncertain (Bartosiewicz, Zapata, and Bonsall 2009). The nearby site of Carding Mill Bay I, excavated by Kenneth D. Connock in the 1980s, also contained a shell midden deposit. Radiocarbon dates for the midden at Carding Mill Bay I range from 5190 ± 85 to 4765 ± 65 BP (ca. 4000–3550 cal BC), suggesting an Early Neolithic context—possibly extending back into the Final Mesolithic (Bonsall and Smith 1992; Connock, Finlayson, and Mills 1993).

Raschoille Cave (56°24'12"N, 5°28'40"W) lies ca. 0.8 kilometer southeast of the Carding Mill Bay sites, at the edge of the (former) Oban embayment, facing northeast. In two brief excavation campaigns in the 1980s (Connock 1985; Sloan 1986), deposits containing marine shells, mammalian and fish bones, and carbonized plant remains were uncovered beneath stony deposits containing Neolithic human remains. Bonsall (1999) obtained AMS ¹⁴C dates on various materials from the site. The dates from the shell-rich deposits range between ca. 7640 and 4880 BP (6470–3650 cal BC), indicating a Late Mesolithic to Early Neolithic context.

A number of other caves and rock-shelters containing shell middens have been recorded in the Oban area since the late 19th century, including MacArthur's Cave and Druimvargie Rockshelter excavated in 1894–1895 and 1897, respectively (Anderson 1895, 1898; Bonsall and Sutherland 1992). Although Armand D. Lacaille (1954) published a presence/absence list of the faunal remains from the sites, few details of the middens and the shell assemblages survive.

COMPARATIVE ANALYSIS OF THE SHELLFISHING STRATEGIES

Identification

Shells were identified by comparison with reference collections held by Archaeology at the University of Edinburgh and by the National Museum of Scotland. A total of 36 distinct species or genera of shellfish were identified at the four midden sites (Table 19.1). Some specimens could not be attributed beyond the level of genus because of the fragmentary and/or abraded condition of the shells. It is likely, therefore, that the total number of species in the shell assemblages is underrepresented.

Closely related species may be ecologically distinct, occupying different habitats and exhibiting discrete patterns of behavior (e.g., Williams 1990b). Identification to species level is thus potentially important for determining harvesting strategies, which may in turn influence interpretation of the economic and cultural significance of shell middens. For example, Veneridae have been identified in three of the assemblages analyzed: Carding Mill Bay II, Raschoille Cave, and Ulva Cave. Eleven species of Veneridae are native to British waters. These species occupy either lower eulittoral (e.g., *Venerupis senegalensis*) or sublittoral zones (e.g., *Timoclea ovata*). Generally, the Veneridae represented in the shell assemblages were fragmented, with significant surface abrasion that had removed the periostracum and distorted species-specific surface sculpturing. Consequently, only three species, *Venerupis senegalensis, Venus verrucosa*, and *Tapes decussatus*, could be attributed with certainty. Each of these species can occupy the low shore to the sublittoral (Fish and Fish 1996). However, it is possible that specimens of sublittoral species are also present.

Three species of *Patella* are native to British waters: the black-footed limpet (*P. depressa*), the China limpet

Table 19.1. Species and common name of shellfish identified in the four shell middens

Species/Genus	Common Name
Aporrhais pespelecani	Common pelican's foot shell
Arctica islandica	Icelandic cyprine
Bittium reticulatum	Needle whelk
Buccinum undatum	Buckie whelk
Calliostoma zizyphinum	Painted topshell
Cerastoderma edule	Common cockle
Cerastoderma glaucum	Lagoon cockle
Chlamys opercularis	Queen scallop
Cingula trifasciata	n/a
Ensis ensis	Common razor shell
Ensis siliqua/Ensis arcuatus	Pod razor shell/Curved razor shell
Epitonium clathrus	Common wentletrap
Gibbula cineraria	Gray topshell
Gibbula umbilicalis	Flat or purple topshell
Haliotis tuberculata	Green ormer
Helcion pellicidum/Helcion laevis	Blue-rayed limpet
Hinia reticulata (syn.*Nassarius reticulatus*)	Netted dogwhelk
Littorina littorea	Common periwinkle
Littorina mariae	Flat periwinkle
Littorina neritoides (syn. *Melarhaphe neritoides*)	Small periwinkle
Littorina obtusata	Flat periwinkle
Littorina saxatilis species-complex	Rough Periwinkle
Littorina spp.	Periwinkles
Mimachlamys varia	Variegated or black scallop
Modiolus modiolus	Horse mussel
Mytilidae	Mussel
Mytilus edulis	Common mussel
Nucella lapillus	Dogwhelk
Osilinus lineatus (syn. *Monodonta lineata*)	Thick top-shell
Ostrea edulis	Common oyster
Patella spp.	Limpet
Pecten maximus	King scallop
Rissoa sp.	Sea snail
Tapes decussatus (syn. *Venerupis decussata*)	Chequered carpet shell
Trivia monacha/Trivia arctica	Cowrie
Trochidae	Topshell
Turritella communis	Auger shell
Veneridae	Venus shell
Venerupis senegalensis (syn. *Venerupis pullastra*)	Pullet carpet shell
Venus verrucosa	Warty venus

Table 19.2. Species representation by minimum number of individuals (MNI)

Species Representation (MNI)	An Corran	Carding Mill Bay II	Rascoille Cave	Ulva Cave
Aporrhais pespelecani				1
Arctica islandica	1			
Bittium reticulatum			1	1
Buccinum undatum		4	12	2
Calliostoma zizyphinum				1
Cerastoderma edule		7	28	1
Cerastoderma glaucum		1		1
Chlamys opercularis				3
Cingula trifasciata		11		1
Ensis ensis				2
Ensis siliqua/Ensis arcuatus				2
Epitonium clathrus				1
Gibbula cineraria		1		21
Gibbula umbilicalis	13	6	1	14
Gibbula sp.	1	1	1	
Haliotis tuberculata				1
Helcion spp.	1			253
Hinia reticulata				1
Littorina littorea	1,714	2,411	855	6,230
Littorina mariae	51	62	24	40
Littorina neritoides	1			2
Littorina obtusata	17	21	53	42
Littorina saxatilis species-complex	25	4	10	25
Littorina spp.			1	150
Mimachlamys varia		1	1	4
Modiolus modiolus	2		3	10
Mytilidae		2	1	53
Mytilus edulis	53	1	30	12
Nucella lapillus	621	13	1	1,597
Osilinus lineatus				3
Ostrea edulis		4	62	6
Patella spp.	27,270	5,782	257	13,873
Pecten maximus	2	2	2	6
Rissoa spp.		2		4
Tapes decussatus			26	16
Trivia spp.	2	1		5
Trochidae				23
Turritella communis				3

Table 19.2. (continued)

Species Representation (MNI)	An Corran	Carding Mill Bay II	Rascoille Cave	Ulva Cave
Veneridae		1	101	17
Venerupis senegalensis		3	85	8
Venus verrucosa			1	2
TOTAL ASSEMBLAGE	29,774	8,341	1,556	22,437

(*P. ulyssiponensis*), and the common limpet (*P. vulgata*). Species-specific attributes occur in the periostracum and/or soft tissues, rendering these species archaeologically indistinguishable (Ebling et al. 1962). Russell, Bonsall, and Sutherland (1995) described *P. vulgata* and/or *P. aspera* as present in the Ulva Cave midden. *P. aspera*, until recently considered synonymous with *P. ulyssiponensis*, is now considered taxonomically and genetically distinct (Weber and Hawkins 2005).

Morphometric analysis of *Patella* spp. specimens from the shell assemblages (Russell, Bonsall, and Sutherland 1995, and see below) demonstrates that limpet shells were collected from all regions of the shore. Sympatric observations of the vertical distribution of *P. ulyssiponensis* and *P. vulgata* have demonstrated that the former dominates lower tidal populations, preferring continuous immersion, whereas the latter, which exhibits greater tolerance of desiccation, is most frequent in mid- to high tidal regions (Ebling et al. 1962; Moore 1934). It can be inferred from this distribution that both *P. vulgata* and *P. ulyssiponensis* are likely represented in the shell middens.

Although widely reported to be a southern species reaching its northernmost distribution in Wales (e.g., Fretter and Graham 1976), recent records document the occurrence of *P. depressa* populations on the west coast of Scotland (Skewes 2003). It is therefore possible that all three species, *P. depressa*, *P. ulyssiponensis*, and *P. vulgata*, are present in the middens.

Similar problems of attribution apply to the two species of *Trivia*, the Arctic cowrie (*Trivia arctica*) and the European cowrie (*T. monacha*), commonly found in British waters, which are indistinguishable in the absence of soft tissues and where the periostracum is degraded (Lebour 1933). Although *T. monacha* is generally larger than *T. arctica* (*T. monacha* grows to 12 millimeters whereas *T. arctica* reaches 10 millimeters), "large" *T. arctica* specimens are a regular component of southern populations (Vayssière 1923); that is, the two species are not morphometrically discrete. Ecologically, however, the two species are

different. Both *T. arctica* and *T. monacha* occupy the low shore and sublittoral zone, but *T. arctica* occurs in higher densities in deeper waters (Lebour 1933).

Quantification

Shells and shell fragments identified to species level were quantified by minimum number of individuals (MNI), by number of identified specimens (NISP), and by weight. In this analysis of the shell assemblages, percentage representation of species by MNI is utilized (Table 19.2). The shell assemblages vary significantly in size with a relatively small sample recovered from Raschoille Cave (n=1,556), and larger samples from An Corran (n=29,774), Carding Mill Bay II (n=8,341), and Ulva Cave (n=22,437). The occurrence of gastropod apices and whichever is the greater of the left or right bivalve umbones were recorded. The presence of fragments of other species, not represented by apex or umbo, was also noted. Differential fragmentation and preservation of the shells both within and between the midden sites investigated, as well as different excavation and recovery techniques, limit the usefulness of NISP counts and shell weights for the purpose of comparative analysis (see Marshall and Pilgrim 1993 and Claassen 1998 for discussion of the analytical worth of the various quantification methods used in archaeomalacology).

Morphometric analysis of the *Patella* spp. was conducted following the procedures adopted by Russell, Bonsall, and Sutherland (1995) to determine the shore regions exploited. All measurements were taken with vernier callipers to the nearest 0.1 millimeter.

DISCUSSION

Human Use of Shellfish

Ethnographic accounts suggest that, traditionally, shellfish have been harvested for five principal purposes, as food, bait, raw material for tool/utensil manufacture, ornamentation, and currency (e.g., Meehan 1983; Stewart 1977; Waselkov 1987). Generally, large common species are collected for food and raw materials, with rarer and extra-local species used for ornamentation and currency. Species representation, harvesting strategies, processing methods, and modification of shells may provide some insight into the intended use of the shellfish recovered from the midden sites.

Species Representation

Each of the assemblages analyzed comprised a similar range of species (Table 19.3), although there is some variation in the occurrence of secondary species. Only two species/genera were abundant, limpets (*Patella* spp.) and periwinkles (*Littorina littorea*), the combined species representation accounting for 97.3 percent of the assemblage at An Corran, 98.2 percent at Carding Mill Bay II, 71.5 percent at Raschoille Cave, and 89.6 percent at Ulva Cave. The greatest number of distinct species/genera was identified at Ulva Cave (35 species/genera are represented). This number may reflect the intensive recovery and processing methods used at this site, as much as taphonomic or environmental factors. Virtually all of the midden material excavated from Ulva Cave was brought back to the laboratory for processing and analysis. The material was wet-sieved through mesh sizes down to at least one millimeter and the residues painstakingly picked over for marine shells/fragments and other items of archaeological interest.

The relative abundance of the predominant species varies both between and within assemblages (Figures 19.2–19.5). *Patella* spp. predominate at An Corran (91.6 percent), Carding Mill Bay II (69.3 percent), and Ulva Cave (61.8 percent). This is a consistent feature of "Obanian" shell assemblages (cf. D. A. Jones 1985). However, although *Patella* spp. are common in the Raschoille Cave assemblage, *L. littorea* dominates (54.9 percent).

Variation in secondary species representation is also evident (Figures 19.2–19.5). The assemblage at Raschoille Cave is distinctive in the relative abundance of bivalves. Ulva Cave is notable for the presence of two species that have a southern distribution today. Thick topshell (*Osilinus lineatus*) is a minor but consistent component of the shell assemblage occurring throughout the lower part of the midden (Russell, Bonsall, and Sutherland 1995). Today *O. lineatus* is restricted to waters south of Anglesey (Crothers 2001; Kendall 1987). Another southern species identified in the midden, the European abalone (*Haliotis tuberculata*), currently reaches the northern limit of its distribution in the Channel Islands. The presence of *O. lineatus* and *H. tuberculata* indicates higher sea temperatures in the Middle Holocene compared to today (Pickard and Bonsall, unpublished data).

Table 19.3. Species occurrence at the four shell midden sites

Species/Genera	An Corran	Carding Mill Bay II	Raschoille Cave	Ulva Cave
Aporrhais pespelecani				■
Arctica islandica	■			
Bittium reticulatum			■	■
Buccinum undatum		■	■	■
Calliostoma zizyphinum				■
Cerastoderma edule		■	■	■
Cerastoderma glaucum		■		■
Chlamys opercularis				■
Cingula trifasciata		■		■
Ensis ensis				■
Ensis siliqua/Ensis arcuatus				■
Epitonium clathrus				■
Gibbula cineraria		■		■
Gibbula umbilicalis	■	■	■	■
Gibbula spp.	■	■	■	
Haliotis tuberculata				■
Helcion spp.	■			■
Hinia reticulata				■
Littorina littorea	■	■	■	■
Littorina mariae	■	■	■	■
Littorina neritoides	■			■
Littorina obtusata	■	■	■	■
Littorina saxatilis species-complex	■	■	■	■
Littorina spp.			■	■
Mimachlamys varia		■	■	■
Modiolus modiolus	■		■	■
Mytilidae		■	■	
Mytilus edulis	■	■	■	■
Nucella lapillus	■	■	■	■
Osilinus lineatus				■
Ostrea edulis		■	■	■
Patella spp.	■	■	■	■
Pecten maximus	■	■	■	■
Rissoa sp.		■		■
Tapes decussatus			■	■
Trivia spp.	■	■		■
Trochidae				■
Turritella communis				■
Veneridae		■	■	■
Venerupis senegalensis		■	■	■
Venus verrucosa			■	■

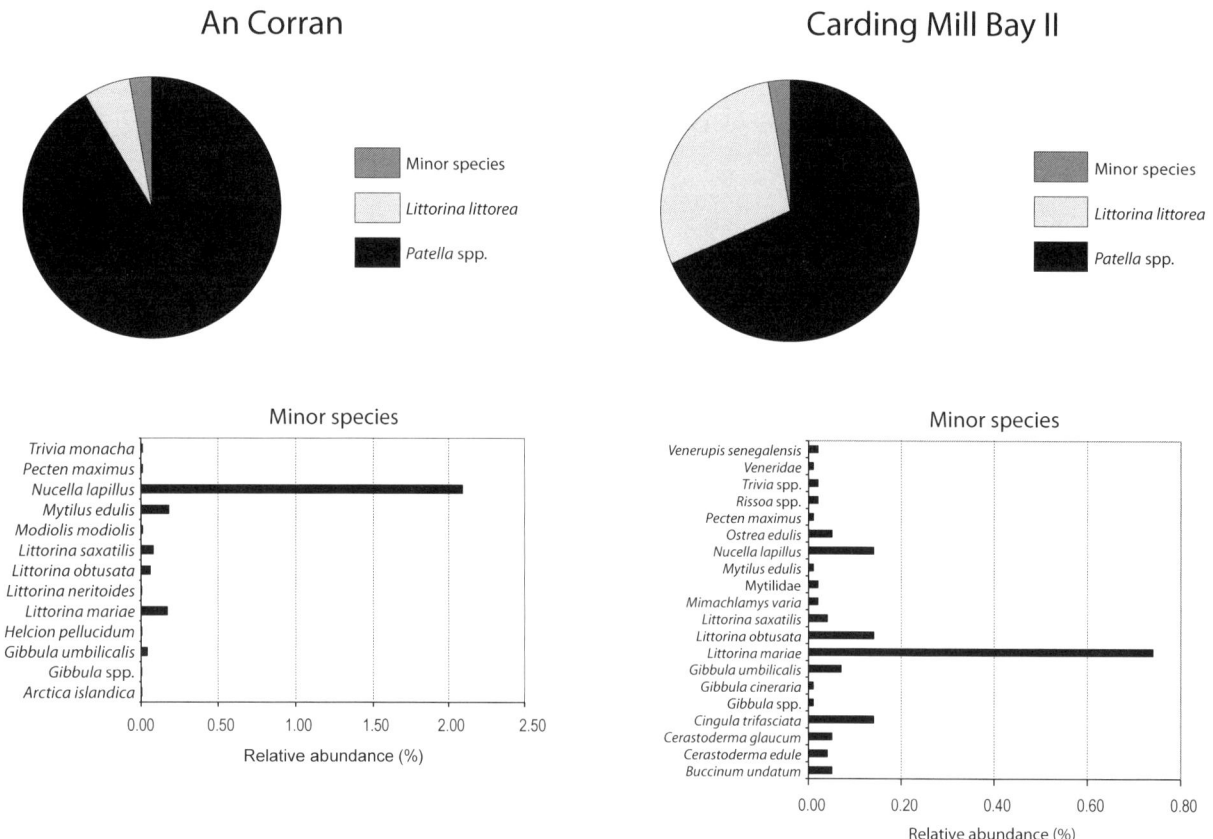

The Ulva Cave assemblage is also idiosyncratic in the proportion of dogwhelk (*Nucella lapillus*) shells (>7 percent). *N. lapillus* is present in very small quantities at An Corran (ca. 2.0 percent) and virtually absent from Raschoille Cave (0.1 percent) and Carding Mill Bay II (0.2 percent). Ecologically, *N. lapillus* favors rocky shores similar to those colonized by *Patella* spp. and *L. littorea*, and as one of the most common species on intertidal stretches of British shores (Freare 1970), *N. lapillus* might be expected to feature in each of the middens. *N. lapillus* was a significant component of the shell assemblages from the Oronsay sites (D. A. Jones 1984), Carding Mill Bay I (Connock, Finlayson, and Mills 1993), and MacArthur Cave (Anderson 1895). Changes in local shore ecology may account for the significant presence of *N. lapillus* at Carding Mill Bay I and its rarity at Carding Mill Bay II, but further discussion of the effect of ecological change on species representation at the Carding Mill Bay sites is constrained by poor chronological/stratigraphic resolution at Carding Mill Bay I (Connock, Finlayson, and Mills 1993) and the

lack of ^{14}C dates for Carding Mill Bay II. *N. lapillus* populations can be restricted on very sheltered shores through predation by crabs (Hughes and Elner 1979). The scarcity of *N. lapillus* at both Carding Mill Bay II and Raschoille Cave may reflect prevailing shore ecology at the time of midden accumulation. However, predation by crabs is seldom so heavy that *N. lapillus* is entirely absent. This leaves open the possibility that some form of cultural selection (resulting in avoidance or overexploitation) was responsible for the scarcity of *N. lapillus* at Carding Mill Bay II and Raschoille Cave. *N. lapillus* is said to have a very distinctive taste that many people today find unpalatable (Crothers 1985), and it is possible that some prehistoric groups were similarly deterred from exploiting dogwhelks as a source of food. Shell morphology in *N. lapillus* has been demonstrated to vary with shore exposure, directly reflecting predation pressures. On sheltered shores, *N. lapillus* populations have a relatively elongated shell and smaller aperture; this form acts to exclude crab chelae, thereby reducing predation (Hughes and Elner 1979). Associated

Raschoille Cave

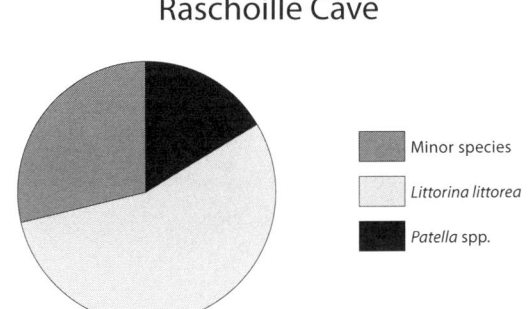

Ulva Cave

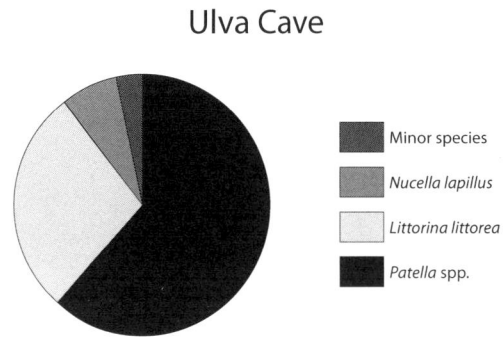

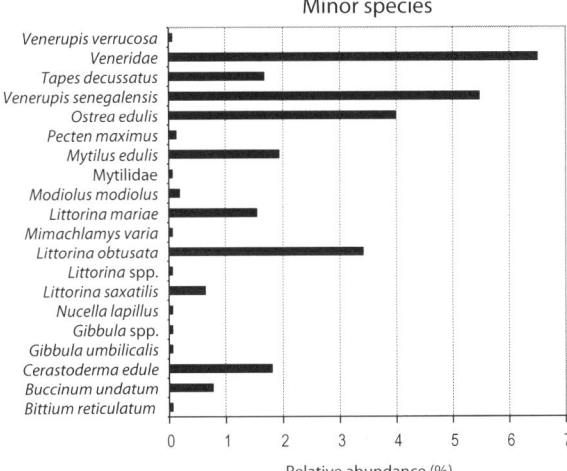

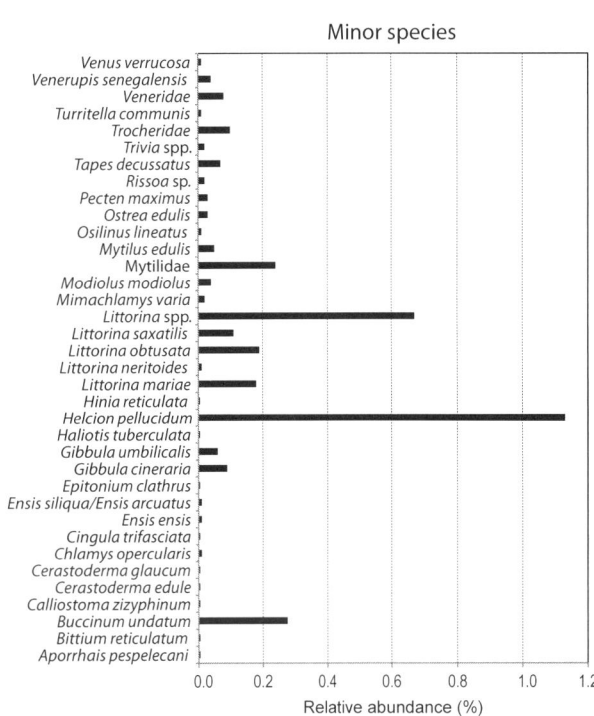

with shell elongation is an increase in wall thickness and consequently a reduction in flesh; these thick shells are "less profitable to crab predators" (Curry and Hughes 1982, 54). This would also be true for human shellfish harvesters. Reduction in animal size and the difficulty of extracting meat from a narrow aperture may have made the harvesting of *N. lapillus* unprofitable on certain very sheltered shores. Since some birds, crustaceans, and fish are known to feed on dogwhelks, it may be that the presence or absence of *N. lapillus* in west Scottish shell middens is related more to the use of this species as bait than as food, reflecting local differences in fishing customs and/or the availability of fish and crustacean species that respond well to dogwhelk bait. Dogwhelk exploitation was not necessarily restricted to use as food or bait. A purple dye can be obtained from the hypobranchial gland of *N. lapillus*, and there was a small-scale dyeing industry in medieval Ireland based on dogwhelks (Cole 1685, cited by Baker 1974). However, there is no evidence for the use of such dyes in Stone Age Scotland.

19.2. (opposite left) An Corran: relative abundance of species by MNI—all species (top), minor species (bottom).

19.3. (opposite right) Carding Mill Bay II: relative abundance of species by MNI—all species (top), minor species (bottom).

19.4. (above left) Raschoille Cave: relative abundance of species by MNI—all species (top), minor species (bottom).

19.5. (above right) Ulva Cave: relative abundance of species by MNI—all species (top), minor species (bottom).

Table 19.4. Summary of species ecology

Species/Genus	Position	Substrate	Vertical Distribution[a]
Chlamys opercularis	epifaunal	firm	intertidal
Ostrea edulis	epifaunal	firm	intertidal
Mimachlamys varia	epifaunal	firm	sublittoral
Cingula trifasciata	epifaunal	mixed	intertidal
Helcion spp.	epifaunal	mixed	low littoral
Rissoa sp.	epifaunal	mixed	mixed
Epitonium clathrus	epifaunal	mixed	sublittoral/low littoral
Trivia monacha/Trivia arctica	epifaunal	mixed	sublittoral/low littoral
Gibbula cineraria	epifaunal	rocky	intertidal
Gibbula umbilicalis	epifaunal	rocky	intertidal
Littorina littorea	epifaunal	rocky	intertidal
Littorina mariae	epifaunal	rocky	intertidal
Littorina neritoides	epifaunal	rocky	intertidal
Littorina obtusata	epifaunal	rocky	intertidal
Littorina saxatilis species-complex	epifaunal	rocky	intertidal
Littorina spp.	epifaunal	rocky	intertidal
Nucella lapillus	epifaunal	rocky	intertidal
Osilinus lineatus	epifaunal	rocky	intertidal
Patella spp.	epifaunal	rocky	intertidal
Trochidae	epifaunal	rocky	intertidal
Calliostoma zizyphinum	epifaunal	rocky	low littoral
Haliotis tuberculata	epifaunal	rocky	low littoral
Hinia reticulata	epifaunal	sands/gravel	intertidal
Buccinum undatum	epifaunal	sands/muds	low littoral
Pecten maximus	epifaunal	sands/muds	sublittoral
Veneridae	infaunal	mixed	mixed
Turritella communis	infaunal	muds/gravels	sublittoral
Tapes decussatus	infaunal	sands/gravel/mud	low littoral
Cerastoderma edule	infaunal	sands/muds	intertidal
Bittium reticulatum	infaunal	sands/muds	low littoral
Cerastoderma glaucum	infaunal	sands/muds	low littoral
Ensis ensis	infaunal	sands/muds	low littoral
Venerupis senegalensis	infaunal	sands/muds	low littoral
Venus verrucosa	infaunal	sands/muds	low littoral
Aporrhais pespelecani	infaunal	sands/muds	sublittoral from 10m
Arctica islandica	infaunal	sands/muds	sublittoral from 10m
Ensis siliqua/Ensis arcuatus	infaunal	soft	low littoral
Mytilus edulis	semi-infaunal	mixed	intertidal
Mytilidae	semi-infaunal	mixed	mixed
Modiolus modiolus	semi-infaunal	mixed	sublittoral

[a] *Vertical distribution* refers to the highest point of the shore from which the species can be harvested, not the vertical range of the species

Harvesting Strategies

Detailed consideration of species ecology may indicate harvesting practices. Shellfish collection strategies may vary depending on:

1. Horizontal distribution—The shore can be subdivided into the *littoral* and the *sublittoral* based on immersion. The littoral is the region between the limits of high and low tides (also known as the intertidal zone); the sublittoral is the region below the low-tide level of the shore. Often the vertical range of a species found in the littoral zone will extend into the sublittoral. However, a number of species occupy the sublittoral zone exclusively and are never fully emersed. While some of these sublittoral species may be collected by hand in near-shore shallows, they often inhabit deeper waters. Systematic harvesting of sublittoral species therefore involves different strategies from the gathering of intertidal species. The latter can be hand-collected in large quantities on the receding tide with little or no specialized equipment, whereas the former would require shellfishing gear such as long-handled rakes or nets, or could be gathered by divers.

2. Vertical distribution—Shellfish can also be categorized according to their vertical position: epifaunal species lie on the substrate surface, infaunal species burrow below the substrate, and semi-infaunal species will be encountered partially buried. Harvesting of infaunal species involves the greatest effort; first, the location of the shellfish must be established; then they must be gathered by digging or dredging.

The ecological preferences of the species/genera identified at the four sites under discussion are given in Table 19.4.

Epifaunal, littoral species dominate the four assemblages analyzed. In spite of the variation in individual species observed between the assemblages, consideration of the ecological preferences of the most abundant species (*Patella* spp., *Littorina* spp., *N. lapillus*, and Trochoidea) indicates that the majority of the shellfish were harvested from rocky shores (see Table 19.4). Moreover *Patella* spp., *Littorina* spp., *N. lapillus*, and Trochoidea are among the most abundant species on intertidal stretches of modern shores (Little and Kitching 1996), suggestive of unselective gathering of the shellfish readily available in the intertidal zone. If shellfishing was largely confined to the intertidal zone, then the collection of cowrie shells from the shore at low tide would likely preferentially select for *T. monacha*,

since *T. arctica* occurs in higher densities in deeper waters (Lebour 1933).

However, it is important to note that shell assemblages may embody time-averaged accumulations; individual shellfishing expeditions may have been more selective than suggested by the shell assemblages. Russell, Bonsall, and Sutherland (1995) noted the presence of pockets of shells of a single species in the Ulva Cave midden. Such pockets may represent individual harvesting episodes. This was also suggested by Joseph Anderson (1895) to account for the single-species concentrations of shells in the MacArthur Cave midden. Targeted harvesting activities are consistent with ethnographic accounts of the shellfishing practices of the Anbarra of Arnhem Land, northern Australia. Betty Meehan (1983) observed that shellfish were gathered by women and children collecting a single predetermined species on each expedition.

D. Aaron Jones (1985) demonstrated that limpet shell morphology (reflected in the length/height ratio) is a useful indicator of the shore zone from which the animal was collected. Shell morphology varies with position on the shore, reflecting emersion time. When not immersed, limpets attach strongly to rock to prevent desiccation and reduce predation risk; in this process muscle exertion causes shells in the upper shore zone to exhibit elongated height relative to overall length.

Russell, Bonsall, and Sutherland (1995) established that the morphology of limpets at Ulva Cave was consistent with collection *mainly* from the middle and lower zones of the littoral.[1] However, further work on midden samples from Ulva Cave indicates that there are areas within the midden where limpet morphology is more heterogeneous than in the samples examined by Russell, Bonsall, and Sutherland (1995)—suggesting some harvesting from the upper shore. Similar heterogeneity was apparent in some samples from An Corran (Pickard and Bonsall 1999). These observations are reinforced by the pattern of occurrence of other shellfish species. A single occurrence of *Littorina neritoides* at Ulva Cave and the more frequent presence of *Littorina saxatilis* at both An Corran and Ulva Cave suggest harvesting of shellfish from the upper shore zone. This is further supported by the co-occurrence of four species of topshell in the Ulva Cave assemblage. Competition for food results in a discrete vertical distribution of the ecologically similar topshell species (Crothers 2001). *C. zizyphinum* and *G. cineraria* inhabit the lower shore, *G. umbilicalis* the middle shore, and *O. lineatus* the upper zone.

It can be inferred from the dominance of epifaunal, littoral species that little specialized technology would have been required for shellfishing, although a wide range of expedient and specialized tools may have been utilized, e.g., digging tools and collecting baskets. As Russell, Bonsall, and Sutherland (1995) note, there has been discussion about the need for some form of hammer to remove limpets from rocks. Limpets attach strongly to rocks when not feeding, making it difficult to pry them from the slight depressions or "home scars" in which they sit. Hundreds of bevel-ended bone and/or stone implements have been recovered from sites such as MacArthur Cave and Caisteal nan Gillean I (Anderson 1898). Anderson (1898) noted the similarity of the larger examples to "limpet hammers" traditionally used to harvest limpets. Experimental limpet harvesting by Russell, Bonsall, and Sutherland (1995) found that removing limpets by direct percussion caused damage to the shell and removal by indirect percussion often resulted in shellfish loss. Janet Griffitts and Bonsall (2001) observed that it was easier to remove limpets when they were just below the waterline or submerged in rock pools. Russell, Bonsall, and Sutherland (1995) noted that limpets are most readily gathered when they are feeding, when it is often possible to remove them by hand. At this time they leave the safety of their home scars in search of food and are only weakly attached to the substrate. Limpet feeding behavior is not directly related to immersion; rather it is temporally restricted to reduce risk of predation by crabs and starfish at high tide and by birds at low tide (Little 1989; Williams et al. 1999). Limpets in the upper reaches of the shore generally feed at night, whereas those occupying the lower shore tend to feed during the day (Little 1989). Temporal variation in the feeding behavior of limpets may have influenced the scheduling of shellfishing expeditions, and nighttime gathering has been widely reported among ethnographically known shellfish gatherers (e.g., Kennedy and Bouchard 1990; Thomas 2007).

Infaunal species and sublittoral species are a consistent but secondary component of each of the middens. Infaunal species comprise a small proportion of the shell assemblages at An Corran (0.2 percent), Carding Mill Bay II (0.2 percent), Raschoille Cave (13.9 percent), and Ulva Cave (0.2 percent). As noted above, the Raschoille Cave assemblage stands out because of the relatively high proportion of infaunal bivalves represented. The presence of significant quantities of these species in conjunction with the predominance of gastropods such as limpets and topshells that have primitive gill systems and consequently are obligate inhabitants of rocky substrates suggests that either (1) a mixed foreshore existed at Raschoille cave (i.e., a combination of soft and firm substrates), or (2) shellfish were

regularly harvested from different shores and then processed and/or deposited at the site. Although Raschoille Cave is now located some distance from the modern shore, in the Middle Holocene the site would have been marginal to a sheltered inlet where a variety of substrate types would have existed near the cave, which favors the former explanation. Although the proportions of shellfish species are distinctive at Raschoille Cave, the harvesting strategy adopted is essentially the same as that observed at the other sites analyzed; in other words, there was an apparently unselective gathering of the shells available in the intertidal zone. This is suggestive of a "least effort" approach to shellfish gathering.

A survey of the distribution and abundance of infaunal bivalves conducted by the Marine Laboratory of Aberdeen reinforces this hypothesis. On average the bivalves inhabiting the coastal waters of Scotland contain more meat per individual than many gastropod species (although admittedly the gastropod *Buccinum undatum* can grow very large). Furthermore, bivalves are widely considered to be more palatable than many gastropods and as such are the primary focus of many modern commercial shellfisheries (e.g., Fernandez-Moreno et al. 2008). Bivalves *might* therefore be expected to be the target of prehistoric shellfish harvesting strategies. The Aberdeen Marine Laboratory survey recovered 39 distinct species of bivalve in Scottish coastal waters (McKay 1992). Surveys of the coastal waters of southwest and northwest Scotland (regions incorporating the sites discussed in this chapter) indicate that several of the most commonly occurring infaunal bivalves (e.g., *Dosinia exoleta, Dosinia lupinus, Lucinoma borealis*, and *Circomphalus casina*), which occupy the lower littoral zone and could have been harvested at low water with the aid of digging sticks, rakes, or nets, are notable by their absence from the middens. Combining the biology and behavior of the species represented in the midden with information on the species that are "missing" from the middens indicates that shellfishing was conducted expediently, with the most accessible and abundant species being targeted.

Of the infaunal species identified at Carding Mill Bay II, Raschoille Cave, and Ulva Cave, e.g., *Cerastoderma* spp., *Tapes decussatus, Venerupis senegalensis*, and *Venus verrucosa*, most occupy habitats a short distance (ca. five–ten centimeters) beneath the substrate surface and can be gathered relatively easily by shallow digging at low tide (Fish and Fish 1996). Razor shells (*Ensis* spp.) may be the exception to this. J. Holden (1979) claims that harvesting razor shells requires considerable skill. Although razor shells can be readily located at low tide from the characteristic keyhole-shaped cast of their burrows left on the surface of the sand, this genus can descend to depths of up to 50 centimeters when disturbed (N. S. Jones 1952) and is anecdotally reported to burrow faster than its pursuer can dig. Traditional methods of collecting razor shells include digging at low tide, salting shores (causing the razor shell to emerge from its burrow), and spearing with a small barbed projectile (Kenchington, Duggan, and Riddell 1998; von Brandt 1984). However, as with other infaunal/sublittoral species, they can sometimes be collected in large numbers on the shore following storms (Darling 1982).

A single specimen of Icelandic cyprine (*Arctica islandica*) is the only infaunal species identified at An Corran, likely reflecting the dominance of rocky and coarse gravel shores in this region of Skye, again suggestive of unselective gathering of intertidal shellfish available in the vicinity of the site. It is conceivable that the *A. islandica* specimen was collected empty from the shore or was transported to the site from elsewhere on Skye with a soft-substrate shore suited to its ecology.

Sublittoral species are surprisingly uncommon, comprising 0.02 percent of the total assemblage at An Corran, 0.04 percent at Carding Mill Bay II, 0.39 percent at Raschoille Cave, and 0.10 percent at Ulva Cave. Many sublittoral species are important commercially exploited foods today and are observed ethnographically to be used for food and raw materials.

Modiolus modiolus is generally reported to be a sublittoral species and is abundant in waters deeper than ten meters. However *Modiolus modiolus* does occupy the very shallow sublittoral at low densities (Dinesen and Ockelmann 2005). The very small quantities of *Modiolus modiolus* recovered are not suggestive of systematic gathering of even shallow sublittoral species.

Two sublittoral species of scallop, king scallop (*Pecten maximus*) and black scallop (*Mimachlamys varia*), also occur in small quantities in each of the shell middens (0.01 percent at An Corran, 0.04 percent at Carding Mill Bay II, 0.19 percent at Raschoille Cave, and 0.04 percent at Ulva Cave). As with *Modiolus modiolus* there is a widely held perception that the distribution of adult *P. maximus* is restricted to waters in excess of ten meters depth (Marshall and Wilson 2009). The Ama of Japan, among the best known traditional divers, regularly dive to collect shellfish, sea urchins, and octopus. Unassisted, the Ama generally dive to depths considerably less than ten meters (Hong et al. 1991; Hong and Rahn 1967). Low temperatures and limited visibility in Scottish coastal waters may have placed further restrictions on free diving; diving for

deeper-water scallops in the early to mid-Holocene in west Scotland is unlikely. However, the current distribution of *P. maximus* in British coastal waters may reflect recent overfishing. Accounts by modern scallop divers suggest that distributions have changed significantly within the last 30 years in the British Isles. Until recently, large scallops were reportedly harvested in waters considerably less than 2.5 meters deep (Mason 1983). Although scallops *may* have been available in the shallow sublittoral at the time of midden accumulation, *regular* diving for sublittoral species still seems unlikely. This is inferred from the relative scarcity of scallop shells in the middens analyzed, reinforced by evidence that some of these at least were collected as empty shells on the shore, presumably for use as raw material (Russell, Bonsall, and Sutherland 1995).

Other sublittoral and infaunal species are very rare in the midden assemblages, which suggests that they were not regularly exploited. Two specimens of common pelican's foot (*Aporrhais pespelecani*) and several tower shells (*Turritella communis*) were identified at Ulva Cave. As with the scallop shells it is possible that these species were gathered empty from the shore. The lack of sublittoral and infaunal species at each of the sites investigated further supports the hypothesis of a "least effort" shellfishing strategy.

INCIDENTAL SPECIES

Russell, Bonsall, and Sutherland (1995) reported the presence of significant numbers of very small shells at Ulva Cave, including those of *L. littorea*, *N. lapillus*, and *Helcion pellucidum*, which they argued were too small to have been collected as food or bait and had probably been transported to the site attached to seaweed.

Helcion (rayed limpets) attach to laminarian species and fucoid seaweeds (Graham and Fretter 1947). The form of *Helcion* varies according to the part of the seaweed to which it attaches. On the basis of this habitat-induced morphological variation, Graham and Fretter (1947) suggested that *Helcion* should be attributed to two species: *H. pellucidum*, which inhabits the fronds of seaweeds and has an oval form with an off-center apex; while *H. laevis*, which occupies the holdfasts of seaweeds, is flatter and more irregular in shape, with a roughly central apex. The two species of *Helcion* also have distinctive shell coloring; *H. laevis* has up to 46 alternating red/brown and green rays whereas *H. pellucidum* has up to 8 blue rays (Graham and Fretter 1947). Although the periostracum (and therefore distinguishing color) is absent, the specimens recovered from Ulva Cave display variable form and both morphs may be represented.

In addition to the incidental species identified by Russell, Bonsall, and Sutherland (1995), there are several other economically unimportant species (i.e., small species or specimens with little flesh that are not particularly rare or decorative) at Ulva Cave and the other sites included in this study. Two species of flat periwinkle (*L. obtusata* and *L. mariae*) fall into this category and, like the rayed limpet, may have found their way onto the sites attached to seaweeds. Small specimens (some as small as three millimeters in length) of flat periwinkles occur consistently throughout the midden deposits at An Corran, Carding Mill Bay II, and Ulva Cave. Both species attach to brown algae on which they feed (Williams 1990a); however, they occupy distinct micro-algal zones (Ekendahl 1995). *L. mariae* attaches to toothed wrack (*Fucus serratus*), whereas *L. obtusata* is found on knotted wrack (*Ascophyllum nodosum*) or bladderwrack (*Fucus vesiculosis*) (Reimchen 1979; Williams 1990b). At Raschoille Cave the relative abundance of flat periwinkle in certain contexts is suggestive of episodic increase in seaweed exploitation. Generally regarded as a species targeted for use as raw material because of the perforated specimens found in abundance at the Oronsay middens (D. A. Jones 1984, 1985), *Trivia* spp. may also have entered the midden deposits on seaweeds; the ascidians on which they feed often attach to seagrasses (*Zostera* spp.) (Lebour 1933). The sea snail *Cingula trifasciata* and other members of the Rissoidae have been found at Carding Mill Bay II, Raschoille Cave, and Ulva Cave. These species are associated with knotted wrack and other algae (Viejo and Aberg 2003). A further small species, the needlewhelk (*Bittium reticulatum*), which was identified at Ulva Cave and Raschoille Cave, is commonly found on eelgrass, *Zostera* spp., and knotted wrack. Thus, on this evidence, a wide range of different seaweeds appears to have been systematically harvested. Russell, Bonsall, and Sutherland (1995) suggested that the seaweed was collected for use in food processing, either as fuel or for wrapping around fish or shellfish prior to baking in open fires. This interpretation was supported by the presence of pieces of vitreous slag in the Ulva Cave midden thought to have resulted from the burning of seaweed.

Not all of the incidental species/specimens identified are associated with seaweeds. Common wentletrap (*Epitonium clathrus*), for example, feeds on sea anemones such as *Anemonia sulcata* (Gittenberger 2003). Generally sublittoral, needlewhelks migrate to the lower shore in spring and summer to breed. Large populations are frequently washed ashore en masse and can be readily gathered in littoral regions at this time (Billiau 2006). Needlewhelks seldom exceed 40 millimeters in length, and as such are economically unimportant; however, they may have been collected for the purple dye they exude when distressed (Keen 1958).

Acorn barnacles, the calcareous plates of which are well represented in each of the shell assemblages discussed, are also likely to have been transported to the site unintentionally, attached to a range of objects such as stones, seaweed, and driftwood as well as shells.

Processing Strategies

Ethnographic and ethnohistoric accounts of processing practices indicate that shellfish intended for human consumption are often cooked. Cooking may not relate directly to palatability and is more often undertaken to extract the shellfish flesh; the easiest way to obtain the meat of bivalves is by heating the shellfish. Many gastropod species (including limpets and periwinkles) are also reported to be easier to remove from their shells if the animal is first killed by immersion in boiling water. The large number of intact periwinkles recovered from each of the assemblages analyzed may reflect cooking to aid meat extraction. Unfortunately the most common forms of cooking recorded, for example boiling, steaming, or baking, are of short duration and generally leave little trace on the shell (Waselkov 1987). Although cooking activities are suggested by the presence of charred shells at An Corran, Carding Mill Bay II, and Ulva Cave, burnt shell constitutes only a very small proportion of the shell assemblages (<1 percent by weight) and as such does not provide evidence for the systematic cooking of shellfish. It is important to note, however, that the majority of the burnt shell fragments at Ulva Cave and Carding Mill Bay II were *Littorina* spp. possibly reflecting the widespread practice of heating these gastropods to facilitate meat extraction. Multiple hearths and burnt lenses of shells attest to cooking activities at the Oronsay shell middens dated to the Late Mesolithic, ca. 5100–4300 cal BC (Mellars 1987). Russell, Bonsall, and Sutherland (1995) reported a "Neolithic cooking pit" at Ulva Cave containing carbonized cereal grains, charcoal, and shell fragments, but new single-entity ^{14}C dates on carbonized cereal grains conflict with a previous radiometric ^{14}C date on charcoal and suggest the pit feature is probably of Medieval date (Bonsall, unpublished data).

As at Ulva Cave (cf. Russell, Bonsall, and Sutherland 1995), *N. lapillus* specimens from An Corran are more fragmented than the shells of *L. littorea*. Often the spires of the *N. lapillus* specimens have been removed. Since dogwhelks generally have thicker, more robust shells than periwinkles, this evidence suggests deliberate breakage of dogwhelks rather than post-depositional damage. D. A. Jones (1984) notes a similar pattern of damage to dogwhelks in the Oronsay assemblages. Breaking the spire is an effective way of accessing the shellfish meat. This is demonstrated on sheltered shores by the approach taken by crabs to exploiting *N. lapillus*; rather than trying to fracture the aperture with their chelae, the crabs attempt to crack open the top of the shell (Hughes and Elner 1979).

Food versus Bait

Shellfish are widely exploited today as both food and bait. Many of the most commercially valuable food species (e.g., *Ensis* spp., *Ostrea edulis*, and *Pecten maximus*) are widely considered to be the most effective baits. *Ensis* spp. are particularly prized for their efficacy in catching a wide range of fish species (Darling 1982). By contrast, the predominant shellfish in Early-Middle Holocene middens in western Scotland, *Patella* spp., are widely perceived today as poor tasting and useful only as fish bait. In traditional Scottish fisheries, limpets and periwinkles are reported to have been commonly used as bait (Fenton 1984), but they are also widely documented to have been used as food (e.g., Fenton 1997), and modern informants who have actually tasted limpets often find them to be very palatable, especially when baked.

Margaret R. Deith (1989) argued that shells intentionally broken to extract the meat were likely to have been used as bait, whereas shells that had been heated were human food. It might be inferred from such a statement that many of the shells found in the middens, such as the fractured dogwhelks at Ulva Cave, were collected for use as bait for fish and crustaceans. As Russell, Bonsall, and Sutherland (1995) point out, recent shellfish processing strategies often involve shucking or breaking of shells to extract meat for human food. Gregory A. Waselkov (1987) noted that shellfish are often consumed with shell fragments left in the meat. Patterns of fracture are therefore not a reliable indicator of intended use.

Two things follow from this: one is that ethnocentric evaluations of shellfish palatability should be treated with caution; the other is that it would be difficult to distinguish intended use on the basis of species representation alone. There are few features that distinguish food assemblages from bait assemblages. Arguably, the shell assemblage from Ulva Cave is more consistent with food use given the evidence for collection of potential fuels (e.g., seaweeds) for on-site cooking activities and the recovery of burnt

shells at the site. Moreover, during the Early-Middle Holocene, Ulva Cave was at least 350 meters from the shoreline in very rugged terrain, and it seems improbable that shellfish intended for bait would have been transported to the cave for processing prior to use, and much more likely that they would have been processed and the shells discarded on the shore.

Use of Shellfish as Raw Material and the Manufacture of Artifacts

Many coast-dwelling communities, both archaeologically and ethnographically documented, made use of shells for the manufacture of artifacts (Stewart 1977; Waselkov 1987). The collection of shells for raw material rather than food or bait can be established in archaeological assemblages by the presence of (1) encrustation of the interior surface of the shell or perforation by carnivorous gastropods, both of which would indicate that the shell had been collected empty, (2) use-wear, and (3) manufacturing traces reflecting deliberate modification for use as utensils or decorative objects. Such evidence occurs relatively infrequently in the shell assemblages analyzed.

It may be inferred from the presence of true sublittoral species (as discussed above) that certain shells were collected empty from the shore. Fragments of common pelican's foot (*A. pespelecani*) were identified in the Ulva Cave assemblage. This species has two subspecies, one of which, *A. pespelecani pespelecani*, is more abundant in southern European waters today; the other, *A. pespelecani bilobatus*, is more commonly found in Boreal Atlantic waters. Both subspecies have been found in the offshore waters of the west coast of Scotland. The remains from Ulva Cave are too fragmentary to identify to subspecies level, particularly given the morphometric variation observed within each subspecies. It is likely, given the species ecology (infaunal at depths of greater than 10 meters), that this shell was collected empty on the shore and may have attracted the attention of prehistoric beachcombers because of its unusual, highly decorative form.

At An Corran two *Trivia* spp. shells were recovered; neither of these specimens was perforated, but it is likely they were collected for use as raw material or introduced attached to seaweed. Perforated examples of *Trivia* spp. were found in the Ulva Cave assemblage. A single example with a double perforation was recovered from the upper part of the midden and a further example with quadruple perforations was identified in the lower midden deposits. Unperforated *Trivia* spp. shells were also present. The quantities of *Trivia* spp. from An Corran and Ulva Cave are insignificant when compared to the much larger numbers reported from the Oronsay sites (Bishop 1914; Mellars 1987), perhaps reflecting differences in behavior patterns between sites.

A. Henderson Bishop (1914) reported the presence in a Mesolithic shell midden on Oronsay of *P. maximus* shells with edges that were worn by use, and interpreted them as having served as scoops or ladles. Similarly, Paul A. Mellars (1987) reported finds of *P. maximus* shells with edge wear and manufacturing traces from other sites on Oronsay; while Anderson (1895) described finds of *P. maximus* shells from MacArthur Cave, which were thought to have been used as scoops. Shells of *P. maximus* were recovered in small quantities from An Corran, Carding Mill Bay II, and Raschoille Cave; however, they are not obviously modified and there is no indication that they were used as tools or utensils. *P. maximus* was more abundant at Ulva Cave but the shells are highly abraded, although several fragments have wear and polish on the edge that may have resulted from use. Similar wear has been observed on the lower valves of *Ostrea edulis* shells at Ulva Cave. A more detailed study of these finds involving microscopic examination of the edges will be necessary in order to determine if and how the shells were used.

As noted above, the single valve of *A. islandica* from the midden deposits at An Corran may also have been collected as raw material. The edges of this specimen are highly abraded, and no obvious traces of use or manufacturing are evident.

CONCLUSIONS

Our synthesis of the data from four coastal shell middens in western Scotland has provided new insights into the human use of shellfish by Mesolithic and Neolithic groups and into the cultural significance of the middens.

The relative abundance of the species identified at each of the four sites analyzed suggests that the focus of shellfishing activities was epifaunal species, unselectively harvested from the intertidal zone of the shore in the vicinity of the site. The rarity of infaunal and sublittoral species at each site analyzed further suggests that shellfishing was a "least effort" foraging strategy.

The systematic collection of seaweeds is suggested by the consistent occurrence of incidental species. Evidence for the use of seaweed as fuel and the presence of charred shells is consistent with heating shellfish to extract meat.

Although shellfish may have been collected as fish bait, it is likely that shellfish transported back to sites such as Ulva Cave, which was located some distance from the contemporaneous shoreline, were collected as food. Processing of shellfish for bait is likely to have taken place at fishing grounds, namely, close to the shore.

Several species of sublittoral shellfish appear to have been collected in small numbers for use as raw material. Only a small proportion of these shells bears traces of modification. None of these species appears to have been systematically harvested, and they were most likely opportunistically gathered during shellfishing expeditions along the foreshore, reinforcing the impression of a least effort gathering strategy.

NOTE

1. Caution must be exercised in the use of shell morphology as an absolute marker of shore position. Populations of *P. ulyssiponensis* and juvenile *P. vulgata* may permanently inhabit rock-pools in mid- and upper-shore regions (Delany, Myers, and McGrath 2002, Noël et al. 2009). In such locations limpets are continuously submerged, and shell morphology might be expected to mimic that of low-shore populations. Moreover, prolonged periods of storminess and strong wave action have elongating effects on shells from the lower- and mid-shore zones (Yonge 1972). Martha V. Andrews and colleagues (1987) identified changes in *N. lapillus* morphology in the Oronsay shell assemblages that were linked to variations in storm frequency during the Holocene, suggesting that shell morphometry may not be a straightforward measure of shore position.

CHAPTER TWENTY

ETHNOARCHAEOLOGY AND RESIDUE ANALYSIS IN FISHER-HUNTER-GATHERER SITES

A Pilot Study

Ivan Briz i Godino, Débora Zurro, Myrian Álvarez, and Marco Madella

SUMMARY

This chapter demonstrates exploratory research carried out in the shell midden context of Lanashuaia from the Beagle Channel (Tierra del Fuego, Argentina), a dwelling of the Yamana hunter-fisher-gatherer group. The aim of this pilot study has been to outline a method for the recovery of different types of residues from lithics. Field sampling methodology and laboratory procedures are discussed. Different techniques, such as use-wear and phytolith analyses, and tests for the identification of blood residues have been applied to an assemblage of 34 lithic artifacts.

INTRODUCTION

The analysis of the dynamics of resource management strategies and processes is one of the keys to understanding the change and the historical trajectories in the socioeconomic organization of fisher-hunter-gatherer groups. Within this approach, we are developing a project that addresses the analysis of the consumption and production strategies and the social organization of hunter-gatherer-fisher groups in Tierra del Fuego, right before and during European colonization. Key issues such as the use of social space, the strategies for managing different resources, or the particular modes in which tools were used are some of the archaeological goals of our research.

The study of tools is a key element for this endeavor. Considering the need of a holistic approach in sampling and in studying a variety of evidence, we propose an integrated methodological framework for the recovery of residues on stone tools that combines several analytical lines that will serve to identify the strategies of resource procurement and consumption by fisher-hunter-gatherer societies of the northern coast of the Beagle Channel.

To reach this goal, technomorphological and use-wear analysis are routine analyses of these materials. Use-wear analysis was first proposed by Sergei Semenov (1964) and remains one of the best methods of identifying the dynamics of production and consumption of resources in past societies, by using a lithic assemblage (Anderson-Gerfaud 1981; Keeley 1980; Mansur-Franchomme 1983; Semenov 1964; among others). According to this methodological framework, the formation of traces of wear is a dynamic and a complex process involving different variables, such as the length of time during which the artifact was used, the humidity present in the contact zone, the type of raw material from which the artifact is made or the material is worked (e.g., Hurcombe 1992; Keeley 1980; Lerner et al. 2007; Mansur 1999). Consequently, a precise recognition of the worked material relies on the interplay of those variables. Thus, this methodology detects the broad types of material worked, such as hide, wood, herbaceous plants, bone, or horn, but it does not distinguish organic materials at a taxonomical level. Furthermore, the action of post-depositional agents may mask the traces of use, preventing an accurate identification of worked materials.

On the other hand, the analysis of residues preserved on tool edges,[1] as well as those preserved in the micro-polished layer, was one of the main directions of research from the very beginning (see for example Anderson-Gerfaud 1980, 1981, 1986; Mansur-Franchomme 1983; Shafer and Holloway 1979; among others). In the past few years, this analytical trend has acquired a new impetus,[2] and it is now combined with a thorough comparative examination of the sediments in which the artifacts were found and the subsequent or parallel analysis of the microtraces of use (Barton, Torrence, and Fullagar 1998; Kealhofer, Torrence, and Fullagar 1999).

In order to improve the sampling method, and also to generate multiple subsamples for each piece (so as to apply various analyses), the pilot study presented here was designed to accomplish the following objectives:

1. Design and test the analytical procedures for recovering residues from lithic materials, and

2. Evaluate and compare the preservation of residues from a small lithic assemblage from a very controlled archaeological site.

The proposed methodology is articulated around four main axes of analysis and interpretation:

• Analysis of the residues by detecting the presence and type of residues on lithic artifacts;

• Use-wear analysis of the lithic assemblage from a techno-economical perspective;

• Identification of correlation/non-correlation between use-wear evidence and residue evidence;

• Testing of the sampling and analysis design.

We discuss the preliminary results of applying this method to a pilot assemblage from the archaeological site of Lanashuaia I, a shell midden located on the coast of the Beagle Channel (Piana, Estévez, and Vila 2000). The final aim is to integrate the methodology as a routine in current protocols for the study of the materials in these contexts, but we also expect to determine criteria to create general routines to be applied elsewhere.

CHANNELS, MIDDENS, AND CANOES: THE SITE OF LANASHUAIA I

Lanashuaia I (54°52'75"S, 67°16'49"W) is situated in the inner Cambaceres Bay, on the northern coast of the Beagle Channel, in the Isla Grande of Tierra del Fuego (Argentina) (Figure 20.1). The area is characterized by islands of different size and waterways that extend from the Beagle Channel and its prolongations right up to the Cape of Horn. It has been inhabited by fisher-hunter-gatherer societies since at least 6000 BP (Orquera and Piana 1999a), ethnographically identified as Yaghán or Yámana, who lived in this area until

the beginning of the 20th century (Gusinde 1986 [1937]; Hyades and Deniker 1891; Lothrop 2002 [1928]).

Lanashuaia I is a typical archaeological site of this coastal area: a ring-shaped shell midden formed by the progressive accumulation of residues of different activities of production and consumption around the habitation unit (Orquera and Piana 1992). The site is part of a remarkable alignment of ring structures that is especially striking because the distance that separates them suggests a pattern possibly linked to the organization of the social space (Figure 20.2). Furthermore, the different structures are situated at the same level above the sea (Piana, Estévez, and Vila 2000). All of these characteristics led to the hypothesis that the structures could be various dwelling units representing a synchronous occupation that could be linked to the processes of exploitation and consumption of a juvenile Minke whale (*Balaenoptera acutorostrata*) (Álvarez et al. 2009; Piana, Estévez, and Vila 2000). Radiocarbon dating carried out recently by the authors gave results of (CNA 301) 1160 ± 70 and (CNA 302) 1160 ± 60 BP.

METHODOLOGY

Field Sampling Strategy

Lanashuaia I was excavated for three seasons in 1995, 1996, and 2005 as part of different projects undertaken in collaboration between Argentinean and Catalan teams.[3] During the first two seasons, the aim was to investigate the socioeconomic dynamics at the beginning of the European contact (19th century). New excavations at Lanashuaia I were undertaken in 2005 to understand the socioeconomic practices that took place inside and outside the habitation unit (e.g., the pattern of management of social space). Lanashuaia I thus offered a starting point for planning and designing the methodological and analytical procedures for the recovery of organic and inorganic remains from archaeological artifacts. The sampling strategy required the selection of both lithic artifacts and control samples of the sediment in which each artifact was contextualized.

Different criteria were employed for selecting the artifacts on which residue analyses would be carried out:

• Spatial location: representative samples were taken from inside and outside the dwelling unit.

• Association: artifacts that might have been part of the same work processes (on the basis of their spatial nearness) were selected.

• Size of the artifacts: only those whose main axis was over 20 millimeters in length were systematically

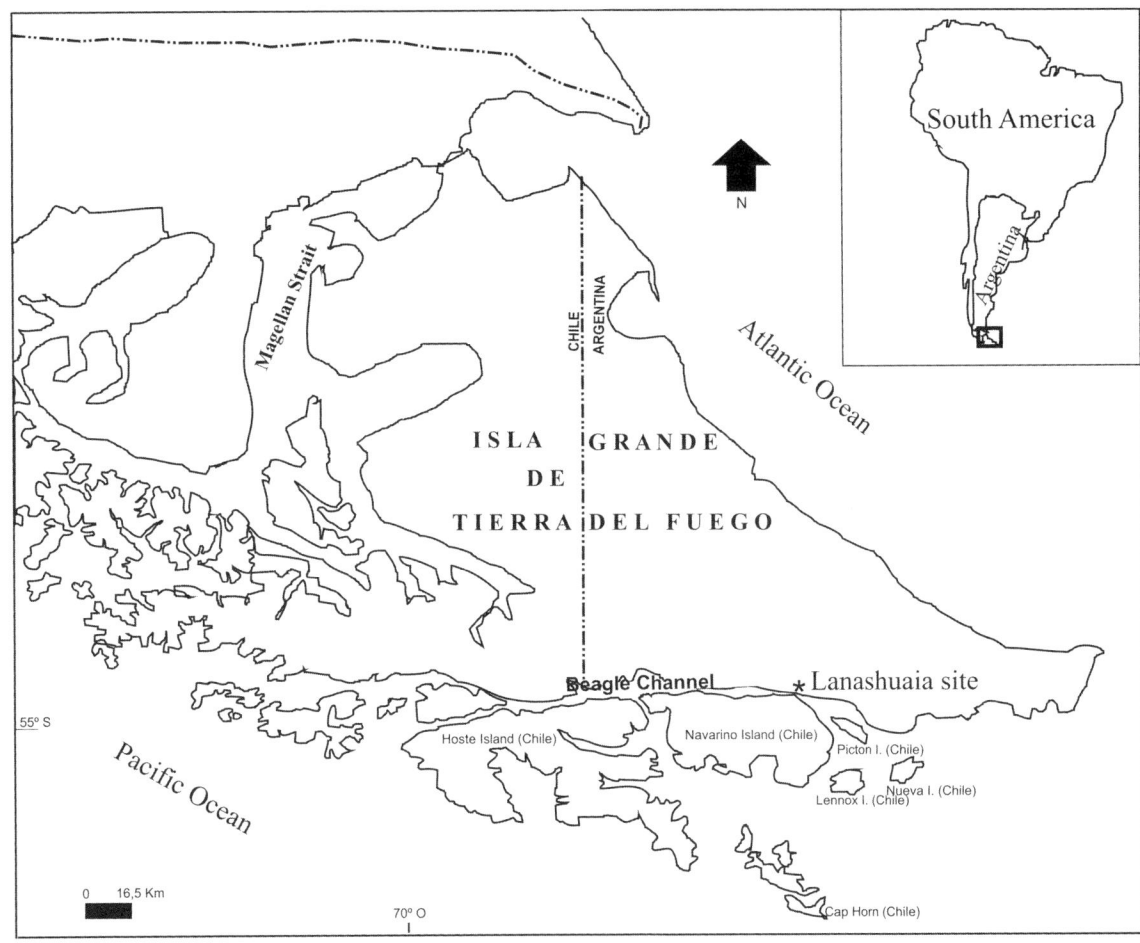

20.1. Map of Tierra del Fuego.

selected for ease of handling at this preliminary stage of the project.

The analysis of residues within an approach that hopes to explore patterns in lithic assemblages depends on the existence of a relationship between the type of residue found on the artifact and the morpho-technical and economical characteristics of the artifact to which it is associated (Álvarez et al. 2009; Briz 2004). For this, it is necessary to be certain that the plant or animal remains recovered from the tool edge of an instrument strictly correspond to the original work process (or to one of them, considering the potential multifunctionality of the tools) and is not the result of a possible contamination (due to the depositional context or to post-depositional phenomena. It is also possible that the tool was laid on the same surface where the processing was taking place, so that the same residue is in the control sample as well as in the tool. For this reason, each artifact was recovered together with a

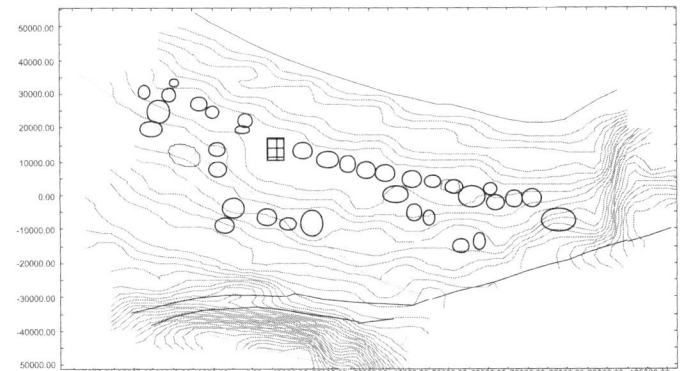

20.2. Alignment of shell middens in Lanashuaia (inner Camba-ceres Bay, Beagle Channel) (topography by J. Estévez). Circles represent the different dwelling units (shell middens) identified in the area. The grid represents the excavation of the site Lanashuaia I. Dotted lines represent the fence next to the site.

Table 20.1. List of lithic artifacts that have been analyzed

Sample	Square[a]	Layer
7006	H7	B2
7007	H7	B2
7010	H7	B2
7013	H7	B2
7015	H7	B2
7020	H7	B2
7021	H7	B2
7027	H7	B2
7432	J10	B800 base over pebble layer
7433	J10	B800 base over pebble layer
7438	J10	B800 base over pebble layer
7446	I11	C200
7452	I11	C200
7475	J12	B900
7581	J12	B900
7582	J12	B900
7583	J10	B900
7584	J10	B900
7585	J10	B900
7586	J10	B900
7587	J10	B900
7589	J10	B900
7590	J10	B900
7591	J10	B900
7604	J11	B900
7605	J11	B900
7606	J11	B900
7607	J11	B900
7608	J11	B900
7609	J11	B900
7610	J11	B900
7616	J11	B900
7617	J11	B900

[a] "Square" shows the location within the grid.

control sample (named "Sample C"[4]) of the sediment in which it was contextualized and that potentially (through contact, treading, or other taphonomic processes) could have contaminated the sample. These samples are kept in case there is the need to contrast results.

The retrieval of the control samples was not a simple task and involved considering beforehand the volume of the sample to be collected, up to what distance from the tool it would be collected, and whether it would come from all around the tool or just from along the used edge.[5] It was decided to determine in an a priori manner the edge that potentially was used, basing the decision on criteria such as the length of the edge and the degree/type of associated secondary trimming, as well as on the basis of previous results of use-wear analysis undertaken in similar contexts in the region (Álvarez 2003; Clemente 1995). Thus the sediment associated with the chosen edge was taken as the control sample. In the case of artifacts for which reasonable doubts existed, samples from various edges were taken. The samples were taken from different depositional units:

- Layers with names starting with "B" are fine-grained deposits of humus composition located around the shell midden ring.
- Layers with names starting with "C" are shell midden (in Spanish, *concheros*) units containing almost entirely shells.

In the following pages we show the methods and results obtained from a first group of 34 cases,[6] from different depositional contexts including layers B2, the base of B800 and B900, and two samples (7446 and 7452) from the shell midden layer C200 (see Table 20.1).

Laboratory Procedure

The laboratory procedure was divided into different stages of processing and analysis, including a first stage to test the existence of residues of animal origin and, in a secondary step, the extraction of phytoliths.

Before undertaking any type of cleaning or treatment that could have affected the conservation of possible residues, a basic exploratory test for contact with soft animal tissues was undertaken (see Table 20.2). The test consisted of the direct application of benzidine ($C_{12}H_{12}N_2/NH_2C_6H_4$-$C_6H_4NH_2$, n° CAS 92-87-5), a chemical reactive that produces a chromatic reaction in contact with blood that is commonly used in forensic investigations.[7]

Table 20.2. Results of blood tests carried out in comparison to use-wear analysis and phytolith analysis results[a]

A. Sample	B. Use-wear Analysis	C. Layer	D. Animal Residue tests	E. Phytoliths on Slide
7446	Hard material cutting	C200	Negative	3
7452	Bone cutting	C200	Negative	0
7475	Unknown worked material	B900	Positive	79 (taph.)
7581	Unknown worked material	B900	Positive	74
7583	Unknown worked material	B900	Positive	154
7584	Non-used	B900	Positive	105
7585	Bone cutting	B900	Negative	273
7586	Non-used	B900	Positive	3.829
7587	Non-used	B900	Negative	472
7589	Bone cutting	B900	Positive	67
7590	Non-used	B900	Positive	38
7605	Non-used	B900	Positive	4 (indet. + taph.)
7606	Non-used	B900	Positive	85
7608	Unknown worked material	B900	Positive	339
7609	Non-used	B900	Negative	72 (indet. + arboreal)
7610	Non-used	B900	Negative	7
7616	Non-used	B900	Positive	78
7617	Non-used	B900	Positive	817

[a] Clear tendencies in the phytolith spectra are shown when possible. In this table blood tests refer to the pseudoperoxidative activity of the hemoglobin and myoglobin. For further information, see Figure 20.3. Column E. shows the number of phytoliths on slide (that is, the whole residue). This result can be achieved through calculating a proportion in those samples that were very rich or through the total screening of the slide surface. Those samples with a particular tendency in the composition of the phytolith assemblage have been labeled.

After this first test, pieces that presented less exfoliation of the edges were selected. The active surface of each artifact was cleaned, spraying it with distilled water. The runoff was then collected as a liquid sample (called Sample M0). Reactive strips were then applied to the samples M0, again so as to detect the possible presence of blood on the basis of the pseudoperoxidative activity of the hemoglobin and myoglobin. Despite the various samples that gave positive results indicating the presence of blood, it is important to underline the strictly exploratory nature of this application from a methodological point of view. This will remain so until we can evaluate the methodology's capabilities vis à vis the results with other analyses. Indeed, the difference in results obtained using the two blood tests is an element that must be taken into consideration when planning this type of work in future excavations.

Once the analysis of residues of animal origin was carried out, the next stage was to explore the presence of plant residues, focusing on the recovery of the phytoliths that were potentially bonded with the active tool edges. In this case, the whole initial set was analyzed. The selected edges of the artifacts were washed using a solution of 10 percent hydrochloric acid in an ultrasound to detach the phytoliths. This liquid suspension was named "Sample A."

These suspensions were placed in 15-milliliter tubes with distilled water and centrifuged at 1,000 revolutions per minute for three minutes for three successive washings in order to eliminate the hydrochloric acid. After this step, we applied a modified version of the phytolith extraction method proposed by Marco Madella and colleagues (1998). First, a solution of 5 percent sodium hexametaphosphate was added in order to deflocculate the sample, after which oxygenated water at 33 percent was added so as to eliminate organic matter. After the addition of each chemical product, the samples were washed following the same procedure described previously for eliminating the HCl. All of the residues were then dried by adding ethanol and were mounted on slides

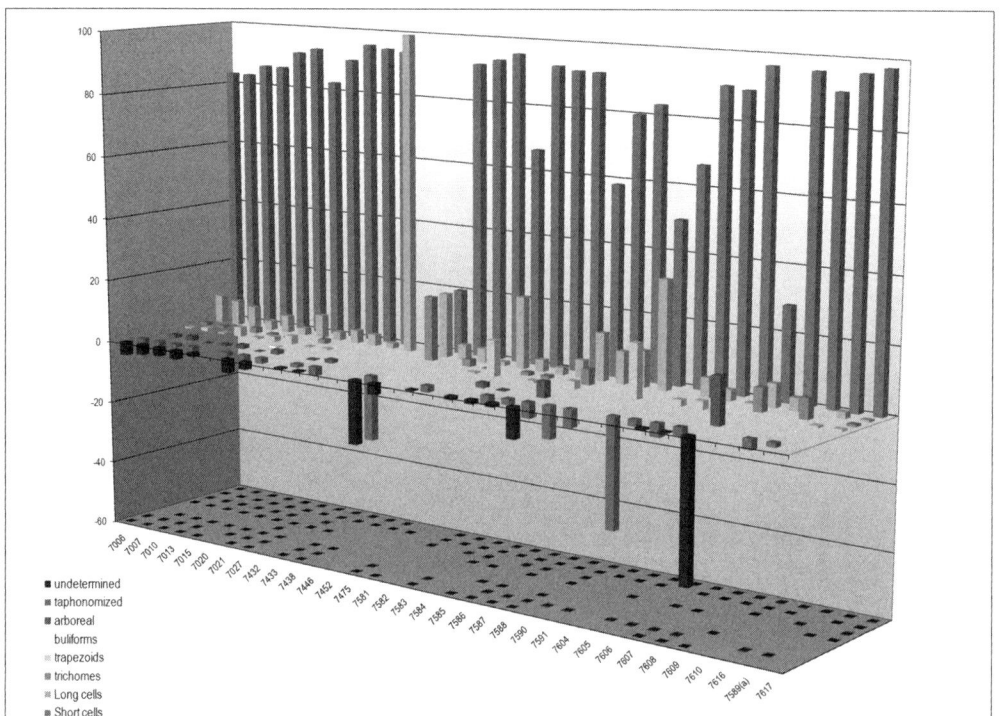

20.3. Phytolith spectra recovered from the samples.

for observation under the microscope (an Olympus BX microscope with a 400x magnification).

At the same time, all the artifacts analyzed for the presence of residues were also observed with an Olympus BHSM optical microscope with a magnification of between 50x and 500x for detecting the presence of macrotraces and microtraces of use (*sensu* Mansur 1999). Before this microscopic examination, it is necessary to clean the artifacts, which were hand-washed with water and mild detergent and were then wiped with ethylic alcohol. This process makes it difficult to select pieces for residue analyses before doing use-wear exploration. Due to the peculiar characteristics of the raw materials used on the north coast of the Beagle Channel, the use-wear analysis followed the guidelines proposed by María Estela Mansur (1999) for crystalline rocks of coarse granulometry. The process of use-wear development on these kinds of rocks is relatively slow compared to flint (Álvarez 2003; Mansur 1999).

RESULTS

By undertaking the proposed analyses on each single artifact, we were able first and foremost to test the possible problems arising from applying the methodology. For instance, some of the artifacts that were part of the sample fractured due to freeze and thaw cycles (i.e., the physicochemical alteration of the structure due to the water

freezing in the microfractures of the rock; Briz 2004; Terradas 1996), so they were unsuitable for part of the residue analysis protocol.

The tests to detect residues of animal origin by using benzidine were all negative. This was somehow expected, since the test was carried out with the sediments still attached to the tool edges, which made the process of applying the chemical to the stone tool extremely difficult. On the other hand, there were some positives for the second blood residue test, which used reactive strips for hemoglobin and myoglobin identification (see Table 20.2).

The microscopic analysis was carried out counting a minimum of 150 phytoliths. For the slides that contained less than 150 phytoliths, a minimum of 10 transects were observed. The phytolith analysis highlighted a large quantitative variability (Figure 20.3). Some interesting trends can be drawn from this study regarding the shell midden contexts of Tierra del Fuego. First, the values of the samples from layer B900 were noticeably less than those of layer B2 and of the base of B800 (see Table 20.1). The only two exceptions are artifacts 7586 and 7617 (both recovered from layer B900), which exhibit a relatively high quantity of phytoliths. In both cases, use-wear analysis demonstrated that these artifacts were not used.

It is also important to underline that phytoliths were almost completely absent from the samples extracted from the shell midden, except for artifacts 7446 and 7452. The fact that only two artifacts tested positive for the presence of phytoliths does not enable us to discuss this residue in any great detail. Indeed, according to microwear traces, artifact 7452 was used for bone cutting, while artifact 7446 was used to cut a hard material. Although the micropolish is not well developed, the relatively intense brightness, the distribution (covering the higher parts of the tool surface), and the notable level of edge-damage are also compatible with bone working. Therefore, it does seem to indicate that the phytoliths were not related to the worked edge of the tool (there seems to be no pattern in this sense) but to the sediment matrix, which acted as a contaminating element. This hypothesis does not, however, explain the enormous variability, both qualitative and quantitative,[8] from layers in which phytoliths were present.[9]

In most samples, the phytolith spectrum (Table 20.3) is characterized by grasses (e.g., long and short cells,[10] bulliforms, trichomes, and trapeziforms), with a much lower presence of types from woody species (Figure 20.3 and Table 20.3). On the contrary, artifact sample 7609 includes 14 percent of phytoliths from an arboreal origin.[11] This artifact also has a high percentage of nonidentified phytoliths. This result is probably due to the fact that phytoliths of arboreal origin often have forms such as blocks and irregular shapes that are difficult to ascribe. Surprisingly, the microscopic analysis of this piece does not reveal the presence of wear traces; on the contrary, the appearance of the edge allows us to infer that it was not used.

The data from indeterminate and strongly taphonomized phytoliths is indicated by "-" markers in Table 20.3.

Table 20.3. Composition of the phytolith spectrum

Sample	Use-wear analysis	undet.		GRASSES												ARBOREAL		taphonomized		TOTAL
				short cells		long cells		bulliforms		trapezoids		trichomes								
7006	Non-used	10	4.3%	21	8.9%	196	83.4%	0	0%	1	0.4%	2	0.9%	0	0%	5	2.1%	**235**		
7007	Non-used	9	3.3%	22	8%	229	83.3%	0	0%	3	1.1%	2	0.7%	3	1.1%	7	2.5%	**275**		
7010	Non-used	8	2.8%	19	6.7%	244	86.2%	0	0%	1	0.4%	4	1.4%	4	1.4%	3	1.1%	**282**		
7013	Non-used	5	2.9%	5	2.9%	147	86.5%	0	0%	5	2.9%	3	1.8%	0	0%	5	2.9%	**170**		
7015	Non-used	2	1.2%	9	5.4%	153	91.6%	0	0%	1	0.6%	1	0.6%	1	0.6%	0	0%	**167**		
7020	Non-used	0	0%	5	2.1%	218	93.2%	0	0%	4	1.7%	1	0.4%	3	1.3%	3	1.3%	**234**		
7021	Non-used	8	4.5%	13	7.3%	148	82.7%	1	0.6%	5	2.8%	0	0%	0	0%	4	2.2%	**179**		
7027	Non-used	13	2.5%	14	2.7%	472	90.2%	0	0%	1	0.2%	7	1.3%	7	1.3%	9	1.7%	**523**		
7432	Non-used	0	0%	9	4.1%	210	95.5%	0	0%	1	0.5%	0	0%	0	0%	0	0%	**220**		
7433	Non-used	2	0.5%	13	3.5%	348	94.6%	0	0%	0	0%	0	0%	1	0.3%	4	1.1%	**368**		
7438	Non-used	1	0.6%	3	1.7%	170	93.9%	0	0%	0	0%	0	0%	2	1.1%	5	2.8%	**181**		
7446	**Hard material cutting**	0	0%	1	100%	0	0%	0	0%	0	0%	0	0%	0	0%	0	0%	**1**		
7452	**Bone cutting**	0	0%	0	0%	0	0%	0	0%	0	0%	0	0%	0	0%	0	0%	**0**		
7475	Post-depositional alteration	1	20%	1	20%	1	20%	0	0%	0	0%	1	20%	0	0%	1	20%	**5**		
7581	Post-depositional alteration	3	3.6%	4	4.8%	77	91.7%	0	0%	0	0%	0	0%	0	0%	0	0%	**84**		
7581	Post-depositional alteration	0	0%	0	0%	5	71.4%	0	0%	0	0%	0	0%	0	0%	2	28.6%	**7**		

Table 20.3. (continued)

Sample	Use-wear analysis	undet.		short cells		long cells		bulliforms		trapezoids		trichomes		ARBOREAL		taphonomized		TOTAL
7582	Hard material cutting	0	0%	2	4.4%	42	93.3%	0	0%	0	0%	1	2.2%	0	0%	0	0%	45
7583	Post-depositional alteration	1	0.4%	3	1.2%	237	95.6%	0	0%	1	0.4%	1	0.4%	0	0%	5	2%	248
7584	Non-used	0	0%	2	22.2%	6	66.7%	0	0%	1	11.1%	0	0%	0	0%	0	0%	9
7585	Non-used	2	1.0%	7	3.7%	177	92.7%	0	0%	0	0%	2	1%	3	1.6%	0	0%	191
7586	Non-used	4	1.3%	7	2.3%	284	91.6%	0	0%	2	0.6%	3	1%	1	0.3%	9	2.9%	310
7587	Non-used	2	1.2%	9	5.5%	151	91.5%	0	0%	0	0%	0	0%	0	0%	3	1.8%	165
7588	Non-used	4	9.8%	6	14.6%	24	58.5%	0	0%	1	2.4%	2	4.9%	2	4.9%	2	4.9%	41
7589	Bone cutting	0	0%	3	1.9%	148	96.1%	0	0%	1	0.6%	0	0%	0	0%	2	1.3%	154
7590	Non-used	0	0%	1	10%	8	80%	0	0%	0	0%	0	0%	0	0%	1	10%	10
7591	Post-depositional alteration	0	0%	2	11.1%	15	83.3%	0	0%	0	0%	0	0%	0	0%	1	5.6%	18
7604	Non-used	0	0%	2	33.3%	3	50%	0	0%	1	16.7%	0	0%	0	0%	0	0%	6
7605	Non-used	0	0%	0	0%	2	66.7%	0	0%	0	0%	0	0%	0	0%	1	33.3%	3
7606	Non-used	0	0%	3	5.9%	46	90.2%	0	0%	1	2%	0	0%	0	0%	1	2%	51
7607	Non-used	1	0.7%	5	3.3%	134	89.3%	0	0%	4	2.7%	0	0%	0	0%	6	4%	150
7608	Post-depositional alteration	1	0.4%	1	0.4%	233	96.7%	0	0%	0	0%	0	0%	0	0%	6	2.5%	241
7609	Non-used	6	42.9%	1	7.1%	4	28.6%	0	0%	0	0%	1	7.1%	2	14.3%	0	0%	14
7610	Non-used	0	0%	1	4%	24	96%	0	0%	0	0%	0	0%	0	0%	0	0%	25
7616	Non-used	0	0%	0	0%	29	90.6%	0	0%	0	0%	2	6.3%	0	0%	1	3.1%	32
7617	Non-used	0	0%	1	0.7%	137	97.9%	0	0%	1	0.7%	1	0.7%	0	0%	0	0%	140

Indeterminate phytoliths include those that cannot be assigned to any category on the basis of morphological criteria, as well as those whose identification is doubtful. On the other hand, taphonomized phytoliths are those that can be identified but that have fractures or surface erosions/dissolution. The amount of taphonomized phytoliths in a sample is an important indicator of local or regional taphonomic processes.

The use-wear analysis was started with a preliminary sample composed of 248 artifacts, which included the 34 pieces selected for this pilot study; this group of artifacts was selected following the aforementioned criteria employed for residue analysis.

One of the remarkable features of the lithic artifacts was that this is the only assemblage so far known in which a significant percentage of pieces were made with schist from the Yaghan Formation (Kranck 1932). In the majority of fisher-hunter-gatherer sites of the north coast of the Beagle Channel, almost 90 percent of artifacts are made from metamorphic rhyolites and fine-grain tuff, and less than 5 percent from schists, despite its high frequency in secondary deposits of fluvio-glacial origin (Álvarez 2003;

Terradas 1996). The reason for this general pattern seems to be the low quality of this material for producing stone tools (Álvarez 2003).[12] Unfortunately, the lithological characteristics of the schists make it difficult to identify traces of use. This difficulty is due in part to the slow rate of formation of traces (a greater volume of work is required to attain a given degree of development), but mainly because of the fragility of the edges, which often appear fractured and exfoliated.

Despite these difficulties, use-wear studies revealed that many of the lithic artifacts formed part of a workshop situated outside the midden/dwelling unit; no traces of use were observed on 83.3 percent of the flakes, while 6.1 percent of the sample showed signs of post-depositional alterations (such as patination, natural gloss, and soil abrasion) that prevented any precise identification. Furthermore, traces could not be analyzed on 3.7 percent of the lithic artifacts because their edges were exfoliated.

However, microtraces were identified on the remaining 6.9 percent of the artifacts. These traces have been linked to the working of different materials including (in order of importance) bone, hard materials, hide, and soft materials (Figure 20.4). Traces linked to cutting activities predominate in the case of hard materials and especially in that of bone, whereas transversal and scraping traces are more common in the case of soft materials and hide (Figure 20.4). These results contrast with those from another site in the same region (Túnel VII), where traces linked to woodworking were more common (Clemente 1995). Nevertheless, these kinds of traces were not observed at Lanashuaia I. Also, there is no evidence of processing of herbaceous plants.

The traces identified and the residues detected (Table 20.2) are relatively associated. Thus, use-wear analyses of artifacts that gave a positive result to the identification of blood traces were used either to work bone or did not give any result (did not show any evidence of having been used). This could provide an interesting data set to evaluate contamination from the general sediment. The absence of phytoliths in the pieces analyzed from the shell midden layers may also indicate possible contamination in the other layer types. In this respect, further analyses are planned to be able to understand this peculiar situation.

FINAL CONSIDERATIONS

The first and very preliminary results of the pilot project on residue analysis have given the possibility for some

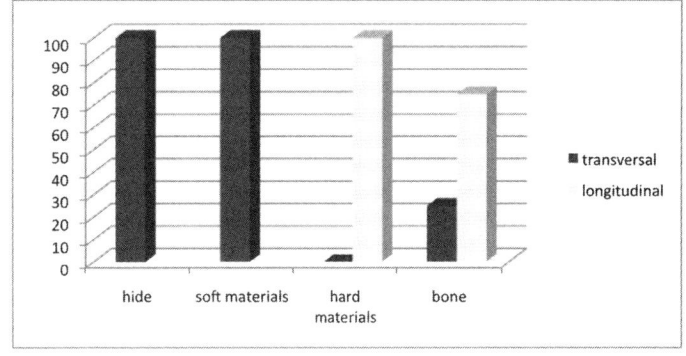

20.4. Results of use-wear analyses.

preliminary interpretations on the methodology and a number of remarks for future research in the area or elsewhere:

• The identification of residues of animal origin requires more sophisticated tests than those applied so far. Furthermore, traces originating from the use of tools on soft material of animal origin form over long and repeated actions. Therefore, it is sometimes difficult to unambiguously identify them. In order to solve this problem, we are currently undertaking an experimental project that strictly controls all the different variables involved.

• The phytolith analysis has highlighted the existence of a high variability in the frequency of phytoliths, not only between samples but also between the analyzed layers (B2, base of B800, B900, and C200). On one hand, the fact that there are fewer phytoliths in the lower levels makes it likely that no vertical mobility or illuviation took place and that they are in situ. The absence of phytoliths in the shell midden (layer C200) is particularly interesting, and it can be explained not only by the absence of a sedimentary matrix, but also because of its formation as a rubbish dump (even if the cleaning of hearths could theoretically have generated an important vegetal input).

• The absence of traces of use related to the working of plant materials makes it difficult to compare the results of the phytolith and the use-wear analyses. However, these results draw attention to the importance of considering and applying both analytical methods in a complementary manner for a deeper understanding of the production-consumption processes carried out in the settlement or in any other given settlement. It seems reasonable that the presence of phytoliths on the stone tool edges is not related to their use as a working tool, but at the same time it turns our attention to new dimensions and discussions, opening interesting lines of research.

Finally, one of the more important remarks that arise from this pilot study, as a general consideration of residue analyses, is the need to evaluate the representativeness of the analyzed assemblage. In this case, the study samples collected for residue analysis should have been higher in number and more representative of the different areas of the social space. Indeed, the inherent variability of each of the analyses is too great when compared to the size of the sample, and it is therefore not possible to attempt a statistical study that would enable a deeper understanding of the data set on the basis of context of origin, tool use, variability of the tests for animal residues, or variability of the phytolith assemblages.

At the same time, this pilot study has shown the need to control variables involved in the production, the conservation, and the recovery of the residues. This need leads to a great difficulty in interpreting results from residue analyses as they usually do not show one-to-one matches. Contamination and mixing of different types of residues seem to be common.

For interpreting the results of residue analyses, it is of paramount importance to understand how lithic tools were used. We must consider that they could have been used for purposes for which they had not been initially manufactured once their useful life was finishing. This would be an added difficulty for uncovering general patterns.

Despite its complexity, the method described in this chapter has shown, in our opinion, to be both applicable and useful as there appear to be no incompatibilities between the different analyses undertaken. Further research, with a deep focus on methodological development, should be carried out in this and other contexts in order to reach a level of maturity in residue analyses that would make analyses more straightforward and productive, avoiding research where the investment of efforts is unbalanced in relation to the results acquired. Residue analyses still need, in this sense, to prove their validity and potential for generating new avenues of research apart from their own methodological development, producing useful archaeological data.

ACKNOWLEDGMENTS

We would like to thank the many people who helped us with this work and in particular the excavation and laboratory team (Victoria Yannito, Joana Boix, Edgard Camarós, Marta Juez, Nélida Pal, and Elsa Puig). This project was funded by the Spanish Council for Scientific Research (CSIC, Spain), the Wenner-Gren Foundation (EUA), and Consejo Nacional de Investigaciones Científicas y Técnicas (CONICET, Argentina). We would also like to acknowledge the reviewer for the valuable comments made on the chapter.

NOTES

1. The term *residue* refers, in this chapter, to the presence of material on a tool that comes either from worked raw materials or from supplementary material(s) used during the work process. The presence of the residue is therefore the result of the interaction between the instrument of work and the material being worked (Briz et al. 2005).

2. We are referring to the rapidly developing area of research mainly known as biomolecular archaeology (the study of blood and protein residues, as well as DNA) (see Craig and Collins 2002; Lowenstein et al. 2005; Loy 1993; Shanks et al. 2001; as well as research where different complementary techniques are used, such as Jahren et al. 1997; Petraglia et al. 1996).

3. Fieldwork at Lanashuaia I was funded through the projects *Marine Resources at the Beagle Channel prior to the Industrial Exploitation: an Archaeological Evaluation* of the European Union (1995–1996) and *The integrity of social space: ethnoarchaeology of settlements in the Beagle Canal (Tierra del Fuego) 2005*, Ministry of Culture, Spain. Lanashuaia I fieldwork was originally directed by J. Estévez, L. Orquera, E. Piana, and A. Vila (1995 and 1996 field seasons) and later by M. Álvarez, I. Briz, and D. Zurro (in 2005).

4. The samples were named as follows:

• Sample Mo: liquid sample obtained by cleaning the selected edges of the artifacts with distilled water.

• Sample A: liquid suspension obtained by cleaning the selected edges of the artifacts using a solution of 10 percent hydrochloric acid in an ultrasound to detach the eventual phytoliths.

• Sample C: soil sample from the sediment surrounding the piece.

5. The analyses of the sediments (control samples—that is, Samples C) are going to be done in a secondary step of the research.

6. Phytolith analysis was done on samples recovered from 34 artifacts. The animal residue tests were done first on the whole assemblage (benzidine test) and second on a selection of 18 pieces (pseudoperoxidative test). Use-wear was done on the whole assemblage as well (34 artifacts).

7. Nonetheless, this type of analysis may result in "false positives" in the presence of chlorophyll (A. Crowther, pers. com.).

8. Data was standardized per gram of residue so as to compare samples following an adaptation of Rosa M. Albert and colleagues (1999).

9. We do not yet consider other data regarding plant resources consumption in the excavation, as macrobotanical remains are currently being studied.

10. Long and short cells are the most common cells in grasses, which are present mainly in stems (see Piperno 2006).

11. It is important to keep in mind that the phytolith production of arboreal species is much less than that of grasses (silica production is ca. 20 times less than grasses).

12. Despite the low quality of schist, in the case of Lanashuaia the existence of a schist quarry next to the site seems to be enough explanation for its use as a raw material.

CHAPTER TWENTY-ONE

MICRO-REMAINS TRAPPED IN DENTAL CALCULUS REVEAL PLANTS CONSUMED BY BRAZILIAN SHELL MOUND BUILDERS

Célia H. C. Boyadjian and Sabine Eggers

SUMMARY

The use of plants by Brazilian shell mound populations is still very unclear. Indirect evidence of plant consumption in prehistoric Brazil has revealed that most shell mound groups show low caries rates, while some show rates compatible with frequent cariogenic food intake. Here we explore an approach in which plant micro-remains such as starch grains and phytoliths are retrieved from human dental calculus (tartar) to shed light on which plant parts were consumed by these ancient populations. Using this approach, we contrast data from the huge coastal shell mound Jabuticabeira II (low caries rate) with that from the small riverine site of Moraes (high caries rate). We conclude that: (a) the site with the higher caries rate shows a much higher proportion of starch grains than the samples from the site with a low caries rate; (b) therefore, diet must have contained more starchy and cariogenic food in Moraes than in Jabuticabeira II; (c) there does not seem to be a correlation, nor an association, between the number of caries and the corresponding starch grain concentration per individual; (d) diet was not homogeneous for all people from one site; (e) a greater variety of plants seems to have been consumed/used by the people from Jabuticabeira II than by those from Moraes; (f) some of the starchy plants consumed were possibly sweet potato (*Ipomoea batatas*), yams (*Dioscorea* sp.), and plants from the Araceae family; and finally, (g) some of the starch grains found are modified grains, suggesting food processing. Although preliminary, these data, and especially this approach, are promising to uncover how plants were used by Brazilian shell mound societies.

INTRODUCTION

People who built shell mounds (*sambaquis*) in Brazil subsisted mainly on fish and shellfish (De Masi 1999; Figuti 1992; Figuti and Plens [chap. 16], Gaspar et al. [chap. 7], and Klokler [chap. 11] in this volume). We still know little about which plants were used to complement their marine diet with carbohydrates, fibers, vitamins, minerals, and non-animal proteins. This is partially due to the bad preservation of noncarbonized plant macro-remains, but also because Brazilian archaeologists were not particularly focused on the systematic recovery of plant remains until recently (Bianchini, Scheel-Ybert, and Gaspar 2007; Scheel-Ybert et al. 2003; Wesolowski et al. 2010), leading to a loss of evidence. The few reports regarding plant use in sambaquis were originally based on indirect evidence such as lithic artifacts interpreted as plant-processing tools (Gaspar 1998; Kneip 1977, 1994; Tenório 1991).

Results of groundbreaking research in the sambaqui context include anthracology (Scheel-Ybert, chap. 22 in this volume), which has shown that a diversity of plants was used as fuel, and might have been used as construction material, and in rituals (Scheel-Ybert 2000, 2001a, 2001b, chap. 22 in this volume; Scheel-Ybert et al. 2003). Also, many of the charred seeds and wood identified correspond to plant taxa that produce edible fruits (Scheel-Ybert 2001a, 2001b). Charred tubers of monocotyledons (e.g., *Dioscorea* sp.—yams) were also found. But does the presence of remains from plants eaten today mean that those plants were actually used as food in the past?

Local climatic conditions influence plant preservation. In arid environments seeds, fibers, and fruits can preserve well, allowing paleodietary reconstruction. In places where plant remains are badly preserved, flotation techniques are essential to systematically explore ancient plant use (Bianchini, Scheel-Ybert, and Gaspar 2007; Pearsall 2000; Scheel-Ybert et al. 2005/2006; Scheel-Ybert, chap. 22 in this volume). Unfortunately, the recovered remains do not necessarily belong to plants that were actually used as food.

Various approaches suggest plant use in ancient diets: (a) discovering edible plant remains in "garbage middens" or on tools and (ceramic) vessels used for food procurement, storage, processing, or cooking (Pearsall 2000); (b) finding plant remains in human coprolites (Reinhard and Bryant 2008); (c) observing high caries rates and rapid growth of carious lesions suggesting a highly cariogenic and thus carbohydrate-rich diet (Lanfranco and Eggers 2010; Turner II 1979); and (d) obtaining stable isotope signatures from bone and teeth revealing consumption of C3 or C4 plants (Ambrose and Krigbaum 2003; Katzenberg 1992).

All of these approaches show certain drawbacks when applied to the sambaquis. Ceramic vessels are extremely rare and not necessarily associated with sambaquis (Gaspar 1998). Coprolites tend not to preserve in tropical and subtropical sites (Reinhard and Bryant 2008). Dental caries are frequent in some and rare in other sambaquis but show no association with the presence of ceramics (Wesolowski 2000). Finally, stable isotope analysis in sambaquis focuses on collagen (reflecting protein intake), as opposed to apatite (that represents the whole diet—Ambrose and Norr 1993; Tieszen and Fagre 1993). In addition, isotopic data give only a very general picture of an ancient people's diet (although they were crucial to confirm that the sambaqui builders' main dish was fish—De Masi 1999).

So, how can we reconstruct the consumption of plants by the sambaqui people and what plants were actually eaten by them?

TRACES LEFT BY PLANTS IN THE ARCHAEOLOGICAL RECORD

Plant micro-remains can be found in sediments, attached to lithic and ceramic instruments, or preserved in coprolites, as well as in dental calculus (tartar) from ancient teeth, though only coprolites and teeth yield results directly linked to diet.

Retrieving micro-remains from these sources has not yet been carried out in most sambaquis. Fortunately, recovering plant micro-residues from the sambaqui builders' teeth located in different institutions is, for most sambaquis

excavated in past years (often neglecting the collection of plant remains in the field), the only way to investigate the importance of plants in these people's diet. The present chapter is the result of one of the only two research projects undertaken until now on this subject in Brazil.

Studying either archeological or ancient plant micro-remains is not easy. There are different protocols for retrieving them (Pearsall 2000; Piperno 2006; Torrence and Barton 2006; Henry and Piperno 2008); different methods for calculating their concentration (Boyadjian, Eggers, and Reinhard 2007; Haslan et al. 2009; Tromp and Dudgeon 2011; Wesolowski et al. 2010); and differences in the classification of some micro-remains (Erra 2010; Rapp and Mulholland 1992). Even the identification of micro-particles is not always simple and straightforward. For example, at first sight, starch grains from different plants may look very similar, causing misidentification. Therefore, different features must be carefully analyzed to distinguish among them (Torrence and Barton 2006). Also, the analysis of micro-remains from dental calculus by itself, despite being a field of research that has gained prestige worldwide, is still relatively recent, requiring more basic research and tests. In the dental calculus, it is possible to find fibers, epidermal cells, and other plant particles (but not exclusively plant micro-remains); however, starch grains and phytoliths are the most commonly present (Reinhard et al. 2001).

Phytoliths: Durable Inorganic Plant Structures

Phytoliths are particles of hydrated silica ($SiO_2.nH_2O$) with specific sizes and shapes that are produced by plants (Lalueza-Fox, Juan, and Albert 1996; Lalueza-Fox, Perez-Perez, and Juan 1994; Piperno 2006; Piperno and Pearsall 1993). Involved in mechanical support, protection against herbivores and fungi, and some physiological functions of the plants (Piperno 2006), they mainly occur in leaves, stems, and seeds (Lalueza-Fox, Perez-Perez, and Juan 1994).

Because phytoliths are very resistant to mechanical and chemical damage (Pearsall 2000; Piperno 1988), they can be found in archaeological contexts where plant macro-remains or even other micro-remains, such as pollen grains, do not preserve well (Piperno 2006; Piperno and Holst 1998).

Starch Grains: Energy Storage for Plants

Starch grains, found abundantly in roots, tubers, fruits, and seeds, are the main form of energy storage in plants (Gott et al. 2006; Lehninger, Nelson, and Cox 1993; Piperno and Holst 1998). Unlike other plant micro-particles, they are directly linked to diet (Torrence 2006), since the storage organs (where they abound) are among the best energy sources for humankind.

They consist of two carbohydrate polymers (amylosis and amylopectine) and grow as those polymers are deposited in layers (lamellae) around the hilum (Gott et al. 2006). When lamellae, the hilum, and the interference cross (formed under polarized light because of birefringence—Gott et al. 2006) are identified in a micro-particle, they indicate it is a starch grain. To discover which plant produced a certain starch grain, it is also necessary to observe features such as size and shape of the grain, the hilum location, and the presence of lamellae, among others (Loy 1994; Torrence 2006).

Starch grains are less resistant than phytoliths. Moisture, temperature, and pH are known to facilitate microorganism attack (Barton and Matthews 2006). Even though they are prone to easy decay, starch grains can last for thousands of years (Torrence 2006) when protected by cracks and depressions in stone tools (Piperno and Holst 1998; Piperno et al. 2004; Ranere et al. 2009), or by the dental calculus matrix (Hardy et al. 2009; Henry, Brooks, and Piperno 2010; Henry and Piperno 2008; Lieverse 1999).

Ancient starch is found as native starch and as modified starch (resulting from taphonomic processes and/or plant manipulation, such as grinding, boiling, and baking— Babot 2006; Gott et al. 2006). These procedures modify the granule's structure, leading to the loss of some important characteristics, sometimes preventing identification. However, the patterns of modification can reveal habits and technologies used by past populations.

HOW DO PLANT MICRO-REMAINS BECOME TRAPPED IN DENTAL CALCULUS?

Dental plaque is a biofilm (Hardy et al. 2009) that covers teeth and gums. In a simplified way, it absorbs minerals from the saliva and the crevicular (gingival) fluid, originating dental calculus (Charlier et al. 2010; Greene, Kuba, and Irish 2005).

During the feeding process, some micro-particles are retained in the dental plaque and, as it mineralizes, they become trapped in the dental calculus, eventually being preserved for thousands of years. Plant micro-particles may get embedded in the dental calculus through food mastication and also during the use of teeth as tools (Hardy 2008). This can occur while holding, chewing, scraping, and scratching plant fibers and other plant structures during the production of ropes, baskets, fishing nets, and the like. Thus,

micro-remains retrieved from dental calculus may reveal ancient diet and also the material used for artifact production. This is possible because many of the micro-particles preserve their morphology and characteristics, allowing taxonomic identification (Henry and Piperno 2008).

RECOVERING PLANT MICRO-REMAINS FROM DENTAL CALCULUS

Dental calculus can be as "hard as bone" (Hardy et al. 2009), but it is possible to process it chemically, dissolving its matrix, for the extraction of micro-remains. The solution obtained is mounted on a microscope slide with glycerol to allow some mobility of the micro-remains, permitting the observation of their three-dimensional configuration, a key element for taxonomic identification.

The quantification and identification of the micro-remains from dental calculus then permit reconstructing diet and the use of plants in the past (Hardy et al. 2009; Henry, Brooks, and Piperno 2010; Henry and Piperno 2008; Juan-Tresserras et al. 1997; Lalueza-Fox, Juan, and Albert 1996; Lalueza-Fox, Perez-Perez, and Juan 1994; Lieverse 1999; Reinhard et al. 2001; Scott Cummings and Magennis 1997; Wesolowski et al. 2010).

When the teeth show large amounts of calculus (Figure 21.1), we use a more "traditional" methodology, consisting of the mechanical detachment of the calculus deposit, followed by its chemical treatment (Henry and Piperno 2008; Hardy et al. 2009; Lalueza-Fox, Juan, and Albert 1996; Reinhard et al. 2001; Wesolowski et al. 2010). For more details, see Célia H. C. Boyadjian and colleagues (2007), and Veronica Wesolowski and colleagues (2010).

Unfortunately, in some archaeological sites, human teeth show only faint dental calculus marks (Figure 21.1), preventing its mechanical detachment. Therefore, an alternative technique called "dental wash" was developed (Boyadjian, Eggers, and Reinhard 2007). Although this technique can damage teeth (Kucera et al. 2011), it efficiently recovers microfossils from faint calculus marks and yields results similar to those obtained with the "traditional" treatment (Boyadjian 2007).

The "dental wash" method consists of the immersion of the tooth crowns into a solution of HCl to dissolve the remaining dental calculus, releasing the micro-particles (see Boyadjian, Eggers, and Reinhard 2007 for more details).

Slide Preparation and Analysis

For this study, we prepared five slides with 10 µl of each

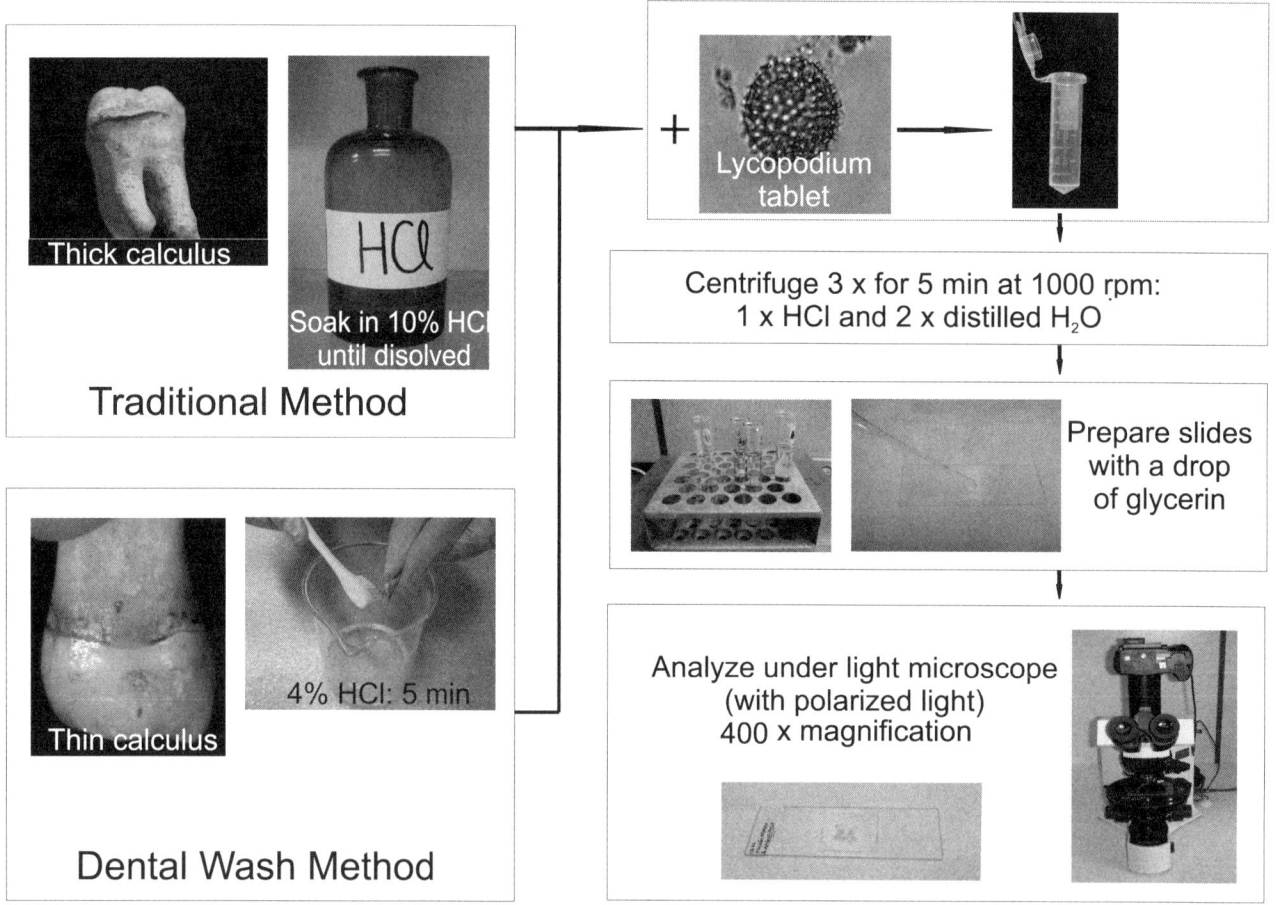

21.1. The two methods applied to recover plant micro-remains from dental calculus.

sample that were analyzed under an optical compound microscope (at 400x magnification) with polarized light (to identify the starch grains). The added marker (*Lycopodium clavatum* spores, necessary for quantification) and the micro-remains were counted, measured, and recorded as digital images and drawings.

Taxonomic Identification of the Dental Calculus Contents

Although starch grain and phytolith reference collections for taxonomic identification exist, they do not include plants typical from the Brazilian shell mound regions. The construction of a reference collection based on native plant material has just been initiated. Therefore, we currently can identify only some of the micro-remains and determine the relative proportion of phytoliths versus starch grains. To obtain the starch grains for our reference collection we processed native fruits, tubers, and seeds according to Judith Field (2006).

HYPOTHESES

The intake of cariogenic carbohydrate-rich food must have been distinct from one sambaqui to the other, because their caries rate and pattern differ significantly (Scheel-Ybert et al. 2003). Did the groups with high caries rates consume more cariogenic plant foods than those with very low rates? Is there a different mosaic of plant micro-remains present in the groups with high caries rates, as opposed to the groups with low rates? If cariogenic food is rich in carbohydrates and these are found abundantly in starchy plants, we should find a higher proportion of starch grains among groups with high caries rates than in those with very low caries rates.

BIOARCHAEOLOGY OF THE STUDIED SAMBAQUIS

Here we compare two shell mound groups to test the abovementioned hypothesis. Jabuticabeira II was chosen because it represents one of the best studied sambaquis in Brazil, showing a low caries rate, while Moraes, the riverine sambaqui with the largest human osteological collection, presents a much higher caries rate (Eggers et al. 2008).

Coastal Sambaqui: Jabuticabeira II

The huge sambaqui Jabuticabeira II (ca. 480,000 cubic meters—Figure 21.2) was constructed between 2890 ± 55 to 1805 ± 65 years BP on the coast of Santa Catarina State, Brazil (DeBlasis et al. 1998; Fish et al. 2000; Giannini et al. 2010). Since chapters 7, 8, 11, and 22 of this volume are dedicated to it (Gaspar et al.; Klokler, Okumura and Eggers; and Scheel-Ybert), here we summarize the bioarchaeological data necessary for the comprehension of its people's diet. Like most coastal sambaquis, Jabuticabeira II is located in a region rich in aquatic resources (DeBlasis et al. 1998; Klokler 2001, 2008; Scheel-Ybert et al. 2003). However, artifacts potentially related to plant processing, such as mortars and pestles, have also been found, although pottery is absent (Scheel-Ybert et al. 2003; Gaspar et al., chap. 7 in this volume). Indeed, anthracological analyses reveal that Jabuticabeira II was located in the *restinga* forest, an ecosystem rich in fruits, seeds, and tubers including plants from the Myrtaceae, Annonaceae, and Arecaceae families (Scheel-Ybert 2000, 2001a, 2001b, chap. 22 in this volume).

The people from Jabuticabeira II show a high degree of dental wear (Storto, Eggers, and Lahr 1999) and a very low frequency of dental decay, where only 0.44 percent of the analyzed teeth are carious (Okumura and Eggers 2005), as is typical for hunter-gatherers (Larsen 1997; Turner II 1979) with a diet rich in abrasive material and hard texture, as well as low in cariogenic food. However, low caries frequency has also been found in rice-consuming agriculturalists, despite their cariogenic diets (Tayles, Domett, and Nelsen 2000). Therefore, a more detailed analysis of the paleodiet is paramount in sambaquis.

The people who built Jabuticabeira II initiated life with some nutritional problems (as seen through the high rates of cribra orbitalia and porotic hyperostosis), and had early, but evenly distributed, mild joint degeneration, with the exception of more severe osteoarthroses in upper limbs among adults (Okumura and Eggers 2005; Scheel-Ybert et al. 2003). Adult stature is small (156 centimeters in males and 146 centimeters in females), as in almost all extant and ancient Amerindians (Storto, Eggers, and Lahr 1999). The frequency of auditory exostosis (23.8 percent), a marker of aquatic activity, resembles that of other sambaqui groups of this region (Okumura, Boyadjian, and Eggers 2007).

21.2. Location of the studied sambaquis.

Considering the huge size of this site and the enormous quantity of people estimated to be buried there (approximately 40,000; Fish et al. 2000), it is not surprising to find evidence of communicable diseases such as treponematoses (De Melo et al. 2010; Okumura and Eggers 2005). Nonetheless, trauma, especially of the violent kind, is very rare (Okumura and Eggers 2005), suggesting that the people from Jabuticabeira II had a relatively pacific way of life.

Inland Riverine Sambaqui: Moraes

Besides coastal sambaquis, there are also inland riverine sambaquis, such as Moraes (Figure 21.2), a small site (ca. 180 cubic meters) located in the Atlantic forest (ca. 35 kilometers inland from the coast of today's São Paulo State), dated from 5895 ± 45 to 4511 ± 32 years BP (Figuti et al. 2004; Figuti and Plens, chap. 16 in this volume). This type of forest contains a high species diversity (Morellato and Haddad 2000), suggesting a varied diet. In fact, zooarchaeological studies suggest a wide range of small terrestrial game, such as small primates, peccary, skunk, and small deer (Figuti et al. 2004; Figuti and Plens, chap. 16 in this volume), confirmed indirectly through stable isotope studies carried out not only in this riverine sambaqui (Plens 2007), but also in another one nearby called Capelinha (Eggers et al. 2011).

The people from Moraes show a high caries frequency associated with a dental wear pattern suggestive of a hunter-gatherer way of life, which must have included cariogenic plants (Eggers et al. 2008). The frequency of 12 percent carious teeth in Moraes is considerably higher than the less than 4 percent found in most coastal sambaquis of south-southeastern Brazil (Neves and Wesolowski 2002; Scheel-Ybert et al. 2003), including Jabuticabeira II. Some rare coastal series of this region, however, do show caries frequencies between 6 and 13 percent, and while not associated with pottery, they suggest a cariogenic diet (Neves and Wesolowski 2002; Scheel-Ybert et al. 2003; Wesolowski 2000). High caries frequencies (ca. 9 percent) were also found among hunter-gatherer Paleoamericans from Central Brazil (Neves and Cornero 1997).

The individuals exhumed from Moraes were very short (males: 141–155 centimeters; females: 130–140 centimeters; Eggers et al. 2008), even in comparison to coastal sambaqui people and other prehistoric and extant Amerindians (156–167 centimeters for males and 148–157 centimeters for females; Okumura and Eggers 2005; Scheel-Ybert et al. 2003; Storto, Eggers, and Lahr 1999), a feature not yet fully understood. Also still mysterious is the reason for the high frequency of auditory exostosis (22 percent; Eggers et al. 2008) that, together with the greater severity of articular degeneration in upper than in lower limbs, suggests aquatic activity. These features could indicate diving in rivers, or conversely, they could support the hypothesis of contact with the coast, including performing activities in the sea. However, "the use of auditory exostoses as an aquatic activity marker in tropical and subtropical regions should be used only cautiously" (Okumura, Boyadjian, and Eggers 2007). In fact, contact of this inland group with coastal sambaqui people is suggested by maritime implements found in Moraes (Figuti et al. 2004; Figuti and Plens, chap. 16 in this volume) and by the similarity of cranial and dental morphology in riverine and coastal sambaqui people (Eggers et al. 2008; Figuti et al. 2004; Neves and Okumura 2005). Further indirect evidence of contact between Moraes people and other more populous groups, perhaps coastal sambaqui groups, is the presence of treponematosis (Eggers et al. 2008), a communicable disease typical of crowded groups that was diagnosed in various pre-Columbian Amerindians and Old World groups (see De Melo et al. 2010 for a review). As found for most coastal sambaquis (Lessa 2005; Lessa and Medeiros 2001; Okumura and Eggers 2005; Scheel-Ybert et al. 2003), the people from Moraes also do not seem to have frequently engaged in

interpersonal conflicts yielding to physical violence and accidents (Eggers et al. 2008). Thus, life in this small inland sambaqui must also have been quite tranquil.

In summary, there are many bioanthropological similarities between the riverine sambaqui Moraes and coastal sambaquis in the south-southeastern part of Brazil, including Jabuticabeira II: (a) auditory exostosis with equally high frequencies (Eggers et al. 2008; Okumura, Boyadjian, and Eggers 2007); (b) significantly more frequent osteoarthrosis in upper rather than in lower limbs among adults (Eggers et al. 2008; Scheel-Ybert et al. 2003); (c) craniometric and non-metric dental similarities (Neves and Okumura 2005); and finally (d) low frequencies, if any, of violent trauma (Lessa 2005; Lessa and Medeiros 2001; Okumura and Eggers 2005; Scheel-Ybert et al. 2003). This is in accordance with cultural similarities found between Moraes and the coastal sambaquis such as the presence of shark teeth, ray spines, hooks, and especially the habit of collecting shells and using them for site construction in both types of site. In contrast, the most striking difference between the bioanthropology of these two sites resides in their distinct caries frequency. The study of the plant micro-remains recovered from dental calculus is able to shed light on this paleodietary puzzle.

Just as in Jabuticabeira II, we still have much to investigate about plant use in Moraes. However, in contrast to Jabuticabeira II, there is no other research focused on the botanical remains of Moraes and, unfortunately, no systematic recovery of plant remains took place during excavation. Therefore, this chapter summarizes the only study on plant consumption by the Moraes group carried out thus far.

WHAT DO PLANT MICRO-REMAINS REVEAL ABOUT DIET IN SAMBAQUI GROUPS WITH LOW (JABUTICABEIRA II) AND HIGH (MORAES) CARIES RATES?

Here we present a comparison of plant micro-remains recovered from dental calculus from adult individuals exhumed from Jabuticabeira II (54 samples) and Moraes (32 samples). In both sites, the total number of starch grains is expressive, suggesting starchy food intake (Figure 21.3A). However, it is not possible at this time to estimate the amount of carbohydrate intake in the sambaqui builders' diet. Nevertheless, the ubiquitous presence of starch granules in most dental calculus samples from the studied sites shows that starchy foods were an essential part of these peoples' diet (Figure 21.3B).

More Starch Grains than Phytoliths

Figure 21.3 shows a much higher proportion of starch grains, as well as a significantly higher (Mann-Whitney p = 0.001) mean concentration of starch in Moraes (93 percent of micro-remains; 44.85 grains/µL) than in Jabuticabeira II (54 percent of micro-remains; 8.24 grains/µL). This result corroborates our hypothesis that caries-prone populations do show a relatively higher content of starch grains in the dental calculus than groups with low caries frequencies. Accordingly, the diet of the people from Moraes must have contained more starchy food than that of the Jabuticabeira II builders. These good sources of energy could, theoretically and in both sites (but to a different extent), include tubers, roots, nuts, seeds, and/or fruits.

In fact, tubers such as *Dioscorea* sp. were found in some coastal shell mounds (Scheel-Ybert 2001a, 2001b, chap. 22 in this volume; Scheel-Ybert et al. 2003). Since Jabuticabeira II is located in the restinga forest, an ecosystem rich in plant resources, including tubers (Scheel-Ybert 2000, 2001a, 2001b, chap. 22 in this volume; Scheel-Ybert et al. 2003), it would not be surprising to discover starch grains from yams in the dental calculus of the Jabuticabeans.

Plants Not Only for Food?

Indeed, our preliminary analysis indicates that some starch grains from our samples are consistent with *Dioscorea* sp. and also with *Ipomoea batatas* (sweet potato), while others are similar to the starch found in the Araceae (arum) family (Figure 21.4; Torrence and Barton 2006; Zeder et al. 2006). Starch from *Dioscorea* sp. and *Ipomoea batatas* clearly indicate the use of starch storage organs as food.

Furthermore, there are Araceae species that are not only used as food today (e.g., *Colocasia esculenta*—taro) but also as medicine, such as *Philodendron bipinnatifidum* (Balbach 1979). Would it be far-fetched to suggest that some of the plants of the highly diverse restinga forest were used for medicinal purposes? Indeed, Moraes people had reasons to search for medicinal plants, since treponematoses, periostitis, osteoarthritis, abscesses, and caries were diagnosed among them (Eggers et al. 2008).

Starchy Food and Caries

Although there is an association of high caries frequency and higher starch proportion when comparing one sambaqui group to the other, we could not find a correlation

nor an association between starch concentrations and the number of caries per person exhumed from Moraes (Figure 21.3D). This finding could be due to the many factors that influence the way and frequency in which dental caries affect people, in which diet is only one of them (Tayles, Domett, and Nelsen 2000). Although it is widely acknowledged that a carbohydrate-rich diet normally causes an increase in caries frequency (Cohen and Armelagos 1984; Kleinberg 2002; Turner II 1979), the dynamics of cariogenicity, as well as the methods used to evaluate caries depth and location, are quite complex (Lanfranco and Eggers 2010). Some diets, like the fluoride- and calcium-rich marine foods, can be cariostatic (Bowen 1994; Hillson 2001). Moreover, marine food can also lead to intense and quick dental wear, eliminating cusps and fissures of teeth, and thereby the areas prone to bacterial attack (Hillson 2001). Thus, the higher the degree of dental wear, the greater the probability that established caries are removed. Even the dental calculus can be a protective barrier against the action of bacteria (Greene, Kuba, and Irish 2005). In fact, the people from Jabuticabeira II do show high degrees of dental wear and huge amounts of dental calculus (Okumura and Eggers 2005). Therefore, there might be a set of factors working together that results in low caries frequencies in Jabuticabeira II, even if people were eating starchy cariogenic food as a complement to their marine-based diet.

Dietary Heterogeneity

The types of food ingested seem to have been quite distinct from person to person at both sites. Although almost all samples contain an expressive concentration of starch grains, only some of them also contain phytoliths (some of them identified as Poaceae—grass family). This is in accordance with studies on other groups (Henry and Piperno 2008; Juan-Tresserras et al. 1997; Lalueza-Fox, Juan, and Albert 1996; Scott Cummings and Magennis 1997), including other sambaquis (Wesolowski et al. 2010). As starch grains are abundant (and phytoliths are rare) in storage organs like tubers and roots, we suggest that some individuals of both sites might have eaten, apart from storage organs, plant parts rich in phytoliths, such as leaves or stems. Alternatively, we cannot discard the possibility that phytolith-rich plant parts were chewed or scraped with the teeth for purposes other than feeding, perhaps in artifact production, or as part of a ritual (Scheel-Ybert, chap. 22 in this volume) or treatment procedure such as using "chew sticks" (made of twigs, stems, or roots) for dental hygiene (Hyson 2003; Rasingam, Jeeva, and Kannan

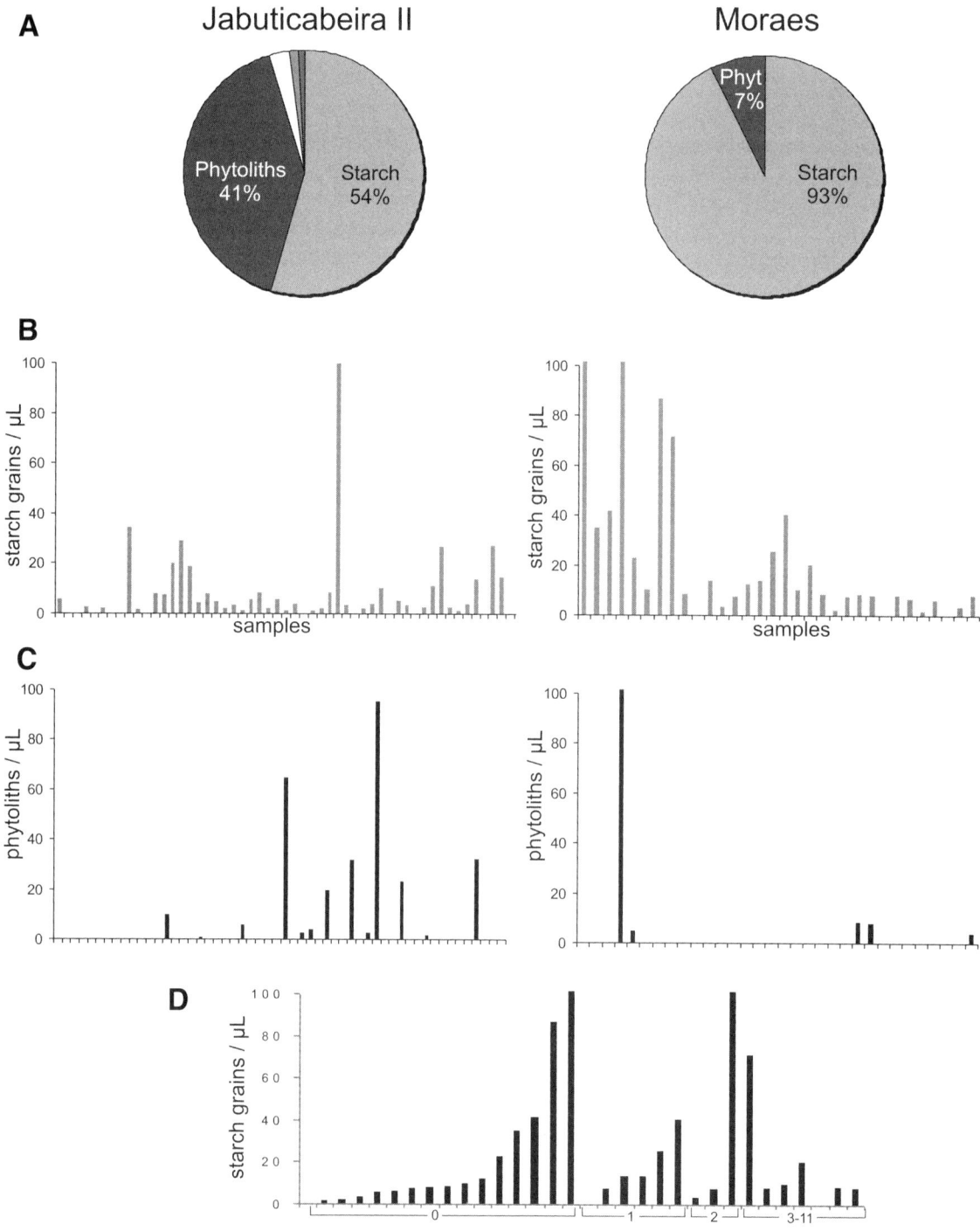

21.3. Comparison of micro-remains found in dental calculus from Jabuticabeira II and Moraes (with 54 and 32 samples, respectively): (A) proportion of starch grains and phytoliths (all samples from each site were taken together); (B) concentration of starch grains (grains/μL) in each sample; (C) concentration of phytoliths (phytoliths/μL) in each sample; and (D) lack of association (Chi-square = 0.3678; p = 0.5442) and correlation (correlation coefficient = 0.039; p = 0.847) of the number of caries and of the concentration of starch grains (grains/μL) per individual from Moraes.

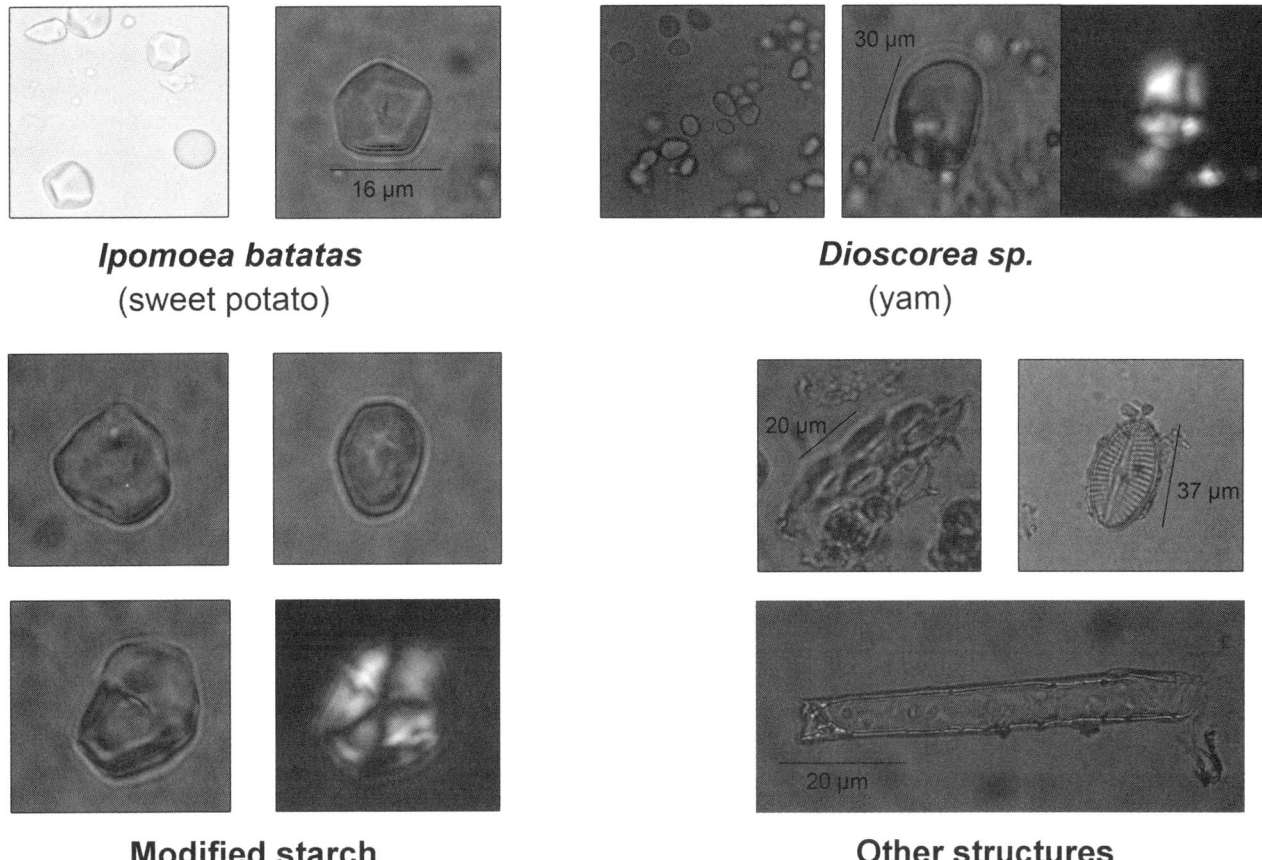

Ipomoea batatas
(sweet potato)

Dioscorea sp.
(yam)

Modified starch

Other structures

21.4. Upper row: starch grains consistent with Dioscorea sp. *and* Ipomoea batatas *from Jabuticabeira II samples (at the right side) compared to the images obtained from the reference material (at the left side). Lower row: examples of modified starch grains and other micro-remains found in the Jabuticabeira II and Moraes samples. 400x magnification.*

2012; Sofrata et al. 2011), a practice that is still common around the world (Elvin-Lewis 1980; Rasingam, Jeeva, and Kannan 2012; Sofrata et al. 2011). However, this practice would mechanically remove dental plaque (Sofrata et al. 2011), thereby preventing calculus formation, which does not seem to have been the case for the Jabuticabeira II group (high calculus index).

Additionally, other micro-particles were observed in Jabuticabeira II, but not in Moraes, including diatoms, epidermis fragments, and plant fibers. While the diatoms could have been ingested with aquatic food, the presence of plant micro-fragments other than starch grains could suggest a greater diversity of plants eaten in Jabuticabeira II than in Moraes (Eggers et al. 2008).

Food Processing

Apart from native starch grains, we noticed many grains with morphological alterations in both sambaquis (Figure 21.4)

that can be attributed to food processing (Henry, Brooks, and Piperno 2010; Henry and Piperno 2008). In fact, certain food-processing techniques remove toxic substances from plants and improve their palatability and nutritional quality (Beck 2006; Carmody and Wrangham 2009). Many starch storage organs are difficult to digest or are even inedible (Beck 2006), and many "seed and root foods" must be cooked or processed in a complex multi-step way (Beck 2006). There is one variety of manioc (*Manihot esculenta*), for example, with high concentrations of hydrocianic acid (Cascudo 2004). To be edible, the roots have to be peeled, ground, and then squeezed through a *tipiti* (a long and narrow flexible implement made of plant fibers). During this process the toxin-containing juice is removed. Only after this treated mass has dried can it be roasted and eaten like a tortilla (Cascudo 2004).

The modified starch grains found in the sambaquis suggest that processing of plant food occurred prior to consumption, especially in Jabuticabeira II where artifacts related to plant processing, such as mortars and pestles, were found. Additionally, dark fragments similar to charcoal were retrieved, which could also be related to food processing with fire (Torrence and Barton 2006).

consumed were probably sweet potato (*Ipomoea batatas*), yams (*Dioscorea* sp.), and plants from the Araceae family; and finally, (g) some of the starch grains found were damaged, and might have resulted from food-processing techniques.

CONCLUSIONS

The data obtained through dental calculus analyses are doubtless evidence of plants eaten by Brazilian shell mound builders. As constructing a reference collection for southern Brazil is a recent endeavor, many starch grains and phytoliths still lack taxonomic identification. This highlights the necessity to continue and amplify the construction of the reference collection, perhaps as an international consortium. However, the great variation of microparticle types suggests a high diversity of plant foods, as also noticed for other sambaquis (Wesolowski et al. 2010). We also conclude that: (a) indeed, the site with the higher caries rate (Moraes) shows a much higher proportion of starch grains than the site with a low caries rate (Jabuticabeira II), confirming our initial hypothesis; (b) therefore, diet must have contained more starchy and cariogenic foods in Moraes than in Jabuticabeira II; (c) there does not seem to be a correlation nor an association between the number of caries and the corresponding starch grain concentration per individual in Moraes, a fact that still needs clarification; (d) diet was not homogeneous among the individuals exhumed from each site; (e) a greater variety of plants and plant parts seems to have been consumed or might have been used for artifact production by the people from Jabuticabeira II; (f) some of the starchy plants

OUTLOOK

The study of micro-remains such as phytoliths and starch grains retrieved from dental calculus is very recent in Brazil. The ongoing construction of reference collections and identification keys for starch grains and phytoliths from modern Brazilian plants that has been started recently will allow better reconstructions of the sambaqui people's way of life. The best approach for this endeavor is investing in joint efforts of various specialists. Experiments especially designed to obtain data on plant food preparation and storage (experimental archaeology) are also welcomed. These approaches, and the optimization of retrieving and analyzing botanical remains, will unravel the diversity of plant usage by sambaqui people.

ACKNOWLEDGMENTS

We would like to thank Mirjana Roksandic, Karl Reinhard, Rita Scheel-Ybert, Paulo DeBlasis, Levy Figuti, Claudia Plens, Fabiana S. Ferreira, Veronica Wesolowski, Cecilia Petronilho, and the anonymous referees whose commentaries greatly improved our manuscript. Financial support: FAPESP (Grants 99/12684-2, 03/02059-0, 04/11038-0, 05/51710-1, 2008/53351-7) and CNPq (Productivity Grant).

CHAPTER TWENTY-TWO

LANDSCAPE AND USE OF PLANTS BY SOUTHERN AND SOUTHEASTERN BRAZILIAN SHELL MOUND BUILDERS

Rita Scheel-Ybert

SUMMARY

Sambaquis, Brazilian shell mounds, are among the best studied sites in the country. While recent research is drastically changing our views about this society, plant use and consumption still remain largely underestimated. Recent archaeobotanical research, however, is gradually changing this scenario. The present chapter synthesizes the current knowledge on the use of plants by sambaqui builders based on anthracological (charcoal) analysis as well as on archaeobotanical analysis. Eight sites were analyzed in southeastern Brazil (Rio de Janeiro State) and two sites were analyzed in southern Brazil (Santa Catarina State). Our results demonstrate that sambaqui people settled in the *restinga* ecosystem, usually near coastal forests and mangroves, and that plants played a much more important role in sambaqui people's subsistence than previously recognized. Plant foods were also a part of ritualistic activities, as we have indications that they were offered in funerary rituals and/or consumed during mortuary feasting. Fire was a central element in sambaqui people's life. The ecofacts studied by anthracology are the remains of countless fireplaces, many of which have been maintained for long periods in honor of the dead. Beyond their social importance, these fires' remains may give us information about a wide range of domestic and ritualistic aspects.

INTRODUCTION

Sambaquis, occurring along almost the entire Brazilian coast and testifying to an occupation dated from at least 8000 until ca. 1000 BP, are among the best studied sites in the country. Recent research, however, is drastically changing our views about these sites, as may be seen in several chapters in this book (e.g., Boyadjian and Eggers [chap. 21]; Figuti and Plens [chap. 16]; Gaspar et al. [chap. 7]; Klokler [chap. 11]; Okumura [chap. 13]; Okumura and Eggers [chap. 8]; and Souza [chap. 12]). In the place of the traditional image, namely that of shell deposits as food residues left behind by small groups of nomadic foragers, emerged the vision of monumental landscape markers constructed by sedentary fishers with a relatively complex organization.

In spite of the fact that questions related to landscape, diet, subsistence, and ceremonial activities have always been among the main interests of sambaqui archaeologists, the importance of plant use and consumption remained, until recently, largely underestimated. This is due to the poor preservation of plant remains in the archaeological record and to the fact that archaeobotany is still a very young field of research in Brazil, but also to the rarity of field research aimed at maximizing the recovery of plant remains through flotation techniques.

Indeed, preservation of noncarbonized botanical macro-remains in these sites is very rare. On the other hand, carbonized macro-remains are generally abundant in sambaqui archaeological sediments. A great deal of information on the abovementioned subjects resides in these charred remains, which until quite recently were collected exclusively for dating purposes.

Anthracology (charcoal analysis and identification based on wood anatomy criteria) provides paleoenvironmental and landscape reconstitutions, as well as paleo-ethnobotanical information concerning plant use. This discipline allows reliable reconstructions of the local

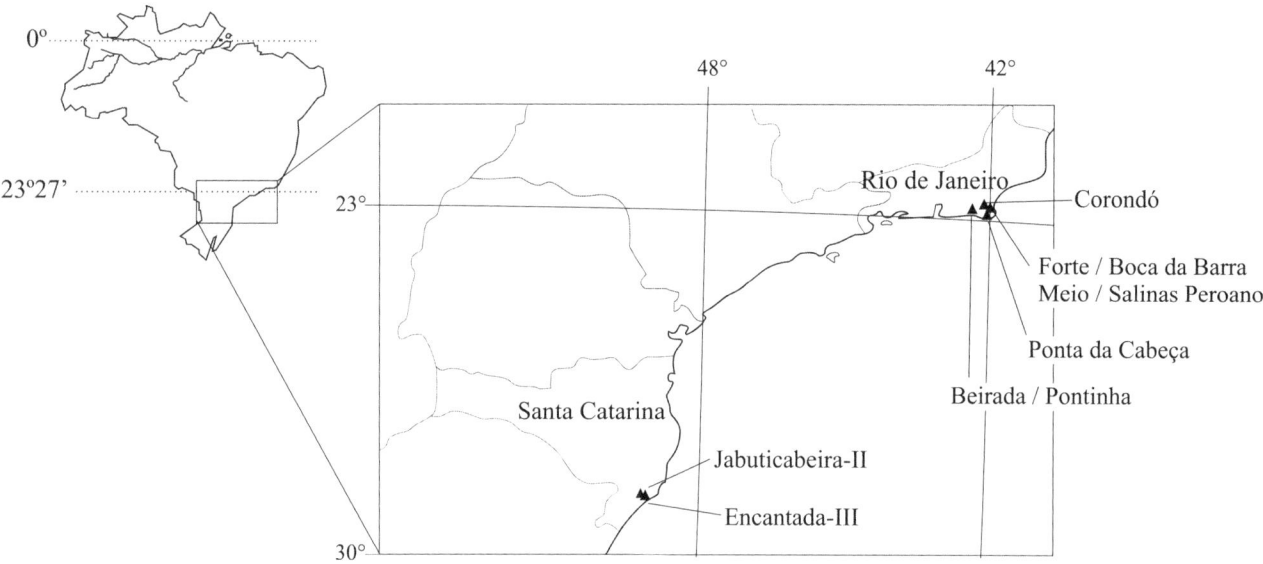

22.1. Geographic location of the studied sites.

woody vegetation, since the correlation with phytosocio-logical data is usually quite direct (Scheel-Ybert 2000). Charred macro-remains of fruits, seeds, tubers, and other dietary items are frequently preserved along with wood charcoal remains, thus providing information about food plants (Di Piazza 1998; Scheel-Ybert 2001a; Tengberg 2002).

In the present chapter, we aim to present a synthesis of the current knowledge on the use of plants by Brazilian sambaqui builders based on anthracological as well as on archaeobotanical analysis. These results disclose the importance of plants for sambaqui populations.

REGIONAL SETTING

Eight sambaquis from Rio de Janeiro State (Forte, Boca da Barra, Salinas Peroano, Meio, Ponta da Cabeça, Corondó, Pontinha, Beirada—22°53'–22°57'S /42°03'–42°33'W), and two sambaquis from Santa Catarina State (Jabuticabeira II, Encantada III—28°36'–28°37'S/48°54'–48°57'W) were studied (Figure 22.1). Their chronology is situated between 6190–5760 and 1380–1180 cal BP. Two of these sites present evidence of short occupations (Meio and Encantada III), but most of them attest to long-standing sedentary settlements (Table 22.1).

In most of the Rio de Janeiro State coastal zone, the climate is tropical: wet, hot, and rainy in summer with a mild dry season in winter. Plant associations, as in a great part of the Brazilian coast, vary according to physiographic conditions and distance from the ocean. The land-sea interface, especially the edges of rivers and lagoons, presents mangrove and saltwater marshes. The restinga ecosystem, a mosaic of vegetation types with diverse physiognomies, occupies the coastal sandy beach ridges. It varies from sparse, open plant communities, such as herbaceous and scrub formations ("open restinga") to dense evergreen forest ("restinga forest") (see Figure 22.2), and is characterized by high percentages of Myrtaceae. Farther from the ocean, low mountains and hills support the Atlantic Rain Forest, although trees may be lower than at higher altitudes.

In Santa Catarina State, the climate is temperate sub-hot, with mild mean-winter temperatures and no dry season. Natural vegetation is almost absent from this region today, but the sites are in the phytosociological domain of the restinga ecosystem. Restinga forest probably dominated the palaeodunes, and flooded restinga forests may have occurred in the plains before deforestation. The Atlantic Rain Forest is situated inland, as is the subtropical forest typical of the high plateaus over 800 meters in altitude.

MATERIALS AND METHODS

In the sambaquis Forte, Boca da Barra, Salinas Peroano, Meio, Pontinha, Beirada, Jabuticabeira II, and Encantada III, charcoal fragments were collected from vertical profiles in excavations of one square meter along the full height of the sambaquis, through a combination of natural archaeological layers and ten-centimeter artificial levels (artificial levels were defined, mostly, when the cultural layers were particularly large, something quite common in sambaquis). For each artificial level, 100 liters of sediments were floated (up to 200 liters in some samples of Forte). For natural layers and features, all the sediment was floated. Either the light or the heavy fractions were then sorted for charcoal recovery. In Jabuticabeira II we also analyzed charcoal samples coming from excavations on large surfaces. In sambaquis Ponta da Cabeça and Corondó, charcoal fragments were collected by dry screening during the archaeological excavations (Tenório, Barbosa, and Portela 1992; Dias and Carvalho 1983). Whenever possible, a minimum of 100 to 200 charcoal pieces were analyzed per sample; in cases with fewer pieces, all of the charcoal pieces from a sample were analyzed (see Table 22.1).

Charcoal pieces were analyzed under reflected light microscopes. The three fundamental sections for wood anatomy were exposed by hand-splitting. Systematic determination was obtained by comparing the anatomical structure observed with that of extant charred samples from a reference collection, and with descriptions and photographs from the literature. All charcoal fragments larger than four millimeters were analyzed, except for samples from Meio and Encantada III, which only presented fragments less than two millimeters.

Conventionally, anthracological results are presented either by ubiquity, by weight, or by count of charcoal fragments. Under tropical conditions, we recommend counting charcoal pieces rather than weighing, because (1) tropical woods present a very wide range of density values (from 0.1 to 1.3 in dry wood) that may distort biomass estimations based on weight; and (2) charcoal fragments, especially from shell mounds, are frequently impregnated with carbonates that increase the sample weight in uncontrollable proportions (Scheel-Ybert 2000).

Although ubiquity supporters argue that counting or weighing fragments is overly influenced by sampling and preservation biases, and therefore does not accurately reflect past vegetation (Willcox 1974; Popper 1988), studies based on the analysis of saturation and Gini-Lorenz curves

Table 22.1. Location and chronology of the analyzed sites, as well as total number of charcoal pieces and number of samples analyzed at each site[a]

Sites	Location	Coordinates	Conventional Ages	Calibrated Ages (2σ)	Charcoal Pieces	Samples
Forte		22°52'53" 42°00'28"	5520 ± 120 BP 2240 ± 70 BP	6180–5630 BP 1990-1670 BP	8101	43S
Salinas Peroano		22°52'49" 42°00'07"	4490 ± 40 BP 1830 ± 45 BP	5280–4870 BP 1820-1570 BP	2052	18
Boca da Barra	Cabo Frio, RJ	22°53'11" 42°00'06"	3760 ± 180 BP 1430 ± 55 BP	4540–3580 BP 1380-1180 BP	698	11
Meio		22°53'03" 42°00'02"	5180 ± 80 BP	5700–5320 BP	9	1
Corondó		22°45'30" 42°03'53"	3010 ± 80 BP 4260 ± 65 BP	2921–3346 BP 4529–4865 BP	851	16
Ponta da Cabeça	Arraial do Cabo, RJ	22°58'23" 42°01'50"	3270 ± 70 BP 2080 ± 40BP	3630–3270 BP 2110-1880 BP	1956	9
Beirada	Saquarema, RJ	22°55'32" 42°32'37"	4520 ± 190 BP 3800 ± 190 BP	5240–4190 BP 4250–3290 BP	519	11
Pontinha		22°55'26" 42°32'35"	2270 ± 190 BP 1790 ± 40 BP	2750–1750 BP 1730–1540 BP	1621	11
Jabuticabeira II	Jaguaruna, SC	28°36S 48°57'W	2890 ± 55 BP 1781 ± 65 BP	3206–2849 BP 1859–1526 BP	4047	54
Encantada-III		28°37'37"S, 48°54'52"W	4320 ± 40 BP 4420 ± 50 BP	4970–4830 BP 4961–4642 BP	265	4

[a] Dates given refer to the latest and to the earliest ages obtained; when only one date is presented, it refers to the base site.

(Scheel-Ybert 2002), as well as the application of multivariate analysis comparing charcoal records to the extant vegetation, have enabled us to demonstrate that the relative proportion of counted charcoal pieces shows a representative image of the surrounding vegetation, provided that a minimum of 100 or 200 charcoal fragments per sample are examined (e.g., Scheel-Ybert 2000).

RESULTS AND DISCUSSION

Landscape Reconstruction

Complete anthracological diagrams have been published previously (Bianchini 2008; Scheel-Ybert 2000, 2001b; Scheel-Ybert and Dias 2007; Scheel-Ybert, Bianchini, and DeBlasis 2009). Summary diagrams, where the different taxa have been grouped by plant formation, are presented for six sites, which are considered to be representative of the studied localities (Figure 22.2). Transversal sections of some of the identified charcoal fragments are presented in Figure 22.3.

A great floristic diversity characterizes all of the charcoal diagrams. Most of the ancient taxa identified (at the taxonomic level of family, genus, or "type") correspond to plant associations presently reported for the region. More than a hundred taxa were identified in these sites, indicating that domestic firewood was not collected on a restrictive basis.

For instance, each anthracological sample studied from the Forte site (corresponding to artificial archaeological levels of 100/200 liters of sediment) or from the Jabuticabeira II funerary area (corresponding to natural archaeological levels) consists of 30 to 50 taxa, a plant diversity that is comparable to what is normally found in phytosociological studies of one hectare of forest (an area considered to be representative of the forest as a whole; e.g., Scherer, Maraschin-Silva, and Baptista 2005; Silva and Scariot 2004).

In spite of all the processes that affect the charcoal sample from the moment of wood gathering until its analysis (physical transformations of charred wood, post-depositional processes, charcoal fragmentation, etc.), our results show that the anthracological assemblage resembles present-day plant associations fairly well (Scheel-Ybert 2000).

Anthracological results from southern and southeastern Brazilian sites demonstrate that sambaqui mound builders settled in the restinga ecosystem. They used to establish themselves in specific ecotones, reasonably close to other plant communities, such as humid coastal forests and mangroves, that were generally inside their site catchment area (Bianchini 2008; Scheel-Ybert 2000, 2001a, 2001b; Scheel-Ybert and Dias 2007; Scheel-Ybert, Bianchini, and DeBlasis 2009), and always in the vicinity of coastal lagoons (DeBlasis et al. 2007).

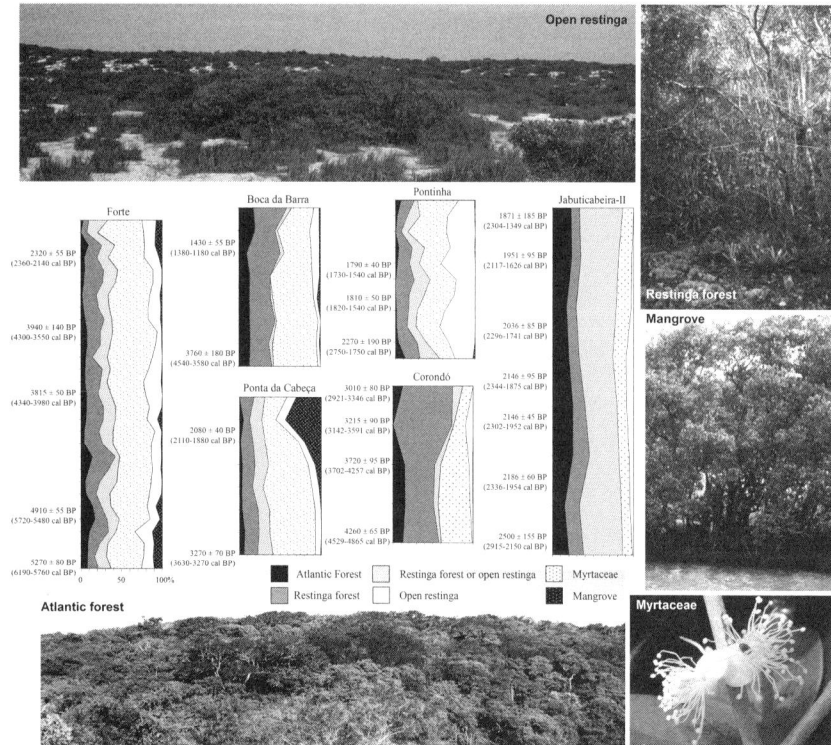

22.2. (left) Selected summary charcoal diagrams showing the most representative sites from Rio de Janeiro State (Forte, Boca da Barra, Pontinha, Ponta da Cabeça, Corondó), and Santa Catarina State (Jabuticabeira II), in percentages of charcoal pieces, and examples of the most important vegetation type. Species are grouped according to the vegetation types (adapted from Scheel-Ybert 2000, 2001b; Scheel-Ybert and Dias, 2007).

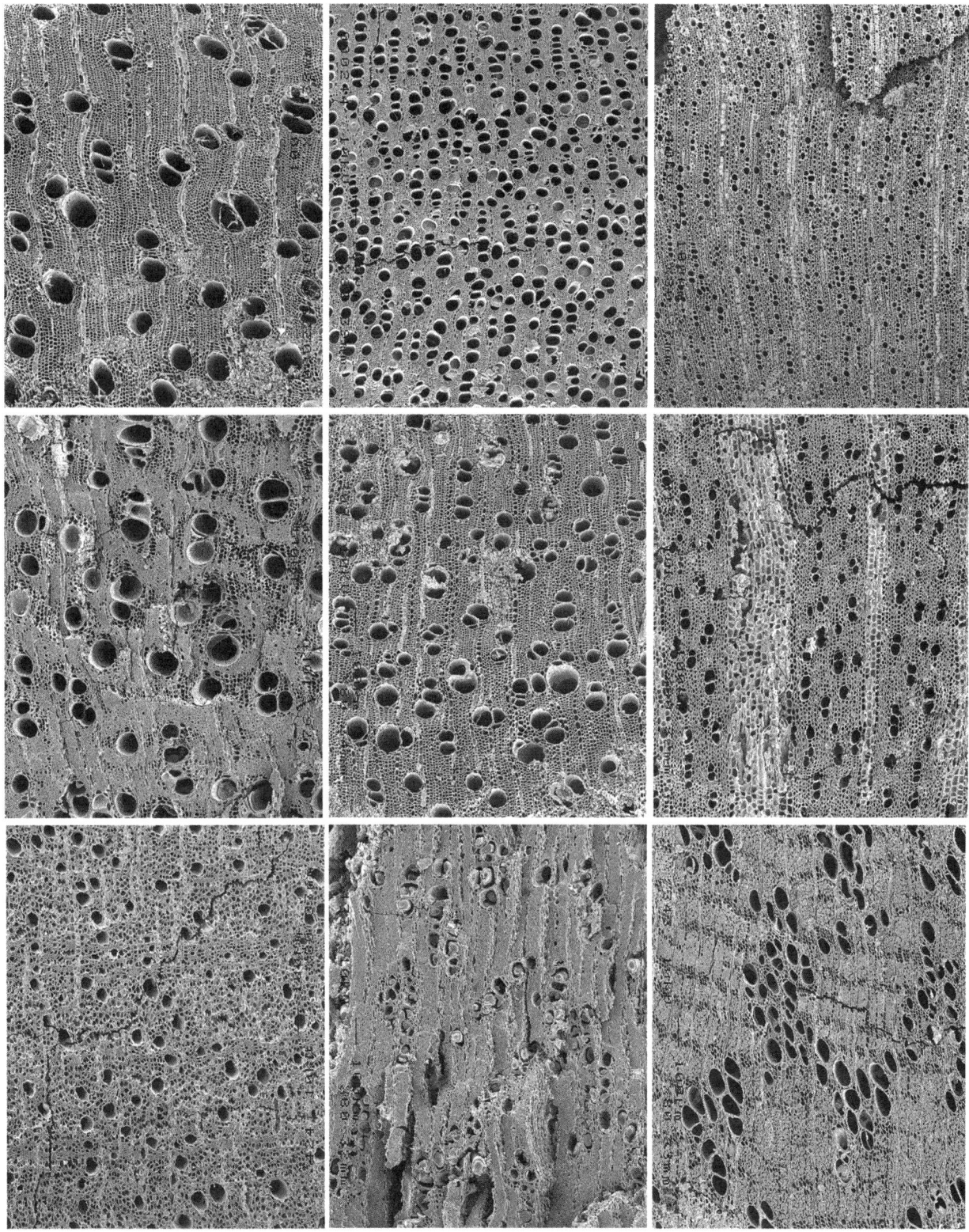

22.3. Transversal plan of some frequently found taxa: (A) cf. Astronium *(Anacardiaceae); (B)* Gochnatia *sp. (Compositae); (C)* Actinostemon *sp. (Euphorbiaceae); (D)* Caesalpinia *cf.* echinata *(Leguminosae, Caesalpinoideae); (E) Melastomataceae; (F)* Myrsine *sp. (Myrsinaceae); (G) Myrtaceae; (H)* Condalia *sp. (Rhamnaceae); (I)* Sideroxylon *cf.* obtusifolium *(Sapotaceae).*

As anthracological spectra reflect the local vegetation, each site presents the predominance of one or another vegetation type, depending on its geographical location (Figures 22.2 and 22.4). Open-restinga taxa predominate in sambaquis Beirada and Pontinha, both situated between the sea and a coastal lagoon, in the phytosociological domain of the open restinga. Open-restinga and restinga-forest taxa prevail in Forte, Ponta da Cabeça, and Jabuticabeira II; the first two sites are presently situated near the sea, but clearly in ecotones; although the latter is situated farther inland, the sea level was higher at the time it was occupied. Anthracological spectra of Salinas Peroano, Boca da Barra, and Corondó, situated farther inland (Corondó) or upon coastal crystalline hills (the other two), present a significant contribution of restinga forest and Atlantic forest taxa. Mangrove elements are present in Forte, Salinas Peroano, Boca da Barra, Ponta da Cabeça, and Beirada (Scheel-Ybert 2000, 2001b). The few charcoal micro-fragments provided by sambaquis Meio and Encantada III showed that a restinga-type vegetation existed near these sites during the occupation period; mangrove was also present at Encantada III (Scheel-Ybert 2000; Scheel-Ybert, Bianchini, and DeBlasis 2009).

The charcoal assemblage at each site did not change significantly during the several centuries of occupation. However, climatic oscillations did occur, at least in the southeastern coast. Oscillations in the mangrove vegetation (Scheel-Ybert 2000), corroborated by modifications of the lagoon salinity recorded by several cores' sediments (Tasayco-Ortega 1996), suggest regional climatic variations during the Holocene. These changes were associated with two more humid episodes (recorded from ca. 5500 to 4900/4500 and from ca. 2300 to 2000 ^{14}C years BP), intercalated by two episodes of increased dryness with increased lagoon salinity (from ca. 4900/4500 to 2300 and from ca. 2000 to 1400 ^{14}C years BP) (Scheel-Ybert 2000).

Note that the absence of significant variation in the land plant associations around sambaquis, which has been pointed to as a *vegetation stability* (Scheel-Ybert 2000), cannot be associated with a stationary or immutable landscape. In addition to the attested climatic variations and to the activities of human populations that inhabited the region for thousands of years, significant sea-level variations changed the coastal outline and the local lagoon conformation (Angulo, Lessa, and Souza 2006; Kneip 2004; Martin, Dominguez, and Bittencourt 2003). What probably happened either in southeastern or in southern Brazil was a retreat of the coastal line and a reorganization of the coastal lagoons' size and distribution, as a consequence of a lower

sea level. In this process, the restinga vegetation advanced inland, changing its distribution in the landscape, but maintaining its structure and floristic composition.

The relative vegetation stability during the late Holocene has been associated with the edaphic character of the coastal vegetation, as the restinga ecosystem is essentially related to sandy soils and to the geomorphologic nature of sandy beach ridges, which results in a greater resilience to climatic change (Scheel-Ybert 2000). In addition to that, however, it is possible that the sambaqui people themselves might have contributed to this landscape construction (Bianchini 2008).

Indeed, the strong contribution of Myrtaceae wood species in all sambaquis' anthracological diagrams is striking. Although common in different communities of Brazilian vegetation, Myrtaceae are typical of restinga formations, particularly in Rio de Janeiro State (Araujo and Henriques 1984). The restinga flora typically presents high species diversity and a great number of individuals from this family, which frequently assumes a strong dominance in this vegetation physiognomy. Many of these species produce edible fruits; a number of them, domesticated or semi-domesticated, are important food items in tropical regions (several species of *Psidium*, *Eugenia*, *Myrciaria*, *Campomanesia*, *Syzygium*, and others). The prominence of Myrtaceae species in southeastern and southern sambaquis demonstrates that these plants were largely used by sambaqui builders, either as firewood or, probably, as food. The presence of Myrtaceae seeds (as well as wood) associated with the funerary ritual in the sambaqui Jabuticabeira II, as will be discussed later, suggests that plants of this family had a high intrinsic value for these people (Bianchini 2008).

It is likely that sambaqui builders may have behaved as dispersal agents for these plants—transporting seeds along their paths, exchanging fruits from their "gardens" or in any way managing them, even if incipiently. These activities would tend to increase these species' importance in the environment (either in terms of species diversity or in number of individuals). Indeed, the increase of plant diversity in a landscape is frequently associated with human activities, either through plant management or by opening clearings, planting trees, or introducing new species (Odum 1983). If that is true, the high frequency of Myrtaceae and the relative stability of the restinga environment would persist not *in spite of* the human occupation, but most likely *because of it*.

It is also possible that sambaqui people managed plants of *Sideroxylon obtusifolium*, a Sapotaceae (Scheel-Ybert 2001a). Trees and shrubs from this species are presently commonly found in the restinga; this wood is quite common in most of the southeastern sambaqui charcoal samples as well. What makes it remarkable, however, is the present association of *Sideroxylon* with sambaquis—these plants are very often found in a site's vicinity and frequently over the mounds. Even if this is a fragile indication, we are now well aware that human intervention has had significant consequences on the structure of the present vegetation. The systematic association of these plants with archaeological sites might be an indication of their ancient use, representing the relict of past human activities related to this plant.

INFERENCES ON WOOD USE

Artifacts or Construction Material

Wood was certainly used in many ways by the sambaqui people as construction material, for artifact manufacturing such as boats and tools, for firewood, and so forth. Wood vestiges, however, are rarely preserved, and wooden artifacts are not likely to be preserved by carbonization. Wood used for construction material, however, has a better chance of being preserved in this way, as houses and fences may be accidentally or intentionally burnt.

The remains of a charred post associated with a funerary context at the site Jabuticabeira II were identified as a Lauraceae species (Bianchini, Scheel-Ybert, and Gaspar 2007), a plant from the cinnamon family. Another sample from this site, coming from a feature in a funerary area where several postholes were identified, presented a particularly high frequency of Lauraceae charcoal pieces. It is possible, although not proven, that this charcoal also comes from carbonized posts (Bianchini 2008).

The little data available does not allow for inferring wood selection or special choice. Yet it is remarkable that this particular wood was used, as these species are known for their distinct features and high wood quality (Bianchini, Scheel-Ybert, and Gaspar 2007). In modern times, this hardwood has been widely exploited in Brazil for its resistance, durability, and essence contents, conferring it a high commercial value (Marques 2001).

Wood as Fuel in Domestic and Ritualistic Activities

There is clear evidence that the main source of firewood for sambaqui builders was opportunistic gathering of dead wood (e.g., Scheel-Ybert 2000). The high floristic diversity of charcoal diagrams points to nonselective wood gathering. Frequent traces of decay and insect larvae attack before charring, interpreted as signs of deadwood

gathering, are an additional demonstration of opportunistic firewood collection.

The great floristic diversity of anthracological assemblages supports the hypothesis that charcoal remains are associated with an extended temporal activity and correspond to the "sampling" of wood in a relatively large area around the site. These are essential premises for reliable paleoecological interpretation based on archaeological charcoal (Chabal 1997).

The wood charcoal preserved in a site, in the case of long-lasting settlements, is evidence of a number of fire events, including domestic firewood burning and specialized activities such as smoking, drying, and ceremonial or ritualistic fires. These different fire events involve either random gathered wood (domestic burning) or possibly selected species (specialized and ritualistic activities). In this situation, it is likely that most of the plant species present in the environment were eventually transported to the settlement site, where they might have a chance of being preserved as charcoal (Théry-Parisot, Chabal, and Chrzavzez 2010). This argument also warrants paleoecological interpretation based on archaeological charcoal. Moreover, it opens a large new field of investigation concerning wood use.

We do not have evidence of quotidian specialized hearths in sambaquis. On the other hand, ritualistic hearths are in the very center of the sambaquis culture. Most sambaquis show an intense relation with fire. Hearths are essential elements of the funerary ritual, being invariably present somewhat close to the body. Numerous and frequently very large hearths occur in many sites.

There is no evidence of wood selection for these hearths. In Jabuticabeira II, the detailed analysis of some of these features demonstrated particularly high wood species diversity, as well as a high frequency of seeds, which will be discussed hereafter (Bianchini 2008). The three hearths associated with a funerary area in Locus 1 presented between 30 and almost 50 taxa per sample of ca. 100 to 200 charcoal pieces. This finding is very significant, as it points to activities that are not restricted in time, but long-lasting.

Hearths that have had a short utilization present only a few taxa, corresponding to the few branches that have been used to set that particular fire. Hearths presenting a high taxonomic diversity correspond to fires that have been repeatedly lit at the same place, or else that have been maintained and continuously fed for a long time. This means Jabuticabeira II funerary hearths represent long-lasting events, suggesting that the mortuary rites of sambaqui people might be very important events persisting for several days.

Nonfunerary layers in ritually constructed sambaquis (e.g., Jabuticabeira II), interpreted as construction material intended to cover the funerary areas in mounded structures ("covering" layers), also contain charcoal fragments. This charcoal is not gathered in hearths, and the sediments and shells around it do not present signs of burning, thus characterizing "dispersed charcoal" (Chabal 1997; Scheel-Ybert 2004). In this precise case, we cannot speak about charcoal naturally dispersed from the ceremonial hearths, as the context of deposition of funerary and covering layers is clearly distinct. Neither is there evidence of dispersal from local fires, as these layers do not contain any archaeological evidence of having been occupational spaces. We might think, therefore, that this charcoal originated from deposits that were accumulated elsewhere in order to provide the "construction material" for these covering layers, and only afterward transported to the sambaqui site, where they composed a different depositional pattern (Villagrán et al. 2010), one in which the different materials are all mixed together and do not present any particular identifiable feature. If this assumption is true, we can logically presume that this accumulation was done in a dumping area or in a domestic context, and therefore that it contains the leftovers of different activities, potentially including food remains (mollusks, fish, and eventually plants) and charcoal. The high diversity of charcoal samples from the shellfish covering layers supports this hypothesis (Scheel-Ybert 2001b), as it points to the residues of a long-duration activity.

On the other hand, it must be considered that in some sambaqui sites, as at Sernambetiba (southeast Brazil), for instance, the shellfish layers are closely alternated with dark carbonized layers associated with very large local hearths, in the base of which field excavations have identified high quantities of fish bones. These layers indicate in situ activities, suggesting that the sites were frequently revisited and that important fire ceremonies were performed at these places. The revisitation of sites outside the funerary ritual has already been proposed for Jabuticabeira II, where it is suggested by fine layers of burnt shells, associated with a significantly higher charcoal diversity (Bianchini 2008; Gaspar 2004).

Wood Selection

Human choices are frequently dictated by cultural beliefs, and these are not always determined by the taxonomic or technological properties of the chosen element. First of all,

we must consider that taxonomic classifications differ in each culture, and that no prehistoric society will classify plants according to our Linnaean system. The concept of "species" itself is relative and varies greatly between traditional societies. Systems of plant classification are innumerable, and they may consider either appearance, usefulness, or any other subjective or objective parameter (Lévi-Strauss 1962).

In addition, technological requirements are also inherent to different cultural groups. When thinking about "wood selection," a modern-society individual might evoke notions such as "good fuel" or "calorific power." In traditional groups, however, the choice of a fuel will vary according to the usage intended for that particular fire: heating, cooking, illuminating, protecting, drying, smoking, communicating, transforming raw matter, cremating, feasting, and so on. And yet, most of the wood fuel properties required for attaining each one of these objectives (e.g., availability, ease of ignition, durability, blazing, smoking ability, smell) can be obtained either by varying the wood species or by varying its diameter, humidity rate, and/or physiological state (healthy or decayed wood) (Théry-Parisot, Chabal, and Chrzavzez 2010).

Cultural and technological choices are thus extremely complex, and not always easy to perceive in the archaeological record. In the case of concentrated charcoal in archaeological features, some choices can be recognized by the repetition of a given pattern: for instance, the reiterated presence of a specific taxon/diameter/physiological state in particular circumstances (e.g., funerary or specific hearths). In the case of dispersed charcoal in the archaeological sediments, choices can be evidenced by discrepancies in the frequencies of a given taxon between the anthracological record and known vegetation types (underrepresentation or overrepresentation of taxa).

In most southeastern sites studied (Forte, Boca da Barra, Salinas Peroano, and Ponta da Cabeça), the high frequencies of *Condalia* sp., a Rhamnaceae species, fit in this criterion (Scheel-Ybert 2000). *Condalia buxifolia*, the only species that occurs in present-day Brazilian coastal vegetation, is a very rare taxon (Silva and Oliveira 1989). It is possible that this species was at least more frequent than it is nowadays (one cannot *choose* a plant that does not *exist*); however, the floristic assemblage of the archaeological charcoal is otherwise very similar to the present vegetation, indicating that no significant environmental change has taken place and that *Condalia* is indeed overrepresented. We can thus conclude that this species was especially selected for cultural reasons that are still

22.4. Histogram showing the number of seeds and tuber fragments in sambaqui Forte, Rio de Janeiro State, along with food remains: wood charcoal ratios. Ratios represent the number of food remains (seeds + palm nuts + tubers) divided by the total number of charcoal pieces in each sample (adapted from Scheel-Ybert 2001a).

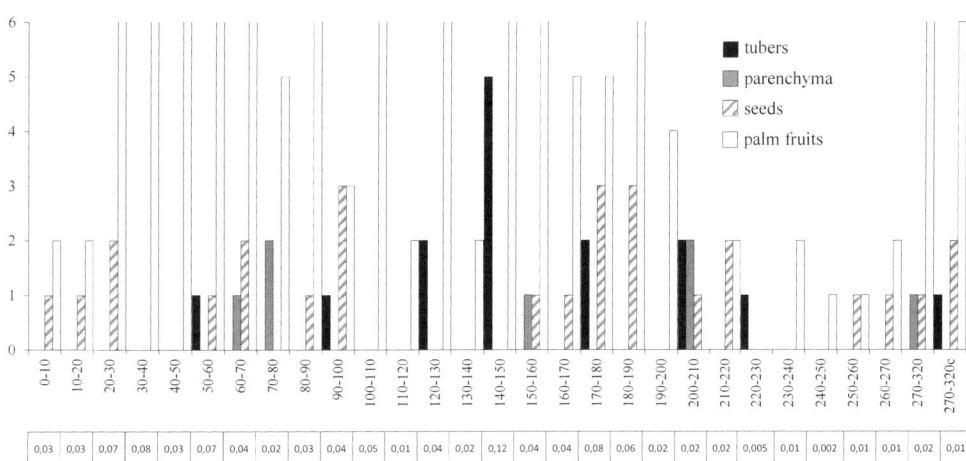

impossible to identify. We can also hypothesize that its scarceness in the present vegetation is a consequence of its overexploitation in the past.

While a ritual utilization of this taxon cannot be discarded, this species selection could also be explained by economic reasons (Scheel-Ybert 2000). Samuel J. Record and Robert W. Hess (1943) report that this wood, considered an excellent combustible, also produces a blue pigment; moreover, the root bark of some species is used as soap or medicine, and the plant bears edible fruits.

FOOD PLANTS

Presently, it is largely accepted that sambaqui builders were fisher-gatherers. The establishment of fishing as their main economic activity was the first important change to the traditional interpretations about this society (Bandeira 1992; De Masi 2001; Figuti 1992, 1993; Figuti and Klokler 1996; see also Gaspar et al. and Klokler, chaps. 7 and 11 in this volume). For many Brazilian archaeologists, however, the notion of "mollusk gatherers" is still implicit in the second part of this expression. But the time when plant consumption could only be indirectly inferred through the existence of lithic artifacts attributed to plant processing (Tenório 1991) has now elapsed. Studies on macro- and micro-botanical remains are once again changing our views about sambaqui builders (Bianchini 2008; Boyadjian 2007; Scheel-Ybert 2001a; Scheel-Ybert et al. 2003, 2009; Wesolowski et al. 2007; Wesolowski et al. 2010; see also Boyadjian and Eggers, chap. 21 in this volume) and demonstrating that plant consumption, even if secondary, certainly played a pivotal part in their diet and way of life.

Palm nuts, probably mostly from *Astrocaryum*, *Bactris*, *Syagrus*, and *Butia*, are frequently found in sambaquis (e.g., Carvalho 1984; Heredia and Beltrão 1980; Kneip and Pallestrini 1987), as opposed to other seeds or tubers. This may be explained by differential preservation. As preservation of plant remains in a tropical climate is achieved almost exclusively by carbonization, it depends on whether or not the plant material is directly exposed to fire. Palm nuts are likely to be thrown into the fire after the edible kernels are removed, and may even be recycled as supplementary fuel. Seeds and tubers, however, are less likely to be preserved by carbonization, as it depends on the way they are prepared to be eaten and on the likeliness of their getting in direct contact with fire (Scheel-Ybert 2001a). For this reason, they are rarely identified in archaeological sites.

The first anthracological/archaeobotanical analysis in sambaquis, however, demonstrated that charred seeds and tuber fragments, besides palm nuts, are relatively frequent (Scheel-Ybert 2001a). The sambaquis Forte, Salinas Peroano, Boca da Barra, Pontinha, and Beirada, in southeastern Brazil, presented vestiges of edible plants within most of their archaeological levels, starting from the beginning of the occupation. Although never abundant, they are a significant part of the archaeological record, and their preservation attests that they were widely used by these populations and that plant gathering greatly contributed to their diet.

The retrieving of these vestiges, however, was only possible because a great investment in charcoal identification was made. We take the sambaqui Forte as an example (Figure 22.4). In this site, 8,887 charred pieces were analyzed; from these, 250 could be attributed to dietary remains, and

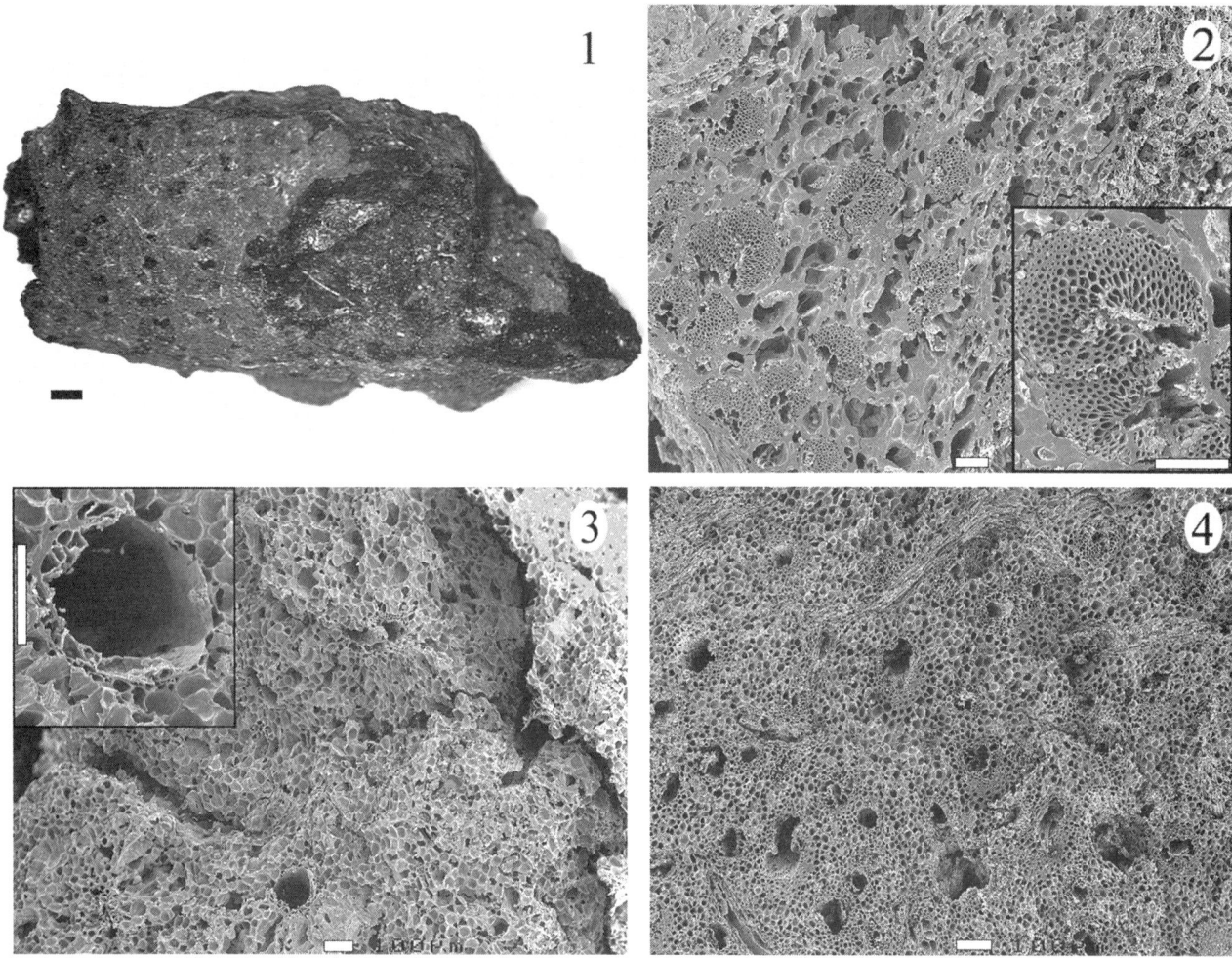

22.5. (1) and (2) cf. Gramineae/Cyperaceae tuber, macroscopic and SEM views. Salinas Peroano (1820–1570 cal BP). (3) Dioscorea tuber. Forte (4340–3980 cal BP). (4) unidentified monocotyledonous tuber. Forte (5720–5480 cal BP). Black scale = 1 mm. White scales = 100 μm (from Scheel-Ybert 2001a). Copyright permission accorded by Elsevier.

only 15 were tuber remains. As already mentioned, this is not a measure of food consumption; rather, it is a direct consequence of differential preservation.

Besides palm nuts (*Syagrus* sp.), one Poaceae or Cyperaceae and several yam (*Dioscorea* spp.) tubers were identified, along with other monocotyledonous tubers and several seeds that remain unidentified (Figure 22.5). The high proportion of indetermination in these analyses may be explained by the difficulties of the determination process, due to high fragmentation and to the scarcity of comparative material.

At Forte, tuber fragments are present starting from the first archaeological layer, dated at 6180–5630 cal BP, until the more recent layer, after 1990–1670 cal BP. It is very interesting to note that, unlike the site Jabuticabeira II,

presented below, in southeastern Brazilian sites dietary remains occur in all archaeological levels (Scheel-Ybert 2001a). However, as all southeastern sites presented here were excavated during the 1980s (cf. Gaspar 1991; Kneip 1980, 1994; Tenório, Barbosa, and Portela 1992), the archaeological context of the analyzed samples is not so well known (see Gaspar et al., chap. 7 in this volume, for the paradigm changes in Brazilian sambaquis archaeology).

On the contrary, Jabuticabeira II is presently one of the best excavated and understood sites in Brazil (cf. Bianchini 2008; DeBlasis et al. 2007; Fish et al. 2000; Klokler 2008; Villagrán et al. 2010). The magnitude of the site itself, with its complex constructive process and rich funerary offerings and features that reflect an elaborated mortuary ritual and ceremonial feastings, point to a special "concern with the body" in this society (Gaspar 2004; Klokler 2008). In these circumstances, we may expect that most of the material integrated into the funerary ritual might have been carefully selected, in agreement with the ideological and/or symbolic universe of the group (Bianchini 2008).

At this site, three cubic meters of sediments from the covering layers of a funerary area in Locus 1 were sampled, producing 1,788 wood charcoal fragments (596 remains/cubic meter) and no food remains (Scheel-Ybert 2001b). Sediments sampled from a funerary area at the same locus corresponded to 0.7 cubic meters, in which 2,193 wood charcoal fragments were retrieved, along with 149 seeds, 115 palm nuts, and one tuber fragment (4,097 remains/cubic meter) (Bianchini 2008). The funerary layers are clearly distinguished from covering layers not only by the presence of seeds, nuts, and tuber remains (Figure 22.6), but also by the floristic composition of samples, even if both ensembles indicate a restinga landscape, with the presence of the Atlantic forest farther away (Figure 22.2). Moreover, funerary and covering layers are intrinsically different in the archaeological contents, as virtually all significant features and artifacts are concentrated in the former (see Gaspar et al. [chap. 7]; Klokler [chap. 7]; and Okumura and Eggers [chap. 8] in this volume).

Currently, 55 food-remains specimens have already been identified. Among these, there was one seed of Cucurbitaceae (probably *Cucurbita*), 17 Myrtaceae, 19 Annonaceae, and 18 Palmae (*Syagrus* sp. and *Butia* sp.) (Figure 22.7), all of which produce fruits that are still used as food in Brazil and other countries (Bianchini 2008).

The abundance of seeds and palm nuts associated with specific features of the mortuary layers such as hearths contrasts with their absence in the covering layers, suggesting that they were an important component of the funerary ritual practiced in Jabuticabeira II (Bianchini 2008). It is likely that fruits were used as offerings or consumed during the funerary rituals or feasting ceremonies. Indeed, the presence of food plants in funerary contexts is frequently associated with the practice of feasting (Pauketat et al. 2002; Rosenswig 2007). This evidence strengthens the hypothesis of funerary feastings (Klokler 2008), while demonstrating that not only animal food was used in these ceremonies, but plant food as well.

It is not possible, at this stage, to recognize if these seeds were the product of gathering, or if they are related to plant management or food production activities. This is a very interesting research subject, as it has been proposed that the first plant domestications and food production might have originated from the intensification of gathering and

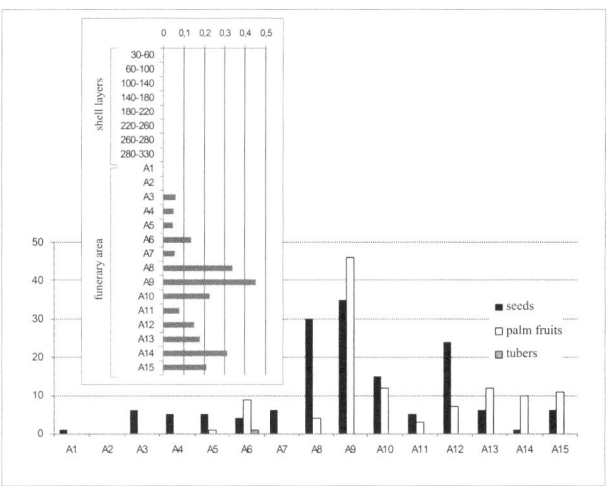

22.6. Bar graph showing the food remains: wood charcoal ratios in Trench T18/Locus 1 of sambaqui Jabuticabeira II (Santa Catarina State) and histogram showing the absolute number of seeds, palm nuts, and tuber fragments in the funerary area (adapted from Bianchini 2008). Levels 30–330 = shellfish-rich covering layers; A1, A2, A3 = shellfish-rich sediments with charcoal—intermediate layers between the covering layers and the funerary area; A4 = sandy sediments with charcoal; A5, A6 = hearths with shells and fish bones; A7 = shellfish-rich sediments with postholes; A8 = hearths with shells and fish bones; A9 = hearths with shells, fish bones, thermal flakes; A10 = hearth next to the burial; A11 = fish bones; A12 = ashes with postholes; A13, A14 = shells; A15 = charred shells

22.7. Seeds from the funerary area in Trench T18/Locus 1 of sambaqui Jabuticabeira II (Santa Catarina State) (A) Cucurbitaceae; (B) Syagrus sp. (Palmae); (C) Annonaceae; (D) Rollinia sp. (Annonaceae); (E) Myrtaceae (adapted from Bianchini 2008).

management processes, especially for food items for which the context of consumption was ritualistic (Hayden 2003). Regardless, however, their presence in this archaeological context surely indicates intentionality and labor investment (Bianchini 2008).

Although we have no evidence of these fruits being consumed in domestic contexts, it is quite probable that they were. Ritual practices and quotidian activities may be intimately related in several aspects (Hodder 2005). Moreover, mortuary rituals are among the routine, strategic engagements through which people reproduce the conditions of their own lives (Barrett 1990).

The absence of vestiges of these seeds in the covering layers is not contradictory with this hypothesis, even if the material that originated them was effectively from a domestic context, as proposed above, because it is likely that the context of fruit consumption in domestic spaces was different from the ritual practices. That is to say, during funerary rituals the seeds might be regularly charred, because in this context they represent an offering; in domestic contexts, however, fleshy fruits like Myrtaceae and Annonaceae are consumed fresh, and therefore have little chance of entering into contact with fire and thus being uncommonly preserved as archaeological vestiges.

CONCLUSIONS

The archaeobotanical research carried out during the last few years in Brazil has greatly improved the understanding of sambaqui builders' settlement and use of plant resources. While this work is still in progress, we have already achieved some important results, especially concerning landscape reconstruction, firewood use in domestic and ritualistic contexts, and plant consumption.

All anthracological results converge in demonstrating that sambaqui people settled in the restinga ecosystem. Their firewood and plant catchment area included the open restinga, the restinga forest, and, less frequently the Atlantic Rain Forest, as well as mangroves, when these existed. It is now important to investigate whether sambaqui mound builders have effectively contributed to the restinga landscape construction, either disseminating, managing, or cultivating Myrtaceae, Sapotaceae, tuber-bearing, and/or other plants. We also expect that new studies will advance our understanding about specific uses that these populations made of plants, including wood selection for special purposes, either economic/technological or ritualistic.

Our results have also contributed to demonstrating the importance of plants to the sambaqui people's subsistence. Yams and other tubers, palm fruits, Myrtaceae, Annonaceae, Cucurbitaceae, and surely many other plant species were making a substantial contribution to their diet. At the same time, these plants played an important role in ritualistic activities, as we have indications that they were offered in funerary rituals and/or were consumed during mortuary feastings. More research is needed on this subject in order to gather a better understanding of the plants that were effectively used, as well as to determine whether food production activities were in practice at any level.

Fire was a central element in the life of sambaqui people. The ecofacts studied by anthracology are the remains of countless fireplaces, many of which were maintained for long periods in honor of the dead. In addition to being monumental constructions, erected to mark the landscape, sambaquis were made even more visible by the blazing of flames upon them. Beyond their social importance, these fire remains may give us information about a wide range of domestic and ritualistic aspects of the lives of sambaqui builders.

ACKNOWLEDGMENTS

The author is deeply indebted to Gina Bianchini, Veronica Wesolowski, Sabine Eggers, Célia Boyadjian, and MaDu Gaspar for so many enriching discussions and contributions that greatly improved the manuscript and were fundamental to shaping it into its present form. I also thank Stephanie Armstrong for language revision and anonymous referees for helpful comments and advice, as well as the National Council of Technological and Scientific Development (CNPq) and the Carlos Chagas Filho Foundation for Research Support of the State of Rio de Janeiro (FAPERJ) for financial support.

Acheson, Steven. 1998. *In the Wake of the ya'áats' xaatgáay [Iron People]: A Study of Changing Settlement Strategies Among the Kunghit Haida.* Oxford: Archeopress, British Archaeological Reports, International Series No. 711.

Adler, Michael A., and Richard H. Wilshusen. 1990. Large-Scale Integrative Facilities in Tribal Societies: Cross-Cultural and Southwestern U.S. Examples. *World Archaeology* 22 (2): 133–46.

Afonso, Marisa C., and Paulo DeBlasis. 1994. Aspectos da Formação de um Grande Sambaqui: Alguns Indicadores em Espinheiros II, Joinville. *Revista do Museu de Arqueologiae Etnologia* 4:21–30.

Albert, Rosa M., Ofer Lavi, Lara Estroff, Steve Weiner, Alexander Tsatskin, Avraham Ronen, and Simcha Lev-Yadun. 1999. Mode of Occupation of Tabun Cave, Mt. Carmel, Israel, During the Mousterian Period: A Study of the Sediments and Phytoliths. *Journal of Archaeological Science* 26 (10): 1249–60.

Alekshin, V. A. 1983. Burial Customs as an Archaeological Source. *Current Anthropology* 24 (2): 137–49.

Allen, Melinda S. 2006. New Ideas About Late Holocene Climate Variability in the Central Pacific. *Current Anthropology* 47:521–35.

Álvarez, Myrian. 2003. Organización Tecnológica en el Canal Beagle. El Caso de Túnel I (Tierra del Fuego, Argentina). PhD diss., Universidad de Buenos Aires, Argentina.

Álvarez, Myrian, Débora Zurro, Ivan Briz, Marco Madella, Margarita Osterrieth, and Natalia Borreli. 2009. Análisis de los Procesos Productivos en las Sociedades Cazadoras-Recolectoras-Pescadoras de la Costa Norte del Canal Beagle (Argentina): el Sitio Lanashuaia. In *Arqueología de la Patagonia. Una Mirada desde el Último Confín*, edited by M. Salemme, F. Santiago, M. Álvarez, E. Piana, M. Vázquez, and E. Mansur, 903–17. Ushuaia, Argentina: Editorial Utopías.

Alvim, Marilia C. de M., and D. P. Mello Filho. 1965. Morfologia Craniana da População do Sambaqui da Cabeçuda (Laguna-SC) e sua Relação com Outras Populações de Paleoameríndios do Brasil. Vol. 2. In *Homenage a Juan Comas en su 65 aniversário*, 359–66. N.p.: Editorial Libros de México.

———. 1967/1968. Morfologia da População do Sambaqui do Forte Marechal Luz (Santa Catarina). *Revista de Antropologia* 15/16:1–12.

Alvim, Marilia C. de M., and Sheila M. F. M. de Souza. 1990. Relações Biológicas entre Populações Indígenas Atuais e Pré-Históricas do Brasil. *Clio* 1 (6): 69–79.

Alvim, Marilia C. de M., Dorath P. Uchôa, and João C. de O. Gomes. 1989. Análise e Interpretação da Hiperostose Porótica em Crânios Humanos do Sambaqui de Cabeçuda (SC—Brasil). *Revista de Pré-História* 7:127–45.

Alvim, Marilia C. de M., Marcus I. Vieira, and Lilia M. C. Machado. 1975. Os Construtores do Sambaqui de Cabeçuda, SC e de Piaçaguera, SP: Estudo Morfológico Comparativo. *Arquivos de Anatomia e Antropologia da Universidade Souza Marques (Rio de Janeiro)* 1:393–406.

Alvim, Pedro, and Mary Jackes. In prep. Reconstructing Moita do Sebastião, The Second Step.

Ambrose, Stanley H., and John Krigbaum. 2003. Bone Chemistry and Bioarchaeology. *Journal of Anthropological Archaeology* 22:193–99.

Ambrose, Stanley H., and Lynette Norr. 1993. Experimental Evidence for the Relationship of the Carbon Isotope Ratios of Whole Diet and Dietary Protein to Those of Bone Collagen and Carbonate. In *Prehistoric Human Bone: Archaeology at the Molecular Level*, edited by J. B. Lambert and G. Grupe, 1–37. New York: Springer-Verlag.

Ames, Kenneth M. 1994. The Northwest Coast: Complex Hunter-Gatherers, Ecology, and Social Evolution. *Annual Review of Anthropology* 23:209–29.

———. 1998. Economic Prehistory of the Northern British Columbia Coast. *Arctic Anthropology* 35 (1): 68–87.

———. 2003. The Northwest Coast. *Evolutionary Anthropology* 12:19–33.

Ames, Kenneth M., and Herbert D. G. Maschner. 1999. *People of the Northwest Coast: Their Archaeology and Prehistory.* London: Thames and Hudson.

Anderberg, Michael R. 1973. *Cluster Analysis for Applications.* San Diego, CA: Academic Press.

Anderson, Atholl. 1981. A Model of Prehistoric Collecting on the Rocky Shore. *Journal of Archaeological Science* 8:109–20.

Anderson, Joseph. 1895. Notice of a Cave Recently Discovered at Oban, Containing Human Remains, and a Refuse-heap of Shells and Bones of Animals, and Stone and Bone Implements. *Proceedings of the Society of Antiquaries of Scotland* 29:211–30.

———. 1898. Notes on the Contents of a Small Cave or Rock-Shelter at Druimvargie, Oban; and of Three Shell mounds in Oronsay. *Proceedings of the Society of Antiquaries of Scotland* 32:298–313.

Anderson-Gerfaud, Patricia. 1980. A Testimony of Prehistoric Tasks: Diagnostic Residues on Stone Tool Working Edges. *World Archaeology* 12 (2): 181–94.

———. 1981. Contribution Méthodologique à L'Analyse des Microtraces d'Utilisation sur les Outils Préhistoriques. PhD diss., Université de Bordeaux I, Talence, France.

———. 1986. A Few Comments Concerning Residue Analysis of Stone Plant-Processing Tools. *Early Man News (Part I, Newsletter for Human Paleoecology)* 9/10/11:69–81.

Andrews, Martha V., David D. Gilbertson, and Martin Kent. 1987. Storm Frequencies Along the Mesolithic Coastline. In *Excavations on Oronsay: Prehistoric Human Ecology on a Small Island*, edited by P. A. Mellars. Edinburgh: Edinburgh University Press.

Andrus, C. Fred T., and Douglas E. Crowe. 2000. Geochemical Analysis of *Crassostrea virginica* as a Method to Determine Season of Capture. *Journal of Archaeological Science* 27:33–42.

Andrus, C. Fred T., and Kelley Whatley Rich. 2008. A Preliminary Assessment of Oxygen Isotope Fractionation and Growth Increment Periodicity in the Estuarine Clam *Rangia cuneata. Geo Marine Letters* 28:301–8.

Angulo, Rodolfo J., Guilherme C. Lessa, and Maria Cristina Souza. 2006. A Critical Review of Mid- to Late-Holocene Sea-Level Fluctuations on the Eastern Brazilian Coastline. *Quaternary Science Review* 25:486–506.

Araújo, Ana Cristina. 2003. Long-Term Change in Portuguese Early Holocene Settlement and Subsistence. In *Mesolithic on the Move: Papers Presented at the Sixth International Conference on the Mesolithic in Europe, Stockholm 2000*, edited by L. Larsson, H. Kindgren, K. Knutsson, D. Loeffler, and A. Akerlund, 569–80. Oxford: Oxbow Books.

Araujo, Astolfo G. M. 2001. Teoria e Método em Arqueologia Regional: Um Estudo de Caso no Alto Paranapanema, Estado de São Paulo. PhD diss., Universidade de São Paulo, Brazil.

Araujo, Dorothy Sue Dunn, and Raimundo P. B. Henriques. 1984. Análise Florística das Restingas do Estado do Rio de Janeiro. In *Restingas: Origem, Estrutura, Processos*, edited by L. D. de Lacerda, D. S. D. Araujo, R. Cerqueira, and B. Turcq, 159–94. Niterói, Brazil: CEUFF.

Arnaud, José Morais. 1987. Os Concheiros Mesolíticos dos Vale do Tejo e do Sado: Semelhanças e Diferenças. *Arqueologia* 15:53–64.

———. 1989. The Mesolithic Communities of the Sado Valley (Portugal) in Their Ecological Setting. In *The Mesolithic in Europe: Papers Presented at the III International Symposium, Edinburgh 1985*, edited by C. Bonsall, 614–31. Edinburgh: John Donald.

Arnold, Jeanne E. 1996. The Archaeology of Complex Hunter-Gatherers. *Journal of Archaeological Method and Theory* 3 (2): 77–126.

———, ed. 2001. *The Origins of a Pacific Coast Chiefdom:*

The Chumash of the Channel Islands. Salt Lake City: University of Utah Press.

Ascadi, György, and János Nemeskeri. 1970. *History of Human Life Span and Mortality*. Budapest: Budapest Akadémiai Kiadó.

Aspillaga, Eugenio, Carlos Ocampo, and Pilar Rivas. 1999. Restos Óseos Humanos de Contextos Arqueológicos del Área de Navarino: Indicadores de Estilo de Vida en Indígenas Canoeros. *Anales del Instituto de la Patagonia* 26:123–36.

Assunção, Danilo C. 2010. Sambaquis da Paleolaguna de Santa Marta: Em Busca do Contexto Regional no Litoral Sul de Santa Catarina. MA diss., Universidade de São Paulo, Brazil.

Atalay, Sonya, and Christine A. Hastorf. 2006. Food, Meals, and Daily Activities: Food Habitus at Neolithic Catalhoyuk. *American Antiquity* 71:283–319.

Aten, Lawrence E. 1999. Middle Archaic Ceremonialism at Tick Island, Florida: Ripley P. Bullen's 1961 Excavations at the Harris Creek Site. *Florida Anthropologist* 52 (3): 131–201.

Babot, María del Pilar. 2006. Damage on Starch from Processing Andean Food Plants. In *Ancient Starch Research*, edited by R. Torrence and H. Barton, 66–97. Walnut Creek, CA: Leaf Coast Press.

Bailey, Geoffrey N. 1975. The Role of Molluscs in Coastal Economies: The Results of Midden Analysis in Australia. *Journal of Archaeological Science* 2:45–62.

———. 1977. Shell Mounds, Shell Middens, and Raised Beaches in the Cape York Peninsula. *Mankind* 11:132–43.

———. 1983. Problems of Site Formation and the Interpretation of Spatial and Temporal Discontinuities in the Distribution of Coastal Middens. In *Quaternary Coastlines and Marine Archaeology: Towards the Prehistory of Land Bridges and Continental Shelves*, edited by P. M. Masters and N. C. Flemming, 559–82. London: Academic Press.

———. 1993. Shell Mounds in 1972 and 1992: Reflections on Recent Controversies at Ballina and Weipa. *Australian Archaeology* 37:1–18.

———. 1994. The Weipa Shell Mounds: Natural or Cultural? In *Archaeology in the North: Proceedings of the 1993 Australian Archaeological Association Conference*, edited by M. Sullivan, S. Brockwell, and A. Webb, 107–29. Darwin: North Australian Research Unit, Australian National University.

———. 1999. Shell Mounds and Coastal Archaeology in Northern Queensland. In *Australian Coastal Archaeology*, edited by J. Hall and I. J. McNiven, 105–12. Canberra: ANH Publications, Department of Archaeology and Natural History, RSPAS, Australian National University.

Bailey, Geoffrey N., and Alan S. Craighead. 2003. Late Pleistocene and Holocene Coastal Palaeoeconomies: A Reconsideration of the Molluscan Evidence from Northern Spain. *Geoarchaeology* 18:175–204.

Bailey, Geoffrey N., Margaret R. Deith, and Nicholas J. Shackleton. 1983. Oxygen Isotope Analysis and Seasonality Determinations: Limits and Potential of a New Technique. *American Antiquity* 48:390–98.

Bailey, Geoffrey N., and Nicky Milner. 2008. Molluscan Archives from European Prehistory. In *Early Human Impact on Megamolluscs*, edited by A. Anctczak and R. Cipriani, 111–34. Oxford: Archaeopress, British Archaeological Reports, International Series No. 1865.

Baker, J. T. 1974. Tyrian Purple: An Ancient Dye, a Modern Problem. *Endeavour* 33:11–17.

Balbach, Alfons. 1979. *A Flora Nacional Na Medicina Doméstica: Plantas Medicinais 2*. Rio de Janeiro: A Edificação do Lar.

Baldus, Herbert, ed. 1979. *Ensaios de Etnologia Brasileira*. São Paulo: Editora Nacional.

Balkwill, Darlene, and Jerome S. Cybulski. 1992. Faunal Remains. In *A Greenville Burial Ground: Human Remains and Mortuary Elements in British Columbia Coast Prehistory*, edited by J. S. Cybulski, 75–111. Hull, QC: Archaeological Survey of Canada, Canadian Museum of Civilization, Mercury Series Paper No. 146.

Bandeira, Dione R. 1992. Mudança na Estratégia de Subsistência do Sítio Arqueológico Enseada I—Um Estudo de Caso. MSc diss., Universidade Federal de Santa Catarina, Brazil.

———. 2004. Ceramistas Pré-Coloniais da Baía de Babitonga, SC: Arqueologia e Etnicidade. PhD diss., Universidade Estadual de Campinas, Brazil.

Barber, Marcus. 2005. Where the Clouds Stand: Australian Aboriginal Relationships to Water, Place, and the Marine Environment in Blue Mud Bay,

Northern Territory. PhD diss., Australian National University.

Barberena, Ramiro. 2002. *Los Límites del Mar*. Buenos Aires: Sociedad Argentina de Antropología.

———. 2004. Arqueología e Isótopos Estables en Tierra del Fuego. In *Temas de Arqueología: Arqueología del Norte de la Isla Grande de Tierra del Fuego*, edited by L. A. Borrero and R. Barberena. Buenos Aires: Dunken.

Barbosa, Márcia. 1999. Reconstituição Espacial de um Assentamento de Pescadores-Coletores-Caçadores. In *Pré-História da Terra Brasilis*, edited by M. C. Tenório, 205–32. Rio de Janeiro: EDUFERJ.

Barbosa-Guimarães, Márcia. 2003. O Lixo e o Luxo: As Premissas Teóricos-Metodológicas e a Noção de Sambaqui. *Boletim do Museu Nacional* 63:1–24.

———. 2007. A Ocupação Pré-Colonial da Região dos Lagos, RJ: Sistema de Assentamento e Relações Intersocietais entre Grupos Sambaquianos e Grupos Ceramistas Tupinambá e da Tradição Una. PhD diss., Universidade de São Paulo, Brazil.

Bar-Oz, Guy, and Tamar Dayan. 2003. Testing the Use of Multivariate Inter-Site Taphonomic Considerations: The Faunal Analysis of Hefzibah in Its Epipalaeolithic Cultural Context. *Journal of Archaeological Science* 30:885–900.

Barreto, Cristiana N. G. B. 1988. A Ocupação Pré-Colonial do Vale do Ribeira de Iguape, SP: Os Sítios Concheiros do Médio Curso. PhD diss., Universidade de São Paulo, Brazil.

———. 2000. A Construção do Passado Pré-Colonial: Uma Breve História da Arqueologia no Brasil. *Revista da USP Dossiê antes de Cabral: Arqueologia Brasileira* 1:32–51.

Barrett, John C. 1990. The Monumentality of Death: The Character of Early Bronze Age Mortuary Mounds in Southern Britain. *World Archaeology* 22 (2): 179–89.

Barron, John A., Linda Heusser, Timothy Herbert, and Mitch Lyle. 2003. High-Resolution Climatic Evolution of Coastal Northern California During the Past 16,000 Years. *Paleoceanography* 18 (1).

Bartel, Brad. 1983. Comment on Alekshin. *Current Anthropology* 24 (2): 145–46.

Barton, Huw, and Peter J. Matthews. 2006. Taphonomy. In *Ancient Starch Research*, edited by R. Torrence and H. Barton, 75–94. Walnut Creek, CA: Leaf Coast Press.

Barton, Huw, Robin Torrence, and Richard Fullagar. 1998.

Clues to Stone Tool Function Re-Examined: Comparing Starch Grain Frequencies on Used and Unused Obsidian Artifacts. *Journal of Archaeological Science* 25:1231–38.

Bartosiewicz, Laszlo, Lydia Zapata, and Clive Bonsall. 2009. A Tale of Two Shell Middens: The Natural versus the Cultural in "Obanian" Deposits at Carding Mill Bay, Oban, Western Scotland. In *Integrating Zooarchaeology and Paleoethnobotany: A Consideration of Issues, Methods, and Cases*, edited by A. M. Van Derwarker and T. M. Peres, 205–25. New York: Springer.

Bar-Yosef Mayer, Daniella E., Bernard Vandermeersch, and Ofer Bar-Yosef. 2009. Shells and Ochre in Middle Palaeolithic Qafzeh Cave, Israel: Indications for Modern Behavior. *Journal of Human Evolution* 56:307–14.

Bass, William M. 1995. *Human Osteology: A Laboratory and Field Manual*. Columbia: Missouri Archaeological Society.

Baxter, M. 1994. *Exploratory Multivariate Analysis in Archaeology*. Edinburgh: Edinburgh University Press.

Bayham, Frank E. 1979. Factors Influencing the Archaic Pattern of Animal Utilization. *Kiva* 44:219–35.

Bayne, Brian. 1973. The Responses of Three Species of Bivalve Mollusc to Declining Oxygen Tension at Reduced Salinity. *Comparative Biochemistry and Physiology Part A: Physiology* 45:793–806.

Beaton, John. 1990. The Importance of Past Population for Prehistory. In *Hunter-Gatherer Demography: Past and Present*, edited by B. Meehan and N. White, 23–40. Sydney: University of Sydney.

Becher, Hans. 1956. *The Surara and Pakidai, Two Yanoama Tribes in Northwest Brazil*. Hamburg: Kommissionsverlag Cram, De Gruyter & Co.

Beck, Anamaria. 1972a. A Variação do Conteúdo Cultural dos Sambaquis—Litoral de Santa Catarina. PhD diss., FFLCH, Universidade de São Paulo, Brazil.

———. 1972b. *A Variação do Conteúdo Cultural dos Sambaquis do Litoral de Santa Catarina*. Erechim, Brazil: Habilis.

———. 1974. O Sambaqui de Enseada I—SC LN 71—Um Estudo sobre Tecnologia Pré-Histórica, Universidade Federal de Santa Catarina, Brazil.

Beck, Wendy. 2006. Australian Aboriginal Food-Processing Technology. In *Ancient Starch Research*, edited by R. Torrence and H. Barton, 75–94. Walnut Creek, CA: Leaf Coast Press.

Becker, Ítala Irene Basile. 1995. O Indio Kaingang no Rio Grande do Sul. *Pesquisas, série Antropologia* 29.

———. 1999. *O Indio Kaingang do Paraná: Subsídios para uma Etno-História*. São Leopoldo, Brazil: Editora Unisinos.

Belém, Fabiana. 2012. Do Seixo ao Zoólito. A Indústria Lítica dos Sambaquis do Sul Catarinense: Aspectos Formais, Tecnológicos e Funcionais. MA diss., Universidade de São Paulo, Brazil.

Belém, Fabiana, and André Penin. 2011. O sistema de assentamento sambaquieiro no litoral sul-catarinense: O caso do sambaqui Lagoa dos Bichos II. Paper read at the XVI Congresso Mundial da UISPP and XVI Congresso da SAB, September 4–10, Florianópolis, Brazil.

Bell, Catherine. 1997. *Ritual: Perspectives and Dimensions*. Oxford: Oxford University Press.

Bendazzoli, Cintia. 2007. O Processo de Formação dos Sambaquis: Uma Leitura Estratigráfica do Sítio Jabuticabeira II, SC. MA diss., Museu de Arqueologia e Etnologia, Universidade de São Paulo, Brazil.

Bense, Judith A. 1969. Excavations at the Bird Hammock Site (8Wa30), Wakulla County, Florida. MA diss., Florida State University, USA.

———. 1992. Santa Rosa–Swift Creek in Northwest Florida. Paper read at 49th Annual Meeting of the Southeastern Archaeological Conference, October 21–24, Little Rock, AR.

———. 1994. Configuration of the Bernath Ring Midden Site (SR986) near Pensacola, Florida: Introduction of a New Explanation for Ring Midden Sites. Paper read at 51st Southeastern Archaeological Conference, November 9–12, Lexington, KY.

———. 1998. Santa Rosa–Swift Creek in Northwestern Florida. In *A World Engraved: Archaeology of the Swift Creek Culture*, edited by M. Williams and D. T. Elliott, 247–73. Tuscaloosa: University of Alabama Press.

Bense, Judith A., and Thomas C. Watson. 1977. A Swift Creek–Weeden Island Village Complex in the St. Andrew Bay System of the Northwest Florida Coast: Analysis and Implications. Tallahassee: Florida Department of State, Division of Historical Resources, Florida Master Site File, Survey 847.

Beriault, John G., Robert S. Carr, Mark Lance, and Steven Bertone. 2003. A Phase I Archaeological Assessment of the Ten Thousand Islands, Collier County, Florida. Tallahassee: Florida Department of State,

Division of Historic Resources Grant No. F0221, Archaeological and Historical Conservancy Technical Report No. 434.

Bernick, Kathryn. 1983. *A Site Catchment Analysis of the Little Qualicum River Site, DiSc 1: A Wet Site on the East Coast of Vancouver Island, B.C.* Ottawa: Archaeological Survey of Canada, Mercury Series Paper No. 118, National Museums of Canada.

Bernick, Kathryn, and Rebecca J. Wigen. 1990. Seasonality of the Little Qualicum River West Site. *Northwest Anthropological Research Notes* 24 (2): 153–59.

Betts, Matthew W. 2005. Seven Focal Economies for Six Focal Places: The Development of Economic Diversity in the Western Canadian Arctic. *Arctic Anthropology* 42 (1): 47–87.

———. 2008. *Subsistence and Culture in the Western Canadian Arctic: A Multicontextual Approach*. Hull, QC: Canadian Museum of Civilization.

Betts, Matthew W., and T. Max Friesen. 2004. Quantifying Hunter-Gatherer Intensification: A Zooarchaeological Case Study from Arctic Canada. *Journal of Anthropological Archaeology* 23:357–84.

Bianchini, Gina. 2008. Fogo e Paisagem: Evidências de Práticas Rituais e Construção do Ambiente a Partir da Análise Antracológica de um Sambaqui no Litoral Sul de Santa Catarina. MSc diss., Universidade Federal do Rio de Janeiro, Brazil.

Bianchini, Gina, Rita Scheel-Ybert, and Maria Dulce Gaspar. 2007. Estaca de Lauraceae em Contexto Funerário (Sítio Jabuticabeira-II, Santa Catarina, Brasil). *Revista do Museu de Arqueologia e Etnologia* 17:223–29.

Bicho, Nuno F., Mary Stiner, John Lindly, and C. Reid Ferring. 2000. O Processo de Neolitização na Costa Sudoeste. In *Actas do 3º Congresso de Arqueologia Peninsular*. Vol. 3, *A Neolitização e o Megalitismo*, 11–22. Porto, Portugal: SPEA.

———. 2003. O Mesolítico e o Neolítico Antigo da Costa Algarvia. In *Muita Gente, Poucas Antas? Origens, Espaços e Contextos do Megalitismo. Actas do II Colóquio Internacional Sobre Megalitismo*, edited by V. S. Gonçalves, 15–22. Lisbon: Instituto Português de Arqueologia (Trabalhos de Arqueologia, 25).

Bicho, Nuno F., Cláudia Umbelino, Cleia Detry, and Telmo Pereira. 2010. The Emergence of Muge Mesolithic Shell Middens in Central Portugal and the 8200 cal yr BP Cold Event. *Journal of Island and Coastal Archaeology* 5:86–104.

Billiau, R. 2006. Een reuzenstranding van levende gewone wenteltrap *Epitonium clathrus* (Linnaeus, 1758) op het strand van De Panne. *De Strandvlo* 26:12–19.

Binford, Lewis. R. 1971. Mortuary Practices: Their Study and Their Potential. In *Approaches to the Social Dimension in Mortuary Practices*, edited by J. A. Brown, 6–29. Washington, DC: Memoirs of the Society of American Archaeology 25.

Bird, Douglas W., and Rebecca Bliege Bird. 2000. The Ethnoarchaeology of Juvenile Foraging: Shellfishing Strategies Among Meriam Children. *Journal of Anthropological Archaeology* 19:461–76.

———. 2002. Children on the Reef: Slow Learning or Strategic Foraging. *Human Nature* 13:269–97.

Bishop, A. Henderson. 1914. An Oransay Shell mound—a Scottish Pre-Neolithic Site. *Proceedings of the Society of Antiquaries of Scotland* 48:52–108.

Blondiaux, Jöel, Armelle Alduc-Le Bagousse, Cécille Niel, Nicholas Gabard, and Erica Tyler. 2006. Relevance of Cement Annulations to Paleopathology. *Paleopathology Newsletter* 135:4–13.

Blondiaux, Jöel, Jean-Pierre Bocquet-Appel, Sheila M. F. M. de Souza, and Stephen Naji. 2009. An Estimated Demographic Profile of Fishermen-Forageurs Using TCA Technique for Aging and Paleodemographic Estimations (Cabeçuda, Lagoa do Imaruí, Santa Catarina, Brazil, 2670 ± 300 Cal BP). Paper read at 78th Annual Meeting of the American Association of Physical Anthropology, March 31–April 1, Chicago, IL.

Bocquet-Appel, Jean-Pierre. 2002. The Paleoanthropological Traces of the Neolithic Demographic Transition. *Current Anthropology* 43:638–50.

Bocquet-Appel, Jean-Pierre, and Claude Masset. 1996. Paleodemography: Expectancy and False Hope. *American Journal of Physical Anthropology* 99:571–83.

Bocquet-Appel, Jean-Pierre, and Stephen Naji. 2006. Testing the Hypothesis of a Worldwide Neolithic Demographic Transition. Corroboration for American Cemeteries. *Current Anthropology* 47 (2): 341–65.

Bolton, Herbert Eugene. 1926. *Historical Memoirs of New California, by Fray Francisco Palou*. Berkeley: University of California Press.

Bonneville, F., M. R. Jacamon, G. Jacquet, and J.-F. Bonneville. 2004. Split Atlas in a Patient with Odontoid Fracture. *Neuroradiology* 46:450–52.

Bonsall, Clive. 1996. The "Obanian" Problem: Coastal Adaptation in the Mesolithic of Western Scotland. In *The Early Prehistory of Scotland*, edited by T. Pollard and A. Morrison, 183–97. Edinburgh: Edinburgh University Press.

———. 1999. Raschoille Cave, Oban. *Discovery and Excavation in Scotland* 1999:112.

Bonsall, Clive, and Christopher A. Smith. 1992. New AMS 14C Dates for Antler and Bone Artifacts from Great Britain. *Mesolithic Miscellany* 13 (2): 28–34.

Bonsall, Clive, and Donald G Sutherland. 1992. The Oban Caves. In *The South-West Scottish Highlands: Field Guide*, edited by M. J. C. Walker, J. M. Gray, and J. J. Lowe, 115–21. Cambridge: Quaternary Research Association.

Bonsall, Clive, Donald G. Sutherland, and Timothy J. Lawson. 1989. Ulva Cave and the Early Settlement of Northern Britain. *Cave Science* 16 (3): 109–11.

———. 1991. Excavations in Ulva Cave, Western Scotland 1987: A Preliminary Report. *Mesolithic Miscellany* 12 (2): 18–23.

Bonsall, Clive, Donald G. Sutherland, Nancy J. Russell, Geraint M. Coles, Christopher R. C. Paul, Jacqui P. Huntley, and Timothy J. Lawson. 1994. Excavations in Ulva Cave, Western Scotland 1990–1991: A Preliminary Report. *Mesolithic Miscellany* 15 (1): 8–21.

Bonsall, Clive, Donald G. Sutherland, Nancy J. Russell, and Timothy J. Lawson. 1992. Excavations in Ulva Cave, Western Scotland 1989: A Preliminary Report. *Mesolithic Miscellany* 13 (1): 7–13.

Booth, Derek B. 1987. Timing and Processes of Deglaciation Along the Southern Margin of the Cordilleran Ice Sheet. In *North America and Adjacent Oceans During the Last Deglaciation: The Geology of North America, K-3*, edited by W. F. Ruddiman and H. E. Wright Jr., 71–90. Boulder, CO: Geological Society of America.

Borges, Caroline. 2006. Analise de Industria Osteodontoquerática Proveniente do Sambaqui Fluvial Capelinha I, Bacia do Rio Jacupiranguinha, Vale do Ribeira de Iguape, São Paulo. São Paulo Research Foundation (FAPESP).

Borrero, Luis A. 1986. La Economía Prehistórica de los Habitantes del Norte de la Isla Grande de Tierra del Fuego. PhD diss, Universidad de Buenos Aires, Argentina.

———. 1993. Site Formation Processes in Patagonia: Depositional Rates and Properties of the Archaeological Record. *Arqueología Contemporanea* 4:107–21.

———. 2001. *El Poblamiento de la Patagonia: Toldos, Milodones y Volcanes*. Buenos Aires: Emecé.

Borrero, Luis A., and Ramiro Barberena. 2006. Hunter-Gatherer Home Ranges and Marine Resources: An Archaeological Case from Southern Patagonia. *Current Anthropology* 47:855–67.

Borrero, Luis A., Ricardo A. Guichón, Robert Tykot, Jennifer Kelly, Alfredo Prieto, and Pedro Cardenas. 2001. Dieta a Partir de Isótopos Estables en Restos Óseos Humanos de Patagonia Austral: Estado Actual y Perspectivas. *Anales del Instituto de la Patagonia. Serie Ciencias Humanas* 29:119–28.

Borrero, Luis A., and A. Sebastián Muñoz. 1999. Tafonomía en el Bosque Patagónico: Implicaciones para el Estudio de su Explotación y Uso por Poblaciones Humanas de Cazadores-Recolectores. Paper read at Soplando el Viento . . . Actas de las Terceras Jornadas de Arqueología de la Patagonia, May 27–31, 1996, San Carlos de Bariloche, Argentina.

Botkin, S. 1980. Effects of Human Predation on Shellfish Populations at Malibu Creek, California. In *Modelling Change in Prehistoric Subsistence Economies*, edited by T. K. Earle and A. L. Christenson, 121–39. New York: Academic Press.

Bourke, Patricia. 2000. Late Holocene Indigenous Economies of the Tropical Australian Coast: An Archaeological Study of the Darwin Region. PhD diss., Northern Territory University, Darwin, Australia.

Bourke, Patricia, Sally Brockwell, Patrick Faulkner, and Betty Meehan. 2007. Climate Variability in the Mid to Late Holocene Arnhem Land Region, North Australia: Archaeological Archives of Environmental and Cultural Change. *Archaeology in Oceania* 42:91–101.

Bovy, Kristine M. 2005. Effects of Human Hunting, Climate Change, and Tectonic Events on Waterbirds Along the Pacific Northwest Coast During the Late Holocene. PhD diss., University of Washington, USA.

———. 2007. Global Human Impacts or Climate Change? Explaining the Sooty Shearwater Decline at the Minard Site, Washington State, USA. *Journal of Archaeological Science* 34 (7): 1087–97.

Bovy, Kristine M., Laura S. Phillips, and Julie K. Stein. 2007. Watmough Bay Site Stabilization Project 45-SJ-280, Descriptive Preliminary Report.

Submitted to Bureau of Land Management, Spokane District, WA.

Bowdler, Sandra. 2006. Mollusks and Other Shells. In *Archaeology in Practice: A Student Guide to Archaeological Analysis*, edited by J. Balme and A. Paterson, 316–37. Oxford: Blackwell Carleton.

Bowen, William H. 1994. Food Components and Caries. *Advances in Dental Research* 8 (2): 215–20.

Bowers, Peter M., and Madonna L. Moss. 2001. The North Point Wet Site and the Subsistence Importance of Pacific Cod on the Northern Northwest Coast. In *People and Wildlife in Northern North America: Essays in Honor of R. Dale Guthrie*, edited by S. C. Gerlach and M. S. Murray. Oxford: Archaeopress, British Archaeological Reports, International Series No. 944.

Boyadjian, Célia H. C. 2007. Microfósseis Contidos no Calculo Dentário como Evidencia do Uso de Recursos Vegetais: os Sambaquis de Jabuticabeira II (SC) e Moraes (SP). MA diss., Universidade de São Paulo, Brazil.

Boyadjian, Célia H. C., Sabine Eggers, and Karl J. Reinhard. 2007. Dental Wash: A Problematic Method for Extracting Microfossils from Teeth. *Journal of Archaeological Science* 34 (10): 1622–28.

Bradley, Richard. 1998. *The Significance of Monuments: On the Shaping of Human Experience in Neolithic and Bronze Age Europe*. New York: Routledge.

———. 2005. The Consecration of the House. In *Ritual and Domestic Life in Prehistoric Europe*, edited by R. Bradley, 41–80. New York: Routledge.

Braje, Todd J., Douglas J. Kennett, Jon M. Erlandson, and Brendan J. Culleton. 2007. Human Impacts on Nearshore Shellfish Taxa: A 7,000 Year Record from Santa Rosa Island, California. *American Antiquity* 72 (4): 735–56.

Brijker, J. M., Simon J. A. Jung, Gerald M. Ganssen, Torsten Bickert, and Dick Kroon. 2007. ENSO Related Decadal Scale Climate Variability from the Indo-Pacific Warm Pool. *Earth and Planetary Science Letters* 253:67–82.

Briz, Ivan. 2004. Dinàmiques Econòmiques de Producció-Consum en el Registre Lític Caçador-Recollector de l'Extrem Sud Americà. La Societat Yàmana. PhD diss., Universitat Autònoma de Barcelona, Spain.

Briz, Ivan, Ignacio Clemente, Jordi Pijoan, Xavier Terradas, and Assumpció Vila. 2005. Stone tools in ethnoarchaeological contexts: Theoretical-methodological inferences. In *Lithic Toolkits in Ethnoarchaeological Contexts. Actts of the XIVth UISPP Congress. Liège, Belgium, 2001*, edited by X. Terradas, 1–7. Oxford: Archaeopress, British Archaeological Reports, International Series No. 1370.

Brochado, José P. 1984. An Ecological Model of the Spread of Pottery and Agriculture into Eastern South America. PhD diss., University of Illinois, USA.

Brockwell, Sally, Patrick Faulkner, Patricia Bourke, Anne Clarke, Christine Crassweller, Daryl Guse, Betty Meehan, and Robin Sim. 2009. Radiocarbon Dates from the Top End: A Cultural Chronology for the Northern Territory Coastal Plains. *Australian Aboriginal Studies* 2:54–76.

Brodie, J. 1970 [1869]. On the Food of Man in Prehistoric Times, and the Methods by Which It Was Prepared. *Proceedings of the Society of Antiquaries of Scotland* 8:177–82.

Broecker, Wallace S., and Tsung-Hung Peng. 1982. *Tracers in the Sea*. Palisades, NY: Eldigio Press.

Broom, M. J. 1982. Analysis of the Growth of *Anadara granosa* (Bivalvia: Arcidae) in Natural, Artificially Seeded and Experimental Populations. *Marine Ecology Progress Series* 9:69–79.

———. 1983. Mortality and Production in Natural, Artificially-Seeded and Experimental Populations of *Anadara granosa* (Bivalvia: Arcidae). *Oecologia* 58 (3): 389–97.

———. 1985. *The Biology and Culture of Marine Bivalve Molluscs of the Genus* Anadara. Manila, Philippines: International Centre for Living Aquatic Resources Management.

Broughton, Jack M. 1994a. Declines in Mammalian Foraging Efficiency During the Late Holocene, San Francisco Bay, California. *Journal of Anthropological Archaeology* 13:371–401.

———. 1994b. Late Holocene Resource Intensification in the Sacramento Valley, California: The Vertebrate Evidence. *Journal of Archaeological Science* 21:501–14.

Brown, Alan K. 1967. The Aboriginal Population of the Santa Barbara Channel. *University of California Archaeological Survey Reports* 69:1–99.

Brown, James A. 1971a. The Dimensions of Status in the Burials at Spiro. In *Approaches to the Social Dimensions of Mortuary Practices*, edited by J. A. Brown, 92–112. Washington, DC: Society of American Archaeology, Memoir No. 25.

———. 1971b. Introduction to *Approaches to the Social Dimensions of Mortuary Practices*, edited by J. A.

Brown, 1–5. Washington, DC: Society of American Archaeology, Memoir No. 25.

Bruseth, James E. 1991. Poverty Point Development as Seen at the Cedarland and Claiborne Sites, Southern Mississippi. In *The Poverty Point Culture: Local Manifestations, Subsistence Practices, and Trade Networks*. Geoscience and Man, vol. 29, edited by K. M. Byrd, 7–26. Baton Rouge: Louisiana State University.

Bruzek, Jaroslav. 2002. A Method for Visual Determination of Sex Using the Human Hip Bone. *American Journal of Physical Anthropology* 117 (2): 157–68.

Bryan, Alan L. 1977. Resumo da Arqueologia do Sambaqui Forte Marechal Luz. *Arquivos do Museu de História Natural (BH)* 2:9–30.

Buckberry, Jo L., and Andrew T. Chamberlain. 2002. Age Estimation from the Auricular Surface of the Ilium: A Revised Method. *American Journal of Physical Anthropology* 119:231–39.

Buddemeir, Robert W., James E. Maragos, and David W. Knutson. 1974. Radiographic Studies of Reef Coral Exoskeletons: Rates and Patterns of Coral Growth. *Journal of Experimental Marine Biology and Ecology* 14:179–99.

Buikstra, Jane E., and Lyle W. Konigsberg. 1985. Paleodemography: Critiques and Controversies. *American Anthropologist* 87:316–33.

Buikstra, Jane E., and Douglas H. Ubelaker. 1994. *Standards for Data Collection from Human Skeletal Remains*. Fayetteville: Arkansas Archaeological Survey.

Bullen, Ripley P., and Adelaide K. Bullen. 1956. Excavations on Cape Haze Peninsula, Florida. Gainesville: Contributions of the Florida State Museum, Social Sciences No. 1.

Burchell, Meghan. 2006. Gender, Status and Grave Goods in British Columbia Burials. *Canadian Journal of Archaeology* 30:252–72.

Burley, David V. 1980. *Marpole: Anthropological Reconstructions of a Prehistoric Northwest Coast Culture Type*. Burnaby, BC: Archaeology Press, Simon Fraser University.

Butler, Virginia L. 2000. Resource Depression on the Northwest Coast of North America. *American Antiquity* 74:649–61.

———. 2001. Changing Fish Use on Mangaia, Southern Cook Islands: Resource Depression and the Prey Choice Model. *International Journal of Osteoarchaeology* 11:88–100.

Butler, Virginia L., and Sarah K. Campbell. 2004.

Resource Intensification and Resource Depression in the Pacific Northwest of North America: A Zooarchaeological Review. *Journal of World Prehistory* 18 (4): 327–405.

Cali, Plácido. 2004. *Cartilha da Cultura*. Ilhabela, Brazil: Secretaria Municipal da Cultura e Fundação Arte e Cultura de Ilhabela.

Calippo, Flavio R. 2004. Os Sambaquis Submersos de Cananéia: Um Estudo de Caso de Arqueologia Subaquática. MA diss., Universidade de São Paulo, Brazil.

———. 2010. Sociedade Sambaquieira, Comunidades Marítimas. PhD diss., Universidade de São Paulo, Brazil.

Calixto, Benedito. 1904. Algumas Notas e Informações Sobre a Situação dos Sambaquis de Itanhaem e de Santos. *Revista do Museu Paulista* 6:490–518.

Calmes, Alan. 1968. Test Excavations at Three Late Archaic Shell-Ring Mounds on Hilton Head Island, South Carolina. *Southeastern Archaeological Conference Bulletin* 8:45–48.

Calvert, Sheila Gay. 1980. A Cultural Analysis of Faunal Remains from Three Archaeological Sites in Hesquiat Harbour, BC. PhD diss., University of British Columbia, Canada.

Calvert, Sheila Gay, and Susan Crockford. 1982. Analysis of Faunal Remains from the Shoemaker Bay Site (DhSe 2). In *Alberni Prehistory: Archaeological and Ethnographic Investigations on Western Vancouver Island*, edited by A. D. McMillan and D. E. St. Claire, 174–219. Penticton, BC: Theytus Books.

Campbell, Sarah K., and Virginia L. Butler. 2010. Archaeological Evidence for Resilience of Pacific Northwest Salmon Populations and the Socioecological System over the Last ~7500 Years. *Ecology and Society* 15 (1): 17.

Cannon, Aubrey. 1991. *The Economic Prehistory of Namu*. Burnaby, BC: Archaeology Press, Simon Fraser University.

———. 2000. Assessing Variability in Northwest Coast Salmon and Herring Fisheries: Bucket-Auger Sampling of Shell Midden Sites on the Central Coast of British Columbia. *Journal of Archaeological Science* 27:725–37.

———. 2001. Was Salmon Important in Northwest Coast Prehistory? In *People and Wildlife in Northern North America: Essays in Honor of R. Dale Guthrie*, edited by S. C. Gerlach and M. S. Murray, 178–87. Oxford: Archaeopress, British Archaeological Reports, International Series No. 944.

———. 2002. Sacred Power and Seasonal Settlement on the Central Northwest Coast. In *Beyond Foraging and Collecting: Evolutionary Change in Hunter-Gatherer Settlement Systems*, edited by B. Fitzhugh and J. Habu, 212–338. New York: Kluwer Academic.

Cannon, Aubrey, and Meghan Burchell. 2009. Clam Growth-Stage Profiles as a Measure of Harvest Intensity and Resource Management on the Central Coast of British Columbia. *Journal of Archaeological Science* 36 (4): 1050–60.

Cannon, Aubrey, Meghan Burchell, and Rhonda Bathurst. 2008. Trends and Strategies in Shellfish Gathering on the Pacific Northwest Coast of North America. In *Early Human Impact on Megamolluscs*, edited by A. Antczak and R. Cipriani, 7–22. Oxford: Archaeopress, British Archaeological Reports, International Series No. 1865.

Cannon, Aubrey, and Dongya Yang. 2006. Early Storage and Sedentism on the Pacific Northwest Coast: Ancient DNA Analysis of Salmon Remains from Namu, British Columbia. *American Antiquity* 71 (1): 123–40.

Capanema, Guilherme S. 1876. Os Sambaquis. *Ensayos Sciencia por Diversos Amadores* 1:79–91.

Caracotche, María S., and Bernardita Ladrón de Guevara. 2008. El Registro Arqueológico Costero de Patagonia: Diagnóstico del Estado Actual y Herramientas para la Conservación. In *Arqueología de la Costa Patagónica: Perspectivas para la conservación*, edited by I. Cruz and M. S. Caracotche, 17–50. Rio Gallegos, Argentina: Universidad Nacional de la Patagonia Austral.

Cardoso, J. L., and Jose M. Rolão. 1999/2000. Prospeções e Escavações nos Concheiros Mesolíticos de Muge e de Magos (Salvaterra de Magos): Contribuição para a História dos Trabalhos Arqueológicos Efectuados. Câmara Municipal de Oeiras. *Estudos Arqueológicos de Oeiras* 8:83–240.

Carefoot, Thomas H. 1977. *Pacific Seashores: A Guide to Intertidal Ecology*. Seattle: University of Washington Press.

Carlson, Catherine C. 2003. The Bear Cove Fauna and the Subsistence History of Northwest Coast Maritime Culture. In *Archaeology of Coastal British Columbia: Essays in Honour of Professor Philip M. Hobler*, edited by R. L. Carlson. Burnaby, BC: Archaeology Press, Simon Fraser University.

Carlson, Roy L. 1970. Excavations at Helen Point on Mayne Island. *BC Studies* 6/7:113–23.

———. 1996. The Later Prehistory of British Columbia. In

Early Human Occupation in British Columbia, edited by R. L. Carlson and L. D. Bona, 215–26. Vancouver, BC: UBC Press.

Carmody, Rachel N., and Richard W. Wrangham. 2009. The Energetic Significance of Cooking. *Journal of Human Evolution* 57:379–91.

Carter, David O., and Mark Tibbett. 2008. Cadaver Decomposition in Soil: Process. In *Soil Analysis in Forensic Taphonomy Principles: Chemical and Biological Effects of Buried Human Remains*, edited by M. Tibett and D. O. Carter, 29–52. New York: Taylor and Francis.

Carter, David O., David Yellowlees, and Mark Tibbett. 2007. Cadaver Decomposition in Terrestrial Ecosystems. *Naturwissenschaften* 94:12–24.

Carter, Richard J. 2001. New Evidence for Seasonal Human Presence at the Early Mesolithic Site of Thatchan, Berkshire, England. *Journal of Archaeological Science* 28:1055–60.

Carvalho, António Faustino. 2008. *A Neolitização do Portugal Meridional. Os Exemplos do Maciço Calcário Estremenho e do Algarve Ocidental*. Faro, Portugal: Universidade do Algarve.

Carvalho, António Faustino, Nuno F. Bicho, Mary C. Stiner, Juan F. Gibaja, Maria João Valente, and Maria A. Masucci. 2005. O Projecto "O Processo de Neolitização no Algarve" (Portugal): Âmbito e Primeiros Resultados. In *III Congreso del Neolítico en La Península Ibérica*, edited by P. Arias, R. Ontañon, and C. García-Moncó, 965–73. Santander, Spain: Universidade de Cantábria.

Carvalho, António Faustino, and Maria João Valente. 2005. Novos Contextos Conquíferos Pré-Históricos na Costa Vicentina. In *Actas do 2.º Encontro de Arqueologia do Algarve (Xelb, 5)*, 9–26. Silves, Portugal: Câmara Municipal de Silves.

Carvalho, António Faustino, Maria João Valente, and Rebecca M. Dean. 2010. O Mesolítico e o Neolítico Antigo do Concheiro da Rocha das Gaivotas (Sagres, Vila do Bispo). In *Actas do 7.º Encontro de Arqueologia do Algarve (Xelb, 10)*, 39–53. Silves, Portugal: Câmara Municipal de Silves.

Carvalho, Cláudia R. 2004. Marcadores de Stress Ocupacional em Populações Sambaquianas. PhD diss., Fundação Oswaldo Cruz, Rio de Janeiro.

Carvalho, Eliana T. 1984. Estudo Arqueológico do Sítio Corondó. Missão de 1978. *Boletim do Instituto de Arqueologia Brasileira* 2:1–243.

Cascudo, Luís da Câmara. 2004. *História da Alimentação no Brasil*. São Paulo: Global.

Catterall, Carla P., and Ian R. Poiner. 1987. The Potential Impact of Human Gathering on Shellfish Populations, with Reference to Some NE Australian Intertidal Flats. *Oikos* 50:114–22.

Chabal, Lucie. 1997. Forêts et Sociétés en Languedoc (Néolithique Final, Antiquité Tardive). L'Anthracologie, Méthode et Paleoécologie. *Documents d'archéologie française, Paris* 63:1–188.

Chagnon, Napoleon A. 1992. *Yąnomamö*. 4th ed. *Case Studies in Cultural Anthropology, Stanford University*. Fort Worth, TX: Harcourt Brace Jovanovich.

———. 2013. *Noble Savages: My Life Among Two Dangerous Tribes—The Yanomamö and the Anthropologists*. New York: Simon and Schuster.

Chamberlain, Andrew. 2006. *Demography in Archaeology*. Cambridge: Cambridge University Press.

Chapman, Robert W., and Klavs Randsborg. 1981. Approaches to the Archaeology of Death. In *The Archaeology of Death*, edited by R. W. Chapman, I. Kinnes, and K. Randsborg, 1–24. Cambridge: Cambridge University Press.

Chappell, John, Eugene G. Rhodes, Bruce G. Thom, and Eugene Wallensky. 1982. Hydro-Isostasy and the Sea Level Isobase of 5500BP in North Queensland, Australia. *Marine Geology* 49:81–90.

Chappell, John, and Bruce. G. Thom. 1977. Sea Levels and Coasts. In *Sunda and Sahul: Prehistoric Studies in Southeast Asia, Melanesia and Australia*, edited by J. Allen, J. Golson, and R. Jones, 275–91. London: Academic Press.

Charlier, Philippe, Isabelle Huynh-Charlier, Olivia Munoz, Michel Billard, Luc Brun, and Geoffroy L. de la Grandmaison. 2010. The Microscopic (Optical and SEM) Examination of Dental Calculus Deposits (DCD): Potential Interest in Forensic Anthropology of a Bio-Archaeological Method. *Legal Medicine Annual* 12:163–71.

Charnov, Eric, Gordon H. Orians, and Kim Hyatt. 1976. Ecological Implications of Resource Depression. *American Naturalist* 110:247–59.

Chernorkian, Robert. 1983. Contribution d'une Étude de Malacofaune à la Connaissance de l'Économie des Amas Coquillier et de la Paléoécologie des Lagunes de Basse Côte-d'Ivoire. Paper read at 1ér Symposium Archéologie Africaine et Sciences de la Nature Appliquées à L'Archéologie, September 25–30, Bordeaux, France.

Childe, Vere Gordon. 1945. Directional Changes in Funerary Practices During 50,000 Years. *Man* 45:13–19.

Chivas, Allan R., Adriana Garcia, Sander van der Kaars,

Martine J. J. Couapel, Sabine Holt, Jessica M. Reeves, David J. Wheeler, Adam D. Switzer, Colin V. Murray-Wallace, Debabrata Banerjee, et al. 2001. Sea-Level and Environmental Changes Since the Last Interglacial in the Gulf of Carpentaria, Australia: An Overview. *Quaternary International* 83–85:19–46.

Chmyz, Igor. 1976. A Ocupação do Litoral dos Estados do Paraná e Santa Catarina por Povos Ceramistas. *Estudos Brasileiros (Curitiba)* 1:7–43.

Christensen, Tina, Jim Stafford, Jennifer Lindberg, and Becky Wigen. 1999. Qay'llnagaay Heritage Center Development, Skidegate Indian Reserve #1, Archaeological Impact Assessment. Victoria, BC: Culture Resource Library, Ministry of Sustainable Resource Management.

Cipriani, Roberto, Andrzeg Antczak, and Maria M. Antczak. 2008. The Study of Ancient Human-Mollusc Interactions as an Interdisciplinary Challenge. In *Early Human Impact on Megamolluscs*, edited by A. Antczak and R. Cipriani, 247–54. Oxford: Archaeopress, British Archaeological Reports, International Series No. 1865.

Claassen, Cheryl. 1986. Shellfishing Seasons in the Prehistoric Southeastern United States. *American Antiquity* 51:21–37.

———. 1991. Normative Thinking and Shell-Bearing Sites. In *Archaeological Methods and Theories*, edited by M. B. Schiffer, 249–98. Tucson: University of Arizona Press.

———. 1996. A Consideration of Social Organization of the Shell Mound Archaic. In *Archaeology of the Mid-Holocene Southeast*, edited by K. E. Sassaman and D. Anderson, 235–58. Gainesville: University of Florida Press.

———. 1998. *Shells*. Cambridge: Cambridge University Press.

———. 2010. *Feasting with Shellfish in the Southern Ohio Valley: Archaic Sacred Sites and Rituals*. Knoxville: University of Tennessee Press.

Clague, John, John R. Harper, Richard J. Hebda, and Don E. Howes. 1982. Late Quaternary Sea Levels and Crustal Movements, Coastal British Columbia. *Canadian Journal of Earth Sciences* 19:597–618.

Clark, George R. 1974. Growth Lines in Invertebrate Skeletons. *Annual Review of Earth and Planetary Science* 9:77–79.

Clark, Robin L., and J. C. Guppy. 1988. A Transition from Mangrove Forest to Freshwater Wetland in the Monsoon Tropics of Australia. *Journal of Biogeography* 15:665–84.

Clark, Terence N. 2000. Prehistoric Culture Change on Southern Vancouver Island: The Applicability of Current Explanations of the Marpole Transition. MA diss., University of Victoria, Canada.

———. 2010. Rewriting Marpole: The Path to Cultural Complexity in the Gulf of Georgia. PhD diss., University of Toronto, Canada.

Clemente, Ignacio. 1995. Instrumentos de Trabajo Líticos de los Yámanas (Canoeros Nómadas de la Tierra del Fuego): Una Perspectiva Desde el Análisis Funcional. PhD diss., Universitat Autònoma de Barcelona, Spain.

Clune, Genevieve, and Rodney Harrison. 2009. Coastal Shell Middens of the Abydos Coastal Plain, Western Australia. *Archaeology in Oceania* Supplement 44:70–80.

Cobb, Hannah L. 2005. Midden, Meaning, Person, Place: Interpreting the Mesolithic of Western Scotland. In *Investigating Prehistoric Hunter-Gatherer Identities in Palaeolithic and Mesolithic Europe*, edited by H. L. Cobb, S. Price, F. Coward, and L. Grimshaw, 69–78. Oxford: Archaeopress.

Cocilovo, Jose A., and Ricardo A. Guichón. 1985/1986. Propuesta para el Estudio de las Poblaciones Aborígenes del Extremo Austral de Patagonia. *Anales del Instituto de la Patagonia. Serie Ciencias Sociales* 16:111–23.

Cockburn, Aidan. 1967. *Infectious Diseases: Their Evolution and Eradication*. Springfield, IL: Thomas.

Cohen, Mark N., and George J. Armelagos. 1984a. *Paleopathology at the Origins of Agriculture*. New York: Academic Press.

———. 1984b. Paleopathology at the Origins of Agriculture: Editor's Summation. In *Paleopathology at the Origins of Agriculture*, edited by M. Cohen and G. Armelagos, 581–601. New York: Academic Press.

Collet, Guy C. 1976. A Arqueologia e Seus Amadores. *Espeleo Tema, São Paulo* 10:1–4.

Collet, Guy C., and André Prous. 1977. Primeiro Informe Sobre Os Sambaquis da Região de Itaóca (SP). 1: Apresentação e Localização. *Arquivos do Museu de História Natural* 2:31–35.

Connock, Kenneth D. 1985. Rescue Excavation of the Ossuary Remains at Raschoille Cave, Oban: An Interim Report. Oban, Scotland: Lorn Archaeological and Historical Society.

Connock, Kenneth D., Bill Finlayson, and Coralie M. Mills. 1993. Excavation of a Shell Midden at Carding Mill Bay, near Oban, Scotland. *Glasgow Archaeological Journal* 17:25–38.

Constantino, Camila. 2009. Análise Zooarqueológica de um Sambaqui Fluvial: O Caso do Sítio Capelinha 1. MA diss., Museu de Arqueologia e Etnologia, Universidade de São Paulo, Brazil.

Correia, Maria Margarida Gomes, Iva Nilce da Silva Brum, and Walter Zwink. 1984. Ocorrências de Crustáceos no Sambaqui da Embratel Guaratiba, Campo Grande, RJ. *Revista de Pré-história* 6:361–70.

Costa, Maria H. F., and Henrique B. Malhano. 1986. Habitação Indígena Brasileira. In *Suma Etnológica Brasileira*. Vol. 2, edited by D. Ribeiro, 27–94. Rio de Janeiro: Vozes.

Coupland, Gary. 1988. Prehistoric Economic and Social Change in the Tsimshian Area. *Research in Economic Anthropology* Supplement 3:211–43.

———. 1998. Maritime Adaptation and Evolution of the Developed Northwest Coast Pattern on the Central Northwest Coast. *Arctic Anthropology* 35 (1): 36–56.

Coupland, Gary, Craig Bissell, and Sarah King. 1993. Prehistoric Subsistence and Seasonality at Prince Rupert Harbour: Evidence from the McNichol Creek Site. *Canadian Journal of Archaeology* 17:59–73.

Coupland, Gary, Roger H. Colten, and Rebecca Case. 2003. Preliminary Analysis of Socioeconomic Organization at the McNichol Creek Site, British Columbia. In *Emerging from the Mist: Studies in Northwest Coast Culture History*, edited by R. G. Matson, G. Coupland, and Q. Mackie, 152–69. Vancouver, BC: UBC Press.

Coupland, Gary, and Kathlyn Stewart. 2005. Do You Never Get Tired of Salmon? Evidence for Extreme Subsistence Specialization at Prince Rupert Harbour, British Columbia. Paper read at 38th Annual Canadian Archaeological Association Conference, May 11–14, Nanaimo, British Columbia.

Coupland, Gary, Kathlyn Stewart, and Katherine Patton. 2010. Do You Never Get Tired of Salmon? Evidence for Extreme Salmon Specialization at Prince Rupert Harbour, British Columbia. *Journal of Anthropological Archaeology* 29:189–207.

Coutts, Peter, and Charles Higham. 1971. The Seasonal Factor in Prehistoric New Zealand. *World Archaeology* 2 (3): 266–77.

Craig, Oliver, and Matthew Collins. 2002. The Removal of Protein from Mineral Surfaces: Implications for Residue Analysis of Archaeological Materials. *Journal of Archaeological Science* 29:1077–82.

Cribb, Roger. 1996. Shell Mounds, Domiculture and Ecosystem Manipulation on Western Cape York Peninsula. In *Archaeology of Northern Australia: Regional Perspectives*, edited by P. Hiscock and P. Veth, 150–74. Brisbane: Anthropology Museum, University of Queensland.

Croes, Dale R. 1992. *Exploring Prehistoric Subsistence Change on the Northwest Coast: Long-Term Subsistence Chance in Prehistoric North America*. Greenwich, CT: JAI Press.

———. 1995. *The Hoko River Archaeological Site Complex: The Wet/Dry Site (45CA213), 3000–1700 B.P.* Pullman: Washington State University Press.

Croes, Dale R., and Steven Hackenberg. 1988. Hoko River Archaeological Complex: Modeling Prehistoric Northwest Coast Economic Evolution. *Research in Economic Anthropology* Supplement 3:19–85.

Cronyn, Janey M. 1990. *The Elements of Archaeological Conservation*. London: Routledge.

Crothers, J. H. 1985. Dog-Whelks: An Introduction to the Biology of *Nucella lapillus* (L.). *Field Studies* 6:291–360.

———. 2001. Common Topshells: An Introduction to the Biology of *Osilinus lineatus* with Notes on Other Species in the Genus. *Field Studies* 10:115–60.

Crowley, Thomas J., and Thomas S. Lowery. 2000. How Warm Was the Medieval Warm Period? *Ambio* 29 (1): 51–54.

Cummings, Vicky. 2003. Mesolithic World-Views of the Landscape in Western Britain. In *Mesolithic on the Move*, edited by L. Larsson, H. Kindgren, K. Knutsson, D. Loeffler, and A. Åkerlund, 74–81. Oxford: Oxbow Books.

Cunha, E., and F. Cardoso. 2001. The Osteological Series from Cabeço Da Amoreira (Muge, Portugal). *Bulletin et Memoire de la Société d'Anthropologie de Paris* 13:321–33.

———. 2002/2003. New Data on Muge Shell Middens: A Contribution to More Accurate Numbers and Dates. *Muge Estudos Arqueológicos* 1:171–83.

Cunha, Manuela C. da. 1992. *História dos Índios do Brasil*. São Paulo: FAPESP/Cia das Letras.

Curle, A. O. 1908. Notice of the Examination of Prehistoric Kitchen Middens on the Archerfield Estate, near Gullane, Haddingtonshire, in November 1907. *Proceedings of the Society of Antiquaries of Scotland* 42:308–19.

Curry, John D., and Roger N. Hughes. 1982. Strength of the Dogwhelk *Nucella lapillus* and the Winkle *Littorina littorea* from Different Habitats. *Journal of Animal Ecology* 51:47–56.

Cushing, Frank H. 1973 [1896]. *Exploration of Ancient Key Dweller's Remains on the Gulf Coast of Florida.* New York: AMS Press.

Cybulski, Jerome S. 1992. *A Greenville Burial Ground: Human Remains and Mortuary Elements in British Columbia Coast Prehistory.* Hull, QC: Archaeological Survey of Canada, Canadian Museum of Civilization, Mercury Series Paper No. 146.

Dallimore, Audrey, Richard E. Thomson, and Miriam A. Bertram. 2005. Modern to Late Holocene Deposition in an Anoxic Fjord on the West Coast of Canada: Implications for Regional Oceanography, Climate and Paleoseismic History. *Marine Geology* 219:47–69.

Dalrymple, C. E. 1866. Notes of the Excavation of Two Shell mounds on the Eastern Coast of Aberdeenshire. *Proceedings of the Society of Antiquaries of Scotland* 6:423–26.

Daniels, Phoebe S. 2009. A Gendered Model of Prehistoric Resource Depression: A Case Study on the Northwest Coast of North America. PhD diss., University of Washington, USA.

Darling, John. 1982. *Shore Fishing.* London: Ward Lock.

Davenport, John, and Tat Meng Wong. 1986. Responses of the Blood Cockle *Anadara granosa* (L.) (Bivalvia: Arcidae) to Salinity: Hypoxia and Aerial Exposure. *Aquaculture* 56:151–62.

DeBlasis, Paulo. 1988. A Ocupação Pré-Colonial do Vale do Ribeira de Iguape, SP: Os Sítios Líticos do Médio Curso. MA diss., Universidade de São Paulo, Brazil.

DeBlasis, Paulo, Suzanne K. Fish, Maria Dulce Gaspar, and Paul R. Fish. 1998. Some References for the Discussion of Complexity Among the Sambaqui Moundbuilders from the Southern Shores of Brazil. *Revista de Arqueologia Americana* 15:75–105.

DeBlasis, Paulo, Suzanne K. Fish, Maria Dulce Gaspar, Paul R. Fish, Marisa C. Afonso, Sabine Eggers, Levy Figuti, Daniela Klokler, Peter J. Pilles, Guadalupe Sanches-Carpenter, and Anne Worthington. 1999. Projeto Arqueológico Camacho (Padrões de Assentamento e Formação de Sambaquis em Santa Catarina). As Campanhas de 1998 e 1999. São Paulo: Unpublished report (FAPESP 98/8114-3).

DeBlasis, Paulo, Maria Dulce Gaspar, Paulo C. Giannini, Levy Figuti, Sabine Eggers, Rita Scheel-Ybert, Marisa C. Afonso, Deise S. Farias, Andreas Kneip, Carlos A. Mendonça, et al. 2004. Processos Formativos nos Sambaquis do Camacho, SC: Padrões Funerários e Atividades Cotidianas. Unpublished report (FAPESP 03/02059-0).

DeBlasis, Paulo, Andreas Kneip, Rita Scheel-Ybert, Paulo Giannini, and Maria Dulce Gaspar. 2007. Sambaquis e Paisagem: Dinâmica Natural e Arqueologia Regional no Litoral Sul do Brasil. *Arqueologia Sudamericana/ Arqueologia Sul-americana* 3 (1): 29–61.

de Boer, Willem F. 1997. Ceremonial Centers from the Cayapas (Esmeraldas, Ecuador) to Chillicothe (Ohio, USA). *Cambridge Archaeological Journal* 7 (2): 225–53.

de Boer, Willem F., and John H. Blitz. 1991. Ceremonial Centers of the Chachi. *Expedition* 33:53–62.

de Boer, Willem F., Tania Pereira, and Almeida Guissamulo. 2000. Comparing Recent and Abandoned Shell Middens to Detect the Impact of Human Exploitation on the Intertidal System. *Aquatic Ecology* 34:287–97.

de Boer, Willem F., and Herbert H. T. Prins. 2002. Human Exploitation and Benthic Community Structure on a Tropical Intertidal Flat. *Journal of Sea Research* 48:225–40.

De Masi, Marco A. N. 1999. Mobility of Prehistoric Hunter-Gatherers on the Southern Brazilian Coast: Santa Catarina Island. PhD diss., Stanford University, USA.

———. 2001. Pescadores Coletores da Costa Sul do Brasil. *Pesquisas* 57:1–136.

De Melo, Fernando L., Joana C. M. de Mello, Ana M. Fraga, Kelly Nunes, and Sabine Eggers. 2010. Syphilis at the Crossroad of Phylogenetics and Paleopathology. *PLoS Neglected Tropical Diseases* 4 (1): e575.

Dean, Rebecca M. 2010. Delicacy or Desperation? Eating Penducular Barnacles in Neolithic Portugal. *Journal of Ethnobiology* 30 (1): 80–91.

Dean, Rebecca M., and António Faustino Carvalho. 2011. Surf and Turf: The Use of Marine and Terrestrial Resources in the Early Neolithic of Coastal Southern Portugal. In *Trekking the Shore: Changing Coastlines and the Antiquity of Coastal Settlement*, edited by N. F. Bicho, J. A. Haws, and L. G. Davis, 291–304. New York: Springer.

Dean, Rebecca M., Maria João Valente, and António Faustino Carvalho. 2012. The Mesolithic/Neolithic Transition on the Costa Vicentina, Portugal. *Quaternary International* 264:100–108.

Deith, Margaret R. 1983. Seasonality of Shell Collecting,

Determined by Oxygen Isotope Analysis of Marine Shells from Asturian Sites in Cantabria. In *Animals and Archaeology: Shell Middens, Fishes and Birds*, edited by C. Grigson and J. Clutton-Brock, 68–76. Oxford: Archaeopress, British Archaeological Reports, International Series No. 183.

———. 1986. Subsistence Strategies at a Mesolithic Campsite: Evidence from Stable Isotope Analyses of Shells. *Journal of Archaeological Science* 13:61–78.

———. 1989. Clams and Salmonberries: Interpreting Seasonality Data from Shells. In *The Mesolithic in Europe*, edited by C. Bonsall, 73–79. Edinburgh: John Donald.

Delany, Jane, Alan A. Myers, and David McGrath. 2002. Recruitment, Immigration and Emigration of Two Coexisting Limpet Species in Mid-shore Tide Pools on the West Coast of Ireland. In *New Survey of Clare Island: Marine Intertidal Ecology*, edited by A. A. Myers, 69–77. Dublin: Royal Irish Academy.

Deo, Jennie N., John O. Stone, and Julie K. Stein. 2004. Building Confidence in Shell: Variations in the Marine Radiocarbon Reservoir Correction for the Northwest Coast over the Past 3,000 Years. *American Antiquity* 69 (4): 771–86.

DePratter, Chester B. 2010. Thoughts on the Late Archaic/Early Woodland Transition on the Georgia and South Carolina Coasts. In *Trend, Tradition, and Turmoil: What Happened to the Southeastern Archaic*, edited by D. H. Thomas and M. C. Sanger, 247–52. New York: American Museum of Natural History, Anthropological Papers of the American Museum of Natural History No. 93.

Dethier, Megan N. 1993. A Baseline Survey and Inventory of Intertidal Communities in San Juan Island National Historic Park. Submitted to the National Park Service.

Dethier, Megan N., and Helen D. Berry. 2008. Decadal Changes in Shoreline Biota in Westcott and Garrison Bays, San Juan County. Olympia, WA: Nearshore Habitat Program, Aquatic Resources Division, Washington State Department of Natural Resources.

Di Piazza, Anne. 1998. Archaeobotanical Investigations of an Earth Oven in Kiribati, Gilbert Islands. *Vegetation History and Archaeobotany* 7:49–154.

Dias, Adriana. S. 2004. Sistemas de Assentamento e Estilo Tecnológico: Uma Proposta Interpretativa para a Ocupação Colonial do Alto Vale do Rio dos Sinos, Rio Grande do Sul. PhD diss., Universidade de São Paulo, Brazil.

Dias, Ondemar F., Jr. 1967/1977. A Evolução da Cultura em Minas Gerais e no Rio de Janeiro. *Anuário de Divulgação Científica (Goiânia)* 3:110–30.

———. 1969. Fase Mucuri (Estado do Rio de Janeiro). Anais do III Simpósio de Arqueologia da Área do Prata. *Pesquisas, Antropologia* 20:113–18.

———. 1972. Síntese da Pré-História do Rio de Janeiro, Uma Tentativa de Periodização. *Revista Histórica* 1 (2): 75–83.

———. 1980. Rio de Janeiro: A Tradição Itaipu e Os Sambaquis. *Anuário de Divulgação Científica* 7:33–42.

———. 1992. A Tradição Itaipu, Costa Central do Brasil. In *Prehistoria Sudamericana: Nuevas Perspectivas*, edited by B. Meggers, 161–76. Washington, DC: Taraxacun.

Dias, Ondemar F., Jr., and Eliana Carvalho. 1983. Um Possível Foco de Domesticação de Plantas no Estado do Rio de Janeiro. RJ-JC-64 (sítio Corondó). *Boletim do Instituto de Arqueologia Brasileira* 1 (1): 1–18.

Dillehay, Tom D. 1990. Mapuche Ceremonial Landscape, Social Recruitment, and Resource Rights. *World Archaeology* 22 (2): 223–41.

———. 1992. Keeping Outsiders Out: Public Ceremony, Resource Rights, and Hierarchy in Historic and Contemporary Mapuche Society. In *Wealth and Hierarchy in the Intermediate Area*, edited by F. W. Lange, 379–421. Washington, DC: Dumbarton Oaks.

———. 1997. ¿Dónde Están los Restos Humanos del Periodo Pleistoceno Tardío? Problemas y Perspectivas en la Búsqueda de los Primeros Americanos. *Boletín de Arqueología PUCP* 1:55–63.

Dinesen, Grete E., and Kurt W. Ockelmann. 2005. Spatial Distribution and Species Distinction of *Modiolus modiolus* and Syntopic Mytilidae (Bivalvia) in Faroese Waters (NE Atlantic). *BIOFAR Proceedings* 2005:125–36.

Donald, Leland. 2003. The Northwest Coast as a Study Area: Natural, Prehistoric, and Ethnographic Issues. In *Emerging from the Mist: Studies in Northwest Coast Culture History*, edited by R. G. Matson, G. Coupland, and Q. Mackie, 289–327. Vancouver, BC: UBC Press.

Doran, Glen H., and Bruce J. Piatek. 1985. Archaeological Investigations at Naval Live Oaks: Studies in Spatial Patterning and Chronology in the Gulf Coast of Florida CX5000-1-1039. Tallahassee, FL: Southeast Archeological Center, National Park Service.

Drayton, John. 1802. *A View of South Carolina, as Respects Her Natural and Civil Concerns.* Charleston, SC: W. P. Young.

Drucker, Philip. 1950. *Northwest Coast.* Berkeley: University of California Press.

———. 1955. *Indians of the Northwest Coast, Anthropological Handbook No. 10.* New York: Bureau of American Ethnology, Smithsonian Institution; McGraw-Hill Book Company.

———. 1965. *Cultures of the North Pacific Coast.* San Francisco, CA: Chandler Publishing Company.

Duarte, Paulo. 1967. O Sambaqui Visto Através de Alguns Sambaquis. *Ciência e Cultura* 19:643–45.

———. 1968. *O Sambaqui Visto Através de Alguns Sambaquis.* São Paulo: Instituto de Pré-História da Universidade de São Paulo.

Duday, Henri. 1978. Archéologie Funéraire et Anthropologie: Application des Relevés et de l'Étude Ostéologiques à l'Interprétation de Quelques Sépultures Pré-et Protohistoriques du Midi de la France. *Cahiers d'Archéologie* 78 (1): 55–101.

———. 1985. Nouvelles Observations sur la Décomposition des Corps dans un Espace Libre. In *Méthode d'Étude des Sépultures*, edited by H. Duday and C. Masset, 6–13. Paris: CNRS.

———. 2006. Archaeothanathology or the Archaeology of Death. In *Social Archaeology of Funerary Remains*, edited by R. Gowland and C. J. Knüsel, 30–56. Oxford: Oxbow Books.

———. 2009. *The Archaeology of the Dead: Lectures in Archaeothanatology.* Oxford: Oxbow Books.

Duday, Henri, Patrice Courtaud, Eric Crubezy, Pascal Sellier, and Anne-Marie Tillier. 1990. L'Anthropologie de "Terrain": Reconnaissance et Interpretation des Gestes Funeraires. *Bulletins et Memoires de la Societe d'Anthropologie de Paris* 2:26–49.

Duer, Douglas, and Nancy Turner. 2005. Introduction: Reassessing Indigenous Resource Management, Reassessing the History of an Idea. In *Keeping It Living: Traditions of Plant Use and Cultivation on the Northwest Coast of North America*, edited by D. Duer and N. Turner, 3–36. Seattle: University of Washington Press.

Dupont, Catherine. 2003. La Malacofaune de Sites Mésolithiques et Néolithiques de la Façade Atlantique de la France: Contribuition à l'Économie et à l'Identité Culturelle des Grupes Concerné. PhD diss., Université Paris I (Sorbonne), France.

Dye, Arthur H., Theresa A. Lasiak, and S. Gabula. 1997. Recovery and Recruitment of the Brown Mussel, *Perna perna* (L.), in Transkei: Implications for Management. *South African Journal of Zoology* 32 (4): 118–23.

Ebling, F. J., J. F. Sloane, J. A. Kitching, and H. M. Davies. 1962. The Ecology of Loch Ine. XII The Distribution and Characteristics of *Patella* Species. *Journal of Animal Ecology* 31:457–70.

Edwards, Howell G. M., Dennis W. Farwell, Dalva L. A. Faria, Ana Maria F. Monteiro, Marisa C. Afonso, Paulo DeBlasis, and Sabine Eggers. 2001. Raman Spectroscopic Study of 3000-Year-Old Human Skeletal Remains from a Sambaqui, Santa Catarina, Brazil. *Journal of Raman Spectroscopy* 32:17–22.

Edwards, William E. 1965. A Preliminary Report on the Sewee Mound Shell Midden, Charleston County, South Carolina. Columbia: U.S. Forest Service. On file, South Carolina Institute of Archaeology and Anthropology, University of South Carolina.

Eggers, Sabine, Maria Parks, Gisela Grupe, and Karl J. Reinhard. 2011. Paleoamerican Diet, Migration and Morphology in Brazil: Archaeological Complexity of the Earliest Americans. *PLoS One* 6 (9): e23962.

Eggers, Sabine, Cecilia C. Petronilho, Katharina Brandt, Camila Jerico-Daminello, José Filippini, and Karl J. Reinhard. 2008. How Does a Riverine Setting Affect the Lifestyle of Shellmound Builders in Brazil? *Homo* 59 (6): 405–27.

Ekendahl, Anette. 1995. Microdistribution in the Field and Habitat Choice in Aquaria by Colour Morphs of *Littorina mariae* Sacchi & Rastelli. *Journal of Molluscan Studies* 61:249–56.

Ellis, David W., and Luke Swan. 1981. *Teachings of the Tides: Uses of Marine Invertebrates by the Manhousat People.* Nanaimo, BC: Theytus Books.

Elvin-Lewis, Memory. 1980. Plants Used for Teeth Cleaning Throughout the World. *American Journal of Preventive Medicine* 6:61–70.

Epstein, Samuel, Ralph Buchsbaum, Heinz A. Lowenstam, and Harold C. Urey. 1953. Revised Carbonate-Water Isotopic Temperature Scale. *Bulletin of the Geological Society of America* 64:1315–26.

Erlandson, Jon M. 1994. *Early Hunter-Gatherers of the California Coast.* New York: Plenum.

———. 2001. The Archaeology of Aquatic Adaptations: Paradigms for a New Millennium. *Journal of Archaeological Research* 9 (4): 287–350.

Erlandson, Jon M., Michael H. Graham, Bruce J. Bourque, Debra Corbett, James A. Estes, and Robert S. Steneck. 2007. The Kelp Highway Hypothesis: Marine Ecology, the Coastal Migration Theory, and the Peopling of the Americas. *Journal of Island and Coastal Archaeology* 2 (2): 161–74.

Erlandson, Jon M., Torben C. Rick, Todd J. Braje, Alexis Steinberg, and René L. Vellanoweth. 2008. Human Impacts on Ancient Shellfish: A 10,000-Year Record from San Miguel Island, California. *Journal of Archaeological Science* 35:2144–52.

Erlandson, Jon M., Torben C. Rick, Todd J. Braje, Molly Casperson, Brendan Culleton, Brian Fulfrost, Tracy Garcia, Daniel A. Guthrie, Nicholas Jew, Douglas J. Kennett, et al. 2011. Paleoindian Seafaring, Maritime Technologies, and Coastal Foraging on California's Channel Islands. *Science* 441:1181–85.

Erlandson, Jon M., Torben C. Rick, Douglas J. Kennett, and Phillip L. Walker. 2001. Dates, Demography, and Disease: Cultural Contacts and Possible Evidence for Old World Epidemics among the Island Chumash. *Pacific Coast Archaeological Society Quarterly* 37 (3): 1–16.

Erlandson, Jon M., Torben C. Rick, and Curt Peterson. 2005. A Geoarchaeological Chronology of Holocene Dune Building on San Miguel Island, California. *Holocene* 15 (8): 1227–35.

Erlandson, Jon M., Torben C. Rick, and René L. Vellanoweth. 2008. *A Canyon Through Time: Archaeology, History, and Ecology of the Tecolote Canyon Area, Santa Barbara County, California.* Salt Lake City: University of Utah Press.

Erlandson, Jon M., Torben C. Rick, René L. Vellanoweth, and Douglas J. Kennett. 1999. Maritime Subsistence at 9300-Year-Old Shell Midden on Santa Rosa Island, California. *Journal of Field Archaeology* 26:255–65.

Erra, Georgina. 2010. Asignación Sistemática e Paleocomunidades Inseridas a Partir del Estúdio Fitolítico de Sedimentos Cuaternarios de Entre Rios, Argentina. *Boletín de La Sociedad Argentina de Botânica* 45 (3–4): 309–19.

Estévez, Jordi, Ernesto L. Piana, Assumpció Shiavini, and Nuria Juan-Muns. 2001. Archaeological Analysis of Shell Middens in the Beagle Channel, Tierra del Fuego Island. *International Journal of Osteoarchaeology* 11:24–33.

Estévez, Jordi, and Assumpció Vila, eds. 1996. *Encuentros en los Conchales Fueguinos.* Madrid-Barcelona: CSIC-UAB, Treballs d'Etnoarqueologia No. 1.

Fabian, Stephen Michael. 1992. *Space-Time of the Bororo of Brazil.* Gainesville: University Press of Florida.

Faria, Luis de C. 1952. Le Probléme des Sambaquis du Brésil: Récents Excavations du Gisement de Cabeçuda (Laguna, Santa Catarina). Paper read at 30th International Congress of Americanists, August 18–23, Cambridge, UK.

Faulkner, Patrick. 2006. The Ebb and Flow: An Archaeological Investigation of Late Holocene Economic Variability on the Coastal Margin of Blue Mud Bay, Northeast Australia. PhD diss., Australian National University.

———. 2008. Patterns of Chronological Variability in Occupation on the Coastal Margin of Blue Mud Bay. *Archaeology in Oceania* 43 (2): 81–88.

———. 2009. Focused, Intense and Long-Term: Evidence for Granular Ark (*Anadara granosa*) Exploitation from Late Holocene Shell Mounds of Blue Mud Bay, Northern Australia. *Journal of Archaeological Science* 36:821–34.

———. 2010. Morphometric and Taphonomic Analysis of Granular Ark (*Anadara granosa*) Dominated Shell Deposits of Blue Mud Bay, Northern Australia. *Journal of Archaeological Science* 37:1942–52.

———. 2013. Life on the Margins: An Archaeological Investigation of Late Holocene Economic Variability, Blue Mud Bay, Northeastern Australia. Canberra: ANU E Press.

Faulkner, Patrick, and Anne Clarke. 2009. Artefact Assemblage Characteristics and Distribution on the Point Blane Peninsula, Blue Mud Bay, Arnhem Land. *Australian Archaeology* 69:21–28.

Fausto, Carlos. 1992. Fragmentos de História e Cultura Tupinambá: da Etnologia Como Instrumento Crítico de Conhecimento Etno-Histórico. In *História dos Índios do Brasil*, edited by M. Carneiro da Cunha, 381–96. São Paulo: FAPESP/Cia das Letras.

———. 2000. *Os Indios Antes do Brasil.* Rio de Janeiro: Jorge Zahar.

Fedje, Daryl W., Rebecca J. Wigen, Quentin Mackie, Cynthia R. Lake, and Ian D. Sumpter. 2001. Preliminary Results from Investigations at Kilgii

Gwaay: An Early Holocene Archaeological Site on Ellen Island, Haida Gwaii, British Columbia. *Canadian Journal of Archaeology* 25:98–120.

Fenton, Alexander. 1984. Notes on Shellfish as Food and Bait in Scotland. In *The Fishing Culture of the World*, edited by B. Gunda, 121–42. Budapest: Akadémiai Kiadó.

———. 1997. *The Northern Isles: Orkney and Shetland*. Edinburgh: Tuckwell Press.

Ferembach, Denise. 1974. *Le Gisement Mésolithique de Moita do Sebastião, Muge, Portugal. II. Anthropologie*. Lisbon: Direção Geral do Assuntos Culturais.

Fernandez-Moreno, Mercedes, Alberto Arias-Perez, Ruth Freire, and Josefina Méndez. 2008. Genetic Analysis of *Aequipecten opercularis* and *Mimachlamys varia* (Bivalvia: Pectinidae) in Several Atlantic and Mediterranean Localities, Revealed by Mitochondrial PCR-RFLPs: A Preliminary Study. *Aquaculture Research* 39:474–81.

Field, Judith. 2006. Methods for Preparing Reference Slides. In *Ancient Starch Research*, edited by R. Torrence and H. Barton, 35–45. Walnut Creek, CA: Left Coast Press.

Figueiral, Isabel, and António Faustino Carvalho. 2006. Rocha das Gaivotas e Vale Boi: Os Restos Vegetais Carbonizados, Vestígios da Vegetação Meno-Neolítica. *Promontoria* 4:81–91.

Figuti, Levy. 1989. Estudos dos Vestígios Faunísticos do Sambaqui Cosipa-3, Cubatão, São Paulo. *Revista de Pré-História* 7:112–26.

———. 1992. Les Sambaquis COSIPA (4200 à 1200 ans BP): Étude de la Subsistance chez les Peuples Préhistoriques de Pêcheurs-Ramasseurs de Bivalves de la Côte Centrale de l'État de São Paulo, Brésil. PhD diss., Museum National d'Histoire Naturelle, Institut de Paleontologie Humaine, Paris, France.

———. 1993. O Homem Pré-Histórico, o Molusco e o Sambaqui: Considerações Sobre a Subsistência dos Povos Sambaquianos. *Revista do Museu de Arqueologia e Etnologia* 3:67–80.

———. 1995. Os Sambaquis Cosipa (4200 a 1200 anos AP): Estudo da Subsistência dos Povos Pescadores Coletores Pré-Históricos da Baixada Santista. *Anais da Revista de Arqueologia* 8:267–83.

———. 2010. Construindo o Sambaqui: a Ocupação e os Processos de Construção do Sítio da Bacia do Canal do Palmital. Santa Catarina. Relatório (01/06/2008 a 30/04/2009). São Paulo: FAPESP.

Figuti, Levy, Sabine Eggers, Carlos A. Mendonça, João L.

Porsani, Eronaldo B. Rocha, Paulo DeBlasis, and Walter M. Bissa. 2004. Investigações Geofísicas e Arqueológicas dos Sambaquis Fluviais do Vale do Ribeira de Iguape, Estado De São Paulo. Museu de Arqueologia e Etnologia, USP Relatório Final de Atividades de Projeto Temático, processo FAPESP n 1999/12684-2, 2004.

Figuti, Levy, and Daniela Klokler. 1996. Resultados Preliminares dos Vestígios Zooarqueológicos do Sambaqui Espinheiros II (Joinville, SC). *Revista do Museu de Arqueologia e Etnologia* 6:169–87.

Filippini, José. 2004. Biodistância entre Sambaquieiros Fluviais e Costeiros: Uma Abordagem Não-Métrica Craniana entre Três Sítios Fluviais do Vale do Ribeira–SP (Moraes, Capelinha e Pavão XVI) e Três Costeiros do Sul e Sudeste do Brasil (Piaçaguera, Jabuticabeira II e Tenório). MSc diss., Universidade de São Paulo, Brazil.

Filippini, José, and Sabine Eggers. 2005. Distância Biológica entre Sambaquieiros Fluviais (Moraes–Vale do Ribeira–SP) e Construtores de Sítios Litorâneos (Piaçaguera e Tenório SP e Jabuticabeira II-SC). *Revista do Museu de Arqueologia e Etnologia* 15/16:165–80.

Fischer, Patricia, Veronica Wesolowski, and Sheila M. F. M. de Souza. 2009. Tratamento Diferenciado de Lactentes: Primeiros Insigths. Paper read at XV Congresso da Sociedade de Arqueologia Brasileira, September 20–23, Belém, Pará, Brazil.

Fish, J. D., and Susan Fish. 1996. *A Student's Guide to the Seashore*. 2nd ed. Cambridge: Cambridge University Press.

Fish, Suzanne, Paulo DeBlasis, Maria Dulce Gaspar, and Paul Fish. 1998. Incremental Events in the Construction of Sambaquis, Southeastern Santa Catarina. *Revista de Arqueologia (SAB)* 10.

———. 2000. Eventos Incrementais na Construção de Sambaquis, Litoral Sul do Estado de Santa Catarina. *Revista do Museu de Arqueologia e Etnologia* 10:69–87.

Fitzhugh, Ben. 2003. *The Evolution of Complex Hunter-Gatherers: Archaeological Evidence from the North Pacific, Interdisciplinary Contributions to Archaeology*. New York: Kluwer-Plenum.

Fladmark, Knut R. 1975. *A Paleoecological Model for Northwest Coast Prehistory*. Ottawa: National Museum of Man, Mercury Series Archaeological Survey of Canada, Paper No. 43.

Flowers, Nancy. 1994. Crise e Recuperação Demográfica:

Os Xavante de Pimentel Barbosa, Mato Grosso. In *Saúde e Povos Indígenas*, edited by R. V. Santos and C. Coimbra Jr., 213–42. Rio de Janeiro: Editora Fiocruz.

Flury, Bernard D. 2006. Principal Components. In *Encyclopaedia of Statistical Sciences Online*. New York: John Wiley and Sons.

Ford, James A. 1966. Early Formative Cultures in Georgia and Florida. *American Antiquity* 31 (6): 781–99.

———. 1969. *A Comparison of Formative Cultures in the Americas: Diffusion or the Psychic Unity of Man*. Washington, DC: Smithsonian Institution Press.

Fournier, J. A., and J. Dewhirst. 1980. Zooarchaeological Analysis of Barnacle Remains from Yuquot, British Columbia. In *The Yuquot Project*. Vol. 2, edited by W. J. Folan and J. Dewhirst, 59–102. Ottawa: National Historic Parks and Sites Branch, Parks Canada.

Fraser, Douglas. 1968. *Village Planning in the Primitive World*. New York: George Braziller.

Freare, Christopher J. 1970. Aspects of the Ecology of an Exposed Shore Population of Dogwhelks *Nucella lapillus* (L.). *Oecologia* 5:1–18.

Frederick, Gay, and Susan Crockford. 2005. Appendix D: Analysis of the Vertebrate Fauna from Ts'ishaa Village, DfSi 16, Benson Island, B.C. In *Ts'ishaa: Archaeology and Ethnography of a Nuu chah nulth Origin Site in Barkley Sound*, edited by A. D. McMillan and D. E. St. Claire. Burnaby, BC: Archaeology Press, Simon Fraser University.

Fretter, Vera, and Alastair Graham. 1976. *The Prosobranch Molluscs of Britain and Denmark*. Part 1, *Pleurotomariacea, Fissurellacea, and Patellacea, the Journal of Molluscan Studies*. Reading, UK: Angus Graham Associates.

Fróes Abreu, S. 1932. A Importância dos Sambaquis no Estudo da Pré-História do Brasil. *Revista da Sociedade Brasileira de Geografia* 35:2–15.

Gagan, Michael K., and John Chappell. 2000. Massive Corals: Grand Archives of ENSO. In *In El Niño— History and Crisis: Studies from the Asia-Pacific Region*, edited by R. H. Grove and J. Chappell, 35–50. Cambridge: White Horse Press.

Gagan, Michael K., Allan R. Chivas, and Peter J. Isdale. 1994. High-Resolution Isotopic Records of the Mid-Holocene Tropical Western Pacific. *Earth and Planetary Science Letters* 121:549–58.

Gagan, Michael K., Erica J. Hendy, Simon G. Haberle, and Wahyoe S. Hantoro. 2004. Post-Glacial Evolution of the Indo-Pacific Warm Pool and El Niño–Southern Oscillation. *Quaternary International* 118–19:127–43.

Gagliano, Sherwood M., and Clarence H. Webb. 1970. Archaic–Poverty Point Transition at the Pearl River Mouth. In *The Poverty Point Culture*, edited by B. J. Broyles and C. H. Webb, 47–72. Morgantown, WV: Southeastern Archaeological Conference, Bulletin 12.

Gallucci, Vincent F., and Betty B. Gallucci. 1982. Reproduction and Ecology of the Hermaphroditic Cockle *Clinocardium nuttallii* (Bivalvia: Cardiidae) in Garrison Bay. *Marine Ecology Progress Series* 7:137–45.

Gamble, Lynn H. 2008. *The Chumash at European Contact: Power, Trade, and Feasting Among Complex Hunter-Gatherers*. Berkeley: University of California Press.

Gamble, Lynn H., Phillip L. Walker, and Glenn S. Russell. 2001. An Integrative Approach to Mortuary Analysis: Social and Symbolic Dimensions of Chumash Burial Practices. *American Antiquity* 66 (2): 185–212.

Garcia, Caio. 1970. Meios de Subsistência de Duas Populações Pré-Históricas no Litoral do Estado de São Paulo. MSc diss., Instituto de Biociências, Universidade de São Paulo, Brazil.

———. 1972. Estudo Comparativo das Fontes de Alimentação duas Populações Pré-Históricas do Litoral Paulista. PhD diss., Instituto de Biociências, Universidade de São Paulo, Brazil.

Garcia, Caio, and Dorath P. Uchôa. 1980. Piaçaguera: um Sambaqui do Litoral do Estado de São Paulo, Brasil. *Revista de Pré-História (São Paulo)* 2:11–84.

Gaspar, Maria Dulce. 1991. Aspectos da Organização Social de um Grupo de Pescadores, Coletores e Caçadores: Região Compreendida entre a Ilha Grande e o Delta do Paraíba do Sul, Estado do Rio de Janeiro. PhD diss., Universidade de São Paulo, Brazil.

———. 1994/1995. Espaços, Ritos Funerários e Identidade Pré-Histórica. *Revista de Arqueologia (São Paulo)* 8 (2): 221–37.

———. 1995. Parâmetros Demográficos Para a Ocupação Pré-Histórica dos Pescadores, Coletores e Caçadores. In *Arqueologia do Estado do Rio de Janeiro*, edited by M. da Conceição Beltrão, 35–42. Rio de Janeiro: Arquivo Público do Estado do Rio de Janeiro/SEJ.

———. 1998. Considerations of the Sambaquis of the Brazilian Coast. *Antiquity* 72:592–615.

———. 2000. *Sambaqui: Arqueologia do Litoral Brasileiro.* Rio de Janeiro: Editora Jorge Zahar.

———. 2003. Aspectos da Organização Social de Pescadores-Coletores: Região Compreendida Entre a Ilha Grande e o Delta do Paraíba do Sul, Rio de Janeiro. *Pesquisas (São Leopoldo)* 59:1–163.

———. 2004. Cultura: Comunicação, Arte, Oralidade na Pré-História do Brasil. *Revista do Museu de Arqueologia e Etnologia, São Paulo* 14:156–68.

Gaspar, Maria Dulce, Débora Barbosa, and Márcia Barbosa. 1994. Análise do Processo Cognitivo de Construção do Sambaqui Ilha da Boa Vista I–RJ. *Clio (Recife)* 1 (10): 104–23.

Gaspar, Maria Dulce, Angela M. Buarque, Jane Cordeiro, and Eliane Escorcio. 2007. Tratamento dos Mortos Entre os Sambaquieiros, Tupinambá e Goitacá Que Ocuparam a Região dos Lagos, Estado do Rio de Janeiro. *Revista do Museu de Arqueologia e Etnologia (São Paulo)* 17:169–90.

Gaspar, Maria Dulce, and Paulo DeBlasis. 1992. Construção de Sambaquis. *Anais da VI Reunião da Sociedade de Arqueologia Brasileira* 2:811–20.

Gaspar, Maria Dulce, Paulo DeBlasis, Suzanne K. Fish, and Paul R. Fish. 2008. Sambaqui (Shell Mound) Societies of Coastal Brazil. In *Handbook of South American Archaeology*, edited by H. Silverman and W. H. Isbell, 319–35. New York: Springer.

Gaspar, Maria Dulce, and Daniela Klokler. 2004. Time to Die, Time to Eat: Ritual in Shell Mounds. Paper read at SAA 69th Annual Meeting, April, Montreal.

———. 2011. Amourins: Same Site, Different Perspectives. Sambaqui Archaeology 30 Years Later. Paper read at SAA 76th Annual Meeting, March 30–April 3, Sacramento, CA.

Gaspar, Maria Dulce, Daniela Klokler, Marisa C. Afonso, Paulo DeBlasis, and Levy Figuti. 2009. Monumental Shell Mounds (Sambaquis) from the Southern Brazilian Coast. Paper read at SAA 74th Annual Meeting, Atlanta, GA.

Gaspar, Maria Dulce, Daniela Klokler, and Paulo DeBlasis. 2011. Traditional Fishing, Mollusk Gathering, and the Shell Mound Builders of Santa Catarina, Brazil. *Journal of Ethnobiology* 31 (2): 188–212.

Geo-Marine Inc. 2006. National Register Eligibility Determinations and Boundary Delineation of Selected Sites on Tyndall Air Force Base, Bay County, Florida. Tallahassee: Tyndall Air Force Base, Florida. On file, Florida Division of Historical Resources, Survey No. 12805.

Giannini, Paulo C. F., Ximena S. Villagrán, Milene Fornari, Daniel do Nascimento Jr., Priscila M. L. Menezes, Ana P. B. Tanaka, Danilo C. Assunção, Paulo DeBlasis, and Paula G. C. do Amaral. 2010. Interações entre Evolução Sedimentar e Ocupação Humana Pré-Histórica na Costa Centro-Sul de Santa Catarina, Brasil. *Boletim do Museu Paraense Emílio Goeldi. Ciências Humanas* 15 (1): 105–28.

Gibson, Jon L. 2001. *The Ancient Mounds of Poverty Point: Place of Rings.* Gainesville: University Press of Florida.

Gifford, Diane P. 1980. Ethnoarchaeological Contributions to the Taphonomy of Human Sites. In *Fossils in the Making: Vertebrate Taphonomy and Palaeoecology*, edited by A. K. Behrenmeyer and A. P. Hill, 94–106. Chicago: University of Chicago Press.

Gillikin, David P., Anne Lorrain, Steven Bouillon, Philippe Wllenz, and Frank Dehairs. 2006. Stable Carbon Isotopic Composition of *Mytilus edulis* Shells: Relation to Metabolism, Salinity, $\delta^{13}C_{DIC}$ and Phytoplankton. *Organic Geochemistry* 37:1371–82.

Gilman, Antonio. 1983. Comment on Alekshin. *Current Anthropology* 24 (2): 146–47.

Gittenberger, Adriaan. 2003. The Wentletrap *Epitonium hartogi* spec. nov. (Gastropoda: Epitoniidae), Associated with Bubble Coral Species, *Plerogyra* spec. (Scleractinia: Euphyllidae), off Indonesia and Thailand. *Zoologische Verhandelingen* 345:139–50.

Glassow, Michael A. 1996. *Purisimeño Chumash Prehistory: Maritime Adaptations Along the Southern California Coast.* Fort Worth, TX: Harcourt Brace College Publishers.

Glassow, Michael A., John R. Johnson, and Jon M. Erlandson. 1986. Mescalitan Island Archaeology and the Canaliño Period of Santa Barbara Prehistory. In *A New Look at Some Old Sites*, 9–20. Salinas, CA: Coyote Press, Archives of California Prehistory No. 6.

Goggin, John M. 1949. The Archaeology of the Glades Area, Southern Florida. New Haven, CT: Unpublished manuscript on file at Yale University Department of Anthropology.

Gonçalves, A. A. Huet d. B. 1986. Inéditos de Rui Serpa Pinto sobre as Escavaçoes Arqueologicas de Muge. *Trabalhos de Antropologia e Etnologia da*

Sociedade Portuguesa de Antropologia e Etnologia 26:211–29.

Goodenough, Ward H. 1965. Rethinking "Status" and "Role": Toward a General Model of the Cultural Organisation of Social Relationships. In *The Relevance of Models for Social Anthropology*, edited by M. Banton, 1–24. London: Tavistock.

Goodman, Alan H., R. B. Thomas, Allan C. Swedlund, and George J. Armelagos. 1988. Biocultural Perspectives on Stress in Prehistoric, Historic and Contemporary Population Research. *Yearbook of Physical Anthropology* 31:169–202.

Goodwin, David H., Bernd R. Schöne, and David L. Dettman. 2003. Resolution and Fidelity of Oxygen Isotopes as Paleotemperature Proxies in Bivalve Mollusk Shells: Models and Observations. *Palaios* 18:110–25.

Gott, Beth, Huw Barton, Delwen Samuel, and Robin Torrence. 2006. Biology of Starch. In *Ancient Starch Research*, edited by R. Torrence and H. Barton, 35–45. Walnut Creek, CA: Leaf Coast Press.

Graham, Alastair, and Vera Fretter. 1947. The Life History of *Patina pellucida* (L.). *Journal of the Marine Biological Association of the United Kingdom* 26:590–601.

Graham, Michael H. 2004. Effects of Local Deforestation on the Diversity and Structure of Southern California Giant Kelp Forest Food Webs. *Ecosystem* 7:341–57.

Grayson, Donald K. 1984. *Quantitative Zooarchaeology: Topics in the Analysis of Archaeological Faunas.* Orlando, FL: Academic Press.

Greene, David L., D. P. Van Gerven, and George J. Armelagos. 1986. Life and Death in Ancient Populations: Bones of Contention in Paleodemography. *Human Evolution* 1:193–207.

Greene, Tammy R., C. L. Kuba, and Joel D. Irish. 2005. Quantifying Calculus: A Suggested New Approach for Recording an Important Indicator of Diet and Dental Health. *Homo* 56:119–32.

Grier, Colin. 2003. Political, Social, and Economic Dimensions of Regional Interaction in the Prehistoric Gulf of Georgia Region. PhD diss., Arizona State University, USA.

Grieve, David. 1872. Notes on the Shell Heaps near Inveravon, Linlithgowshire. *Proceedings of the Society of Antiquaries of Scotland* 9:45–52.

Griffitts, Janet, and Clive Bonsall. 2001. Experimental Determination of the Function of Antler and Bone "Bevel-Ended" Tools from Prehistoric Shell Middens in Western Scotland. In *Crafting Bone: Skeletal Technologies Through Time and Space, Proceedings of the 2nd Meeting of the (ICAZ) Worked Bone Research Group, Budapest, 31 August–5 September 1999*, edited by A. M. Choyke and L. Bartosiewicz, 207–20. Oxford: Archaeopress, British Archaeological Reports, International Series No. 937.

Grøn, Ole. 1991. A Method for Reconstruction of Social Structure in Prehistoric Societies and Examples of Prehistorical Application. In *Social Space: Human Spatial Behavior in Dwellings and Settlements, Proceedings of an Interdisciplinary Conference*, edited by O. Grøn, E. Englestad, and I. Lindblom, 100–117. Odense, Denmark: Odense University Press.

Gualberto, Luis. 1924. Os Casqueiros de Santa Catarina ou Sambaquis. *Revista do Instituto Histórico e Geográfico Brasileiro* 96 (150): 287–304.

Guerra, Antonio T. 1950. Apreciação Sobre o Valor dos Sambaquis como Indicadores de Variações do Nível dos Oceanos. *Boletim Geográfico* 8 (91): 850–53.

Guichón, Ricardo A., Ramiro Barberena, and Luis A. Borrero. 2001. ¿Dónde y Cómo Aparecen los Restos Óseos Humanos en Patagonia Austral? *Anales Instituto Patagonia, Serie Ciencias Humanas* 29:103–18.

Guichón, Ricardo A., Isabel Marti, Eugenio Aspillaga, Jose A. Cocilovo, and Francisco Rothhammer. 1989/1990. El Poblamiento Tardío de Tierra del Fuego. *Runa* 19:27–39.

Guichón, Ricardo A., A. Sebastián Muñoz, and Luis A. Borrero. 2000. Datos para una Tafonomía de Restos Óseos Humanos en Bahía San Sebastián, Tierra del Fuego. *Relaciones de la Sociedad Argentina de Antropología* 25:297–313.

Guichón, Ricardo A., and Jorge A. Suby. 2011. Estudio Bioarqueológico de los Restos Óseos Humanos Recuperados por Anne Chapman en Caleta Falsa, Tierra del Fuego. *Magallania* 39 (1): 163–77.

Guichón, Ricardo A., Jorge A. Suby, Romina Casali, and Martín H. Fugassa. 2006. Health at the Time of Native-European Contact in Southern Patagonia. *Memorias do Instituto Oswaldo Cruz* 101, Supplement 2:97–105.

Guichón, Ricardo A., Jorge A. Suby, and Martín H. Fugassa. 2008. El Registro Biológico Humano en Patagonia Austral: Algunas Líneas de Análisis. In *Arqueología de la Costa Patagónica: Perspectivas para su conservación*, edited by I. Cruz and M. S. Caracotche, 232–48. Rio Gallegos, Argentina: Universidad Nacional de la Patagonia Austral.

Gunther, Ema. 1927. *Klallam Ethnography*. Seattle: University of Washington Press.

Gusinde, Martin. 1986 [1937]. *Los Indios de Tierra del Fuego, IIIT*. Buenos Aires: Centro Argentino de Etnología Americana, Consejo Nacional de Investigaciones Científicas y Técnicas.

Guy, Hervé, Claude Masset, and Charles-Albert Baud. 1997. Infant Taphonomy. *International Journal of Osteoarchaeology* 7:221–29.

Haberle, Simon G., and Bruno David. 2004. Climates of Change: Human Dimensions of Holocene Environmental Change in Low Latitudes of the PEPII Transect. *Quaternary International* 118–19:165–79.

Habu, Junko. 2004. *Ancient Jomon of Japan*. Cambridge: Cambridge University Press.

Haines, Peter W., David J. Rawlings, I. P. Sweet, B. A. Pietsch, Kenneth A. Plumb, Thomas L. Madigan, and Andrew A. Krassay. 1999. 1:250 000 Geological Map Series, Explanatory Notes: Blue Mud Bay SD53-7. Darwin: Department of Mines and Energy, Northern Territory Geological Survey, Australian Geological Survey Organisation.

Hallmann, Nadine, Meghan Burchell, Bernd R. Schöne, Gail V. Irving, and David Maxwell. 2009. High-Resolution Sclerochronological Analysis of the Bivalve Mollusk *Saxidomus gigantea* from Alaska and British Columbia: Techniques for Revealing Environmental Archives and Archaeological Seasonality. *Journal of Archaeological Science* 36:2353–64.

Ham, Leonard. 1982. Seasonality, Shell Midden Layers, and Coast Calish Subsistence Activities at the Crescent Beach Site, DgRr 1. PhD diss., University of British Columbia, Canada.

Hamell, George R. 1992. The Iroquois and the World's Rim: Speculations on Color, Culture and Contact. *American Indian Quarterly* 16 (4): 451–69.

Hanson, Diane K. 1991. Late Prehistoric Subsistence in the Strait of Georgia Region of the Northwest Coast. PhD diss., Simon Fraser University, Burnaby, BC, Canada.

Hardy, Karen. 2008. Prehistoric String Theory: How Twisted Fibers Helped to Shape the World. *Antiquity* 82:271–80.

Hardy, Karen, Tony Blakeney, Les Copeland, Jennifer Kirkham, Richard Wrangham, and Matthew Colins. 2009. Starch Granules, Dental Calculus and New Perspectives on Ancient Diet. *Journal of Archaeological Science* 36 (2): 248–55.

Hardy, Karen, and Caroline R. Wickham-Jones. 2003. Scotland's First Settlers: An Investigation into Settlement, Territoriality and Mobility During the Mesolithic in the Inner Sound, Scotland, First Results. In *Mesolithic on the Move*, edited by L. Larsson, H. Kindgren, K. Knutsson, D. Loeffler, and A. Åkerlund, 369–81. Oxford: Oxbow Books.

Harrison, Geoffrey A. 1988. Seasonality and Human Population Biology. In *Coping with Uncertainty in Food Supply*, edited by I. De Garine and G. A. Harrison, 26–31. Oxford: Clarendon Press.

Harrison, Rodney. 2009. The Archaeology of the Port Hedland Coastal Plain and Implications for Understanding the Prehistory of Shell Mounds and Middens in Northwestern Australia. *Archaeology in Oceania* 44, Supplement:81–98.

Harrison, William M., and Edith S. Harrison. 1966. An Archaeological Sequence for the Hunting People of Santa Barbara, California. *Annual Reports of the University of California Archaeological Survey* 8:1–89.

Harrold, Christopher, and John S. Pearse. 1987. The Ecological Role of Echinoderms in Kelp Forests. In *Echinoderm Studies*, edited by M. Jangoux and J. M. Lawrence, 137–233. Rotterdam: A. A. Balkema.

Hartt, Charles F. 1885. Contribuições Para a Ethnologia do Valle do Amazonas. *Arquivos do Museu Nacional (Rio de Janeiro)* 6:1–14.

Haslan, Michael, Gail Robertson, Alison Crowther, Sue Nugent, and Luke Kirkwood. 2009. *Archaeological Science Under a Microscope: Studies in Residue and DNA Analyses in Honor of Thomas H. Loy*. Canberra: Australian National University E Press.

Hassan, Fekri. 1981. *Demographic Archaeology*. New York: Academic Press.

Hauser, Gertrud, and Gian F. De Stefano. 1989. *Epigenetic Variants of the Human Skull*. Stuttgart: E. Schweizerbart'sche Verlagsbuchhandlung.

Hay, Murray B., Audrey Dallimore, Richard E. Thomson, Stephen E. Clavert, and Reinhard Pienitz. 2007. Siliceous Microfossil Record of Late Holocene Oceanography and Climate Along the West Coast of Vancouver Island, British Columbia (Canada). *Quaternary Research* 67:33–49.

Hayden, Brian. 1981. Research and Development in the Stone Age: Technological Transitions Among Hunter-Gatherers. *Current Anthropology* 22 (5): 519–48.

———. 2001. Fabulous Feasts. A Prolegomenon to the Importance of Feasting. In *Feasts: Archaeological and Ethnographic Perspectives on Food, Politics, and Power*, edited by M. Dietler and B. Hayden, 23–64. Washington, DC: Smithsonian Institution Press.

———. 2003. Were Luxury Foods the First Domesticates? Ethnoarchaeological Perspectives from Southeast Asia. *World Archaeology* 34 (3): 458–69.

Hayden, Brian, and Aubrey Cannon. 1983. Where the Garbage Goes: Refuse Disposal in the Maya Highlands. *Journal of Anthropological Archaeology* 2:117–63.

Healy, John M., and Fred. E. Wells. 1998. Superfamily Cerithioidea. In *Mollusca: The Southern Synthesis. Fauna of Australia, Vol. 5, Part B*, edited by P. L. Beesley, G. J. B. Ross, and A. Wells, 707–33. Melbourne: CSIRO.

Heaton, T. J., Paul G. Blackwell, and Caitlin E. Buck. 2009. A Bayesian Approach to the Estimation of Radiocarbon Calibration Curves: The IntCal09 Methodology. *Radiocarbon* 51 (4): 1151–64.

Heckenberger, Michael J. 1996. War and Peace in the Shadow of Empire: Sociopolitical Change in the Upper Xingu of Southeastern Amazonia, AD 1400–2000. PhD diss., University of Pittsburgh, USA.

———. 2005. *The Ecology of Power: Culture, Place, and Personhood in the Southern Amazon, A.D. 1000–2000*. New York: Routledge.

Heide, Gregory, and Michael Russo. 2003. Investigation of the Coosaw Island Shell Ring Complex (38BU1866). Tallahassee, FL: South Carolina Department of Natural Resources, Heritage Trust Program, Columbia. On file, Southeast Archeological Center, National Park Service.

Heikkinen, Olavi. 1984. Dendrochronological Evidence of Variation of Coleman Glacier, Mt. Baker, Washington. *Arctic and Alpine Research* 16 (1): 53–64.

Hemmings, E. Thomas. 1970. Preliminary Report of Excavations at Fig Island, South Carolina. *Notebook* 2 (9): 9–15.

Hendy, Erica J., Michael K. Gagan, Chantal A. Alibert, Malcolm T. McCulloch, Janice M. Lough, and Peter J. Isdale. 2002. Abrupt Decrease in Tropical Pacific Sea Surface Salinity at End of Little Ice Age. *Science* 295:1511–14.

Henry, Amanda G., Alison S. Brooks, and Dolores R. Piperno. 2010. Microfossils in Calculus Demonstrate Consumption of Plants and Cooked Foods in Neanderthal Diets (Shanidar III, Iraq; Spy I and II, Belgium). *Proceedings of the National Academy of Sciences* 10.1073/pnas.1016868108.

Henry, Amanda G., and Dolores R. Piperno. 2008. Using Plant Microfossils from Dental Calculus to Recover Human Diet: A Case Study from Tell Al-Raqaí, Syria. *Journal of Archaeological Science* 35:1943–50.

Heredia, Osvaldo R., and Maria da Conceição Beltrão. 1980. Mariscadores e Pescadores Pré-Históricos do Litoral Centro-Sul Brasileiro. *Pesquisas* 31:101–19.

Hering, Alexandre. 2005. Estudo da Indústria Osteodontomalacológica do Sambaqui Jabuticabeira II, Jaguaruna, SC. São Paulo: Museu de Arqueologia e Etnologia, Universidade de São Paulo, Brazil.

Hertz, Robert. 2006. A Contribution to the Study of the Collective Representation of Death. In *Death, Mourning and Burial: A Cross-Cultural Reader*, edited by A. C. G. Robben, 197–212. Malden, MA: Blackwell.

Hill, Erica. 2000. The Contextual Analysis of Animal Interments and Ritual Practice in Southwestern North America. *Kiva* 65 (4): 361–98.

Hill, J. D. 1996. The Identification of Ritual Deposits of Animals: A General Perspective from a Specific Study of "Special Animal Deposits" from the Southern English Iron Age. In *Ritual Treatment of Human and Animal Remains*, edited by S. Anderson and J. Boyle, 17–32. Oxford: Oxbow Books.

Hillson, Simon W. 2001. Recording Dental Caries in Archaeological Human Remains. *International Journal of Osteoarchaeology* 11:249–89.

Hintze, Jerry. 2007. NCSS [Number Cruncher Statistical System] 2007. Kaysville, UT: NCSS, LCC.

Hiscock, Peter. 1997. Archaeological Evidence for Environmental Change in Darwin Harbour. In *The Marine Flora and Fauna of Darwin Harbour, Northern Territory, Australia: Proceedings of the Sixth International Marine Biological Workshop*, edited by J. R. Hanley, G. Caswell, D. Megirian, and H. K. Larson, 445–49. Darwin, Australia: Museum and Art Galleries of the Northern Territory and the Marine Sciences Association.

———. 1999. Holocene Coastal Occupation of Western Arnhem Land. In *Australian Coastal Archaeology*, edited by J. Hall and I. J. McNiven, 91–103. Canberra: ANH Publications, Department of Archaeology and Natural History, RSPAS, Australian National University.

———. 2008. *Archaeology of Ancient Australia*. London: Routledge.

Hiscock, Peter, and Patrick Faulkner. 2006. Dating the Dreaming? Creation of Myths and Rituals for Mounds Along the Northern Australian Coastline. *Cambridge Archaeological Journal* 16 (2): 209–22.

Hodder, Ian. 1982. *Symbols in Action*. Cambridge: Cambridge University Press.

———. 2005. Socialization and Feasting at Çatalhöyük: A Response to Adams. *American Antiquity* 70 (1): 189–91.

Hogg, Robert S. 1985. An Investigation into the Aboriginal Subsistence Patterns in the Eastern Queen Charlotte Strait. Victoria: Department of Anthropology, University of Victoria.

Holdaway, Simon, Patricia Fanning, Martin Jones, Justin Shiner, Dan C. Witter, and Geoff Nicholls. 2002. Variability in the Chronology of Late Holocene Aboriginal Occupation on the Arid Margin of Southeastern Australia. *Journal of Archaeological Science* 29:351–63.

Holdaway, Simon, Patricia Fanning, and Justin Shiner. 2005. Absence of Evidence or Evidence of Absence? Understanding the Chronology of Indigenous Occupation of Western New South Wales, Australia. *Archaeology in Oceania* 40:33–49.

Holden, J. 1979. *Shorefishing*. London: Faber.

Hong, Suk K., J. Henderson, Albert Olszowka, William E. Hurford, Konrad J. Falke, J. Qvist, Peter Radermacher, K. Shiraki, M. Mohri, H. Takeuchi, et al. 1991. Daily Diving Pattern of Korean and Japanese Breath-hold Divers (Ama). *Undersea Biomedical Research* 18:433–43.

Hong, Suk K., and Hermann Rahn. 1967. The Diving Women of Korea and Japan. *Scientific American* 216:34–43.

Horwitz, Liora K. 2001. Animal Offerings in the Middle Bronze Age: Food for the Gods, Food for Thought. *Palestine Exploration Quarterly* 133:78–90.

Hrdlicka, Ales. 1922. *The Anthropology of Florida*. De Land: Florida State Historical Society.

Hudson, Charles. 1976. *The Southeastern Indians*. Knoxville: University of Tennessee Press.

Hughen, Konrad A., Mike G. L. Baillie, Edouard Bard, Alex Bayliss, J. Warren Beck, Chanda J. H. Bertrand, Paul G. Blackwell, Caitlin E. Buck, George S. Burr, K. B. Cutler, et al. 2004. Marine04 Marine Radiocarbon Age Calibration, 26–0 ka BP. *Radiocarbon* 46:1059–86.

Hughes, Roger N., and Robert W. Elner. 1979. Tactics of a Predator, *Carcinus maenas*, and Morphological Responses of the Prey, *Nucella lapillus*. *Journal of Animal Ecology* 48:65–78.

Hurcombe, Linda. 1992. *Use-Wear Analysis and Obsidian Theory, Experiments and Results*. Sheffield, UK: Equinox Publishing, Sheffield Archaeological Monographs No. 4.

Hurt, Wesley R., and Oldemar Blasi. 1960. *O Sambaqui do Macedo, A 52 B, Paraná, Brasil*. Curitiba, Brazil: Centro de Ensino e Pesquisas Arqueológicas.

Hutson, Scott R., and Travis W. Stanton. 2007. Cultural Logic and Practical Reason: The Structure of Discard in Ancient Maya Houselots. *Cambridge Archaeological Journal* 17 (2): 123–44.

Hyades, Paul, and J. Deniker. 1891. *Mission Scientifique du Cap Horn 1882–1883. Anthropologie et Ethnographie*. Paris: Ministères de la Marine et de l'Instruction Publique, Gauthier-Villars et Fils.

Hyson, John M., Jr. 2003. History of the Toothbrush. *Journal of the History of Dentistry* 51 (2): 73–80.

IGeoE. 2007. 1:25 000 Folha 378 Raposa (Almeirim), Edição 3. Lisbon: Serviço Cartográfico do Exército.

IGP. 1960. 1:2000. Lisbon: Instituto Geográfico Português.

Ihering, Hermann. 1903. As Origens dos Sambaquis. *Revista do Instituto Histórico e Geográfico de São Paulo* 8:446–57.

Isbell, Raymond F. 1983. Kimberley—Arnhem—Cape York (III). In *Soils: An Australian Viewpoint*, 189–99. Melbourne: CSIRO.

Ives, Ryan S., and Sara L. Walker. 2003. Site 45SJ165. In *Archaeological Investigations at Sites 45SJ165 and 45SJ169, Decatur Island, San Juan County, Washington*, edited by S. L. Walker, 33–59. Cheney: Eastern Washington University, Reports in Archaeology and History 100–118.

Jackes, Mary. 2009. Teeth and the Past in Portugal: Pathology and the Mesolithic-Neolithic Transition. In *Comparative Dental Morphology*. Vol. 13, edited by T. Koppe, G. Meyer, and K. W. Alt, 167–72. Basel, Switzerland: Karger.

———. 2011. Representativeness and Bias in Archaeological Skeletal Samples. In *Handbook of Social Bioarchaeology, Blackwell Studies in Global Archaeology*, edited by S. C. Agarwal and B. Glencross, 107–46. Chichester, UK: Wiley-Blackwell.

————. In press. Muge Mesolithic Heterogeneity: Comparing Moita do Sebastião and Cabeço da Arruda. In *Proceedings of the Eighth Conference on the Mesolithic in Europe*, edited by A. Cabal, M. C. Pablo, and M. Á. Fano. *Use-Wear Analysis and Obsidian Theory, Experiments and Results.* Oxford: Oxbow Books.

Jackes, Mary, and Pedro Alvim. 2006. Reconstructing Moita do Sebastião, The First Step. In *Do Epipalaeolítico ao Calcolítico na Península Iberica. Actas do IV Congresso de Arqueologia Peninsular, vol. Promontoria Monográfica*, edited by N. F. Bicho and H. Verissimo, 13–25. Faro, Portugal: Universidade do Algarve.

Jackes, Mary, Pedro Alvim, and Maria J. Cunha. In press. Reconstructing Cabeço da Amoreira, 1930–1933. In *Proceedings of the Eighth Conference on the Mesolithic in Europe*, edited by A. Cabal, M. C. Pablo, and M. Á. Fano. Oxford: Oxbow Books.

Jackes, Mary, and David Lubell. 1996. Dental Pathology and Diet: Second Thoughts. In *Nature et Culture: Actes du Colloque International de Liège, 13–17 decembre 199.* Vol. 68, *Etudes et Recherches Archéologiques*, edited by M. Otte, 457–80. Liège, Belgium: Université de Liège.

————. 2012. Mortuary Archaeology of the Muge Shell Middens. In *Funerary Practices in the Iberian Peninsula from the Mesolithic to the Chalcolithic*, edited by J. F. Gibaja, A. F. Carvalho, and P. Chambon, 67–76. Oxford: Archaeopress, British Aarchaeological Reports, International Series No. 2417.

Jackes, Mary, and Christopher Meiklejohn. 2004. Building a Method for the Study of the Mesolithic-Neolithic Transition in Portugal. *Documenta Praehistorica* 31:89–111.

————. 2008. The Paleodemography of Central Portugal and the Mesolithic-Neolithic Transition. In *Recent Advances in Paleodemography: Data, Techniques, Patterns*, edited by J. P. Bocquet-Appel, 209–58. New York: Springer-Verlag.

Jackes, Mary, Ana Maria Silva, and Joel Irish. 2001. Dental Morphology: A Valuable Contribution to Our Understanding of Prehistory. *Journal of Iberian Archaeology* 3:97–119.

Jahren, A. Hope, Nicholas Toth, Kathy Schick, J. Desmond Clark, and Ronald Amundsen. 1997. Determining Stone Tool Use: Chemical and Morphological Analyses of Residue on Experimentally Manufactured Stone Tools. *Journal of Archaeological Science* 24:245–50.

James, Frances C., and Charles E. McCulloch. 1990. Multivariate Analysis in Ecology and Systematics—Panacea or Pandora Box? *Annual Review of Ecology and Systematics* 21:129–66.

Jamieson, Glen S. 1993. Marine Invertebrate Conservation: Evaluation of Fisheries Over-Exploitation Concerns. *American Zoology* 33:551–67.

Jerardino, Antonieta. 1997. Changes in Shellfish Species Composition and Mean Shell Size from a Late-Holocene Record of the West Coast of Southern Africa. *Journal of Archaeological Science* 24:1031–44.

————. 1998. Excavations at Pancho's Kitchen Midden, Western Cape Coast, South Africa: Further Observations into the Megamidden Period. *South African Archaeological Bulletin* 55 (167): 16–25.

Johnson, Allen W., and Timothy Earle. 1987. *The Evolution of Human Societies.* Stanford, CA: Stanford University Press.

Johnson, Donald L. 1972. Landscape Evolution on San Miguel Island, California. PhD diss., University of Kansas, USA.

Johnson, John R. 1982. An Ethnohistoric Study of the Island Chumash. MA diss., University of California, Santa Barbara, USA.

————. 1988. Chumash Social Organization: An Ethnohistoric Perspective. PhD diss., University of California, Santa Barbara, USA.

Johnson, John R., Thomas W. Stafford, Henry O. Ajie, and Don P. Morris. 2002. Arlington Springs Revisited. In *Proceedings of the Fifth California Islands Symposium*, edited by D. Browne, K. Mitchell, and H. Chaney, 541–45. Santa Barbara, CA: Santa Barbara Museum of Natural History.

Johnson, Lucy L., and Clive Bonsall. 1999. Mesolithic Adaptations on Offshore Islands: The Aleutians and Western Scotland. In *Den Bogen spannen . . . Festschrift für Bernhard Gramsch*, edited by E. Cziesla, T. Kersting and S. Pratsch, 107–15. Weißbach, Germany: Beier and Beran.

Johnston, Francis E. 1962. Growth of the Long Bones of Infants and Young Children at Indian Knoll. *Human Biology* 33:66–81.

Johnstone, Dave. 1991. The Function(s) of a Shellmidden Site from the Southern Strait of Georgia. MA diss., Simon Fraser University, Burnaby, BC, Canada.

Jones, D. Aaron. 1984. An Ecological Interpretation of

Mesolithic Shellfish Remains on the Island of Oronsay, Inner Hebrides. PhD diss., University of Sheffield, UK.

———. 1985. Ecological Investigation of Marine Molluscs: An Examination of Changes in Body Weight and Shape as Aids to the Interpretation of the Mesolithic Shell Middens of the Island of Oronsay, Inner Hebrides. In *Palaeobiological Investigations: Research Design, Methods and Data Analysis*, edited by N. J. R. Fieller, D. D. Gilbertson, and N. G. A. Ralph, 209–20. Oxford: Archaeopress, British Archaeological Reports.

Jones, Norman S. 1952. The Bottom Fauna and the Food of Flatfish off the Cumberland Coast. *Journal of Animal Ecology* 21:182–205.

Jones, Phillip M. 1956. Archaeological Investigation on Santa Rosa Island in 1901. Edited by R. G. Heizer and A. B. Elsasser. *University of California Anthropological Records* 17 (2): 201–80.

Jorge, Filipe. 2005. *Algarve Visto do Céu*. Lisbon: Argumentum.

Jorgensen, Joseph G. 1980. *Western Indians*. San Francisco, CA: W. H. Freeman.

Juan-Tresserras, Jordi, Carles Lalueza, Rosa M. Albert, and Manuel Calvo. 1997. Identification of Phytoliths from Prehistoric Human Dental Remains from the Iberian Peninsula and the Balearic Islands. In *Primer Encuentro Europeo sobre el Estudio de Fitolitos*, edited by A. Pinilla, J. Juan-Tresserras, and M. J. Machado, 197–203. Madrid: Gráficas Fersán.

Kaplan, Hilard S., and Kim Hill. 1992. The Evolutionary Ecology of Food Acquisition. In *Evolutionary Ecology and Human Behavior*, edited by E. A. Smith and B. Winterhalder, 167–202. Hawthorne, NY: Aldine de Gruyter.

Karl, Rick. 2000. The Relative Chronology of Cultural Episodes at the Coastal Sambaqui, Jabuticabeira II, in Santa Catarina, Brazil. MA diss., University of Arizona, USA.

Katzenberg, M. Anne. 1992. Advances in Stable Isotope Analysis of Prehistoric Bones. In *Skeletal Biology of Past Peoples, Research Methods*, edited by S. A. Saunders and M. A. Katzenberg, 105–19. New York: Wiley-Liss.

Kealhofer, Lisa, Robin Torrence, and Richard Fullagar. 1999. Integrating Phytoliths Within Use-Wear/Residue Studies of Stone Tools. *Journal of Archaeological Science* 26:527–46.

Keegan, William F., Roger W. Portell, and John Slapcinsky. 2003. Changes in Invertebrate Taxa at Two Pre-Columbian Sites in Southwestern Jamaica, AD 800–1500. *Journal of Archaeological Science* 30:1607–17.

Keeley, Lawrence. 1980. *Experimental Determination of Stone Tool Uses: A Microwear Analysis*. Chicago: University of Chicago Press.

Keen, A. Myra. 1958. *Sea Shells of Tropical West America*. Stanford, CA: Stanford University Press.

Keen, S. D. 1979. *The Growth Rings of Clam Shells from Two Pentlach Middens as Indicators of Seasonal Gathering*. Victoria, BC: Archaeology Division, Heritage Conservation Branch.

Kelly, Robert L., Lin Poyer, and Bram Tucker. 2005. An Ethnoarchaeological Study of Mobility, Architectural Investment, and Food Sharing Among Madagascar's Mikea. *American Anthropologist* 107 (3): 403–16.

———. 2006. Mobility and Houses in Southwestern Madagascar: Ethnoarchaeology Among the Mikea and Their Neighbors. In *Archaeology and Ethnoarchaeology of Mobility*, edited by F. Sellet, R. Greaves and P.-L. Yu, 75–107. Gainesville: University Press of Florida.

Kenchington, Ellen, R. Duggan, and T. Riddell. 1998. *Early Life History Characteristics of the Razor Clam (Ensis directus) and the Moonsnails (Euspira spp.) with Applications to Fisheries and Aquaculture*. Dartmouth, NS: Bedford Institute of Oceanography, Canadian Technical Report of Fisheries and Aquatic Sciences No. 2223.

Kendall, Michael A. 1987. The Age and Size Structure of Some Northern Populations of the Trochid Gastropod *Monodonta lineata. Journal of Molluscan Studies* 53:213–22.

Kennedy, Dorothy, and Randy Bouchard. 1990. Northern Coast Salish. In *Handbook of North American Indians: Northwest Coast*, edited by W. Suttles, 441–52. Washington, DC: Smithsonian Institution Press.

Kennedy, Michael A. 2003. An Investigation of Hunter-Gatherer Shellfish Foraging Practices: Archaeological and Geochemical Evidence from Bodega Bay, California. PhD diss., University of California, Davis, USA.

Kennedy, W. J. 1980. Manuscript Map: Reed Mound (originally drawn, 1966). In *Cultural Resource Reconnaissance of Hobe Sound National Wildlife*

Refuge, Martin County, Florida, by Mildred L.
Fryman, David Swindell III, and James J. Miller,
43. Tallahassee: Interagency Archeological
Services Division, National Park Service, Atlanta.
Contract A-55034(79). On file, Florida Division of
Archives, History, and Records Management.

Kennett, Douglas J. 2005. *The Island Chumash: Behavioral
Ecology of a Maritime Society.* Berkeley: University
of California Press.

Kennett, Douglas J., B. Lynn Ingram, Jon M. Erlandson,
and Phillip Walker. 1997. Evidence for Temporal
Fluctuations in Marine Radiocarbon Reservoir
Ages in the Santa Barbara Channel, Southern
California. *Journal of Anthropological Archaeology*
24:1051–59.

Kennett, Douglas J., and Barbara Voorhies. 1996. Oxygen
Isotopic Analysis of Archaeological Shells to
Detect Seasonal Use of Wetlands on the Southern
Pacific Coast of Mexico. *Journal of Archaeological
Science* 23:689–704.

Kennett, Douglas J., Barbara Voorhies, and Dean Martorana. 2006. An Evolutionary Model for the Origins
of Agriculture on the Pacific Coast of Southern
Mexico. In *Behavioral Ecology and the Transition
to Agriculture,* edited by D. J. Kennett and B.
Winterhalder, 103–36. Berkeley: University of
California Press.

Kent, Susan. 1992. Studying Variability in the Archaeolog-
ical Record: An Ethnoarchaeological Model for
Distinguishing Mobility Patterns. *American
Antiquity* 57 (4): 635–60.

Keough, Michael J., Gerald P. Quinn, and Alice King.
1993. Correlations Between Human Collecting and
Littoral Mollusc Populations on Rocky Shores.
Conservation Biology 7:378–90.

Kershaw, A. Peter. 1995. Environmental Change in Greater
Australia. *Antiquity* 69:656–75.

Kershaw, A. Peter, and Henry A. Nix. 1988. Quantitative
Palaeoclimatic Estimates from Pollen Taxa Using
Bioclimatic Profiles of Extant Species. *Journal of
Biogeography* 15:589–602.

Killingley, John S. 1981. Seasonality of Mollusk Collecting
Determined from O-18 Profiles of Midden Shells.
American Antiquity 46:152–58.

King, Chester D. 1975. The Names and Locations of
Historic Chumash Villages (Assembled by Thomas
Blackburn). *Journal of California Anthropology*
2:171–79.

Kirby, Michael X., Thomas M. Sonait, and Howard J.

Spero. 1998. Stable Isotope Sclerochronology of
Pleistocene and Recent Oyster Shells (*Crassostrea
virginica*). *Palaios* 13:560–69.

Kleinberg, Israel. 2002. Mixed-Bacteria Ecological
Approach to Understanding the Role of Oral
Bacteria in Dental Caries Causation: An Alterna-
tive to Streptococcus Mutans and Specificplaque
Hypothesis. *Critical Reviews of Oral Biology and
Medicine* 13:108–25.

Klokler, Daniela 2001. Construindo ou Deixando um
Sambaqui? Análise de Sedimentos de um Samba-
qui do Litoral Meridional Brasileiro: Processos
Formativos, Região De Laguna, SC. MA diss.,
Universidade de São Paulo, Brazil.

———. 2003. Vida Ritual dos Sambaquieiros. Paper read at
XII Reunião Científica da Sociedade de Arqueologia Brasileira, São Paulo.

———. 2006. Eating With the Dead. Funerary Feasting
and Shell Mound Construction Along the Southern Brazilian Coast. Paper read at ICAZ International Conference, August 23–28, Mexico City.

———. 2008. Food for Body and Soul: Mortuary Ritual in
Shell Mounds (Laguna-Brazil). PhD diss., University of Arizona, USA.

Klokler, Daniela, Maria Dulce Gaspar, and Paulo DeBla-
sis. 2009. Cemitérios e/ou Palcos: Sambaquis e o
Teatro da Morte. Paper read at XV SAB Congress,
September 20–23, Belém, Brazil.

Klokler, Daniela, Ximena Villagrán, Paulo Giannini,
Silvia Peixoto, and Paulo DeBlasis. 2010. Juntos na
Costa: Zooarqueologia e Geoarqueologia de
Sambaquis do Litoral Sul Catarinense. *Revista do
Museu de Arqueologia e Etnologia* 20:53–76.

Kneip, Andreas. 2004. O Povo da Lagoa: Uso do SIG Para
Modelamento e Simulação na Área Arqueológica
do Camacho. PhD diss., Universidade de São
Paulo, Brazil.

Kneip, Lina M. 1974. Identificação Espacial das Atividades
Humanas e suas Implicações (Cabo Frio, RJ,
Brasil). MA diss., Universidade de São Paulo,
Brazil.

———. 1977. Pescadores e Coletores Pré-Históricos do
Litoral de Cabo Frio, RJ. *Arqueologia* 5:7–169.

———. 1980. A Sequência Cultural do Sambaqui do
Forte—Cabo Frio, Rio de Janeiro. *Pesquisas*
31:87–100.

———. 1994. Cultura Material e Subsistência das Populações Pré-Históricas de Saquarema, RJ. *Documento
de Trabalho, sér. Arqueologia* 2:1–120.

———. 1998. Os Pescadores, Coletores e Caçadores Pré-Históricos da Área Arqueológica de Saqua-rema, RJ. *Revista de Arqueologia Americana* 15:57–73.

Kneip, Lina M., A. C. S. Coelho, Fausto L. de S. Cunha, and Elisa M. B. Mello. 1975. Informações Prelimi-nares Sobre a Arqueologia e a Fauna do Sambaqui do Forte, Estado do Rio de Janeiro, Brasil. *Revista do Museu Paulista* 22:89–108.

Kneip, Lina M., and Lilia M. C. Machado. 1993. Os Ritos Funerários das Populações Pré-Históricas de Saquarema, RJ: Sambaquis da Beirada, Moa e Pontinha. *Documentos de Trabalho, Série Arqueo-logia, Museu Nacional* 1:1–76.

Kneip, Lina M., and Luciana Pallestrini. 1987. Arqueolo-gia: Estratigrafia, Cronologia e Estruturas do Sambaqui Zé Espinho. In *Coletores e Pescadores Pré-Históricos de Guaratiba, Rio de Janeiro*, edited by L. M. Kneip, 89–141. Rio de Janeiro: Museu Nacional.

Kneip, Lina M., Luciana Pallestrini, Filomena Crâncio, and Lilia M. C. Machado. 1991. As Estruturas e Suas Interrelações em Sítios de Pescadores-Coletores Pré-Históricos do Litoral de Saquarema, RJ. *Boletim do Instituto de Arqueologia Brasileira (Rio de Janeiro)* 5:1–42.

Knight, Vernon James, Jr. 2001. Feasting and the Emer-gence of Platform Mound Cermonialism in Eastern North America. In *Feasts: Archaeological and Ethnographic Perspectives on Food, Politics, and Power*, edited by M. Dietler and B. Hayden, 239–54. Washington, DC: Smithsonian Institution Press.

Knudson, Gary D. 1979. Partial Cultural Resource Inventory of Tyndall Air Force Base, Florida C5917(79). Tallahassee: Interagency Archeological Services, National Park Service, Atlanta. On file, Southeast Archeological Center, National Park Service.

Kobayashi, Tatsuo. 2004. *Jomon Reflections: Forager Life and Culture in the Prehistoric Japanese Archipel-ago*. Edited by S. Kaner and O. Nakamura. Oxford: Oxbow Books.

Koch, Johannes, Brian Menounos, John J. Clague, and Gerald D. Osborn. 2004. Environmental Change in Garibaldi Provincial Park, Southern Coast Mountains, British Columbia. *Geoscience Canada* 31:127–35.

Koch, Johannes, Gerald D. Osborn, and John J. Clague.

2007. Pre-"Little Ice Age" Glacier Fluctuations in Garibaldi Provincial Park, Coast Mountains, British Columbia, Canada. *Holocene* 17 (8): 1069–78.

Kohler, Timothy Alan. 1978. The Social and Chronological Dimensions of Village Occupation at a North Florida Weeden Island Period Site. PhD diss., University of Florida, USA.

Koike, H., and M. Okamura. 1994. Times-Scaling of Successively Accumulated Shell Layers for Exploitation Dairy Analysis. *ArchaeoZoologia* 6 (2): 23–36.

Kopperl, Robert E. 2001. Herring Use in Southern Puget Sound: Analysis of Fish Remains at 45-K-437. *Northwest Anthropological Research Notes* 35 (1): 1–20.

Kozloff, Eugene N. 1990. *Invertebrates*. Philadelphia: Saunders College Publications.

———. 1993. *Seashore Life of the Northern Pacific Coast: An Illustrated Guide to Northern California, Oregon, Washington, and British Columbia*. Seattle: University of Washington Press.

Kranck, Ernst. 1932. Geological Investigations in the Cordillera of Tierra del Fuego. *Acta Geographica* 4:1–231.

Kruskal, Joseph B. 1964. Multidimensional Scaling by Optimizing Goodness of Fit to a Nonmetric Hypothesis. *Psychometrika* 29:1–27.

Kruskal, Joseph B., and Myron Wish. 1978. *Multidimen-sional Scaling*. Beverly Hills, CA: Sage.

Kucera, Matthias, Doris Pany-Kucera, Célia H. Boyadjian, Karl J. Reinhard, and Sabine Eggers. 2011. Efficient but Destructive: A Test of the Dental Wash Technique Using Secondary Electron Microscopy. *Journal of Archaeological Science* 38:119–35.

Kyle, R., B. Pearson, P. J. Fielding, W. D. Robertson, and S. L. Birnie. 1997. Subsistence Shellfish Harvesting in the Maputaland Marine Reserve in Northern KwaZulu-Natal, South Africa: Rocky Shore Organisms. *Biological Conservation* 82 (2): 183–92.

Laboratório de Paleodemografia e Paleopatologia. 2003. *Cabeço da Amoreira 2002: Relatório Antropológico*. Coimbra, Portugal: University of Coimbra.

Lacaille, Armand D. 1954. *The Stone Age in Scotland*. London: Oxford University Press.

Lacerda, José B., and R. Peixoto. 1876. Contribuição para o Estudo Antropológico das Raças Indígenas do Brasil. *Arquivos do Museu Nacional* 1:47–74.

Lalueza-Fox, Carles. 1995. Recuperación de DNA

Mitocondrial y Caracterización de Variabilidad en Poblaciones Antiguas. PhD diss., Universidad de Barcelona, Spain.

Lalueza-Fox, Carles, Jordi Juan, and Rosa M. Albert. 1996. Phytoliths Analysis on Dental Calculus, Enamel Surface, and Burial Soil: Information About Diet and Paleoenvironment. *American Journal of Physical Anthropology* 101 (1): 101–13.

Lalueza-Fox, Carles, Alejandro Perez-Perez, and Jordi Juan. 1994. Dietary Information Through the Examination of Plant Phytoliths on the Enamel Surface of Human Dentition. *Journal of Archaeological Science* 21 (1): 29–34.

Lambert, Patricia M. 1997. Patterns of Violence in Prehistoric Hunter-Gatherer Societies of Coastal Southern California. In *Troubled Times: Violence and Warfare in the Past*, edited by D. L. Martin and D. W. Frayer, 77–109. Amsterdam: Gordon and Breach Publishers.

Lanfranco, Luis N. Pezo, and Sabine Eggers. 2010. The Usefulness of Caries Frequency, Depth, and Location in Determining Cariogenicity and Past Subsistence: A Test on Early and Later Agriculturalists from the Peruvian Coast. *American Journal of Physical Anthropology* 143 (1): 75–91.

Larsen, Clark Spencer. 1997. *Bioarchaeology. Interpreting Behaviour from the Human Skeleton.* Cambridge: Cambridge University Press.

Lasiak, Theresa A. 1992. Contemporary Shellfish-Gathering Practices of Indigenous Coastal People in Transkei: Some Implications for Interpretation of the Archaeological Record. *South African Journal of Science* 88:19–28.

Lebour, Marie V. 1933. The British Species of *Trivia: T. arctica* and *T. monacha. Journal of the Marine Biological Association of the United Kingdom* 18:477–84.

Lees, Brian G. 1992. Geomorphological Evidence for Late Holocene Climatic Change in Northern Australia. *Australian Geographer* 23 (1): 1–10.

Lees, Brian G., John Stanner, David M. Price, and Lu Yanchou. 1995. Thermoluminescence Dating of Dune Podzols at Cape Arnhem, Northern Australia. *Marine Geology* 129:63–75.

Lefèvre, J. 1973. Étude Odontologique des Hommes de Muge. *Bulletins et Mémoires de la Société d'Anthropologie de Paris* 10:301–33.

Legendre, Pierre, and Louis Legendre. 1998. *Numerical Ecology.* New York: Elsevier.

Legoupil, Dominique. 1993/1994. El Archipiélago del Cabo de Hornos y la Costa sur de la Isla Navarino: Poblamiento y Modelos Económicos. *Anales del Instituto de la Patagonia. Serie Ciencias Sociales* 22:101–22.

Lehninger, Albert L., David L. Nelson, and Michael M. Cox. 1993. *Principles of Biochemistry.* New York: Institute of Electrical and Electronics Engineering.

Lerner, Harry, Xiandong Du, Andre Costopoulos, and Martin Ostoja-Starzewski. 2007. Lithic Raw Material Physical Properties and Use-Wear Accrual. *Journal of Archaeological Science* 34:711–22.

Leroi-Gourhan, Andre. 1981. *Pré-História.* São Paulo: Universidade de São Paulo.

Lessa, Andrea. 2005. Paleoepidemiologia dos Traumas Agudos em Grupos Atacamenhos: A Violência sob Uma Perspectiva Diacrônica. PhD diss., Fundação Oswaldo Cruz (FIOCRUZ), Brazil.

———. 2009. Daily Risks: A Biocultural Approach to Acute Trauma in Pre-Colonial Coastal Populations from Brazil. *International Journal of Osteoarchaeology* 21 (2): 159–72.

Lessa, Andrea, and Izaura S. Coelho. 2010. Lesões Vertebrais e Estilos de Vida Diferenciados em dois Grupos Sambaquieiros do Litoral Fluminense. *Revista do Museu de Arqueologia e Etnologia (São Paulo)* 20:77–89.

Lessa, Andrea, and João C. Medeiros. 2001. Reflexões Preliminares Sobre a Questão Violência em Populacões Construtoras de Sambaquis: Análise Dos Sítios Cabeçuda (SC) e Arupuã (RJ). *Revista do Museu de Arqueologia e Etnologia* 11:77–94.

Lévi-Strauss, Claude. 1962. *La Pensée Sauvage.* Paris: Plon.

Lieberman, Daniel E. 1993. The Rise and Fall of Seasonal Mobility Among Hunter-Gatherers: The Case of the Southern Levant. *Current Anthropology* 34:599–631.

Lieverse, Angela R. 1999. Diet and the Aetiology of Dental Calculus. *International Journal of Osteoarchaeology* 9:219–32.

Lightfoot, Kent G., and Robert M. Cerrato. 1988. Prehistoric Shellfish Exploitation in Coastal New York. *Journal of Field Archaeology* 15:141–49.

Lightfoot, Kent G., and Edward M. Luby. 2006. Shell Mounds and Mounded Landscapes in the San Francisco Bay Area: An Integrated Approach. *Journal of Island and Coastal Archaeology* 1 (2): 191–214.

Lima, Tania A. 1991. Dos Mariscos aos Peixes: Um Estudo

Zooarqueológico de Mudança de Subsistência na Pré-História do Rio de Janeiro. PhD diss., Universidade de São Paulo, Brazil.

———. 1999/2000. Em Busca dos Frutos do Mar: os Pescadores-Coletores do Litoral Centro-Sul do Brasil. *Revista da Universidade de São Paulo (São Paulo)* 44:270–332.

Lima, Tania A., and Jose Lopez Mazz. 2000. La Emergencia de Complejidad entre los Cazadores Recolectores de la Costa Atlantica Meridional Sudamericana. *Revista de Arqueologia Americana* 17–19:129–75.

Lima, Tania A., Kita D. Macário, Roberto M. Anjos, Paulo R. S. Gomes, Melayne M. Coimbra, and David Elmore. 2002. The Antiquity of the Prehistoric Settlement of the Central-South Brazilian Coast. *Radiocarbon* 44:733–38.

Lima, Tania A., Kita D. Macário, Roberto M. Anjos, Paulo R. S. Gomes, Melayne M. Coimbra, and David Elmore. 2004. The Earliest Shellmounds of the Central-South Brazilian Coast. *Nuclear Instruments and Methods in Physics Research* 223/224:691–94.

Little, Colin. 1989. Factors Governing Patterns of Foraging Activity in Littoral Marine Herbivorous Molluscs. *Journal of Molluscan Studies* 55:273–84.

Little, Colin, and J. A. Kitching. 1996. *The Biology of Rocky Shores*. Oxford: Oxford University Press.

Liu, W., A. O. Alabi, and Christopher M. Pearce. 2008. Fertilization and Embryonic Development in the Basket Cockle, *Clinocardium nuttallii*. *Journal of Shellfish Research* 27 (2): 393–97.

Loefgren, Alberto. 1908. Os Sambaquis. *Revista do Instituto Histórico e Geográfico* 8:458–65.

Losey, Robert J. 2002. Communities and Catastrophe: Tillamook Response to the AD 1700 Earthquake and Tsunami, Northern Oregon Coast. PhD diss., University of Oregon, USA.

Lothrop, Samuel. 2002 [1928]. *The Indians of Tierra del Fuego*. Ushuaia, Argentina: Zagier and Urruty Publications.

Lourandos, Harry. 1983. Intensification: A Late Pleistocene–Holocene Archaeological Sequence from Southwestern Victoria. *Archaeology in Oceania* 18:81–94.

Lowenstein, Jerold, Joshua Reuther, Darden Hood, Gary Scheuenstuhl, Craig Gerlach, and Douglas Ubelaker. 2005. Identification of Animal Species by Protein Radioimmunoassay of Bone Fragments and Bloodstained Stone Tools. *Forensic Science International* 159 (2–3): 182–88.

Lowie, Robert H. 1946. The Bororo. In *Handbook of South American Indians*, edited by J. Steward, 419–34. Washington, DC: Smithsonian Institution Press.

Loy, Thomas H. 1993. The Artifact as a Site: An Example of the Biomolecular Analysis of Organic Residues on Prehistoric Tools. *World Archaeology* 25 (1): 44–63.

———. 1994. Methods in the Analysis of Starch Residues on Prehistoric Stone Tools. In *Tropical Archaeobotany: Applications and New Developments*, edited by J. G. Hather, 86–114. London: Routledge.

Lozano, Pedro. 1974 [1873]. *Historia de la Conquista del Paraguay: Río de la Plata y Tucumán. Biblioteca del Río de la Plata*. Vol. 1. Buenos Aires: Andres Lamas.

Lubell, David. 2004. Prehistoric Edible Land Snails in the Circum-Mediterranean. In *Petits Animaux et Sociétés Humaines: Du Complément Alimentaire aux Ressources Utilitaires. XXIVe Rencontres Internationales d'Archéologie et d'Histoire d'Antibes*, edited by J.-P. Brugal and J. Desse, 77–98. Antibes, France: Éditions APDCA.

Lubell, David, Mary Jackes, Peter Sheppard, and Peter Rowley-Conwy. 2007. The Mesolithic-Neolithic in the Alentejo: Archaeological Investigations, 1984–1986. In *From the Mediterranean Basin to the Portuguese Atlantic Shore: Papers in Honor of Anthony Marks*, edited by N. F. Bicho, 209–29. Faro, Portugal: Universidade do Algarve.

Luby, Edward M., and Mark F. Gruber. 1999. The Dead Must Be Fed: Symbolic Meanings of the Shellmounds of the San Francisco Bay Area. *Cambridge Archaeological Journal* 9 (1): 95–108.

Lull, Vicente. 2000. Death and Society: A Marxist Approach. *Antiquity* 74:576–80.

Lyman, R. Lee. 1994. *Vertebrate Taphonomy*. Cambridge: Cambridge University Press.

———. 2003. Appendix C: Zooarchaeology of Sites 45SJ169 and 45SJ165. In *Archaeological Investigations at Sites 45SJ165 and 45SJ169, Decatur Island, San Juan County, Washington*, edited by S. L. Walker, 235–74. Cheney: Eastern Washington University, Reports in Archaeology and History 100–118.

———. 2008. *Quantitative Paleozoology*. Cambridge: Cambridge University Press.

MacArthur, Robert H., and Eric R. Pianka. 1966. On the Optimal Use of a Patchy Environment. *American Naturalist* 100:603–9.

Macchiarelli, Roberto, Luca Bondioli, Arnaud Mazurier, Gildas Merceron, and Ernesto L. Piana. 2006. The Oldest Human Remain from the Beagle Channel Region, Tierra del Fuego. *International Journal of Osteoarchaeology* 15 (1): 1–10.

Machado, Lilia M. C. 1983. Análise Dos Remanescentes Arqueológicos do Sítio Corondó, RJ: Aspectos Biológicos e Culturais. PhD diss., Universidade De São Paulo, Brazil.

———. 1992. Paleodemografia e Saúde em Perspectiva Populacional. In *Paleopatologia and Paleoepidemiologia. Estudos Multidisciplinares*, edited by A. J. Gomes de Araújo and L. F. Ferreira, 87–94. Rio de Janeiro: Escola Nacional de Saúde Pública.

———. 2006. Paleodemografia e Saúde em Perspectiva Populacional. *Boletim do Instituto de Arqueologia Brasileira (Rio de Janeiro)* 12:194–198.

———. 2006. Biologia de Grupos Indígenas Pré-Históricos do Sudeste do Brasil. As Tradições Itaipu e Una. *Boletim do Instituto de Arqueologia Brasileira* 12:100.

Macintosh, Donald J. 1982. Fisheries and Aquaculture Significance of Mangrove Swamps, with Special Reference to the Indo-West Pacific Region. In *Recent Advances in Aquaculture*, edited by J. F. Muir and R. J. Roberts, 5–85. Sydney: Croom Helm.

Mackie, Quentin. 2003. Location-Allocation Modelling of Shell Midden Distribution on the West Coast of Vancouver Island. In *Emerging from the Mist: Studies in Northwest Coast Culture History*, edited by R. G. Matson, G. Coupland, and Q. Mackie, 261–88. Vancouver, BC: UBC Press.

Madella, Marco, Alix Power-Jones, and Martin Jones. 1998. A Simple Method of Extraction of Opal Phytoliths from Sediments Using a Non-Toxic Heavy Liquid. *Journal of Archaeological Science* 25:801–3.

Madsen, David B., and Dave N. Schmitt. 1998. Mass Collecting and the Diet Breadth Model: A Great Basin Example. *Journal of Archaeological Science* 25:445–57.

Malinowski, Bronislaw. 1929. *The Sexual Life of Savages in North-Western Malaysia*. New York: Horace Liveright.

Manizer, Henrich H. 1919. Les Botocudos d'Après les Observations Recueillies pendant un Séjour chez eux en 1915. *Archivos do Museu Nacional do Rio de Janeiro* 22:234–73.

———. 2006. *Os Kaingang de São Paulo*. Campinas, Brazil: Editora Curt Nimuendaju.

Manly, Bryan F. J. 1994. *Multivariate Statistical Methods: A Primer*. Boca Raton, FL: Chapman and Hall/CRC.

Mannino, Marcello A., Baruch F. Spiro, and Kenneth D. Thomas. 2003. Sampling Shells for Seasonality: Oxygen Isotope Analysis of Shell Carbonates of the Inter-tidal Gastropod *Monodonta lineata* (da Costa) from Populations Across Its Modern Range and from a Mesolithic Site in Southern Britain. *Journal of Archaeological Science* 30:667–79.

Mannino, Marcello A., and Kenneth D. Thomas. 2001. Intensive Mesolithic Exploitation of Coastal Resources? Evidence from a Shell Deposit on the Isle of Portland (Southern England) for the Impact of Human Foraging on Populations of Intertidal Rocky Shore Molluscs. *Journal of Archaeological Science* 28:1101–14.

Mannino, Marcello A., and Kenneth D. Thomas. 2002. Depletion of a Resource? The Impact of Prehistoric Human Foraging on Intertidal Mollusc Communities and Its Significance for Human Settlement, Mobility, and Dispersal. *World Archaeology* 33 (3): 452–74.

Mansur, María Estela. 1999. Análisis de Instrumental Lítico: Problemas de Formación y Deformación de Rastros de Uso. Paper read at XII Congreso Nacional de Arqueología Argentina, La Plata.

Mansur-Franchomme, María Estela. 1983. Traces d'Utilisation et Technologie Lithique: Exemple de Patagonie. PhD diss., Université de Bordeaux I, France.

Marinho, Anderson N. R., Newton C. Miranda, Valéria Braz, Ândrea K. Ribeiro dos Santos, and Sheila M. F. M. de Souza. 2006. Paleogenetic and Taphonomic Analysis of Human Bones from Moa, Beirada, and Zé Espinho Sambaquis, Rio de Janeiro, Brazil. *Memorias do Instituto Oswaldo Cruz* 101, Supplement 2:1–9.

Marquardt, William H. 1992. *Culture and Environment in the Domain of the Calusa*. Gainesville, FL: Institute of Archaeology and Paleoenvironmental Studies.

———. 2010a. Shell Mounds in the Southeast: Middens, Monuments, Temple Mounds, Rings, or Works? *American Antiquity* 75 (3): 551–70.

———. 2010b. Mounds, Middens, and Rapid Climate Change During the Archaic-Woodland Transition in the Southeastern United States. In *Trend, Tradition, and Turmoil: What Happened to the Southeastern Archaic?* edited by D. H. Thomas and

M. C. Sanger, 253–71. New York: American Museum of Natural History.

Marques, Carlos Alexandre. 2001. Importância Econômica da Família Lauraceae. *Floresta e Ambiente* 8 (1): 195–206.

Marrinan, Rochelle A. 1975. Ceramics, Molluscs, and Sedentism: The Late Archaic Period on the Georgia Coast. PhD diss., University of Florida, USA.

———. 2010. Two Late Archaic Period Shell Rings, St. Simons Island, Georgia. In *Trend, Tradition, and Turmoil: What Happened to the Southeastern Archaic?* edited by D. H. Thomas and M. C. Sanger, 71–102. New York: American Museum of Natural History.

Marshall, Charlotte E., and Emily Wilson. 2009. *Pecten maximus. Great Scallop. Marine Life Information Network: Biology and Sensitivity Key Information Sub-programme.* Marine Biological Association of the United Kingdom. http://www.marlin.ac.uk/species/pectenmaximus.htm. Accessed April 8, 2009.

Marshall, Fiona, and Tom Pilgram. 1993. NISP vs. MNI in Quantification of Body-Part Representation. *American Antiquity* 58:261–69.

Marshall, L. G. 1989. Bone Modification and the "Laws of Burial." In *Bone Modification*, edited by R. Bonnichsen and M. H. Sorg, 7–24. Orono: University of Maine, Center for the Study of the First Americans, Institute for Quaternary Studies.

Martin, Fabiana M. 2004. Tendencias Tafonómicas en el Registro Óseo Humano del Norte de Tierra del Fuego. In *Temas de Arqueología: Arqueología del Norte de la Isla Grande de Tierra del Fuego*, edited by L. A. Borrero and R. Barberena, 107–33. Buenos Aires: Dunken.

Martin, Fabiana M., Ramiro Barberena, and Ricardo A. Guichón. 2004. Erosión y Huesos Humanos: El Caso de la Localidad Chorrillos, Tierra del Fuego. *Magallania* 32:125–42.

Martín, Fernando D. 2005. *El Largo Viaje. Arqueología de los Orígenes Humanos y las Primeras Migraciones.* Barcelona: Bellaterra.

Martin, Louis, José Maria Landim Dominguez, and Abilio C. S. P. Bittencourt. 2003. Fluctuating Holocene Sea Levels in Eastern and Southeastern Brazil: Evidence from Multiple Fossil and Geometric Indicators. *Journal of Coastal Research* 19 (1): 101–24.

Maschner, Herbert D. G. 1991. The Emergence of Cultural Complexity on the Northern Northwest Coast. *Antiquity* 65:924–34.

———. 1992. The Origins of Hunter and Gatherer Sedentism and Political Complexity: A Case Study from the Northern Northwest Coast. PhD diss., University of California, Santa Barbara, USA.

———. 1997. Settlement and Subsistence in the Later Prehistory of Tebenkof Bay, Kuiu Island, Southeast Alaska. *Arctic Anthropology* 34 (2): 74–99.

Maschner, Herbert D. G., and Jeffrey W. Stein. 1995. Multivariate Approaches to Site Location on the Northwest Coast of North America. *Antiquity* 69:61–73.

Mason, James. 1983. *Scallop and Queen Fisheries in the British Isles.* Farnham, UK: Fishing News Books.

Matson, R. G. 1974. Clustering and Scaling of Gulf of Georgia Sites. *Syesis* 7:101–14.

———. 1983. Intensification and the Development of Cultural Complexity: The Northwest Versus the Northeast Coast. In *The Evolution of Maritime Cultures on the Northeast and Northwest Coasts of America*, edited by R. J. Nash, 125–48. Burnaby, BC: Archaeology Press, Simon Fraser University.

———. 1992. The Evolution of Northwest Coast Subsistence. *Research in Economic Anthropology* Supplement 6:367–428.

Matson, R. G., and Gary Coupland. 1995. *The Prehistory of the Northwest Coast.* San Diego, CA: Academic Press.

Matson, R. G., D. Ludowicz, and W. Boyd. 1980. Excavations at Beach Grove in 1980. Victoria, BC: Culture Library, Ministry of Natural Resource Operations.

Maxwell, David 2003. Growth Colouration Revisited: Assessing Shell Fishing Seasonality in Coastal British Columbia. In *Archaeology of Coastal British Columbia: Essays in Honour of Professor Philip M. Hobler*, edited by R. L. Carlson, 175–88. Burnaby, BC: Archaeology Press, Simon Fraser University.

Mayewski, Paul A., Eelco E. Rohling, J. Curt Stager, Wibjörn Karlen, Kirk A. Maasch, L. David Meeker, Eric A. Meyerson, Francoise Gasse, Shirley van Kreveld, Karin Holmgren, et al. 2004. Holocene Climate Variability. *Quaternary Research* 62 (3): 243–55.

McCarthy, Frederick D., and Frank M. Setzler. 1960. The Archaeology of Arnhem Land. In *Records of the American-Australian Scientific Expedition to*

Arnhem Land. Vol. 2, *Anthropology and Nutrition,* edited by C. P. Mountford, 215–95. Melbourne: Melbourne University Press.

McConnaughey, Ted A. 1989. ^{13}C and ^{18}O Isotopic Disequilibrium in Biological Carbonates: I. Patterns. *Geochimica et Cosmochimica Acta* 53:151–62.

McConnaughey, Ted A., Jim Burdett, Joseph F. Whelan, and Charles K. Paull. 1997. Carbon Isotopes in Biological Carbonates: Respiration and Photosynthesis. *Geochimica et Cosmochimica Acta* 61:611–22.

McConnaughey, Ted A., and David P. Gillikin. 2008. Carbon Isotopes in Mollusk Shell Carbonates. *Geo Marine Letters* 28:287–99.

McCrae, Jean. 1994. Oregon Development Series: Cockle Clam *Clinocardium nuttallii.* Salem: Oregon Department of Fish and Wildlife.

McKay, David W. 1992. Report on a Survey around Scotland of Potentially Exploitable Burrowing Bivalve Molluscs. In *Fisheries Research Services Collaborative/Contract Reports.* Aberdeen: Marine Laboratory, Fisheries Research Services Report No 1/9.

McKinley, William. 1873. Mounds in Georgia. *Annual Report to the Board of Regents, Smithsonian Institution* 22:422–28.

McMillan, Alan D. 1999. *Since the Time of the Transformers: The Ancient Heritage of the Nuu-chah-nulth, Ditidaht, and Makah.* Vancouver, BC: UBC Press.

McMillan, Alan D., Iain McKechnie, Denis E. St. Claire, and Sheila Gay Frederick. 2008. Exploring Variability in Maritime Resource Use on the Northwest Coast: A Case Study from Barkley Sound, Western Vancouver Island. *Canadian Journal of Archaeology* 32 (2): 214–38.

McMillan, Alan D., and Denis E. St. Claire. 1982. *Alberni Prehistory: Archaeological and Ethnographic Investigations on Western Vancouver Island.* Penticton, BC: Theytus Books.

———. 2005. *Ts'ishaa: Archaeology and Ethnography of a Nuu chah nulth Origin Site in Barkley Sound.* Burnaby, BC: Archaeology Press, Simon Fraser University.

Means, Bernard K. 2007. *Circular Villages of the Monongahela Tradition.* Tuscaloosa: University of Alabama Press.

Meehan, Betty. 1982. *Shell Bed to Shell Midden.* Canberra: Australian Institute of Aboriginal Studies.

———. 1983. A Matter of Choice? Some Thoughts on Shell Gathering Strategies in Northern Australia. In *Animals and Archaeology.* Vol. 2, *Shell Middens, Fishes and Birds,* edited by C. Grigson and J. Clutton-Brock, 3–17. Oxford: Archaeopress, British Archaeological Reports.

Meggers, Betty, Clifford Evans, and Emilio Estrada. 1965. *Early Formative Period of Coastal Ecuador: The Valdivia and Machalilla Phases.* Washington, DC: Smithsonian Institution Press.

Mellars, Paul A., ed. 1987. *Excavations on Oronsay: Prehistoric Human Ecology on a Small Island.* Edinburgh: Edinburgh University Press.

———. 2004. Mesolithic Scotland, Coastal Occupation, and the Role of the Oronsay Middens. In *Mesolithic Scotland and Its Neighbours,* edited by A. Saville, 167–83. Edinburgh: Society of Antiquaries of Scotland.

Métraux, Alfred. 1946a. Ethnography of the Chaco. In *Handbook of South American Indians.* Vol 1, edited by J. Steward, 197–370. Washington, DC: Smithsonian Institution Press.

———. 1946b. The Botocudo. In *Handbook of South American Indians.* Vol. 1, edited by J. H. Steward, 531–40. Washington, DC: Smithsonian Institution Press.

———. 1947. Mourning Rites and Burial Forms of the South American Indians. *America Indigena (México City)* 7:7–44.

———. 1948. The Guarini. In *Handbook of South American Indians.* Vol. 2, edited by J. H. Steward, 69–94. Washington, DC: Smithsonian Institution Press.

———. 1949. Religion and Shamanism. In *Handbook of South American Indians.* Vol 5, edited by J. Steward, 559–99. Washington, DC: Smithsonian Institution Press.

Métraux, Alfred, and Herbert Baldus. 1946. The Guayaki. In *Handbook of South American Indians,* edited by J. H. Steward, 435–44. Washington DC: Smithsonian Institution Press.

Meyer, Joseph, Prentice M. Thomas Jr., and Merrill Dicks. 2001. Field Investigations. In *Mitigative Data Recovery at the Horseshoe Bayou Site, 8WL36, Sandestin Beach Resorts Inc., Walton County, Florida,* edited by P. M. Thomas Jr., L. J. Campbell, and C. Cannon, 22–53. Ft. Walton, FL: Prentice Thomas and Associates.

Michie, James L. 1979. *The Bass Pond Dam Site: Intensive Archaeological Testing at a Formative Period Base Camp on Kiawah Island, South Carolina.* Columbia:

South Carolina Institute of Archaeology and Anthropology, University of South Carolina.

Middaugh, Douglas P. 2009. Putative Structures and Salinity Gradients at the Sewee Shell Ring, South Carolina: Evidence for Ancient Control of Freshwater Resources. *Journal of the North Carolina Academy of Science* 125 (3): 87–102.

Mikell, Gregory. 1992. 8OK5: A Coastal Weeden Island Village in Northwest Florida. *Florida Anthropologist* 45 (3): 195–220.

———. 1996. Bone Tools and Implements. In *Controlled Excavation at 8WL58, the Old Homestead Site: Completing the Compliance Process at Eglin Air Force Base, Okaloosa, Santa Rosa, and Walton Counties*, edited by P. M. Thomas Jr., M. L. Schleidt Peñalva, L. J. Campbell, and M. Cox, 119–31. Ft. Walton, FL: Prentice Thomas and Associates.

Miket, Roger, and Alan Saville. 1994. An Corran Rock Shelter, Skye: A Major New Mesolithic Site. *PAST* 8:9–10.

Milanich, Jerald T. 1994. *Archaeology of Precolumbian Florida*. Gainesville: University Press of Florida.

Milanich, Jerald T., Ann S. Cordell, Vernon James Knight Jr., Timothy Alan Kohler, and Brenda J. Sigler-Lavelle. 1984. *McKeithen Weeden Island: The Culture of North Florida, A.D. 200–900*. Orlando, FL: Academic Press.

Milner, Nicky. 2005. Seasonal Consumption Practices in the Mesolithic: Economic, Environmental, Social or Ritual? In *Mesolithic Studies at the Beginning of the 21st Century*, edited by N. Milner and P. Woodman, 57–68. Oxford: Oxbow.

Milner, Nicky, James Barrett, and Jon Welsh. 2007. Marine Resource Intensification in Viking Age Europe: The Molluscan Evidence from Quoygrew, Orkney. *Journal of Archaeological Science* 34:1461–72.

Mitchell, Donald H. 1981a. DcRu 78: A Prehistoric Occupation of Fort Rodd Hill National Historic Park. *Syesis* 14:131–50.

———. 1981b. Test Excavations at Randomly Selected Sites in Eastern Queen Charlotte Strait. *BC Studies* 48:103–23.

———. 1988. Changing Patterns of Resource Use in the Prehistory of Queen Charlotte Strait, British Columbia. *Research in Economic Anthropology* Supplement 3:245–90.

Mitchell, Peter. 2002. Hunter-Gatherer Archaeology in Southern Africa: Recent Research, Future Trends. *Before Farming* 1 (3): 1–36.

Moberg, Anders, Dmitry M. Sonechkin, Karin Homgren, Nina M. Datsenko, and Wibjörn Karlén. 2005. Highly Variable Northern Hemisphere Temperatures Reconstructed from Low- and High-Resolution Proxy Data. *Nature* 433:613–17.

Monks, Gregory G. 1976. Quantitative Comparison of Glenrose Components with the Marpole Component from Site DhRt 3. In *The Glenrose Cannery Site*, edited by R. G. Matson, 267–80. Ottawa: National Museum of Man, Mercury Series, Archaeological Survey of Canada Paper No. 52.

———. 1977. An Examination of Relationships Between Artifact Classes and Food Resource Remains at Deep Bay, DiSe 7. PhD diss., University of British Columbia, Canada.

———. 1981. Seasonality Studies. In *Advances in Archaeological Methods and Theory*, edited by M. B. Schiffer, 177–293. New York: Academic Press.

———. 1987. Prey as Bait: The Deep Bay Example. *Canadian Journal of Archaeology* 11:119–42.

———. 2006. The Fauna from Ma'acoah (DfSi–5), Vancouver Island, British Columbia: An Interpretive Summary. *Canadian Journal of Archaeology* 30 (2): 272–301.

Monks, Gregory G., and R. Johnston. 1993. Estimating Season of Death from Growth Increment Data: A Critical Review. *Archaeozoologica* 2:17–40.

Moore, Clarence B. 1897. Certain Aboriginal Mounds of the Georgia Coast. *Journal of the Academy of Natural Sciences of Philadelphia* 2:71–73.

———. 1898. Certain Aboriginal Mounds of the Coast of South Carolina. *Journal of the Academy of Natural Sciences* 11, 2nd series.

———. 1900. Certain Antiquities of the Florida West Coast. *Journal of the Academy of Natural Sciences of Philadelphia* 11:349–94.

———. 1902. Certain Aboriginal Remains of the Northwest Florida Coast (Part II). *Journal of the Academy of Natural Sciences of Philadelphia* 12:127–355.

———. 1905. Miscellaneous Investigations in Florida. *Journal of the Academy of Natural Sciences of Philadelphia* 13:299–325.

———. 1907. Notes on the Ten Thousand Islands. *Journal of the Academy of Natural Sciences of Philadelphia* 13:458–70.

———. 1918. The Northwestern Florida Coast Revisited. *Journal of the Academy of Natural Sciences of Philadelphia* 16:515–81.

———. 1919. Notes on the Archaeology of Florida. *American Anthropologist* 21:400–402.

Moore, Hilary B. 1934. The Relation of Shell Growth to Environment in *Patella vulgata*. *Proceedings of the Malacological Society of London* 21:217–22.

Morellato, L. Patrícia C., and Célio F. B. Haddad. 2000. Introduction: The Brazilian Atlantic Forest. *Biotropica* 32:786–92.

Morrison, Michael. 2003. Old Boundaries and New Horizons: The Weipa Shell Mounds Reconsidered. *Archaeology in Oceania* 38 (1): 1–8.

———. 2010. The Shell Mounds of Albatross Bay: An Archaeological Investigation of Late Holocene Production Strategies near Weipa, North Eastern Australia. PhD diss., Flinders University, South Australia.

Moss, Madonna L. 1993. Shellfish, Gender, and Status on the Northwest Coast: Reconciling Archeological, Ethnographic, and Ethnohistorical Records of the Tlingit. *American Anthropologist* 95 (3): 631–52.

———. 2004. *Archaeological Investigation of Cape Addington Rokshelter: Human Occupation of the Rugged Seacoast on the Outer Prince of Wales Archipelago, Alaska*. Eugene: University of Oregon, Anthropological Paper No. 63.

———. 2008. Outer Coast Maritime Adaptations in Southern Southeast Alaska: Tlingit or Haida? *Arctic Anthropology* 45 (1): 41–60.

———. 2012. Understanding Variability in Northwest Coast Faunal Assemblages: Beyond Economic Intensification and Cultural Complexity. *Journal of Island and Coastal Archaeology* 7 (1): 1–22.

Moss, Madonna L., and Jon M. Erlandson. 1995. Reflections on North American Pacific Coast Prehistory. *Journal of World Prehistory* 9 (1): 1–45.

Mowat, Fiona. M. 1995. Variability in Western Arnhem Land Shell Midden Deposits. MA diss., Northern Territory University, Australia.

Muñoz, A. Sebastián, María S. Caracotche, and Isabel Cruz. 2009. Cronología de la Costa al Sur del Río Santa Cruz: Nuevas Dataciones Radiocarbònicas en Punta Entrada y Parque Nacional Monte León (Provincia de Santa Cruz, Argentina). *Magallania* 37 (1): 19–38.

Museu dos Serviços Geológicos de Portugal. 1982. *Guia Descritivo de Sala de Arqueologia Pré-Histórica Texto de Autoria de O. da Veiga Ferreira*. 2nd ed. Lisbon: Museu dos Serviços Geológicos de Portugal.

Nagaoka, Lisa. 2002. Explaining Subsistence Change in Southern New Zealand Using Foraging Theory Models. *World Archaeology* 34:84–192.

Nagaoka, Tomohito, and Kazuaki Hirata. 2007. Reconstruction of Paleodemographic Characteristics from Skeletal Age at Death Distribution: Perspectives from Hitoshubati, Japan. *American Journal of Physical Anthropology* 134:301–11.

Nakamura, Yasuo, and Yumi Shinotsuka. 2007. Suspension Feeding and Growth of Ark Shell *Anadara granosa*: Comparison with Ubiquitous Species *Scapharca subcrenata*. *Fisheries Science* 73:889–986.

Nakiboglu, S. Mete, Kurt Lambeck, and Paul Aharon. 1983. Postglacial Sea-Levels in the Pacific: Implications with Respect to Deglaciation Regime and Local Tectonics. *Tectonophysics* 91:335–58.

Nanfro, Claire Elizabeth. 2004. An Analysis of Faunal Remains from the Bird Hammock Site (8Wa30). MA diss., Florida State University, USA.

Neel, Joseph V., and Francisco M. Salzano. 1967. Further Study on the Xavante Indians. Some Hypothesis-Generalizations Resulting from These Studies. *American Journal of Human Genetics* 19:554–74.

Nelson, Ben A., J. Andrew Darling, and David A. Kice. 1992. Mortuary Practices and the Social Order at La Quemada, Zacatecas, Mexico. *Latin American Antiquity* 3 (4): 298–315.

Nelson, Nels C. 1909. Shellmounds of the San Francisco Bay Region. *University of California Publications in American Archaeology and Ethnology* 7:309–56.

Netto, Ladislau. 1890. *Instruções Sobre a Preparação e Remessa das Colleções que lhe Forem Destinadas*. Rio de Janeiro: Imprensa Nacional.

Neves, Walter A. 1984a. Estilo de Vida e Osteobiografia: A Reconstituição do Comportamento Pelos Ossos Humanos. *Revista de Pré-História* 6:287–91.

———. 1984b. Antropologia Física e Padrões de Subsistência no Litoral Norte de Santa Catarina, Brasil. *Revista de Pré-história* 6:467–77.

———. 1988. Paleogenética dos Grupos Pré-Históricos do Litoral Sul do Brasil (Paraná e Santa Catarina). *Pesquisas* 43:1–178.

Neves, Walter A., Danilo V. Bernardo, and Mercedes Okumura. 2007. A Origem do Homem Americano Vista a Partir da América do Sul: Uma ou Duas Migrações? *Revista de Antropologia* 50 (1): 9–44.

Neves, Walter A., and Mark Blum. 1998. Afinidades Biológicas Entre Populações Pré-Históricas do Centro-Sul Brasileiro: uma Análise Multivariada. *Fronteiras—Revista de História da Universidade Federal de Mato Grosso do Sul (Cuiabá)* 2:143–69.

Neves, Walter A., and Jose A. Cocilovo. 1984. Componentes Craneofuncionales y Microdiferenciación de las Poblaciones Prehistóricas del Litoral Centro-Sur de Brasil. *Ciência e Cultura* 41:1071–85.

Neves, Walter A., and Silvia Cornero. 1997. What Did South American Paleoinidans Eat? *Current Research in the Pleistocene* 14:93–96.

Neves, Walter A., Mark Hubbe, Mercedes Okumura, Rolando Gonzales Jose, Levy Figuti, Sabine Eggers, and Paulo DeBlasis. 2005. A New Early Holocene Human Skeleton from Brazil: Implications for the Settlement of the New World. *Journal of Human Evolution* 48:403–15.

Neves, Walter A., and Mercedes Okumura. 2005. Afinidades Biológicas de Grupos Pré-Históricos do Vale do Rio Ribeira de Iguape (SP): Uma Análise Preliminar. *Revista de Antropologia* 48:525–58.

Neves, Walter A., P. Unger, and Carlos A. M. Scaramuzza. 1984. Incidência de Cáries e Padrões de Subsistência no Litoral Norte de Santa Catarina. *Revista de Pré-História* 6:371–80.

Neves, Walter A., and Veronica Wesolowski. 2002. Economy, Nutrition, and Disease in Prehistoric Coastal Brazil: A Case Study from the State of Santa Catarina. In *The Backbone of History: Health and Nutrition in the Western Hemisphere*, edited by R. H. Steckel and J. C. Rose, 376–405. Cambridge: Cambridge University Press.

Newell, Raymond R., Trinette S. Constandse-Westermann, and Christopher Meiklejohn. 1979. The Skeletal Remains of Mesolithic Man in Western Europe: An Evaluative Catalogue. *Journal of Human Evolution* 8:1–228.

Nilsson, Liv. 1998. Dynamic Cadavers: A Field-Anthropological Analysis of the Skateholm II Burials. *Lund Archaeological Review* 1998:5–17.

Nilsson Stutz, Liv. 2003. *Embodied Rituals and Ritualized Bodies: Tracing Ritual Practices in Late Mesolithic Burials*. Lund, Sweden: Wallin and Dalholm Boktryckeri AB.

———. 2006. Unwrapping the Dead: Searching for Evidence of Wrappings in the Mortuary Practices at Zvejnieki. In *Back to the Origin: New Research in the Mesolithic-Neolithic Zvejnieki Cemetery and Environment, Northern Latvia*, edited by L. Larsson and I. Zagorska, 217–33. Stockholm: Almquiest and Wiksell International.

Nishida, Paula. 2007. A Coisa Ficou Preta: Estudo do Processo de Formação da Terra Preta do Sítio Arqueológico Jabuticabeira II. PhD diss., Museu de Arqueologia e Etnologia, Universidade de São Paulo, Brazil.

Noël, Laure M.-L. J., Steve J. Hawkins, Stuart R. Jenkins, and Richard C. Thompson. 2009. Grazing Dynamics in Intertidal Rockpools: Connectivity of Microhabitats. *Journal of Experimental Marine Biology and Ecology* 370:9–17.

Norton, Helen. 1985. Women and Resources of the Northwest Coast: Documentation from the 18th and Early 19th Centuries. PhD diss., University of Washington, USA.

Nunn, Patrick D. 2000. Environmental Catastrophe in the Pacific Islands around A.D. 1300. *Geoarchaeology* 15 (7): 715–40.

Ocampo, Carlos, and Pilar Rivas. 2000. Nuevos Fechados C14 de la Costa Norte de la Isla Navarino, Costa sur del Canal de Beagle, Provincia Antartica Chilena, Región de Magallanes. *Anales Instituto Patagonia, Serie Ciencias Humanas* 28:197–214.

O'Connor, Sue. 1999. A Diversity of Coastal Economies: Shell Mounds in the Kimberley Region in the Holocene. In *Australian Coastal Archaeology*, edited by J. Hall and I. J. McNiven, 37–50. Canberra: ANH Publications, Department of Archaeology and Natural History, RSPAS, Australian National University.

Odum, Eugene P. 1983. *Ecologia*. Rio de Janeiro: Editora Guanabara.

Okumura, Mercedes. 2007. Diversidade Morfológica Craniana, Micro-Evolução e Ocupação Pré-Histórica da Costa Brasileira. PhD diss., Universidade de São Paulo, Brazil.

———. 2008. Diversidade Morfológica Craniana, Micro-evolução e Ocupação Pré-Histórica da Costa Brasileira. *Pesquisas* 66.

Okumura, Mercedes, Célia H. C. Boyadjian, and Sabine Eggers. 2007. Auditory Exostoses as an Aquatic Activity Marker: A Comparison of Coastal and Inland Skeletal Remains from Tropical and Subtropical Regions of Brazil. *American Journal of Physical Anthropology* 132 (4): 558–67.

Okumura, Mercedes, and Sabine Eggers. 2005. The People of Jabuticabeira II: Reconstruction of the Way of Life in a Brazilian Shellmound. *Homo* 55 (3): 263–81.

———. 2008. Natural and Cultural Formation Processes in the Archaeological Record: A Case Study Regarding Skeletal Remains from a Brazilian Shellmound. In *Archaeology Research Trends*, edited by A. R. Suárez and M. N. Vásquez, 1–39. New York: Novascience.

———. 2011. Grupos de Afinidade no Sambaqui Jabuti-cabeira II (SC): O que diz a Morfologia Craniana? Paper read at XVI Congresso Mundial da UISPP and XVI Congresso da SAB, September 4–10, Florianópolis, Brazil.

Orchard, Trevor J. 2007. Otters and Urchins: Continuity and Change in Haida Economy During the Late Holocene and Maritime Fur Trade Periods. PhD diss., University of Toronto, Canada.

———. 2009. *Otters and Urchins: Continuity and Change in Haida Economy During the Late Holocene and Maritime Fur Trade Periods.* Oxford: Archaeopress, British Archaeological Reports, International Series No. 2027.

Orchard, Trevor J., and Terence Clark. 2005. Multidimensional Scaling of Northwest Coast Faunal Assemblages: A Case Study from Southern Haida Gwaii, British Columbia. *Canadian Journal of Archaeology* 29:88–112.

Orquera, Luis A. 2005. Mid-Holocene Littoral Adaptation at the Southern End of South America. *Quaternary International* 132:107–15.

Orquera, Luis A., Dominique Legoupil, and Ernesto L. Piana. 2011. Littoral Adaptation at the Southern End of South America. *Quaternary International* 239:61–69.

Orquera, Luis A., and Ernesto L. Piana. 1992. Un Paso Hacia La Resolución del Palimpsesto. In *Análisis Espacial en la Arqueología Patagónica*, edited by L. Borrero and J. L. Lanata, 21–52. Buenos Aires: Búsqueda de Ayllu, S.R.L.

———. 1999a. *La Vida Material y Social de los Yámana.* Buenos Aires: Eudeba.

———. 1999b. *Arqueología de la Región del Canal Beagle.* Buenos Aires: Sociedad Argentina de Antropología.

———. 2001. Composición de Conchales de la Costa del Canal de Beagle (Tierra del Fuego, Republica Argentina). Segunda Parte. *Relaciones, Sociedad Argentina de Antropología* 16:345–68.

Orr, Phil C. 1968. *Prehistory of Santa Rosa Island.* Santa Barbara, CA: Santa Barbara Museum of Natural History.

Orsich, Adam de S. 1977. O Sambaqui do Araújo II—Nota Prévia. *Cadernos de Arqueologia (Curitiba)* 2 (2): 11–60.

O'Shea, John M. 1984. *Mortuary Variability: An Archaeological Investigation.* Orlando, FL: Academic Press.

Owens, D'Ann, and Brian Hayden. 1997. Prehistoric Rites of Passage: A Comparative Study of Transegalitarian Hunter-Gatherers. *Journal of Anthropological Archaeology* 16:121–61.

Owsley, Douglas W., and William M. Bass. 1979. A Demographic Analysis of Skeletons from the Larson Site (39WW2), Willworth County, South Dakota—Vital Statistics. *American Journal of Physical Anthropology* 51:145–54.

Pagliaro, Heloisa, Marta M. Azevedo, and Ricardo V. Santos. 2005. *Demografia dos Povos Indígenas do Brasil.* Rio de Janeiro: ABEP/Fiocruz.

Pallestrini, Luciana, and José L. Morais. 1980. *Arqueologia Pré-Histórica Brasileira.* Fundo de Pesquisas: Universidade de São Paulo, Museu Paulista.

Parker Pearson, Michael. 1999. *The Archaeology of Death and Burial.* College Station: Texas A&M University Press.

Partlow, Megan A. 2000. Salmon Intensification and Changing Household Organization in the Kodiak Archipelago. PhD diss., University of Wisconsin-Madison, USA.

———. 2006. Sampling Fish Bones: A Consideration of the Importance of Screen Size and Disposal Context in the North Pacific. *Arctic Anthropology* 43 (1): 67–79.

Pathansali, D. 1966. Notes on the Biology of the Cockle, *Anadara granosa* L. *Proceedings of the Indo-Pacific Fisheries Council* 11 (2): 84–98.

Pathansali, D., and M. K. Soong. 1958. Some Aspects of Cockle (*Anadara granosa* L.) Culture in Malaya. *Proceedings of the Indo-Pacific Fisheries Council* 8 (2): 26–31.

Pauketat, Timothy R., Lucretia S. Kelly, Gayle J. Fritz, Neil H. Lopinot, Scott Elias, and Eve Hargrave. 2002. The Residues of Feasting and Public Ritual at Early Cahokia. *American Antiquity* 67 (2): 257–79.

Peacock, Evan. 2000. Assessing Bias in Archaeological Shell Assemblages. *Journal of Field Archaeology* 27:183–96.

Pearsall, Deborah M. 2000. *Paleoethnobotany: A Handbook of Procedures.* New York: Academic Press.

Peixoto, Silvia A. 2008. Pequenos aos Montes: Uma Análise dos Processos de Formação dos Sambaquis de Pequeno Porte do Litoral Sul de Santa Catarina. MA diss., Universidade Federal do Rio de Janeiro, Brazil.

Penin, André. 2005. Análise dos Processos Formativos do Sítio Capelinha—Estabelecimento de um Contexto

Microrregional. MA diss., Universidade de São Paulo, Brazil.

Penton, Daniel Troy. 1970. Excavations in the Early Swift Creek Component at Bird Hammock (8Wa30). MA diss., Florida State University, USA.

Percy, George W., and David S. Brose. 1974. Weeden Island Ecology, Subsistence, and Village Life in North-west Florida. Paper read at 39th Annual Meeting of the Society for American Archaeology, May, Washington, DC.

Pereira da Costa, Francisco A. 1865. Da Existencia do Homen em Epochas Remotas no Valle do Tejo. *Commissão Geologica de Portugal*, 3–58.

Peterson, Charles H., and Fred E. Wells. 1998. Molluscs in Marine and Estuarine Sediments. In *Mollusca: The Southern Synthesis. Fauna of Australia*. Vol. 5, *Part A*, edited by P. L. Beesley, G. J. B. Ross, and A. Wells, 36–46. Melbourne: CSIRO.

Peterson, Nicolas. 1971. Open Sites and the Ethnographic Approach to the Archaeology of Hunter-Gatherers. In *Aboriginal Man and Environment in Australia*, edited by D. J. Mulvaney and J. Golson, 239–48. Canberra: Australian National University Press.

Petraglia, Michael, Dennis Kneeper, Petar Glumac, Margaret Newman, and Carole Sussman. 1996. Immunological and Microwear Analysis of Chipped-Stone Artifacts from Piedmont Contexts. *American Antiquity* 61:127–35.

Piana, Ernesto L., Jordi Estévez, and Assumpció Vila. 2000. Lanashuaia: Un Sitio de Canoeros del Siglo Pasado en la Costa Norte del Canal Beagle. In *Desde el País de Los Gigantes. Perspectivas Arqueológicas en Patagonia, Tomo II*, 455–69. Rio Gallegos, Argentina: Universidad Nacional de la Patagonia Austral.

Piana, Ernesto L., Augusto Tessone, and Atilio F. Zangrando. 2006. Contextos Mortuorios en la Región del Canal Beagle . . . del Hallazgo Fortuito a la Búsqueda Sistemática. *Magallania* 34 (1): 103–17.

Piatek, Bruce J. 1981. *Effect of Firebreak Construction on Sites 8-SR-66 and 8-SR-67, Naval Live Oaks Reservation, Gulf Islands National Seashore*. Tallahassee: Southeast Archaeological Center, National Park Service.

Piazza, Walter. 1966. Estudos de Sambaquis (nota prévia). *Série Arqueologia* 2:6–22.

Pickard, Catriona, and Clive Bonsall. 1999. Preliminary Report on the Marine Molluscs from An Corran, Staffin, Isle of Skye. Edinburgh: Department of Archaeology, University of Edinburgh, manuscript on file.

———. 2009. Some Observations on the Mesolithic Crustacean Assemblage from Ulva Cave, Inner Hebrides, Scotland. In *Understanding the Past, Papers Offered to Stefan K. Kozłowski*, edited by J. M. Burdukiewicz, K. Cyrek, P. Dyczek, and K. Szymczak, 305–14. Warsaw: Warsaw University Press.

———. 2012a. A Different Kettle of Fish: Food Diversity in Mesolithic Scotland. In *Food and Drink Archaeology 3*, edited by D. Collard, J. Morris and E. Perego, 76–88. Totnes, UK: Prospect Books.

———. 2012b. The Marine Molluscs. In *An Corran, Staffin, Skye: A Rockshelter with Mesolithic and Later Occupation*, edited by A. Saville, K. Hardy, R. Miket, and T. Ballin, 62–69. Scottish Archaeological Internet Reports 51. http://www.sair.org.uk/sair51/.

Pickering, Thomas M. 1998. The Identification of the Processes of Formation and Diagenesis of a Shell-Bearing Habitation Site. MA diss., University of Houston, USA.

Piggott, Stuart. 1973. Problems in the Interpretation of Chambered Tombs. In *Megalithic Graves and Rituals: III Atlantic Colloquium*, edited by G. Daniel and P. Kjaertum, 9–15. Moesgard, Denmark: Jutland Archaeological Society.

Piperno, Dolores R. 1988. Paleothnobotany in the Neotropic from the Microfossils: New Insights into Ancient Plant Use and Agricultural Origins in the Tropical Forest. *Journal of World Prehistory* 12 (4): 393–449.

———. 2006. *Phytoliths: A Comprehensive Guide for Archaeologists and Paleoecologists*. Lanham, MD: AltaMira Press.

Piperno, Dolores R., and Irene Holst. 1998. The Presence of Starch Grains on Prehistoric Stone Tools from the Humid Neotropics: Indications of Early Tuber Use and Agriculture in Panama. *Journal of Archaeological Science* 25:765–76.

Piperno, Dolores R., and Deborah M. Pearsall. 1993. The Nature and Status of Phytolith Analysis. In *Current Research in Phytolith Analysis: Applications in Archaeology and Paleoecology*, edited by D. M. Pearsall and D. R. Piperno, 9–18. Philadelphia: University Museum of Archaeology and Anthropology, University of Pennsylvania.

Piperno, Dolores R., Ehud Weiss, Irene Holst, and Dani

Nadel. 2004. Processing of Wild Cereal Grains in the Upper Paleolithic Revealed by Starch Grain Analysis. *Nature* 430:670–73.

Plens, Claudia R. 2007. Sitio Moraes, Uma Biografia Não Autorizada: Análise do Processo de Formação de um Sambaqui Fluvial. PhD diss., Museu de Arqueologia e Etnologia, Universidade de São Paulo, Brazil.

Plens, Claudia R., Sabine Eggers, Paulo DeBlasis, and Levy Figuti. 2001. Um Sepultamento de 9,000 Anos: Saúde, Culturra e Atividade. Paper read at Annual Meeting for the Sociedade de Arquologia, Brasileira, São Paulo, September 23–29, São Paulo.

Pluckhahn, Thomas J. 2003. *Kolomoki: Settlement, Ceremony, and Status in the Deep South, A.D. 350 to 750.* Tuscaloosa: University of Alabama Press.

Popper, Virginia S. 1988. Selecting Quantitative Measurements in Paleoethnobotany. In *Current Paleoethnobotany: Analytical Methods and Cultural Interpretation of Archaeological Plant Remains*, edited by C. A. Hastorf and V. S. Popper, 53–71. Chicago: University of Chicago Press.

Portnoy, Alice. 1981. A Microarchaeological View of Human Settlement Space and Function. In *Modern Material Culture: The Archaeology of Us*, edited by R. A. Gould and M. B. Schiffer, 213–24. New York: Academic Press.

Poutiers, Jean-Maurice. 1998. Bivalves (Acephala, Lamellibranchia, Pelecypoda). In *The Living Marine Resources of the Western Central Pacific*. Vol. 1, *Seaweeds, Corals, Bivalves and Gastropods*, edited by K. E. Carpenter and V. H. Niem, 124–362. Rome: Food and Agriculture Organization of the United Nations, FAO Species Identification Guide for Fishery Purposes.

Prebble, Matiu, Robin Sim, Jan Finn, and David Fink. 2005. A Holocene Pollen and Diatom Record from Vanderlin Island, Gulf of Carpentaria, Lowland Tropical Australia. *Quaternary Research* 64:357–71.

Price, T. Douglas. 2003. Emerging Ideas about Complexity Emerging. In *Theory, Method and Practice in Modern Archaeology*, edited by R. J. Jeske and D. K. Charles, 51–67. Westport, CT: Praegar.

Price, T. Douglas, and James A. Brown. 1985. Aspects of Hunter-Gatherer Complexity. In *Prehistoric Hunter-Gatherers*, edited by T. D. Price and J. A. Brown, 3–20. Orlando, FL: Academic Press.

Prieto, Alfredo. 1993/94. Algunos Datos en Torno a los Enterratorios Humanos de la Region Continental de Magallanes. *Anales del Instituto de la Patagonia. Serie Ciencias Humanas* 22:91–100.

Prokopetz, A. Wayne. 1975. *Evaluation of Archeological Sites for National Register Nomination: Gulf Islands National Seashore*. Tallahassee: Southeast Archeological Center, National Park Service.

Prous, André. 1977. Les Sculptures Zoomorfes du Sud Brésilien et de l'Uruguay. Paris: Cahiers d'Archéologie d'Amérique du Sud 5.

———. Arqueologia Brasileira. Brasília, Brazil: Editora Universidade de Brasília.

Prous, André, and Walter Piazza. 1977. Documents pour la Préhistoire du Brésil Méridional 2: l'Etat de Santa Catarina. Paris: Cahiers d'Archéologie d'Amérique du Sud 4.

Raab, L. Mark. 1992. An Optimal Foraging Analysis of Prehistoric Shellfish Collecting on San Clemente Island, California. *Journal of Ethnobiology* 18:63–80.

Rabassa, Jorge, Andrea Coronato, Gustavo Bujalesky, Monica Salemme, Claudio Roig, Andres Meglioli, Calvin Heusser, Sandra Gordillo, Fidel Roig, Ana Borromei, and Mirta Quattrocchio. 2000. Quaternary of Tierra del Fuego, Southernmost South America: An Updated Review. *Quaternary International* 68–71:217–40.

Ramos, Arthur. 1951. *Introdução à Antropologia Brasileira: As Culturas Não-Européias*. Rio de Janeiro: Coleção Estudos Brasileiros.

Randall, Asa. 2008. Archaic Shell Mounds of the St. Johns River, Florida. *SAA Archaeological Record* 8 (5): 13–17.

Ranere, Anthony J., Dolores R. Piperno, Irene Holst, Ruth Dickau, and José Iriarte. 2009. The Cultural and Chronological Context of Early Holocene Maize and Squash Domestication in the Central Balsas River Valley, Mexico. *Proceedings of the National Academy of Sciences* 106 (13): 5014–18.

Raposo, Luís. 1994. O Sítio de Palheirões do Alegra e a "Questão do Mirense." In *Arqueologia en el Entorno del Bajo Guadiana (Huelva, 1992)*, edited by J. M. Campos, A. Pérez, and F. Gómez, 55–69. Huelva, Spain: Universidade de Huelva y Junta de Andalucia.

Rapp, George, Jr., and Susan C. Mulholland. 1992. *Phytolith Systematics: Emerging Issues*. New York: Plenum Press.

Rasingam, L., Solomon Jeeva, and Doraipandian Kannan. 2012. Dental Care of Andaman and Nicobar Folks:

Medicinal Plants Use as Tooth Stick. *Asian Pacific Journal of Tropical Biomedicine* 2 (2): S1013–16.

Rath, Carlos. 1968 [1875]. *Algumas Palavras Etnológicas e Paleontológicas a Respeito da Província de São Paulo, cited in Duarte, Paulo, O Sambaqui Visto Através de Alguns Sambaquis.* São Paulo: Instituto de Pré-História-USP.

Rauth, José W. 1962. *O Sambaqui de Saquarema, S-10.B Paraná, Brasil.* Curitiba, Brazil: Conselho de Pesquisas/Universidade Federal do Paraná.

———. 1968. O Sambaqui do Gomes S.11.B, Paraná, Brasil. *Arqueologia (Curitiba)* 4:1–99.

———. 1976. Subsídios para a Arqueologia dos Sambaquis. *Boletim do Museu de Antropologia e Arqueologia Cornélio Procópio* 1:49–54.

Raymond, J. Scott. 2003. Social Formations in the Western Lowlands of Ecuador During the Early Formative. In *Archaeology of the Early Formative*, edited by J. S. Raymond and R. L. Burger, 33–68. Washington, DC: Dumbarton Oaks.

Record, Samuel J., and Robert W. Hess. 1943. *Timbers of the New World.* New Haven, CT: Yale University Press.

Reeder, Leslie A., Torben C. Rick, and Jon M. Erlandson. 2011. Our Disappearing Past: A GIS Analysis of the Vulnerability of Coastal Archaeological Resources in California's Santa Barbara Channel Region. *Journal of Coastal Conservation* 16 (2): 187–97. doi: 10.1007/s11852-010-0131-2.

Reichel-Dolmatoff, Geraldo. 1972. The Cultural Context of Early Fiber-Tempered Pottery in Northern Columbia. In *Fiber-Tempered Pottery in the Southeastern United States and Northern Columbia: Its Origins, Context, and Significance*, edited by R. P. Bullen and J. B. Stoltman, 1–8. Gainesville: Florida Anthropological Society, Publication No. 6.

Reimchen, Thomas E. 1979. Substratum Heterogeneity, Crypsis, and Colour Polymorphism in an Intertidal Snail (*Littorina mariae*). *Canadian Journal of Zoology* 57:1070–85.

Reimer, Paula J., Mike G. L. Baillie, Edouard Bard, Alex Bayliss, J. Warren Beck, Paul G. Blackwell, C. Bronk Ramsey, Caitlin E. Buck, George S. Burr, R. Lawrence Edwards, et al. 2009. Intcal09 and Marine09 Radiocarbon Age Calibration Curves, 0–50,000 Years Cal BP. *Radiocarbon* 51 (4): 1111–50.

Reimer, Paula J., and Ron W. Reimer. 2000. *Marine Reservoir Correction Database.* http://calib.qub.ac.uk/marine. Accessed January 7.

Reinhard, Karl J., and Vaughn M. Bryant Jr. 2008. Pathoecology and the Future of Coprolite Studies. In *Reanalysis and Reinterpretation in Southwestern Bioarchaeology*, edited by A. W. M. Stodder, 199–216. Tempe: Arizona State University Press.

Reinhard, Karl J., Sheila F. M. de Souza, Cláudia Rodrigues, Erin Kimmerle, and Sheila Dorsey-Vinton. 2001. Microfossils in Dental Calculus: A New Perspective on Diet and Dental Disease. In *Human Remains: Conservation, Retrieval and Analysis* [proceedings of a conference held in Williamsburg, VA, Nov. 7–11, 1999], edited by E. Williams. Oxford: Archeopress, British Archaeological Reports, International Series No. 934.

Reitz, Elizabeth J., and Elizabeth S. Wing. 1999. *Zooarchaeology.* Cambridge: Cambridge University Press.

Rhoads, Donald C., and Giorgio Pannella. 1970. The Use of Molluscan Shell Growth Patterns in Ecology and Paleoecology. *Lethaia* 3:143–61.

Rhodes, Eugene G. 1980. Models of Holocene Coastal Progradation, Gulf of Carpentaria. PhD diss., Australian National University.

Ribeiro, Carlos. 1884. Les "Kjoekkenmoeddings" de la Vallée du Tage. Comptes Rendues de la 9éme du Congrès International d'anthropologie et d'archéologie Préhistoriques (Lisbon, 1880), 279–90. Lisbon: Typographie de l'Académie des Sciences.

Richardson, C. A. 1987. Microgrowth Patterns in the Shell of the Malaysian Cockle *Anadara granosa* (L.) and Their Use in Age Determination. *Journal of Experimental Marine Biology and Ecology* 111 (1): 77–98.

Rick, Torben C. 2007. *The Archaeology and Historical Ecology of Late Holocene San Miguel Island.* Los Angeles: Cotsen Institute of Archaeology, UCLA.

Rick, Torben C., and Jon M. Erlandson, eds. 2008. *Human Impacts on Ancient Marine Ecosystems: A Global Perspective.* Berkeley: University of California Press.

Rick, Torben C., Jon M. Erlandson, Todd J. Braje, James A. Estes, Michael H. Graham, and René L. Vellanoweth. 2008. Historical Ecology and Human Impacts on Coastal Ecosystems of the Santa Barbara Channel Region, California. In *Human Impacts on Ancient Marine Ecosystems: A Global Perspective*, edited by T. C. Rick and J. M. Erlandson, 77–102. Berkeley: University of California Press.

Rick, Torben C., Jon M. Erlandson, René L. Vellanoweth, and Todd J. Braje. 2005. From Pleistocene Mariners to Complex Hunter-Gatherers: The Archaeology of the California Channel Islands. *Journal of World Prehistory* 19:169–228.

Rick, Torben C., and Michael A. Glassow. 1999. Middle Holocene Fisheries of the Central Santa Barbara Channel, California: Investigations at CA-SBA-53. *Journal of California and Great Basin Anthropology* 21:236–56.

Ricketts, E. F., J. Calvin, and J. W. Hedgpeth. 1968. *Between Pacific Tides.* 4th ed. Stanford, CA: Stanford University Press.

Roberts, Andrew. 1991. An Analysis of Mound Formation at Milingimbi, NT. M.Litt diss., University of New England, Armidale, NSW, Australia.

Robinson, Scott W., and George Thompson. 1981. Radiocarbon Corrections for Marine Shell Dates with Application to Southern Pacific Northwest Coast Prehistory. *Syesis* 14:45–57.

Roche, Jean. 1951. *L'Industrie Préhistorique du Cabeço d'Amoreira (Muge).* Porto, Portugal: Imprensa Portuguesa.

———. 1952. Les Fouilles des Amas Coquilliers de Muge. *Boletim da Sociedade Geológica de Portugal* 10:145–50.

———. 1964/1965. Notes sur la Stratigraphie de l'Amas Coquillier Mésolithiques de Cabeço de Amoreira (Muge). *Comunicações dos Serviços Geológicos de Portugal* 48:5–13.

———. 1965. Observations sur la Stratigraphie et la Chronologie des Amas Coquilliers Mésolithiques de Muge (Portugal). *Bulletin de la Société Préhistorique Française* 62:130–38.

———. 1967. Seconde Note sur la Stratigraphie de l'Amas Coquillier Mésolithique de Cabeço de Amoreira (Muge). *Comunicações dos Serviços Geológicos de Portugal* 51:243–52.

———. 1972a. *Le Gisement Mésolithique de Moita do Sebastião: Muge, Portugal. I, Archéologie.* 2nd ed. Lisbon: Instituto de Alta Cultura.

———. 1972b. Les Amas Coquilliers (Concheiros) Mésolithique de Muge (Portugal). *Die Anfänge des Neolithikums vom Orient bis Nordeuropa Westliches Mittelmeergebiet und Britische Inseln. Fundamenta* 8:72–107.

———. 1989. Spatial Organization in the Mesolithic Sites of Muge, Portugal. In *The Mesolithic in Europe: Papers Presented at the Third International Symposium*, edited by C. Bonsall, 607–13. Edinburgh: John Donald.

Roche, Jean, and Octávio da Veiga Ferreira. 1967. Les Fouilles Récentes dans les Amas Coquilliers Mésolithiques de Muge (1962–1965). *O Arqueólogo Português* 1:19–41.

Rogers, David B. 1929. *Prehistoric Man of the Santa Barbara Coast, California.* Santa Barbara, CA: Santa Barbara Museum of Natural History, Special Publications 1.

Rohr, João A. 1977a. *O Sítio Arqueológico do Pântano do Sul SC-F-10.* Florianópolis, Brazil: Imprensa Oficial do Estado de Santa Catarina.

———. 1977b. Terminologia Queratosseodontomalacológica. *Anais do Museu de Antropologia da UFSC* 9 (10): 5–81.

Roksandic, Mirjana. 2002. Position of Skeletal Remains as a Key to Understanding Mortuary Behaviour. In *Advances in Forensic Taphonomy. Method, Theory, and Archaeological Perspectives*, edited by W. D. Haglund and M. H. Sorg, 99–118. London: CRC Press.

———. 2003. New Standardized Visual Forms for Recording the Presence of Human Skeletal Elements in Archaeological and Forensic Contexts. *Internet Archaeology* 13. http://intarch.ac.uk/journal/issue13/roksandic_index.html. Accessed January 2, 2013.

———. 2006. Analysis of Burials from the New Excavations of the Sites Cabeço da Amoreira and Arruda (Muge, Portugal). In *Do Epipapelolítico ao Calcolítico na Península Ibérica. Actas do IV Congresso de Arqueologia Peninsular*, edited by N. Bicho and H. Verissimo, 43–54. Faro, Portugal: University of Algarve Press.

Roksandic, Mirjana, and Stephanie D. Armstrong. 2011. Using the Life History Model to Set the Stage(s) of Growth and Senescence in Bioarchaeology and Paleodemography. *American Journal of Physical Anthropology* 145:337–47.

Rolão, José M., and Mirjana Roksandic. 2007. The Muge Mesolithic Complex: New Results from the Excavations of Cabeço da Amoreira 2001–2003. In *Shell Middens in Atlantic Europe*, edited by O. E. Craig and G. N. Bailey, 158–64. Oxford: Oxbow Books.

Roosevelt, Anna C., R. A. Housley, Maura Imazio da Silveira, Silvia Maranca, and R. Johnson. 1991. Eighth Millennium Pottery from a Prehistoric

Shell Midden in the Brazilian Amazon. *Science* 254:1621–24.

Rosenswig, Robert M. 2007. Beyond Identifying Elites: Feasting as a Means to Understand Early Middle Formative Society on the Pacific Coast of Mexico. *Journal of Anthropological Archaeology* 26:1–27.

Roth, Walter E. 1901. *Food: Its Search, Capture and Preparation*. Brisbane, Australia: Government Printer.

Rowland, Michael J. 1983. Aborigines and Environment in Holocene Australia: Changing Paradigms. *Australian Aboriginal Studies* 2:62–77.

———. 1994. Size Isn't Everything: Shells in Mounds, Middens and Natural Deposits. *Australian Archaeology* 39:118–24.

Rudy, Paul, Jr., and Lynn H. Rudy. 1983. *Oregon Estuarine Invertebrates: An Illustrated Guide to the Common and Important Invertebrate Animals*. Bay St. Louis, MS: National Coastal Ecosystems Team, Office of Biological Services, Fish and Wildlife Service, U.S. Dept. of the Interior.

Russell, Nancy J., Clive Bonsall, and Donald G. Sutherland. 1995. The Exploitation of Marine Molluscs in the Mesolithic of Western Scotland: Evidence from Ulva Cave, Inner Hebrides. In *Man and Sea in the Mesolithic*, edited by A. Fischer, 273–88. Oxford: Oxbow Books.

Russo, Michael. 1991. Archaic Sedentism on the Florida Coast: A Case Study from Horr's Island. PhD diss., University of Florida, USA.

———. 1994. Why We Don't Believe in Archaic Ceremonial Mounds and Why We Should: The Case from Florida. *Southeastern Archaeology* 13:93–108.

———. 1996. Southeastern Archaic Mounds. In *Archaeology of the Mid-Holocene Southeast*, edited by K. Sassaman and D. Anderson, 259–87. Gainesville: University of Florida Press.

———. 2002. Architectural Features at Fig Island. In *The Fig Island Ring Complex (38CH42): Coastal Adaptation and the Question of Ring Function in the Late Archaid*, edited by R. Saunders, 98–140. Report submitted to the South Carolina Department of Archives and History under grant #45-01-16441.

———. 2004. Measuring Shell Rings for Social Inequality. In *Signs of Power: The Rise of Cultural Complexity in the Southeast*, edited by J. L. Gibson and P. J. Carr, 26–70. Tuscaloosa: University of Alabama Press.

———. 2006. Archaic Shell Rings of the Southeast U.S.: National Historic Landmark, National Register of Historic Places Historic Context Study. Tallahassee: National Register of Historic Places, National Historic Landmark Survey, Washington. Southeast Archeological Center, National Park Service.

———. 2008. Late Archaic Shell Rings and Society in the Southeast U.S. *SAA Archaeological Record* 8 (5): 18–22.

———. 2010. Shell Rings and Other Settlement Features as Indicators of Cultural Continuity Between the Late Archaic and Woodland Periods of Coastal Florida. In *Trend, Tradition, and Turmoil: What Happened to the Southeastern Archaic?* edited by D. H. Thomas and M. C. Sanger, 149–72. New York: American Museum of Natural History.

Russo, Michael, Ann S. Cordell, and Donna L. Ruhl. 1993. *The Timucuan Ecological and Historic Preserve, Phase III Final Report*. Gainesville: Florida Museum of Natural History.

Russo, Michael, Craig Dengel, and Jeffrey Shanks. 2013. Woodland Mounds and Rings: The Sacred and the Not-So Secular. In *New Histories of PreColumbian Florida*, edited by Neil Wallis and Asa Randall. Gainesville: University Press of Florida.

Russo, Michael, Carla Hadden, and Craig Dengel. 2009. Archeological Investigations of Mounds and Ring Middens at Hare Hammock, Tyndall Air Force Base. Tallahassee: Southeast Archeological Center, National Park Service. Submitted to Tyndall Air Force Base, Florida.

Russo, Michael, and Gregory Heide. 2002. The Joseph Reed Shell Ring (8Mt13). *Florida Anthropologist* 55 (2): 67–87.

———. 2003. Mapping the Sewee Shell Ring. Tallahassee: Francis Marion and Sumter National Forests, South Carolina. Tallahassee, FL: Southeast Archaeological Center, National Park Service, on file.

Russo, Michael, Gregory Heide, and Vicki Rolland. 2002. The Guana Shell Ring. Tallahassee: Northeast Florida Anthropological Society, Historic Preservation Grant F0126, Florida Department of State, Division of Historical Resources. On file, Bureau of Archaeological Resources.

Russo, Michael, and Charles F. Lawson. 2007. Preliminary Report, Hare Hammock Survey. Tallahassee: Southeast Archeological Center, National Park Service. Submitted to Tyndall Air Force Base, Florida.

Russo, Michael, and Rebecca Saunders. 1999. Identifying the Early Use of Coastal Fisheries and the Rise of Social Complexity in Shell Rings and Arcuate Middens on Florida's Northeast Coast. Tallahassee: Southeast Archaeological Center, National Park Service. Submitted to National Geographic Society.

Russo, Michael, Margo Schwadron, and Emily M. Yates. 2006. Archeological Investigation of the Bayview Site (8By137): A Weeden Island Ring Midden. Tallahassee: Southeast Archeological Center, National Park Service. Submitted to Tyndall Air Force Base, Florida.

Russo, Michael, Jeffrey Shanks, Craig Dengel, and Thadra Stanton. 2011. Investigations of Stranges Mound (8By26), Bakers Mound (8By29), and Associated Ring Middens (8By1355, 8By1357). Tallahassee: Southeast Archeological Center, National Park Service. Submitted to Tyndall Air Force Base, Florida.

Ryder, June M. 1987. Neoglacial History of the Stikine-Iskut Area, Northern Coast Mountains, British Columbia. *Canadian Journal of Earth Sciences* 24:1294–1301.

———. 1989. Holocene Glacier Fluctuations (Canadian Cordillera). In *Quaternary Geology of Canada and Greenland*, edited by R. J. Fulton, 74–76. Ottawa: Geological Survey of Canada.

Saint-Hilaire, A. 1838. *Voyage dans l'Interieur du Brésil: Voyage dans le District des Diamants et sur le Littoral du Brésil—1830–1833*. Vol. 2. Paris: N.p.

Salemme, Monica, Fernando Santiago, Jorge A. Suby, and Ricardo A. Guichón. 2007. Arqueología Funeraria en el Norte de Tierra del Fuego. Paper read at XVI Congreso Nacional de Arqueología Argentina, October 8–12, San Salvador de Jujuy, Argentina.

San Román, Manuel. 2010. La Explotación de Recursos Faunísticos en el Sitio Punta Santa Ana 1: Estrategias de Subsistencia de Grupos de Cazadores Marinos Tempranos de Patagonia Meridiona. *Magallania* 38 (1): 183–98.

Sanger, Matthew C. 2010. Leaving the Rings: Shell Ring Abandonment and the End of the Late Archaic. In *Trend, Tradition, and Turmoil: What Happened to the Southeastern Archaic*, edited by D. H. Thomas and M. C. Sanger, 201–16. New York: American Museum of Natural History, Anthropological Papers No. 93.

Sanger, Matthew C., and David Hurst Thomas. 2010. The Two Rings of St. Catherines Island: Some Preliminary Results from the St. Catherines and McQueen Shell Rings. In *Trend, Tradition, and Turmoil: What Happened to the Southeastern Archaic*, edited by D. H. Thomas and M. C. Sanger, 45–70. New York: American Museum of Natural History, Anthropological Papers No. 93.

Sanghvi, L. D. 1953. Comparison of Genetical and Morphological Methods for a Study of Biological Distances. *American Journal of Physical Anthropology* 11:385–404.

Santiago, Fernando, Monica Salemme, Jorge A. Suby, and Ricardo A. Guichón. 2011. Restos Óseos Humanos en el Norte de Tierra del Fuego. Aspectos Contextuales, Dietarios y Paleopatológicos. *Intersecciones en Antropología* 12:147–62.

Sassaman, Kenneth E. 2003. *St. Johns Archaeological Field School 2000–2001: Blue Spring and Hontoon Island State Parks*. Gainesville: Laboratory of Southeastern Archaeology, Department of Anthropology, University of Florida, Technical Report 4.

———. 2004. Complex Hunter-Gatherers in Evolution and History: A North American Perspective. *Journal of Archaeological Research* 12 (3): 227–80.

———. 2008. The New Archaic: It Ain't What It Used to Be. *SAA Archaeological Record* 8 (5): 6–8.

Saunders, Nicholas J. 1999. Biographies of Brilliance: Pearls, Transformation of Matter and Being, c. AD 1492. *World Archaeology* 31 (2): 243–57.

Saunders, Rebecca. 2002a. Previous Archaeological Research. In *The Fig Island Ring Complex (38CH42): Coastal Adaptation and the Question of Ring Function in the Late Archaic*, edited by R. Saunders and M. Russo, 43–63. Report submitted to the South Carolina Department of Archives and History under Grant #45-01-16441.

———. 2002b. Field Excavations: Methods and Results. In *The Fig Island Ring Complex (38CH42): Coastal Adaptation and the Question of Ring Function in the Late Archaic*, edited by R. Saunders and M. Russo, 98–140. Columbia: South Carolina Department of Archives and History.

———. 2003. Feast or Quotidian Fare? Rollins Shell Ring and the Question of Ring Function. Tallahassee: Submitted to the Florida Department of Archives and History for Grant 1A-32 9697.04.

———. 2004a. Stratigraphy at the Rollins Shell Ring Site: Implications for Ring Function. *Florida Anthropologist* 57 (4): 249–70.

———. 2004b. Spatial Variation in Orange Culture Pottery: Interaction and Function. In *Early Pottery: Technology, Function, Style, and Interaction in the Lower Southeast*, edited by R. Saunders and C. T. Hays, 1–22. Tuscaloosa: University of Alabama Press.

———. 2010. Rollins Redux: Rings, Ringlets, and Really Big Pits. Report submitted to the Florida Department of Archives and History for Permit 0304.38.

Saunders, Rebecca, and Michael Russo, eds. 2002. *The Fig Island Ring Complex (38CH42): Coastal Adaptation and the Question of Ring Function in the Late Archaic*. Columbia: South Carolina Department of Archives and History.

———. 2011. Coastal Shell Middens in Florida: A View from the Archaic. In *Shell Middens as Archives of Past Environments, Human Dispersal and Specialized Resource Management: Quaternary International* 239:38–50.

Saunders, Rebecca, and Margaret Wrenn. 2011. Crafting Pottery in Early Florida: Production and Distribution. In *54th Annual Meeting of the Southeastern Archaeological Conference*. Jacksonville, FL: Southeastern Archaeological Conference.

Saunders, Rebecca, John Wrenn, William Krebs, and Vaughn M. Bryant. 2009. Coastal Dynamics and Cultural Occupations on Choctawhatchee Bay, Florida. *Palynology* 33 (2): 135–56.

Scheel-Ybert, Rita. 2000. Vegetation Stability in the Southeastern Brazilian Coastal Area from 5500 to 1400 14C yr BP Deduced from Charcoal Analysis. *Review of Palaeobotany and Palynology* 110:111–38.

———. 2001a. Man and Vegetation in the Southeastern Brazil During the Late Holocene. *Journal of Archaeological Science* 28:471–80.

———. 2001b. Vegetation Stability in the Brazilian Littoral During the Late Holocene: Anthracological Evidence. *Revista Pesquisas em Geociências* 28 (2): 315–23.

———. 2002. Evaluation of Sample Reliability in Extant and Fossil Assemblages. In *Charcoal Analysis: Methodological Approaches, Palaeoecological Results and Wood Uses*, edited by S. Thiébault, 9–16. Oxford: Archaeopress, British Archaeological Reports, International Series No. 1063.

———. 2004. Teoria e Métodos em Antracologia. 2. Técnicas de Campo e de Laboratório. *Arquivos do Museu Nacional* 62 (4): 343–56.

Scheel-Ybert, Rita, Gina Faraco Bianchini, and Paulo DeBlasis. 2009. Registro de Mangue em um Sambaqui de Pequeno Porte do Litoral Sul de Santa Catarina, Brasil, a Cerca de 4900 Anos cal BP, e Considerações sobre o Processo de Ocupação do Sítio Encantada-III. *Revista do Museu de Arqueologia e Etnologia, São Paulo* 19:103–18.

Scheel-Ybert, Rita, and Ondemar F. Dias Jr. 2007. Corondó: Palaeoenvironmental Reconstruction and Palaeoethnobotanical Considerations in a Probable Locus of Early Plant Cultivation (South-Eastern Brazil). *Environmental Archaeology* 12:129–38.

Scheel-Ybert, Rita, Sabine Eggers, Veronica Wesolowski, Cecilia C. Petronilho, Célia H. C. Boyadjian, Paulo DeBlasis, Márcia Barbosa-Guimarães, and Maria Dulce Gaspar. 2003. Novas Perspectivas na Reconstituição do Modo de Vida dos Sambaquieiros: Uma Abordagem Multidisciplinar. *Revista de Arqueologia da Sociedade de Arqueologia Brasileira* 16:109–37.

Scheel-Ybert, Rita, Sabine Eggers, Veronica Wesolowski, Cecilia C. Petronilho, Célia H. C. Boyadjian, Maria Dulce Gaspar, Márcia Barbosa-Guimarães, Maria Cristina Tenório, and Paulo DeBlasis. 2009. Subsistence and Lifeway of Coastal Brazilian Moundbuilders. In *La Alimentación en la América Precolombina y Colonial: Una Aproximación Interdisciplinaria*, edited by A. Capparelli, A. Chevalier, and R. Piqué, 37–53. Madrid: Consejo Superior de Investigaciones Cientificas, Treballs d'Etnoarqueologia 7.

Scheel-Ybert, Rita, Daniela Klokler, Maria Dulce Gaspar, and Levy Figuti. 2005/2006. Proposta de Amostragem Padronizada para Macro-Vestígios Bioarqueológicos: Antracologia, Arqueobotânica, Zooarqueologia. *Revista do Museu de Arqueologia e Etnologia* 15 (6): 139–63.

Schenck, W. Egbert. 1926. The Emeryville Shellmound Final Report. *University of California Publications in American Archaeology and Ethnology* 23:150–282.

Scherer, Adriano, Fabiana Maraschin-Silva, and Luis Rios de Moura Baptista. 2005. Florística e Estrutura do Componente Arbóreo de Matas de Restinga Arenosa no Parque Estadual de Itapuã, RS, Brasil. *Acta Botanica Brasilica* 19 (4): 717–26.

Schiffer, Michael B. 1987. *Formation Processes of the Archaeological Record*. Albuquerque: University of New Mexico Press.

Schmidt, Morgan. 2010. Reconstructing Tropical Nature: Prehistoric and Modern Anthrosols (Terra Preta) in the Amazon Rainforest, Upper Xingu River, Brazil. PhD diss., University of Florida, USA.

Schmitt, Dave N., David B. Madsen, and Karen D. Lupo. 2004. The Worst of Times, the Best of Times: Jackrabbit Hunting by Middle Holocene Human Foragers in the Bonneville Basin of Western North America. In *Colonisation, Migration, and Marginal Areas: A Zooarchaeological Approach*, edited by M. Mondini, S. Munoz, and S. Wickler, 86–95. Oxford: Oxbow Books.

Schmitz, Pedro I. 1984. *Caçadores e Coletores da Pré-História do Brasil*. São Leopoldo, Brazil: Instituto Anchietano de Pesquisas.

———. 1987. Prehistoric Hunters and Gatherers of Brazil. *Journal of World Prehistory* 11:53–126.

Schmitz, Pedro I., and Ana V. Bitencourt. 1996. O Sítio Arqueológico do Pântano do Sul, S.C. *Pesquisas* 53:77–123.

Schoenherr, Allan A., C. Robert Feldmeth, and Michael J. Emerson. 1999. *Natural History of the Islands of California*. Berkeley: University of California Press.

Schöne, Bernd R. 2008. The Curse of Physiology: Challenges and Opportunities in the Interpretation of Geochemical Data from Mollusk Shells. *Geo Marine Letters* 28:269–85.

Schöne, Bernd R., Antuane D. Freyre Castro, Jens Fiebig, Stephen D. Houk, Wolfgang Oschmann, and Ingrid Kroncke. 2004. Sea Surface Temperatures Over the Period 1884–1983 Reconstructed from Oxygen Isotope Ratios of a Bivalve Mollusk Shell (Arctic *islandica*, Southern North Sea). *Palaeogeography, Palaeoclimatology, Palaeoecology* 212:215–32.

Schöne, Bernd R., Elena Dunca, Jens Feibig, and Miriam Pfeiffer. 2005. Mutvei's Solution: An Ideal Agent for Resolving Microgrowth Structures of Biogenic Carbonates. *Palaeogeography, Palaeoclimatology, Palaeoecology* 228:149–66.

Schwadron, Margo. 2010. Landscapes of Maritime Complexity: Prehistory Shell Work Sites of the Ten Thousand Islands, Florida. PhD diss., University of Leicester, UK.

Scott Cummings, Linda, and Ann Magennis. 1997. Phytolith and Starch Record of Food and Grit in Mayan Human Tooth Tartar. In *Primer Encuentro Europeo sobre el Estudio de Fitolitos*, edited by J. Juan-Tresserras and M. J. Machado, 211–18. Madrid: Gráficas Fersán.

Semenov, Sergei. 1964. *Prehistoric Technology*. Wiltshire, UK: Moonraker Press.

Sepez, Jennifer. 2001. Political and Social Ecology of Contemporary Hunting, Fishing, and Shellfish Collecting Practices. PhD diss., University of Washington, USA.

Serrano, Antonio. 1946. The Sambaquis of the Brazilian Coast. In *Handbook of South American Indians*, edited by J. Steward, 401–7. Washington, DC: Smithsonian Institution.

Service, Elman R. 1971. *Os Caçadores*. Rio de Janeiro: Zahar Editores.

Seyferth, Giralda. 1985. A Antropologia e a Teoria do Branqueamento da Raça no Brasil: A Tese de João Batista de Lacerda. *Revista do Museu Paulista* 30:81–98.

———. 1995. A Invenção da Raça e o Poder Discriminatório dos Estereótipos. *Anuário Antropológico. Edição Tempo Brasileiro*, 175–204.

Shackleton, Judith C., and Tjeerd H. van Andel. 1986. Prehistoric Shore Environments, Shellfish Availability, and Shellfish Gathering at Franchthi, Greece. *Geoarchaeology* 1 (2): 127–43.

Shackleton, Nicholas J. 1973. Oxygen Isotope Analysis as a Means of Determining Season of Occupation of Prehistoric Midden Sites. *Archaeometry* 15:133–41.

Shafer, Harry, and Richard Holloway. 1979. Organic Residue Analysis in Determining Stone Tool Function. In *Lithic Use-Wear Analysis*, edited by B. Hayden, 385–99. New York: Academic Press.

Shanks, Orin, Robson Bonnichsen, Anthony Vella, and Walter Ream. 2001. Recovery of Protein and DNA Trapped in Stone Tool Microcracks. *Journal of Archaeological Science* 28:965–72.

Shennan, Susan E. 1975. The Social Organization at Branc. *Antiquity* 49:279–87.

Shulmeister, James. 1992. A Holocene Pollen Record from Lowland Tropical Australia. *Holocene* 2:107–16.

———. 1999. Australasian Evidence for Mid-Holocene Climate Change Implies Precessional Control of Walker Circulation in the Pacific. *Quaternary International* 57/58:81–91.

Shulmeister, James, and Brian Lees. 1992. Morphology and Chronostratigraphy of a Coastal Dunefield; Groote Eylandt, Northern Australia. *Geomorphology* 5:521–34.

Silva, Carlos Tavares, and Joaquina Soares. 1997. Economias Costeiras na Pré-História do Sudoeste

Português: O Concheiros de Montes de Baixo. *Setúbal Arqueológica* 11–12:69–108.

Silva, Janie Garcia, and Arline S. Oliveira. 1989. A Vegetação de Restinga no Município de Maricá, RJ. *Acta Botanica Brasílica* Suppl. 3:253–72.

Silva, Luciana A., and Aldicir Scariot. 2004. Comunidade Arbórea de uma Floresta Estacional Decídua sobre Afloramento Calcário na Bacia do Rio Paraná. *Revista Árvore* 28 (1): 61–67.

Skewes, Marie. *Patella depressa. Black-Footed Limpet. Marine Life Information Network: Biology and Sensitivity Key Information Sub-programme.* Marine Biological Association of the United Kingdom 2003. http://www.marlin.ac.uk/species/ Patelladepressa.htm. Accessed April 8, 2009.

Sloan, Derek. 1986. Raschoille Cave, Oban: Preliminary Sample Assessment and Recommendations. Edinburgh: Department of Archaeology, University of Edinburgh, manuscript on file,

Smith, Eric A., and Bruce Winterhalder. 1992. Natural Selection and Decision Making: Some Fundamental Principles. In *Evolutionary Ecology and Human Behavior*, edited by E. A. Smith and B. Winterhalder, 25–60. New York: Aldine de Gruyter.

Soares, António Monge, and João M. Alveirinho Dias. 2006. Coastal Upwelling and Radiocarbon-Evidence for Temporal Fluctuations in Ocean Reservoir Effect off Portugal During the Holocene. *Radiocarbon* 48 (1): 45–60.

Soares, Joaquina, and Carlos Tavares Silva. 1993. Na Transição Plistocénico-Holocénico: Marisqueio na Pedra do Patacho. *Al-Madan* 2:21–29.

———. 2003. A Transição para o Neolítico na Costa Sudoeste Portuguesa. In *Muita Gente, Poucas Antas? Origens, Espaços e Contextos do Megalitismo. Actas do II Colóquio Internacional Sobre Megalitismo*, edited by V. S. Gonçalves, 45–56. Lisbon: Instituto Português de Arqueologia (Trabalhos de Arqueologia, 25).

———. 2004. Alterações Ambientais e Povoamento na Transição Mesolítico-Neolítico na Costa Sudoeste. In *Actas Do Congresso Evolução Geohistórica do Litoral Português e Fenómenos Correlativos: Geologia, História, Arqueologia e Climatologia*, edited by A. A. Tavares, M. J. F. Tavares, and J. L. Cardoso, 397–424. Lisbon: Universidade Aberta.

Sofrata, Abier, Fernanda Brito, Meshari Al-Otaibi, and Anders Gustafsson. 2011. Short Term Clinical Effect of Active and Inactive *Salvadora persica*

Miswak on Dental Plaque and Gingivitis. *Journal of Ethnopharmacology* 137 (3): 1130–34.

Souza, Alfredo A. C. M. de. 1977. Pré-História de Parati. *Nheengatu. Cadernos Brasileiros de Arqueologia e Indigenismo (Rio de Janeiro)* 1 (2): 47–90.

———. 1981/1982. Um Modelo Etnográfico Para Estimativas Paleodemográficas. *Arquivos do Museu de História Natural da Universidade Federal de Minas Gerais (Belo Horizonte)* 6/7:329–58.

———. 1991. História da Arqueologia Brasileira. *Pesquisas (São Leopoldo)* 46:1–157.

Souza, Alfredo A. C. M. de, and Sheila M. Ferraz. 1974. Paleopatologia do Homem do Sambaqui. Paper read at IX International Congress of Archaeological and Ethnological Sciences, St. Louis.

Souza, Sheila M. F. M. de. 1991. Aplicação de Função Discriminante em Estimativas de Sexo em Ossos Humanos Pré-Históricos. MSc diss., Universidade Federal do Rio de Janeiro, Brazil.

———. 1992/1993. Paleodemografia da População do Grande Abrigo de Santana do Riacho: Uma Hipótese Para Verificação. *Arquivos do Museu de História Natural da Universidade Federal de Minas Gerais (Belo Horizonte)* 18 (2): 161–71.

———. 1995. Estresse, Doença e Adaptabilidade: Estudo Comparativo de Dois Grupos Pré-Históricos em Perspectiva Biocultural. PhD diss., Escola Nacional de Saúde Pública, Fundação Oswaldo Cruz, Brazil.

———. 1999. Anemia e Adaptabilidade em um Grupo Costeiro Pré-Histórico: Uma Hipótese Patocenótica. In *Pré-História de Terra Brasilis*, edited by M. C. Tenório, 171–88. Rio de Janeiro: Universidade Federal do Rio de Janeiro.

———. 2010. O Silêncio Bioarqueológico da Amazonia. Entre o Mito da Diluição Demográfica e o da Diluição Biológica na Floresta Tropical. In *Arqueologia Amazonica*. Vol. 1, edited by E. Pereira and V. Guapindaia, 427–45. Belém, Brazil: Museu Paraense Emilio Goeldi/IPHAN/SECULT.

Souza, Sheila M. F. M. de, Diana M. de Carvalho, and Andrea Lessa. 2003. Paleoepidemiology: Is There a Case to Answer? *Memórias do Instituto Oswaldo Cruz (Rio de Janeiro)* 98 (S1): 21–27.

Souza, Sheila M. F. M. de, and Alfredo A. C. M. de Souza. 1980. *Tentativa de Interpretação Paleoecológica do Sambaqui do Rio das Pedrinha –Magé–RJ*. Rio de Janeiro: Instituto Superior de Cultura Brasileira.

———. 1981/1982. Pescadores e Recoletores do Litoral do

Rio de Janeiro. *Arquivos do Museu de História Natural da Universidade Federal de Minas Gerais (Belo Horizonte)* 6/7:109–31.

Souza, Sheila M. F. M. de, Veronica Wesolowski, and Claudia Rodrigues-Carvalho. 2009. Teeth, Nutrition, Anemia, Infection, Mortality: Costs of Lifestyle of the Coastal Brazilian Sambaquis. *British Archaeological Reports (Oxford)* 2026:33–40.

Spenneman, Dirk H. R. 1987. Availability of Shellfish Resources on Prehistoric Tongatapu, Tonga: Effects of Human Predation and Changing Environment. *Archaeology in Oceania* 22 (3): 81–96.

Spielmann, Katherine A. 2008. Crafting the Sacred: Ritual Places and Paraphernalia in Small-Scale Societies. *Research in Economic Anthropology* 27:37–72.

Stearns, Stephen C., and Jacob C. Koella. 2008. *Evolution in Health and Disease*. Oxford: Oxford University Press.

Stein, Julie K., ed. 1992. *Deciphering a Shell Midden*. San Diego, CA: Academic Press.

———. 2000. *Exploring Coast Salish Prehistory: The Archaeology of San Juan Island*. Seattle: University of Washington Press.

Stein, Julie K., Jennie N. Deo, and Laura S. Phillips. 2003. Big Sites—Short Time: Accumulation Rates in Archaeological Sites. *Journal of Archaeological Science* 30 (3): 297–316.

Stein, Julie K., Kimberly D. Kornbacher, and J. L. Tyler. 1992. British Camp Shell Midden Stratigraphy. In *Deciphering a Shell Midden*, edited by J. K. Stein, 95–134. San Diego: Academic Press.

Stephenson, Keith, Judith A. Bense, and Frankie Snow. 2002. Aspects of Deptford and Swift Creek of the South Atlantic and Gulf Coastal Plain. In *The Woodland Southeast*, edited by D. G. Anderson and R. C. Mainfort Jr., 318–51. Tuscaloosa: University of Alabama Press.

Steponaitis, Vincas P. 1986. Prehistoric Archaeology in the Southeastern United States, 1970–1985. *Annual Review of Anthropology* 15:363–404.

Steward, Julian. 1949. South American Cultures: An Interpretive Summary. In *Handbook of South American Indians*. Vol 5, edited by J. Steward, 669–767. Washington, DC: Smithsonian Institution.

Stewart, Hilary. 1977. *Indian Fishing. Early Methods on the Northwest Coast*. Seattle: University of Washington Press.

Stine, Scott. 1994. Extreme and Persistent Drought in California and Patagonia During Medieval Time. *Nature* 369:546–49.

Stiner, Mary C. 1999. Paleolithic Mollusc Exploitation at Ripario Mochi (Balz Rossi, Italy): Food and Ornaments from the Aurignacian Through Epigravettian. *Antiquity* 73:735–54.

———. 2003. Zooarchaeological Evidence for Resource Intensification in Algarve, Southern Portugal. *Promontoria* 1 (1): 27–61.

Stiner, Mary C., Nuno F. Bicho, John Lindly, and C. Reid Ferring. 2003. Mesolithic to Neolithic Transitions: New Results from Shell middens in the Western Algarve, Portugal. *Antiquity* 77 (1): 75–86.

Stodder, Ann L. W. 2008. Taphonomy and the Nature of Archaeological Assemblages. In *Biological Anthropology of the Human Skeleton*, edited by M. A. Katzenberg and S. R. Saunders, 71–114. New York: Wiley-Liss.

Storto, Camila, Sabine Eggers, and Marta Lahr. 1999. Estudo Preliminar das Paleopatologias da População do Sambaqui Jabuticabeira II, Jaguaruna, SC. *Revista do Museu de Arqueologia e Etnologia* 9:61–71.

———. 2001. Os Construtores do Sambaqui de Jabuticabeira II. In *Arqueologia do Brasil Meridional*, edited by A. A. Kern and K. Hilbert. Porto Alegre, Brazil: Pontifícia Universidade Católica do Rio Grande do Sul (CD ROM).

Stothert, Karen. 2003. Expressions of Ideology in the Formative Period of Ecuador. In *Archaeology of the Early Formative*, edited by J. S. Raymond and R. L. Burger, 337–442. Washington, DC: Dumbarton Oaks.

Straus, Lawrence G., Jesus Altuna, and Bradley Vierra. 1990. The Concheiro at Vidigal: A Contribution to the Late Mesolithic of Southern Portugal. In *Contributions to the Mesolithic of Europe: Papers Presented at the IV International Symposium (Leuven, 1990)*, edited by P. M. Vermeersch and P. Van Peer, 463–74. Leuven, Belgium: Leuven University Press.

Strauss, André. 2010. As Práticas Mortuárias dos Caçadores-Coletores Pré-Históricos da Região de Lagoa Santa (MG): Um Estudo de Caso do Sítio Arqueológico "Lapa do Santo." MSc diss., Universidade de São Paulo, Brazil.

Stuiver, Minze, and Paula J. Reimer. 1993. Extended 14C Database and Revised CALIB Radiocarbon Calibration Program. *Radiocarbon* 35:215–30.

Suby, Jorge A. 2007. Propiedades Estructurales de Restos Óseos Humanos y Paleopatología en Patagonia Austral. PhD diss., University of Mar del Plata, Argentina.

Suby, Jorge A., and Ricardo A. Guichón. 2007. Análisis de Restos Bioarqueológicos de la Costa Meridional de Santa Cruz: Octavas Jornadas de Antropología Biológica de la Republica Argentina. *Revista Argentina de Antropología Biológica* 9:103.

———. 2010. Los Restos Óseos Humanos de la Colección de la Misión "La Candelaria" (Rio Grande, Tierra del Fuego). *Magallania* 38 (2): 121–33.

Suby, Jorge A., Ricardo A. Guichón, and Atilio F. Zangrando. 2009. El Registro Biológico Humano de la Costa Meridional de Santa Cruz. *Revista Argentina de Antropología Biológica* 11:109–24.

Sumpter, Ian D. 1999. 1998 Archaeological Investigations, Site 922T, Gunlai Kin (Hotspring Island), Gwaii Haanas. Victoria, BC: Parks Canada, Cultural Resource Services.

Suttles, Wayne. 1987. *Coast Salish Essays.* Seattle: University of Washington Press.

———. 1990. Environments. In *Handbook of North American Indians: Northwest Coast 7,* edited by W. Suttles, 16–29. Washington, DC: Smithsonian Institution.

Swadling, Pamela 1976. Changes Induced by Exploitation in Prehistoric Shellfish Populations. *Mankind* 10:156–62.

Swanton, John R. 1979 [1946]. *The Indians of the Southeastern United States.* Washington, DC: Smithsonian Institution Press.

Tait, L. 1868. Notes on the Shell Mounds, Hut-Circles and Kistvaens of Sutherland. *Proceedings of the Society of Antiquaries of Scotland* 7:525–32.

Tan, Francis C. 1989. Stable Carbon Isotopes in Dissolved Inorganic Carbon in Marine and Estuarine Environments. In *Handbook of Environmental Isotope Geochemistry.* Vol 3, edited by P. Fritz and J. C. Fontes, 171–90. New York: Elsevier.

Tasayco-Ortega, Luis A. 1996. Variations Paléohydrologiques et Paléoclimatiques d'une Région d'Upwelling au Cours de l'Holocène: Enregistrement dans les Lagunes Côtières de Cabo Frio (État de Rio de Janeiro, Brésil). PhD diss., Université Pierre et Marie Curie, France.

Tayles, Nancy, Kate Domett, and Kirsten Nelsen. 2000. Agriculture and Dental Caries? The Case of Rice in Prehistoric Southeast Asia. *World Archaeology* 32 (1): 68–83.

Taylor, Amanda K., Julie K. Stein, and Stephanie A. E. Jolivette. 2011. Big Sites, Small Sites, and Coastal Settlement Patterns in the San Juan Islands, Washington, USA. *Journal of Island and Coastal Archaeology* 6 (2): 287–313.

Tengberg, Margareta. 2002. Vegetation History and Wood Exploitation in the Oman Peninsula from the Bronze Age to the Classical Period. In *Charcoal Analysis: Methodological Approaches, Palaeoecological Results and Wood Uses,* edited by S. Thiébault, 151–57. Oxford: Archaeopress, British Archaeological Reports, International Series No. 1063.

Tenório, Maria Cristina. 1991. A Importância da Coleta no Advento da Agricultura. MA diss., Universidade Federal do Rio de Janeiro, Brazil.

Tenório, Maria Cristina, Márcia Barbosa, and Teresa Portela. 1992. Pesquisas Arqueológicas no Sítio Ponta de Cabeça, Arraial do Cabo, Rio de Janeiro. Paper read at 4th Annual Meeting for the Sociedade de Arqueologia Brasileira, Rio de Janeiro.

Terradas, Xavier. 1996. La Gestió dels Recursos Minerals entre les Comunitats Caçadores-Recollectores. Vers una Representació de les Estratègies de Proveïment de Matèries Primeres. PhD diss., Universitat Autònoma de Barcelona, Spain.

Tesar, Louis. 1973. *Archaeological Survey and Testing of the Gulf Islands National Seashore. Part 1, Florida.* Tallahassee: Southeast Archaeological Center, National Park Service.

Tessone, Augusto, Atilio F. Zangrando, Susana Valencio, and Héctor O. Panarello. 2003. Análisis de Isótopos en Restos Óseos Humanos en la Región del Canal Beagle (Isla Grande de Tierra del Fuego). *Revista Argentina de Antropología Biológica* 5 (2): 33–43.

Théry-Parisot, Isabelle, Lucie Chabal, and Julia Chrzavzez. 2010. Anthracology and Taphonomy, from Wood Gathering to Charcoal Analysis: A Review of the Taphonomic Processes Modifying Charcoal Assemblages, in Archaeological Contexts. *Palaeogeography, Palaeoclimatology, Palaeoecology* 291:142–53.

Thom, Brian D. 1992. An Investigation of Interassemblage Variability Within the Gulf of Georgia Phase. *Canadian Journal of Archaeology* 16:24–31.

Thomas, David Hurst. 2008. Radiocarbon Dating on St.

Catherines Island. In *Native American Landscapes of St. Catherines Island, Georgia*, edited by D. H. Thomas, 345–71. New York: American Museum of Natural History, Anthropological Papers of the American Museum of Natural History No. 88 (nos. 1–3).

———. 2010. What Happened to the Southeastern Archaic? A Perspective from St. Catherines. In *Trend, Tradition, and Turmoil: What Happened to the Southeastern Archaic?* edited by D. H. Thomas and M. C. Sanger, 173–99. New York: American Museum of Natural History, Anthropological Papers of the American Museum of Natural History No. 93.

Thomas, David Hurst, and Matthew C. Sanger, eds. 2010. *Trend, Tradition, and Turmoil: What Happened to the Southeastern Archaic?* New York: American Museum of Natural History, Anthropological Papers of the American Museum of Natural History No. 93.

Thomas, Frank R. 2007. The Behavioral Ecology of Shellfish Gathering in Western Kiribati, Micronesia 1: Prey Choice. *Journal of Human Ecology* 35:179–94.

Thomas, Kenneth D., and Marcello A. Mannino. 2001. The Exploitation of Invertebrates and Invertebrate Products. In *Handbook of Archaeological Sciences*, edited by D. R. Brothwell and A. M. Pollard, 427–40. Chichester UK: Wiley.

Thomas, Prentice M, Jr. 1983. Management Report: Summary of Cultural Resources Investigations, Eglin Air Force Base, Florida. 1982–1983. New World Research, Ft. Walton, Florida, CX5000-Z-0497. Atlanta, GA: Archeological Services Branch, National Park Service.

———. 1985. Management Report: Summary of Cultural Resources Investigations, Eglin Air Force Base, Florida, 1982–1985. New World Research, Ft. Walton, Florida, CX5000-Z-0497. Atlanta, GA: Archeological Services Branch, National Park Service.

Thomas, Prentice M., Jr., and L. Janice Campbell. 1985. Cultural Resources Investigation at Tyndall Air Force Base, Bay County, Florida. New World Research, Ft. Walton, Florida, Report of Investigations 84-4, CX5000-4-0499. Atlanta, GA: Archeological Services Branch, National Park Service.

———. 1993. Eglin Air Force Base: Historic Preservation Plan, Technical Synthesis of Cultural Investigations at Eglin, Santa Rosa, Okaloosa, and Walton Counties, Florida. New World Research, Ft. Walton, Florida, Report of Investigations No. 192, CX5000-2-0497. Atlanta, GA: National Park Service, Southeast Region.

———. 1996. Interpretations. In *Controlled Excavation at 8WL58, the Old Homestead Site: Completing the Compliance Process at Eglin Air Force Base, Okaloosa, Santa Rosa, and Walton Counties*, edited by P. M. Thomas Jr., M. L. Schleidt Peñalva, L. J. Campbell, and M. Cox, 148–66. Ft. Walton, FL: Prentice Thomas and Associates.

Thomas, Prentice M., Jr., L. Janice Campbell, and Charlotte Cannon, eds. 2001. *Mitigative Data Recovery at the Horseshoe Bayou Site, 8WL36, Sandestin Beach Resorts, Inc., Walton County, Florida*. Ft. Walton, FL: Prentice Thomas and Associates.

Thomas, Prentice M., Jr., Maria L. Schleidt Peñalva, L. Janice Campbell, and Mathilda Cox, eds. 1996. *Controlled Excavation at 8WL58, the Old Homestead Site: Completing the Compliance Process at Eglin Air Force Base, Okaloosa, Santa Rosa, and Walton Counties*. Ft. Walton, FL: Prentice Thomas and Associates.

Thompson, Victor D. 2006. Questioning Complexity: The Prehistoric Hunter-Gatherers of Sapelo Island, Georgia. PhD diss., University of Kentucky, USA.

———. 2007. Articulating Activity Areas and Formation Processes at the Sapelo Island Shell Ring Complex. *Southeastern Archaeology* 26:91–107.

Thompson, Victor D., and C. Fred T. Andrus. 2011. Evaluating Mobility, Monumentality, and Feasting at the Sapelo Island Shell Ring Complex. *American Antiquity* 76 (2): 315–44.

Thompson, Victor D., and Thomas J. Pluckhahn. 2010. History, Complex Hunter-Gatherers, and the Mounds and Monuments of Crystal River, Florida: A Geophysical Perspective. *Journal of Island and Coastal Archaeology* 5 (1): 33–51.

Thomson, Donald F. 1949. *Economic Structure and the Ceremonial Exchange Cycle in Arnhem Land*. Melbourne, Australia: Macmillan.

Tieszen, Larry L., and Tim Fagre. 1993. Carbon Isotopic Variability in Modern and Archaeological Maize. *Journal of Archaeological Science* 20:25–40.

Tilley, Christopher. 2004. *The Materiality of Stone: Explorations in Landscape Phenomenology*. Oxford: Berg.

Torrence, Corbett McPherson. 1996. From Objects to the Cultural System: A Middle Archaic Columella

Extraction Site on Useppa Island, Florida. MA diss., University of Florida, USA.

Torrence, Robin. 2006. Starch and Archaeology. In *Ancient Starch Research*, edited by R. Torrence and H. Barton, 17–34. Walnut Creek, CA: Leaf Coast Press.

Torrence, Robin, and Huw Barton, eds. 2006. *Ancient Starch Research*. Walnut Creek, CA: Leaf Coast Press.

Trigger, Bruce G. 1990. Monumental Architecture: A Thermodynamic Explanation of Symbolic Behaviour. *World Archaeology* 22 (2): 119–32.

Trinkley, Michael B. 1985. The Form and Function of South Carolina's Early Woodland Shell Rings. In *Structure and Process in Southeastern Archaeology*, edited by R. S. Dickens Jr. and H. T. Ward, 102–18. Tuscaloosa: University of Alabama Press.

———. 1997. The Gradual Accumulation Theory: The Lighthouse Point and Stratton Place Shell Rings. In *South Carolina Archaeology Week: Shell Rings of the Late Archaic*. Columbia: South Carolina Institute of Archaeology and Anthropology, University of South Carolina.

Tromp, Monica, and John Dudgeon. 2011. SEM-EDS as an Effective Tool for Population-Level Analysis of Microfossils Extracted from Prehistoric Human Dental Calculus. Paper read at 76th Meeting of the Society for American Archaeology, March 30–April 3, Sacramento, California.

Tudhope, Alexander W., Colin P. Chilcott, Malcolm T. McCulloch, Edward R. Cook, John Chappell, Robert M. Ellam, David W. Lea, Janice M. Lough, and Graham B. Shimmield. 2001. Variability in the El Niño-Southern Oscillation Through a Glacial-Interglacial Cycle. *Science* 291:1511–17.

Tunnicliffe, Verena, J. M. O'Connell, and Melissa R. McQuoid. 2001. A Holocene Record of Marine Fish Remains from the Northeastern Pacific. *Marine Geology* 174:197–210.

Turner II, Christy G. 1979. Dental Anthropological Indications of Agriculture Among the Jomon People of Central Japan. *American Journal of Physical Anthropology* 51:619–36.

Turner, Terence. 1992. Os Mebengokre Kayapó: História e Mudança Social de Comunidades Autônomas para a Comunidade Interétnica. In *História dos Índios do Brasil*, edited by M. Carneiro da Cunha, 311–38. São Paulo: FAPESP/Cia das Letras/SMC.

Ubelaker, Douglas H. 1978. *Human Skeletal Remains. Excavation, Analysis and Interpretation*. Washington, DC: Smithsonian Institution.

———. 1989. *Human Skeletal Remains: Excavation, Analysis, Interpretation*. 2nd ed. Washington, DC: Taraxacum.

Uchôa, Dorath P. 2007 [1973]. *Arqueologia de Piaçaguera e Tenório: Análise de Dois Sítios Pré-Cerâmicos do Litoral Paulista*. Florianópolis, Brazil: Sociedade de Arqueologia Brasileira.

Uchôa, Dorath P., and Marilia C. de M. Alvim. 1989. Demografia Esqueletal dos Construtores do Sambaqui de Piaçaguera, São Paulo-Brasil. *Dédalo (São Paulo)* 1:455–72.

Ucko, Peter J. 1969. Ethnography and Archaeological Interpretation of Funerary Remains. *World Archaeology* 1:262–81.

Ulm, Sean. 2006a. *Coastal Themes: An Archaeology of the Southern Curtis Coast, Queensland*. Canberra: Pandanus Books, Research School of Pacific and Asian Studies, Australian National University.

———. 2006b. Australian Marine Reservoir Effects: A Guide to ΔR Values. *Australian Archaeology* 63:57–60.

Umbelino, Cláudia. 2006. Outros Sabores do Passado. As Análises de Oligoelementos e de Isótopos Estáveis na Reconstituição da Dieta das Comunidades Humanas do Mesolítico Final e do Neolítico Final / Calcolítico do Território Português. PhD diss., Universidade de Coimbra, Portugal.

Valente, Maria João. 2008. As Últimas Sociedades de Caçadores-Recolectores no Centro e Sul de Portugal (10,000–6,000 anos BP): Aproveitamento dos Recursos Animais. PhD diss., Universidade do Algarve, Portugal.

———. 2010. O Barranco das Quebradas (Vila do Bispo, Portugal) no Contexto dos Concheiros Mesolíticos do Sudoeste Português. In *Actas do 7.º Encontro de Arqueologia do Algarve (Xelb, 10)*, 15–38. Silves, Portugal: Câmara Municipal de Silves.

Valente, Maria João, and António Faustino Carvalho. 2009. Recent Developments in Early Holocene Hunter-Gatherer Subsistence and Settlement: A View from South-Western Iberia. In *Mesolithic Horizons: Papers Presented at the Seventh International Conference on the Mesolithic in Europe, Belfast 2005*, edited by S. McCartan, R. Schulting, G. Warren, and P. Woodman, 312–17. Oxford: Oxbow Books.

Van Beck, John C., and Linda M. Van Beck. 1965. The Marco Midden, Marco Island, Florida. *Florida Anthropologist* 18:1–20.

Van der Schriek, Tim, David G. Passmore, Anthony C. Stevenson, and Jose M. Rolão. 2007. The Palaeo-geography of Mesolithic Settlement-Subsistence and Shell Midden Formation in the Muge Valley, Lower Tagus Basin, Portugal. *Holocene* 17:369–86.

Van Derwarker, Amber M. 1999. Feasting and Status at the Toqua Site. *Southeastern Archaeology* 18 (1): 24–34.

Van Neer, Wim, Anton Ervynck, Loes J. Bolle, and Richard S. Millner. 2004. Seasonality Only Works in Certain Parts of the Year: The Reconstruction of Fishing Seasons Through Otolith Analysis. *International Journal of Osteoarchaeology* 14:457–64.

Vass, Arpad A., William M. Bass, Jeffrey D. Wolt, J. E. Foss, and John T. Ammons. 1992. Time Since Death Determinations of Human Cadavers Using Soil Solution. *Journal of Forensic Sciences* 37:1236–53.

Vayssière, A. 1923. Recherches Zoologiques et Anato-miques sur les Mollusques de la Famille des Cypræidés. *Annales du Musee d'Histoire Naturelle de Marseille, Zoologie* 18:1–120.

Veitch, Bruce. 1999. What Happened in the Mid-Holocene? Archaeological Evidence for Change from the Mitchell Plateau, Northwest Kimberley, Western Australia. PhD diss., University of Western Australia.

Viejo, Rosa M., and Per Aberg. 2003. Temporal and Spatial Variation in the Density of Mobile Epifauna and Grazing Damage on the Seaweed *Ascophyllum nodosum*. *Marine Biology* 142:1229–41.

Vierra, Bradley J. 1995. *Subsistence and Stone Tool Technology: An Old World Perspective*. Tempe: Arizona State University.

Vilaça, Aparecida. 1996. Quem Somos Nós: Questões da Alteridade no Encontro dos Wari com os Brancos. PhD diss., Universidade Federal do Rio de Janeiro, Brazil.

Villagrán, Ximena. 2008. Análise de Arqueofácies na Camada Preta do Sambaqui Jabuticabeira II. MA diss., Museu de Arqueologia e Etnologia, Universidade de São Paulo, Brazil.

Villagrán, Ximena, Andrea L. Balbo, Marco Madella, Assumpció Vila, and Jordi Estévez. 2011a. Experimental Micromorphology in Tierra del Fuego (Argentina): Building a Reference Collection for the Study of Shell Middens in Cold Climates. *Journal of Archaeological Science* 38:588–604.

Villagrán, Ximena, Daniela Klokler, Silvia Peixoto, Paulo DeBlasis, and Paulo Giannini. 2011b. Building Coastal Landscapes: Zooarchaeology and Geoarchaeology of Brazilian Shell Mounds. *Journal of Island and Coastal Archaeology* 6:211–34.

Villagrán, Ximena, Paulo Giannini, and Paulo DeBlasis. 2009. Archaeofacies Analyses: Using Depositional Attributes to Identify Anthropic Processes of Deposition in a Monumental Shell Mound of Santa Catarina State (Southern Brazil). *Geoarchaeology* 24:311–35.

Villagrán, Ximena, Daniela Klokler, Paula Nishida, Maria Dulce Gaspar, and Paulo DeBlasis. 2010. Lecturas Estratigráficas: Arquitectura Funerária y Deposi-tación de Resíduos en el Sambaquí Jabuticabeira II. *Latin American Antiquity* 21:195–227.

von Brandt, A. 1984. *Fish Catching Methods of the World*. 3rd ed. Farnham, UK: Fishing News Books.

Voorhies, Barbara. 2004. *Coastal Collectors in the Holocene: The Chantuto People of Southwest Mexico*. Gainesville: University Press of Florida.

Voorhies, Barbara, and Janine Gasco. 2004. *Postclassic Soconusco Society: The Late Prehistory of the Coast of Chiapas, Mexico*. Albany: State Uuniversity of New York-Albany, IMS Monographs, Institute for Mesoamerican Studies Monograph 14.

Waldron, Tony. 1994. *Counting the Dead. The Epidemiology of Skeletal Populations*. Chichester, UK: Wiley and Sons.

Walker, Karen Jo. 1992. The Zooarchaeology of Charlotte Harbor's Prehistoric Maritime Adaptations: Spatial and Temporal Perspectives. In *Culture and Environment in the Doman of the Calusa*, edited by W. H. Marquardt, 265–366. Gainesville: University Press of Florida.

Walker, Sara L. 2003. Site 45SJ169. In *Archaeological Investigations at Sites 45SJ165 and 45SJ169, Decatur Island, San Juan County, Washington*, edited by S. L. Walker. Cheney: Eastern Washington University, Reports in Archaeology and History 100–118.

Walker, William H. 1995. Ceremonial Trash? In *Expanding Archaeology*, edited by J. Skibo, W. H. Walker, and A. Nielsen, 67–79. Salt Lake City: University of Utah Press.

———. 2001. Ritual Technology in an Extranatural World. In *Anthropological Perspectives on Technology*, edited by M. B. Schiffer, 87–106. Albuquerque: University of New Mexico Press.

Ward, Joe H. 1963. Hierarchical Grouping to Optimize an

Objective Function. *Journal of the American Statistical Association* 58:236–44.

Waring, Antonio J., Jr. 1968. The Archaic Hunting and Gathering Cultures: The Archaic and Some Shell Rings. In *The Waring Papers: The Collected Works of Antonio J. Waring, Jr.*, edited by S. B. Williams, 243–46. Cambridge, MA: Peabody Museum of Archaeology and Ethnology.

Waring, Antonio J., Jr., and Lewis H. Larson. 1968. The Shell Ring on Sapelo Island. In *The Waring Papers: The Collected Works of Antonio J. Waring, Jr.*, edited by S. B. Williams, 263–78. Cambridge, MA: Peabody Museum of Archaeology and Ethnology.

Warner, W. Lloyd. 1969. *A Black Civilization: A Social Study of an Australian Tribe.* Gloucester, MA: Peter Smith.

Waselkov, Gregory A. 1987. Shellfish Gathering and Shell Midden Archaeology. *Advances in Archaeological Method and Theory* 10:93–210.

Wasson, R. J. 1986. Geomorphology and Quaternary History of the Australian Continental Dunefields. *Geographical Review of Japan* 59B:55–67.

Weber, Laura I., and Stephen J. Hawkins. 2005. *Patella aspera* and *P.-ulyssiponensis*: Genetic Evidence of Speciation in the North-east Atlantic. *Marine Biology* 147:153–62.

Wefer, Gerold, and Wolfgang H. Berger. 1991. Isotope Paleontology: Growth and Composition of Extant Calcareous Species. *Marine Geology* 100:207–48.

Weiss, Kenneth M. 1972. On the Systematic Bias in Skeletal Sexing. *American Journal of Physical Anthropology* 37:239–49.

Wesolowski, Veronica. 2000. A Prática da Horticultura Entre os Construtores de Sambaquis e Acampamentos Litorâneos da Região da Baía de São Francisco, Santa Catarina: Uma Abordagem Bio-Antropológica. MSc diss., Universidade de São Paulo, Brazil.

———. 2007. Cáries, Desgaste, Cálculos Dentários e Micro-Resíduos da Dieta entre Grupos Pré-Históricos do Litoral Norte de Santa-Catarina: É Possível Comer Amido e Não Ter Cárie? PhD diss., Fundação Oswaldo Cruz (FIOCRUZ), Brazil.

Wesolowski, Veronica, Sheila M. F. M. de Souza, and Patricia Fischer. 2009. Sepultamentos no Sambaqui do Cubatão I: Antropologia de Terreno e Interpretação Arqueológica. Paper read at XV Congresso da Sociedade de Arqueologia Brasileira, September 20–23, Belém, Pará, Brazil.

Wesolowski, Veronica, Sheila M. F. M. de Souza, Karl J. Reinhard, and Gregório Ceccantini. 2007. Grânulos de Amido e Fitólitos em Cálculos Dentários Humanos: Contribuição ao Estudo do Modo de Vida e Subsistência de Grupos Sambaquianos do Litoral Sul do Brasil. *Revista do Museu de Arqueologia e Etnologia* 17:191–210.

———. 2010. Evaluating Microfossil Content of Dental Calculus from Brazilian Sambaquis. *Journal of Archaeological Science* 37:1326–38.

Wessen, Gary C. 1988. The Use of Shellfish Resources on the Northwest Coast: The View from Ozette. In *Prehistoric Economies of the Pacific Northwest Coast, Research in Economic Anthropology,* Supplement 3, edited by B. L. Isaac, 179–207. Greenwich, CT: JAI Press.

Wheeler, Ryan, C. I. Newman, and Ray M. McGee. 2000. A New Look at the Mount Taylor and Bluffton Sites, Volusia County, with an Outline of the Mount Taylor Culture. *Florida Anthropologist* 53 (2/3): 133–57.

White, Tim D., and Pieter A. Folkens. 1991. Human Osteology. 1st ed. San Diego: Academic Press.

Widmer, Randolph J. 1988. *The Evolution of the Calusa: A Nonagricultural Chiefdom on the Southwest Florida Coast.* Tuscaloosa: University of Alabama Press.

———. 1989. Archaeological Research Strategies in the Investigation of Shellbearing Sites, a Florida Perspective. Paper read at the 1989 SAA meeting, Charleston, South Carolina.

———. 1996. Recent Excavations at the Key Marco Site, 8Cr48, Collier County, Florida. *Florida Anthropologist* 49:10–25.

———. 2002. The Woodland Archaeology of South Florida. In *The Woodland Southeast*, edited by D. G. Anderson and R. C. Mainfort Jr., 373–97. Tuscaloosa: University of Alabama Press.

Wiener, Carlos. 1876. Estudos Sobre os Sambaquis do Sul do Brasil. *Arquivos do Museu Nacional* 1:1–20.

Wiessner, Polly. 1974. A Functional Estimator of Population from Floor Area. *American Antiquity* 39:343–49.

Wigen, Rebecca J. 1980. A Faunal Analysis of Two Middens on the East Coast of Vancouver Island. MA diss., University of Victoria, Canada.

———. 1990. Identification and Analysis of Vertebrate Fauna from Eighteen Archaeological Sites on the Southern Queen Charlotte Islands. Victoria: British Columbia Heritage Trust.

———. 1999. Appendix A: Analysis of Bone from 922T Hotspring Island, Units 7 and 9. In *1998 Archaeological Investigations, Site 922T, Gunlai Kin (Hotspring Island), Gwaii Haanas*, edited by I. D. Sumpter. Victoria, BC: Parks Canada, Cultural Resource Services.

———. 2003. Appendix D: Fish Remains from Sites 45SJ165 and 45SJ169. In *Archaeological Investigations at Sites 45SJ165 and 45SJ169, Decatur Island, San Juan County, Washington*, edited by S. L. Walker, 275–308. Cheney: Eastern Washington University, Reports in Archaeology and History 100–118.

Wilcoxon, Larry R. 1993. Subsistence and Site Structure: An Approach for Deriving Cultural Information from Coastal Shell Middens. In *Archaeology on the Northern Channel Islands of California*, edited by M. A. Glassow, 137–50. Salinas, CA: Coyote Press.

Wilcoxon, Larry R., Jon M. Erlandson, and David F. Stone. 1982. Intensive Cultural Resources Survey for the Goleta Flood Protection Program, Santa Barbara County, California. Los Angeles: US Army Corps of Engineers.

Wiles, Gregory C., David J. Barclay, and Parker E. Calkin. 1999. Tree-Ring-Dated "Little Ice Age" Histories of Maritime Glaciers from Western Prince William Sound, Alaska. *Holocene* 9:163–73.

Wiles, Gregory C., David J. Barclay, Parker E. Calkin, and Thomas V. Lowell. 2008. Century to Millennial-Scale Temperature Variations for the Last Two Thousand Years Inferred from Glacial Geologic Records of Southern Alaska. *Global and Planetary Change* 60:115–25.

Willcox, George H. 1974. A History of Deforestation as Indicated by Charcoal Analysis of Four Sites in Eastern Anatolia. *Journal of the British Institute of Archaeology at Ankara* 24:117–33.

Willey, Gordon R. 1949a. *Archaeology of the Florida Gulf Coast*. Washington, DC: Smithsonian Institution, Miscellaneous Collections 113.

———. 1949b. *The Archaeology of Southeast Florida*. New Haven: Yale University.

Williams, Gray A. 1990a. *Littorina mariae*—A Factor Structuring Low Shore Communities? *Hydrobiologia* 193:139–46.

———. 1990b. The Comparative Ecology of the Flat Periwinkles, *Littorina obtusata* (L.) and *L. mariae* Sacchi et Rastelli. *Field Studies* 7:469–82.

Williams, Gray A., Colin Little, David Morritt, Penny Stirling, Linda Teagle, Alison Miles, Graham Pilling, and Mireille Consalvey. 1999. Foraging in the Limpet *Patella vulgata*: The Influence of Rock Slope on the Timing Activity. *Journal of the Marine Biological Association of the United Kingdom* 79:881–89.

Williams, John. 2007. *Clam Gardens: Aboriginal Mariculture on Canada's West Coast*. Vancouver, BC: New Star Books.

Wing, Elizabeth. 1965. Animal Bones Associated with Two Indian Sites on Marco Island, Florida. *Florida Anthropologist* 18:21–28.

Wood, James W., George R. Milner, Henry C. Harpending, and Kenneth M. Weiss. 1992. The Osteological Paradox. *Current Anthropology* 33:343–70.

Woodroffe, Colin D. 1988. Changing Mangrove and Wetland Habitats over the Last 8000 Years, Northern Australia and South-East Asia. In *Floodplains Research. Northern Australia: Progress and Prospects*. Vol. 2, edited by D. Wade-Marshall and P. Loveday, 1–33. Darwin: Australian National University, North Australian Research Unit.

———. 1995. Response of Tide-Dominated Mangrove Shorelines in Northern Australia to Anticipated Sea-Level Rise. *Earth Surface Processes and Landforms* 20:65–85.

Woodroffe, Colin D., John Chappell, Bruce G. Thom, and Eugene Wallensky. 1986. *Geomorphological Dynamics and Evolution of the South Alligator Tidal River and Plains, Northern Territory*. Darwin: Australian National University, North Australian Research Unit.

Woodroffe, Colin D., and M. E. Mulrennen. 1993. *Geomorphology of the Lower Mary River Plains, Northern Territory*. Darwin: Australian National University, North Australian Research Unit.

Woods, David J., and Diane Woods. 2005. Ancient Sea Gardens. In *Mystery of the Pacific Northwest*. Toronto: Aquaculture Pictures Inc.

Wright, Cynthia A., Audrey Dallimore, Richard E. Thomson, R. Timothy Patterson, and Daniel M. Ware. 2005. Late Holocene Paleofish Populations in Effingham Inlet, British Columbia, Canada. *Paleogeography, Palaeoclimatology, Paleoecology* 224:367–84.

Wright, Richard V. S. 1971. Prehistory in the Cape York Peninsula. In *Aboriginal Man and Environment in Australia*, edited by D. J. Mulvaney and J. Golson,

133–40. Canberra: Australian National University Press.

Wyman, Jeffries. 1875. Fresh-Water Shell Mounds of the St. Johns River, Florida. *Peabody Academy of Science Memoir 4*.

Yesner, David R., Maria J. Figuerero Torres, Ricardo A. Guichón, and Luis A. Borrero. 2003. Stable Isotope Analysis of Human Bone and Ethnohistoric Subsistence Patterns in Tierra del Fuego. *Journal of Anthropological Archaeology* 22:279–91.

Yokoyama, Yusuke, Anthony Purcell, Kurt Lambeck, and Paul Johnston. 2001. Shore-Line Reconstruction Around Australia During the Last Glacial Maximum and Late Glacial Stage. *Quaternary International* 83–85:9–18.

Yonge, C M. 1972. *The Seashore*. London: Fontana.

Zangrando, Atilio F., Augusto Tessone, Susana Valencio, Héctor O. Panarello, María E. Mansur, and Monica Salemme. 2004. Isótopos Estables y Dietas Humanas en Ambientes Costeros. In *Avances en Arqueometría 2003*, edited by J. F. Ortega, J. M. Calleja, C. E. Sanchez, C. Fernandez Lorenzo, P. Martinez Brell, A. Gil Montero, and R. Puerto, 91–97. Cádiz, Spain: Universidad de Cádiz.

Zeder, Melinda A., Daniel G. Bradley, Eve Emshwiller, and Bruce D. Smith. 2006. *Documenting Domestication: New Genetic and Archaeological Paradigms*. Berkeley: University of California Press.

Zilhão, João. 2000. From the Mesolithic to the Neolithic in the Iberian Peninsula. In *Europe's First Farmers*, edited by T. D. Price, 144–82. Cambridge: Cambridge University Press.

Zohar, Irit, and Miriam Belmarker. 2005. Size Does Matter: Methodological Comments on Sieve Size and Species Richness in Fishbone Assemblages. *Journal of Archaeological Science* 32:635–41.

Myrian Álvarez (PhD, archaeology, Universidad de Buenos Aires, Argentina) is a researcher of Centro Austral de Investigaciones Científicas (Ushuaia) of the Consejo Nacional de Investigaciones Científicas y Técnicas of Argentina (CONICET). She is a specialist in use-wear analysis in lithics and in shell middens, and she is working on hunter-fisher-gatherer societies from the Beagle Channel, Tierra del Fuego, Argentina. myrianalvarez@gmail.com.

Pedro Alvim (PhD candidate, University of Durham; MA, archaeology, University of Évora, Portugal) is an archaeologist member of CHAIA research center (University of Évora) and has been researching prehistoric monuments and architecture for fifteen years. pdro.alvim@gmail.com.

José Antonio Anacleto has worked at the Geological Museum, Lisbon, since 2000 and is studying environmental sciences at the Open University, Lisbon. jose.moita@lneg.pt.

Célia Helena Cezar Boyadjian (PhD, biology [genetics], Universidade de São Paulo [USP], Brazil) is a researcher at Laboratorio de Antropologia Biologica, in USP and a visiting researcher at Max-Planck-Institute for Evolutionary Anthropology. She specializes in the analysis of modern and ancient plant micro-remains (pollen grains and phytoliths but mainly starch grains), and also of dental calculus contents. Her research interests include reconstruction of ancient diets and food processing, use of plants in the past, subsistence changes, and origins and dispersion of agriculture in South America, shell

mound-builders subsistence, and studies of paleopathology and paleoparasitology.

Clive Bonsall is a professor of early prehistory at the University of Edinburgh, Scotland. His research interests include hunter-gatherer societies, the transition to farming in Europe, the reconstruction of ancient diets, and human-environment interactions. He has conducted fieldwork in northern Britain, Romania, and Slovenia, and is a corresponding member of the Romanian Academy of Scientists. Clive.Bonsall@ed.ac.uk.

Todd J. Braje (PhD, anthropology, University of Oregon, USA) is an assistant professor of anthropology at San Diego State University. His research interests include the historical ecology of coastal hunter-gatherers and the application of deep historical data to modern fisheries management. tbraje@mail.sdsu.edu.

Meghan Burchell (PhD, anthropology, McMaster University, Canada), is an assistant professor at Memorial University of Newfoundland. Her research interests include improving seasonality methods for archaeological interpretation thorough high-resolution stable isotope sclerochronology and the archaeology of hunter-gatherer settlement, and subsistence strategies. mburchell@mun.ca.

Aubrey Cannon (PhD, archaeology, University of Cambridge, UK), is a professor in the Department of Anthropology, McMaster University. His research areas include hunter-gatherer settlement and subsistence and marine-based economies in British Columbia and Tonga, as well mortuary practices and material fashion in both the prehistoric and Victorian eras. cannona@mcmaster.ca.

António Faustino Carvalho (PhD, archaeology Universidade do Algarve, Portugal), is an assistant professor at the Universidade do Algarve. Research interests include the origins of the early farming societies in the Mediterranean world and their development. afcarva@ualg.pt.

Terence N. Clark (PhD, anthropology, University of Toronto, Canada) is curator of western Canadian archaeology at the Canadian Museum of Civilization, and a research associate at the Institute of Archaeology, University College London. He has extensive archaeological field experience across the Northwest Coast, Plateau, and Western Subarctic culture areas. His current research projects focus on the rise of intensive shellfishing, the development of social complexity, contact-period archaeology, and statistical methods. terence.clark@civilisations.ca.

Phoebe S. Daniels (PhD, anthropology, University of Washington, USA) currently works for the University of Washington Press. Her research is focused on three interrelated themes in archaeology: adapting foraging models to include gender, explaining the effects of human foraging and Holocene climate change on shellfish populations in the central Northwest Coast, and applying the archaeological record to contemporary issues. phoebesdaniels@gmail.com.

Rebecca Dean (PhD, anthropology, University of Arizona, USA) is an associate professor at the University of Minnesota, Morris. She specializes in the analysis of animal bones from archaeological sites, and her research is focused on early farming societies in southern Arizona and the Mediterranean, particularly the spread and development of farming and the impact that agricultural societies had on their landscapes. rdean@morris.umn.edu.

Paulo DeBlasis (Post-PhD, archaeology, University of Arizona, USA; DSc archaeology, University of São Paulo, Brazil) is a professor at the University of São Paulo and a researcher associated with the Museum of Archaeology and Ethnology. In addition to conducting research on a variety of topics in Brazilian archaeology, he has vast experience in cultural heritage management. deblasis@usp.br.

Sabine Eggers (PhD in medical genetics, University of São Paulo [USP], Brazil; MSc in human biology, University

of Vienna, Austria) is a professor at the USP, Brazil. Her main research interests are biocultural and evolutionary causes (and effects) of disease patterns in past and present populations; and diverse trajectories to social complexity and subsistence change in ancient South American coastal groups. saeggers@gmail.com.

Jon M. Erlandson (PhD, anthroplogy, University of California–Santa Barbara, USA) is the director of the University of Oregon Museum of Natural and Cultural History. His research interests include the historical ecology of hunter-gatherers, the history of maritime migrations, and the peopling of the New World. jerland@uoregon.edu.

Patrick A. Faulkner (PhD, archaeology, Australian National University) is a lecturer in the Department of Archaeology, School of Philosophical and Historical Inquiry, Faculty of Arts and Social Sciences, University of Sydney, Australia. His research focuses on human-environment interactions in coastal environments and hunter-gatherer palaeoeconomies. patrick.faulkner@sydney.edu.au

Levy Figuti (PhD, prehistory, geology, and paleontology, Muséum national d'Histoire naturelle, Paris, France; BA, biology, University of São Paulo, Brazil) is an archaeozoologist who has worked for years in faunal remains of shell mounds. He is a senior researcher at the Museu de Arqueologia e Etnologia da USP. lfiguti@usp.br.

Maria Dulce Gaspar (PhD, University of São Paulo, Brazil) is a professor at the National Museum, Federal University of Rio de Janeiro, and a CNP researcher. She works on shell-matrix sites in Brazil and is directing a study on their dimensions and social significance, funded by FAPERJ. madugaspar@terra.com.br.

Ivan Briz i Godino (PhD, prehistorical archaeology, Universitat Autònoma de Barcelona, Spain) is an ICREA researcher at Institució Milà i Fontanals-Spanish Council for Scientific Research (CSIC) and associated researcher in the Department of Archaeology, University of York. He is a specialist in form-function analysis in lithics as well as in shell midden archaeology. At the moment he is working on new archaeological methods from ethnoarchaeology. ibrizgodino@gmail.com.

Ricardo A. Guichón (PhD, biological anthropology, Universidad de Buenos Aires, Argentina), is a CONICET independent researcher and director of the project Paleopathology and Paleopidemiología of Southern Patagonia. He is a member of the Human Evolutionary Ecology Laboratory of Quequen (Facultad de Cs. Sociales de la Universidad Nacional del Centro de la Provincia de Buenos Aires, Argentina), and the Department of Biology (Facultad de Cs. Ex. y Naturales de la Universidad Nacional de Mar del Plata, Argentina). ricardoguichon@hotmail.com.

Nadine Hallmann (PhD, paleontology, University of Mainz, Germany) is a postdoctoral researcher at the Centre Européen de Recherche et d'Enseignement de Géosciences de l'Environnement in Aix-en-Provence, France. Her research interests include the reconstruction of Late Holocene sea-level changes in French Polynesia, South-Central Pacific, based on coral reef records. hallmann@cerege.fr.

Mary Jackes (PhD, University of Toronto, Canada) is an adjunct associate professor at the University of Waterloo, Ontario, and has been studying Portuguese human skeletons since 1984. mkjackes@uwaterloo.ca.

Daniela Klokler (PhD, anthropology, University of Arizona, USA) is a professor in archaeology at the Universidade Federal de Sergipe, Brazil. She has worked in Brazilian shell middens since 1996. Her main research interests are zooarchaeology and the formation processes in sambaquis, coastal adaptations, and ritual practice. dklokler@gmail.com.

Marco Madella (PhD, archaeology, University of Cambridge, UK) is an ICREA research professor in environmental archaeology at the Spanish Council for Scientific Research (CSIC, Institució Milà i Fontanals-Barcelona). He is the coordinator of the SimulPast Consolider Ingenio2010 project of the government of Spain. marco.madella@icrea.es.

Mercedes Okumura (PhD, University of São Paulo, Brazil) is a former curator in the Leverhulme Centre of Human Evolutionary Studies, University of Cambridge, UK, and now a postdoctoral fellow at the Museu de Arqueologia e Etnologia, University of São Paulo. Her main research interests are the biological and cultural diversity of past populations in Southern Brazil explored through the application of evolutionary theory. okumuram@usp.

Trevor J. Orchard (PhD, anthropology, University of Toronto, Canada) is a lecturer in the Department of Interdisciplinary Studies, Lakehead University, Orillia, Canada. He has been actively involved in field and laboratory research in the northeastern Pacific Rim for approximately 14 years with a particular focus on zooarchaeology. trevorjorchard@gmail.com.

Catriona Pickard (PhD, archaeology, University of Edinburgh, Scotland; BSc, Physics, University of Aberdeen, Scotland) lectures in archaeological science and manages the laboratory facilities of the School of History, Classics and Archaeology at the University of Edinburgh. Her research interests focus on early prehistory, coastal archaeology, palaeodietary reconstruction, and archaeogenetics. Catriona.Pickard@ed.ac.uk.

Claudia Plens (PhD and MSc, archaeology, Museu de Arqueologia e Etnologia da USP, Brazil; BA, archaeology, Universidade Estácio de Sá, Rio de Janeiro, Brazil) does research and teaching at the Universidade Federal do Estado de São Paulo.

Torben C. Rick (PhD, anthropology, University of Oregon, USA) is a curator of North American Archaeology at the National Museum of Natural History, Smithsonian Institution. Dr. Rick's research focuses on the interactions of ancient people with coastal and terrestrial ecosystems, from California's Channel Islands to the Chesapeake Bay. rickt@si.edu.

Mirjana Roksandic (PhD, Simon Fraser University, Canada) is an associate professor and coordinator of biological anthropology, University of Winnipeg. Her research attention is divided between the human evolution in Pleistocene Europe and burial ritual among sedentary hunter-gatherers in Southern Europe and the Caribbean. m.roksandic@uwinnipeg.ca.

Michael Russo (PhD, anthropology, University of Florida, USA) is an archaeologist with the U.S. National Park Service, Southeast Archeological Center, Tallahassee, Florida. Russo's research has included the development of shell seasonality metrics and distributional mapping as related to social, cosmologic, and environmental component analysis. He is currently working on growth analysis of the Banded Mystery Snail (*Viviparus georgianus*) and development of wireless digital penetrometry for recording the depth and density of shell deposits. mike_russo@nps.gov.

Rebecca Saunders (PhD, University of Florida, USA) is an associate professor in the Department of Geography and Anthropology, Louisiana State University, and curator of anthropology at the Louisiana State University Museum of Natural Science. Her research interests include prehistoric and early historic Native American sites in the southeastern United States, coastal adaptations, pottery technology and style, and forensic archaeology. rsaunde@lsu.edu.

Rita Scheel-Ybert (PhD, biology of populations and ecology, Université Montpellier-II, France) is an associate professor of archaeology at the Federal University of Rio de Janeiro State, Brazil. She is an archaeobotanist, the first specialist in anthracology for tropical regions. scheelybert@mn.ufrj.br, rita@scheel.com.br.

Bernd R. Schöne (PhD, University of Göttingen, Germany) is a professor in the Department of Applied and Analytical Paleontology, University of Mainz, and is the director of the INCREMENTS (International Center for the Reconstruction of Environmental Conditions archived in Marginal-growing Biological Entities) research group. His research focuses on high-resolution climate and seasonality reconstructions from mollusk shells using sclerochronology, trace elements, and stable isotopes. schoeneb@uni-mainz.de.

Henry Schwarcz (PhD, geology, California Institute of Technology, USA) is university professor emeritus in the School of Geography and Earth Sciences, McMaster University and fellow of the Royal Society of Canada (FRSC). His research interests include stable isotope geochemistry, paleodiet, and the ultrastructure and mineralogy of bone. schwarcz@mcmaster.ca.

Sheila Mendonça de Souza (PhD, University of Rio de Janeiro, Brazil) was born and educated in Rio de Janeiro, and worked part time as a physician. She has been teaching for 20 years in the first faculty of archaeology in Brazil, doing research in bioarchaeology in different museums and institutions inside and outside the country. She is now a senior researcher in ENSP/Focruz. sferraz@ensp.fiocruz.br.

Jorge A. Suby (PhD and BA in biological sciences, Mar del Plata University, Argentina) is a researcher of the National Research Council (CONICET-Argentina), working in paleopathology of human populations of Southern Patagonia. He is a member of the Laboratorio de Ecología Evolutiva Humana, Archaeology Department, Universidad Nacional del Centro de la Provincia de Buenos Aires, Argentina. jasuby@hotmail.com.

Maria João Valente (PhD, archaeology and zooarchaeology, Universidade do Algarve, Portugal) is an assistant professor at Universidade do Algarve. Her research is focused on subsistence studies and animal resources (mammals and mollusks) in several periods from the Paleolithic to the Medieval. mvalente@ualg.pt.

Randolph J. Widmer (PhD, anthropology, Pennsylvania State University, USA) is an associate professor of anthropology at the University of Houston. His research interests include coastal adaptation along the U.S. Gulf Coast and craft specialization in Mesoamerica with emphasis on their roles in sociocultural development. rwidmer@uh.edu.

Débora Zurro (PhD, prehistorical archaeology, Universitat Autònoma de Barcelona, Spain) is a specialized technician at Institució Milà i Fontanals-Spanish Council for Scientific Research (CSIC, Institució Milà i Fontanals-Barcelona). She is specially focused on the visibility of plant resources consumption in hunter-gatherer contexts. debora@imf.csic.es.